THE DEFINITIVE ILLUSTRATED ENCYCLOPEDIA
Jazz & Blues

Publisher and Creative Director: Nick Wells

Project Editor: Sara Robson

Picture Researchers: Melinda Revesz and Julia Rolf

Art Director and Layout Design: Mike Spender

Digital Design and Production: Chris Herbert

Special thanks to: Chelsea Edwards, Victoria Lyle, Theresa Maynard, Geoffrey Meadon, Cliff O'Dea, Julie Pallot, Lucy Robins, Helen Tovey, Claire Walker and Gemma Walters

First published 2007 by

FLAME TREE PUBLISHING

Crabtree Hall, Crabtree Lane,

Fulham, London SW6 6TY

United Kingdom

www.flametreepublishing.com

Music information site: www.musicfirebox.com

11 10

5 7 9 10 8 6 4

Flame Tree is part of The Foundry Creative Media Company Limited

The CIP record for this book is available from the British Library.

Hardback ISBN: 978-1-84786-273-0

Hardback Special ISBN: 978-1-84786-732-2

Paperback ISBN: 978-1-84786-728-5

Every effort has been made to contact copyright holders. We apologize in advance for any omissions and would be pleased to insert the appropriate acknowledgment in subsequent editions of this publication.

Printed in China

THE DEFINITIVE ILLUSTRATED ENCYCLOPEDIA Jazz & Blues

General Editor: Julia Rolf
Foreword by Jeff 'Tain' Watts

FLAME TREE
PUBLISHING

Contents

THE FIFTIES

THE SIXTIES

THE SEVENTIES

THE EIGHTIES

THE CONTEMPORARY ERA

THE STYLES

HOW TO USE THIS BOOK

The Definitive Illustrated Encyclopedia of Jazz and Blues takes the reader on a journey through these extraordinary musical genres, their decades of success and those marked by hardship, and explores the numerous styles to have emerged as well as the artists who made it all happen. The detailed Sources & Sounds sections explore the interplay between social and political factors and their impact upon musicians of the day.

Taking a chronological view of the music, the book glides through the roots of both genres and moves on through the 1920s, the decade dubbed the 'Jazz Age', onto the poverty-ridden 1930s and the war-scarred world of the 1940s, before arriving at one of the most significant periods for jazz and blues: the 1950s. The momentum of this booming decade carried on into the next decade, but the disappointment of its unfulfilled promise was realized in the 1970s. The technology of the 1980s aided new recording techniques, but jazz and blues continued to be overshadowed by other types of popular music. Concluding the first section with the contemporary era, the book examines the place of jazz and blues today, and begs the question 'where do we go from here?' The second section of the book examines both jazz and blues music in terms of the individual styles to have emerged from each genre's rich musical heritage.

INTRODUCTIONS

Each chapter is introduced and set in its cultural context, giving a glimpse into what was going on behind the scenes and how that influenced the musical highs and lows of each decade.

SOURCES & SOUNDS

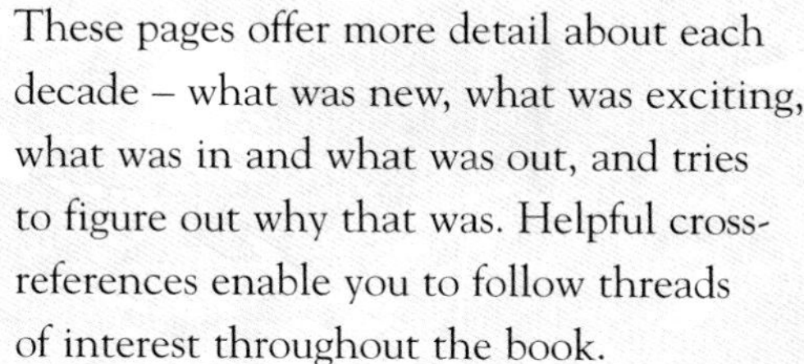

These pages offer more detail about each decade – what was new, what was exciting, what was in and what was out, and tries to figure out why that was. Helpful cross-references enable you to follow threads of interest throughout the book.

KEY ARTISTS

These artists carry the musical torch for their generation and so are the main focus of each decade. Classic recordings, key album covers and great quotes help to get under the skin of the artists' music.

A–Z OF ARTISTS

Although they did not quite make it into the Key Artists pages, these are the artists that formed the musical backbone of each decade.

LIST OF ARTISTS

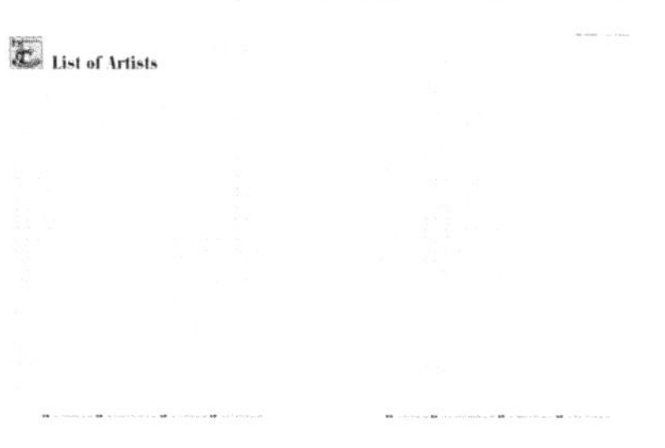

Found at the end of each decade, these pages offer a comprehensive list of all the major jazz and blues artists, from those included in the Key Artists and A–Z sections, to the many others who contributed to the sounds of each era. The list gives a idea of each artist's origins, instruments and main period of influence.

Foreword

It is my pleasure to welcome you to this encyclopedia, and thank you in advance for your interest in these vital art forms. Hopefully, some of the information contained herein will enlighten and fortify your appreciation and enjoyment of jazz and blues, thereby further enriching your life.

As a youngster growing up in urban Pittsburgh, I took these musics for granted. My background in pop and R&B (which would later expand to include rock and classical music), offered me little evidence or reason to dig any deeper into American music. Jazz and blues were certainly all around me, but I'm sure that I subconsciously filed them away as 'old people's music', with no obvious connection to artists more prevalent on my radio. The collecting of records was not a big priority in my household.

Later, in my mid-teens, my brother's job at a college record store would spur him to expose me to Seventies jazz-fusion. Thus would begin an ongoing backtracking process, as Herbie Hancock would lead me to Miles Davis, and eventually to artists like Charlie Parker. Soon, I began to connect the dots, and swelled with pride to discover almost daily the pioneering, predominantly African-American virtuosi who were the foundation of much that I, and music lovers worldwide, enjoyed as the soundtracks of their lives.

My subsequent study of music, and life as a touring performer would shape me even further, broadening my scope, and giving me appreciation for artists not from the States, admiring their respectful takes on America's gift to the world. This process made me less provincial, yet more beholden to the source material than ever. My career on stage, in the studio, and in television led me to be blessed with sharing the energy and spirit of some pretty seminal artists. In jazz these include Dizzy Gillespie, Sonny Rollins, McCoy Tyner, Milt Hinton, Ron Carter, George Benson, Sarah Vaughan, Betty Carter and Alice Coltrane. I have also gotten to work with such blues legends as John Lee Hooker, B.B. King, Buddy Guy, Little Richard, Albert Collins and Miss Linda Hopkins. I was uniformly touched by their sound, drive and conviction.

There should be no argument when it comes to the overwhelming relevance and importance of the classic artists and their works. But, in recent years, I have been made aware of a sort of movement, mostly sincere on the part of artists, but perhaps not without a sense of home-grown commerce on the marketing end. I am both sympathetic and welcoming of an increasing emphasis on folk-based hybrids that have roots in the traditional songs of European and other nations supplanting American artists on jazz festivals in both Europe and the States. Detractors stateside bemoan both the potential loss of employment, and whether or not these musical genres have the right to bear the names of their national treasures. The mantles of jazz and blues come attached with years of association with the negative. At times, there can exist a stigma with the question of who has the right to dance with the girl once deemed so ugly.

But, of course, art is far greater than any man or label; it is to be celebrated and respected. Thus making the information contained here more important than ever, as a living document and template for the architecture and development of the songs our descendants will play and sing. Enjoy!

Jeff 'Tain' Watts
2007

Jeff 'Tain' Watts started out playing with the Marsalis brothers and has become one of the foremost drummers of his generation.

Introduction

Every book, even an illustrated encyclopedia of music, tells a story. Ours concerns 100 years of jazz and blues – enduring, artful, popular musics created by vivid characters during turbulent times.

Our history of these musics, which bear both irrevocable kinship and fundamental differences, begins where they were born: the United States of America. The blues' prime movers were descendants of African-American slaves. They played music for themselves and nearby neighbours, toured lowly venues as restless loners or in barnstorming troupes, and occasionally ascended to a theatre stage. Jazz was engendered by self-taught black American instrumentalists, more formally-trained Creole and Latin American musicians, and odd individuals of general lower, upper and middle, immigrant, labouring and dilettante classes as they jostled together in the burgeoning ports, river cities, labour camps and industrial centres of early twentieth-century America.

From the start, Europe embraced and forwarded the movement of jazz and blues. African-American globetrotters such as James Reese Europe, Sam Wooding, Josephine Baker, Louis Armstrong, Sidney Bechet and Duke Ellington captured the fancies of London, Paris, Berlin, St. Petersburg and other cosmopolitan capitals (as well as South America and eventually Africa, the Middle East and Asia), attracting enthusiastic audiences and coteries of adherents. Blues and jazz have always been embraced by aficionados and the uninitiated alike, recognized as universal forms of art capable of expressing all of human experience.

Life's dramas involve love, loss, honour, regret, festivity, commitment, rootlessness, devotion, depravity, setbacks and victory – conditions evoked and enacted, in nuanced detail, by blues and jazz. Furthermore, these musics have evolved to be both flexible and firm. Jazz and blues can accept, celebrate and assimilate the most profound effects of their most singular innovators, yet remain arts unto themselves. Bessie Smith influenced the blues forever, but the blues is not Bessie Smith; Miles Davis will exert an enormous influence on jazz for evermore, but there is jazz besides Miles.

Blues and jazz were ideally suited or readily tailored for the sound recording and broadcast technologies that developed in the twentieth century. They were the first musics disseminated as documents of the spontaneous creativity of charismatic virtuosi, rather than as artifacts of fixed interpretations of printed scores. Jazz and blues records were snatched up, but they merely whetted appetites for live appearances by heroes celebrating the immediate eternal moment. Was it mere coincidence that international interest in jazz and blues tied in with the rise of faster, easier and cheaper international travel?

In truth, blues and jazz are best when they are heard live; live performance demonstrates a music's vitality genuinely, and first-hand witnesses are usually more able transplanters of imported arts. Jazz and blues scattered seeds wherever they landed, and those seeds took root everywhere.

From our perspective, blues and jazz are self-perpetuating gifts to the world coming from deep in the heart of post-slavery America, a historic place and state-of-mind in which rustic and regional traditions are transformed to suit the global digitopolis of today. Musicians well beyond the US and Europe, enthralled with jazz and blues, model songs on the musical styles but with their own unique vocabularies, inflections and dialects. The musics' strains, strategies and structures have been pressed to serve many cultures' and peoples' needs; given the space explorations of artists such as Sun Ra, being beyond the rainbow may be swinging, too.

So other histories of jazz and blues could be, and should be, told – the all-too-often overlooked women; the considerable influences exerted by Hispanola, the Mediterranean and the Caribbean isles; the investigation of the links between concert-hall compositions and sounds shaped by improvisation, the better to fulfil the imperatives of the brothels, street parades, barrooms, dancehalls and smoky dives from which the music originated.

The Definitive Illustrated Encyclopedia of Jazz & Blues touches on those topics, but its focus is elsewhere. We don't claim to be exhaustive, but hope that our selectivity represents breadth and inclusivity. We acknowledge the diverse forces, decade by decade, that shaped all peoples' activities, understanding that blues and jazz musicians are as prey to the influence of circumstance as anyone else. But we highlight, over all, those individuals who made this music.

Here they are, the musicians, year after year, page after page, many captured in the heat of action. Always, their photos and attendant graphic ephemera are illustrative, revealing: even when they've been posed, jazz and blues musicians make their points, directing the narrative. Read all about them. See what they chose to show.

Blues crystallizes images of strength against adversity; jazz expands upon insights, whims and systems of the imagination. Our *Definitive Illustrated Encyclopedia* points to a world off the page – go out and hear how the music sounds. And know that the story of jazz and blues has not ended. We believe it has just begun.

THE EARLY YEARS

Jazz and blues are rooted in the enormous technological and social transformations affecting the USA and Western Europe at the turn of the twentieth century. The most striking changes were the advent of easier and cheaper travel; better communications; electric lighting; improvements in audio recording and moving pictures; increased urbanization; and the rise of the US, concurrent with the fall of the UK, as the world's leading military, economic and cultural power. The budding empowerment of African-Americans, who no longer faced slavery, had more impact on the development of new forms of music than any other engine of change. The abolishment of slavery was the beginning of the end of white performers in blackface impersonating Negroes in minstrel shows. African-Americans in the US still may not have been treated equally, but they could gather more freely, and engage in group amusements without censure. Loose threads of African retentions, Scotch-Irish ballads, Christian hymns, vaudeville themes, Spanish dance rhythms, marching-band fanfares and idiosyncratic expression began to be woven together by musicians who were either seeking their fortunes adrift from their childhood homes, or were immigrants exiled from age-old traditions.

After the First World War, the US tried to regain its isolationist past. But newly efficient production methods and the rapid growth of cities lent the economy unbridled power. Money, speed, relocation and youth were ascendant – blues and jazz sang their anthems. Blues and jazz were themselves flexible enough to adapt to changes that continued at seemingly ever-faster rates, swallowing all prior conventions, throughout the twentieth century.

MAPLE LEAF RAG.
By King of Ragtime writers
Scott Joplin.
CAPITOL
DO NOT STAND IN FRONT OF ORCHESTRA

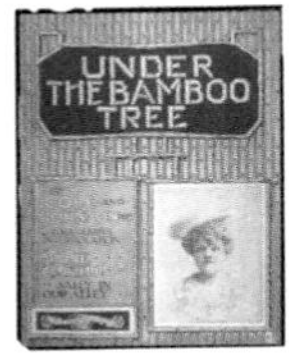

Sources & Sounds

KEY ARTISTS

Kid Ory

Charley Patton

Ma Rainey

Clarence Williams

Throughout their long histories, jazz and blues have been fundamentally linked – at some points more closely than others, certainly, but their intertwining roots in the post-Civil War African-American communities, among people liberated from slavery but still living under jim crow repression, mean that there will always be common ground between the two genres.

Echoes Of Distant Cultures

The blues was shaped by African culture, the experience of slavery and many other influences, but it emerged as a distinct form only around the turn of the twentieth century – some four decades after the abolition of slavery and several generations removed from the mother continent. African retentions in timbres, tones and rhythms, and in the functional nature of music in daily life by people who were not necessarily professional musicians, interacted in America with European musical traditions, including Scotch-Irish fiddle tunes, English ballads, Christian songs and marching bands. Slaves with musical talent learned to entertain whites at plantation dances, performing the popular dances and songs of the day. The work songs and hollers of those labouring in the fields often harked back to the chants of their African ancestors, while in the churches Protestant hymns took on an African-American character to emerge as 'Negro spirituals'. Africanisms survived in the work and game songs, call-and-response patterns, vocal and instrumental phrasings, syncopations, oral traditions, folk customs and beliefs, pentatonic scales and flattened 'blue notes', as well as in instrumentation.

'In the beginning, Adam had the blues, 'cause he was lonesome. So God helped him and created a woman. Now everybody's got the blues.'

Willie Dixon

Minstrels And Spirituals

After America's Civil War, itinerant songsters and travelling minstrel show troupes spread their music far and wide. Early forms of music that would become the blues began to develop not only on the plantations, where former slaves and their descendants now toiled as sharecroppers, but also in towns and cities along the Mississippi and Ohio Rivers and elsewhere. The music makers' repertoires variously included 'jump-ups' (unrelated lines sung over simple chorded accompaniments), ditties, old plantation melodies, breakdowns (uptempo dance pieces), church songs, bad man or folk hero ballads and derogatory 'coon songs' (sung in minstrel shows by blackface performers), as well as popular white music, show tunes and – in some areas, as black musicians acquired formal training – classical works. The jubilee singing of black spiritual ensembles drew national and international attention, and the ragtime craze that swept the country from the 1890s to the First World War established America's fascination with the secular music of African-Americans.

The blues drew from many sources to give voice to an African-American identity. The lyrics often expressed a desire to move on to a better place or a better mate; songs of lost love and mistreatment sometimes had a double meaning – as codified protests or commentary secretly directed towards the white boss man and his social order. Risqué sexual double entendres also abounded, as blues inherited the vulgar side of ragtime's early notoriety as low-class and disreputable, denounced by churchgoers as the 'devil's music'. It may have been born

Right
In Alabama and other parts of the Deep South, the blues developed as a form of dance music.

of sorrow and hardship, consigned to the margins of society, yet blues sought not to wallow in pain and misery but to raise the spirits in cathartic release, often with humour or irony – to get rid of the blues by singing them.

The Blues Begins To Spread

Blues took hold in Mississippi, Texas, Georgia, Louisiana, Missouri, the Carolinas and several other southern states. Waves of northward migration would eventually establish Chicago as the blues capital, but in earlier years St. Louis and Memphis were more significant urban blues centres. The cotton plantation system of the Mississippi Delta spawned an especially concentrated and prolific blues subculture, as workers sought weekend release from their toils at house parties, juke joints, country suppers, fish fries and picnics, or in the nearest towns' cafés, saloons, barrelhouses, nightclubs and brothels.

A primary function of the blues was as dance music, played by banjoists, mandolinists and guitarists; string bands with fiddles; harmonica blowers and washboard, fife and drum, pianists and jug bands. Most blues performers also worked as fieldhands or labourers, but some made a living from their music, playing for workers on plantations or in levee and lumber camps. In towns and cities black musicians were also able to join brass bands, mandolin clubs, singing quartets and dance orchestras.

Evidence Of Early Blues Songs

While most such recollections – including those of bluesmen such as Big Bill Broonzy (1893–1958) from Mississippi and Leadbelly (1888–1949) from northwest Louisiana – were published decades after the fact, a few researchers did file more timely reports of early blues or blues-like songs. Charles Peabody, a Harvard archeologist working on an excavation at the Stovall Plantation in the Mississippi Delta in 1901, wrote of the 'autochthonous music' he heard the black workers singing; folklorist Howard Odum collected a number of blues songs in Georgia and Mississippi, from both local musicians and travelling performers between 1905 and 1908, as well as some from North Carolina. Besides this, songs dating back to 1890 were collected by Gates Thomas in Texas. Various compositions published in the 1890s and early 1900s contained some structural or lyrical resemblance to blues, although the blues form had yet to congeal; 'I Got The Blues' by New Orleans violinist Antonio Maggio – the 1908 instrumental that was perhaps the earliest such number to use blues in the title – was advertised as an 'up-to-date rag'.

CLASSIC TRACKS

1898
Black Alfalfa: 'Black Alfalfa's Jail-House Shouting Blues'

1899
Scott Joplin: 'Maple Leaf Rag'

1901
Porter Steele: 'High Society'

1902
Robert Cole, James W. and J. Rosamond Johnson: 'Under The Bamboo Tree'
Belle Davis: 'The Honeysuckle And The Bee'

1903
W.C. Handy: 'Joe Turner Blues', 'Yellow Dog Rag'

1908
Antonio Maggio: 'I Got The Blues'
Bessie McCoy: 'Yama Yama Man'

1912
W.C. Handy: 'Memphis Blues'

1914
W.C. Handy: 'St. Louis Blues'
James Reese Europe: 'Castle House Rag'

1915
Jelly Roll Morton: 'Original Jelly Roll Blues'

1917
The Original Dixieland Jass Band: 'Bluin' The Blues', 'Tiger Rag'

Above
The beginnings of Delta blues can be traced back to the Mississippi cotton plantations.

see Daddy Stovepipe pp 31 *see* Big Bill Broonzy pp 104 *see* Leadbelly pp 116 *see* Work Songs pp 414

Few recordings of black performers were made in the earliest eras of cylinders, piano rolls and 78-rpm discs; of those that were made, most were spirituals, coon songs or comedy routines. The primary dissemination of black music was still done via sheet music (including 'ballits' sold on the streets by itinerant songwriters) and public performances. Blues had yet to make a name for itself and was in fact only just beginning to be called 'blues' – some early bluesmen remembered the songs being called 'reels' or 'reals'. But a folk blues repertoire was forming (although not yet being recorded) from songs such as 'Make Me A Pallet On The Floor', 'Joe Turner Blues', 'East St. Louis', 'Stack O' Lee' and 'John Henry', along with other southern airs noted by W.C. Handy (1873–1958) – whose own blues compositions would also become jazz standards.

Right
The 'father of the blues', composer and music collector W.C. Handy.

The Blues Meets Ragtime

'Jazz started in New Orleans,' Jelly Roll Morton (*c.* 1890–1941) declared in his monumental 1938 oral autobiography for the Library of Congress. Jazz also

Below
Canal Street, New Orleans, *c.* 1900, as jazz music was developing.

see Introduction pp 12 *see* Key Artists pp 22 *see* A–Z of Artists pp 26 *see* List of Artists pp 32

started in many other places across America; a new wave of musical sound, melded from turn-of-the-century African-American rivulets of song in the ragtime and the blues styles, reached middle America by the 1910s with the force of revelation. But in New Orleans, the music was fertilized and nurtured by a vibrant culture of many nationalities and ethnic groups: a melting pot of cultures from across the South.

Ragtime was a jubilant, rhythmically propulsive music in syncopated march time, and when forged together with the blues, these gifts from the African-American soul created a new music that rapidly circled the globe and became a primary expression of the modern American spirit. The world entered a new age, dancing and singing to the sounds of jazz. By 1918, the emerging new music had been named 'jass' (a slang term for sex) – or 'jazz', 'jaz', 'jas', even 'jazs' – by listeners fascinated by its manic energy and emotional exuberance. It fused the hot rhythms and lively animation of ragtime with the plangent harmonies and lyrical depth of the blues.

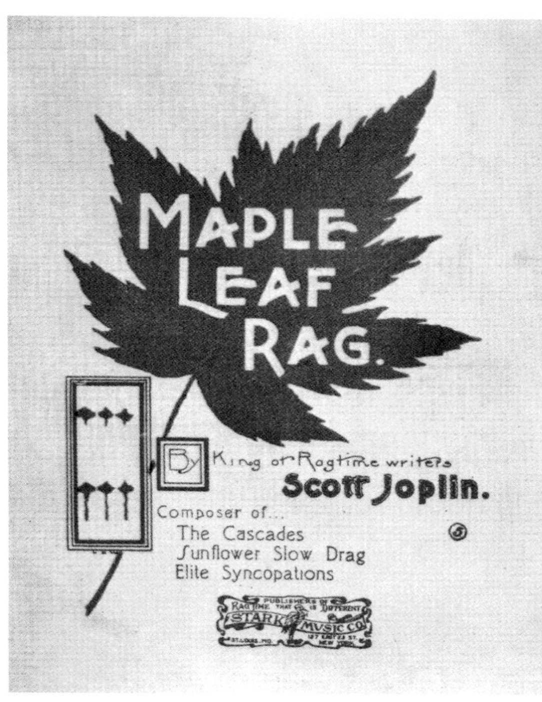

Left
The sheet music for 'Maple Leaf Rag'.

A Missouri pioneer and entrepreneur named John Stark heard black pianists playing their own works and decided to use his small music-publishing firm to proselytize America with their enticing, melodic music. In 1899, he published a piece by Scott Joplin (1868–1917), an up-and-coming young ragtime pianist who arrived in Missouri by way of Texas and Arkansas. It was named after a rough and ready Sedalia bar, the Maple Leaf Club. Joplin's 'Maple Leaf Rag' was a nationwide sensation, selling upwards of a million copies of Stark's sheet-music score.

The Many Sounds Of New Orleans

New Orleans had long, fertile traditions preserving all forms of black music. In Congo Square in the nineteenth century, generations of African-Americans gathered to sing, dance and drum, maintaining a lifeline to their homeland traditions. Strains of Creole music from the gumbo of New Orleans' mixed culture – French, Spanish, American-Indian and African-American – emerged and blended with the more formal ballroom music from south of the city (Cuban, Caribbean and Latin-American rhythms such as the habañera and the tango).

New Orleans, a city of constant, organized festivities teeming with social clubs, fraternal orders and non-stop partying, required the brash urgency of brass-band music. Bands were in demand for lawn parties, parades, holiday celebrations and funerals, while circuses, travelling minstrel/tent shows, revival meetings, medicine shows and carnivals all featured bands in which New Orleans musicians apprenticed themselves. Trumpeters like William Geary 'Bunk' Johnson (1889–1949) and Ernest 'Kid Punch' Miller (1894–1971) hit the circus-band circuit and brought

Below
The Mississippi riverboat SS *Capitol*.

see Jelly Roll Morton pp 60 *see* Punch Miller pp 80 *see* Ragtime pp 378 *see* New Orleans Jazz pp 380

back more new music. Musicians could also find work on the Mississippi riverboats, such as in the band of pianist Fate Marable (1890–1947), in which many future stars developed their skills.

A Swelling Flood Of Music

Various founts of new music fed the surging tide of jazz in the teens. In Storyville, the few square blocks set aside for licensed prostitution (known locally as 'the District'), piano 'professors' played dance tunes, blues, bawdy songs, Creole badinage and pop music. While brass bands, dance bands, ragtime pianists and blues singers retailed new and exciting musical forms, they inevitably traded and reconfigured them, absorbing the harmonies and rhythms heard in the dance halls, on riverboats and in the streets. Music for the larger bands was produced by publishers like John Stark, whose *Red Backed Book of Rags* gathered work by Joplin and other 'classic ragtime' writers and arranged them for small orchestras, giving the tunes a wider accessibility.

Similarly, blues made a leap forward into the public consciousness of America in 1912, when Baby Seals, Hart Wand and W.C. Handy became the first composers to publish blues sheet music, or at least to register blues with the copyright office. Many more 'blues' were to follow, often from the pens of New York songwriters. Not all compositions named 'blues' were actually blues in structure or feel – many such songs of the era were rags, vaudeville tunes or Tin Pan Alley pop pieces, with 'blues' fashionably attached to the end of the title. The real breakthrough for blues came with Handy's 'St. Louis Blues', which incorporated traditional folk and blues elements, along with a touch of habañera. In the years following its first publication in 1914, it became one of the most widely recorded compositions of all time and topped the sales lists for sheet music and piano rolls.

As much early jazz derived from musical scores as from invented or overheard music; in the city, musicians distinguished between readers ('musicianers') and illiterate improvisers ('routiners'). One white entrepreneur-agent, hustler and midwife to jazz was 'Papa' Jack Laine (1873–1966), a sometime drummer who ran a stable of brass bands and dance groups in New Orleans' thriving white jazz community. These white musicians rubbed elbows with African-American players and quickly adopted their musical styles and traditions, bringing with them lyrical strains of Italian and French operas, folk ditties, the sounds of Mediterranean bands and dance music from old Europe, all transposed into jazz time.

America Moves Forward

In the teens of the twentieth century, science, industry, technology and commerce were reshaping American culture. Women were within grasp of the vote,

Below
Bandleader Fate Marable (seated at the piano) with his Capitol Revue.

see Introduction pp 12 *see* Key Artists pp 22 *see* A–Z of Artists pp 26 *see* List of Artists pp 32

temperance forces were starting the country on a vast experiment with Prohibition, troops returning from Europe were unwilling to return to the farms, and rapidly expanding cities and suburbs absorbed rural communities. Ford's Model T personalized transportation forever, aircraft were becoming familiar sights overhead, women's hair got shorter – and their skirts did too. Popular music was also beginning to shift. White listeners learned blues harmonies for the first time; phonographs and piano rolls delivered more music to more homes. Language loosened and took on an African-American hue.

Jazz Music Comes Of Age

As the 1920s approached, jazz was maturing in New Orleans. Young players like cornettist Joseph 'Buddie' Petit (*c.* 1890–1931) developed flexible and infectious styles. The younger men recalled the earliest years of jazz in the city, when Charles 'Buddy' Bolden (1877–1931) led what was then called a 'ragtime' band and entranced the city with his powerful tone, his ability to swing both fast stomps and slow-drag blues, and his charisma as a soloist. But the golden standard of music during the years of the First World War was the Oliver-Ory band, which performed both for

Above

'Papa' Jack Laine – entrepreneur, drummer and bandleader.

see Kid Ory pp 22 *see* Eagle Band pp 28 *see* King Oliver pp 62 *see* Ragtime pp 378

dancing and as a brass band. It was led by Edward 'Kid' Ory (1886–1973), the first great trombonist in jazz, and by Joe 'King' Oliver, at that time still largely unchallenged for the cornet crown. Veterans remember how vigorous, inventive and solid this band was; it employed many upcoming 1920s jazz stars: Louis Armstrong (1901–71), cornet; Johnny Dodds (1892–1940), clarinet; and Warren 'Baby' Dodds (1898–1959), drums.

The largest landmark of the decade, however, was the 1917 advent of the Original Dixieland Jass Band, a vaudeville-touring quintet of white New Orleanians. The band opened in Reisenweber's Café in New York and cut landmark (and bestselling) records such as 'Livery Stable Blues', 'Tiger Rag', 'Ostrich Walk' and 'Bluin' the Blues', before branching out to tour in England and take London by storm. Thus, the Jazz Age was launched by a crew of young white men from the rough Irish Channel district of New Orleans.

The Blues On Wax

Blues music had already found its way into the recording studio by the time the Original Dixieland Jass Band cut their first sides. Prior to the record industry's discovery that there was a niche market for blues and jazz among black buyers – sparked by the success of Mamie Smith's (1883–1946) recording of 'Crazy Blues' in 1920 – what little black music was recorded was done so with white audiences in mind. The first singers to record any of Handy's blues in 1914 were white, in fact, and so were many other vaudeville singers who began to incorporate the blues (something of a novelty at the time) into their repertoires, including the young star billed as 'Queen of the Blues',

Below
The only known photograph of Buddy Bolden (standing second from left), *c.* 1895.

see Introduction pp 12 *see* Key Artists pp 22 *see* A–Z of Artists pp 26 *see* List of Artists pp 32

Above

New York City, *c.* 1917, where the arrival of the Original Dixieland Jass Band helped to launch the Jazz Age.

Marion Harris, and even Sophie Tucker. In New York, the most famous of the early black vaudevillians, Bert Williams, was in the nineteenth year of his recording career when he finally waxed 'I'm Sorry I Ain't Got It, You Could Have Had It If I Had It Blues' in 1919, followed by two blues in 1920.

Another black act, Dan Kildare's string band, featuring two banjos, had recorded 'St. Louis Blues' in 1917 in London, where they were entertaining white Britons at clubs and dance halls; they were billed as Ciro's Club Coon Orchestra. The guitar would supplant the banjo as blues came to fruition, but even so the record labels were late in bringing Sylvester Weaver, the first recorded blues guitarist, to the studio in 1923, and later still in rounding up the first generation of great blues singer-guitarists such as Blind Lemon Jefferson (c. 1897–1929), Lonnie Johnson (c. 1894–1970), Blind Blake (c. early 1890s–c. 1933) and Charley Patton (c. 1891–1934). Seminal figures such as Henry 'Ragtime Texas' Thomas (1874–1930), Frank Stokes and banjoists Gus Cannon (1885–1979) and Papa Charlie Jackson (c. 1890–1938) only began to record in the 1920s, but their music obviously echoed sounds from the dawn of the blues and before. The most extensive recording of early black ballads, pre-blues, and work and game songs was done by Leadbelly at the behest of folklorists John (1867–1948) and Alan (1915–2002) Lomax, but not until the 1930s and 1940s; such music held little appeal for commercial recording concerns.

The Early Blues Divas

Even from its emergence, blues was a multi-faceted phenomenon, developing both as a grassroots folk music in local community environments and as a professional entertainment medium on a more commercial level. It also continued to influence and be affected by musicians from other genres, within or outside the African-American culture – from jazz and gospel to old-time country and pop. The blues' first proven stars atop the black showbusiness ladder were the divas who travelled the vaudeville circuit co-ordinated by the Theater Owners Booking Association (TOBA, founded in Memphis in 1909); these included Ma Rainey (1886–1939), Sara Martin (1884–1955), Ida Cox (1896–1967) and a young Bessie Smith (1894–1937), among others. That they were advertised not just as singers but as 'comediennes' underscored the nature of their art; they could turn tears into laughter and survive in the face of adversity. When the doors to the recording industry opened to them in the 1920s, they were already on centre stage.

see Ma Rainey pp 24 *see* Sara Martin pp 29 *see* Original Dixieland Jass Band pp 31 *see* Johnny Dodds pp 72

Kid Ory

Key Artists

CLASSIC RECORDINGS

1926
Louis Armstrong's Hot Five: 'Muskrat Rumble', 'Hotter Than That'
Jelly Roll Morton's Red Hot Peppers: 'Smokehouse Blues', 'Doctor Jazz'

1926–27
King Oliver's Dixie Syncopators: 'Snag It', 'Every Tub'

1927
Louis Armstrong's Hot Seven: 'Potato Head Blues'

1944–45
Kid Ory's Creole Jazz Band: 'Ory's Creole Trombone'

1953
Kid Ory's Creole Jazz Band: 'Milenberg Joys', 'The Girls Go Crazy'

Above
New Orleans trombonist Kid Ory, with his Original Creole Jazz Band.

Edward 'Kid' Ory was born in LaPlace, Louisiana in 1886. He learned trombone and led a group of young musicians, the Woodland Band, which he took to New Orleans around 1908. He played with veteran jazzmen in the following years and gained a reputation as a powerful ensemble player and inspired soloist, especially where the blues were concerned.

'When we made those records we didn't have any expectation that they would be so successful'
Kid Ory on Louis Armstrong's Hot Five and Seven recordings

From Lala's To LA

In the teens, Ory worked at Pete Lala's Café and developed a partnership with Joe 'King' Oliver, the top trumpet man and leader in the city. The Ory-Oliver bands showcased rising talents, including the Dodds brothers, Jimmie Noone and Bill Johnson. When Oliver left for Chicago, Ory migrated to Los Angeles, where he assembled a group of musicians who followed him throughout his long career – bassist Ed 'Montudie' Garland, guitarist Arthur 'Bud' Scott, trumpeter Thomas 'Mutt' Carey and clarinetist Wade Whaley were all Ory loyalists, even during the periods in which the band was beset by feuds. Later stalwarts included pianist Albert Wesley 'Buster' Wilson and drummer Minor 'Ram' Hall. In 1922, Ory's band made history as the first African-American New Orleans jazz band to record, cutting sides for the tiny Sunshine label in LA; they accompanied blues singers and made instrumentals including a trick trombone speciality, 'Ory's Creole Trombone'.

Chicago Beckons

Ory left for Chicago in the mid-1920s, becoming a star with King Oliver's Dixie Syncopaters and with Louis Armstrong's Hot Five and Hot Seven. With Oliver and Armstrong, Ory became the model for the traditional 'tailgate' players of the era. Tailgate playing describes a jazz trombone style in which the instrument fulfils a largely rhythmic and riff-tagging role beneath the more melodic cornets and trumpets. This remained the norm until virtuoso players such as Jack Teagarden came along and reinvented the trombone as a lead instrument. The name itself derives from the trombone player's position at the back of the bandwagons, where the instrument's slide would not be in the way of the other musicians.

Ory also recorded with the New Orleans Wanderers and the New Orleans Bootblacks, as well as participating in Jelly Roll Morton's brilliant first Red Hot Peppers recordings. In the 1930s Ory, like many veteran jazzmen, found work too scarce to continue as a musician. He returned to California, where he was traced by Orson Welles in the early 1940s and brought back to prominence via radio and recordings. A central figure in the revival of New Orleans-style jazz in the 1940s to 1960s, Ory led bands in California, touring and recording prolifically with many old cohorts to the end of his days in 1973.

see Introduction pp 12 *see* Sources & Sounds pp 14 *see* A–Z of Artists pp 26

Charley Patton

Although not really the 'Founder of the Delta Blues', as one reissue album title touted, Charley Patton more than anyone defined not only the genre but also the image of the hard-living, rambling Delta bluesman, leaving trouble in his wake as he rolled from plantation to plantation and woman to woman. His rough vocal timbre – combined with the poor sound quality of the few surviving Paramount 78s he recorded – may have caused some listeners to regard him as primitive, yet even guitarists such as John Fahey, who wrote the first book on Patton, have been awed by both the power and the complexity of his music.

A Formidable Bluesman

Under the influence of an older guitarist named Henry Sloan on the Dockery Plantation, Patton, probably born in 1891 in Bolton, Mississippi, developed into the most famous and formidable Delta bluesman of the early twentieth century. By his biographers' accounts, he was leading the way long before his belated recording debut in 1929. Patton, of mixed black, white and Native-American ancestry, was an animated performer who clowned with the guitar and beat on the instrument for percussive effects. He taught or influenced guitarists such as Tommy Johnson, Willie Brown, Roebuck 'Pops' Staples and Howlin' Wolf during his stays in the Dockery area, and later, further north in the Delta, added Son House, Robert Johnson and others to the list. Tommy Johnson used some of Patton's themes on his own Victor recording debut in 1928.

Patton's Lasting Influence

Patton's first Paramount disc, 'Pony Blues'/'Banty Rooster Blues', was his biggest hit. His recorded repertoire drew from traditional black folk songs, white pop tunes, religious songs, dance pieces and frolics, as well as his own creative wellspring as a composer and storyteller. His records are noteworthy for his descriptions of topical events, such as the great Mississippi River flood of 1927, and for the local lore and real-life characters that he worked into songs such as 'Tom Rushen Blues' and 'High Sheriff Blues'. He died in 1934, but his influence persists into the twenty-first century; Bob Dylan included a tribute song – 'High Water Everywhere (For Charley Patton)' – on his 2001 album *Love And Theft*.

CLASSIC RECORDINGS

1929
'Banty Rooster Blues', 'Down The Dirt Road', 'High Water Everywhere', 'Pony Blues', 'Screamin' And Hollerin' The Blues', 'Shake It And Break It', 'Tom Rushen Blues'

1930
'Dry Well Blues'

1934
'High Sheriff Blues', 'Stone Pony Blues'

'If I were going to record for just my pleasure I would only record Charley Patton songs.'
Bob Dylan

Left
Charley Patton, the first great Delta bluesman and a key influence on all who followed.

see Tommy Johnson pp 29 *see* Louis Armstrong pp 44 *see* Willie Brown pp 121 *see* Jack Teagarden pp 136

Ma Rainey

CLASSIC RECORDINGS

1923
Madame 'Ma' Rainey (with Lovie Austin and her Blues Serenaders): 'Bo-Weavil Blues', 'Barrel House Blues'

1924
Ma Rainey: 'Shave 'Em Dry Blues'
Ma Rainey (with her Georgia Jazz Band): 'See See Rider Blues', 'Toad Frog Blues'

1925–27
Ma Rainey (with her Georgia Band): 'Blues Oh Blues', 'Ma Rainey's Black Bottom', 'Yonder Comes The Blues'

1926–28
Ma Rainey: 'Mountain Jack Blues', 'Daddy Goodbye Blues'

Gertrude 'Ma' Rainey, the 'Mother of the Blues', had been singing the blues for some two decades before she commenced her influential series of recordings for the Paramount label in 1923. She even laid claim to naming the music 'the blues' after hearing the singing of a young girl in Missouri in 1902, where Rainey was performing with a tent show.

Assassinators Of The Blues

Born Gertrude Pridgett on 26 April 1886, Rainey began performing in her native Columbus, Georgia as a schoolgirl, before joining a number of travelling revues and minstrel shows, working southern theatres, circuses, carnivals and other venues. She teamed with William 'Pa' Rainey, whom she married in 1904, to perform as 'Rainey and Rainey, Assassinators of the Blues'. Known for her flamboyant stage shows, jewelled attire and colourful lifestyle, she was already one of the best-known blues singers in the South when recruited by Paramount.

'When she opened her mouth, she was fascinating, and she made you forget everything.'
Jack Dupree

A Versatile Performer

Rainey helped to shape the character, style and presentation of blues in its formative years, and her role and stature in the blues genre escalated during her brief but prolific career (1923–28). Her records were noted not only for the powerful majesty of her singing, but also for the variety of outstanding accompaniment by acclaimed jazz, blues and jug-band musicians. Ma Rainey possessed an earthier, more downhome southern style than most of the early blues queens, and was effective working with bluesmen such as Tampa Red, Georgia Tom Dorsey and Blind Blake, as well as with jazz musicians. She retired in 1935 and died four years later, but her influence is evident in the work of her protégé Bessie Smith and many others. Among Rainey's classics were the original version of 'See See Rider', 'Bo-Weavil Blues', 'Moonshine Blues' and 'Ma Rainey's Black Bottom' (also the title of an award-winning play written in the 1990s by August Wilson, with a Rainey studio recording session as its setting).

Right
Ma Rainey, a flamboyant blues singer with a powerful voice who mentored others, including Bessie Smith.

see Introduction pp 12 *see* Sources & Sounds pp 14 *see* A–Z of Artists pp 26

Clarence Williams

Clarence Williams was born in 1898 in Plaquemine, Louisiana, migrating to New Orleans in the teens to play piano in the District and begin a long career as a composer, bandleader and musical promoter. He was manager of two early jazz venues – the Big 25 Club and Pete Lala's Café – hiring the best musicians in the city. He opened a publishing business with Armand J. Piron, the leader of a popular dance band operating at the Lake Pontchartrain resorts. In 1919 he partnered with the savvy publisher-writer Spencer Williams (no relation). They gathered, annotated and copyrighted musical numbers that were floating in the air around the dance halls, bars and brothels of the city, publishing such enduring mega-hits as 'None Of My Jelly Roll' and 'Royal Garden Blues'.

The Blue Five

Williams left for Chicago around 1917, pursuing publishing and becoming an agent for recording companies. In the 1920s he shifted to New York City as it became a hub for hot music. He assembled bands of friends from New Orleans for OKeh and Columbia Records, including the seminal Blue Five group, which united a young Louis Armstrong, just emerging as the most innovative soloist in jazz, and Sidney Bechet, who was beginning his long reign as king of the soprano saxophone. Williams featured his wife, Eva Taylor, as vocalist on many blues and pop numbers. Among important songs he recorded were 'Cakewalking Babies From Home', 'Papa De Da Da', 'Of All The Wrongs', 'Coal Cart Blues' and 'Texas Moaner Blues'. He also cut a series of Washboard Band recordings, including numbers from his ill-fated musical comedy, *Bottomlands* (1927), which he promoted in New York.

In The Studio

In his long career, Williams' gift for spotting fresh talent and potential musical hits was renowned. Among the first-rate musicians he assembled were trumpeters such as King Oliver, Jabbo Smith, Henry Allen, Ed Allen, Bubber Miley and Louis Metcalf. He recorded clarinetists such as Buster Bailey, Arville Harris and Albert Nicholas and trombonists Charlie Irvis and Ed Cuffee. He was the session piano player on many recordings – for example, he can be heard playing piano on Bessie Smith's classic track 'Nobody Knows You When You're Down And Out' – but he was most comfortable as a musical director for OKeh Records, and an arranger and composer of jazz and pop tunes.

With a fine ear for both novelty jazz material and songs that bridged the gap between pure jazz and pure pop, Williams was an important transmitter of New Orleans traditions to the East Coast musicians he met in his recording and publishing roles. In the 1930s, during the squeeze of the Depression, Williams closed his publishing office, turned to radio promotion and went on to run an antique store in Harlem. He died in 1965, having sold his vast catalogue to Decca Records in 1943.

CLASSIC RECORDINGS

1923–24
Clarence Williams' Blue Five: 'Cakewalking Babies From Home', 'Everybody Loves My Baby', 'Kansas City Man Blues', 'Mandy Make Up Your Mind', 'Texas Moaner Blues', 'Wildcat Blues'

1927
Clarence Williams & his Washboard Band: 'Cushion Foot Stomp', 'P.D.Q. Blues'

1928
Clarence Williams' Orchestra: 'Organ Grinder Blues', 'Wildflower Rag'

'He was very important in coaching and teaching and working on our artists. He could somehow manage to get the best out of them, and to this day hasn't received the credit he really deserves.'

Frank Walker

Above
Pianist, composer, arranger and musical director Clarence Williams (back left) with one of his bands.

see Georgia Tom Dorsey pp 27 *see* Bessie Smith pp 64 *see* Sidney Bechet pp 69 *see* James 'Bubber' Miley pp 79

A-Z of Artists

Above

Jazz great Papa Celestin, leader of the Original Tuxedo Jazz Orchestra.

Gus Cannon

(Vocals, banjo, jug, kazoo, guitar, fiddle, piano, 1885–1979)

A pioneering bluesman who became a central figure in the Memphis jug band scene, Gus Cannon may have been the first blues recording artist, if tales of music he recorded as early as 1898 are true. However, no documentary evidence of Cannon recordings has been retrieved prior to his Paramount sides of 1927; furthermore, if he did record almost 30 years earlier the music may not have been blues at all, for his repertoire also drew from pre-blues black and white folk and minstrel traditions. Cannon performed as Banjo Joe on medicine shows in the teens and 1920s and recorded his first sides under that name.

Inspired by the success of the Memphis Jug Band, Cannon reconfigured his act into Cannon's Jug Stompers and signed with Victor in 1928. Among the Cannon songs reworked by latter-day folk revivalists is 'Walk Right In', which became a number-one pop hit in the US for the Rooftop Singers in 1963. The notoriety enabled Cannon to record an album for Stax Records in 1963, although his participation in the blues revival of the 1960s was limited.

Papa Celestin

(Trumpet, vocals, 1884–1954)

Oscar 'Papa' Celestin was a much-loved New Orleans fixture, who started out with the Algiers Brass Band, under Henry Allen Sr. at the turn of the century. In 1910 he founded the Original Tuxedo Jazz Orchestra with trombonist William 'Baba' Ridgley. Celestin recorded with OKeh and Columbia in the mid-1920s, and his recordings of 'Original Tuxedo Rag' and 'Black Rag' stand up well as sizzling hot jazz or dance music in comparison with the recordings that King Oliver made at the time with his Creole Jazz Band.

Unlike many of his peers, Celestin stayed in New Orleans. After the glory days of the Original Tuxedo Jazz Orchestra, he led bands on Bourbon Street, made records and played regularly for radio broadcasts on a national ABC network show, 'Dixieland Jambake'. He was a sweet-toned trumpeter and a frog-voiced singer, vigorously selling sure-fire tunes like 'Li'l Liza Jane', 'Mama Don't Allow' and 'Bill Bailey'. His band featured elders including Alphonse Picou (clarinet), Bill Mathews (trombone), Ricard Alexis (bass) and Christopher 'Black Happy' Goldston (drums).

see Introduction pp 12 *see* Sources & Sounds pp 14 *see* Key Artists pp 22

Will Marion Cook

(Composer, arranger, violin 1869–1944)

Will Marion Cook was a highly educated musician, studying at Oberlin Conservatory and the Berlin Hochschule für Musik with virtuoso Joseph Joachim (he also studied briefly with Antonín Dvorák). He worked as a composer with Bob Cole's All-Star Stock Company, a seminal force in early African-American musical comedy production. (The group later employed the Johnson brothers – J. Rosamund and James Weldon – to write pioneering all-black musicals such as *The Shoo-fly Regiment*, 1907 and *The Red Moon*, 1909.) At this time, African-American musical comedy was performed on and off Broadway, but only fragments or sections were recorded, despite the popularity of many of the shows.

Cook dreamed of working with the stellar African-American vaudeville team of (Bert) Williams and (George W.) Walker. In 1898, together with poet Paul Lawrence Dunbar, he wrote *Clorindy*, or *The Origin Of The Cakewalk*. This innovative show starred popular singer-composer Ernest Hogan, as well as a cast of 40 singers and dancers. Very successful, *Clorindy* set a new course for black musicals. This success assured Cook of his dream – he worked for Williams and Walker for more than a decade, while continuing to collaborate with Dunbar on *In Dahomey* (1903), *In Abyssina* (1906) and *In Bandanna Land* (1908). In 1918, Cook formed the New York (or American) Syncopated Orchestra, with settings for the new jazz music. In the 1920s he led Clef Club ensembles and worked with many important musicians, including pioneer big-band leader Fletcher Henderson and singer-actor Paul Robeson. Cook's musical *Swing Along* (1929) displayed his earlier work.

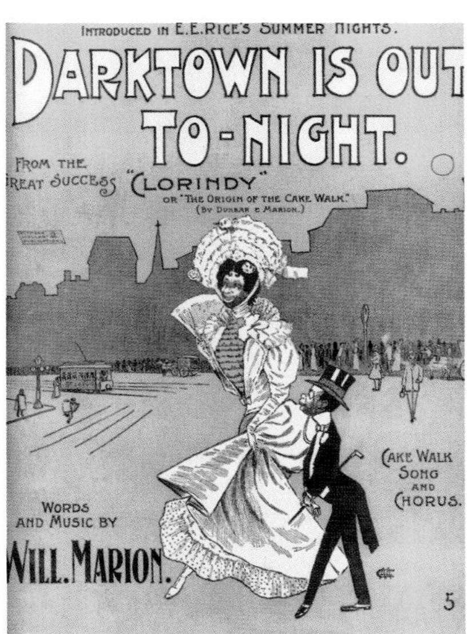

Left
The music for a song from Will Marion Cook's *Clorindy*, or *The Origin Of The Cakewalk*.

Georgia Tom Dorsey

(Vocals, piano, 1899–1993)

Thomas A. Dorsey earned his greatest fame as the 'Father of Gospel Music' after leaving his blues career behind in 1932, but in his early days he was an important blues performer, songwriter, arranger and studio musician. In his youth in ragtime-era Atlanta and in Chicago from 1916, Dorsey developed his piano-playing skills at barrelhouses and rent parties. He also worked with jazz orchestras and Ma Rainey's band before teaming up with Tampa Red in 1928. Dorsey composed songs for the duo as well as material for Ma Rainey and others, and had a special knack for the risqué double entendre – ironic for a man best known for religious classics such as 'Precious Lord (Take My Hand)'.

Dorsey achieved his greatest success as a music publisher and was founder of the National Convention of Gospel Choirs and Choruses, Inc. Despite his stature in religious circles, Dorsey continued to give credit to the blues, both as a valid expression of the human condition and as a contributing element in the development and acceptance of gospel music.

Below
The multi-talented Georgia Tom Dorsey (third from left) with Ma Rainey's band.

see Ma Rainey pp 24 *see* King Oliver pp 62 *see* Fletcher Henerson pp 74 *see* Tampa Red pp 135

Eagle Band

(Instrumental group, 1900–17)

The Eagle Band, originally led by Buddy Bolden, was an extremely popular and influential New Orleans ensemble. Frankie Duson (or Dusen) (1880–1940), a powerful tailgate trombonist, joined the band in 1906 and went on to take over the band when Bolden suffered a mental collapse the following year. Subsequently, Duson employed various Bolden alumni – guitarists Lorenzo Staulz and Brock Mumford, clarinetist Frank Lewis and cornettist Edward Clem. He also chose younger sidemen who became major jazz stalwarts – Bunk Johnson, Joe Oliver, Sidney Bechet, Johnny Dodds and 'Big Eye' Louis Nelson. Drummers Baby Dodds, Henry Zeno and Abbey 'Chinee' Foster also played with the band.

Duson was associated with the raggy and bluesy music of Bolden, and in the song 'Buddy Bolden's Blues', retailed by Jelly Roll Morton in the 1930s to celebrate the Bolden legend, Duson's name was mentioned: 'I thought I heard Frankie Duson shout,/Gal, give me that money,/Or I'm gonna to beat it out….' The Eagle Band itself sported a simple and catchy motto: 'The Eagles fly high/And never lose a feather./If you miss this dance,/You'll have the blues forever.' Unfortunately for jazz history, Duson's bands never recorded.

Below
Formidable guitar picker and gentle folk blues narrator Mississippi John Hurt.

Mississippi John Hurt

(Vocals, guitar, 1892–1966)

A songster and fingerpicking guitarist from Avalon, Mississippi, John Hurt excelled in the pre-blues black folk ballad tradition as well as in blues, gospel and dance instrumentals. He spent most of his life working on farms and entertaining at local parties and functions for both blacks and whites. His first opportunity to record came in 1928, when the white Mississippi fiddle/guitar duo of Narmour and Smith informed OKeh Records of a talented black guitar picker that they knew.

Hurt not only contributed songs such as 'Candy Man' and 'Avalon Blues' to the blues canon, but also reinvigorated the folk legends of Casey Jones, Frankie & Albert and Stack O' Lee. Hurt enjoyed a new career on the folk-blues circuit from 1963 until his death, recording several excellent albums and charming festival and coffeehouse audiences with his gentle nature and warm, captivating music.

Bunk Johnson

(Trumpet, 1889–1949)

William Geary 'Bunk' Johnson, a New Orleans trumpeter with good reading and improvising skills, said that he played in Buddy Bolden's pioneer band before 1900. He was certainly associated with Frankie Duson and other Bolden cohorts, and was famous as a showy, lyrical soloist. Johnson's nickname rose from his loquacity, and he was an inveterate self-promoter (he claimed to have mentored Louis Armstrong, among others). He played with Adam Olivier's orchestra in the city and then worked mainly in western Louisiana, and on the road with tent shows and other itinerant outfits. Johnson left music in 1933 after an affray in which bandleader Evan Thomas was murdered. He was rediscovered in New Iberia, Louisiana by William Russell and his co-authors of the influential *Jazzmen* (among the first serious jazz histories) in the late 1930s.

After correspondence, in which Johnson claimed he could play again if he were equipped with false teeth and a trumpet, Russell and friends rehabilitated Johnson and set him on the path to a new career with other New Orleans jazz veterans. In the early 1940s, Johnson led bands, recorded steadily for Russell's American Music label and toured, with a long stand in New York City from 1945–46. The band he led continued for decades under the leadership of clarinetist George Lewis, exerting a worldwide impact on the jazz revival.

Johnson generated controversy, epitomizing the acrimony between early jazz advocates ('Mouldy Figs') and zealots for the emerging modern jazz ('Modernists'). His example inspired the jazz revival of ensuing decades, and he joined the pantheon of New Orleans trumpet stars that included Bolden, King Oliver, Louis

see Introduction pp 12 *see* Sources & Sounds pp 14 *see* Key Artists pp 22

Above

Trumpeter Bunk Johnson, shown here playing with Leadbelly.

Armstrong and others. Struggling with alcoholism, Johnson declined in the late 1940s, leaving one final recording session with a hand-picked band of New York musicians which shows his personal concept of hot jazz.

Tommy Johnson

(Vocals, guitar, c. 1896–1956)

Johnson was a highly influential early blues artist due to the impact of his three 1928 records for Victor, which earned him a niche as Mississippi's first black recording star. Johnson recorded only three more 78s after that, for Paramount, plus a few unissued sides, but the songs he recorded for Victor (including 'Cool Drink Of Water', 'Big Road Blues', 'Maggie Campbell Blues' and 'Canned Heat Blues') became entrenched in the repertoires of many bluesmen to follow.

Inspired by Charley Patton, Johnson developed a unique approach, employing falsetto accents and hypnotic guitar riffs. He learned from an older brother, LeDell, who later told folklorist David Evans a tale of Tommy selling his soul to the devil at a crossroads – a story associated today with Robert Johnson (no relation). Johnson's reputation as a great bluesman was equalled perhaps only by his notoriety as a drinker, which no doubt contributed to his quick decline. He ceased recording after 1929 and spent his remaining years playing streets and house parties in Mississippi.

Sara Martin

(Vocals, 1884–1955)

Martin, an early classic blues singer, was signed by Clarence Williams for OKeh Records in 1922, at the beginning of the blues craze. While she was a pop-style singer, she was also able to pitch the blues in a rough-and-ready way. She recorded with Williams-led jazz groups, with such illustrious accompanists as King Oliver and Sidney Bechet (on some sessions she sang as 'Margaret Johnson' or 'Sally Roberts').

Martin was often accompanied by Thomas Morris (cornet) and Charlie Irvis (trombone), both blues specialists. On 'Death Sting Me Blues' (1928), Martin matches Joe Oliver's intensity, and on 'Atlanta Blues' (1923) she delivers the old folk melody with great dignity. Her diction was clear, and she had a good ear for plangent blues that were not over-worn. In 1929, she appeared on film with the immortal Bill 'Bojangles' Robinson in *Hello Bill*. She left showbusiness in the Depression and returned to Louisville.

see Charley Patton pp 23 *see* Clarence Williams pp 25 *see* Johnny Dodds pp 72 *see* George Lewis pp 77

New Orleans Rhythm Kings

(Instrumental group, 1922–25)

The New Orleans Rhythm Kings (NORK) were one of the major white groups in early New Orleans jazz; after a run at Chicago's Friar's Club in 1922, they recorded with Paul Mares (trumpet), George Brunis (trombone), Leon Roppolo (clarinet), Jack Pettis (alto sax), Elmer Schoebel (piano), Lew Black (banjo), Steve Brown (bass) and Frank Snyder (drums). Mares was a skilful, Oliver-esque lead, Roppolo a highly gifted clarinetist, Schoebel a fine arranger and composer, and Brown a top-flight bassist. Sometime associates were drummer (and future bandleader) Ben Pollack, pianist Mel Stitzel and others.

The NORK's sound was different from the Original Dixieland Jass Band (ODJB), with slow blues and relaxed, mid-tempo tunes that swung. They emulated Joe Oliver's style, and recorded some of his music ('Sweet Lovin' Man'), some from the ODJB book ('Tiger Rag') and some basic New Orleans material ('Maple Leaf Rag'). They also recorded standards still played: 'She's Cryin' For Me' and 'Angry'. In 1923 the NORK made history, playing with Jelly Roll Morton on piano to create the first interracial band recording session on sides that included 'Sobbin' Blues'.

Original Creole Orchestra

(Instrumental group, 1912–18)

Freddie Keppard's Original Creole Orchestra toured extensively during the teens as an early harbinger of authentic New Orleans jazz, reaching big-time vaudeville's prestigious Orpheum circuit. Powerful pioneer trumpeter Keppard (1889–1933) had with him Creole clarinetists George Baquet, 'Big Eye' Louis Nelson and Jimmie Noone, pioneer bassist Bill Johnson and multi-instrumentalist Dink Johnson as a drummer.

The band created a sensation among vaudeville audiences well before the ODJB hit New York. Keppard reputedly refused to record for fear of rival trumpeters 'stealing his stuff'. While the band did not record, Sidney Bechet appropriated a piece of mock-orientalia from Keppard, 'Egyptian Fantasy' (drawn from Abe Olman's 1911 piano rag 'Egyptia'), and recorded the track. The band broke up during 1918 and Bill Johnson set about finding a replacement for Keppard; after contacting Buddy Petit, Johnson settled on King Oliver. Keppard went to Chicago in the 1920s, playing with important orchestras run by Charles 'Doc' Cook. He recorded with the Cook big band and with a small washboard band, demonstrating hot styles from wah-wah to plunger blues to a stirring open horn of startling volume.

see Introduction pp 12 *see* Sources & Sounds pp 14 *see* Key Artists pp 22

Original Dixieland Jass Band

(Instrumental group, 1917–25)

The Original Dixieland Jass (or Jazz) Band were five young white musicians from working-class uptown New Orleans – Nick LaRocca (cornet), Larry Shields (clarinet), Eddie Edwards (trombone), Tony Spargo (real name Sbarbaro, drums) and Henry Ragas (piano). All alumni of 'Papa' Jack Laine's stable of bands, they went to Chicago and then to New York, where their music created a sensation. The word 'jazz' or 'jass' was not spoken in polite circles (it was a slang term for sex), but their frenetic and wild music made it suddenly acceptable.

After making important recordings – including 'Livery Stable Blues'/'Dixie Jass One Step' (1917), the first jazz recording released – and conquering New York society, in 1919 the band went on to a stand in Britain (with Billy Jones on piano), before returning to the US and to further tours and recordings. They disbanded in the mid-1920s but were reunited briefly (with ragtimer J. Russel Robinson on piano) in 1936, making a *March Of Time* short film and cutting new recordings of the ODJB standards, including 'Clarinet Marmalade', 'Skeleton Jangle' and 'Original Dixieland One-Step'. They also recorded with a large swing band backing them.

Daddy Stovepipe

(Vocals, harmonica, guitar, 1867–1963)

Daddy Stovepipe – a.k.a. Mobile, Alabama native Johnny Watson – is an obscure figure, with only a scattering of recording sessions to his credit, but he represents an important era of blues and pre-blues music. He was not only one of the first downhome blues performers to record (in 1924), but his 1867 birth date is the earliest yet documented for any artist in the blues discographies: he was, in fact, decades older than the blues genre itself.

His recorded work has much in common with the jug-band melodies of Memphis, a similarity enhanced by the addition of his wife, Mississippi Sarah, on vocals and jug during the 1930s. Watson performed as a one-man band on streets and in medicine shows in Mississippi, Texas and elsewhere, before going to Chicago, where he played for tips on Maxwell Street. He was one of at least three pre-war bluesmen to record using the name Stovepipe, either in reference to the stovepipe hat or a stovepipe used as a musical instrument.

Far Left

Trumpeter Freddie Keppard, leader of the Original Creole Orchestra.

Below

The Original Dixieland Jass Band *c.* 1916 with the line-up that preceded their recording career: l–r Tony Spargo, Eddie Edwards, Nick LaRocca, Alcide 'Yellow' Nunez, Henry Ragas.

see Jelly Roll Morton pp 60 *see* Sidney Bechet pp 69 *see* Jimmie Noone pp 81 *see* Ben Pollack pp 81

List of Artists

Entries appear in the following order: name, music style, year(s) of popularity, instruments, country of origin.

Baquet, George, Traditional Jazz; New Orleans Jazz, 1910s–1940s, Clarinet, American
Beaman, Lottie, Classic Blues, 1910s–1930s, Vocals, American
Bigeou, Esther, Delta Blues, 1910s–1930s, Vocals, American
Bocage, Peter, Dixieland; Big Band; New Orleans Jazz, 1900s–1960s, Cornet, violin, American
Bolden, Buddy, Traditional Jazz; New Orleans Jazz, 1900s–1930s, Cornet, bandleader, American
Bradford, Perry, Traditional Jazz, 1910s–1930s, Piano, composer, producer, American
Brown, Lillyn, Ragtime, 1890s–1930s, Vocals, American
Brown, Richard 'Rabbit', New Orleans Blues, c. 1900s–1930s, Vocals, American
Brown, Tom, Dixieland, 1900s–1950s, Trombone, bass, American
Cannon, Gus, Country Blues, 1910s–1960s, Vocals, banjo, jug, kazoo, guitar, fiddle, piano, American
Carey, Mutt, New Orleans Jazz, 1910s–1940s, Trumpet, American
Celestin, Papa Oscar, New Orleans Jazz, 1910s–1950s, Trumpet, bandleader, American
Christian, Emile, Traditional Jazz; New Orleans Jazz, 1910s–1960s, Trombone, American
Connolly, Dolly, Ragtime, 1900s–1920s, Vocals, American
Cook, Will Marion, Ragtime; Vaudeville, 1910s–1930s, Composer, arranger, violin, American
Daddy Stovepipe, Zydeco, Mississippi Blues Downhome Blues, 1910s–1960s, Guitar, harmonica, American
Dorsey, Georgia Tom, Country Blues, 1910s–1930s, Vocals, piano, composer, American
Dunn, Johnny, Traditional Jazz, 1910s–1930s, Trumpet, bandleader, American
Eagle Band, New Orleans Jazz, 1900s–1910s, Various instruments, American
Europe, Jim, Ragtime, 1900s–1910s, Bandleader, entrepreneur, songwriter, American
Garland, Ed 'Montudi', New Orleans Jazz, 1900s–1970s, Bass, American
Gottschalk, Louis Moreau, Ragtime, 1890s, Piano, composer, American
Goudie, Frank 'Big Boy', New Orleans Jazz, 1910s–1960s, Saxophone, clarinet, trumpet, American
Handy, W.C., Delta Blues, 1900s–1920s, Vocals, composer, American
Harney, Ben, Ragtime, 1890s–1900s, Piano, composer, Austrian
Hill, Chippie, Chicago Jazz, 1910s–1940s, Vocals, American
Hogan, Ernest, Ragtime, 1890s–1900s, Composer, American
Howard, Darnell, Delta Blues, 1910s–1960s, Clarinet, violin, saxophone, American
Hurt, Mississippi John, Country Blues; Work Songs, 1910s–1940s; 1960s, Guitar, vocals, composer, American
Jackson, Jim, Country Blues, 1910s–1930s, Guitar, American
Jackson, Tony, New Orleans Jazz, 1890s–1920s Piano, vocals, American
Johnson, Bill, New Orleans Jazz, 1900s–1970s, Bass, guitar, banjo, American
Johnson, Bunk, New Orleans Jazz, 1910s–1940s, Trumpet, American
Johnson, Tommy, Delta Blues; Country, 1910s–1930s, Guitar, vocals, composer, American
Jones, Davey, Swing; New Orleans Jazz, 1910s–1950s, Trumpet, mellophone, horn, drums, saxophone, American
Joplin, Scott, Ragtime, 1900s–1910s, Piano, composer, American
Jordan, Luke, Country Blues, 1910s–1940s, Vocals, American
Kelly, Chris, New Orleans Jazz, 1910s–1920s, Trumpet, American
Laine, Papa Jack, Ragtime, 1880s–1910s, Drums, horn, leader, American
Lewis, Ted, Traditional Jazz, 1910s–1960s, Clarinet, vocals, American
Marable, Fate, New Orleans Jazz, 1910s–1940s, Piano, calliope, leader, American
Marrero, Lawrence, New Orleans Jazz, 1910s–1950s, Banjo, guitar, American
Martin, Sara, Country Blues; New Orleans Jazz, 1910s–1930s, Vocals, American
Nelson, Louis 'Big Eye', New Orleans Jazz, 1900s–1940s, Clarinet, American
New Orleans Rhythm Kings, New Orleans Jazz, 1910s–1920s, Various instruments, American
Numez, Alcide 'Yellow', New Orleans Jazz, 1900s–1930s, Clarinet, American
Original Creole Orchestra, New Orleans Jazz, 1910s, Various instruments, American
Original Dixieland Jass Band, New Orleans Jazz, 1910s–1950s, Various instruments, American
Ory, Kid, New Orleans Jazz, 1910s–1960s, Trombone, vocals, composer, American
Palmer, Roy, New Orleans Jazz; Chicago Jazz, 1910s–1930s, Trombone, American
Parenti, Tony, New Orleans Jazz, 1910s–1970s, Clarinet, saxophones, American
Patton, Charley, Delta Blues; Country Blues, 1910s–1930s, Guitar, vocals, composer, American
Perez, Manuel, New Orleans Jazz, 1900s–1940s, Cornet, American
Picou, Alphonse, New Orleans Jazz, 1890s–1950s, Clarinet, composer, American
Piron, Armand, Swing, 1910s–1940s, Violin, composer, American
Rainey, Ma, Delta Blues, 1910s–1930s, Vocals, American
Rena, Kid, New Orleans Jazz, 1910s–1940s, Trumpet, American
Roberts, Luckey, Ragtime, 1910s–1960s, Piano, composer, American
Robertson, Zue, New Orleans Jazz; Chicago Jazz, 1910s–1940s, Trombone, American
Robichaux, John, New Orleans Jazz, 1890s–1930s, Violin, bass, drums, accordion, leader, American
Signorelli, Frank, Dixieland; Swing, 1910s–1950s, Piano, composer, American
Spargo, Tony, Dixieland, 1910s–1960s, Drums, kazoo, American
Spikes Brothers, Swing; Big Band, 1900s–1920s, Entrepreneurs, American
Stokes, Frank, Country Blues, 1910s–1920s, Guitar, American
Sweatman, Wilbur, Ragtime, 1900s–1930s, Clarinet, leader, composer, American
Thomas, George, Texas Blues, 1910s–1920s, Composer, piano, American
Tio Jr., Lorenzo, New Orleans Jazz, 1900s–1930s, Clarinet, saxophone, arranger, oboe, American
Turpin, Tom, Ragtime, 1890s, Composer, American
Walker, Willie, Ragtime, 1910s–1930s, Guitar, American
Williams, Clarence, New Orleans Jazz; Swing, 1910s–1940s, Piano, vocals, arranger, bandleader, composer, American
Williams, Spencer, Swing, 1900s–1950s, Composer, piano, vocals, American

DO NOT STAND IN FRONT OF ORCHESTRA

see Introduction pp 12 *see* Sources & Sounds pp 14 *see* Key Artists pp 22 *see* A–Z of Artists pp 26

see Papa Celestin pp 26 *see* Eagle Band pp 28 *see* New Orleans Rhythm Kings pp 30 *see* Original Creole Orchestra pp 30

THE TWENTIES

The 1920s was, without doubt, the Jazz Age. Workers and the newly burgeoning middle class turned into consumers due to relatively higher wages. The international political advantages that came from having just won a major war buttressed a 'lost generation' of artistic types, who took up residence in Europe. New moral codes, sophistication and cynicism abounded. Some African-Americans benefited from the prosperity, but far from all of them. It was the age of the Harlem Renaissance, of black sports heroes, black revues on Broadway and exotic 'jungle music' in New York and abroad. Yet the Great Migration brought tens of thousands of former farm workers from the southern US to northern industrial areas, seeking jobs and fairer treatment. Although in many ways conditions were better than they had been back home, racist oppression did not end. Corrupt urban governments and landlords exploited the new immigrant population, while employers and labour unions prevented black workers from earning wages equivalent to those of their white counterparts. Meanwhile, back in the South, with the Ku Klux Klan trumpeting white supremacy, it sometimes seemed as though conditions were scarcely better than they had been under slavery.

Against the backdrop of new wealth juxtaposed with poverty and desperation, blues and jazz grew and took root as never before among African-Americans, white Americans and audiences overseas. Advances in the recording industry and radio broadcasts made them fully fledged popular musics. From acoustic guitar pickers on the streets of Texas towns to the 'classic blues' that women sang in well-appointed theatres backed by jazz musicians, from New Orleans orphan trumpeters to would-be Dukes from black Washington, listeners and dancers responded to a newly charged atmosphere of interchange, creativity and inspiration.

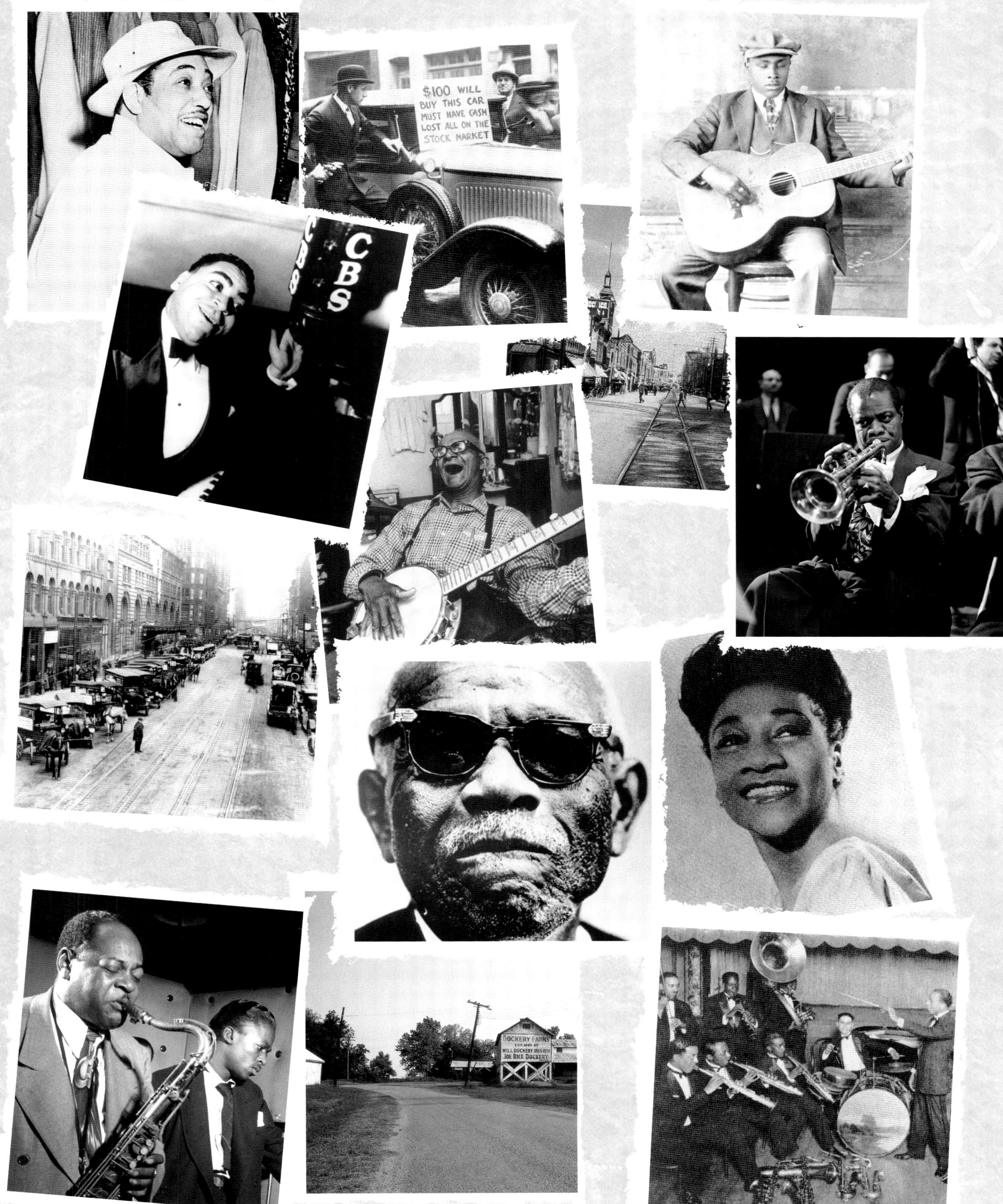
$100 WILL
BUY THIS CAR
MUST HAVE CASH
LOST ALL ON THE
STOCK MARKET
CBS
DOCKERY FARMS
JOE RICE DOCKERY

Sources & Sounds

KEY ARTISTS

Louis Armstrong
Bix Beiderbecke
Leroy Carr
Duke Ellington
Blind Lemon Jefferson
Lonnie Johnson
Jelly Roll Morton
King Oliver
Bessie Smith

The 1920s saw the shift of both jazz and blues music from their bases in particular communities to more widespread audiences, through touring, migration, the more frequent recording and increased circulation of jazz and blues records, and radio broadcasts.

With many seminal jazz figures heading north, the epicentre of jazz moved from its birthplace in New Orleans to Chicago. One of the events that caused this mass exodus of pioneering musicians from the Crescent City was the official closing of Storyville, the city's red-light district, in 1917. In 1898, in an attempt to control prostitution, alderman Sidney Story had proposed a city ordinance to confine illegal trafficking to an area of New Orleans bordered on the north by Robertson and on the south by Basin Street. He was determined that such vice would be contained within this area, which became known as Storyville. It flourished as a red-light district for 20 years, providing many musicians with gainful employment in the various sporting houses that flourished there. In 1898, there were about 2,200 registered prostitutes working and advertising their services in Storyville, but by 1917, that number had dwindled to 388 and so the employment possibilities for jazz musicians were severely diminished. Storyville was eventually closed for good by the Navy on the grounds that it was illegal to operate houses of prostitution within five miles of a military institution.

'Chicago was really jumping around that time [1923]. The Dreamland was in full bloom. The Lincoln Gardens, of course, was still in there. The Plantation was another hot spot at that time. But the Sunset, my boss' place, was the sharpest of them all, believe that.'

Louis Armstrong

From Crescent City To Windy City

Clarinet great Sidney Bechet (1897–1959) was among the first to leave the Crescent City and travel north. In 1917, just as New Orleans' stringent vice laws came into effect, he hooked up with the Bruce & Bruce Stock Company for a whirlwind tour of the Midwest, ending up in Chicago in November of that year. Meanwhile, trombonist and prominent bandleader Edward 'Kid' Ory (1886–1973) went west in 1919 – probably for medical reasons – and ended up in Los Angeles, where in 1922 he led the first African-American New Orleans group to make a record (under the name Spike's Seven Pods of Pepper Orchestra). Cornettist Joe 'King' Oliver (1885–1938), formerly a sideman in Ory's New Orleans group, also left to seek his fortune in Chicago in February 1919 and formed his own seminal band, followed in 1923 by itinerant musician Jelly Roll Morton (1890–1941) who would record there with his Red Hot Peppers; both became key figures on the Windy City's burgeoning hot jazz scene.

Right
New Orleans clarinet virtuoso Sidney Bechet.

Far Right Top
1920s Chicago, which became the thriving centre of jazz music.

Far Right Bottom
Louis Armstrong (second from right) with Erskine Tate's Band at Chicago's Vendome Theater.

see Introduction pp 34 *see* Key Artists pp 44 *see* A–Z of Artists pp 68 *see* List of Artists pp 88

CLASSIC RECORDINGS

1920
Mamie Smith: 'Crazy Blues'

1922
Fats Waller: 'Ain't Misbehavin''

1923
James P. Johnson: 'Charleston'

1926
Louis Armstrong's Hot Five: 'Muskrat Rumble'
Blind Lemon Jefferson: 'That Black Snake Moan'
Bessie Smith: 'Young Woman's Blues'

1927
Duke Ellington Orchestra: 'Black and Tan Fantasy'

1928
Scrapper Blackwell: 'Kokomo Blues'
Blind Willie McTell: 'Statesboro Blues'
Pine Top Smith: 'Pine Top's Boogie-Woogie'

The Jazz Age Begins

Chicago held the promise of a new life for the southern black population, which left behind the cotton fields for the blast furnaces, factories and slaughterhouses of the big northern cities; an estimated half million southern blacks arrived in Chicago before 1920. A centrally located transportation link between Los Angeles and New York, Chicago was also an attractive destination for working jazz and, in later years, blues musicians, many of whom worked in the gangster-owned speakeasies created in reaction to the Volstead Act of 1919 outlawing the manufacture and sale of alcohol in the United States. What followed was the 'Roaring Twenties', a decade marked by prosperity and a new vitality and spirit of experimentation in the wake of the First World War; the period was underscored by a prevailing air of good times, in spite of the repressive era of Prohibition. The Jazz Age was a time when young, uninhibited people, fuelled by a new permissiveness, sought illegal booze, unregulated revelry and hot music.

In Chicago, jazz matured at the hands of its finest composers and practitioners, including Bechet, Ory, Oliver, Morton, Louis Armstrong (1901–71) and others who held forth on the city's predominantly black South Side, on a nine-block stretch of State Street known as 'The Stroll'. There, jazz lovers could choose between the Lincoln Gardens, Pekin Inn, Dreamland

see **Kid Ory pp 22** *see* **Jelly Roll Morton pp 60** *see* **Sidney Bechet pp 69** *see* **Chicago Jazz pp 380**

Right
Dockery's plantation in Mississippi, where Charley Patton honed his craft.

Far Right
Blind Willie McTell was among the blues musicians based along the Eastern Seaboard.

Below
Banjo player Gus Cannon, whose knowledge of blues music came largely from the radio.

Ballroom, Plantation Café, Elite Café, Vendome, Apex Club, Sunset Café and other spots where hot jazz flowed nightly. It was in this black neighbourhood that the young, white jazz-seeking teenagers who attended Austin High School on Chicago's white, middle-class West Side congregated at the Lincoln Gardens to hear King Oliver's Creole Jazz Band, featuring the exceptional talents of Louis Armstrong and Johnny Dodds (1892–1940). By 1923, Chicago had become the centre of the jazz universe. The traditional, easy-going attitude underlying the New Orleans sound was slowly being replaced with a more energetic, fast-paced and competitive edge that surviving in the big city required.

The Blues As Folk Music

While jazz spread northwards and found new strongholds, blues retained its rural roots in some respects, while it simultaneously began to infiltrate more urban areas. Although one still often hears the term 'folk music' – a label that implies rustic simplicity, ingenuous lack of artifice and a hand-to-hand passing down of ideas from mentor to student – to describe much of the blues played and recorded during the 1920s, the reality and the music itself were far more complex than that. No doubt there were strong regional and local traditions that might be described as 'folk', some centred around southern plantations like Dockery's, where Charley Patton (c. 1891–1934) had

see Introduction pp 34 *see* Key Artists pp 44 *see* A–Z of Artists pp 68 *see* List of Artists pp 88

learned from older guitarists such as Henry Sloan; others more broadly based, such as along the Eastern Seaboard between Georgia and the Carolinas, where Blind Blake (*c.* early 1890s–*c.* 1933), Blind Willie McTell (1901–59), Blind Boy Fuller (1908–41), Rev. Gary Davis (1896–1972) and others interacted and shared ideas. Certainly, many blues songs' lyrical content, as well as their harmonic and melodic structures, rhythms and even, arguably, the 12-bar form itself, could be traced to traditions that extended back for generations.

But at the same time, even in remote, rural areas in the 1920s, people were listening to radios and purchasing (or at least hearing) records. One need only listen to the ragtime-influenced guitar patterns played by a 'folk' blues artist such as Blind Blake, or the melange of blues, pop tunes, vaudeville-like comedy routines and novelty songs purveyed by the Mississippi Sheiks to know that these were artists who had a keen ear for 'mainstream' popular entertainment, and who worked diligently and consciously to create music that would please listeners and dancers who shared those tastes. When Gus Cannon (1885–1979) was discovered working as a yard man in Memphis in the early 1960s, his awestruck young admirers asked him where he had learned his material. 'From the radio,' he answered, instantly shattering virtually all the preconceptions they had entertained about him.

The First Blues Recording Session And Its Aftermath

At the very least, the most important event in terms of recorded blues in the 1920s occurred in a decidedly urban, and urbane, context. On 10 August 1920, a vaudeville singer and Harlem nightclub chanteuse named Mamie Smith (1883–1946) entered a New York recording studio and cut a song called 'Crazy Blues', the first recording by an African-American singer to be billed specifically as a 'blues'. Her band was a classy one, anchored by stride piano genius Willie 'The Lion' Smith (1897–1973) and possibly featuring cornettist Johnny Dunn (although Willie 'The Lion' remembered the horn man as Addington Major, and many discographers agree with him).

Clearly, songwriter Perry Bradford, who had urged OKeh to do the session and probably also assembled the band, had a pop hit on his mind when he planned the date. But it was Bradford's genius to figure out that a song like 'Crazy Blues', which reflected the vernacular culture, language and tastes of mainstream,

see Gus Cannon pp 26 *see* Blind Blake pp 70 *see* Johnny Dodds pp 72 *see* Mamie Smith pp 82

Above
A 1926 Charleston competition; the jazz dance craze took 1920s society by storm.

working-class African-Americans despite (or alongside) its jazzy uptown setting, might tap into a market of potential listeners that, until then, virtually no one in the recording industry had sought to infiltrate.

'Crazy Blues' sold upwards of a million copies in its first six months, and in its wake a new genre was born. These days that genre is usually referred to as 'classic blues', a name that neither does it justice nor describes it very well. At its best, it combined the sophisticated improvisational musicianship of 1920s-era jazz with the earthy vocal declamations of women singers whose material did, indeed, often invoke 'folk' traditions or portray the day-to-day lives and struggles of urban and rural African-Americans with a hardscrabble, lyric vividness that had never before been heard on record. But the musical context (often a single pianist, but not infrequently an ensemble graced with skilled soloists, occasionally even big names such as Louis Armstrong) was strictly first class, or was at least staged to look that way.

The 'Race' Records Craze

The record companies were forced to acknowledge that there was a huge market for recordings by African-American artists, and their catalogues began to include 'race' record listings. The records sold well with both black and white audiences, and jazz and blues artists were being signed up and ushered into studios at a

see Introduction pp 34 *see* Key Artists pp 44 *see* A–Z of Artists pp 68 *see* List of Artists pp 88

phenomenal rate as the labels sought to take advantage of this new and seemingly limitless money making opportunity. Jazz and blues records could soon be heard blaring out of clubs, cafés and juke joints across the US.

Radio broadcasts also played an important role in the increasing popularity of 'race' records. From the earliest days of jazz and blues, and certainly by the early 1920s, artists such as Kid Ory, Bessie Smith (1894–1937), Fletcher Henderson (1897–1952), Clarence Williams (1989–1965) and Duke Ellington (1899–1974) were making regular broadcasts, bringing their live shows to diverse listeners nationwide and neatly side-stepping constraining issues such as segregated venues.

The Harlem Renaissance

As the Chicago jazz scene thrived, the continuing mass migration of blacks from the South also fed the growth of population in Harlem, Mamie Smith's stamping ground in uptown New York City. This influx of people helped to create the Harlem Renaissance, a period of unprecedented creative activity among African-Americans in all fields of art. From 1920–30, great works were done by writers and poets such as Langston Hughes, Countee Cullen and Zora Neale Hurston; painters William H. Johnson, Palmer Hayden and Lois Mailous Jones; composer-bandleaders Noble Sissle (1889–1975), Eubie Blake (1883–1983), Duke Ellington and Fletcher Henderson; and entertainment icons Bill 'Bojangles' Robinson, Paul Robeson, Ethel Waters (1896–1977), Josephine Baker (1906–75) and Bert Williams.

Alongside established Harlem venues such as the Savoy Ballroom, new nightclubs began to spring up to cater for the increasing population, employing jazz and blues musicians and African-American dancers, and bearing names that recalled the South, such as the Cotton Club and the Kentucky. Other clubs, such as Connie's Inn, were run for white customers but remained useful venues in which jazz bands could perfect their performances. Two jazz geniuses who came up in Harlem during this incredibly rich period in African-American history, and emerged fully fledged stars by the end of the decade, were Thomas 'Fats' Waller (1904–43) and Louis Armstrong. They were good friends whose paths crossed frequently in Chicago and New York, socially and professionally, throughout the 1920s.

Waller And Armstrong

Fats, a charismatic entertainer and an exponent of the 'Harlem stride' piano style in the tradition of Eubie Blake and James P. Johnson (1894–1955), first met Louis in 1924 while the two musicians were both moonlighting with Clarence Williams' Blue Five band at the Hoofer's Club in Harlem. They appeared together on live radio broadcasts and at late-night jams at Connie's Inn. In 1925, before Armstrong went back to Chicago to record his revolutionary Hot Five sessions, they appeared together on a recording date for Vocalion by Perry Bradford's Jazz Phools. In 1927, the two kindred spirits met up again in Chicago for a series of gigs at the Vendome Theater with Erskine Tate's band. During his brief stay in the Windy City, Waller also sat in on several late-night jam sessions at the Sunset Café with Armstrong's band, which by 1927 included pianist Earl Hines (1903–83).

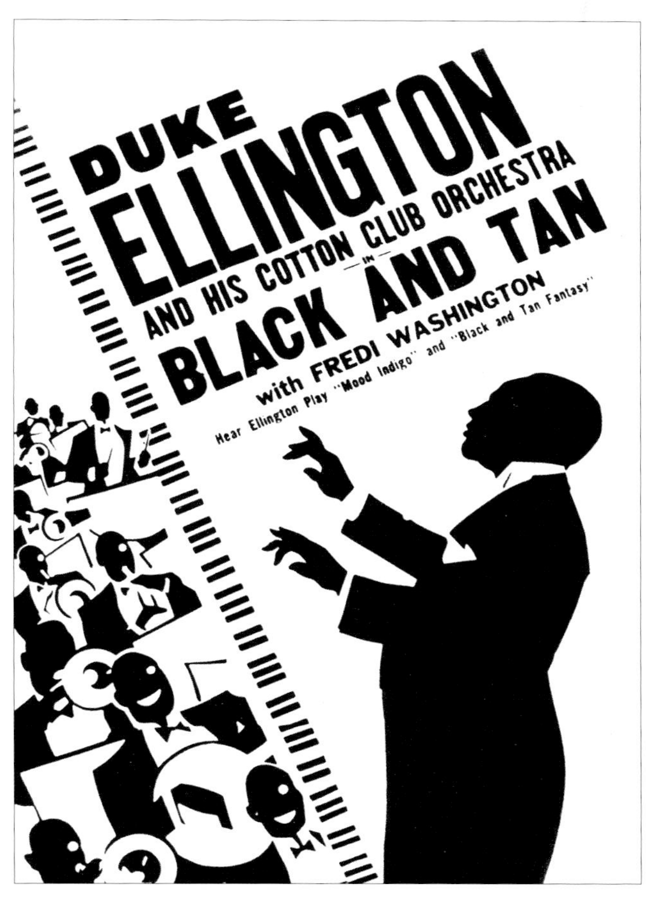

Above
A 1929 poster advertising Duke Ellington's band at the Cotton Club.

Evolution And Growth

While jazz musicians in this period tended to amalgamate in particular cities, many blues performers had been honing their sound and building up the world of black showbusiness during their relentless touring. The 'classic blues' sound promoted by Mamie Smith's release was similar to that which countless blues singers had been doing in live performance, especially in the South, for some time. Many if not most of them either got their start or spent significant amounts of time performing in tent shows, minstrel revues and along the rugged Theater Owners' Booking Association (TOBA) African-American vaudeville circuit. The shows that they took out on the road after recording

see Clarence Williams pp 25 *see* Louis Armstrong pp 44 *see* Fletcher Henderson pp 74 *see* Fats Waller pp 85

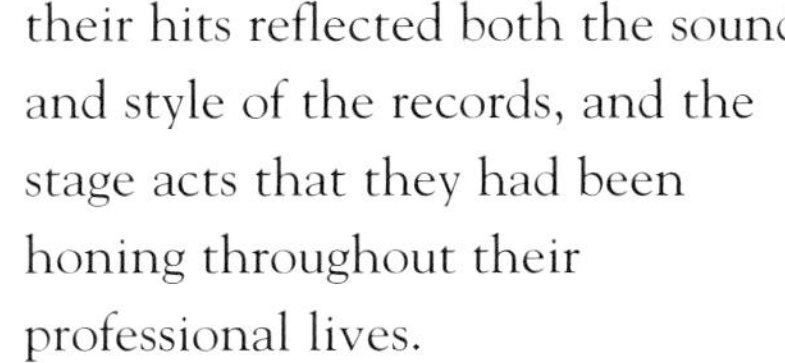

their hits reflected both the sound and style of the records, and the stage acts that they had been honing throughout their professional lives.

These shows, and the songs that their stars recorded, also had an important (and too often under-recognized) influence on the southern guitarists, pianists and harmonica players who comprise the other half of what might be called the 'blues dialectic' of the 1920s and 1930s. Often, southern acoustic blues and 'classic blues' are portrayed as parallel genres that evolved at the same time but were relatively untouched by each other. Musical evidence, however, suggests that the various blues forms developing during these years were the products of a complex, and still not fully understood, pattern of cross-pollination and influence.

Right
As the blues grew in popularity, the genre began to dominate 1920s record catalogues.

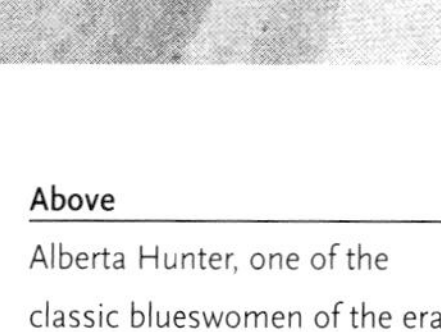

Above
Alberta Hunter, one of the classic blueswomen of the era.

Two-Way Streets And Fuzzy Categories

As already mentioned, ragtime, jazz and/or vaudeville influences can be heard not only in the sophisticated musical backings and well-tempered diction that characterize most of the 'classic blues' singers' recorded output (and, one assumes, their performances), but also in the work of some of the most putatively 'pure' folk bluesmen of the era.

For that matter, some of those 'folk' artists were, in fact, city-born or came of musical age in an urban environment. Even that prototypical 'country' bluesman Blind Lemon Jefferson (*c.* 1897–1929) cut his teeth among the barrelhousers, ragtimers, pimps and hustlers of Dallas's notorious Deep Ellum district. Conversely, even at their most musically refined, 'classic blues' women such as Ida Cox (1896–1967), Victoria Spivey (1906–76), Ma Rainey (1886–1939) and the various unrelated Smiths often dealt in material with lyrics as nasty and uncompromisingly funk-drenched as anything that might have emanated from a plantation juke (or a backstreet urban gin mill) on a Saturday night.

None of this is to suggest that there is anything inauthentic or faked about the blues recorded and performed in the 1920s, be it 'classic blues' backed by a single pianist or a full jazz orchestra, or the downhome stylings of a lone Mississippi guitar picker. That records may be recorded and sold as commodities, or that music may be played and sung for profit, does not detract from either's artistic worth or legitimacy – the 'folk'/'commercial' dichotomy is, in this context, arbitrary and false. Whether performed in a backwoods shack or a big-city theatre, blues did (and does) express the deepest emotional and aesthetic truths of its purveyors, both as a people and as individuals.

The Jazz Scene Relocates Again

By the end of the 1920s, the centre of jazz had shifted once more, taking advantage of the cultural regeneration in Harlem and moving from Chicago to New York. Here, Duke Ellington was leading the way with the 'jungle music' created by his sophisticated Cotton Club Orchestra, while Armstrong, who returned to New York in 1929, and Bix Beiderbecke (1903–31), also fresh from Chicago, were setting the pace for up-and-coming young trumpeters Jabbo Smith (1908–91), Henry 'Red' Allen (1908–67), Jimmy McPartland (1907–91) and Red Nichols (1905–65). Meanwhile, the stock market crash of 29 October 1929 signalled a symbolic end to the raucous, freewheeling, thrill-seeking Jazz Age. As the Great Depression loomed, Americans would soon turn to the ebullient dance music of the swing era to heal their woes.

While Ellington and Armstrong would spearhead a transition from jungle music and classic jazz into the new swing era, others such as Jelly Roll Morton, King Oliver and Kid Ory would fall out of favour in the 1930s, their New Orleans jazz, with its dependence on ragtime rhythms, now perceived as archaic and corny by the thrill-seeking swing set.

Blues From The Heart

It is the abiding genius of blues music that it is at once culturally specific – rooted in a particular epoch and cultural milieu – and grandly universal, voicing desires, dreams, joys and frustrations common across the human condition. In the 1920s, it evolved to new levels of sophistication and popularity as well as artistic and emotional honesty, setting the context and the standards for the developments that would transpire in the decades that lay ahead. The Great Depression and inevitable financial difficulties that this caused within the recording industry would naturally have an adverse affect on many blues performers, but the beautiful, melancholy simplicity of blues music would touch many souls during those dark days, and in some ways would sum up the feelings of a nation.

Above

A typical image of the sudden poverty that followed the 1929 stock market crash.

see Duke Ellington pp 52 *see* Blind Lemon Jefferson pp 56 *see* Ida Cox pp 71 *see* Jimmy McPartland pp 78

Louis Armstrong

CLASSIC RECORDINGS

1925–28
Louis Armstrong & his Hot Five: 'Cornet Chop Suey', 'Hotter Than That', 'Struttin' With Some Barbecue'

1927
Louis Armstrong & his Hot Seven: 'Potato Head Blues'

1928
Louis Armstrong & his Savoy Ballroom Five: 'Basin Street Blues', 'Tight Like This', 'Weather Bird', 'West End Blues'

1929
Louis Armstrong & his Orchestra: 'Ain't Misbehavin'', 'St. Louis Blues'

'What he does is real, and true, and honest, and simple, and even noble. Every time this man puts his trumpet to his lips, even if only to practice three notes, he does it with his whole soul.'

Leonard Bernstein

Above
The Colored Waif's Home band, featuring Louis Armstrong (back row, indicated by a white arrow).

An incomparable figure in the history of jazz, Armstrong played with an unprecedented virtuosity and bravura, while retaining an individual tone and a deceptively laid-back style. In the early 1920s, he shifted the emphasis of jazz from ensemble playing to a soloist's art form, while setting new standards for trumpeters worldwide. The sheer brilliance of his playing is best exemplified by his epochal masterworks from the 1920s, such as 'Potato Head Blues', 'West End Blues', 'Muggles', 'Hotter Than That', 'Tight Like This', 'Cornet Chop Suey' and 'Weather Bird' – all marked by a passionate, robust attack, dramatic, slashing breaks and a remarkable flexibility and range. As Miles Davis put it, 'You can't play anything on your horn that Louis hasn't already played'.

The Making of a Star

Born in New Orleans on 4 August 1901, Armstrong began playing cornet after being sent to the Colored Waif's Home in 1913. Nicknamed 'Dippermouth' or 'Satchelmouth' (shortened to Satchmo) because of his wide, toothy grin, Armstrong came up playing in parade bands and bars around Storyville. In late 1918, he replaced his mentor Joe 'King' Oliver in Kid Ory's band and honed his skills in that outfit until Ory's relocation to California in 1919 caused the band to split up.

see Introduction pp 34 *see* Sources & Sounds pp 36 *see* A–Z of Artists pp 68

Armstrong remained in New Orleans, joining Fate Marable's band and playing on the Mississippi riverboats. The experience that Armstrong gained during this period was instrumental in his passage from an amateur jobbing musician to a professional jazz artist. Apart from the opportunities for travel that the riverboats offered, the performance and rehearsal schedule for the band was a gruelling one, and Armstrong had to strengthen his embouchure, sharpen his improvisational skills and learn to read music. Marable's band was also home to many future stars and Armstrong collaborators, including bass player Pops Foster, banjoist Johnny St. Cyr, clarinetist Johnny Dodds and his brother, percussionist Warren 'Baby' Dodds.

Satchmo Joins King Oliver

On 8 August 1922, Armstrong accepted an invitation to play second cornet to King Oliver in Oliver's Creole Jazz Band in Chicago, alongside the Dodds brothers, trombonist Honoré Dutrey and pianist Lil Hardin, who became Armstrong's second wife. The band had a residency at Lincoln Gardens, where they had built up a reputation as the hottest ticket in Chicago. Louis made his recording debut with the Creole Jazz Band for Gennett on 6 April 1923, although as second cornet he took few solos, tending to remain more in the background of Oliver's lead (notable exceptions to this can be heard on 'Chimes Blues' and 'Froggie Moore'). He remained with Oliver's band throughout that year before moving to New York in early 1924 to join Fletcher Henderson's band during its residency at the Roseland Ballroom.

Moving East

Henderson had seen Armstrong play during a visit to New Orleans in 1922; he had been impressed and had invited Louis to join his band there and then, but the offer was turned down. This time, however – possibly at the encouragement of his ambitious new wife – Armstrong accepted. His virtuosic playing gained him immediate respect with the other band-members, and Henderson's inspired arrangements enabled Armstrong to shine out in solos and lead parts. In 'Sugarfoot Stomp', a version of the 'Dippermouth Blues' that Armstrong recorded with the Creole Jazz band, the young player's progress from background player to confident soloist can be clearly heard. It was also in the Fletcher Henderson band that Armstrong began to develop his vocal skills, regularly singing onstage and revelling in the positive reactions from the audience. This experience would go on to influence the direction that his career took in later years.

As his reputation spread, Armstrong became more and more in demand as a session musician in New York. The sides he recorded with the blues stars

Above
The house in Perdido Street, New Orleans in which Armstrong grew up.

Left
Perhaps jazz music's most emblematic star, Louis Armstrong.

see Kid Ory pp 22 see King Oliver pp 62 see Fletcher Henderson pp 74 see Johnny St. Cyr pp 84

of the day such as Ma Rainey, Clara Smith and, in particular, Bessie Smith show his ability as an attentive and sensitive accompanist, responding to the other musicians and allowing the singer to take centre stage. He also worked as a sideman, notably for the New Orleans-raised pianist, composer, publisher and bandleader Clarence Williams in his Red Onion Jazz Babies and Blue Five, sometimes alongside the formidable Sidney Bechet, which triggered energetic cutting contests that led to some of the hottest jazz recordings of all time.

Above

Armstrong's virtuosic trumpet solos changed the emphasis of jazz from ensemble to solo playing.

Armstrong continued to gain musical knowledge while with Fletcher Henderson's band, and at the same time his own playing style was catching on and being assimilated by the New York musicians. Traces of his solos would appear in the work of others, and elements of swing began to infiltrate the sounds of Harlem, as the spirit of New Orleans jazz moved in. However, by late 1925 Armstrong was tiring of the Henderson band, and was persuaded by Lil to return to Chicago.

The Rosetta Stone Of Jazz

After returning to Chicago in 1925, Armstrong began playing with Erskine Tate's Orchestra at the Vendome, where he regularly took solo spots. It was also at this time that he recorded the first of his historic Hot Five sessions for Okeh Records with Lil Hardin Armstrong, Kid Ory, Johnny Dodds and Johnny St. Cyr. There followed some Hot Seven sessions in 1927, featuring Armstrong's home-town friend Baby Dodds on drums, and a second Hot Five session in 1928 with Earl Hines replacing Hardin on piano. Often referred to as 'the Rosetta Stone of Jazz', the Hot Five and Hot Seven recordings are the most exciting and influential in jazz music, if not in the entire twentieth century. Armstrong's all-star ensembles set the ground rules for the direction jazz was to take, establishing it as a basis for improvisation and virtuosic solo playing within a group. He also introduced wordless 'scat' singing and steered jazz towards the more fluid rhythms of swing – perhaps best illustrated by the beautifully crafted improvised passage that forms the introduction to 'West End Blues'.

Following these revolutionary recordings, Armstrong returned to New York and began gradually to focus on entertainment at the expense of art. His work in the Chicago clubs had encouraged him to experiment further with singing and dancing, and he enjoyed the relationship that this type of performance enabled him to form with the audience. Even within the confines of his more serious music from the same period, he had hinted at a more good-humoured direction with his ribald, vaudevillian playfulness on the introduction to 'Tight Like This' and in his frisky repartee with pianist Earl Hines that started off 'A Monday Date', both from his Hot Seven recordings of 1928. It was a direction that stern jazzophiles would come to view with increasing indignation over the years.

In 1929, Armstrong gave a crowd-pleasing performance in *Hot Chocolates*, which had its initial

see Introduction pp 34 *see* Sources & Sounds pp 36 *see* A–Z of Artists pp 68

Above

Armstrong was a charismatic performer who loved to entertain the crowd.

run at Connie's Inn in Harlem before moving to the Hudson Theatre on Broadway. It was in that show that Satchmo introduced 'Ain't Misbehavin'', the Fats Waller-Andy Razaf tune that became his first big hit. Armstrong was featured with Leroy Smith's group, at first performing from the pit but eventually taking his spot on stage, to the delight of audiences. His gravel-throated charisma helped to make *Hot Chocolates* the phenomenal success that it became.

Armstrong Follows A New Route

In that same pivotal year of 1929 Armstrong cut the pop song 'I Can't Give You Anything But Love', charting a new course away from the cutting-edge Hot Fives and Hot Sevens, and steering more toward the mainstream entertainment by emphasizing his signature vocals. He played with a variety of big bands throughout the 1930s and 1940s, under leaders such as Luis Russell and Joe Garland, and toured extensively in the US and Europe, where he helped to bring jazz music to a wider audience. Under the guidance of manager Joe Glaser, who recognized the money making potential of Louis' popularity, Armstrong then continued to pursue his career as a vocalist and all-round entertainer throughout the 1950s and 1960s, with various aggregations of his All-Stars band. By then he had become a beloved yet sometimes controversial icon, a featured player in movies – including *Paris Blues* (in which he appeared with Duke Ellington), *High Society* (hamming it up as a grinning bandleader in a stellar cast that included Grace Kelly, Bing Crosby and Frank Sinatra) and *Hello, Dolly* – and a worldwide ambassador of jazz. His last big hit was 'What A Wonderful World', released in 1968, although he continued to tour and perform for another two years. After his death from kidney and heart failure in 1971, his home in Queens, New York was preserved as an archive and museum.

see Bessie Smith pp 64 *see* Warren 'Baby' Dodds pp 72 *see* Lil Hardin Armstrong pp 73 *see* Earl Hines pp 126

Bix Beiderbecke

CLASSIC RECORDINGS

1924
Wolverine Orchestra: 'Jazz Me Blues', 'Royal Garden Blues', 'Tiger Rag'

1925
Bix & his Rhythm Jugglers: 'Davenport Blues'

1927
Bix Beiderbecke: 'In A Mist'
Frankie Trumbauer Orchestra: 'Riverboat Shuffle', 'Singing The Blues'

1927–29
Paul Whiteman Orchestra: 'Marie', 'Mississippi Mud', 'Sweet Sue'

The most strikingly original and authoritative voice on cornet since Louis Armstrong, Leon 'Bix' Beiderbecke set the example for a generation of aspiring white jazz players during the 1920s. His meteoric rise to fame was followed by a dramatic fall from grace that led to his ultimate death from alcoholism at the age of just 28 in 1931.

A Self-Taught Genius

Born in Davenport, Iowa on 10 March 1903, Beiderbecke rebelled against his strait-laced parents and his own upper-middle-class upbringing by becoming a jazz musician, a path that his parents found abhorrent. Inspired by recordings of the Original Dixieland Jass Band from New Orleans (and particularly the playing of the group's trumpeter and bandleader Nick LaRocca), Beiderbecke began playing cornet aged 15. Completely self-taught, he developed a distinctive tone and biting attack along with flawless intonation, a natural sense of swing and an uncanny command of blue notes. Contemporaries such as Hoagy Carmichael later said that the notes coming out of Beiderbecke's horn sounded like they were hit rather than blown, like a mallet striking a chime.

'Bix's breaks were not as wild as Armstrong's, but they were hot and he selected each note with musical care. He showed me that jazz could be musical and beautiful as well as hot.'

Hoagy Carmichael

In 1923 Bix joined the Indiana-based Wolverines (named after Jelly Roll Morton's 'Wolverine Blues'), and in 1924 they cut a series of classic sides for the Gennett label, including 'Tiger Rag', 'Royal Garden Blues', 'Jazz Me Blues', 'Copenhagen' and Hoagy Carmichael's first tune, 'Free Wheeling'. Those recordings were absorbed and analyzed note for note by a group of jazz-hungry young Chicagoans collectively known as the Austin High School Gang, whose ranks included cornettist Jimmy McPartland, saxophonist Bud Freeman, clarinetist Frank Teschemacher, drummer Dave Tough and trombonist Jim Lannigan. It also included other young Windy City players such as trumpeter Muggsy Spanier, drummer Gene Krupa, clarinetist Benny Goodman and banjoist Eddie Condon.

Bix And Tram

In 1925 Beiderbecke moved to Chicago and began sitting in with all the great New Orleans players there, including King Oliver, Jimmy Noone and Louis Armstrong, whom Beiderbecke had first heard playing on a riverboat in 1920 with Fate Marable's band, in his hometown of Davenport. In the early part of 1926, Bix joined a band led by C-melody saxophonist Frankie 'Tram' Trumbauer at the Arcadia Ballroom in St. Louis, and by summer of that year the two were playing in Jean Goldkette's Orchestra at the Graystone Ballroom in Detroit. In late 1927, Bix and Tram were recruited by Paul Whiteman, who led the most successful dance band of the day. Though unworthy of his moniker 'King of Jazz', Whiteman did respect the superb artistry that Beiderbecke demonstrated with his horn and featured him frequently on recordings from 1927–29. Bix's brief eight-bar statements within the context of popular Whiteman fare such as 'Marie', 'Louisiana', 'Sweet Sue' and 'Mississippi Mud' were brilliant gems of well-constructed, lyrical improvisation.

At his peak, around 1927–28, Bix was fêted by his fellow jazz musicians, white and black alike. Perhaps his most famous and most widely imitated solo

Above
Jazz cornet genius Bix Beiderbecke, who took Chicago by storm.

see Introduction pp 34 *see* Sources & Sounds pp 36 *see* A–Z of Artists pp 68

came on a 1927 Trumbauer-led small group recording of Bix's 'Singin' The Blues', which trumpeters of the day studied assiduously. Louis Armstrong refused to record the track himself, believing that Bix's solo could not be improved upon. Beiderbecke's other famous compositions included 'Davenport Blues' and a Debussy-inspired solo piano piece, 'In A Mist' – one of two such works that he recorded.

The Alcohol Takes Its Toll

In the autumn of 1929, Beiderbecke had a nervous collapse; he was sent back to Davenport and entered a sanatorium to help him with his alcohol problems. Off the Whiteman payroll by the spring of 1930, he tried making a comeback with some recordings as a leader but died of pneumonia, exacerbated by alcoholism, on 6 August 1931. Seven years after his death, Beiderbecke was the inspiration for *Young Man With A Horn*, a novel by Dorothy Baker that was adapted for a 1950 Warner Bros. film starring Kirk Douglas.

Left
Bix (left) with his good friend and musical collaborator, saxophonist Frankie 'Tram' Trumbauer, in 1928.

Below
Bix (seated far right) in his first group – the Wolverines.

see Original Dixieland Jass Band pp 31 *see* Bud Freeman pp 72 *see* Frankie Trumbauer pp 84 *see* Paul Whiteman pp 86

Leroy Carr

CLASSIC RECORDINGS

1928–29
'How Long, How Long Blues', 'Low Down Dirty Blues', 'Prison Bound Blues', 'Truthful Blues'

1930
'Sloppy Drunk Blues'

1934–35
'Blues Before Sunrise', 'Bobo Stomp', 'I Believe I'll Make A Change', 'Mean Mistreater Mama', 'Shady Lane Blues'

Vocalist/pianist Leroy Carr's life and career belie the myth that pre-war acoustic blues artists were necessarily 'rural' or 'primitive'. Carr was born not on a plantation but in Nashville, Tennessee on 27 March 1905. His father worked as a porter at Vanderbilt University. After his parents separated, his mother brought him and his sister to Indianapolis (known in the vernacular as 'Naptown'), which at the time was a major nexus of the US automotive industry.

Carr's Musical Match

Young Leroy taught himself piano and left school at an early age to go out into the world and seek his fortune; he travelled with a circus, he spent time in the military, he worked as a meat packer and as a bootlegger. But by the mid-1920s he was a professional entertainer, performing at private parties and in clubs around Indiana Avenue, Indianapolis's primary black nightlife strip. Some time during these years he met guitarist Francis 'Scrapper' Blackwell (1903–62), who shared his urbane, somewhat wistful musical sensibilities. The two developed an uncanny musical telepathy; they could interweave melodies of pristine delicacy one moment, then charge into a drive-'em-down barrelhouse stomp the next, goading the patrons back on to the dance floor.

'I am in love with Leroy Carr; I can play his stuff all night and not give a damn if people like it!'
Barrelhouse Chuck

A Successful Formula

In 1928 the duo had their first recording session for Vocalion. 'How Long, How Long Blues', their debut release, turned out to be their most successful. A melancholy pastiche of images of loss and resignation – lonesome train whistles, departed lovers, desolate mountain vistas – set to a pop-tinged melody line of eight bars, it was sophisticated in feel, yet 'country' enough in its lyric content to strike a familiar chord in listeners downhome. In Mississippi, Robert Johnson became a devotee; plenty of others shared his tastes, and the team of Carr and Blackwell quickly became one of the most popular acts in blues. They followed up their first hit with a series of sides, almost all of them featuring Carr's understated yet emotionally rich vocals – 'Naptown Blues', 'Rocks In My Bed', 'We're Gonna Rock', 'Mean Mistreater Mama', 'Blues Before Sunrise' – which may not have sold quite as well as 'How Long …', but were more than sufficient to maintain their careers for the next seven years or so.

The Liquor Takes Its Toll

The blues life has never been an easy one, and both Carr and Blackwell (who had also been a bootlegger before he became a bluesman) were heavy drinkers. Their last session together was in February 1935; less than two months later, Carr died from the effects of acute alcoholism. His partner soldiered on for a while, but he was devastated by the loss and eventually dropped out of music. He was 'rediscovered' in 1959, and enjoyed a brief comeback until his death a few years later.

Right
Vocalist and pianist Leroy Carr, who died from alcoholism at the age of 30.

see Introduction pp 34 *see* Sources & Sounds pp 36 *see* A–Z of Artists pp 68

Despite his undeniable influence on Robert Johnson and others (Johnson's 'Love In Vain' carries distinct echoes of both 'How Long ...' and another Carr/Blackwell song, 'When The Sun Goes Down'), and despite the popularity the Carr/Blackwell duo enjoyed in their heyday (among male blues singers, only Blind Lemon Jefferson could claim as many admirers), Leroy Carr is under-recognized today. Perhaps his location in a northern city outside of Chicago or Detroit is a hindrance; maybe his style remains too subtle for those who still insist on associating blues only with sledge-hammer emotions or gutbucket 'primitivism'. But in his own quiet way, Leroy Carr earned himself an honoured place in the pantheon next to Jefferson, Lonnie Johnson, Bessie Smith and the others who helped to codify modern blues in the 1920s.

Above
Carr's friend and musical soul mate, guitarist Scrapper Blackwell.

see **Blind Lemon Jefferson pp 56** *see* **Lonnie Johnson pp 58** *see* **Scrapper Blackwell pp 70** *see* **Robert Johnson pp 112**

Duke Ellington

CLASSIC RECORDINGS

1924
Duke Ellington Orchestra: 'Choo Choo (Gotta Hurry Home)', 'Rainy Nights (Rainy Days)'

1926–29
'Black And Tan Fantasy', 'Creole Love Call', 'East St. Louis Toodle-Oo', 'Jubilee Stomp', 'The Mooche'

1929–31
'Mood Indigo', 'Rockin' In Rhythm', 'Wall Street Wail'

Right
Duke Ellington – pianist, composer, bandleader and one of jazz music's most important figures.

Universally acknowledged as one of the twentieth century's emblematic composers, Edward Kennedy 'Duke' Ellington used his long-standing touring orchestra as a tool to create wholly unique tonal colours and a distinctive harmonic language in jazz. His career was characterized by the close and long-lasting relationships that he struck up with particular musicians and other figures from the music business, which brought a certain stability to his various periods of creativity. From the late 1920s to the early 1970s he composed many tunes that have become standards, as well as exquisite three-minute jazz concertos, dance-band repertoire, popular suites, sacred concerts, revues, tone poems and film soundtracks. His most famous titles – including 'Mood Indigo', 'Satin Doll', 'Sophisticated Lady' and 'It Don't Mean A Thing (If It Ain't Got That Swing)' – have become embedded in the English language.

'I like any and all of my associations with music – writing, playing, and listening. We write and play from our perspective, and the audience listens from its perspective. If and when we agree, I am lucky.'
Duke Ellington

The Duke Makes His Name

Born in Washington, DC on 29 April 1899, Ellington enjoyed a stable, middle-class upbringing that gave no hint of his future as one of the pivotal figures in jazz music. His childhood piano lessons were abandoned due in part to his unwillingness to learn to read music, and of all the arts it was at painting that he excelled. When he began to take an interest in music, in his later high-school years, he found that he could get by with a mixture of his own intelligence, inventiveness and the little piano schooling he had received. Nicknamed 'Duke' for his dapper appearance, he composed his first pieces – 'Soda Fountain Rag' and the risqué blues 'What You Gonna Do When The Bed Breaks Down?' – as a teenager and in 1919 formed his first group, the Duke's Serenaders.

The beginnings of the Ellington band began to take shape under the leadership of banjo player Elmer Snowden. As the ripples of the Harlem Renaissance began to spread, Ellington felt the call of New York as the newly established centre of burgeoning black culture, and the hub of creative opportunity. His first visit there proved unsuccessful, but on the second attempt a chance meeting with a fellow Washington, DC musician resulted in a gig at Barron's, and by 1923 Ellington had settled in Harlem. From Barron's the band, which included drummer Sonny Greer and saxophonist Otto Hardwick, moved on to a residency at the Hollywood Inn, a club on Times Square where the clientele was of a higher calibre and the pay packets decidedly more substantial.

The Jazz Influence Creeps In

Although the Duke's background was not in jazz, he began to absorb influences from ragtime piano players and other popular performers of the day, including

see Introduction pp 34 *see* Sources & Sounds pp 36 *see* A–Z of Artists pp 68

Above

Ellington recorded prolifically throughout his career.

Willie 'The Lion' Smith and James P. Johnson, the father of Harlem stride piano. Still, the repertoire of the Washingtonians, as they had named themselves, was centred mainly around pop and dance numbers until the sound of New Orleans was also introduced to the band during their time at the Hollywood Club – in the form of James 'Bubber' Miley, who joined the band after original trumpeter Arthur Whetsol left. Miley had styled his playing after King Oliver, having seen the Creole Jazz Band play at Chicago's Dreamland in 1921. His growling, muted trumpet brought a fierce blues edge to the band's music and forced New York to sit up and take notice. Jazz great Sidney Bechet also played with the band for a brief period around this time and imparted a lasting influence, especially concerning the musicians' understanding of jazz phrasing.

Following a pay dispute in 1924, Snowden was ousted from the band and Ellington took over as leader, securing a new post at the Kentucky Club in midtown Manhattan. He formed a fruitful partnership with Irving Mills, a music publisher and promoter, in which both men received a percentage of the royalties from what were mainly Ellington's compositions. However, Mills was able to set Duke up with a recording contract and provide him with the connections that he needed to make his next move. His first recordings with the group in 1924 were 'Choo Choo (Gotta Hurry Home)' and 'Rainy Nights (Rainy Days)'.

A Golden Opportunity In Harlem

A pivotal year in Ellington's career was 1927, when he took over residency at the Cotton Club in Harlem, a lucrative and high-profile gig that had been unwisely turned down by King Oliver. The band provided music for dancing, accompanied solo performers and also played the background music for erotic stage shows. Mills came up with the term 'jungle music' to describe the band's growling, vaguely sinister sound, and the mini-genre came to be defined by a string of early Ellington masterpieces, recorded that same year: 'Black and Tan Fantasy', based on a New Orleans funeral march, 'East St. Louis Toodle-Oo', which developed from a Bubber Miley riff, and 'Creole Love Call', which owed much to King Oliver's 'Camp Meeting Blues'. Another signature 'jungle music piece was 'The Mooche', recorded in 1928 and marked by Miley's distinctive trumpet and the plunger-mute trombone work of Joseph 'Tricky Sam' Nanton. CBS radio broadcasts of the Cotton Club's music ensured that the Duke's reputation soon began to spread.

Ellington remained at the Cotton Club until 1930, then took his orchestra to Hollywood to appear in the Amos 'n' Andy film *Check And Double Check*. The subsequent decade saw Ellington's flowering, as he produced hundreds of recordings, played countless concerts and broadcasts and became a sophisticated international figure – in his terms, 'beyond category'. He also took his band to London in 1933, where he was to discover that his music had made a bigger

see Sidney Bechet pp 69 *see* James P. Johnson pp 76 *see* James 'Bubber' Miley pp 79 *see* Willie 'The Lion' Smith pp 134

Above
The hugely popular Duke Ellington Orchestra, shown here in Chicago in 1934.

impact than he could ever have imagined, and that he was regarded as a key contemporary composer.

Key to Ellington's art was his use of specific musicians – including baritone saxophonist Harry Carney, alto saxophonist Johnny Hodges, trumpeters Cootie Williams (following Bubber Miley's departure from the band in 1929) and Rex Stewart, trombonist Juan Tizol, bassist Jimmy Blanton, drummer Sonny Greer, and clarinetists Barney Bigard, Jimmy Hamilton and Russell Procope – as individual tones on his compositional palette. He often transformed improvised riffs or half-baked themes into enduring, full-blown works, and despite the rise in the 1930s of the big white swing orchestras, such as those of Benny Goodman and Paul Whiteman, Ellington's band managed to hold its own.

Moving Ever Onward

As his partnership with Irving Mills drew to a close, the Duke was ready to begin a new phase in his career. In 1938 he initiated a remarkable close collaboration with co-composer Billy Strayhorn, who had similar musical sensibilities to Duke and furnished the band with the piece that would become their signature tune

see Introduction pp 34 *see* Sources & Sounds pp 36 *see* A–Z of Artists pp 68

during the 1940s, 'Take the "A" Train'. The addition of tenor saxophonist Ben Webster around this time altered the band's sound by filling in a middle-register role that had remained empty since the group's conception. While Webster was undeniably a fine musician, some felt that this detracted from the trademark Ellington style.

The 1940s were a difficult time in the American recording industry; a recording ban destroyed the livelihoods of many bands, and Ellington lost a number of musicians as a result. In the years immediately following the war, the economy had taken a downturn and it was difficult for musicians to make a living; the band became somewhat downsized. However, Ellington typically continued to look forward throughout the decade, premiering ambitious works, such as 'Black, Brown And Beige' – a musical history of African-Americans – at New York's Carnegie Hall.

A Long And Varied Career

Although not immune from industry-wide downturns and changes in band personnel as well as audience tastes, Ellington toured and recorded prolifically throughout the 1950s and 1960s, filling his orchestra with new soloists – such as trumpeter Clark Terry, drummer Louie Bellson, trombonist Quentin Jackson and tenor saxophonist Paul Gonslaves – when his longtime sidemen died, retired or moved on. His appearance at the 1956 Newport Jazz Festival led to a *Time* magazine cover, a new contract with Columbia Records and the bestselling *Ellington At Newport*, which featured Gonslaves' fabled 27-chorus solo on 'Diminuendo And Crescendo In Blue'. Ever the open-minded modernist, Ellington recorded with John Coltrane, Max Roach and Charles Mingus in the 1960s. He also provided the score for the 1961 film, *Paris Blues*. Duke's later masterpieces included 'The Far East Suite' (1966), marked by modal and Asian-inflected motifs, the 'New Orleans Suite' (1970) and a series of sacred works inspired by his increasing interest in religion. Ellington was revered worldwide as a genius and giant of contemporary music long before his death in 1974.

Above
Ellington found international fame and recognition in his lifetime.

Left
Harlem's Cotton Club, where Duke Ellington's Orchestra held a three-year residency.

see Benny Goodman pp 110 *see* Rex Stewart pp 135 *see* Ben Webster pp 185 *see* Charles Mingus pp 230

Blind Lemon Jefferson Key Artists

CLASSIC RECORDINGS

1926–29
'Bed Springs Blues', '(That) Black Snake Moan', 'Careless Love', 'Hangman's Blues', ''Lectric Chair Blues', 'Jack O'Diamond Blues', 'Match Box Blues', 'One Dime Blues', 'See That My Grave Is Kept Clean', 'Tin Cup Blues'

Although he is often cited as the first 'folk' bluesman to record, Blind Lemon Jefferson was actually much more than that: he was America's first male blues pop star. On the strength of his recordings for the Paramount label – some of which are said to have sold upwards of 100,000 copies – Jefferson became a celebrity throughout the southern blues circuit and beyond.

From Couchman To Deep Ellum

Jefferson was born in Couchman, Texas, most likely in 1897. 'Lemmon' was probably his given name. He may have been partially sighted, at least as a youth. He taught himself guitar early on, and by his mid-teens he had travelled as far as Dallas to perform. There he sang on street corners and in the jukes and whorehouses that lined Deep Ellum, the wide-open entertainment district that ran along Elm Street in the city's African-American quarter. He teamed up with Huddie 'Leadbelly' Ledbetter for a while, before Leadbelly went to prison in 1918.

In 1925, someone – possibly pianist Sammy Price – recommended him to a Paramount Records talent scout. For Paramount, Jefferson recorded approximately 100 sides (counting alternate versions), of which 42 were issued. In 1927 he also paid a brief visit to the OKeh label, for whom he cut a version of his already popular '(That) Black Snake Moan', as well as the first incarnation of 'Match Box Blues', which he soon re-cut for Paramount. He became such a celebrity that Paramount adorned some of his discs with a designer label featuring that now-famous photo of him, surrounded by bright lemon-yellow trim.

'Lemon was fat, dirty, dissolute, but his singing was perhaps the most exciting country blues singing of the 1920s.'

Samuel Charters

Above
Blind Lemon Jefferson, an inventive guitarist and one of the biggest blues stars of his day.

'Don't Play Me Cheap!'

By all accounts, he carried himself like the star he was. He usually travelled alone – or at least without a personal guide – and he comported himself like a dandy, decked out in suits, demanding respect and appropriate remuneration everywhere he went (one of his favourite catchphrases was 'Don't play me cheap!').

Although many of his best-known songs – 'Tin Cup Blues', ''Lectric Chair Blues', 'Match Box Blues' – portrayed a man suffering under oppressive conditions, his musical persona was that of a resolute survivor. His voice was high-pitched and supple, his diction and enunciation crisp and sure. His lyrics expressed the desires, passions and day-to-day struggles of working-class black people with an unadorned yet poetic directness that had never before been captured on disc.

As a guitarist he was superbly inventive within the confines of the 12-bar form, to which he generally adhered – at least on record (Leadbelly recalled him crooning ballads like 'Careless Love' in performance).

see Introduction pp 34 *see* Sources & Sounds pp 36 *see* A–Z of Artists pp 68

Creating separate voices with his bass lines and his trademark high-treble arpeggios, and sometimes interrupting the rhythmic flow for a bar or two of unaccompanied single-string solo work, his playing reflected the two-handed contrapuntal attack of the pianists he'd no doubt heard as a young man in the gin mills of Deep Ellum.

'See That My Grave Is Kept Clean'

In December of 1929, Jefferson was found dead on a sidewalk in Chicago, apparently having lost his way in a snowstorm and suffered a heart attack. Pianist Will Ezell took him back to Texas, where he was buried in Wortham Cemetery, not far from where he was born.

Not long afterwards, Rev. Emmet Dickinson recorded what was probably the first 'tribute' record in the history of blues muisc – a sermon entitled 'The Death Of Blind Lemon Jefferson'. That an artist whose recording career spanned less than half a decade would receive such an encomium is remarkable; that a Christian minister would record it is even more so – in those days, church-going Christians were advised to shun the blues. But Dickinson's words eloquently captured the feelings of the many who had listened to Jefferson's records and danced at his shows over the years: 'Blind Lemon Jefferson is dead, and the world today is mourning over this loss ... there is a vacancy in our hearts that will never be replaced.'

Below

Deep Ellum – Elm Street in Dallas, Texas – as it would have looked in the days when Blind Lemon Jefferson played there.

see Leadbelly pp 116 *see* Sammy Price pp 182 *see* Texas Blues pp 419

Lonnie Johnson

CLASSIC RECORDINGS

1925
'Mr. Johnson's Blues'

1927
'Handful O'Keys', 'Steppin' On The Blues'

1928
'Careless Love', 'Playing With The Strings', 'Way Down That Lonesome Road', 'Wrong Woman Blues'

1930
'Don't Drive Me From Your Door', 'I Got The Best Jelly Roll In Town, Pts 1 and 2'

1932
'Cat You Been Messin' Around'

Above
New Orleans *c.* 1900, where Johnson grew up.

'Lonnie Johnson is one of my favorite guitar players ... he kind of bridged the gap between blues and jazz.'
Catfish Keith

Alonzo 'Lonnie' Johnson will probably be forever classified as a 'blues' guitarist, and – at least in his later years – he seemed to accept the label, albeit somewhat gruffly. But in fact he was a consummate musician, deft enough to move between jazz, pop and blues stylings with ease, and inventive enough to imbue everything he touched with new angles of vision and fresh improvisational ideas.

A Musical Upbringing

Johnson was born into a musical New Orleans family on 8 February, probably in 1894. At a young age he began performing around town (on violin and piano) with his parents and siblings. In 1917, the year he purchased his first guitar, he landed an overseas tour with Will Marion Cook's Syncopated Orchestra. When he returned home, he discovered that his entire family, except his brother James, had died in the flu epidemic of 1918. He and James left for St. Louis, where they played in the riverboat bands of Fate Marable and Charlie Creath, with whom Johnson recorded in 1925.

A Prolific Recording Career

Also in 1925, Johnson won a blues contest sponsored by OKeh Records, the first prize for which was a recording contract. He ended up cutting, by his own recollection, 572 sides for the label, many (but not all) of which were 12-bar blues. He also worked, and sometimes recorded, with such jazz stalwarts as Eddie Lang, Louis Armstrong and Duke Ellington.

As a bluesman, Johnson sang in a fluttery, somewhat thin voice, which was nonetheless effective in delivering his sometimes violently misogynistic lyrics. His apparent lack of emotion heightened the threat as

see Introduction pp 34 *see* Sources & Sounds pp 36 *see* A–Z of Artists pp 68

he drawled out ultimatums like 'Woman, get out of my face/or I'll take my fist and knock you down' (from 'Cat You Been Messin' Around') with dead-eyed, murderous serenity. Even on ballads such as 'Careless Love' ('I'm goin' to shoot you and shoot you four, five times/And stand over you until you finish dyin"), he sounded like a man hurt beyond all caring. Meanwhile, his lithe guitar lines and horn-like phrasing amplified (and sometimes mercifully tempered) such lyric themes with improvisational *élan* and an ever-present sense of swing.

Echoes Of Johnson's Influence

In 1948 Johnson hit the R&B charts with 'Tomorrow Night', a sentimental ballad that he followed up with several other pop-styled hits. He was nonetheless billed as a 'blues singer' when he toured overseas in 1952. The vicissitudes of the music industry forced him to take a day job shortly thereafter. In the early 1960s, upon his 'rediscovery', he often found himself playing coffeehouses and being booked on 'folk blues' packages with the likes of Muddy Waters and Big Joe Williams. He is said to have been rather imperious in such settings, but audiences enjoyed his slicked-up versions of traditional blues and pop themes. He made his last recordings for Folkways in 1967.

Following a 1969 automobile accident, Lonnie Johnson suffered a stroke; he died on 6 June 1970. Although he was inducted into the Blues Hall Of Fame in 1997, he is still not often mentioned in the same breath as Blind Lemon Jefferson, Charley Patton or Robert Johnson, yet his influence was at least as important as theirs. Robert Johnson, in fact, was so enamoured of him that it is said he sometimes tried to pass himself off as a relative. Echoes of Lonnie's fusion of blues themes with a jazz-like harmonic and rhythmic sensibility resonate through the work of fretmen such as Charlie Christian, T-Bone Walker and many others, including Walker devotees such as B.B. King. Johnson was undeniably a blues trailblazer and an important figure in the evolution of mainstream American popular music.

Above

Lonnie Johnson (right), a highly influential guitarist.

see Will Marion Cook pp 27 *see* Eddie Lang pp 76 *see* Robert Johnson pp 112 *see* T-Bone Walker pp 168

Jelly Roll Morton

CLASSIC RECORDINGS

1923
Jelly Roll Morton with the New Orleans Rhythm Kings: 'Milenburg Joys', 'Mr. Jelly Lord', 'Sobbin' Blues'

1923–26
Piano Solos: 'Grandpa's Spells', 'King Porter Stomp', 'The Pearls', 'Wolverine Blues'

1926–28
Jelly Roll Morton & his Red Hot Peppers: 'Black Bottom Stomp', 'Dead Man Blues', 'The Chant'

Ridiculed as a braggart, pimp, card shark and pool hustler, the audacious, self-proclaimed inventor of jazz Jelly Roll Morton was also hailed as a pioneering composer, gifted arranger, dazzling pianist and the greatest entertainer that New Orleans ever produced. He was one of the first jazz musicians to strike a perfect balance between composition and collective improvisation, bridging the gap between ragtime and jazz.

Above
The multi-talented Jelly Roll Morton.

Ferdinand Lamothe Becomes Mr. Jelly Roll

Born on 20 October 1890, Ferdinand Joseph Lamothe was a Creole of mixed French and African ancestry. He was among the earliest piano players in the bordellos of the Storyville district, where he mixed elements of ragtime, minstrel and marching-band music, foxtrots and French quadrilles, opera and salon music along with Latin American-influenced rhythms, which he called 'the Spanish tinge'.

'He was fussy on introductions and endings and he always wanted the ensemble his way but he never interfered with the solo work.... His own playing was remarkable and kept us in good spirits.'
Omer Simeon

By 1907, after re-christening himself 'Jelly Roll Morton', he began to travel the black vaudeville circuit around the Gulf Coast. By 1911 his travels had brought him up to New York, and the following year he made trips through Texas and the Midwest. Morton settled in Chicago in 1914 and remained in this new centre of hot jazz until 1917, during which time he composed and published his earliest numbers, including 'Jelly Roll Blues', 'New Orleans Blues' and 'Winin' Boy Blues'.

Morton's Red Hot Peppers

Morton travelled to California during the summer of 1917 and remained there throughout 1922, working his way up and down the West Coast from Tijuana to Vancouver with pick-up bands. By May of 1923 he was back in Chicago and in June made his first recordings – 'Big Fat Ham' and 'Muddy Water Blues' – for the Paramount label. In July, he cut sides with the New Orleans Rhythm Kings ('Sobbin' Blues', 'Mr. Jelly Lord', 'Milenburg Joys' and 'London Blues'), along with some solo piano pieces ('Wolverine Blues', 'New Orleans Joys', 'Grandpa's Spells', 'The Pearls' and 'King Porter Stomp'), for Gennett Records. In 1924, Morton recorded two piano-cornet duets, 'Tom Cat Blues' and 'King Porter Stomp', with his New Orleans colleague King Oliver. Morton recorded prolifically throughout 1926–27 with two different editions of his Red Hot Peppers, cutting classic New Orleans-flavoured sides such as 'The Chant', 'Black Bottom Stomp', 'Sidewalk Blues', 'Dead Man Blues', 'Jelly Roll Blues' and 'Grandpa's Spells' in 1926 with a group featuring Kid Ory, Omer Simeon and Johnny St. Cyr, and 'The Pearls', 'Jungle Blues' and 'Wild Man Blues' in 1927 with a band that included both Johnny and Baby Dodds.

see Introduction pp 34 *see* Sources & Sounds pp 36 *see* A–Z of Artists pp 68

When the centre of jazz shifted to New York, Morton relocated there and from 1928–30 recorded several sides for the Victor label, including lesser-known tunes such as 'Low Gravy', 'Deep Creek', 'Tank Town Bump' and 'Smilin' The Blues Away'. For these New York sessions, Morton recorded with a new edition of the Red Hot Peppers, featuring trumpeters Henry 'Red' Allen and Bubber Miley, trombonists Geechie Fields and J.C. Higginbotham, clarinetists Omer Simeon and Albert Nicholas, bassist Pops Foster and drummers Paul Barbarin and Zutty Singleton.

A Jazz Musician's Testament

By 1930, Morton's style was considered old-fashioned and his work opportunities declined. He moved to Washington, DC in 1935 – the same year in which Benny Goodman's rendition of Morton's 'King Porter Stomp', arranged by Fletcher Henderson, ushered in the swing era – but throughout the decade Morton laboured with little success to regain his earlier status. Although his compositions were performed regularly, he did not receive royalties. In 1938, folklorist Alan Lomax recorded a series of interviews for the Library of Congress in which Morton reminisced about his New Orleans upbringing and his colourful career, while also providing examples of various piano styles. Lomax later used these interviews for an oral biography of Morton, which was released posthumously as *Mister Jelly Lord*. In 1939, Morton recorded eight sides for Bluebird in an all-star session that included New Orleans musicians Sidney Bechet, Sidney de Paris, Zutty Singleton, Henry 'Red' Allen and Albert Nicholas. He made his last recordings in January 1940 and died in poverty and obscurity at the age of 50 in Los Angeles on 10 July 1941.

Below

The mid-1920s recordings of Morton's Red Hot Peppers are classics, combining the spirit of New Orleans with the modernism of Chicago Jazz.

see New Orleans Rhythm Kings pp 30 *see* Henry 'Red' Allen pp 68 *see* George 'Pops' Foster pp 72 *see* Johnny St. Cyr pp 84

King Oliver

CLASSIC RECORDINGS

1923
King Oliver's Creole Jazz Band: 'Canal Street Blues', 'Chimes Blues', 'Dippermouth Blues', 'Froggie Moore', 'Mabel's Dream', 'Sobbin' Blues'

1924
King Oliver with Jelly Roll Morton: 'Tom Cat Blues'

1925
King Oliver's Dixie Syncopators: 'Snag It', 'Sugar Foot Stomp', 'West End Blues'

One of the cornet kings of early New Orleans – along with Buddy Bolden, Freddie Keppard and Bunk Johnson – Joseph 'King' Oliver helped to define the bravura spirit of hot jazz through his work in Chicago during the 1920s with his Creole Jazz Band. He is said to have earned the sobriquet 'King' by besting Keppard in a cutting contest one night in Storyville.

A King And His Mute

Born in Abend, Louisiana on 11 May 1885, Joseph Oliver began working around New Orleans as a cornettist in 1907 with the Onward Brass Band and later with the Eagle Band. By 1917, he became the star cornettist in a popular band led by Kid Ory. One of the early masters of the mute, Oliver created a whole lexicon of vocal effects on his horn during his two-year stint with Ory's band, which influenced a generation of musicians including trumpeter Bubber Miley and trombonist Tricky Sam Nanton – both of whom would play decisive roles in the Duke Ellington Orchestra in the 1930s. When Oliver went north to Chicago in February 1919, Ory hired his 18-year-old protégé Louis Armstrong as his replacement on cornet (Armstrong idolized Oliver and always referred to him as 'Papa Joe').

'Joe would stand there fingering his horn with his right hand and working his mute with his left, and how he would rock the place….'
George Wettling

Oliver Rocks Lincoln Gardens

In Chicago, Oliver established himself in Bill Johnson's band at the Dreamland Ballroom. Following a year-long stay in California, he returned to Chicago in June 1922 and started playing regularly with his Creole Jazz Band at the Lincoln Gardens on Chicago's South Side. The original line-up of the Creole Jazz Band included trombonist Honoré Dutrey, bassist Bill Johnson, clarinetist Johnny Dodds, drummer Baby Dodds and pianist Lil Hardin. In July he sent for Louis Armstrong, who joined the group in Chicago on 8 August. Oliver's Creole Jazz Band made its first recordings in April 1923 at the Richmond, Indiana studios of Gennett Records. Included in the batch of Oliver originals that they cut that day were 'Snake Rag', 'Zulu's Ball', 'Just Gone', 'Chimes Blues', 'Canal Street Blues' and 'Dippermouth Blues', which showcases Oliver's wah-wah technique.

Right
King Oliver, who taught Louis Armstrong the basics of ensemble cornet playing and improvisation.

see Introduction pp 34 see Sources & Sounds pp 36 see A–Z of Artists pp 68

Above
King Oliver (centre) with his band and assorted musical instruments.

Oliver Loses His Protégé

Lil Hardin and Louis Armstrong were married in February 1924 and Hardin had plans for her new husband, advising him on various matters and ultimately convincing him to leave his mentor's side and join Fletcher Henderson's Orchestra in New York. Shortly after Armstrong's exit, the Creole Jazz Band fell apart; in December 1924 Oliver recorded a pair of piano-cornet duets ('King Porter Stomp' and 'Tom Cat Blues') with Jelly Roll Morton for the Autograph label. In 1925, he took over Dave Peyton's band, which had a residency at the Plantation Café, and renamed it the Dixie Syncopators. From 1927–28, the Dixie Syncopators recorded prolifically for the Vocalion and Brunswick labels, and when the Plantation Café was destroyed by fire in 1929, the band went to New York and worked at the Savoy Ballroom. Oliver unwisely turned down an offer to become the house band at the Cotton Club in Harlem (the gig went to Duke Ellington's Orchestra, which became famous via the club's radio broadcasts) and Luis Russell later took over Oliver's band, renaming it the Luis Russell Orchestra.

Oliver's last recordings as a leader were in 1931 for the Victor, Brunswick and Vocalion labels, although he was suffering from a gum disease and rarely played himself, hiring other cornet players for the sessions. The New Orleans jazz legend spent his last years touring the South and finally settled in Georgia, where he worked as a janitor in a pool hall up until his death in 1938.

see Kid Ory pp 22 *see* Louis Armstrong pp 44 *see* Jelly Roll Morton pp 60 *see* Warren 'Baby' Dodds pp 72

Bessie Smith

CLASSIC RECORDINGS

1923
'Ain't Nobody's Business If I Do', 'Chicago Bound Blues', 'Down Hearted Blues', 'Gulf Coast Blues'

1925
'St. Louis Blues', 'You've Been A Good Ole Wagon'

1928
'Empty Bed Blues', 'It Won't Be You'

1929
'Nobody Knows You When You're Down And Out'

1930
'New Orleans Hop Scop Blues'

Bessie Smith was one of the greatest vocalists of the twentieth century; her emotional delivery and exquisite phrasing has been an influence on instrumentalists as well as innumerable singers, both male and female. Many of her records, including 'Gimmie a Pigfoot', 'Woman's Trouble Blues', 'St. Louis Blues' and the song that became an anthem of the Great Depression, 'Nobody Knows You When You're Down And Out', are still considered classics in both jazz and blues circles. Bessie worked for years in vaudeville and tent shows, and her versions of popular songs such as 'Alexander's Ragtime Band', as well as her potential as a swing artist evident in the sides from her final recording session, show that she was a more versatile performer than she is often given credit for.

Life On The Road

Born into crushing poverty in Chattanooga, Tennessee on 15 April 1894, Bessie Smith sang on street corners for tips as a girl, and in her teens she danced in a minstrel show; also performing in the show was Ma Rainey, who recognized Bessie's potential and encouraged her to sing the blues. While honing her craft and expanding her territory, Bessie worked extensively in travelling shows and relocated to several different cities. By the early 1920s she was starring in her own revue, touring the Theater Owners' Booking Association (TOBA) circuit along the Eastern Seaboard and through the South. In 1922 she met and fell in love with Jack Gee, a night watchman; they would marry the following year, although the union would be far from a happy one.

'We had a lot of great singers back then … Ethel Waters, Ida Cox, Sippie Wallace, Clara Smith, Trixie Smith – they were great singers but they couldn't reach Bessie.'

Little Brother Montgomery

Above
The 'Empress Of The Blues', Bessie Smith.

Far Right
Smith's confidence, determination and integrity, as well as her massive talent, contributed to her success.

Street Fighting Woman

Following a failed audition with Okeh records, at which it was reportedly declared that Bessie's voice sounded 'too rough', pianist Clarence Williams

accompanied her to a recording session at Columbia Records in New York on 15 February 1923. When Gee discovered that Williams was siphoning off the majority of the money made from Bessie's initial recordings, he severed the business arrangement, and Bessie signed a contract with Frank Walker at Columbia. Although she still recorded Williams' compositions, she now relied on Fletcher Henderson for piano accompaniment.

Her second session with Columbia resulted in 'Ain't Nobody's Business If I Do', a street-savvy declaration of defiance that became one of her theme songs, and which remains a classic of the genre. On the strength of that record and her subsequent releases,

see Introduction pp 34 see Sources & Sounds pp 36 see A–Z of Artists pp 68

Smith garnered national fame and toured widely, not just in the South but in northern cities where African-American migrants were pouring in, seeking jobs and better living conditions than they had been able to find back home. It was for these audiences that Bessie Smith crafted her music and her persona as a tough-talking, urbane woman of power who nonetheless retained memories of her southern roots.

The lyrics of the songs Smith recorded dealt uncompromisingly with the harsh realities of African-American life, although their overall themes – love, loss, betrayal, defiance and perseverance in the face of hard times – were universal. Even at her most mournful she undergirded her sorrow with steely resolve, as if determined to shout down suffering with the pure force of will and determination.

The Empress Of The Blues

Although her vocal range was limited, Smith employed a broad variety of vocal effects – growls, sobs, burnished hollers, church-like ascents and moans – that heightened her appeal for sophisticated jazz aficionados as well as the working-class blues audience that remained her core listenership. In 1925 she recorded some sessions with Louis Armstrong, who responded to her vocal lines on fare such as 'You've Been A Good Old Wagon' and 'St. Louis Blues' with unerring zest – he obviously treated her as a musical equal, and he riffed off her leads as though she were a fellow horn player. Bessie recorded with many of the key jazz and blues artists of the day, including Lonnie Johnson, Tommy Ladnier, James P. Johnson, Don Redman and the then fledgling blues singer Clara Smith, who was no relation – although the two women sometimes pretended to be sisters.

The Gees' marriage was proving to be a tempestuous one; extra-curricular liaisons by both parties, Bessie's gruelling schedule, disputes over money and the clashing of stubborn personalities and violent tempers resulted in the relationship finally coming to and end in spring 1929. Shortly afterwards, at W.C. Handy's suggestion, Bessie was cast in a short film based around the track 'St. Louis Blues'. In a sketchy plot that mirrored real life perhaps rather too closely for comfort, Smith played a woman who catches her man with another woman, before turning to drink and wailing the blues.

see Ma Rainey pp 24 *see* Clarence Williams pp 25 *see* James P. Johnson pp 76 *see* Don Redman pp 82

Above
The room where Smith died at the Riverside Blues Hotel, a former hospital near Clarksdale, Mississippi.

Far Right
Janis Joplin, who greatly admired Bessie Smith and helped to finally mark her grave with a tombstone in 1970.

Nobody Knows You When You're Down And Out

As the Great Depression hit America, work began to slow down for Bessie, as it did for many people. Audience figures were falling on the TOBA circuit and she performed her last tour with them in 1930. She began recording again with Clarence Williams, but Columbia were going through tough times, and dropped her from the label in 1931. Meanwhile, Bessie had found a new lover – Richard Morgan, a bootlegger and long-standing friend from Chicago who admired and respected her as both a person and an artist, and began acting as her manager.

In 1933, Bessie met John Hammond, who arranged a recording session for her at Okeh, a subsidiary label of Columbia. The band that Hammond had put together for the occasion included Jack Teagarden on trombone and Leon 'Chu' Berry on tenor saxophone, while clarinetist Benny Goodman, who happened to be recording in the same building, also contributed to 'Gimmie A Pigfoot'.

Successful appearances at prestigious New York venues (the Apollo Theater and Connie's Inn) in late 1935 and early 1936 suggested that Bessie Smith's star may have been about to rise again; she also had her ticket into the swing era working with Benny Goodman's band alongside Lionel Hampton, who was Morgan's nephew. Sadly, however, fate intervened.

A Tragic End On 'Blues Alley'

In the early morning of 26 September 1937, Smith was travelling along Highway 61, just outside of Clarksdale, Mississippi. The car in which she was riding sideswiped a truck. She was severely injured, with one of her arms

see Introduction pp 34 *see* Sources & Sounds pp 36 *see* A–Z of Artists pp 68

torn nearly loose at the elbow. A white physician stopped to help her; after he loaded her into his car, that car was also hit. The ambulance that finally arrived took her to Clarksdale's 'colored' hospital (the legend that she was refused admittance at a 'white' institution has no basis in fact), where she died, primarily from loss of blood.

So ended the life of one of the blues' most monumental talents. Bessie Smith represented not just the crowning glory of the 'classic blues' style, or of 1920s-era African-American popular music, or even of the blues as a whole. She was, and is, an artist against whom all others, male and female, black and white, in all areas of entertainment and popular art, continue to be judged.

The Legacy Of The Empress

Bessie had became known during her lifetime as the 'Empress Of The Blues', but even that title doesn't come close to truly reflecting her importance. Like her erstwhile contemporary Ma Rainey, and like other 'race heroes', such as Jack Johnson, Joe Louis, Jesse Owens and Paul Robeson, as well as such latter-day figures as Muhammad Ali, Aretha Franklin and James Brown, she came to symbolize more than mere excellence in her chosen field. With her air of brazen self-confidence, her apparently fearless strutting of her appetites (sexual and otherwise), her defiant refusal to compromise her selfhood or her integrity (at least in public), even her flair for ostentation and conspicuous consumption, she became a role model and heroine for African-American admirers who saw in her success a vision of what 'the race' might some day be able to achieve.

Smith's legacy has been strong and wide-ranging, particularly among female vocalists; artists as diverse as Billie Holliday, Janis Joplin, Dinah Washington and Mahalia Jackson have cited her as a key influence. Columbia's major reissue of her recordings in 1970 raised awareness of the fact that her grave was still unmarked. A letter to the *Philadelphia Inquirer* prompted a plea for donations, and the cost of a gravestone was divided between Janis Joplin and Juanita Green, a former maid of Bessie's. The stone was unveiled on 7 August, and the epitaph read: 'The Greatest Blues Singer in the World Will Never Stop Singing'.

see Benny Goodman pp 110 *see* John Hammond pp 125 *see* Dinah Washington pp 185 *see* Janis Joplin pp 274

A-Z of Artists

Above
Trumpet great Henry 'Red' Allen (second from left) with (l–r) trombonists J.C. Higginbotham and Lou McGarity, and saxophonist Lester Young.

Texas Alexander

(Vocals, 1900–54)

Alger 'Texas' Alexander's broad-toned, pugnacious vocal delivery recalled older work songs and field hollers, while his themes evoked the hard-travelling lives of migrant workers and hoboes. His recordings on OKeh in the 1920s paired him with sophisticated instrumentalists such as Clarence Williams, Lonnie Johnson and King Oliver. In his later years, he often worked alongside his cousin, vocalist-guitarist Lightnin' Hopkins; the pair recorded for Aladdin in 1947.

Henry 'Red' Allen

(Trumpet, 1908–67)

The son of bandleader Henry Allen Sr., Henry 'Red' Allen was one of the greatest trumpeters to come out of New Orleans, although he remained eternally in the shadow of Louis Armstrong. He moved to New York in 1927 to join King Oliver's Dixie Syncopators and in 1929 the Victor label signed him as an answer to rival OKeh's Armstrong.

Allen played with Luis Russell's Orchestra from 1929–32, then in 1933 joined Fletcher Henderson's Orchestra for a year, during which he appeared alongside Coleman Hawkins on influential recordings such as 'King Porter Stomp' and 'Down South Camp Meeting'. Following a stint with the Mills Blue Rhythm Band (1934–37), Allen returned to the Russell Orchestra, which by 1937 had become Armstrong's backing band. He then led his own bands through the 1940s and 1950s, participated in the 1957 CBS TV special *The Sound of Jazz* and toured Europe in 1959 with Kid Ory. Allen experienced a renaissance in the 1960s before succumbing to cancer.

Deford Bailey

(Vocals, harmonica, guitar, 1899–1982)

Deford Bailey was a member of the original Grand Ole Opry and was its first big star, until he was dismissed from the troupe in 1941 because allegedly he either could not or would not learn new material. His 'Pan American Blues', a harmonica train imitation, was one of the early Opry's most readily identifiable themes. Bailey recorded for both Brunswick and Victor, and while a member of the Opry he also toured with the show. A drive is currently underway to induct him into the Country Music Hall Of Fame, an institution that seldom, if ever, embraces black artists.

Right
Harmonica player Deford Bailey was one of the original stars of the Grand Ole Opry.

Far Right
Prolific composer Irving Berlin (left) discusses one of his songs with actor, dancer and singer Fred Astaire.

see Introduction pp 34 see Sources & Sounds pp 36 see Key Artists pp 44

Josephine Baker

(Vocals, dancer, 1906–75)

Born Freda Josephine McDonald, the St. Louis-born entertainer danced in the 1921 Sissle/Blake musical *Shuffle Along* before gaining a bigger role in their *Chocolate Dandies* in 1924, leading to appearances at the Cotton Club. The following year, she introduced 'le jazz hot' to Paris in *La Revue Négre* (also featuring Sidney Bechet) with her exotic dancing and uninhibited onstage sexuality. After working with the Red Cross and French Resistance during the Second World War – and adopting 12 children – she staged a major comeback in 1973, culminating in a 1975 performance at New York's Carnegie Hall.

Barbecue Bob

(Vocals, guitar, 1902–31)

Barbecue Bob Hicks was a mainstay of the 1920s Atlanta scene. His 12-string guitar technique featured percussive, banjo-like flailing and sometimes a bottleneck slide, instead of the rag-style fingerpicking often associated with the Southeast. Hicks recorded over 60 sides for Columbia, including his trademark 'Barbecue Blues' (he had a day job at a barbecue stand). He remained a popular entertainer in Atlanta jukes until his death.

Sidney Bechet

(Soprano saxophone, clarinet, 1897–1959)

A child prodigy who left school at the age of 16 and worked with various bands around New Orleans, the Creole clarinetist thrilled audiences and players alike with his soaring tone, forceful attack, penetrating solos, dazzling facility and unusually fast vibrato. In 1917, Bechet and King Oliver played together briefly in Kid Ory's band until Bechet relocated to Chicago. The following year, while on a European tour with Will Marion Cook's Southern Syncopated Orchestra, Bechet discovered the instrument with which he would eventually make jazz history: the unsual straight soprano saxophone.

Bechet made his first recordings in 1923 with the Clarence Williams Blue Five and continued to record prolifically throughout the 1920s and 1930s, scoring a hit in 1938 with his bluesy rendition of George Gershwin's 'Summertime'. The New Orleans revival of the 1940s made him an international star and he lived out his final years in France, where he was fêted as a national hero.

Irving Berlin

(Piano, songwriter, 1888–1989)

Born Israel Beilin in Siberia, Berlin's family relocated in 1893 to New York, where he broke into vaudeville. He published his first song in 1907 and in 1911 had his first major hit with 'Alexander's Ragtime Band'. One of America's most prolific melodicists, Berlin wrote hundreds of tunes that became standards, including 'Always', 'Cheek To Cheek', 'White Christmas' and 'There's No Business Like Show Business' from his successful musical *Annie Get Your Gun*. His songs have been interpreted by musicians from Bessie Smith to Charlie Parker to Cassandra Wilson.

see King Oliver pp 62 see Coleman Hawkins pp 74 see Lightnin' Hopkins pp 224 see Cassandra Wilson pp 367

Scrapper Blackwell

(Vocals, guitar, 1903–62)

Francis 'Scrapper' Blackwell is best known as Leroy Carr's musical partner, but he was also a gifted artist in his own right. In 1928 he recorded 'Kokomo Blues', which Kokomo Arnold covered as 'Original Old Kokomo Blues', before Robert Johnson retooled it as 'Sweet Home Chicago'. After Carr died in 1935, Blackwell retired from music until 1959, when he was 'rediscovered' by photographer Duncan Scheidt. In the midst of a somewhat tentative comeback, he was shot to death in an Indianapolis alley.

Below

Blind Blake, a virtuoso guitarist whose personal life remains a mystery.

Blind Blake

(Vocals, guitar, c. early 1890s–c. 1933)

Among the most influential instrumentalists in the blues, Blind Blake remains a mystery man in terms of his personal life. Born either Arthur Blake or Arthur Phelps, probably in Florida (Jacksonville or Tampa), he purveyed a ragtime-influenced, polyrhythmic picking technique that combined jaw-dropping technical virtuosity with an impeccably crafted symmetry. He approached his fretboard like a piano or even an entire orchestra, balancing themes, tonal attack, inflections and cadences, yet never losing either his improvisational flair or his seemingly limitless capacity for speed.

He recorded about 80 sides for Paramount (some with jazz clarinetist Johnny Dodds); after the label folded in 1932 he disappeared from sight. He is generally thought to have died about a year later. Generations of guitarists, from Rev. Gary Davis on down, owe much of their inspiration and their art to his genius.

Eubie Blake

(Piano, composer, 1883–1983)

A long-surviving link to the ragtime era, James Hubert Blake wrote his first piece, 'The Charleston Rag', in 1899. The Baltimore native started out playing piano in sporting houses and with travelling medicine shows in the early 1900s. He also worked with bandleader-composer James Reese Europe before teaming up on the vaudeville circuit with lyricist Noble Sissle in 1915 – they were billed as 'The Dixie Duo'. In 1921 they collaborated on the first all-black musical, *Shuffle Along*, which produced the hit song 'I'm Just Wild About Harry' and paved the way for several other all-black productions during the 1920s and 1930s.

After three decades of inactivity, Blake emerged with a triumphant two-record set on Columbia, *The Eighty-Six Years of Eubie Blake* (1969), which sparked a Blake revival and led to the highly successful 1978 Broadway musical revue, *Eubie* (which subsequently travelled to London). Blake continued performing until he was 98.

Garvin Bushell

(Clarinet, bassoon, 1902–91)

Jazz's first double-reed specialist on bassoon, Bushell played with Mamie Smith's Jazz Hounds before a two-year stint with Sam Wooding's Orchestra (1925–27). In 1928 he formed the Louisiana Sugar Babies with Fats Waller and Jabbo Smith, and he later worked with

see Introduction pp 34 *see* Sources & Sounds pp 36 *see* Key Artists pp 44

Otto Hardwick (1931), Fess Williams (1933), Fletcher Henderson (1935–36), Cab Calloway (1936–37) and Chick Webb (1938). In 1959 he replaced Omer Simeon in Wilbur de Paris's New Orleans Jazz Band, and in 1961 recorded live in a large ensemble with John Coltrane at the Village Vanguard.

Eddie Condon

(Banjo, guitar, 1905–73)

Originally from Indiana, Condon became associated with Chicago's Austin High School Gang, a group of white West-Side teenagers who emulated King Oliver's Creole Jazz Band and created their own take on hot jazz. In 1927, Condon co-led a band with William 'Red' McKenzie (which also included Bud Freeman, Frank Teschemacher, Gene Krupa and Jimmy McPartland) that helped to define the driving, freewheeling Chicago jazz sound of the Roaring Twenties. Condon also worked with Red Nichols & his Five Pennies and with McKenzie's Mound City Blue Blowers during the late 1920s.

Condon's considerable wit and charm made him an ideal spokesperson for the 1940s revival of traditional jazz. His all-star concerts in New York's Town Hall were broadcast weekly on the radio from 1944–45. He opened his own club, Condon's, in New York in 1945 and in 1949–50 hosted the first jazz television show, *Eddie Condon's Floor Show*. Condon continued to record, tour, write about and promote jazz until his death.

Ida Cox

(Vocals, 1896–1967)

An important figure in the so-called 'classic blues' genre, Ida Cox (née Prather) performed in minstrel and tent shows as a teenager. She had already become a vaudeville star when she began to record for the Paramount label in 1923. Apart from her gifts as a vocalist, she was an independent spirit who wrote much of her own material and managed several touring companies (e.g. Darktown Scandals and Raisin' Cain).

She was one of the relatively few 'classic blues' singers who continued to prosper during the Depression. In 1939 she appeared at John Hammond's landmark Spirituals To Swing concert in Carnegie Hall, but the market for her style of music dwindled in subsequent years and she suffered a stroke in the mid-1940s. Nevertheless, she continued to record and perform, on and off, until her death. Her final recording, from 1961, featured Coleman Hawkins on tenor sax.

Above

Eddie Condon was a key figure in the desegregation of jazz and helped to move the music into higher profile venues.

Left

Ida Cox, who remained a largely independent performer and wrote many of her own songs.

see Leroy Carr pp 50 *see* Noble Sissle pp 82 *see* Robert Johnson pp 112 *see* Rev. Gary Davis pp 173

Cow Cow Davenport

(Vocals, piano, c. 1894–1955)

Charles Davenport's best-known recording is 1928's 'Cow Cow Blues', a barrelhouse workout that kicks off with a chiming stop-time intro before plunging into a proto-boogie-woogie theme. Davenport recorded over 30 sides for various labels, and he worked in venues ranging from vaudeville theatres to house rent parties. Although slowed by a stroke in 1938, he continued to perform sporadically (sometimes as just a vocalist) until his death almost 20 years later.

Right
Johnny Dodds – possibly the finest clarinetist in New Orleans jazz.

Johnny Dodds

(Clarinet, 1892–1940)

The premier New Orleans clarinetist of the 1920s, Dodds played in Kid Ory's band from 1912–19 and then alongside Louis Armstrong and his own brother, Warren 'Baby' Dodds, in Fate Marable's riverboat band. Dodds left New Orleans in January 1921 to join King Oliver's Creole Jazz Band in Chicago, taking part in that influential band's classic 1923 recordings for Gennett.

Dodds played a key role in Armstrong's legendary Hot Five and Hot Seven sessions from 1925–27, and his virtuoso solos and distinctive, liquid tone also grace recordings by Jelly Roll Morton's Red Hot Peppers, the New Orleans Wanderers, the Chicago Footwarmers and his own Black Bottom Stompers, featuring Armstrong. He worked regularly in Chicago throughout the 1930s while also running a cab company with Baby Dodds. He led his final session on 5 June 1940, before passing away two months later.

Warren 'Baby' Dodds

(Drums, 1898–1959)

The grandfather of jazz drumming, Baby Dodds played in Fate Marable's riverboat band from 1918–21 before joining King Oliver's Creole Jazz Band and relocating to Chicago. He remained there for the rest of his career, collaborating with Jelly Roll Morton's Red Hot Peppers and Armstrong's Hot Seven, as well as trombonists Kid Ory and Miff Mole, trumpeter Bunk Johnson and clarinetists Jimmie Noone, Sidney Bechet and Dodds' brother Johnny. His soloist style influenced countless drummers, including Gene Krupa, Max Roach and Roy Haynes.

George 'Pops' Foster

(Bass, 1892–1969)

Known for his powerful, slap-bass sound and signature solos, Foster worked with the Magnolia Band and A.J. Piron before playing in Fate Marable's riverboat band (1918–21) and collaborating with Kid Ory and others during the 1920s. In 1928 he played with King Oliver's Dixie Syncopators in New York and then joined the Luis Russell Orchestra for an 11-year stint. Foster was in demand during the 1940s New Orleans revival and from 1956–61 he played with Earl Hines in San Francisco. Foster remained active into the mid-1960s.

Bud Freeman

(Tenor saxophone, clarinet, 1906–91)

Freeman was one of the Austin High School Gang, a group of white, jazz-seeking teenagers who were inspired by New Orleans Rhythm Kings records and obsessed with the hot jazz scene on Chicago's South Side. He recorded in 1927 with the McKenzie-Condon Chicagoans, then moved to New York to work with Red Nichols' Five Pennies. He eventually developed his own style on the tenor saxophone that offered a fresh alternative to Coleman Hawkins and Lester Young, as demonstrated by his masterful showcase on a 1933 Eddie Condon-led recording of 'The Eel'. Freeman became a swing star with the Tommy Dorsey band in 1936 and the Benny Goodman Orchestra in 1938. He was also the house saxophonist at Commodore Records in the 1930s. Freeman reunited with Eddie Condon in 1945

see Introduction pp 34 *see* Sources & Sounds pp 36 *see* Key Artists pp 44

and continued to play freewheeling Chicago-style jazz with the World's Greatest Jazz Band (1968–71) and as a leader into the early 1980s.

George Gershwin

(Piano, composer, 1898–1937)

One of the most enduringly popular composers of the twentieth century, Gershwin composed such enduring melodies as 'Summertime', 'Embraceable You' and 'Let's Call The Whole Thing Off'. His tuneful songs with their rich harmonic progressions are ideal for improvisation and were popular with jazz musicians including Louis Armstrong, Art Tatum, Oscar Peterson, Coleman Hawkins and Miles Davis.

A self-taught pianist, 15-year-old Gershwin was the youngest songwriter on Tin Pan Alley. He and his lyricist brother Ira scored their first big hit in 1919 with 'Swanee' for Al Jolson. From 1919–33 they produced a succession of musicals, including the first Pulitzer Prize-winning musical comedy, *Of Thee I Sing* (1931). In 1924, George wrote *Rhapsody In Blue* as a concerto for piano and the Paul Whiteman Orchestra. His success with this work led to the 1928 tone poem *An American In Paris* and his 1935 'folk opera' *Porgy & Bess*. The Gershwins went to Hollywood in 1936 but George died of a brain tumour the following year. Ira continued to work as a lyricist until retiring in 1960.

Edmond Hall

(Clarinet, 1901–67)

Raised in a musical family (his father Edward also played clarinet), Hall played around New Orleans during the early 1920s before departing to New York in 1928 to work with Alonzo Ross. He worked with Claude Hopkins, Lucky Millinder, Joe Sullivan and Zutty Singleton in the 1930s; with Teddy Wilson and Eddie Condon through the 1940s; and toured with Louis Armstrong's All-Stars from 1955–58. He reunited with Condon in the 1960s and made his final recording in 1967 at John Hammond's New York Spirituals To Swing concert.

Left
A publicity poster for Gershwin's 1935 'folk opera' *Porgy & Bess*.

Lil Hardin Armstrong

(Piano, vocals, arranger, 1898–1971)

Memphis-born pianist Lillian Hardin joined King Oliver's Creole Jazz Band in Chicago during the summer of 1921 and married fellow band member Louis Armstrong in 1924. She played on Armstrong's Hot Five and Hot Seven recordings and also received some composer credits. The couple separated in 1931 and were divorced in 1938. Lil subsequently worked as the house pianist at Decca Records and recorded up until 1961, remaining active on the Chicago club scene. She died during a performance of 'St. Louis Blues' at a Louis Armstrong memorial concert in Chicago.

Below
Jazz pianist Lil Hardin Armstrong, who married Louis Armstrong in 1924.

see Louis Armstrong pp 44 *see* Eddie Condon pp 71 *see* Lester Young pp 118 *see* Max Roach pp 182

Above
Saxophonist Coleman Hawkins, shown here with Miles Davis in the 1940s.

Coleman Hawkins

(Tenor saxophone, 1904–69)

'Hawk' played with Mamie Smith's Jazz Hounds in 1922 before joining Fletcher Henderson's band in New York. Louis Armstrong's presence in the band had a major effect on Hawkins' playing; by marrying a swing feel to his heavy tone, informed by his advanced understanding of harmony and chords, Hawkins became a star soloist and the pre-eminent saxophonist of his time.

Returning to the US in 1939 following a sojourn in Europe (during which he worked with Django Reinhardt and Stephane Grappelli), Hawkins recorded 'Body And Soul' – a masterpiece of melodic improvisation and one of the first pure jazz recordings to become a commercial hit. Hawkins was the first prominent swing-era artist to make the transition to bebop, playing with Thelonious Monk, Dizzy Gillespie and Don Byas. In 1948 Hawk made another milestone recording, 'Picasso', a stunning, unaccompanied solo. He recorded prolifically in the 1950s and 1960s with John Coltrane, Roy Eldridge, Duke Ellington, Max Roach, Sonny Rollins and Pee Wee Russell, among others.

Fletcher Henderson

(Piano, arranger, bandleader, 1897–1952)

The Georgia native came to New York in 1920 and worked at a music publishing company owned by Harry Pace and W.C. Handy. When Pace left in 1921 to form the Black Swan record label, Henderson followed as house pianist and arranger. In 1923 Henderson's session band, which included young talents such as Coleman Hawkins, landed a steady gig at the Club Alabam, and in 1924 began an engagement at the Roseland Ballroom; Louis Armstrong joined the same year.

From 1925–28, Henderson's swinging ensemble was among the finest in jazz, but the Depression took its toll and by 1935 Henderson was writing crack arrangements for the Benny Goodman Orchestra that essentially helped to launch the swing era. Henderson led his own small groups during the 1940s and in 1950 co-led a sextet with Lucky Thompson before being sidelined by a stroke.

Right
The Fletcher Henderson Orchestra in 1924. Henderson is seated behind the bass drum; Coleman Hawkins is second from the left with Louis Armstrong behind him, while Don Redman is on the far right.

see Introduction pp 34 *see* Sources & Sounds pp 36 *see* Key Artists pp 44

Peg Leg Howell

(Vocals, guitar, 1888–1966)

James Barnes 'Peg Leg' Howell, who lost his right leg after being shot when he was about 21 years old, led a three-man band – Peg Leg Howell & his Gang – in Atlanta during the mid- to late 1920s. He recorded for Columbia between 1926 and 1929 and continued to perform locally until the mid-1930s. He was 'rediscovered' in the blues revival of the early 1960s and in 1963 cut an album on Testament.

Alberta Hunter

(Vocals, 1895–1984)

Memphis-born Alberta Hunter ran away to Chicago as a young girl to seek her fortune as an entertainer. She survived the cutthroat world of early twentieth-century jazz long enough to establish herself as a front-line vocalist, albeit in a somewhat less-declamatory style than that favoured by some of her contemporaries. She recorded (sometimes using pseudonyms) for Black Swan, Paramount and other labels; she also appeared in several musical stage revues.

She toured overseas with the play *Showboat* (starring Paul Robeson) in the late 1920s, and in the 1930s she expanded her touring territory to include both Russia and the Middle East. Hunter retired in the mid-1950s and became a registered nurse in New York, but in the early 1960s she began to record again. In 1977, at the age of 82, she returned to performing and continued as a beloved and still-potent purveyor of dusky jazz and blues torch songs and ballads, mostly in upscale nightclub and concert settings, until her death.

Jack Hylton

(Piano, bandleader, 1892–1965)

Prominent British bandleader and booking agent Hylton began recreating the 'symphonic jazz' of Paul Whiteman's Orchestra in 1920. His band's popularity grew in England and France through the 1920s and early 1930s. In 1933 Hylton booked the Duke Ellington Orchestra to tour Europe for the first time. He toured the US with American musicians in 1935, reformed his British band in 1936 and toured through the 1930s before disbanding in 1940.

Papa Charlie Jackson

(Vocals, banjo, c. 1890–1938)

New Orleans-born Charlie Jackson brought a jazzman's sophistication to an instrument still too often overlooked by blues historians. He alternated single-string solos with percussive chording and dexterous fingerpicking, allowing him to bridge styles and genres with rare facility. He released more than 60 sides of his own, and he also recorded with Freddie Keppard, Tiny Parham and Kid Ory, as well as both Ma Rainey and Ida Cox.

Below
British bandleader Jack Hylton (centre) famously booked the Duke Ellington Orchestra to tour Europe for the first time.

see Duke Ellington pp 52 *see* Paul Whiteman pp 86 *see* Benny Goodman pp 110 *see* Thelonious Monk pp 208

Blind Willie Johnson

(Vocals, guitar, c. 1902–47)

Texas-born Willie Johnson, a purveyor of sacred material who would probably have been appalled at being categorized as a 'blues' artist, was blinded at the age of seven when his stepmother threw lye in his face after being beaten by his father. He sang in a hoarse, declamatory voice and his fretwork combined tonal purity and pinpoint accuracy (even when using a pocket-knife slide) with an emotional intensity unsurpassed by any acoustic guitarist, regardless of genre.

His masterpiece, the instrumental 'Dark Was The Night (Cold Was The Ground)', invokes soul-chilling existential dread, and was once described by guitarist Ry Cooder as 'the most transcendent piece in all American music'. Other works – 'Jesus Make Up My Dying Bed', 'Keep Your Lamp Trimmed And Burning' – are testament to his faith and the resolute certainty with which he held it. Johnson, who recorded 30 sides for Columbia in 1927–30, died after contracting pneumonia, having spent a night sleeping in wet clothes after his house burned down.

Below

Blind Willie Johnson coloured the sacred music he recorded with exquisite slide guitar.

James P. Johnson

(Piano, composer, 1894–1955)

The seminal figure among the Harlem stride pianists, Johnson was a mentor to Fats Waller and composer of 'The Charleston', which launched a Jazz Age dance craze. Count Basie, Duke Ellington and Art Tatum were also directly influenced by Johnson's skilful stride and compositions, including 'You've Got To Be Modernistic' – an evolutionary leap from ragtime. His 'Carolina Shout' became proving ground for other stride pianists of the day. Johnson also composed music for the 1923 Broadway show *Runnin' Wild*.

Tommy Ladnier

(Cornet, trumpet, 1900–39)

A stylistic descendant of King Oliver, Ladnier learned under Bunk Johnson and played in various bands around New Orleans. Around 1917 he moved to Chicago, where he became part of the hot jazz scene and worked with Jimmie Noone and King Oliver. In 1925 he toured Europe with Sam Wooding's band and the following year joined Fletcher Henderson in New York. In 1932, Ladnier formed the New Orleans Feetwarmers with Sidney Bechet before dropping off the scene, re-emerging in 1938 with Mezz Mezzrow until his premature death from a heart attack.

Eddie Lang

(Guitar, 1902–33)

Philadelphia native Salvatore Massaro joined the Mound City Blue Blowers in 1924 and by the mid-1920s had become jazz's first in-demand session guitarist, backing various blues and popular singers. A single-note virtuoso, he was also jazz's first guitar hero.

see Introduction pp 34 *see* Sources & Sounds pp 36 *see* Key Artists pp 44

younger-generation aficionados throughout his post-1959 'rediscovery' period. In 1975 he had a cameo alongside Burt Reynolds in the film *W.W. And The Dixie Dance Kings*.

George Lewis

(Clarinet, alto saxophone, 1900–68)

Lewis (born George Louis Francis Zeno) led bands in New Orleans in the 1920s, but he remained in the Crescent City while many of his colleagues headed north to Chicago, where the Jazz Age was being forged on the city's South Side. Lewis did not record until the 1940s (in sessions that teamed him with New Orleans trumpeter Bunk Johnson) and he later became a prominent figure in the New Orleans revivalist movement of the 1950s.

Left
Guitar virtuoso Eddie Lang, who formed a fruitful musical partnership with violinist Joe Venuti.

Below
Following a background in medicine shows, Furry Lewis became a popular entertainer.

In 1926, Lang teamed up with high-school pal Joe Venuti for some classic guitar-violin duet sessions that predated Stephane Grappelli's work with Django Reinhardt. Lang recorded prolifically during 1927, appearing on commercial sessions and also playing in more jazz-oriented settings with Jean Goldkette, Frankie Trumbauer, Red Nichols and Bix Beiderbecke. In 1928 he teamed up with fellow guitarist Lonnie Johnson for some historic duet recordings and in 1929 joined Paul Whiteman's Orchestra, which featured a young Bing Crosby. When Crosby left to launch his solo career in 1932, Lang became his full-time accompanist. The guitarist's career came to an end with his untimely death the following year.

Furry Lewis

(Vocals, guitar, 1893–1981)

Born in Greenwood, Mississippi, Walter 'Furry' Lewis played medicine shows as a young man. After moving to Memphis, he recorded 23 sides for Vocalion and Victor between 1927 and 1929. Despite a somewhat chaotic guitar technique, he was an indefatigable entertainer and he became a beloved figure among

see Bunk Johnson pp 28 *see* Joe Venuti pp 85 *see* Sam Wooding pp 87 *see* Art Tatum pp 135

Above
McKinney's Cotton Pickers, who recorded some of the tightest ensemble playing in 1920s jazz.

McKinney's Cotton Pickers

(Instrumental group, 1926–34)

Formed in 1926 by drummer Bill McKinney (1895–1969), this Ohio-based big band improved significantly after hiring arranger Don Redman from Fletcher Henderson's band in the summer of 1927. For the next four years, until Redman left in 1931, McKinney's Cotton Pickers rivalled both Henderson's and Duke Ellington's orchestras for ensemble precision. The band's trumpeter and principal soloist John Nesbitt (a close friend of Bix Beiderbecke) also contributed potent arrangements throughout the 1920s.

Jimmy McPartland

(Trumpet, 1907–91)

Part of the Chicago-based Austin High School Gang, along with Bud Freeman, Frank Teschemacher, Jim Lannigan and Dave Tough, McPartland was inspired by recordings of the New Orleans Rhythm Kings and Bix Beiderbecke, who he replaced in the Wolverines in 1925. He joined Ben Pollack's band in 1927 and recorded with the McKenzie-Condon Chicagoans that same year. McPartland worked steadily through the 1930s in Chicago and continued leading Dixieland sessions for the next four decades.

see Introduction pp 34 *see* Sources & Sounds pp 36 *see* Key Artists pp 44

Blind Willie McTell

(Vocals, guitar, 1901–59)

A skilled purveyor of the ragtime-influenced Piedmont fingerpicking style, Atlanta-based Blind Willie McTell incorporated pop songs and novelty numbers, as well as blues, into his repertoire – befitting an entertainer who got his start in tent shows, medicine shows and carnivals. His voice was unusually tender and expressive for a musician who made his living as a street singer, adding depth and poignancy to deftly crafted meditations on infatuation and loss like his now-standard 'Statesboro Blues'.

His recording career extended (with some significant interruptions) from 1927–56 and his style remained the same throughout. His gift of conveying intense emotion through low-key, intimate vocals rather than flamboyant shouting – as well as his vivid lyric imagery and piano-like, contrapuntal picking artistry on both six- and 12-string guitars (he also played harmonica, accordion and fiddle) – have made him one of the most revered of the south-eastern acoustic blues artists.

Memphis Jug Band

(Vocal/instrumental group, 1927–34)

They did not invent the style, but guitarist/harpist Will Shade (a.k.a. Son Brimmer) and his rollicking aggregation were among the most popular and influential of the jug and string bands that proliferated around Memphis and Louisville, as well as in the Mississippi Delta, during the 1920s and 1930s. With various personnel coming and going, the Jug Band included instruments such as violin, jug, kazoo, piano, mandolin, banjo, guitar, harmonica and washtub bass, and recorded nearly 60 sides for Victor.

Their members over the years included such luminaries as Furry Lewis, harpist Big Walter Horton and guitarist Casey Bill Weldon, as well as occasional female guest vocalists. Their repertoire included some blues, but their speciality was tightly arranged pop and novelty numbers, some of which (e.g. 'Stealin', Stealin'') have become standards, and all of which they performed with a theatrical, vaudevillian flair. Although the Jug Band disbanded in the 1930s, Shade himself soldiered on with various reincarnated versions until his death in 1966.

James 'Bubber' Miley

(Trumpet, 1903–32)

A key figure in the Duke Ellington Orchestra of 1926–28, Miley played a lead role on such classic pieces of early Ellingtonia as 'East St. Louis Toodle-Oo', 'Black And Tan Fantasy' and 'Creole Love Call'. His uniquely expressive, growling trumpet style was influenced by the plunger mute approach of King Oliver, and served as one of the signatures of Ellington's 'jungle sound'. Miley formed his own band in 1930 but shortly afterwards died of tuberculosis, aged 29.

Below

Cornettist Jimmy McPartland was a soldier during the Second World War, and took part in the 1944 D-Day invasion of Normandy.

see Bix Beiderbecke pp 48 see Furry Lewis pp 77 see Ben Pollack pp 81 see Don Redman pp 82

Punch Miller

(Trumpet, cornet, 1894–1971)

One of the leading New Orleans cornettists during the 1920s, Ernest 'Punch' Miller moved to Chicago in 1926 and found work with fellow New Orleanians Freddie Keppard and Jelly Roll Morton, as well as with Tiny Parham and Albert Wynn's Gutbucket Five. He spent the 1930s in New York before returning to Chicago. In 1956, Miller returned to New Orleans; he recorded his last sessions in the mid-1960s with trombonist George Lewis.

Below

Virtuoso trombonist Miff Mole (second from right) playing with the Original Memphis Five.

Mississippi Sheiks

(Vocal/instrumental group, 1926–35)

The Mississippi Sheiks were Lonnie Chatmon (guitar, violin) and Walter Vinson (guitar), sometimes joined by Chatmon's brothers Sam (guitar, violin) and Armenter (a.k.a. Bo Carter, guitar), as well as Charlie McCoy (banjo, mandolin); the vocals were shared between the group members. Their repertoire blended blues themes with contemporary pop/novelty tunes, similar to a jug band's but somewhat less hokey in its delivery. According to Sam Chatmon's recollections, they played mostly for white audiences. They recorded for OKeh and Bluebird; their 'Sitting On Top Of The World' has become a standard, subsequently interpreted by Howlin' Wolf and Cream, among many others.

Right

The name Red Nichols gave his groups, 'Five Pennies', was a play on his surname (five cents/pennies make a nickel) and often had more than five members.

Far Right

A photo card for Ben Pollack's Park Central Hotel Orchestra, which included Jack Teagarden and Benny Goodman.

Miff Mole

(Trombone, 1898–1961)

A vital figure of the 1920s, Irving Milfred Mole was among the earliest trombonists with the virtuosity to express fully developed musical lines on an instrument largely still relegated to glissandos and rhythm accents. Mole elevated the instrument to first-chair status on hundreds of records and solos, many recorded with Red Nichols. He left jazz to work in radio after 1929, played in various traditional groups after the Second World War, and was reunited with Nichols in 1956 on the television show *This Is Your Life*.

Sam Morgan

(Trumpet, 1895–1936)

An early practitioner of New Orleans jazz, Morgan travelled the Bay St. Louis-Pensacola-Mobile circuit and played Crescent City venues, including the Savoy on Rampart Street, before suffering a stroke in 1925. He recovered and in 1927 made recordings at the Werlein's Music Store on Canal Street for the Columbia label, including 'Mobile Stomp', 'Bogalousa Strut' and his vocal feature, 'Short Dress Gal'. Morgan continued to play until he had a second stroke in 1932.

'Hambone' Willie Newbern

(Vocals, guitar, 1899–1947)

A resident of Brownsville, Tennessee, Willie Newbern had only one recording session, for OKeh in Atlanta in 1929. Although he was not widely known outside his area, he influenced quite a few musicians: he recorded the first known version of 'Roll And Tumble Blues' and is said to have taught it to Charley Patton, among others. Allegedly he was killed while serving time in prison.

Red Nichols

(Cornet, 1905–65)

As a child, Nichols played in his father's brass band. After moving to New York in 1923 he teamed up with trombone player Miff Mole, and this marked the start of a long musical partnership. With Mole, Nichols recorded various line-ups under different names, the most common of which was Red Nichols & his Five Pennies. He worked prolifically on Broadway and radio as well as on tour and in the studio; a film was made about his life in 1959.

see Introduction pp 34 *see* Sources & Sounds pp 36 *see* Key Artists pp 44

Jimmie Noone

(Clarinet, 1895–1944)

The most fluid and graceful of the classic New Orleans clarinetists, Noone worked with trumpeter Freddie Keppard (1914) and also with the Young Olympia Band (1916) before following Keppard to Chicago in 1917. A member of King Oliver's first Creole Jazz Band (1918–20), he also played in Doc Cooke's Dreamland Orchestra (1920–26) before forming his popular Apex Club Orchestra (featuring Earl Hines) in 1928. Noone led bands throughout the 1930s and joined Kid Ory in 1944.

Ben Pollack

(Drums, 1903–71)

A member of the Chicago-based New Orleans Rhythm Kings, Pollack formed his own band in 1926 and by 1928 was employing such promising young players as Benny Goodman, Jimmy McPartland, Jack Teagarden and Glenn Miller. When Pollack's orchestra disbanded in 1934, its membership became the core group for Bob Crosby's orchestra. Pollack became the musical director for Chico Marx in the early 1940s and continued to play Dixieland music with his Pick-A-Rib Boys into the 1960s.

see Charley Patton pp 23 *see* Jack Teagarden pp 136 *see* Glenn Miller pp 180 *see* Howlin' Wolf pp 225

Below

New Orleans drummer Zutty Singleton, whose versatility enabled him to play both traditional and developing styles of jazz, as well as blues music.

Far Right Top

Victoria Spivey in a 1920s photograph signed by the blues star to bandleader Luis Russell.

Far Right Bottom

Mamie Smith with her Jazz Hounds in 1922. Note Bubber Miley on trumpet and a youthful Coleman Hawkins on saxophone.

Don Redman

(Alto saxophone, clarinet, vocals, composer, arranger, 1900–64)

Renowned for crafting the polished sound of the mid-1920s Fletcher Henderson Orchestra, Redman's innovative arrangements pre-dated the swing era by a decade. His sophisticated compositions were significantly affected by the driving, swinging trumpet work of Louis Armstrong, who played in Henderson's orchestra throughout 1924. The conservatory-trained arranger left Henderson's band in 1927 to become musical director of McKinney's Cotton Pickers for four years, then led his own big band from 1931–41.

Zutty Singleton

(Drums, 1898–1975)

Arthur 'Zutty' Singleton was one of the first New Orleans drummers, along with Baby Dodds, to develop a melodic approach to the kit and the concept of the extended drum solo. He played in the second configuration of Louis Armstrong's Hot Five, appearing on OKeh recordings cut in 1928 (including the landmark 'West End Blues'), and then moved to New York the following year. In the 1930s he played with Fats Waller, Eddie Condon and Bubber Miley, while also leading his own band.

After moving to Los Angeles in 1943, he demonstrated his versatility by working with a variety of artists including bluesman T-Bone Walker, Dixielander Wingy Manone and jivester Slim Gaillard (appearing on 'Slim's Jam' with bebop icons Charlie Parker and Dizzy Gillespie). He spent the early 1950s in Europe working with Hot Lips Page, and through the 1960s could be found playing drums at Jimmy Ryan's club in New York.

Noble Sissle

(Vocals, composer, bandleader, 1889–1975)

Sissle worked with bandleader James Reese Europe from 1916–19, before teaming up with Eubie Blake; together Sissle and Blake wrote hits for Sophie Tucker and the successful all-black musicals *Shuffle Along* (1921) and *Chocolate Dandies* (1924). Sissle led his own bands in Europe during the late 1920s before returning to America in 1931 and forming a new group that featured singer Lena Horne. Between 1938 and 1950, Sissle's orchestra held forth at Billy Rose's Diamond Horseshoe Club in New York.

Jabbo Smith

(Trumpet, 1908–91)

This Georgia-born trumpeter (real name Cladys Smith) was on the New York scene by the age of 17 in 1925, working with Charlie Johnson's house band at Small's Paradise. In 1927 he played on Duke Ellington's 'Black And Tan Fantasy' and later that year joined James P. Johnson and Fats Waller in Chicago for a production of *Keep Shufflin'*. By 1929, Smith was being touted as competition for Louis Armstrong on the strength of recordings with his Rhythm Aces for Brunswick.

Mamie Smith

(Vocals, 1883–1946)

Mamie Smith's first recording session, for OKeh in 1920, resulted in a pair of nondescript pop songs, but her manager Perry Bradford then talked the label into recording her as a blues singer. On 10 August 1920, fronting a band dubbed the Jazz Hounds – featuring stride pianist Willie 'The Lion' Smith (no relation) and possibly also cornettist Johnny Dunn – Smith cut the first record ever billed as a 'blues': 'Crazy Blues'. It sold upwards of a million copies, and in support she toured with a flamboyant show that featured trapeze artists, comedians, dancers and other embellishments from her vaudeville past.

Despite her horn-like vocal timbre and emotional delivery, Smith was not really a blues singer: her rhythmic sense was pedestrian, her intonation stiff. But 'Crazy Blues' virtually defined the genre – at least as a recorded popular music – for a generation of women vocalists who followed, each one of whom came in through the door that Mamie Smith had opened.

see Introduction pp 34 *see* Sources & Sounds pp 36 *see* Key Artists pp 44

Pine Top Smith

(Piano, vocals, 1904–29)

A seminal figure in the development of boogie-woogie piano, self-taught Clarence 'Pine Top' Smith was raised in Birmingham, Alabama and worked the southern club and vaudeville circuit during the early 1920s. In 1928 he relocated to Chicago, where he roomed with fellow boogie-woogie piano pioneers Meade 'Lux' Lewis and Albert Ammons. Smith recorded his signature 'Pine Top's Boogie-Woogie' for Vocalion in 1928. The following year he was shot in a Chicago dance hall and died aged just 25.

Trixie Smith

(Vocals, 1895–1943)

Atlanta-born Trixie Smith was a vaudeville trouper when, in 1922, she cut her first records on Black Swan. Although she did not have the vocal prowess of front-line blues stars like Bessie Smith (no relation), she recorded steadily until 1926 – often with top-flight jazz orchestras such as Fletcher Henderson's – and sporadically thereafter. In the 1930s, after her recording career slackened off, she continued in showbusiness, appearing in musical revues and films.

Victoria Spivey

(Vocals, piano, 1906–76)

Houston native Victoria Spivey cut her first sides for OKeh in 1926 and she was soon one of the most popular artists of the 'classic blues' era. An eloquent lyricist alongside her vocal gifts, Spivey worked steadily into the 1940s; in 1962 she emerged from retirement as the head of blues label Spivey Records, on which she recorded herself and other 'rediscovered' blues artists (along with a guest appearance by a youthful Bob Dylan). She continued to record and perform, based in New York City, until her death.

see Eubie Blake pp 70 see Warren 'Baby' Dodds pp 72 see Fletcher Henderson pp 74 see Hot Lips Page pp 131

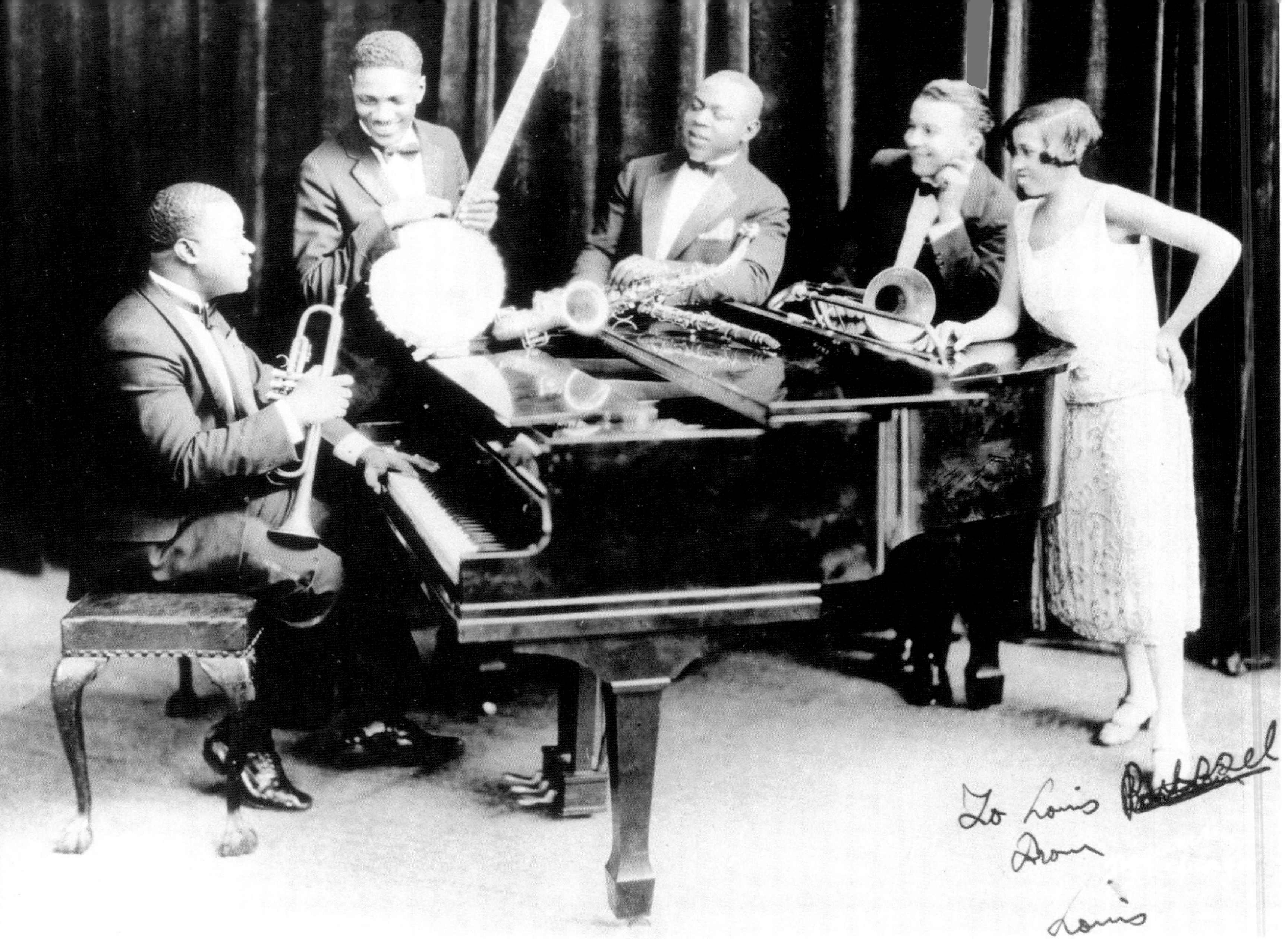

Above
Johnny St. Cyr (second from left) in Louis Armstrong's original Hot Five line-up with (l–r) Armstrong, Johnny Dodds, Kid Ory and Lil Hardin Armstrong.

Far Right
Harlem-based stride pianist and hugely popular entertainer Fats Waller.

Johnny St. Cyr

(Guitar, banjo, 1890–1966)

Johnny St. Cyr played around New Orleans as a teenager with A.J. Piron and the Superior, Olympia and Tuxedo bands. He joined Kid Ory's band in 1918 and later played in Fate Marable's riverboat band. In 1923 he moved to Chicago, where he joined King Oliver's Creole Jazz Band. He played on Armstrong's historic Hot Five and Hot Seven sessions (1925–27) and also recorded with Jelly Roll Morton's Red Hot Peppers (1926). St. Cyr led a small Dixieland band at Disneyland from 1961 until his death.

Henry Thomas

(Vocals, quills, guitar, 1874–1930)

A son of former slaves, Henry 'Ragtime' Thomas specialized in the quills, a panpipe-like instrument made from hollow reeds. He was itinerant for most of his life, a fact reflected in songs such as 'Railroadin'', in which Thomas names train stops from Fort Worth to Chicago. His 'Bull Doze Blues', renamed 'Goin' Up The Country', became a 1960s hit for Canned Heat, who recreated his quills intro note for note.

Frankie Trumbauer

(C-melody and alto saxophone, 1901–56)

Known as 'Tram' by his colleagues, Trumbauer was a player of impeccable technique who had a major influence on many saxophonists in the 1920s (notably Benny Carter and Lester Young). He first recorded in 1923 with the popular Benson Orchestra of Chicago and by 1926 was playing alongside cornettist and kindred spirit Bix Beiderbecke in Jean Goldkette's Orchestra at the Graystone Ballroom in Detroit.

see Introduction pp 34 *see* Sources & Sounds pp 36 *see* Key Artists pp 44

Bix and Tram – the two greatest white instrumentalists of the period – were reunited as star soloists in Paul Whiteman's orchestra in 1927. Trumbauer remained until 1932, during which time he was also on the bandstand with Eddie Lang, Joe Venuti, Andy Secrest, Mildred Bailey and Bing Crosby. His second hitch with Whiteman lasted four years, from 1933–36, and was followed by a stint with the Three Ts, featuring Charlie and Jack Teagarden. Trumbauer continued to record both as a sideman and a leader in the early 1950s.

Joe Venuti

(Violin, 1903–78)

Venuti teamed up with guitarist Eddie Lang in 1926 for some classic duet sessions on OKeh. They reprised their intimate chemistry on 1928 sessions and worked together through the 1920s and 1930s on recordings for Jean Goldkette, Paul Whiteman, Red McKenzie and Roger Wolfe Kahn. In 1933 Venuti led small group sessions and in 1935 fronted a big band. He experienced a major comeback in the 1970s. Venuti was a great practical joker and is fondly remembered in amusing anecdotes from many of his colleagues.

Fats Waller

(Piano, vocals, composer, 1904–43)

Thomas Wright 'Fats' Waller developed his playing style during the early 1920s under the tutelage of Harlem stride pianists James P. Johnson and Willie 'The Lion' Smith. The son of a Baptist preacher, he began playing in the church and by the age of 15 was the house organist at the Lincoln Theatre. He first recorded for OKeh aged 18 and shortly thereafter met lyricist Andy Razaf, who became a key collaborator on popular tunes such as 'Honeysuckle Rose', 'Ain't Misbehavin'' and '(What Did I Do To Be So) Black And Blue' as well as successful musicals *Keep Shufflin'* and *Hot Chocolates*.

By 1924 Fats was well known for his piano rolls, radio broadcasts and extroverted, off-the-cuff, jivey performance style. He also flaunted dazzling piano work on many instrumentals, including 'A Handful Of Keys', 'Smashing Thirds' and 'Jitterbug Waltz'. Waller recorded with a sextet in the mid-1930s and by 1940 was a household name.

see Bix Beiderbecke pp 48 *see* Eddie Lang pp 76 *see* Benny Carter pp 122 *see* Willie 'The Lion' Smith pp 134

Above

Ethel Waters surrounded by dancers at the Cotton Club show in Harlem, New York.

Ethel Waters

(Vocals, 1896–1977)

Ethel Waters' most significant blues releases, on Cardinal and Black Swan, were recorded in the early 1920s. Versatile and ambitious, she soon moved into a more pop-oriented direction, and she also began to work in films and theatrical productions. It was in theatre that she eventually made her greatest mark, but after a mid-1950s religious conversion she joined evangelist Billy Graham's crusade, with which she remained until her death.

Paul Whiteman

(Violin, bandleader, 1890–1967)

Erroneously dubbed 'The King Of Jazz' by press agents, Whiteman led his first dance band in San Francisco in 1918. Arriving in New York in 1920, he assembled some of the city's top musicians and gained popularity with hits such as 'Japanese Sandman' and 'Whispering'. In 1924 his orchestra premiered George Gershwin's *Rhapsody In Blue*. Whiteman's best band (1927–30) included such superb soloists as Frankie Trumbauer, Bix Beiderbecke, Eddie Lang and Joe Venuti, and launched crooner Bing Crosby's career.

see Introduction pp 34 *see* Sources & Sounds pp 36 *see* Key Artists pp 44

Rev. Robert Wilkins

(Vocals, guitar, 1896–1987)

Mississippi-born Robert Wilkins' blues style, as evidenced on records he made for Victor, Brunswick and Vocalion from 1928–35, featured vivid lyric imagery couched in asymmetrical verses, laid over rudimentary strumming. After being ordained in the 1930s, Wilkins quit the blues for religious music. 'Prodigal Son' on the Rolling Stones' *Beggars Banquet* (1968) was a cover of Wilkins' 'That's No Way To Get Along' – ironically, a blues that the Stones recast in a more biblical light.

Sam Wooding

(Piano, arranger, bandleader, 1895–1985)

Wooding led his Society Syncopators in the early 1920s before travelling to Berlin in 1925 with the *Chocolate Kiddies* revue. One of the first wave of expatriate American jazz musicians to live abroad, he spent the remainder of the 1920s in Europe playing with bands that featured star soloists such as Doc Cheatham and Tommy Ladnier. He returned to the United States in 1935 but had little success swimming against the tide of the swing era.

Below

Bandleader Paul Whiteman, whose orchestral line-up at various times included Bix Beiderbecke, Eddie Lang and Bing Crosby.

see Frankie Trumbauer pp 84 *see* Joe Venuti pp 85 *see* Doc Cheatham pp 122 *see* Rolling Stones pp 278

List of Artists

Entries appear in the following order: name, music style, year(s) of popularity, instruments, country of origin.

Abbey, Leon, Traditional Jazz; Big Band, 1920s–1960s, Violin, bandleader, American
Ahola, Sylvester, Traditional Jazz, 1920s–1970s, Trumpet, American
Akers, Garfield, Delta Blues, 1920s–1930s, Guitar, vocals, American
Alexander, Alger 'Texas', Country Blues, 1920s–1950s, Vocals, American
Allen, Ed, New Orleans Jazz; Traditional Jazz, 1920s–1960s, Trumpet, American
Allen, Henry 'Red'. New Orleans Jazz; Swing; Chicago Jazz; Dixieland, 1920s–1960s, Trumpet, vocals, composer, American
Alvin, Danny, Traditional Jazz, 1920s–1950s, Drums, bandleader, American
Anthony, Eddie, Country Blues, 1920s–1930s, Violin, American
Ardoin, Amadie, Country Blues, 1920s–1930s, Vocals, accordion, American
Armstrong, Louis, New Orleans Jazz; Swing; Chicago Jazz, 1920s–1970s, Trumpet, vocals, American
Austin, Lovie, Swing; Traditional Jazz, 1920s–1960s, Piano, American
Bacon, Louis, Swing; Traditional Jazz, 1920s–1940s, Trumpet, American
Bailey, Buster, Big Band; Swing; Traditional Jazz, 1920s–1960s, Clarinet, saxophone, American
Bailey, Deford, Country Blues, 1920s, Harmonica, American
Bailey, Kid, Mississippi Blues, 1920s, Vocals, American
Bailey, Mildred, Country Blues; Swing, 1920s–1950s, Vocals, American
Baker, Edythe, Boogie-Woogie, 1920s, Vocals, American
Baker, Josephine, Swing, 1920s; 1970s, Vocals, dancer, American
Baker, Willie, Country Blues, 1920s–1960s, Vocals, guitar, American
Barbeque Bob, Country Blues, 1920s–1930s, Guitar, American
Barnes, Polo, Traditional Jazz; Swing; New Orleans Jazz, 1920s–1970s, Clarinet, saxophone, American
Barrelhouse Buck, Country Blues, 1920s–1960s, Piano, vocals, American
Batts, Will, Country Blues, 1920s–1950s, Violin, leader, American
Bauduc, Ray, New Orleans Jazz; Big Band, 1920s–1980s, Drums, American
Baxter, Andrew and Jim, Country Blues, 1920s, Violin, guitar, American
Beale Street Sheiks, Delta Blues, 1920s, Various instruments, American
Bechet, Sidney, Chicago Jazz; New Orleans Jazz, 1920s–1950s, Clarinet, soprano saxophone, American
Beiderbecke, Bix, New Orleans Jazz; Traditional Jazz, 1920s–1930s, Cornet, piano, American
Bell, Edward 'Ed', Country Blues, 1920s–1960s, Guitar, American
Benford, Tommy, Swing; Traditional Jazz, 1920s–1980s, Drums, American
Bennett, Cuban, Swing; Bebop, 1920s–1940s, Trumpet, American
Benson, Ivy, Swing, 1920s–1980s, Bandleader, saxophone, keyboard, British
Bentley, Gladys, Country Blues, 1920s–1940s, Vocals, piano, American
Berlin, Irving, Ragtime; Vaudeville, 1920s–1960s, Piano, songwriter, Russian
Berton, Vic, Big Band; Traditional Jazz, 1920s–1940s, Drums, American
Bigard, Barney, New Orleans Jazz; Swing, 1920s–1970s, Clarinet, saxophone, American
Bishop, Wallace, Swing; Traditional Jazz; Bebop, 1920s–1980s, Drums, American
Black Ace, Country Blues; Texas Blues, 1920s–1940s, Guitar, American
Blackwell, Scrapper, Chicago Blues, 1920s–1930s; 1950s–1960s, Guitar, vocals, American
Blake, Eubie, Ragtime, 1920s–1980s, Piano, composer, American
Bland, Jack, Traditional Jazz, 1920s–1940s, Guitar, banjo, American
Blind Blake, Country Blues, 1920s–1930s, Guitar, vocals, American
Blind Boy Fuller, Folk Blues; Country Blues 1920s–1940s, Guitar, vocals, American
Blythe, Jimmy, Traditional Jazz, 1920s–1930s, Piano, American
Bogan, Lucille, Country Blues, 1920s–1930s, Vocals, American
Bonano, Sharkey, Chicago Jazz, 1920s–1960s, Trumpet, vocals, bandleader, American
Bonds, Son, Country Blues, 1920s–1940s, Guitar, American
Bose, Stirling, Traditional Jazz; Big Band; Chicago Jazz, 1920s–1950s, Trumpet, cornet, American
Boswell Sisters, The, Swing, 1920s–1930s, Various instruments, American
Bracey, Ishman, Delta Blues, 1920s–1930s, Guitar, American
Braud, Wellman, Big Band; Swing, 1920s–1960s, Bass, American
Briggs, Arthur, Traditional Jazz; British Jazz, 1920s–1940s, Trumpet, American
Brown, Bessie, Ragtime, 1920s–1930s, Vocals, American
Brown, Henry, Country Blues, 1920s–1970s, Piano, American
Brown, Vernon, Swing; Big Band, 1920s–1970s, Trombone, American
Brunies, Abbie, New Orleans Jazz; Traditional Jazz; Dixieland Jazz, 1920s–1960s, Cornet, American
Brunies, Georg, New Orleans Jazz; Traditional Jazz; Dixieland Jazz; Ragtime, 1920s–1970s, Trombone, American
Brunies, Merritt, New Orleans Jazz; Traditional Jazz; Dixieland Jazz, 1920s–1960s, Cornet, trombone, American
Brunis, Georg, Chicago Jazz, 1920s–1960s, Trombone, vocals, American
Bunn, Teddy, Swing; Traditional Jazz, 1920s–1970s, Guitar, American
Burse, Charlie, Swing; Country Blues, 1920s–1960s, Banjo, guitar, American
Bushell, Garvin, New Orleans Jazz, 1920s–1960s, Clarinet, bassoon, American
Butterbeans & Susie, Country Blues, 1920s–1930s, Various instruments, American
Caldwell, Happy, Chicago Jazz; Swing; Big Band, 1920s–1940s, Saxophone, clarinet, American
California Ramblers, Traditional Jazz, 1920s–1930s, Various instruments, American
Call, Bob, Country Blues, 1920s–1950s, Piano, American
Calloway, Blanche, Swing, 1920s–1970s, Vocals, bandleader, American
Campbell, Gene, Country Blues, 1920s–1930s, Vocals, guitar, American
Cannon's Jug Stompers, Country Blues, 1920s–1930s, Various instruments, American
Carmichael, Hoagy, Traditional Jazz, 1920s–1960s, Piano, vocals, composer, American
Carney, Harry, Swing; Big Band, 1920s–1970s, Saxophone, American
Carr, Leroy, Boogie-Woogie, 1920s–1930s, Piano, vocals, composer, American
Carter, Bo, Country Blues, 1920s–1940s, Guitar, vocals, American
Casa Loma Orchestra, Swing; Big Band, 1920s–1960s, Various instruments, American
Challis, Bill, Traditional Jazz; Swing, 1920s–1980s, Arranger, American
Chittison, Herman 'Ivory', Traditional Jazz, 1920s–1960s, Piano, American
Christian, Buddy, New Orleans Jazz, 1920s, Banjo, American
Clark Sisters, The, Gospel, 1920s–1940s, Vocals, American
Clay, Sonny, Traditional Jazz, 1920s–1960s, Piano, drums, bandleader, American
Clayborn, Reverend Edward, Country Blues, 1920s, Vocals, guitar, American
Clayton, John, Big Band; Swing, 1920s–, Bass, composer, arranger, bandleader, American
Cobb, Junie, Big Band; Traditional Jazz, 1920s–1960s, Clarinet, saxophone, banjo, piano, violin, American
Coleman, Bill, Traditional Jazz; Swing, 1920s–1980s, Trumpet, American
Coleman, Jaybird, Country Blues, 1920s–1930s, Harmonica, American
Collins, Lee, New Orleans Jazz; Traditional Jazz, 1920s–1950s, Trumpet, bandleader, American
Collins, Sam, Country Blues, 1920s–1940s, Guitar, American
Condon, Eddie, Chicago Jazz; Swing; Big Band, 1920s–1970s, Guitar, banjo, bandleader, American
Coon-Sanders Nighthawks, Traditional Jazz, 1920s–1930s, Various instruments, American
Cooper, Harry, Swing, 1920s–1940s, Trumpet, American
Copeland, Martha, Classic Blues, 1920s, Vocals, American
Corley, Dewey, Country Blues, 1920s–1970s, Harmonica, kazoo, American
Cox, Ida, Country Blues. 1920s–1960s, Vocals, American
Crawley, Wilton, New Orleans Jazz; Swing, 1920s–1940s, Clarinet, American
Crosby, Bing, Swing; Traditional Jazz, 1920s–1970s, Vocals, American
Crosby, Bob, Swing; Traditional Jazz; Big Band; Dixieland, 1920s–1990s, Vocals, bandleader, American
Crump, Jesse, Country Blues, 1920s–1960s, Piano, organ, American
Dandridge, Putney, Swing, 1920s–1940s, Piano, vocals, American
Daniels, Joe, Swing, 1920s–1950s, Drums, bandleader, American
Daniels, Julius, Country Blues, 1920s–1940s, Guitar, vocals, American
Darby, Blind Teddy, Country Blues, 1920s–1930s, Guitar, American
Davenport, Charles 'Cow Cow', Boogie-Woogie, 1920s–1950s, Piano, American
Davenport, Jed, Memphis Blues, 1920s–1960s, Harmonica, guitar, trumpet, American
Davis, Walter, Country Blues, 1920s–1940s, Vocals, piano, American
Davison, Wild Bill, Dixieland Revival, 1920s–1980s, Cornet, American
DeBerry, Jimmy, Memphis Blues, 1920s–1950s, Ukulele, banjo, guitar, American
DeParis, Sidney, Chicago Jazz, 1920s–1960s, Trumpet, tuba, vocals, American
DeParis, Wilbur, Traditional Jazz; Dixieland, 1920s–1970s, Trombone, bandleader, American
Dickerson, Carroll, New Orleans Jazz; Swing; Chicago Jazz, 1920s–1950s, Violin, leader, American
Dixon, Mary, Texas Blues, 1920s, Vocals, American
Dodds, Baby, New Orleans Jazz, 1920s–1950s, Drums, American
Dodds, Johnny, New Orleans Jazz, 1920s–1940s, Clarinet, American
Dominique, Natty, New Orleans Jazz, 1920s–1950s, Trumpet, American
Dranes, Arizona, Country Blues, 1920s, Vocals, piano, American
Dunbar, Scott, Country Blues, 1920s–1960s, Guitar, vocals, American
Duncan, Hank, Swing; New Orleans Jazz, 1920s–1960s, Piano, American
Durham, Eddie, Swing; Big Band, 1920s–1980s, Trombone, guitar, arranger, American
Dutrey, Honoré, New Orleans Jazz, 1920s–1930s, Trombone, American
Edwards, Cliff 'Ukulele Ike', Traditional Jazz, 1920s–1970s, Vocals, ukulele, American
Edwards, Moanin' Bernice, Memphis Blues, 1920s–1930s, Piano, vocals, American
Edwards, Susie, Country Blues, 1920s–1960s, Vocals, American
Elizade, Fred, British Jazz, 1920s, Piano, composer, leader, American
Ellington, Duke, Swing, 1920s–1970s, Piano, arranger, composer, American
Etting, Ruth, Traditional Jazz, 1920s–1950s, Vocals, American
Evans, Stump, Chicago Jazz, 1920s, Saxophones, American
Ezell, Will, Boogie-Woogie, 1920s, Piano, American
Fosdick, Dudley, Chicago Jazz, 1920s–1950s, Mellophone, American
Foster, George 'Pops', New Orleans Jazz, 1920s–1960s, Bass, American
Freeman, Bud, Swing, 1920s–1980s, Saxophone, clarinet, composer, American
Garber, Jan, Big Band, 1920s–1970s, Violin, bandleader, American
Garland, Joe, Swing; Chicago Jazz, 1920s–1950s, Saxophones, arranger, American
Gershwin, George, Ragtime, 1920s–1930s, Piano, composer, American
Gibson, Clifford, Country Blues, 1920s–1930s, Guitar, American
Glinn, Lillian, Texas Blues, 1920s, Vocals, American
Goldkette, Jean, Traditional Jazz, 1920s–1960s, Bandleader, French
Gonella, Nat, Dixieland, 1920s–1970s, Trumpet, vocals, British
Gowans, Brad, Swing, 1920s–1950s, Trombone, clarinet, cornet, saxophones, American
Grant, Coot, Country Blues, 1920s–1940s, Vocals, American
Graves, Blind Roosevelt, Country Blues, 1920s–1930s, Guitar, vocals, American
Green, Charlie 'Big', Traditional Jazz, 1920s–1930s, Trombone, American
Green, Leothus Lee, Country Blues, 1920s–1930s, Piano, American
Greer, Sonny, Swing, 1920s–1940s, Drums, American
Guarente, Frank, New Orleans Jazz; New York Jazz, 1920s–1940s, Trumpet, Italian
Guy, Fred, Swing, 1920s–1960s, Guitar, banjo, American
Hall, Adelaide, Swing, 1920s–1940s, Vocals, American

Hall, Edmond, New Orleans Jazz; Swing, 1920s–1960s, Clarinet, saxophone, American
Hanshaw, Annette, Traditional Jazz, 1920s–1930s, Vocals, American
Hardin Armstrong, Lil, Swing; Traditional Jazz, 1920s–1970s, Piano, vocals, composer, American
Hardwick, Otto, Bebop; Hard Bop, 1920s–1940s, Saxophone, American
Harris, William, Delta Blues, 1920s, Vocals, guitar, American
Harrison, Jimmy, Swing; Chicago Jazz, 1920s–1930s, Trombone, vocals, American
Hart, Hattie, Memphis Blues, 1920s–1940s, Vocals, American
Hawkins, Coleman, Swing; Bebop, 1920s–1960s, Saxophone, American
Hawkins, Walter 'Buddy Boy', Ragtime, 1920s, Guitar, vocals, American
Hayes, Clancy, Chicago Jazz, 1920s–1970s, Banjo, drums, vocals, composer, American
Hayes, Clifford, Traditional Jazz, 1920s–1930s, Violin, bandleader, American
Hegamin, Lucille, Country Blues, 1920s–1930s: 1960s, Vocals, American
Henderson, Fletcher, Swing; Big Band, 1920s–1950s, Piano, arranger, bandleader, composer, American
Henderson, Rosa, Classic Blues, 1920s–1930s, Vocals, American
Heywood, Eddie, Swing, 1920s–1980s, Piano, composer, American
Hicks, Edna, Country Blues, 1920s, Vocals, American
Higginbotham, J.C., Swing; New Orleans Jazz, 1920s–1960s, Trombone, American
Hill, Bertha 'Chippie', Country Blues, 1920s, Vocals, American
Hill, Teddy, Bebop; Swing, 1920s–1970s, Saxophone, bandleader, American
Hokum Boys, Hokum, 1920s–1930s, Various instruments, American
Holland, Peanuts, Swing; Big Band, 1920s–1970s, Trumpet, vocals, composer, American
Holmes, Charlie, Swing, 1920s–1980s, Saxophone, clarinet, oboe, flute, American
Howell, Peg Leg, Country Blues, 1920s–1930s, Vocals, composer, American
Hunter, Alberta, Rhythm & Blues, 1920s–1980s, Vocals, American
Hutchison, Frank, Country Blues, 1920s–1930s, Harmonica, guitar, American
Hylton, Jack, Swing; Big Band, 1920s–1930s, Piano, bandleader, British
Irvis, Charlie, Big Band, 1920s–1930s, Trombone, American
Jackson, Bo Weavil, Chicago Blues, 1920s, Vocals, guitar, American
Jackson, Cliff, Swing, 1920s–1970s, Piano, American
Jackson, Papa Charlie, Country Blues, 1920s–1930s, Banjo, American

Jackson, Peg Leg Sam, Country Blues, 1920s–1970s, Harmonica, American
Jackson, Preston, New Orleans Jazz, 1920s–1930s, Trombone, American
Jarrett, Pigmeat, Chicago Blues, 1920s–1990s, Piano, American
Jaxon, Frankie 'Half Pint', East Coast Blues, 1920s–1940s, Vocals, American
Jefferson, Blind Lemon, Country Blues; Texas Blues, 1920s, Guitar, vocals, American
Jefferson, Hilton, Big Band; Swing, 1920s–1960s, Saxophone, American
Johnson, Blind Willie, Texas Blues, 1920s–1940s, Guitar, vocals, American
Johnson, Charlie, Swing, 1920s–1950s, Piano, bandleader, American
Johnson, Edith, Delta Blues, 1920s–1960s, Piano, vocals, American
Johnson, James P., Ragtime, 1920s, Piano, arranger, composer, American
Johnson, Lonnie, Country Blues, 1920s–1960s, Guitar, vocals, banjo, American
Johnson, Mary, Delta Blues, 1920s–1930s, Vocals, American
Johnson, Pete, Boogie-Woogie, 1920s–1960s, Piano, American
Jones, Claude, Chicago Jazz, 1920s–1950s, Trombone, vocals, American
Jones, Dennis 'Little Hat', Country Blues, 1920s–1930s, Vocals, guitar, American
Jones, Isham, Traditional Jazz, 1920s–1940s, Saxophones, bass, American
Jones, Moody, Chicago Blues, 1920s–1950s, Guitar, American
Jones, Richard M., New Orleans Jazz, 1920s–1940s, Piano, vocals, composer, arranger, American
Jordan, Charley, Country Blues, 1920s–1940s, Vocals, guitar, American
Kahn, Roger Wolfe, Dixieland; Swing, 1920s–1930s, Leader, multi-instrumentalist, American
Kelly, Guy, Chicago Jazz, 1920s–1930s, Trumpet, American
Kelly, Jack, Memphis Blues, 1920s–1950s, Vocals, songwriter, American
Keppard, Freddie, New Orleans Jazz, 1920s–1930s, Cornet, American
Kirk, Andy, Swing; Big Band, 1920s–1950s, Saxophones, tuba, American
Klein, Manny, Swing; Big Band; Chicago Jazz, 1920s–1990s, Trumpet, American
Kress, Carl, Swing; Traditional Jazz, 1920s–1960s, Guitar, American
Lacy, Rube, Country Blues, 1920s, Vocals, guitar, American
Ladnier, Tommy, Traditional Jazz, 1920s–1930s, Trumpet, American
Lamare, Nappy, Dixieland; Swing, 1920s–1960s, Guitar, banjo, vocals, American
Lambert, Donald, Swing, 1920s–1960s, Piano, American
Lang, Eddie, Swing, 1920s–1930s, Guitar, American
Laury, Lawrence 'Booker T', Boogie-Woogie, 1920s–1950s, Piano, American

Levine, Henry 'Hot Lips', Dixieland; New Orleans Jazz, 1920s–, Trumpet, British
Lewis, Furry, Delta Blues, 1920s; 1960s–1970s, Guitar, vocals, American
Lewis, George, New Orleans Jazz, 1920s–1960s, Clarinet, saxophone, American
Lewis, Noah, Country Blues, 1920s–1960s, Harmonica, American
Lewis, Willie, Traditional Jazz; Swing, 1920s–1940s, Saxophone, clarinet, vocals, American
Lincoln, Abe, Swing; Dixieland, 1920s–1970s, Trombone, American
Lincoln, Charley, Country Blues, 1920s–1930s, Guitar, American
Marshall, Kaiser, Swing, 1920s–1940s, Drums, American
McConough, Dick, Swing, 1920s–1930s, Guitar, banjo, American
McCoy, Charlie 'Mississippi Muddler', Country Blues; Delta Blues, 1920s–1930s, Vocals, guitar, mandolin, American
McCoy, Joe, Country Blues, 1920s–1930s, Guitar, vocals, American
McCoy, Viola, Country Blues, 1920s–1930s, Vocals, American
McCracken, Bob, Swing; Chicago Jazz, 1920s–1960s, Clarinet, saxophone, American
McKenzie, Red, Swing; Chicago Jazz; Big Band, 1920s–1940s, Vocals, kazoo, American
McKinney, Bill, Swing, 1920s–1940s, Drums, leader, American
McKinney's Cotton Pickers, Big Band; Swing, 1920s–1930s, Various instruments, American
McPartland, Jimmy, Chicago Jazz; Dixieland, 1920s–1930s, Trumpet, American
McTell, Blind Willie, East Coast Blues; Country Blues, 1920s–1950s, Guitar, vocals, American
Memphis Jug Band, Country Blues, 1920s–1930s, Various instruments, American
Metcalf, Louis, Swing, 1920s–1950s, Trumpet, vocals, American
Mezzrow, Mezz, Dixieland, 1920s–1950s, Saxophone, clarinet, American
Miles, Lizzie, Country Blues, 1920s–1930s, Vocals, American
Miley, Bubber, Big Band, 1920s, Trumpet, composer, American
Miller, Punch, New Orleans Jazz; Chicago Jazz, 1920s–1970s, Trumpet, vocals, American
Mississippi Sheiks, Country Blues, 1920s–1930s, Various instruments, American
Mole, Miff, Chicago Jazz, 1920s–1950s, Trombone, American
Moore, Alex 'Whistling', Country Blues; Texas Blues, 1920s–1980s, Vocals, piano, composer, American
Moore, Monette, Country Blues, 1920s–1950s, Piano, vocals, American
Morand, Herb, Chicago Jazz, 1920s–1940s, Trumpet, vocals, American
Morehouse, Chauncey, Dixieland; Swing, 1920s–1970s, Drums, percussion, American
Morgan, Sam, New Orleans Jazz, 1920s–1930s, Trumpet, American
Morton, Benny, Swing; Big Band, 1920s–1980s, Trombone, American
Morton, Jelly Roll, New Orleans Jazz, 1920s–1940s, Piano, vocals, arranger, composer, American
Mosley, Snub, Swing, 1920s–1970s, Trombone, saxophone, vocals, American
Moten, Bennie, Big Band, 1920s–1930s, Piano, composer, bandleader, American
Murray, Don, New Orleans Jazz; Traditional Jazz, 1920s, Clarinet, saxophone, violin, American
Nanton, Joe 'Tricky Sam', Swing, 1920s–1940s, Trombone, American
Napoleon, Phil, Traditional Jazz; Dixieland, 1920s–1990s, Trumpet, bandleader, American
Nelson, Romeo, Country Blues, 1920s, Vocals, piano, American
Newbern, 'Hambone' Willie, Country Blues, 1920s, Guitar, vocals, American
Newton, Frankie, Swing, 1920s–1950s, Trumpet, American
Nicholas, Albert, New Orleans Jazz, 1920s–1970s, Clarinet, saxophone, American
Nichols, Red, Chicago Jazz, 1920s–1960s, Cornet, American
Nixon, Hammie, County Blues, 1920s–1980s, Vocals, mandolin, guitar, American
Noble, Ray, Swing; Big Band, 1920s–1970s, Composer, leader, British
Noone, Jimmie, New Orleans Jazz, 1920s–1930s, Clarinet, saxophones, American
O'Brien, Floyd, Chicago Jazz, 1920s–1960s, Trombone, American
O'Bryant, Jimmy, Traditional Jazz, 1920s, Clarinet, American
Oliver, King, New Orleans Jazz, 1920s–1930s, Cornet, composer, American
Parham, Tiny, Chicago Jazz, 1920s–1930s, Piano, organ, arranger, composer, American
Partch, Harry, World Fusion, 1920s–1970s, Composer, American
Paul, Emmanuel, New Orleans Jazz, 1920s–1980s, Saxophone, banjo, vocals, American
Peer, Ralph, Country Blues, 1920s–1930s, Producer, American
Phillips, Sid, Dixieland Revival, 1920s–1960s, Clarinet, saxophone, piano, arranger, leader, British
Phillips, Washington, Country Blues, 1920s, Vocals, dulceola, American
Pierce, Billie, New Orleans Jazz, 1920s–1970s, Piano, vocals, American
Pollack, Ben, Dixieland; Swing, 1920s–1960s, Drums, bandleader, American
Polo, Danny, Cool Jazz, 1920s–1940s, Clarinet, saxophone, American
Poston, Joe, New Orleans Jazz, 1920s–1940s, Saxophone, clarinet, vocals, American
Powell, Rudy, Swing, 1920s–1970s, Saxophone, clarinet, American
Procope, Russell, Swing, 1920s–1970s, Saxophone, clarinet, American
Purvis, Jack, Swing; Big Band, 1920s–1930s, Trumpet, trombone, vocals, piano, multi-instrumentalist, composer, American
Rank, Bill, Swing; Big Band; Jump Blues, 1920s–1970s, Trombone, American
Redman, Don, Swing, 1920s–1950s, Saxophones, vocals, arranger, composer, American
Reynolds, Blind Joe, Mississippi Blues, 1920s–1960s, Vocals, American

see Introduction pp 34 *see* Sources & Sounds pp 36 *see* Key Artists pp 44 *see* A–Z of Artists pp 68

Rhodes, Walter, Memphis Blues, 1920s–1930s, Vocals, accordion, American
Rich, Fred, Swing, 1920s–1950s, Piano, composer, leader, Polish
Robichaux, Joseph, New Orleans Jazz; Traditional Jazz, 1920s–1960s, Piano, American
Robinson, Ikey, Traditional Jazz, 1920s–1990s, Banjo, guitar, vocals, American
Robinson, Jim, New Orleans Jazz; Free Jazz, 1920s–1960s, Trombone, American
Robinson, Willard, New Orleans Jazz, 1920s–1960s, Composer, American
Rodgers, Jimmie, Country Blues, 1920s–1930s, Vocals, guitar, composer, American
Rodin, Gil, Swing; Big Band, 1920s–1970s, Saxophone, clarinet, flute, Russian
Rollini, Adrian, Traditional Jazz, 1920s–1950s, Saxophone, American
Roppolo, Leon, New Orleans Jazz, 1920s–1940s, Clarinet, composer, American
Roth, Lillian, East Coast Blues, 1920s–1970s, Vocals, American
Sampson, Edgar, Swing, 1920s–1960s, Saxophone, violin, arranger, composer, American
Sane, Dan, Country Blues, 1920s–1930s, Guitar, American
Schutt, Arthur, Chicago Jazz; Swing, 1920s–1960s, Piano, arranger, American
Scott, Cecil, Traditional Jazz, 1920s–1950s, Clarinet, saxophone, American
Scott, James, Ragtime, 1920s, Piano, American
Secrest, Andy, Big Band; Traditional Jazz, 1920s–1950s, Trumpet, cornet, American
Seward, Alec, Ragtime, 1920s–1960s, Vocals, guitar, American
Shade, Will, Country Blues, 1920s–1960s, Harmonica, vocals, guitar, American
Simeon, Omer, New Orleans Jazz; Swing, 1920s–1950s, Clarinet, American
Singleton, Zutty, Swing; Big Band, 1920s–1970s, Drums, American
Sissle, Noble, Traditional Jazz, 1920s–1950s, Vocals, composer, bandleader, American
Smith, Bessie, Country Blues, 1920s–1930s, Vocals, American
Smith, Buster, Swing, 1920s–1990s, Saxophone, arranger, composer, American
Smith, Clara, Country Blues, 1920s–1930s, Vocals, American
Smith, Ivy, Country Blues, 1920s–1930s, Vocals, American
Smith, Jabbo, Bebop, 1920s–1970s, Trumpet, trombone, vocals, American
Smith, Joe, Swing, 1920s–1930s, Trumpet, American
Smith, Laura, Country Blues, 1920s, Vocals, composer, American
Smith, Mamie, Country Blues, 1920s, Vocals, American
Smith, Pinetop, Boogie-Woogie, 1920s, Piano, American
Smith, Russell, Swing; Big Band, 1920s–1950s, Trumpet, American
Smith, Trixie, Country Blues, 1920s–1930s, Vocals, American
Snow, Valaida, Swing; Big Band, 1920s–1950s, Trumpet, vocals, American
Snowden, Elmer, Traditional Jazz, 1920s–1960s, Guitar, banjo, bandleader, American
South, Eddie, Swing, 1920s–1950s, Violin, American
Spand, Charlie, Country Blues, 1920s–1930s, Vocals, piano, American
Speckled Red, Boogie-Woogie, 1920s–1930s, Piano, American
Speir, H.C., Delta Blues; Country Blues, 1920s–1930s, Talent scout, American
Spivey, Victoria, Country Blues, 1920s–1930s, Vocals, American
Spruell, Freddie, Country Blues, 1920s–1930s, Vocals, guitar, American
St Cyr, Johnny, New Orleans Jazz, 1920s–1930s, Banjo, guitar, American
Stark, Bobby, Swing; Big Band, 1920s–1940s, Trumpet, American
State Street Ramblers, Traditional Jazz, 1920s–1930s, Various instruments, American
Stuckey, Henry, Delta Blues; Country Blues, 1920s–1930s, Guitar, vocals, American
Taggart, Blind Joe, Country Blues, 1920s–1930s, Guitar, American
Taylor, Eva, Country Blues, 1920s–1940s, Vocals, American
Taylor, Montana, Chicago Blues, 1920s–1930s, Piano, American
Teagarden, Charlie, Swing; Chicago Jazz, 1920s–1960s, Trumpet, American
Teagarden, Norma, Dixieland Revival, 1920s–1980s, Piano, American
Teschemacher, Frank, Traditional Jazz, 1920s–1930s, Clarinet, saxophone, American
Thomas, Henry 'Ragtime Texas', Country Blues, 1920s–1930s, Guitar, vocals, composer, American
Thomas, Hersal, Country Blues, 1920s, Piano, American
Thomas, Hociel, Country Blues, 1920s–1940s, Vocals, American
Thomas, Joe, Swing; Big Band; Chicago Jazz, 1920s–1950s, Saxophone, clarinet, vocals, American
Thomas, Ramblin', Country Blues, 1920s–1930s, Guitar, American
Tough, Dave, Chicago Jazz, 1920s–1940s, Drums, American
Townsend, Henry, Country Blues, 1920s–1980s, Guitar, American
Trent, Aslphonso E., Swing, 1920s–1950s, Piano, leader, American
Trumbauer, Frankie, Big Band; Traditional Jazz; New Orleans Jazz, 1920s–1950s, Saxophone, multi-instrumentalist, vocals, American
Tucker, Bessie, Country Blues; Delta Blues, 1920s, Vocals, American
Tucker, Sophie, Ragtime, 1920s–1960s, Vocals, American
Valentine, Kid Thomas, New Orleans Jazz, 1920s–1970s, Trumpet, American
Venuti, Joe, Swing, 1920s–1970s, Violin, American
Vinson, Walter, Delta Blues, 1920s–1940s; 1960s–1970s, Guitar, American
Waller, Fats, Swing, 1920s–1940s, Piano, vocals, American
Waters, Ethel, Swing; Country Blues, 1920s–1960s, Vocals, American
Weatherford, Teddy, New Orleans Jazz; Chicago Jazz, 1920s–1940s, Piano, American
Weaver, Curley, Country Blues, 1920s–1930s; 1950s, Guitar, American
Weaver, Sylvester, Country Blues, 1920s, Guitar, vocals, American
Webb, Speed, Swing; Big Band, 1920s–1940s, Leader, drums, vocals, American
Weldon, Casey Bill, Country Blues, 1920s–1940s, Guitar, vocals, American
Wells, Dicky, Swing, 1920s–1980s, Trombone, American
Wettling, George, Chicago Jazz, 1920s–1950s, Drums, American
Whiteman, Paul, Big Band; Traditional Jazz, 1920s–1960s, Bandleader, violin, American
Wiggs, Johnny, New Orleans Jazz, 1920s–1960s, Cornet, American
Wilcox, 'Spiegle', Traditional Jazz; Swing; Big Band, 1920s–1970s, Trombone, American
Wilkins, Rev. Robert, Country Blues, 1920s–1930s, Guitar, vocals, American
Williams, Claude 'Fiddler', Swing, 1920s–2000s, Violin, guitar, vocals, American
Williams, J. Mayo 'Ink', Country Blues; Chicago Blues, 1920s–1940s, Producer, American
Williams, Mary Lou, Swing; Bebop, 1920s–1970s, Piano, arranger, composer, American
Williams, Sandy, Swing; Big Band, 1920s–1950s, Trombone, American
Wilson, Edith, Country Blues, 1920s–1960s, Vocals, American
Winston, Edna, Country Blues, 1920s, Vocals, American
Winters, Tiny, Swing; Bebop, 1920s–1990s, Bass, vocals, leader, British
Wooding, Sam, Swing, 1920s–1960s, Piano, arranger, American
Yancey, Jimmy, Boogie-Woogie, 1920s–1940s, Piano, American

see Leroy Carr pp 50 *see* Blind Lemon Jefferson pp 56 *see* McKinney's Cotton Pickers pp 78 *see* Zutty Singleton pp 82

THE THIRTIES

As if at the convenience of history, the stock market crash in the final weeks of 1929 severed the 1920s from the 1930s. The breach was economic but its consequences were pervasive, sweeping away economic values and social illusions, and affecting all aspects of life for Americans and Europeans alike. America's compliant 1920s middle class became the 1930s 'new poor'. Rural African-Americans were pitched back into conditions akin to slavery; those in the urban North and West after the Great Migration struggled anew to adapt. Poverty's ubiquity lent it unusual moral standing, reflected in movies and songs. Businessmen lost status; the wealthy were subjected to cultural ridicule and liberal reform unleashed by one of their own, President Franklin D. Roosevelt. Clashes over small-town and big-city values were replaced by battles over wages and hours between capital and labour.

Popular culture found easy ways forth. Network radio, paid for by advertisers, took hold; outlets competed for local and niche audiences, hiring bluesmen to host shows aimed at African-American listeners, for example. The record industry almost expired, but live music, especially for dancers, thrived. Movies, combining social realism and romantic fantasy, offered the decade's most iconic imagery. Within 10 years, movies and touring bands displaced theatre and vaudeville as transmitters of a popular culture, available for the first time to millions simultaneously, sea to sea – and beyond. That culture was centred on jazz, steeped in the blues, immersed in transition. In April 1939 the New York World's Fair opened a vision to a future dominated by technology, which 1930s music and art had essentially come to represent. Five months later the decade ended with the beginning of the Second World War. Music and art were to face another wild ride.

Sources & Sounds

KEY ARTISTS

Albert Ammons
Count Basie
Big Bill Broonzy
Charlie Christian
Roy Eldridge
Benny Goodman
Robert Johnson
Leadbelly
Lester Young

The early part of the 1930s was dominated by one major event: the collapse of American financial institutions that led to what is known as the 'Great Depression'. The disaster was underway as the decade began, and hit its lowest point in 1932. Significantly, in the final quarter of that year, there was not a single blues recording session anywhere in America. The Depression hung over America like a dark cloud and economic conditions improved very slowly. While the government instituted many reforms and programmes to help the unemployed, it could do only so much. It would take a wartime economy in the next decade to pull the country out of the doldrums.

Right
The shadow of the Great Depression hung over 1930s America.

Political Change

The 1930s also saw a rise in radical political activity. Critics of capitalism found eager followers, workers banded together in labour unions, and artists and intellectuals were drawn to Marxism as a solution to the problems of America. The infamous trials of the Scottsboro Boys in Alabama, involving rape charges by two white women against eight black men, dominated the news pages during 1931–32 and the Communist Party (CP) was in the middle of that battle. The National Association for the Advancement of Colored People (NAACP), founded in 1909, had been working to expose the racial injustice of the country through traditional methods and was moving cautiously; however, it was upstaged by the CP, which organized marches, demonstrations and letter-writing campaigns. Lawyers from the CP-controlled International Labor Defense represented the defendants and won an appeal of the initial guilty verdict. The second, third and fourth trials were rife with CP attempts to bribe witnesses and manipulate the situation. It was the NAACP that prevailed in its work through the legal system to gain limited victories for some of the defendants. Throughout the remainder of the decade, the CP would be at the forefront of the racial struggle.

'Piano dominated blues music in the twenties and thirties and 'til the late forties. See, acoustic blues that original Sonny Boy Williamson was playing, Big Bill Broonzy, and Memphis Minnie, they all used piano.'

Billy Boy Arnold

Far Right Top
During the Great Depression, the American unemployed were forced to queue for their bread.

Far Right Bottom
Labourers gamble their cotton money in a juke joint, a place where blues musicians could often find work.

The New Record Labels

The welcome repeal of the Volstead Act in 1933 meant that Americans could once more legally consume alcoholic beverages, while the rise of the new jukebox industry helped to fuel the revival of the record business. Such race record stalwarts of the 1920s as Paramount and Gennett had found it impossible to survive the change in economic conditions; total record sales in 1932 were about six per cent of what they had been in 1920. But the void was quickly filled by Victor's new Bluebird imprint; the revived American Record Corporation (ARC), which by 1934

see Introduction pp 90 see Key Artists pp 100 see A–Z of Artists pp 120 see List of Artists pp 140

The Virtuosos Take Over Jazz

While the blues was beginning gradually to find a new respectability, jazz music entered the 1930s as a clunky, two-cylinder Model A and soared out a stainless-steel zephyr gliding on the wind. Three factors shaped this spectacular transformation: an aggressive quest for virtuosity, the power of mass public acclaim and a conscious spirit of modernity.

Much of the evolution of jazz in the 1930s can be explained in terms of a steeply rising arc of instrumental virtuosity. Jazz players had become conscious during the previous decade of the possibilities that instrumental technique could bring to

CLASSIC RECORDINGS

1930
Son House: 'Preachin' The Blues'

1933
Benny Carter: 'Lonesome Nights'
Art Tatum: 'Tiger Rag'

1934
Kokomo Arnold: 'Milk Cow Blues'

1935
Big Joe Williams: 'Baby Please Don't Go'

1937
Bukka White: 'Shake 'Em On Down'
Sonny Boy Williamson: 'Good Morning Little School Girl'

1939
Artie Shaw & his Orchestra: 'Carioca'

had consolidated the Vocalion, OKeh and Columbia catalogues; and the brand new Decca label. The vast majority of great jazz and blues records would appear on those labels for the remainder of the decade.

Geographically, Chicago became a primary location for blues recording by all three labels. Mississippi artists tended to record there, while Piedmont-area performers were more likely to record in New York; in some cases artists would record in both places. In terms of public performance, much of the country blues was played on street corners or at private functions such as parties, fish fries and picnics; this work was generally done for tips and was described as 'streets and functions'. The pianists tended to work indoors, playing in brothels, barrelhouses, taverns and clubs, and while there would be a kitty jar for tips, they were more likely to be hired. By the end of the decade, brothels and barrelhouses were a less frequent destination and for all blues players of reputation, the tavern and nightclub became a more frequent source of work.

see Big Bill Broonzy pp 104 *see* Benny Goodman pp 110 *see* Pete Johnson pp 128 *see* Sonny Boy Williamson pp 138

Above
Forward-thinking pianist Art Tatum stretched the limits of piano playing with his innovative style.

the music. Louis Armstrong (1901–71) had shown that beautifully wrought high notes, growing out of a carefully plotted emotional logic, could bring stately dramatic power to a simple blues. In the 1930s instinct was inspired by skill, which searched for new hills to climb. Armstrong turned away from the blues and applied himself to the more challenging medium of popular song. The best younger players, previously in awe of Armstrong's technique, promptly mastered it and then extended it. With the high notes achieved, faster and more fluid notes chasing more daring ideas became the norm. In the 1930s the legato eighth-note replaced the hammered quarter-note as the centre of jazz phrasing. Roy Eldridge (1911–89) and Harry James (1916–83) showed that one could create a totally original and modern voice within the Armstrong model and take it to new places. Eldridge and Charlie Shavers brought a fresh and ferocious precision to their playing that became the benchmark of virtuosity in the 1940s and formed a technical foundation without which bebop's complexities could not have been mastered.

On piano Art Tatum (1909–56) brought to bear a level of technique so colossal that it would be a generation before others caught up; Teddy Wilson (1912–86) provided a more practical route into the future for most. Tatum and Wilson made their first records in 1933, and each made his right hand the primary focus of his style, playing single-note lines that complemented the rhythmic fluency of swing. But Wilson's gentler, more symmetrical virtuosity made his music more accessible and, accordingly, more directly influential.

The Rise Of Boogie-Woogie

There were also other new trends developing in the music of the 1930s. Boogie-woogie, which had its roots in ragtime and was heard in the blues and jazz of the 1920s, developed into a national phenomenon in the 1930s. Its great exponents, such as Albert Ammons (1907–49), Pete Johnson (1904–67) and Meade 'Lux' Lewis (1905–64), would become stars of radio and movies. The style also spread into the jazz market, where it was embraced by big-band leaders such as Tommy Dorsey (1905–56), Earl Hines (1903–83) and Count Basie (1904–84). Originally a piano music, it proved easily adaptable to other instruments, especially the guitar.

Above
Meade 'Lux' Lewis was among the main exponents of the burgeoning boogie-woogie piano style.

In contrast to the augmenting jazz ensembles in the 1930s, most blues artists of the era were recorded with a fairly minimal accompaniment. There were many solo performances and rarely would a recording session involve more than guitar, harmonica, piano and bass. But with the migration to Chicago by so many artists, changes began to occur. Tampa Red (1904–81) was a catalyst for new ideas among Chicago musicians and among those in his circle were Big Bill Broonzy (1893–1958), Memphis Minnie (1897–1973), John Lee 'Sonny Boy' Williamson (1914–48) and 'Big Maceo' Merriweather (1905–53). Washboard Sam (1910–66)

see **Meade 'Lux' Lewis pp 128** *see* **Memphis Minnie pp 130** *see* **Tampa Red pp 135** *see* **Art Tatum pp 135**

Above
Bandleaders such as Benny Goodman and Harry James (on trumpet) were set to change the character of American music.

was the pioneer of blues percussion, but when artists such as Minnie and Broonzy used drums for some of their 1937 recordings, new vistas began to open. Some would be slow to adopt this new sound, but those who did explore it were able to move towards new audiences, such as those attracted to the big-band swing craze that was sweeping America.

The Reign Of The Big Bands

When Benny Goodman (1909–86) combined his clarinet virtuosity with the arranging skills of Fletcher Henderson (1897–1952), big-band jazz swiftly became the dominant popular music of the late 1930s. Big bands had occupied a major place in popular music since the end of the First World War but, except those led by Duke Ellington (1899–1974), Henderson, Earl Hines and a few others, most were white bands conducted by entertainers who played instruments only incidentally, if at all. Goodman changed much of that in 1935–36. Perhaps the most fundamental shift he wrought was using jazz to turn popular music towards a true meritocracy. For the first time, the power and the glory began to flow from entertainers towards musicians playing the real thing. By 1939, Goodman had opened the door for a procession of bandleader virtuosos that changed the character of American music. They included Artie Shaw (1910–2004), Count Basie, Tommy Dorsey, Jimmy Dorsey (1904–57), Harry James, Gene Krupa (1909–73), Benny Carter (1907–2003), Bunny Berigan (1908–42), Chick Webb (1909–39), Woody Herman (1913–87), Teddy Wilson, Glenn Miller (1904–44) and others – all serious, often brilliant players whose names became the great musical brands of the decade.

The First Jazz Record Labels

While the big swing units reached mass audiences, a self-proclaimed jazz elite that was distrustful of success held itself apart. Rejecting big bands as commercial distortions of the real thing, they insisted that the only true jazz was improvised small-group music with roots in the blues-infused style of the late 1920s. Commodore Records became home to this alternative, as well as the first label founded exclusively to record jazz. Formed in 1938 by record store owner Milt Gabler, it concentrated on spirited Dixieland sessions and drew from a stock company that included Eddie Condon (1905–73), Pee Wee Russell (1906–69), Wild Bill Davison, Bud Freeman

see Introduction pp 90 *see* Key Artists pp 100 *see* A–Z of Artists pp 120 *see* List of Artists pp 140

Above
Three of the great innovators in jazz during the 1930s – (l–r) Teddy Wilson, Jo Jones and Lester Young – reuniting at a Norman Granz session in 1956.

(1906–91), Bobby Hackett (1915–76), Georg Brunis and Max Kaminsky. A year later Blue Note Records became the country's second jazz-only label, emphasizing traditional black artists such as Sidney Bechet (1897–1959) and Meade 'Lux' Lewis. Blue Note remains an important jazz record label to this day.

These labels, with their retro mission, were part of a larger trend – a rising recognition that jazz had a history before 1935. Two music magazines in America (*Down Beat* and *Metronome*) and one in England (*Melody Maker*) became the most influential publications guiding contemporary taste and exploring jazz roots. The first generation of college-educated critics and historians who wrote regularly and articulately about jazz included John Hammond (1910–86), George Simon, George Frazier, Otis Ferguson, Marshall Stearns and Helen Oakley, plus Leonard Feather and Stanley Dance in England and Hughes Panissie in France. *Down Beat* ran a series of articles throughout 1936–38 by Stearns that assembled the first comprehensive (although rough) history of the music. As fans read about jazz history, they grew curious about listening to it as well. At Columbia Records in 1940 George Avakian produced the first series of jazz reissue albums (four 78-rpm records), starting with long out-of-print performances by Armstrong, Henderson, Bessie Smith (1894–1937) and Bix Beiderbecke (1903–31).

see Count Basie pp 102 *see* Benny Goodman pp 110 *see* Tommy Dorsey pp 123 *see* Artie Shaw pp 135

The Blues Arrives At Carnegie Hall

In December 1938, John Hammond organized a concert at Carnegie Hall in New York entitled 'From Spirituals To Swing, An Evening Of American Negro Music'. It was dedicated to the memory of Bessie Smith and was sponsored by a CP magazine, *New Masses*. The concert was a huge success, with almost 3000 people in attendance. There were jazz and gospel performers featured – including Sister Rosetta Tharpe (1915–73) – and the blues was well represented by Sonny Terry (1911–86), Broonzy (a replacement for Robert Johnson, 1911–38), Joe Turner (1911–85) and boogie-woogie piano stars Ammons, Lewis and Johnson. The event generated universal praise in the press and made stars out of most of its participants. It was the first time that many of them had appeared at a mainstream venue like Carnegie Hall, or before a mostly white audience.

Above

New York's Carnegie Hall – the venue for John Hammond's seminal Spirituals To Swing concert, featuring blues, gospel and jazz music.

In the aftermath of the concert, a new nightclub called Café Society opened in New York's Greenwich Village, catering to integrated audiences and performances of black jazz, blues and gospel music. Most of the concert's performers appeared there at one time or another. Another 'Spirituals To Swing' concert was held a year later and featured Broonzy, Terry and Ida Cox (1896–1967) as the blues performers. As a result of these concerts, jazz and blues became closely linked, as they had been before in the jazz accompaniment provided to the vaudeville blues of the 1920s, and would be again.

Jazz Music Gains Wider Recognition

Towards the end of the 1930s, jazz became increasingly conscious of itself as a 'serious' art form. It was no longer a simple folk art of self-taught primitives, its (mostly white) promoters argued. Thus, it deserved a place at the table among the higher arts – a claim based partly on the notion that the best jazz musicians now commanded a level of virtuosity equal to the finest classical players. Mainstream music critics were called upon to recognize jazz on a par with the European masters. At least one classical critic, Winthrop Sargeant of the *New Yorker*, took up the task. His *Jazz, Hot And Hybrid*, published in 1938, was the first serious musicological study of jazz. By the end of the decade, Fred Ramsey and Wilder Hobson had extended jazz's bibliography.

Among the most fundamental changes that made many of these advances possible was an early shift in the rhythm section, which changed the inner clock of jazz and enabled it to swing. By 1932 the banjo and tuba were disappearing, replaced with the more supple sounds of guitar and string bass. Drummers began to untie the rigidity of 1920s two-beat rhythm, giving the pulse a lightness and swiftness

see Introduction pp 90 *see* Key Artists pp 100 *see* A–Z of Artists pp 120 *see* List of Artists pp 140

that was essential to a swing feel. In the Henderson band, as early as 1932, Walter Johnson began to shift time-keeping from the snare to the elastic swish of the hi-hat cymbal. By the mid-1930s, jazz's rhythm engine was revving out its lumpy two-beat tradition to a driving 4/4 swing, revising the most basic laws of motion in jazz.

The Jazz Age Meets The Machine Age

It is here that we find jazz and blues connecting with one of the great controlling sensibilities of the decade, one that touched not only music but also art, architecture, design, cinema and virtually every aspect of the cultural environment. The spirit of the 1930s was dominated by new possibilities of technology and was manifested in notions of speed, structural integration and futuristic, aerodynamic shapes. Beyond their functions, these technological achievements were also expressions of an empirical technocracy that was irresistibly bright and optimistic. In one brief 18-month period from 1934–36 America saw its first diesel streamliners, the Chrysler Airflow car, the space-age shells that turned steam engines into projectiles on rails, the DC-3 aircraft, the Golden Gate Bridge and the polished, Brancusian lines of Jean Harlow captured in iconic MGM publicity stills.

In the midst of this fixation with stylized modernity and motion, the smooth, rhythmic momentum of swing became an extension of the same spirit of efficiency that found beauty in sleek designs born from the physics of velocity and speed. In jazz terms, swing reached a perfection of form by 1939 with the Count Basie band, particularly in its principal tenor saxophone soloist Lester Young (1909–59) and the drumming of Jo Jones (1911–85), of whom it was said, 'he played like the wind'. It was a fitting allegory for the streamlined 1930s.

These cultural developments also had an effect on blues music; despite the fact that great country blues would continue to be performed and recorded, it was clear that around this time the momentum in blues music was moving in the direction of a more urban sound. The changes begun in blues in the late 1930s would come to fruition in the next decade; in time, some blues influence would play a part in most styles of American music, including gospel and country.

Blues Takes A Back Seat

If these relationships seem abstract and intangible, they soon assumed more concrete expressions as jazz spilled out into daily life through radio, movies, advertising and the new dance styles created to follow the music. The top white swing bands, in addition to being heard on sustaining broadcasts from hotels, played on their own radio shows sponsored by major advertisers – often cigarette companies eager to reach young audiences. In Hollywood, swing quickly found its way on to the screen. Louis Armstrong appeared in *Pennies From Heaven* (1936), *Artists And Models* (1937) and *Going Places* (1938). Benny Goodman's music mingled with the Art Deco modernism of Paramount's *Big Broadcast of 1937* and Warner Bros.' *Hollywood Hotel* of the same year, and at MGM the link between jazz and the jitterbug dance fad became the basis for Artie Shaw's first film, *Dancing Co-Ed* (1939). In this convergence of modernistic expressions lies perhaps the best explanation of why jazz managed to swiftly become the popular music of America. As the big swing bands now formed at the forefront of American showbusiness, blues began to take a back seat – although many of the key players such as Basie and Duke Ellington had used the blues as a basis for much of what they performed.

Above
Manhattan's magnificent Chrysler Building typified the streamlined forms that dominated modern design in the US during the 1930s.

see Albert Ammons pp 100 *see* Robert Johnson pp 112 *see* Lester Young pp 118 *see* Sister Rosetta Tharpe pp 136

Albert Ammons

CLASSIC RECORDINGS

1936
Albert Ammons & his Rhythm Kings: 'Barrelhouse Blues', 'Blues In The Groove', 'Boogie Woogie Stomp', 'Early Mornin' Blues', 'Jammin' The Blues'

1938
Albert Ammons, Pete Johnson & Meade 'Lux' Lewis: 'Calvacade Of Boogie'

1939
Albert Ammons: 'Bass Goin' Crazy', 'Boogie Woogie Blues', 'Suitcase Blues'

1946
Albert Ammons & his Rhythm Kings: 'Swanee River Boogie'

Above
Albert Ammons (right) with Pete Johnson – two of the great boogie-woogie masters.

'...I listened to Albert Ammons this morning and it was everything. It was sex, it was life, it was truth. It was marvellous.'
Jools Holland

Albert Clifton Ammons was born in Chicago, Illinois in March 1907. As a young man he learned from Jimmy Yancey, who cast a long shadow over Chicago blues pianists through his work at rent parties, social functions and after-hours jobs. Ammons came to know other pianists and the blues specialists gathered together in Chicago to create a coterie, echoing what was happening with the stride pianists in Harlem. Among the Chicago group, in addition to Yancey, were Clarence 'Pine Top' Smith, Jimmy Blythe, Cripple Clarence Lofton, Hersal Thomas and Ammons' close friend Meade 'Lux' Lewis. Ammons was the youngest of these men and he learned from all of them. He also drew inspiration from stride-piano great Fats Waller, a major star in black entertainment circles. Lewis and Smith had recorded boogie in the 1920s, and among blues pianists boogie-woogie, with its eight-beats-to-the-bar pattern in the left hand, became an adjunct to the basic style.

Ammons' Big Break

Ammons worked at jobs outside music, led his own swing combos and played with other bandleaders until his big break: a residency at the Club DeLisa, the most important nightspot on Chicago's South Side. This engagement, which began in 1935, led to his discovery by John Hammond and his first recordings, for Decca, in February 1936.

In 1938, Ammons was invited to appear in New York for Hammond's Spirituals To Swing concert at Carnegie Hall. He served as accompanist to Sister Rosetta Tharpe and Big Bill Broonzy, and had his own feature number, 'Boogie Woogie'. He was also teamed

see Introduction pp 90 *see* Sources & Sounds pp 92 *see* A–Z of Artists pp 120

with Lewis and Kansas City pianist Pete Johnson for two selections, 'Jumpin' Blues' and 'Cavalcade Of Boogie'. The audience response, which can be heard on the Vanguard recording of the event, was a clear indicator that boogie-woogie had arrived. The occasion also served as a launch pad for this trio of pianists.

The Boogie-Woogie Trio

Ammons, Johnson and Lewis were linked for several years; they appeared in duo or trio settings, occasionally with the addition of vocalist Joe Turner, and recorded for Vocalion, Blue Note and Victor. They toured the US, using Café Society in New York as a base, and also appeared in movies and on radio broadcasts. In the autumn of 1941, Ammons and Johnson had two half-hour radio shows per week on WABC in New York.

The Rhythm Kings

In 1944, during his final extended New York engagement, Albert Ammons recorded two sessions for the Commodore label. One was a solo date, while the other involved an all-star aggregation billed as Albert Ammons & his Rhythm Kings – the same name that Ammons had used on his first recording session. When he returned to Chicago the following year, he signed with the brand-new Mercury label and began a new series of Rhythm Kings recordings. Until this time, the thematic material used in boogie-woogie was usually the blues or simple, riff-based melodies; Ammons, however, began to adapt his thundering left-hand patterns to pop songs. It is here that we get fresh treatments of standards such as 'Deep In The Heart Of Texas', 'Roses Of Picardy' and 'Swanee River' (the latter was used by Fats Domino as the basis of his 'Swanee River Hop'). Ammons made it clear that, in his hands, a boogie-woogie approach could be applied to any musical source.

Ammons made his final Mercury session just before the start of the second American Federation of Musicians recording ban in January 1948. No doubt the future would have held much for this giant of piano blues but, shortly after appearing at the Inaugural Ball for President Truman, he contracted a mysterious disease – later diagnosed as congestive heart failure – which eventually led to his death in December 1949.

Below
Albert Ammons with his band in the Club DeLisa, Chicago in 1936.

see Fats Waller pp 85 *see* Pete Johnson pp 128 *see* Meade 'Lux' Lewis pp 128 *see* Jimmy Yancey pp 139

Count Basie

CLASSIC RECORDINGS

1929–32
Basie Beginnings, 'Moten Swing', 'The Blue Room', 'The Count'

1936–52
America's # 1 Band!, 'Lady Be Good', 'Lester Leaps In', 'Taxi War Dance'

1937–39
The Complete Decca Records, 'One O'Clock Jump', 'Jumpin' At The Woodside'

1938
Count Basie Live At The Famous Door, 'King Porter Stomp', 'Time Out'

Above
Accomplished pianist and revolutionary bandleader Count Basie.

If swing in its most characteristic form was a hot and hard-driving music, William 'Count' Basie showed that there was a cooler and softer side to the music, an alter ego that even at swift tempos could move with a relaxed, almost serene restraint that subliminally mirrored the streamlined design forms of the Machine Age, in which science and art seemed to mingle.

'Count is … just about the best piano player I know for pushing a band and comping for soloists. I mean the way he makes different preparations for each soloist and the way, at the end of one of his solos, he prepares an entrance for the next man.'
Freddie Greene

For Basie this was surely an outcome of chance, not intent. He was born in Red Bank, New Jersey on 21 August 1904 and never finished high school, preferring a life in showbusiness and music. He arrived in New York in 1924 and came to know the reigning Harlem pianists of the day – James P. Johnson, Willie 'The Lion' Smith and Fats Waller – mastering their dense, two-handed stride style. But for his own style to emerge he needed to escape those powerful influences. Stranded in Kansas City, Basie joined the Blue Devils, led by bassist Walter Page, in 1927.

The Kansas City Scene

The American Southwest was a jazz environment unto itself, alive with regional bands that worked from Chicago to Texas. In the Blue Devils Basie met the core of players who would be with him in Chicago and New York. In 1929 Basie joined the Bennie Moten Orchestra. He had recorded nine sessions with Moten by the end of 1932, none of which provide a clue to the pianist that would emerge when he next recorded in 1936.

A lot happened during that four-year blackout. After Moten's sudden death in 1935, Basie took a job at the Reno Club in Kansas City, hiring players from the old Moten unit as well as former Blue Devils. By early 1936 many of the key men were in place, including Walter Page, Jo Jones and Lester Young. Broadcasting nightly from Kansas City, the signals found their way north through the cold night air to Chicago, where they caught the ear of critic John Hammond. Writing in *Down Beat*, he called the band 'far and away the finest in the country' with a rhythm

see Introduction pp 90 see Sources & Sounds pp 92 see A–Z of Artists pp 120

section 'more exciting than any in American orchestral history'.

That summer Hammond drove to Kansas City and was not disappointed. The band was soon on its way to Chicago, where Hammond recorded a small Basie unit featuring Lester Young in the landmark 'Lady Be Good'. Suddenly here was the spacious, minimalist Basie piano style, always implying more notes than were played and allowing the rhythm section to shine through with a transparent clarity.

Basie Rhythm

Rhythm guitarist Freddie Greene joined Jones and Page to complete the unique Basie rhythm team. Page and Greene became the quiet pulse keepers. With a rhythm section so subtle and implicit, the arrangements often held back, offering it space. Many of the band's most characteristic charts would begin softly with a chorus or two of rhythm and Basie's see-through piano, then unfold in steadily expanding layers of riffs (e.g. 'One O'Clock Jump'). The band reached New York in January 1937 and hit its stride in the summer of 1938 during an engagement at the Famous Door. Basie's group recorded more than 60 sides for Decca, then moved to Columbia in 1939 where it remained until after the war. This forms the collective body of work on which the Basie reputation continues to rest.

The Basie Sound Develops

In the early 1950s many of the players who had given the band its voice had left and Basie reformed in 1952 with a new band whose book institutionalized the essence of the Basie sound, but without relying on the cult of the irreplaceable soloist. It became an arrangers' band, in which brilliant writers such as Neal Hefti, Ernie Wilkins, Frank Foster, Thad Jones and Sammy Nestico set the pace. Yet the 'new testament' Basie band would host many fine players and enjoy a steadily growing success from the 1950s through the 1980s. During that time the band recorded extensively for Verve, Roulette and Pablo as Basie watched his fame ascend into legend. The band has continued to tour successfully, under leaders including Thad Jones, Frank Foster, Grover Mitchell and since 2004 Bill Hughes – all alumni of the 1950s Basie bands.

Above
The Count Basie Band moved to Chicago and then to New York, where they accumulated an extensive following.

Left
Kansas City in the 1930s, where Count Basie's band caught the attention of music critic John Hammond.

see Lester Young pp 118 *see* Jo Jones pp 128 *see* Walter Page pp 132 *see* Willie 'The Lion' Smith pp 134

Big Bill Broonzy

CLASSIC RECORDINGS

1932
'Bull Cow Blues', 'Mistreatin' Mama Blues'

1934
'Friendless Blues'

1935
'Keep Your Hands Off Of Her'

1937–40
'Good Time Tonight', 'Just A Dream (On My Mind)', 'Louise, Louise Blues'

1941
'All By Myself', 'Key To The Highway', 'Keep Your Hand On Your Heart'

The parents of William Lee Conley Broonzy were born into slavery. He was born in June 1893 in Scott, Mississippi, one of 17 children. Raised on a farm in Arkansas, Broonzy's first musical instrument was a home-made violin, which he played at church and social functions. In the early teens he was an itinerant preacher, while also working as a country fiddler. He served in the US Army from 1918–19, and shortly after his discharge moved to Chicago. At first he worked as a baggage handler, performing music on a casual basis; it was in Chicago that he first learned to play the guitar.

The Early Recordings

Broonzy worked with Papa Charlie Jackson in 1924 and soon became an accompanist in demand. He made his recording debut for Paramount in 1927 and by 1930 was recording for Gennett/Champion and Perfect/Banner under a variety of pseudonyms, such as Sammy Sampson and Big Bill Johnson. In 1931, he recorded for Paramount and the resulting tracks were issued by 'Big Bill Broomsley'. By this time, Big Bill Broonzy was a professional entertainer.

'As a warm, entertaining blues singer, he had no equal.'
Sam Charters

Broonzy worked theatres and taverns in Chicago and northern Indiana during this period and toured in a show with Memphis Minnie. Broonzy did not record during 1933 and when he resumed in 1934, for ARC and Bluebird, the records were issued simply as Big Bill. This began a period of prolific recording activity for Broonzy. From 1936, he recorded exclusively for ARC (later Columbia), an arrangement that lasted until the end of 1947. By 1937, performance opportunities had slowed and Broonzy was living on his Arkansas farm, commuting to Chicago three or four times a year to make records.

Spirituals To Swing

In 1938 Broonzy was part of the cast for the John Hammond production 'Spirituals To Swing', a concert held at Carnegie Hall in New York City. He made the most of the opportunity and renewed his career as an entertainer, shortly afterwards appearing at major clubs

Big Bill Blues
WILLIAM BROONZY'S STORY
as told to
YANNICK BRUYNOGHE

with 9 pages of half-tone illustrations and four drawings by
PAUL OLIVER

THE JAZZ BOOK CLUB
by arrangement with
CASSELL & COMPANY LIMITED

Above Right
Big Bill Blues – Broonzy's biography, published in 1955.

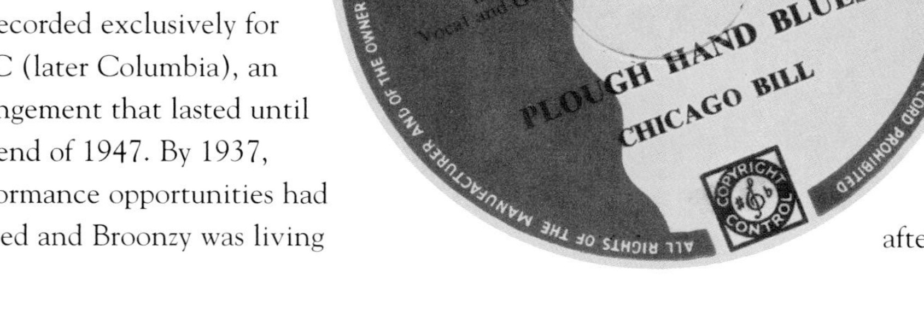

Right
'Plough Hand Blues', a Big Bill Broonzy track recorded for Melodisc under the pseudonym Chicago Bill.

Far Right
Blues and folk singer Big Bill Broonzy, during his 1956 tour of the UK.

see Introduction pp 90 *see* Sources & Sounds pp 92 *see* A–Z of Artists pp 120

in New York as well as Chicago. He appeared in the movie *Swingin' The Dream* in 1939, toured with Lil Green during 1941–42 and had theatre dates in New York and Los Angeles in the early 1940s. He released records on a regular basis and by the end of his career he had written and recorded hundreds of songs.

European Tours

For some time, Broonzy's record dates had alternated between the spare accompaniment of piano and bass, and larger ensembles often featuring two horns. As time wore on, the country aspects of his recording sessions were given scant attention. When he signed with Mercury in 1949, his recording began to take on the flavour of the emerging R&B sound. While he continued to record he was, for a time, employed as a janitor at Iowa State University, but things changed markedly when he made his first overseas tour. He toured England, France and Germany as a solo artist during September and October 1951; he made recordings in each country and proved to be extremely popular.

Another tour in early 1952 came immediately after his final sessions for Mercury. From this point forward, Broonzy would revert to his country blues origins and record prolifically for a variety of European labels. In 1955 his autobiography, *Big Bill Blues*, was published. Further European appearances came during 1955–57 but after the shows Big Bill Broonzy was diagnosed with cancer, from which he died in August 1958 in Chicago.

see Papa Charlie Jackson pp 75 *see* John Hammond pp 125 *see* Memphis Minnie pp 130

Charlie Christian

CLASSIC RECORDINGS

1939–41
Genius Of The Electric Guitar, 'Airmail Special', 'Seven Come Eleven', 'Solo Flight', *Solo Flight Live*, 'AC DC Current', 'Benny's Bugle', 'Soft Winds', *First Master Of The Electric Guitar*, 'Breakfast Feud', 'Flying Home', 'I Got Rhythm'

1941
The Immortal Charlie Christian At Minton's, 'Swing Yo Bop'

Charlie Christian was the last great figure to emerge from the jazz scene of the 1930s. He not only brought a perfectly formed approach to his music, but also an entirely new musical platform – the electric guitar. His career in the big time was brief, but Christian was a lighthouse whose beam still illuminates anyone with serious intentions on the instrument.

Charles Henry Christian was born on 29 July 1916 in Dallas, Texas to Clarence and Willie Mae Christian, both professional musicians. When Clarence lost his sight in 1918, he turned to playing the guitar, which he also taught to his three sons. By the time Charlie was 10 his father had died and the family had moved to Oklahoma City, where he began working part-time as a pianist. During his teens his future looked grim: at 15 Christian was a lanky high-school dropout and at 16 he was an unexpected father, trying to get by in the dust bowl of the Great Depression. But beneath the bashful, diffident exterior stirred an emerging savant of whom it was said that he could hear around corners with flawless logic. In Oklahoma City he was able to make his way, landing regular jobs in clubs.

'If Charlie had lived, he would have been real modern.'
Kenny Clarke

Christian Joins Benny Goodman

Sometime in the mid-1930s Christian bought a Gibson ES150 electric guitar. No recordings exist by which to chart his development, but there is no question that travelling musicians took notice as Christian worked for $2.50 a night in Oklahoma City. One of the players who heard him while passing through in 1939 was Mary Lou Williams, pianist with the Andy Kirk Orchestra.

Meanwhile, Benny Goodman was eager to reinvigorate his band. He was clearly intrigued by the possibilities of the electric guitar and tried out several players on his radio programme, but none was up to the clarinetist's virtuosity. That summer Williams told critic John Hammond about Christian. Hammond flew out to see him, was astonished and shortly afterwards brought him to Los Angeles, where Goodman was playing. In August Christian first sat in with Goodman's quintet. Nothing could have prepared Goodman for what he heard. Christian was immediately hired and for the rest of his short career, the Benny Goodman Sextet and Septet were his professional homes.

He could not have found a more perfect environment. Goodman and vibraphonist Lionel Hampton were brilliant players who recognized one of their own and the Sextet, with its openness to developing original material, offered an ideal creative mandate. Furthermore, Goodman reached a vast national audience and gave his protégé a generous spotlight. Within weeks, both Christian and the electric guitar were famous. His solos were so inventive in concept and flawless in performance that they seemed to foreclose all future alternatives in one sweeping, inclusive stroke. As 1940 began he

Right
Jazz pianist Mary Lou Williams heard Christian play in Oklahoma City and spread the news of his talents.

see Introduction pp 90 *see* Sources & Sounds pp 92 *see* A–Z of Artists pp 120

stood like a lone colossus on the commanding heights of a dawning, electrified instrumental empire.

Christian's Style

Except for the use of accent chords or recurring triads in his largely set solo on 'Stardust', Christian was a horn-like soloist who played through chords, creating single-note contours that would climb and ebb with a gliding, unbroken flow. He might punctuate with a slicing glissando or unexpectedly riff on a tone pair, i.e. a single note alternating two strings for a variation in timbre. He was also frighteningly prolific at tossing off concise musical figures, many of which became the basis for the classic pieces originating in the Goodman groups: 'Air Mail Special', 'Seven Come Eleven', 'Shivers', 'A Smooth One' and others. Away from the Goodman Sextet, Christian's appetite for the jam session was voracious. Several warm-ups were caught during his Columbia sessions, and he took part in a dazzling jam at Carnegie Hall with Count Basie, Lester Young and others in December 1939. He was also recorded playing long solos at Minton's Playhouse in Harlem in 1941, performances that catch him at his most relaxed and unguarded. He died in March 1942 from tuberculosis. Almost immediately, a group of direct disciples emerged: Barney Kessel, Herb Ellis, Remo Palmieri, Irving Ashby and Les Paul. Today, distinguished contemporary players such as Russell Malone and Howard Alden carry on the Christian line.

Below
Electric guitar virtuoso Charlie Christian, who found fame with the Benny Goodman quintet.

see Count Basie pp 102 *see* Benny Goodman pp 110 *see* Lionel Hampton pp 125 *see* Barney Kessel pp 178

Roy Eldridge

CLASSIC RECORDINGS

1935–40
Little Jazz, 'After You've Gone', 'Florida Stomp', 'Heckler's Hop', 'Knock Me A Kiss', 'Rockin' Chair', 'Twilight Time', 'Wabash Stomp'

1939
At The Arcadia Ballroom, 'Mahogany Hall Stomp', 'Minor Jive', 'Shine'

Right
Dizzy Gillespie (left) was greatly influenced by the innovative playing of Roy Eldridge.

'When I was growing up, all I wanted to play was swing. Eldridge was my boy. All I ever did was try to play like him but I never quite made it.'
Dizzy Gillespie

While Louis Armstrong remained a pre-eminent jazz symbol in the public mind through the 1930s, and inspired many imitators (Taft Jordan, Hot Lips Page, Wingy Manone), younger and better-schooled musicians were coming up who could navigate the trumpet with great agility and dexterity. They would break through the perimeters that Armstrong had established in the 1920s and take the music to new places. In the 1930s no player consolidated those advances or expanded their possibilities more spectacularly than Roy Eldridge, known throughout his career as 'Little Jazz' because of his short stature and high power.

Far Right
Exuberant trumpeter Roy Eldridge, who battled it out with Louis Armstrong in Fletcher Henderson's band.

Eldridge's Heroes

Born in Pittsburgh, Pennsylvania on 30 January 1911, David Roy Eldridge came to music with great youthful exuberance, first on drums and then trumpet. In his eagerness to progress, he played by ear at first. It was his older brother Joseph who disciplined his progress and instructed him in matters of theory and the logic of chord sequences, which the young trumpeter acquired by learning the basics of the piano. During his formative years in the late 1920s he avoided the influence of Armstrong, preferring instead to master the speed and precision of saxophonist Coleman Hawkins. Although he began playing professionally around 1927, Eldridge's development as a player is not documented until 1935, when he recorded with Teddy Hill and on three Teddy Wilson-Billie Holiday sessions.

see Introduction pp 90 see Sources & Sounds pp 92 see A–Z of Artists pp 120

Here he emerges as a seasoned player with a big, clean sound and sharp attack.

An Exuberant Playing Style

In 1935 he joined Fletcher Henderson in Chicago and not only showed what he could do, but let loose unimagined possibilities for the trumpet. Starting with Armstrong's sense of dramatic pacing, Eldridge added a wildly exuberant recklessness that threw fast, complex phrasing and penetrating high notes together with meticulous precision. Eldridge was a competitive player and thrived on the stimulation of the encounter. The Henderson band gave him his first important foil: tenor saxophonist Chu Berry. On a simple riff piece, 'Jangled Nerves', Berry solos with swift, glancing eighth notes, setting a rapid pace. Then Eldridge bores in with a ferociously suppressed intensity that soon explodes into stabbing high notes, seasoned with a striking dissonance. In the late 1930s it made musicians' heads spin, including that of a young Dizzy Gillespie, who soon showed Eldridge's impact in his first recorded solos.

Faster, Higher!

After leaving Henderson, Eldridge remained in Chicago and formed his own band, which unleashed the full force of his virtuosity. A number of live radio performances from the Three Deuces in Chicago (1937) and the Arcadia in New York (1939) have survived, which offer some of the most breathtaking trumpet solos ever recorded. Interestingly, he performed several Armstrong showpieces, including 'Shine' and 'Mahogany Hall Stomp'. They were homages to the past but also parodies, serving notice that a new generation of elite virtuosos, eager for risk, was now in charge.

Eldridge broke up his band in late 1939, freelanced on record dates, then joined Gene Krupa in 1941, where he gained national prominence (finally topping *Down Beat*'s Readers' Poll in 1942). But he also found his talents restricted to a few showcase numbers. One of them, the beautiful 'Rocking Chair', became one of his most requested pieces. He worked with Artie Shaw in 1944–45 before bebop marginalized him for a period late in the decade. In the 1950s he became part of Norman Granz's Jazz at the Philharmonic tours, recording frequently for Granz's Verve label, and was featured on *The Sound Of Jazz* with Billie Holiday et al. He later recorded with Pablo Records in the 1970s and 1980s, before health problems forced him to give up playing. Roy Eldridge died in February 1989.

see Fletcher Henderson pp 74 *see* Chu Berry pp 121 *see* Gene Krupa pp 128 *see* Billie Holiday pp 156

Benny Goodman

CLASSIC RECORDINGS

1935–39
The RCA Victor Years, 'Bugle Call Rag', 'Stompin' At The Savoy'

1937–38
'King Porter Stomp', 'Roll 'Em'

1938
Famous 1938 Carnegie Hall Jazz Concert, 'Avalon', 'One O'Clock Jump', 'Sing Sing Sing'

1939–41
Genius Of The Electric Guitar by Charlie Christian, 'Airmail Special', 'Seven Come Eleven', 'Solo Flight'

Benny Goodman was the first of the great bandleader virtuosos of the 1930s to achieve global success. Through a combination of personal connections, nerve, enormous talent and sheer luck, he parlayed a sequence of opportunities in 1934–35 into a payoff that changed American music. After forming his first band in New York in 1934, he won a coveted place on NBC's weekly Let's Dance radio show late that year, and then a record contract with RCA Victor. In 1935 a national tour took him to the Palomar Ballroom in California, where his music finally caught the ear of America and the world.

Benjamin David Goodman was born on 30 May 1909 in Chicago, Illinois and took up the clarinet when he was 10. His progress was so swift that by the age of 13 he had a union card and was soon earning $58 a week playing in the Jules Herbeveaux Orchestra. Goodman's first recordings, made with Ben Pollack's orchestra in December 1926, find him self-assured with a smooth, powerful attack and sparkling sound. Although he was part of the Chicago jazz scene and influenced by its heat, his prodigious technique gave him professional choices that many of his jazz contemporaries lacked. He could rip into raw, hard-driving solos influenced by Johnny Dodds and Frank Teschemacher but also, when the job required, play polite solo interludes with restraint.

'It wasn't just that his own improvisation was marvelous, the spirit, the verve, the vitality, even humor he played with, but the sheer technical mastery. He played that thing like it was a yo-yo.'

Mel Powell

New York Beckons

Moving to New York in 1928, Goodman prospered in radio, theatre and recording work. He was making such a good living by the early 1930s that he had little incentive to fight a growing public indifference to jazz. If Goodman was not committed to 'the cause', however, a young critic and producer named John Hammond was. He approached Goodman in 1933 and provided him with moral support, frequent jazz recording dates and a sense of renewed confidence to pursue the jazz route.

Swing's The Thing

Throughout 1934–35 Benny Goodman became the first white bandleader to bring the swinging spirit of the great black orchestras – Chick Webb, Benny Carter, Duke Ellington and Fletcher Henderson – to a mass audience. He used the Henderson model, bought many of Henderson's arrangements and sharpened the intonation and attack without suffocating any of the rhythmic energy. To this he added his own brilliant clarinet solos. Suddenly jazz music sounded fresh and new to millions of young dancers, who started to listen. By the time Goodman reached Chicago in December, the whole country was talking about 'swing'.

The arrival of swing awakened a sustained consciousness about jazz and, indirectly, about race. The Goodman tide lifted all boats, black and white, and also became a wedge of direct social progress. More than a decade before Jackie Robinson broke the colour line in baseball, Goodman integrated music by bringing Teddy Wilson (1935), Lionel Hampton (1936) and Charlie Christian (1939) into his small groups. Before the end of the decade Fletcher Henderson joined the full Goodman band on piano,

Right
(l–r) Artie Shaw, Benny Goodman, Duke Ellington, Chick Webb (back), George Hall and Raymond Scott.

see Introduction pp 90 *see* Sources & Sounds pp 92 *see* A–Z of Artists pp 120

Above
Important bandleader and clarinet virtuoso Benny Goodman (right) jams with Stan Getz and others.

becoming the first black musician ever to play as a regular member of a white orchestra. Although politically liberal, Goodman's instincts were musical, not ideological.

Jazz Goes Legit

In January 1938 Goodman's famous concert in Carnegie Hall seemed to sanctify jazz with a new status and 'legitimacy'. Although Carnegie Hall was the crowning event of Goodman's prime years, other accomplishments would follow: the brilliant sextets and big band of 1939–41 with Charlie Christian and Cootie Williams, innovative new charts by Eddie Sauter and Mel Powell, and the late-wartime sextet with Red Norvo. After the Second World War Goodman attempted to embrace bebop and performed a clarinet concerto written for him by Aaron Copeland, before wisely returning to the style in which he was most comfortable. From the 1950s into the 1980s he worked when he liked, in a state of semi-retirement.

As a soloist he never fell into set routines, which led to some inconsistency. But an indifferent performance at one concert was often repaid at the next with inspired solos that seemed to surprise Goodman as much as they did the audience.

Musically active until the end, Benny Goodman died in New York in June 1986. His private papers and recordings are archived at Yale University.

see Johnny Dodds pp 72 *see* Charlie Christian pp 106 *see* Lionel Hampton pp 125 *see* Swing pp 384

Robert Johnson

CLASSIC RECORDINGS

1936
'Come On In My Kitchen', 'Cross Road Blues', 'I Believe I'll Dust My Broom', 'Kindhearted Woman Blues', 'Preaching Blues', 'Walking Blues'

1937
'From Four Till Late', 'Hellhound On My Trail', 'Little Queen Of Spades', 'Stones In My Passway'

While blues music has produced dozens of great, innovative musicians, vocalists and songwriters, the continuing influence of Robert Johnson over the years has shown that no other performer has succeeded in combining all the elements in quite the exceptional way that he did. The fascination that Johnson holds for so many people lies not only in his extraordinary playing, but also in the shroud of supernatural legend that envelops his short and enigmatic life. Many blues singers, Tommy Johnson and Peetie Wheatstraw among them, claimed to have more than a nodding acquaintance with the Devil, but when Johnson wails 'Me and the Devil Blues' it does not sound like mere masculine posing, but as if the fear and despair rising from this Satanic connection is consuming him.

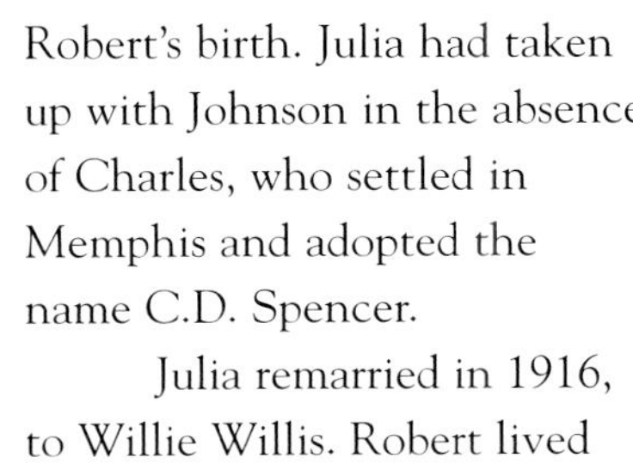

'Amongst all of his peers I felt he was the one that was talking from his soul without really compromising for anybody.'

Eric Clapton

Johnson's intricate guitar style blended boogie-inspired bass lines with a rhythmic, chordal middle register and slide-laced melodies in the treble, while his vocals were delivered with a nervous energy that further intensified his sound. While his music was largely based around the simple country blues emanating from the Mississippi plantations, the directness and inherent urgency of his performances looked forward to the citified Chicago blues of the post-war era.

An Unstable Childhood

Johnson was born Robert Leroy Johnson in May 1911 in Hazelhurst, Mississippi to Julia Dodds and Noah Johnson. Julia Dodds was the wife of Charles Dodds Jr., a farmer forced to leave Mississippi a few years prior to Robert's birth. Julia had taken up with Johnson in the absence of Charles, who settled in Memphis and adopted the name C.D. Spencer.

Julia remarried in 1916, to Willie Willis. Robert lived with them in Robinsonville, Mississippi and was raised as Robert Spencer. It wasn't until his early teens that he was informed about his real father and began to call himself Robert Johnson. Little is known for definite about his upbringing, although he probably worked on the land; however, having to accept three different father figures must have been, at the very least, confusing to the young Johnson. It is suggested that he did not get on with Willis and, whether or not as a direct consequence, turned to music. Starting out on the Jew's harp before progressing to the harmonica, Johnson soon began to take an interest in the guitar; he built a rack for his harmonica and tried picking out accompaniments on the guitar to his harp and voice. He came under the tutelage of Willie Brown, then living in Robinsonville, who introduced him to a wider range of chords and fingerings. Another mentor around this time was Charley Patton, a regular visitor of Brown's, and a frequent performer at the area juke joints. Johnson would follow Brown and Patton and watch their performances – both solo and in duet – with a keen interest.

Johnson married Virginia Travis in Penton, Mississippi in February 1929. The couple moved in with Robert's half-sister on a plantation in the Robinsonville area. Robert worked as sharecropper, while continuing his interest in music, and Virginia became pregnant. Reportedly, Robert was a loving husband, and who knows which way his life may have turned, had his wife not died in childbirth, along with the couple's child, in April 1930.

Above
Blues guitar legend Robert Johnson.

see Introduction pp 90 *see* Sources & Sounds pp 92 *see* A–Z of Artists pp 120

Above

Lonnie Johnson's recordings were one of Robert Johnson's many diverse influences.

Music As A Full-Time Occupation

Within weeks of this tragedy, Son House moved to Robinsonville to work with Willie Brown prior to his recording debut for Paramount in late May 1930. During this brief time, Robert became fascinated by Son House and his music, which was characterized by an intense vocal delivery and a sparkling slide-guitar accompaniment. However, the older man regarded Robert as little more than a beginner, and Patton, Brown and House were not above ridiculing the seemingly omnipresent Johnson. Before the end of 1930, Robert Johnson decided to devote himself completely to music, and headed back to Hazelhurst.

It is generally accepted that Robert remarried around this time, and was supported by his new wife when he met Ike Zinnerman, an Alabama bluesman who became his next mentor. The two men worked the area around Hazelhurst, occasionally encountering artists such as Johnny Temple or Tommy Johnson, and Robert began to blossom. He was working street corners, juke houses, lumber camps – wherever he could make money. Significantly, he travelled not only in the South, but also made excursions around the East Coast and Midwest; the diverse influences that he assimilated during these travels were the key to creating a style that stood out among those of other, more locally schooled Mississippi performers. Johnson also took inspiration from recording artists, including Leroy Carr, Elmore James, Lonnie Johnson, Kokomo Arnold and Skip James; some of Johnson's own records are directly based on those of others, such as 'Love In Vain' (ostensibly Carr's 'When The Sun Goes Down

see Charley Patton pp 23 *see* Willie Brown pp 121 *see* Son House pp 126 *see* Skip James pp 127

(In the Evening)') and 'Sweet Home Chicago' (based on Arnold's 'Old Original Kokomo Blues').

In time Johnson returned to the Mississippi Delta area. On a trip back to Robinsonville he encountered Willie Brown and Son House, who were astonished at how well he could play – and so was born the delicious blues legend of how Johnson sold his soul to the devil in return for his guitar-playing abilities. Johnson soon settled in Helena, Arkansas, which remained his main base of operations for the rest of his life.

Rambling Man

By 1934 Robert Johnson had become a constant traveller. His reputation spread and he had a large following throughout Mississippi and Tennessee. He relied on women to care for him in his constant travels, but he longed to make records. His quest led him to H.C. Speir in Jackson, Mississippi. Speir was a talent scout for ARC records and he passed his recommendation up the line to fellow talent scout and salesman Ernie Oertle. Evidently Oertle was impressed with what he heard, as a recording session was swiftly arranged; following the onset of the Great Depression, the field recordings that had captured the work of so many blues and folk singers for posterity had ceased to prove profitable. Moreover, sides by Mississippi Delta guitarists were not generating significant sales, and the public seemed to prefer the more sophisticated, urban sound of the East Coast and Midwest musicians, many of whom were recording with bands by the mid- to late 1930s. Oertle must, therefore, have recognized something special in Johnson's performance, as in

see Introduction pp 90 *see* Sources & Sounds pp 92 *see* A–Z of Artists pp 120

November 1936 Johnson was on his way to San Antonio, Texas, where he recorded 16 titles in the space of a week. The following June in Dallas, Texas he recorded 13 more.

These 29 songs are the Johnson legacy. 'Terraplane Blues'/'Kindhearted Woman Blues', the first record to be released, was his bestselling track but was still only a modest success. The first LP of this material, *King Of The Delta Blues Singers*, was issued by Columbia in 1961 and inspired a whole new generation of blues musicians including Alexis Korner, the Rolling Stones, Eric Clapton, Jimi Hendrix, Robert Plant and Johnny Winter, many of whom would go on to cover his songs. When the Robert Johnson CD box-set, *The Complete Recordings*, was released in 1990, the worldwide public was finally ready for Johnson's genius and it became an enormous hit.

An Appointment With The Devil

As with his life, the circumstances surrounding Johnson's death are sketchy and mysterious. In August 1938 he was booked to appear at a house party near Greenwood, Mississippi and, according to various witnesses, made a nuisance of himself, drinking too much and flirting with the lady of the house. One poisoned whisky later, the life of the most influential blues guitarist of all time was brought to a premature end. Whether or not this version of events is true is up for discussion; Johnson's death certificate cites 'natural causes'.

Only months later, blues and jazz impresario John Hammond began to make enquiries as to the whereabouts of Robert Johnson; he had heard his records, been greatly impressed and wanted Johnson to appear as part of the 'Spirituals to Swing' concert at New York's Carnegie Hall, the first celebration of African-American music to be staged at such a major venue. Involvement in this event would undoubtedly have propelled Johnson into a prosperous career, and it can only be imagined in what directions his capacity for experimentation and innovation may have led blues music had he lived. However, Johnson's stepson Robert Lockwood, Jnr. also pursued a career as a blues musician, carrying on where Johnson left off and following the blues through into the electric era.

Above
Robinsonville, where Johnson grew up.

Far Left
Johnson's interest in Son House and his music sparked his decision to pursue a musical career.

see **John Hammond pp 125** *see* **Jimi Hendrix pp 273** *see* **Robert Lockwood Jr. pp 276** *see* **Rolling Stones pp 278**

Leadbelly

CLASSIC RECORDINGS

1935
Leadbelly: 'Shorty George', 'You Don't Know My Mind'

1939
Huddie Ledbetter: 'Frankie And Albert', 'The Bourgeois Blues'

1940
Leadbelly & the Golden Gate Quartet: 'Midnight Special'
Huddie Ledbetter: 'Good Morning Blues', 'New York City'

1942
Huddie Ledbetter: 'Rock Island Line', 'Take This Hammer'

1943
Leadbelly & Guitar: 'Goodnight Irene'

Huddie Ledbetter was born in January 1888 in Mooringsport, Louisiana. He was exposed to music from an early age and began playing guitar before he was in his teens. The music he performed was composed of shouts, hollers and Native American songs, as well as ballads, religious songs and dance tunes from a variety of traditions. He became a popular entertainer at functions in his community, which was almost entirely black. By 1901 he had left home and he spent time in the red-light district of Shreveport. It was here that he first encountered early blues songs such as 'The Dirty Dozens'. By the time he was 15, he had his own guitar and his own pistol – both gifts from his father.

In 1910 he was playing in the Deep Ellum area of Dallas and it was probably in 1912 that he met Blind Lemon Jefferson, the Dallas street singer. This is also about the time Huddie acquired his 12-string guitar. Ledbetter and Jefferson worked together over the next three years and Ledbetter absorbed much from the younger man, including his slide guitar technique.

'Leadbelly was a man who decided he was going to be a champion in life. Everything he did, he did it with his whole personality: sing, dance, fight, work.'
Alan Lomax

Leadbelly Serves Time

In December 1917, Ledbetter killed his cousin's husband, for which he was convicted and received a sentence of seven to 30 years in jail. He served his time at the Central State Prison Farm, commonly known as Sugarland, near Houston, Texas. During his time in prison, Huddie picked up the nickname 'Leadbelly'. He was frequently called upon to entertain Governor Pat Neff during his visits to Sugarland. On one occasion in 1924, Leadbelly created an impromptu blues, which – legend has it – so impressed Neff that he promised to pardon him. He was set free in January 1925, but after his release he continued to exhibit violent behaviour. In January 1930, in Mooringsport, he knifed a white man and was sentenced to six to 10 years' hard labour at Angola State Penitentiary.

Lomaxes To The Rescue

As luck would have it, folklorists John and Alan Lomax visited Angola in July of 1933 as part of John's quest to document American folk songs and ballads using portable disc-recording equipment. Leadbelly recorded for them at Angola; among the songs were 'Ella Speed',

Right
Alan Lomax, second-generation American musicologist.

see Introduction pp 90 see Sources & Sounds pp 92 see A–Z of Artists pp 120

'Frankie And Albert' and a gentle waltz called 'Goodnight Irene'. When it became known that John Lomax was returning to Angola in July 1934, Leadbelly saw an opportunity. As his petition for release was being ignored, he recorded his song 'Governor O.K. Allen'. Lomax brought it to the governor's office and Leadbelly was released in August 1934.

At the end of the year, Lomax arranged for Leadbelly to perform at a dinner given by the Modern Language Association in Philadelphia. Within days, the two visited New York and were written up in the *New York Herald Tribune*. This led to Leadbelly's first commercial recording sessions (for ARC) in early 1935. He also continued to record for John – and later John's son Alan – Lomax for the Library of Congress.

An Acrimonious Split

Financial disagreements caused Leadbelly to split from John Lomax and instead reach an arrangement with Mary Elizabeth Barnicle, a professor who introduced Leadbelly to the liberal and radical community that provided much of his growing audience. He made no commercial recordings from 1936–38 and his last association with John Lomax came when *Negro Folk Songs As Sung By Leadbelly* was published in November 1936. The book received favourable reviews and Leadbelly was profiled in *Life* magazine, after which he appeared on a radio series and began to write new songs.

He was arrested again for felonious assault in 1939. Alan Lomax, trying to raise money for his defence, contacted Musicraft Records to arrange a recording session. The songs Leadbelly recorded were issued on an album titled *Negro Sinful Songs*. He was convicted and served eight months. In 1940 Leadbelly recorded for RCA Victor and by the summer of 1941 he had begun a lengthy association with Moses Asch. With the exception of some 1944 recordings for Capitol, the remainder of his recordings were released on Asch/Stinson/Folkways. He continued to be a popular attraction on the folk circuit until his death in 1949.

Left
Huddie 'Leadbelly' Ledbetter – murderer, convict and undisputed blues hero.

Below
Leadbelly with session pianist Paul Mason Howard playing the dolceola, a type of fretless zither.

see Blind Lemon Jefferson pp 56 *see* John & Alan Lomax pp 129

Lester Young

CLASSIC RECORDINGS

1933–44
Complete Billie Holiday On Columbia, 'Easy Living', 'I Must Have That Man', 'When You're Smiling'

1936–52
America's # 1 Band! by Count Basie, 'Lady Be Good', 'Lester Jumps In'

1937–39
The Complete Decca Records by Count Basie, 'John's Idea', 'Jumpin' At The Woodside', 'One O'Clock Jump'

1944–49
The Complete Savoy Recording, 'How High The Moon', 'Neenah'

Of all the great solo architects of the 1930s, none personified the smooth, penetrating sweep through space and time more ideally or organically than tenor saxophonist Lester Young. His fluid, unforced phrasing and undulating attack were matched to a cool, satin skin of sound that seemed to dispel all friction by decompressing the emotional density of the prevailing tenors into a piping, almost hollow echo. Young's streamlined contours would have risen to the top in any context, but when joining with the elegant modernity of the Count Basie rhythm section in 1936, Young found his perfect soul mate; he defined the essence of swing at its most pure and became one of the most influential jazz voices of the decade.

A Musical Background

Born in Woodville, Mississippi on 27 August 1909, Lester Willis Young grew up in a musical family that toured and performed together. He experimented with the trumpet, violin and drums as a boy before finally focusing on the tenor saxophone by 1922. Four years later the Young family relocated to Minneapolis, Minnesota, but Lester grew restless working under his father's hand. When he turned 18 he went out on his own, touring with a variety of regional bands in the upper Midwest. He worked briefly with the Blue Devils in 1930 and with Basie for the first time in the Bennie Moten Band in 1934. But Young didn't stay long; he moved through several other groups, then returned to Basie in 1936, just as the bandleader was on the verge of being discovered by John Hammond.

'When Lester plays, he almost seems to be singing; one can almost hear the words.'
Billie Holiday

Above Right
Young with his patron and organizer of 'Jazz At The Philharmonic', Norman Granz.

Right
Bennie Moten's (seated right) band, shown here in 1929, was where Young met bandleader Count Basie (seated left).

Early Records

Young's career rose swiftly with Basie's, and vice versa. His record debut, made with a small Basie group in October 1936, produced two of the great swing classics of the decade – 'Lady Be Good' and 'Shoe Shine Boy' – and there would be more where that came from. A steady stream of Basie band records poured out, plus many small group

see Introduction pp 90 *see* Sources & Sounds pp 92 *see* A–Z of Artists pp 120

sessions, produced by Hammond, that brought Young together with Billie Holiday, Teddy Wilson, Benny Goodman, Charlie Christian and others. The 54 sides made with Holiday between January 1937 and November 1938 carried a particular and persistent fascination – and not merely because the records caught both artists at the peak of their powers. They also seemed to capture a quality of looming melancholy in the relationship of two gentle but flawed temperaments, for whom doom due to fragility seemed written on the wind. The music survives in a nimbus of legend.

Young's dry, feathery lyricism and fluid laws of motion immediately set him apart from the flock, as the other musicians recognized a new and original tenor voice. His ideas were oblique and unexpected. He would spread a phrase out over several bars, then suddenly pause over a lingering, out-of-tempo note, or interrupt himself with an impulsive arching swoop. In a broadcast performance of 'I Got Rhythm' from the Southland Café, Young bounces along on a sleek, unbroken F over four continuous bars of rhythmic variations. By the end of the 1930s Young had not only become the first serious alternative to the big-toned, romantic tenor; he also seemed to have opened a door into post-war modernism, where the hot would soon make room for the cool.

Leaving Basie

Young left Basie in 1940, returned briefly in 1944, and was then drafted into the army. During basic training he was caught in possession of marijuana and confined to military prison until December 1945. Although he seemed to recover much of his pre-war form in a series of Jazz At The Philharmonic (JATP) concerts in the spring of 1946, it was soon apparent that Young's sound had taken on a thicker, denser texture. Also, his easy fluency seemed to settle into a series of set signature phrases and figures.

Fans and critics disagree on the merits of Young's later work, but there is little dispute that a younger generation of light-toned players based their style and sound largely on his innovations in the 1930s. Although they continued to revere him, they passed him by to become the stars of the post-war cult of the cool: Al Cohn, Zoot Sims, Alan Eager, Dexter Gordon and above all Stan Getz. Norman Granz became Young's most consistent patron, despite the fact that Young's declining health had an increasingly severe impact on his playing. After the mid-1950s his performances were unquestionably a shadow of their former selves. A final reunion with Billie Holiday in December 1957 on *The Sound Of Jazz*, a CBS Television special, would acquire in the years ahead a special poignancy. Today many feel that they see in the performance the star-crossed character of their brief lives, caught with a touching transparency. Young died on 15 March 1959 in New York.

Above
Tenor saxophone great Lester Young, one of the most influential jazz soloists of the 1930s.

see Count Basie pp 102 *see* Billie Holiday pp 156 *see* Zoot Sims pp 233 *see* Stan Getz pp 272

A–Z of Artists

Kokomo Arnold

(Guitar, vocals, 1901–68)

Born and raised in Georgia, James Arnold was taught to play guitar by his cousin. He moved to Buffalo, New York in his late teens and to Chicago in 1929. He worked outside music, making bootleg whiskey, but also played occasional jobs. He first recorded for Victor in 1930 as Gitfiddle Jim and was signed to Decca in September 1934, scoring an instant hit with 'Milk Cow Blues'/'Old Original Kokomo Blues'. The former was a song covered by artists as diverse as Bob Wills, Elvis Presley and George Strait, while the flip side – written about a brand of coffee – provided Arnold with a lifelong nickname.

A left-handed, bottleneck stylist who had 76 sides issued on Decca, Arnold recorded for the last time in 1938. He mainly worked outside music after 1940, although he did play some Chicago dates during the folk music revival of the early 1960s.

Above

Top jazz trumpeter Bunny Berigan's career was cut short by his alcohol-related death at 33.

Billy Banks

(Vocals, 1908–67)

A crooner and scat singer, Billy Banks was a protégé of agency impresario Irving Mills. He headlined a handful of legendary records in 1932 by the Rhythmakers – less interesting for his vocals than for the punchy, eccentric work of the all-star band, which included Henry 'Red' Allen, Pee Wee Russell, Fats Waller, Eddie Condon, Pops Foster, Tommy Dorsey and Zutty Singleton. Banks also recorded with the Mills Blues Rhythm Band in the 1930s before leaving for Europe in 1952. He later settled in Tokyo, where he ran a club.

Danny Barker

(Banjo, guitar, educator, 1909–94)

Daniel Moses Barker carried forth the musical traditions of New Orleans, playing with a number of traditional bands in the 1920s and 1930s before marrying Louise Dupont (a.k.a. Blue Lu Barker) in 1930. They recorded several sides together in 1938, including Barker's own song 'Don't You Make Me High', revived in the 1970s by Maria Muldauer. After working with several big bands in the 1930s (including those of Lucky Millinder and Cab Calloway), he was a New Orleans revival activist, leading a youth band that included Wynton Marsalis.

Bunny Berigan

(Trumpet, vocals, 1908–42)

Rowland Bernard Berigan's warm sound and fluent style made him a major figure of the swing era. To some extent, his alcohol-related death at 33 has unduly enhanced his legacy, lifting a solid talent to the level of tortured artist-genius. Berigan arrived in New York in 1929 and became a sought-after session player. He played in Benny Goodman's 1935 band, leaving memorable solos on 'King Porter Stomp' and 'Sometimes I'm Happy'.

With Tommy Dorsey in 1937 he scored two more classics – 'Marie' and 'Song Of India'. Berigan assembled his own band and recorded his most famous showpiece, 'I Can't Get Started'. His solo began with a series of reflective breaks and then broke into a majestic high note statement, before falling to a low-register denouement and epilogue. Laid out with strong dramatic pacing, it shows Berigan's debt to Louis Armstrong. In 1939 Berigan dissolved his band, rejoined Dorsey briefly in 1940, and then resumed with his own orchestra.

see Introduction pp 90 *see* Sources & Sounds pp 92 *see* Key Artists pp 100

Left
Tenor saxophonist Chu Berry (right) with drummer Cozy Cole.

Big Maceo

(Piano, vocals, 1905–53)

Major Merriweather was born in Georgia and taught himself to play piano. He moved to Detroit in 1924 and worked at the Ford Motor Company, also playing jobs, mostly as a soloist, before moving to Chicago. There he developed a friendship with Tampa Red and they recorded for Bluebird in 1941. His 'Worried Life Blues' is a blues standard, while 'Chicago Breakdown' is an instrumental blues masterpiece. He suffered a stroke in 1946, following which his career was sharply curtailed.

Willie Brown

(Guitar, vocals, 1900–52)

An associate of Charley Patton, Brown was a part of the Mississippi blues scene in the early 1920s. While he started out playing with Patton and Tommy Johnson, he teamed up with Son House in 1926 and accompanied his Paramount session in May 1930, also cutting four songs of his own. Brown played with Robert Johnson frequently in the years prior to Johnson's death. He recorded for the Library of Congress in 1941 but then left the music business.

Chu Berry

(Tenor saxophone, 1908–41)

Inspired by Coleman Hawkins' big sound, Leon 'Chu' Berry honed a more rapid, streamlined tenor attack. He recorded with Benny Carter in 1933 and joined Fletcher Henderson three years later. In 1937 he topped *Down Beat*'s first national poll of leading musicians and joined Cab Calloway's orchestra, where he remained until his death. Berry also participated in numerous small groups. A versatile musician, he was equally at home skating over the beat at fast tempos, surging effortlessly through mid-tempos or playing romantic ballads in the Hawkins tradition.

Below
Pianist Big Maceo, whose 'Worried Life Blues' became a blues standard.

see Fats Waller pp 85 *see* Robert Johnson pp 112 *see* Cab Calloway pp 122 *see* Tommy Dorsey pp 123

Cab Calloway

(Bandleader, vocals, entertainer, 1907–94)

Cabell Calloway's orchestra was one of the most successful black bands of the 1930s and by the end of the decade it was home to some of the finest jazz soloists. He arrived in Chicago in the late 1920s and found his niche as a singer, then went to New York, where the band that he fronted replaced Duke Ellington's at the Cotton Club.

Above

Bandleader Cab Calloway, who took over Duke Ellington's slot at the Cotton Club.

He cultivated a jive-talking persona that appealed to a mixed racial audience; in the broad spectrum of American Negro iconography, Calloway represents a key transitional image between nineteenth-century minstrelsy and contemporary hip hop. After 1935 he reflected the trend towards jazz by bringing in a succession of important soloists (Ben Webster, Chu Berry and Dizzy Gillespie), but his vocals remained the focus of the band's sound. From 1939–41 his band was one of the finest in the country, but after the war he gave it up to concentrate on club, theatre and movie work until the end of his life.

Benny Carter

(Alto saxophone, arranger, trumpet, vocals, 1907–2003)

One of the great arrangers and soloists in jazz history, Bennett Lester Carter wrote some of the first big-band music to fully realize the flowing, legato ensemble of the coming swing movement. His saxophone ensembles were smooth projections of his solo style. 'Lonesome Nights' and 'Symphony In Riffs' were so advanced when Carter recorded them in 1933 that they still sounded at home in the late 1930s and early 1940s when Artie Shaw, Tommy Dorsey, Gene Krupa and Cab Calloway recorded their versions.

Carter worked in Europe during 1935–38 and returned to lead a series of excellent bands. He had a rich, poised alto sound that complemented the relaxed elegance of his phrasing, as illustrated in his 1937 versions of 'Crazy Rhythm' with Coleman Hawkins. After settling in California in 1942, Carter prospered in film and worked to integrate musicians in Hollywood. He continued to record and perform at a high level into his 90s.

Doc Cheatham

(Trumpet, vocals, 1905–97)

Adolphus Cheatham played in countless bands and small groups in the 1920s, before settling in the Cab Calloway orchestra in 1931. He remained with Calloway until 1939, after which he resumed work with a variety of bands. He didn't emerge as a soloist until the 1960s, working with George Wein, Benny Goodman and others. His singing style – like the man himself – was polite, courtly and gentle, suited to both cabaret and jazz clubs; he performed regularly in New York throughout the rest of his long life.

Right

Benny Carter, a hugely influential player but a relatively unsung hero of jazz music.

see Introduction pp 90 *see* Sources & Sounds pp 92 *see* Key Artists pp 100

Left

Tommy (left) and Jimmy Dorsey (right) with drummer Buddy Rich.

Jimmy Dorsey

(Bandleader, alto saxophone, clarinet, 1904–57)

Thoroughly educated in music as a child, Jimmy Dorsey freelanced in New York in the early 1930s, recording frequently with brother Tommy as the Dorsey Brothers Orchestra. They formed a working band in 1934 but split up in 1935. Jimmy carried on, backing Bing Crosby on radio and recording prolifically for Decca. He came into his own in the 1940s, largely on the popularity of his two vocalists, Bob Eberle and Helen O'Connell. In 1957 he scored an unexpected hit with 'So Rare'.

Tommy Dorsey

(Bandleader, trombone, trumpet, 1905–56)

With the break-up of the Dorsey Brothers Orchestra, Tommy Dorsey quickly hired the Joe Haymes Orchestra en masse and built a new band to his specifications. For all the talent it would attract, however, it would always be built around the leader's warm trombone sound and flawless perfection on ballads. The Dorsey band of 1935–39 drew its identity from the muscle-loosening swing of drummer Dave Tough, soloists Bud Freeman, Bunny Berigan, Yank Lawson and Johnny Mince, and singers Jack Leonard and Edythe Wright.

Late in 1939, Sy Oliver came over from Jimmie Lunceford as arranger and reinvented the Dorsey band for the 1940s. It became a precision showboat of talent (artists included Frank Sinatra, Jo Stafford, Buddy Rich and Ziggy Elman), which covered everything from hard-swinging originals ('Well Get It') to imaginatively mounted pop tunes ('Without A Song'). In 1953 the Dorsey brothers reunited and combined their books into a single band. Early in 1956 the Dorsey Brothers *Stage Show* introduced Elvis Presley to a national television audience.

Sleepy John Estes

(Guitar, vocals, 1899–1977)

John Adams Estes was born in Ripley, Tennessee. He teamed up with mandolinist Yank Rachell to work the area from 1919 until the late 1920s. His first recordings were made for Victor in 1929 and included his celebrated 'Divin' Duck Blues'. He left Brownsville for Chicago in 1931.

With harmonica player Hammie Nixon, Estes worked medicine shows, fish fries and hobo camps, touring much of the country in the late 1930s. He recorded six sides for Champion in 1935, including 'Drop Down Mama', and he later recorded for Decca from 1937–40. After two sessions for Bluebird in 1941 he returned to Brownsville and left the music scene, with the exception of two recording sessions for Sun in 1952. He had completely lost his sight by 1950. 'Rediscovered' in 1962, he recorded for several labels and began an extensive comeback, which included at least one album of electric blues with younger musicians. He toured the US, Europe and Japan steadily until his death.

see Benny Goodman pp 110 *see* Gene Krupa pp 128 *see* Dizzy Gillespie pp 152 *see* Yank Rachell pp 278

Above

The Quintet of the Hot Club of France, with Django Reinhardt (second from left) and Stephane Grappelli (second from right).

Ella Fitzgerald

(Vocals, 1917–96)

Sixteen-year-old Ella Fitzgerald joined Chick Webb's band in 1934 and became its biggest attraction. After Webb's death in 1939 she became titular leader of the orchestra, which continued until 1942; she then worked as a solo artist. After the war Fitzgerald revealed an uncanny talent for bebop scat singing; it drew the attention of Norman Granz, who began adding her to his Jazz At The Philharmonic shows. He became her manager in 1953 and took over her recording career. Under Granz's guidance she rose to become the reigning interpreter of twentieth-century American songs.

Blind Boy Fuller

(Guitar, vocals, 1908–41)

Fuller was born Fulton Allen in Wadesboro, North Carolina and was one of 10 children. He learned to play guitar as a teenager and by the mid-1920s was working for tips around Rockingham, North Carolina. He had lost his sight by 1928. He teamed up with artists such as Gary Davis, Bull City Red and Sonny Terry and worked the area around Durham, North Carolina in the mid-1930s.

He first recorded for ARC in 1935 and, with the exception of two sessions for Decca in 1937, recorded for ARC/Vocalion/OKeh until June 1940. He cut well over 100 sides during that time. Fuller was known for the wide variety of music he played, including pop songs, religious material, ragtime and blues, and because of that range he is considered a unique figure in the pantheon of Carolina blues stylists. He underwent kidney surgery in 1940 and suffered blood poisoning, which ultimately killed him.

Stephane Grappelli

(Violin, piano, 1908–97)

Largely self-taught, Stephane Grappelli's virtuosity came to the attention of the world in 1934 through records with Django Reinhardt and the Quintet of the

see Introduction pp 90 *see* Sources & Sounds pp 92 *see* Key Artists pp 100

Hot Club of France. His refined sound was decorative on ballads but could push with an alert and driving attack of formidable power on jazz standards such as 'Tiger Rag', 'Shine' and 'I've Found A New Baby'.

In Paris and London Grappelli recorded with many visiting American players, including violinist Eddie South in 1937. Their repertoire, which ranged from Gershwin to Bach, produced some of the most dazzling and intriguing violin duets ever recorded. The Quintet never appeared in America, although it was heard on several radio broadcasts. Grappelli lived in London during and after the war, but his reputation faded. In 1969 George Wein brought him to the Newport Jazz Festival for his American debut. Still at the top of his form, he continued to tour and record for another 28 years.

Bobby Hackett

(Trumpet, cornet, guitar, 1915–76)

After Bobby Hackett was praised in *Down Beat* by Boston critic George Frazier in 1937, he headed to New York and settled into a group of neo-traditional players loosely associated with Eddie Condon. Although a lifelong fan of Louis Armstrong, Hackett's gentle, fluid lyricism made him a more logical descendent of Bix Biederbecke, whom he represented in a historical section of Benny Goodman's 1938 Carnegie Hall concert. Hackett recorded with his own big band in 1939. His association with Condon brought him into an informal stock company of players who recorded for Dixieland-oriented Commodore Records.

He joined Glenn Miller in 1941 and played the famous cornet bridge on 'String Of Pearls'. During the 1940s he divided his time between radio staff work and jazz. Hackett's placid improvisations found a large audience in the 1950s as the featured solo voice on many mood music albums conducted by Jackie Gleason. He also worked prominently with Goodman, singer Tony Bennett and Vic Dickenson in his later years.

John Hammond

(Critic, producer, 1910–86)

John Hammond was the most influential jazz critic, producer and social activist of the politically charged 1930s. A Vanderbilt descendant raised in social prominence and luxury on New York's East Side, Hammond rebelled against his class, producing jazz records and pressing for racial integration. He played a key role in the careers of Fletcher Henderson, Benny Goodman, Billie Holiday, Lionel Hampton, Count Basie and Charlie Christian – bringing them together on occasions – and later Aretha Franklin, Bob Dylan and Bruce Springsteen.

Lionel Hampton

(Vibraphone, drums, piano, 1908–2002)

Before jazz became highbrow, musicians were cheered, not censured, for being entertainers; Lionel Hampton embraced that model. The more one did, he believed, the more one made. So Hampton was always doing more. During his early years he worked as a drummer. He began experimenting with the vibraphone around 1930, but few bandleaders wanted its unorthodox sound.

In 1936 Benny Goodman heard Hampton, was impressed and immediately invited him to join Gene Krupa and Teddy Wilson, making the Goodman Trio a quartet. Hampton infused Goodman's groups with enormous inspiration and energy. In 1937 he began a parallel series of remarkable sessions under his own name on Victor that would involve most of the greatest soloists of the period. After leaving Goodman in 1940 Hampton formed his own band, which recorded his definitive version of 'Flying Home' in 1942, featuring tenor saxophonist Illinois Jacquet. He continued leading bands and touring the world well into the 1990s, always a combination of brilliant musician, talent scout and antic showman.

Above
Lionel Hampton playing the vibraphone in Benny Goodman's Quartet.

see Bix Beiderbecke pp 48 *see* Benny Goodman pp 110 *see* Django Reinhardt pp 132 *see* Chick Webb pp 137

Earl Hines

(Piano, bandleader, 1903–83)

Earl 'Fatha' Hines was the key transitional figure between the early ragtime and stride styles and the essentials of modern piano. He stripped away much of the density of 1920s piano, replacing it with more linear octaves and edgy single-note lines with the right hand – his 'trumpet style' – while softening the rhythmic accompaniment with the left.

Below
Earl Hines emerged in Louis Armstrong's company, introducing 'trumpet-style' piano.

Hines established his reputation in Chicago in the late 1920s, recording solos and classics such as 'Weather Bird' and 'West End Blues' with Louis Armstrong. He led the house band at Chicago's Grand Terrace Café from 1928–40. Hines turned it into a first-class orchestra, largely on the basis of arrangements by Jimmy Mundy ('Cavernism', 'Mad House'), whom he discovered and mentored. The band's peak years came on its Victor recordings (1939–42). Hines gave up the band in 1947, toured with Louis Armstrong until 1951 and then fell in to obscurity. In 1964 a New York solo concert returned him to prominence; for the next 19 years he toured and recorded prolifically.

Johnny Hodges

(Alto and soprano saxophones, 1907–70)

Saxophonist Johnny Hodges was fortunate enough to forge an early relationship with Sidney Bechet; while playing at Club Bechet in New York he won the attention of Duke Ellington, who signed him in 1928. Hodges' sweeping tone and scooping glissandos remained a vital part of Ellington's orchestra for around 40 years, with only a few periods of absence as he experimented with small groups and other ventures. Hodges was admired by many other saxophonists, including Ben Webster and John Coltrane.

Son House

(Guitar, vocals, 1902–88)

The son of a musician, Eddie James House Jr. was born in Riverton, Mississippi. House was preaching sermons by his mid-teens and travelled widely in the 1920s. He did not learn guitar until the age of 25, but soon thereafter was torn between his faith and his love of the blues. After killing a man in a Lyon juke joint and serving two years in jail, House encountered Charley Patton, whose connections at Paramount Records landed him a recording session in 1930.

The intensity and passion of House on songs such as the two-part 'Preachin' The Blues' have rarely been approached in the blues field. However, the records sold poorly and House worked functions in the Delta, often in the company of Willie Brown, for much of the 1930s. He recorded for the Library of Congress in 1941–42, before leaving music in 1943 and moving

see Introduction pp 90 *see* Sources & Sounds pp 92 *see* Key Artists pp 100

to Rochester, New York. Rediscovered in 1964, he recorded for a number of labels and toured widely for the rest of the decade.

Spike Hughes

(Bass, bandleader, critic, 1908–87)

As editor for *Melody Maker* and producer at British Decca, Spike Hughes recorded many dance and novelty sides during 1930–32 but had ambitions in jazz. During a New York visit in 1933 he augmented Benny Carter's band with Coleman Hawkins and recorded 14 of his own arrangements as Spike Hughes & his Negro Orchestra. Notwithstanding Hughes' many excellent solos, John Hammond wrote that he 'could not write music that swung'. At this, Hughes decided to return to journalism and producing, and never recorded again.

Skip James

(Vocals, guitar, 1902–69)

Born in Bentonia, Mississippi and raised on a nearby plantation, Nehemiah 'Skip' James played the guitar professionally from a young age and also taught himself to play the piano. His distinctive E-minor guitar tuning, three-finger picking technique and melancholy, high-pitched vocals gave him a unique sound, and his recording session for Paramount in 1931 resulted in some of the most affecting and haunting country blues ever recorded. Songs such as 'Devil Got My Woman', 'I'm So Glad' and '22-20 Blues' still stand out as masterpieces of their genre.

In the 1930s James drifted away from the music scene to concentrate on a career in the church, before being 'rediscovered' in the 1960s, along with Son House and various other blues artists. He performed at the 1964 Newport Folk Festival and recorded a handful of albums for Takoma, Melodeon and Vanguard, while his 'I'm So Glad' was covered by the British blues-rock band Cream. Skip James' revived career was unfortunately cut short by his death from cancer in 1969.

Left
Son House, whose role in the development of blues in the genre's early days was significant.

Left
Skip James, whose haunting vocals evoked the desolation of the Mississippi Delta.

see Charley Patton pp 23 *see* Louis Armstrong pp 44 *see* Duke Ellington pp 52 *see* Benny Carter pp 122

Bottom Right
One of the great boogie-woogie pianists Meade 'Lux' Lewis had a hit with 'Honky Tonk Train Blues'.

Far Right
Jimmie Lunceford's band was renowned for its elaborate stage shows.

Pete Johnson

(Piano, 1904–67)

Born in Kansas City, Missouri, Kermit Holden Johnson teamed up with Joe Turner at the Sunset Café in the early 1930s and went to New York for the Spirituals To Swing concert in 1938. He recorded with Turner for Vocalion (the famous 'Roll 'Em Pete'), as well as alone and with Albert Ammons and Meade 'Lux' Lewis. Beginning in 1944, he recorded for Brunswick, National, Apollo and Swingtime, and was often featured with Turner. He suffered a heart attack in 1958 and was only sporadically active after that.

Jo Jones

(Drums, 1911–85)

Few players have defined a big band from the drum chair as strongly as Jonathon 'Jo' Jones did with Count Basie. When the first Basie records came out in 1937, their rhythm section was both a revelation and a revolution – and brought jazz drumming into a new, more sleek modernity. A master of the steely hi-hat cymbal, Jones coaxed from it a supple, relaxed whoosh, sliding accents slightly to either side of the beat. It swung with an uncanny crackle and power and became the principle mainspring of his time.

Jones had first worked with Basie in the Blue Devils in 1929. He joined the Basie band in Kansas City and remained during its prime years from 1936–44, during which he also recorded many dates with Teddy Wilson and Billie Holiday. Jones returned to Basie in 1946, by which time new drummers were carrying his innovations into bebop. From the 1950s onwards he freelanced and taught an army of young students, becoming known as 'Papa' Jo Jones in his later years.

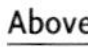

Above
Jo Jones revolutionized jazz drumming, from the bass drum to the hi-hat cymbal.

Jonah Jones

(Trumpet, vocals, 1909–2000)

By the time Jonah Jones came to prominence on New York's 52nd Street, he had developed a fierce, intense attack that suggested Roy Eldridge without the high notes. He played and recorded with Stuff Smith from 1936–40 and on sessions with Teddy Wilson, Billie Holiday and Lionel Hampton. He worked with Cab Calloway from 1941–52. In 1957 he began recording for Capitol and had several hits, including 'Baubles, Bangles And Beads' and 'On The Street Where You Live', which combined a shuffle rhythm with his muted trumpet.

Gene Krupa

(Drums, 1909–73)

Possibly the most famous jazz drummer, Gene Krupa played in the 'press roll' style of Chicago, where he first recorded in 1927. He was a traditionalist and kept time largely on the snare, with either sticks or brushes, playing two-beat on bass drum. He joined Benny Goodman in 1934 and became a key factor in the band's historic success. Krupa could 'kick' a band in a way that few white drummers had managed before him.

As a soloist, he combined technique, imagination and flash that made him the centre of attention. Much of that technique infused Goodman's trio and quartet pieces. But his *tour de force* would forever be 'Sing Sing Sing', a nine-minute collage of riffs linked by Krupa's rock-solid tom-toms and recurring solo interludes. He left Goodman in 1938 to form his own band, which became a great success in the 1940s with Roy Eldridge and Anita O'Day. Krupa scaled back to a trio in 1951 and worked in that format for the next 20 years.

Meade 'Lux' Lewis

(Piano, 1905–64)

Born in Chicago and inspired by Jimmy Yancey, Meade Anderson 'Lux' Lewis recorded an early boogie-woogie masterpiece, 'Honky Tonk Train Blues', for Paramount in 1927 (the song was also recorded for Parlophone, 1935 and Victor, 1937). He recorded for Decca in 1936 ('Yancey Special') and Vocalion,

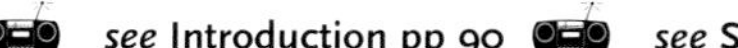

see Introduction pp 90 *see* Sources & Sounds pp 92 *see* Key Artists pp 100

Blue Note and Solo Art throughout 1941, almost always as a soloist or with Albert Ammons and Pete Johnson. He recorded for many other labels between 1944–61.

John & Alan Lomax

(Folklorists, John Avery Lomax 1867–1948; Alan Lomax 1915–2002)

John Lomax was born in Goodman, Mississippi and raised near Fort Worth, Texas. Although his initial interest lay in cowboy songs, a pre-teen friendship with a servant named Nat Blythe sparked an interest in black music. With the 1910 publication of *Cowboy Songs And Other Frontier Ballads*, his reputation was established. His work on black music took root with a consultancy to the Library of Congress in 1933.

Alan Lomax was 18 when he joined his father to record musicians and singers in their natural habitat. In July 1933, the Lomaxes arrived at Angola Penitentiary, where they discovered Leadbelly. Alan continued his father's essential fieldwork, most notably by finding Son House and discovering Muddy Waters in 1941. Much of Alan's best field recordings were released commercially on Atlantic Records (*The Songs Of The South*, which contained Fred McDowell's first recordings). His 1993 memoir, *The Land Where The Blues Began*, recounts all of these adventures.

Jimmie Lunceford

(Bandleader, arranger, 1902–47)

While working as a music teacher in Memphis, Mississippi-born Lunceford formed a band called the Chicksaw Syncopators. They first recorded in 1930 and after four years of touring gained a residency at the Cotton Club and became the Jimmie Lunceford Orchestra. Renowned for its polished stage presence, the band was nevertheless musically tight and trumpeter Sy Oliver's arrangements secured a signature 'Lunceford sound'. Pay disputes split the original line-up in the early 1940s, but Lunceford continued to lead the orchestra until his death.

see Albert Ammons pp 100 see Count Basie pp 102 see Leadbelly pp 116 see Jimmy Yancey pp 139

Wingy Manone

(Trumpet, vocals, 1900–82)

Born in New Orleans, Joseph 'Wingy' Manone's rousing trumpet and gravelly vocals were (as with his fellow Italian-American, Louis Prima) confidently cast from the Armstrong matrix. After scoring a hit with 'Isle Of Capri' in 1935, he became a fixture on New York's 52nd Street before moving to California in 1940 to join Bing Crosby's circle of cronies. His 1930 disc 'Tar Paper Stomp' is the first recorded appearance of the blues riff that would become familiar in 1939 as Glenn Miller's 'In The Mood'.

Below
Mississippi Fred McDowell, who was an unknown amateur until the blues revival of the 1960s.

Mississippi Fred McDowell

(Guitar, vocals, 1904–72)

Self-taught as a guitarist, music was only a sideline for McDowell for the first 60 years of his life. He worked in the Memphis area before settling in Como, Mississippi to work as a farmer in 1929; he didn't own a guitar until 1940. Discovered and recorded by Alan Lomax in 1959, McDowell's first recordings were issued on Atlantic and Prestige/International.

A bottleneck specialist, McDowell was recorded in 1964 by Chris Strachwitz for Arhoolie Records. This provided a springboard to prominence for McDowell, who soon moved into regular appearances at festivals and on the folk-music circuit. From that point until 1971, he recorded regularly and appeared in three films, including the documentary *Fred McDowell* (1969). He was championed by younger performers such as the Rolling Stones, who covered McDowell's tune 'You Got To Move' on their 1971 album *Sticky Fingers*.

Irving Mills

(Music publisher, producer, manager, 1884–1985)

Publisher Irving Mills was early to recognize the potential in black music. He formed Mills Music, Inc. with his brother in 1919 and enjoyed a business relationship with Duke Ellington from 1926–39 that brought a procession of Ellington songs into the Mills catalogue. He also formed the Mills Blue Rhythm Band in 1931 and developed it into a fine orchestra before it evolved into the Lucky Millinder Band in 1938. Mills Music, Inc. was sold in 1965.

Memphis Minnie

(Guitar, vocals, 1897–1973)

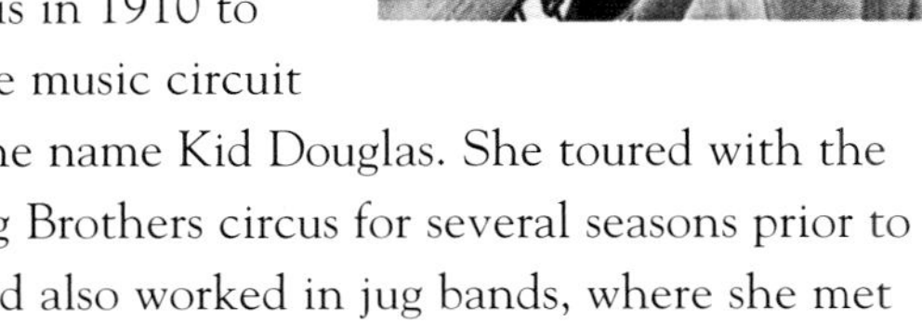

Right
Memphis Minnie, one of the finest female blues guitarists of all time.

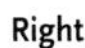

Lizzie Douglas was born in Algiers, Louisiana but was raised in Walls, Mississippi. She learned banjo and guitar at a young age and ran away to Memphis in 1910 to work the music circuit under the name Kid Douglas. She toured with the Ringling Brothers circus for several seasons prior to 1920 and also worked in jug bands, where she met and married 'Kansas' Joe McCoy.

They made their recording debut as Kansas Joe and Memphis Minnie for Columbia in 1929, and recorded for Victor in 1930 and Vocalion during 1930–34. Minnie moved to Chicago in the early 1930s and divorced McCoy in 1935. She recorded for Decca and Bluebird before returning to Vocalion/OKeh/Columbia from 1935–49. She teamed with her third husband, Ernest 'Little Son Joe' Lawlers, in 1939. Minnie then ran a vaudeville company before leaving the music business in the mid-1950s.

Little Brother Montgomery

(Piano, vocals, 1906–85)

Eurreal Wilford Montgomery was born in Louisiana and taught himself piano, dropping out of school to work functions and juke joints. He first recorded for Paramount in 1930 ('Vicksburg Blues'/'No

 *see* Introduction pp 90  *see* Sources & Sounds pp 92 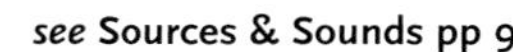 *see* Key Artists pp 100 

Special Rider') and then for Bluebird and ARC in 1935–36. Often featured with traditional jazz bands in addition to his primary work as a soloist, Montgomery settled in Chicago in 1942 and worked as a sideman for other recording artists. He continued to tour and record throughout the 1960s and 1970s.

Hot Lips Page

(Trumpet, vocals, 1908–54)

Oran Thaddeus Page surfaced in the Bennie Moten Band as a powerful blues player, often using a plunger mute. He was with the as-yet unknown Count Basie in 1936 and might soon have left Kansas City as one of that fabled band of brothers had he not been approached by Joe Glaser. Glaser was Louis Armstrong's manager, and he saw in Page's playing and singing another Armstrong; he signed him and took him to New York.

In 1938 Page fronted a band and recorded two sessions for Victor that showcased him as an Armstrong clone. Page's solos were polished, regal and majestic, using many of the spectacular glissandos and dramatic breaks familiar on Armstrong's Decca records. But stardom never came and the band soon broke up. He joined Artie Shaw for five months in 1941–42, reaching his biggest audiences and posting some of his best performances ('There'll Be Some Changes Made'). He freelanced in traditional and small swing groups in the 1940s.

Above
Hot Lips Page (left) plays with Freddie Moore (back left), Sidney Bechet (right) and Lloyd Phillips (back right) in New York.

see **Louis Armstrong pp 44** *see* **John & Alan Lomax pp 129** *see* **Artie Shaw pp 133** *see* **Glenn Miller pp 180**

Walter Page

(Tuba, bass, 1900–57)

By the end of the 1930s Walter Page had brought the usually subordinate roll of the bass to a position of critical importance without substantially expanding its time-keeping function. As a component of the unique Count Basie 'all-American' rhythm section from 1936–42, he produced a large, round but never percussive attack, whose ringing tone would remain a Basie hallmark. He also presaged an expanded melodic roll for the bass in 'Pagin' The Devil', made in 1938 with a Basie contingent a year before the arrival of virtuoso bassist Jimmy Blanton.

Below

Belgian gypsy guitarist Django Reinhardt, who created his own unique playing style.

Django Reinhardt

(Guitar, 1910–53)

One of the reasons that Django Reinhardt dominated conversations about the guitar so completely in the 1930s was his fortunate timing. He arrived on the world jazz scene through the Quintet of the Hot Club of France in 1934 – a year after the death of Eddie Lang and five years before the arrival of Charlie Christian. Belgian by birth, he became a jazz star without ever going to the United States. Reinhardt travelled in a gypsy caravan, yet absorbed American jazz pop and jazz standards, including 'Avalon', 'The Sheik Of Araby' and dozens more.

The Hot Club Quintet had a salonish, continental quality with a tightly packed, chugging rhythm section of two guitars and bass (with no drums). It was an ideal anchor for the improvisations of Reinhardt, whose trajectories had a swift, spun-glass delicacy full of notes quivering with an intense vibrato that was equal parts emotion and ethnic flavouring. After the war he made his only trip to the US, recording with Duke Ellington in 1946.

Jimmy Rushing

(Vocals, 1899–72)

James Andrew Rushing was born in Oklahoma City into a musical family. He worked in California in the mid-1920s as a pianist and vocalist, joined Walter Page's Blue Devils in Oklahoma City in 1927 and made his recording debut with the band in 1929. He played with the Bennie Moten Band in Kansas City from 1929, before joining the first Count Basie Band in 1935. He stayed with Basie until 1950 and recorded more than 50 songs, including his signature song 'Mister Five By Five'.

Luis Russell

(Bandleader, pianist, 1902–63)

Luis Russell first worked in New Orleans, then in Chicago with King Oliver, where he began moving the New Orleans sound towards a big-band format. Between 1929–31 he led one of the best early swing-oriented bands in the country. Its major soloists were J.C. Higginbotham and Henry 'Red' Allen, who also recorded with the band separately under his name in a number of Armstrong-inspired pieces. In 1935 Armstrong himself took over, effectively ending the Russell band as an independent entity.

see Introduction pp 90 *see* Sources & Sounds pp 92 *see* Key Artists pp 100

Pee Wee Russell

(Clarinet, 1906–69)

Great musicians are often judged by the reach of their influence on others, but Charles Ellsworth Russell's clarinet was one of a kind, so personal and eccentric that it offered little to any would-be disciples. He arrived in New York in 1927 from the Midwest, where he had played with Bix Beiderbecke and other Chicago-area musicians. There he built a solid reputation playing a relatively standard hot clarinet with Red Nichols.

By the time he joined Louis Prima on 52nd Street in 1935, however, his tone had taken on a tart growl and his phrasing swung with a lumpy, off-centre quirkiness that seemed to thumb its nose at notions of virtuosity. It gave his playing an 'authentic' quality that appealed to renegade jazz fans in rebellion against the professionalism of swing. From the late 1930s on, he was part of Eddie Condon's stock company of traditionalists. He made his most characteristic records for Commodore from 1938–45.

Artie Shaw

(Clarinet, bandleader, composer, 1910–2004)

If the 1930s comes down to about half a dozen great brand names, Artie Shaw's is surely one of them. After much freelancing in the early 1930s and several years of band-building, Shaw (née Arthur Arshawsky) hit his stride just as Benny Goodman peaked in 1938. But no one ever confused these two unique, clarinet-playing masters. Shaw had a big, broad-shouldered lyricism that could turn diamond-hard in high registers.

His lines were long, bobbing and eloquently fluent. Many clarinetists committed his 'Stardust' solo to memory. When drummer Buddy Rich joined in 1939, the band acquired a supercharged power. But if Shaw loved music and the perquisites of stardom, he disliked the spotlight. He abandoned music in a huff at the end of 1939, returning sporadically between bouts of writing and well-publicized marriages and leading the Gramercy Five in 1953–54. Ultimately, and still in his prime, he disowned the clarinet itself in 1955.

Above
Artie Shaw was a unique clarinet player and influential bandleader who loved music but not the spotlight.

Left
Clarinetist Pee Wee Russell (bottom right) was a member of jazz supergroup the Rhythmakers, who recorded a legendary session in 1932.

see Henry 'Red' Allen pp 68 *see* Eddie Condon pp 71 *see* Count Basie pp 102 *see* Buddy Rich pp 182

Stuff Smith

(Violin, 1909–67)

Inspired by Joe Venuti in the 1920s, Joe Hezekiah Leroy Smith and his sextet (with Jonah Jones) became a sensation on 52nd Street early in 1936. In contrast to the polish of Venuti, Smith turned the violin in a more barrelhouse direction, making it swing with an unremitting swagger. He was also the first to play amplified violin and is remembered for his comic homage to marijuana, 'You'se a Viper'. Norman Granz re-introduced Smith successfully in 1957.

Willie 'The Lion' Smith

(Piano, 1897–1973)

In the 1920s Willie 'The Lion' Smith was an obscure master of Harlem stride (a virtuoso style that evolved out of ragtime after 1919) whose brilliant technique influenced countless young pianists who heard him in person. His legend began to emerge in 1935 as stride was fading into nostalgia and he started to record regularly. For the next four decades, he would be celebrated as a living piece of jazz history – derby and cigar intact. His compositions, such as 'Echoes of Spring' and 'Passionette', show an unexpected, impressionistic strain.

Muggsy Spanier

(Cornet, 1906–67)

Francis Joseph Spanier was an early part of the group of young white Chicagoans who in the late 1920s opened up and amended the original New Orleans styles that had come north during the Roaring Twenties. He had a hot, jabbing, poking attack, often coloured by the use of a plunger mute. When Spanier recorded a number of Commodore sessions in 1939–40 with his own Dixieland group, he helped to restore traditional jazz to prominence.

see Introduction pp 90 *see* Sources & Sounds pp 92 *see* Key Artists pp 100

Rex Stewart

(Cornet, 1907–67)

After honing a vocabulary of unorthodox trumpet techniques with Fletcher Henderson between 1926–33, Rex William Stewart switched to cornet and joined Duke Ellington. In an orchestra of distinctive voices, his was among the most unique. He played with a sharp, biting attack in the middle register. His tone had a slightly sour, almost sarcastic attitude, capable of some bizarre extremes. A typical solo on Henderson's 'Underneath The Harlem Moon' (1933) ended with an odd, sub-tone exclamation.

Seven years later, on 'Menelk' with Ellington, he built that into a long, onomatopoeic interlude evoking the sense of a lurking lion. His most famous trademark was squeezing notes through half-depressed valves, which gave his phrasing on 'Boy Meets Horn' (1938) and other pieces an impacted, almost crushed sense of implosion. But he could also swing with a relentless drive, nowhere more so than on his famous exchanges with Cootie Williams on 'Tootin' Through The Roof' (1939). He left Ellington in 1946 for freelancing and a later career as memoirist and critic for *Down Beat*.

Roosevelt Sykes

(Piano, vocals, 1906–83)

Born in Elmar, Arkansas and raised in St. Louis, Sykes taught himself piano. He made his recording debut for OKeh in 1928 but also recorded for Paramount (as Dobby Bragg) and Victor (as Willie Kelly) from 1929–33. He settled in Chicago in 1931 and created the blues standards '44 Blues', 'Driving Wheel Blues' and 'Night Time Is The Right Time'. Sykes' powerful, lusty style adapted well to modern trends and he remained a prolific recording artist well into his 70s.

Tampa Red

(Guitar, piano, kazoo, vocals, 1904–81)

Hudson Woodbridge was born in Smithville, Georgia; he changed his surname to Whittaker when he went to Tampa, Florida to live with his maternal grandmother. A self-taught musician, he worked juke joints throughout Florida in the early 1920s, before moving to Chicago in 1925. He made his recording debut as Tampa Red for Paramount in 1928. He then teamed with Georgia Tom Dorsey, later a major gospel songwriter, and recorded extensively for Vocalion until 1932, creating blues standards such as 'It's Tight Like That'.

Red also recorded as a soloist, in a successful duo with pianist Big Maceo Merriweather and in jug-band settings. He recorded for Bluebird in 1934 and remained with Bluebird/RCA Victor until 1953, cutting more than 220 titles including the blues standard 'It Hurts Me Too'. Devastated by the death of Frances, his wife and manager, in the mid-1950s, Tampa Red lost interest in music but did make two solo LPs for Prestige/Bluesville in 1960.

Art Tatum

(Piano, 1909–56)

In the arms race of virtuosity that drove jazz in the 1930s, no player was more dazzling than Art Tatum. The piano had a history of virtuosos, but none approached the levels of sheer athletic aptitude that Tatum tossed off with such nonchalance. It came so naturally that he often seemed bored by his own wizardry, hurtling through a procession of sharp contrasts in tempo and style that changed every few bars, under a hail of arpeggios that dropped like confetti.

Tatum, born in Toledo, Ohio with only partial vision, came out of the stride tradition but extended it in so many directions as to create a comprehensive keyboard vocabulary that continues to astonish. His solo showpieces, such as 'Tiger Rag', were intended to intimidate if not terrorize, and in the 1930s he was heard on record and radio mostly in a solo setting. But he was a consummate ensemble player, working with a trio in the 1940s. In the 1950s he recorded a huge body of solo and ensemble work for Norman Granz.

Above
Tampa Red and Big Maceo enjoyed a relaxed musical dialogue similar to that of Leroy Carr and Scrapper Blackwell in the 1920s.

Far Left
Stride pianist Willie 'The Lion' Smith influenced many younger musicians who heard him play.

see Georgia Tom Dorsey pp 27 see Fletcher Henderson pp 74 see Joe Venuti pp 85 see Big Maceo pp 121

Above
Trombonist Jack Teagarden, who revolutionized the instrument's status within jazz music.

Jack Teagarden

(Trombone, vocals, 1905–64)

Arguably the greatest trombonist in jazz history, Jack Teagarden might have been the dominant player of the 1930s. He made his reputation in the late 1920s with Ben Pollack and Red Nichols, but a lack of ambition and desire for security led him to decline the invitation of an obscure clarinetist launching a new band and choose instead a five-year contract with Paul Whiteman. Within months, Benny Goodman had become destiny's child and Teagarden was watching from the sidelines.

His soft sound spoke with a rolling fluidity and ease that no one had ever heard in the trombone, and he was also blessed with one of the best white blues voices of all time, effortlessly singing classics such as 'Basin Street Blues' in a melodic, laid-back drawl. In 1939 he formed his own big band, then in 1940–45 made some of his finest records with small swing groups. He toured with Louis Armstrong from 1947–51 and played with his own groups thereafter.

Sister Rosetta Tharpe

(Guitar, vocals, 1915–73)

Born in Arkansas, Rosetta Nubin was the daughter of a missionary. She had learned to play guitar by the age of six and accompanied her mother at church functions. The family moved to Chicago and Tharpe signed with Decca in 1938. She was essentially a gospel performer, but with Lucky Millinder's Orchestra (1941–43) she recorded blues as well as spirituals. In 1944 she teamed up with blues pianist Sammy Price and made hit records including 'Strange Things Are Happening Every Day'.

Sippie Wallace

(Vocals, 1898–1986)

Beaulah Thomas was raised in Houston, Texas. From an early age she sang in church and worked with her pianist brother Hersal Thomas. She moved to Chicago in 1923 and recorded for OKeh, creating blues standards such as 'Up The Country Blues' and 'I'm A Mighty Tight Woman'. She moved to Detroit in 1929 and joined the church, where she played piano and sang. 'Rediscovered' in 1966, she recorded two albums prior to a 1970 stroke. Her final album, *Sippie* (1983), received a W.C. Handy award and a Grammy nomination.

Washboard Sam

(Washboard, vocals, 1910–66)

Robert Brown was born in Walnut Ridge, Arkansas and was the half-brother of Big Bill Broonzy. He left home to play with street singers in the Memphis area in the mid-1920s. In 1932 he moved to Chicago and teamed up with Sleepy John Estes and Hammie Nixon. He made his recording debut for Bluebird in 1935 and stayed with Bluebird/RCA until 1949; he recorded more than 150 titles, many of which featured Broonzy on guitar.

see Introduction pp 90 *see* Sources & Sounds pp 92 *see* Key Artists pp 100

Left
Flamboyant drummer Chick Webb's big band introduced singer Ella Fitzgerald to the world.

Chick Webb

(Drums, bandleader, 1909–39)

Associated with the Savoy Ballroom from 1927, the Chick Webb band built a large audience in Harlem. In the 1930s arranger Edgar Sampson became the chief architect of its swinging style, which was propelled by Webb's dynamic drumming and flashy solos, crackling with rim shots. He inspired Gene Krupa, Buddy Rich and other white big-band drummers. When Ella Fitzgerald joined in 1934, she became the band's principal attraction, expanded its audience and took over after Webb's early death.

Peetie Wheatstraw

(Piano, vocals, 1902–41)

William Bunch was born in Tennessee but raised in Arkansas. He played guitar and piano in his youth, left home in the mid-1920s and settled in East St. Louis, Illinois. He made his recording debut in 1930 for Vocalion as Peetie Wheatstraw. A popular and prolific recording artist for Decca and Vocalion until his death, Wheatstraw was billed as 'The Devil's Son-In-Law'. His recordings often also featured a prominent guitarist such as Kokomo Arnold or Lonnie Johnson. He died in an automobile accident less than a month after his final recording session.

Left
Peetie Wheatstraw recorded with guitarists such as Kokomo Arnold and Lonnie Johnson.

see Big Bill Broonzy pp 104 *see* Kokomo Arnold pp 120 *see* Ella Fitzgerald pp 124 *see* Sammy Price pp 182

Bukka White

(Guitar, piano, vocals, 1906–77)

Booker T. Washington White was raised on a farm outside Houston, Texas; his father taught him guitar in 1915. Two years later he learned piano and by 1921 he was working barrelhouses and honky tonks in St. Louis. Inspired by a meeting with Charley Patton, he hoboed through the South for much of the 1920s. He made his recording debut for Victor in 1930 as Washington White.

White was athletic and at various times he was a boxer and played baseball for the Birmingham Black Cats. He recorded 'Shake 'Em On Down' for Vocalion in 1937 and the record was a considerable hit. White recorded 12 titles for Vocalion in March 1940, which are among the finest examples of pre-war country blues. He served in the US Navy during the Second World War and retired from music, until being 'rediscovered' in 1963.

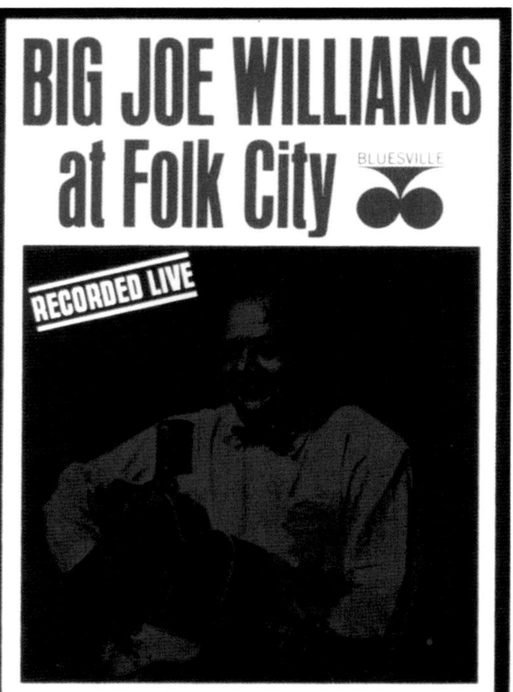

Right
Big Joe Williams, renowned for his nine-string guitar, was inducted into the W.C. Handy Blues Hall of Fame in 1994.

Below
Josh White recorded a variety of blues, gospel and folk music under various pseudonyms.

Josh White

(Guitar, vocals, 1908–69)

Joshua Daniel White was born in Greenville, South Carolina, to a preacher father and a mother who sang in church. He worked in tandem with street singers such as Blind Blake and Blind Joe Taggart for much of the 1920s. His recording debut was made for Paramount in 1928 but his work for Banner/ARC beginning in 1932 is considered to be his most important. He recorded sacred music (as 'Joshua White, The Singing Christian') in addition to blues under his own name or as 'Pinewood Tom'. After 1940, he was increasingly involved with folk music, where he was promoted to white audiences.

Big Joe Williams

(Guitar, vocals, 1903–82)

Joe Lee Williams was born in Crawford, Mississippi to tenant farmer parents and by the age of five he was playing a homemade guitar. He left home in 1915 to hobo through the South. Williams worked tent shows and medicine shows with a jug band and as a soloist from 1918–24. Often accompanied by Little Brother Montgomery, he played brothels, labour camps and barrelhouses throughout Mississippi and Louisiana during the 1920s.

He made his recording debut for Bluebird in 1935 and one of his early recordings, 'Baby Please Don't Go', became a blues standard. He frequently recorded with Robert Nighthawk and Sonny Boy Williamson on Bluebird sessions in the late 1930s. Although Williams played both six- and 12-string guitars, he is most famous for playing a nine-string instrument of his own construction. He toured constantly and recorded into his late 70s.

Sonny Boy Williamson

(Harmonica, vocals, 1914–48)

John Lee Williamson was born in Jackson, Tennessee. He taught himself harmonica at an early age and left home in his mid-teens to hobo with Yank Rachell and Sleepy John Estes through Tennessee and Arkansas. He settled in Chicago in 1934 and made his recording debut for Bluebird in 1937. His first song, 'Good Morning Little School Girl', became a blues standard.

Williamson was friendly with Big Bill Broonzy and frequently worked Chicago clubs with him. During the years 1939–45 he worked Chicago's Maxwell Street for tips, but in 1947 his record 'Shake The Boogie' became a number-four hit on the Race charts. Williamson was the most gifted and influential harmonica stylist of the pre-war era and was very much

see Introduction pp 90 *see* Sources & Sounds pp 92 *see* Key Artists pp 100

in demand to play on recordings by other artists. He was murdered coming home from a job in 1948, after which his name and reputation were taken on by harmonica player Rice Miller – or 'Sonny Boy Williamson II', as he became known.

Teddy Wilson

(Piano, 1912–86)

Although the physical brilliance of Art Tatum may have eluded most pianists in the 1930s, the more practical possibilities offered by Teddy Wilson made him the most influential pianist of the decade. Softening Earl Hines' emphasis on the beat still further, Wilson's style was centred almost wholly in his right hand, which spun smooth, bobbing, single-note lines and tranquil arpeggios, bringing him into perfect alignment with the sleek aerodynamics of swing. This was evident in his first recordings with Benny Carter (1933).

But Wilson found his ideal companionship in the clean rigour of the Benny Goodman Trio and Quartet, which brought him national fame in 1935 and a parallel recording career under his own name that produced a number of jazz classics, several with Billie Holiday. Wilson left Goodman in 1939, formed an excellent but short-lived big band and recorded prolifically during the 1940s, often with Goodman, Edmond Hall and Red Norvo; he continued to perform and record until the end of his life.

Jimmy Yancey

(Piano, 1898–1951)

James Edward Yancey was born in Chicago and toured the vaudeville circuit as a dancer in his childhood. He learned piano from his brother Alonzo in 1915 and was soon working rent parties and small clubs around Chicago. He made his recording debut in 1939 for Solo Art and continued to record intermittently, often in the company of his wife, singer Estella Yancey. Yancey was especially adept at slow blues and had a unique ability to develop his own left-hand bass lines.

Left
Teddy Wilson's accessible yet highly original piano style made him a very influential musician.

see Charley Patton pp 23 *see* Blind Blake pp 70 *see* Benny Goodman pp 110 *see* Benny Carter pp 122

List of Artists

Entries appear in the following order: name, music style, year(s) of popularity, instruments, country of origin.

Addison, Bernard, Swing; Traditional Jazz, 1930s–1990s, Guitar, American
Alabama Shiekhs, Country Blues, 1930s, Various instruments, American
Aleman, Oscar, Swing; Traditional Jazz, 1930s–1960s, Guitar, Argentinian
Altheimer, Joshua, Country Blues, 1930s–1940s, Piano, American
Ammons, Albert, Boogie-Woogie, 1930s–1940s, Piano, American
Ammons, Gene, Bebop; Hard Bop, 1950s–1970s, Saxophone, American
Anderson, Ivie, Swing; Big Band, 1930s–1940s, Vocals, American
Anderson, Pink, Country Blues, 1930s–1960s, Guitar, American
Archey, Jimmy, Swing; Traditional Jazz, 1930s–1960s, Trombone, American
Armstrong, Howard 'Louie Bluie', Country Blues; Swing, 1930s–1990s, Vocals, mandolin, fiddle, guitar, American
Arnold, Kokomo, Chicago Blues, 1930s–1940s, Guitar, vocals, American
Asmussen, Svend, Swing; Traditional Jazz, 1930s–, Violin, vocals, Danish
Auld, Georgie, Swing; Big Band; Bebop, 1930s–1980s, Saxophone, bandleader, Canadian
Autrey, Herman, Swing; Traditional Jazz, 1930s–1970s, Trumpet, vocals, American
Avakian, George, All Jazz Styles, 1930s–, Producer, critic, Armenian
Bailey, Pearl, Swing, 1930s–1970s, Vocals, American
Baker, Shorty, Swing; Modern Jazz, 1930s–1960s, Trumpet, American
Banks, Billy, Traditional Jazz, 1930s–1950s, Vocals, American
Barbee, John Henry, Country Blues; Delta Blues, 1930s, Vocals, American
Barbour, Dave, Traditional Jazz; Big Band, 1930s–1960s, Guitar, American
Barefield, Eddie, Swing; Big Band, 1930s–1970s, Saxophone, clarinet, American
Barker, Blue Lu, East Coast Blues, 1930s–1980s, Vocals, American
Barker, Danny, New Orleans Jazz; Swing, 1930s–1990s, Guitar, banjo, composer, American
Barnes, George, Swing, 1930s–1970s, Guitar, American
Barroso, Ary, Brazilian Jazz; Latin Jazz, 1930s–1970s, Composer, Brazilian
Bascomb, Dud, Modern Jazz; Swing; Big Band, 1930s–1960s, Trumpet, American
Bascomb, Paul, Swing; Big Band, 1930s–1980s, Saxophone, American
Basie, Count, Swing; Big Band, 1930s–1980s, Piano, bandleader, American
Bell, Jimmie, New Orleans Jazz, 1930s–1980s, Piano, American
Beneke, Tex, Swing; Big Band, 1930s–1980s, Saxophone, vocals, American
Bennett, Buster, Swing; Traditional Jazz, 1930s–1940s, Saxophones, piano, bandleader, American
Berigan, Bunny, Swing, 1930s–1940s, Trumpet, vocals, American
Bernhardt, Clyde, Swing; Traditional Jazz; Big Band, 1930s–1980s, Trombone, vocals, bandleader, American
Berry, Chu, Swing, 1930s–1940s, Saxophone, American
Berry, Emmett, Swing; Big Band, 1930s–1970s, Trumpet, American
Best, Johnny, Swing, 1930s–1980s, Trumpet, American
Black Bob, Country Blues, 1930s, Piano, American
Black Boy Shine, Delta Blues; Country Blues, 1930s, Piano, American
Black Ivory King, Delta Blues; Country Blues, 1930s, Piano, vocals, American
Blanton, Jimmy, Swing; Big Band, 1930s–1940s, Bass, American
Blowers, Johnny, Dixieland, 1930s–1960s, Drums, percussion, American
Borum, Willie, Delta Blues, 1930s–1960s, Guitar, harmonica, American
Bowman, Dave, Dixieland; Traditional Jazz, 1930s–1960s, Piano, American
Boy, Andy, Texas Blues, 1930s–1950s, Piano, American
Bradley, Will, Swing; Big Band; Boogie-Woogie, 1930s–1950s, Trombone, bandleader, American
Bradshaw, Tiny, Jump Blues; Rhythm & Blues, 1930s–1950s, Vocals, drums, American
Broonzy, Big Bill, Country Blues; Chicago Blues, 1930s–1950s, Vocals, guitar, American
Brown, Boyce, Big Band; Traditional Jazz, 1930s–1950s, Saxophone, clarinet, American
Brown, Cleo, Swing; Traditional Jazz, 1930s–1980s, Piano, vocals, American
Brown, Gabriel, Country Blues, 1930s–1970s, Guitar, vocals, American
Brown, Lawrence, Big Band; Swing, 1930s–1980s, Trombone, American
Brown, Lee, East Coast Blues; Boogie-Woogie, 1930s–1940s, Guitar, American
Brown, Les, Big Band, 1930s–2000s, Bandleader, arranger, composer, American
Brown, Olive, Rhythm & Blues, 1930s–, Vocals, American
Brown, Pete, Bebop; Swing, 1930s–1960s, Saxophone, bandleader, American
Brown, Willie, Mississippi Blues, 1930s, Guitar, American
Brunner, Eddie, Traditional Jazz; Swing, 1930s–1950s, Saxophone, clarinet, Swiss
Bryant, Beulah, Swing; Bebop, 1930s–1970s, Vocals, American

Bryant, Willie, Big Band, 1930s–1950s, Vocals, leader, American
Buckner, Teddy, Dixieland; Chicago Jazz, 1930s–1980s, Trumpet, flugelhorn, vocals, American
Bull City Red, Country Blues; East Coast Blues, 1930s, Washboard, guitar, American
Bumble Bee Slim, Country Blues; West Coast Blues, 1930s–1950s, Guitar, vocals, American
Burleson, Hattie, Texas Blues, 1930s–1950s, Entrepreneur, American
Bushkin, Joe, Traditional Jazz; Swing, 1930s–2000s, Piano, trumpet, American
Butler, Jacques, Swing, 1930s–, Trumpet, vocals, American
Butterfield, Billy, Chicago Jazz; Swing, 1930s–1980s, Trumpet, flugelhorn, American
Byas, Don, Swing; Bebop, 1930s–1970s, Saxophone, American
Caceres, Ernie, Swing, 1930s–1970s, Clarinet, saxophone, American
Caiazza, Nick, Big Band, 1930s–1960s, Saxophone, clarinet, American
Callicott, Joe 'Mississippi', Country Blues, 1930s; 1960s, Vocals, guitar, American
Calloway, Cab, Swing, 1930s–1980s, Vocals, bandleader, American
Carlisle, Una Mae, Swing, 1930s–1950s, Piano, vocals, composer, American
Carter, Benny, Swing, 1930s–1990s, Saxophone, trumpet, arranger, composer, American
Carver, Wayman, Swing, 1930s–1960s, Saxophone, flute, American
Casey, Al, Swing, 1930s–, Guitar, American
Castle, Lee, Big Band; Swing, 1930s–1980s, Trumpet, bandleader, American
Chambers, Henderson, Big Band; Swing, 1930s–1960s, Trombone, American
Chatmon, Sam, Delta Blues, 1930s–1980s, Guitar, American
Cheatham, Doc, Swing; Chicago Jazz, 1930s–1990s, Trumpet, American
Christian, Charlie, Swing; Bebop, 1930s–1940s, Guitar, American
Claes, Johnny, Traditional Jazz, 1930s–1940s, Trumpet, British
Clayton, Buck, Swing, 1930s–1990s, Trumpet, arranger, composer, American
Clayton, Peter 'Doctor', Chicago Blues, 1930s–1940s, Vocals, composer, American
Cless, Rod, Traditional Jazz, 1930s–1940s, Clarinet, American
Clinton, Larry, Traditional Jazz; Big Band, 1930s–1940s, Trumpet, arranger, composer, bandleader, American
Cobb, Arnett, Soul Jazz; Jump Blues, 1930s–1980s, Saxophone, American
Cole, Cozy, Swing, 1930s–1970s, Drums, American
Colignon, Raymond 'Coco', Traditional Jazz, 1930s–1950s, Piano, Belgian
Collins, John, Swing; Modern Jazz, 1930s–2000s, Guitar, American
Collins, Shad, Swing, 1930s–1960s, Trumpet, American
Combelle, Alix, Swing, 1930s–1970s, Saxophone, clarinet, French
Conniff, Ray, Big Band, 1930s–, Trombone, arranger, bandleader, American
Cooper, Al, Swing, 1930s–1940s, Saxophone, clarinet, bandleader, American
Cottrell, Louis, New Orleans Jazz; Traditional Jazz, 1930s–1970s, Clarinet, saxophone, American
Coughlan, Frank, Swing, 1930s–1970s, Trombone, trumpet, arranger, vocals, bandleader, Australian
Council, Floyd 'Dipper Boy', Country Blues, 1930s, Vocals, guitar, American
Crawford, Jimmy, Swing, 1930s–1970s, Drums, American
Crosby, Israel, Cool Jazz; Swing, 1930s–1960s, Bass, American
Cugat, Xavier, Latin Jazz, 1930s–1960s, Violin, bandleader, Spanish
Curtis, James 'Peck', Memphis Blues, 1930s–1960s, Drums, American
Cutshall, Cutty, Chicago Jazz; Swing, 1930s–1960s, Trombone, American
D'Amico, Hank, Swing, 1930s–1960s, Clarinet, saxophone, American
Daily, Pete, Big Band; Dixieland Revival, 1930s–1970s, Cornet, saxophone, tuba, American
Dance, Stanley, All Jazz Styles, 1930s–1990s, Author, critic, British
Dash, Julian, Swing, 1930s–1970s, Saxophone, composer, American
Davis, Blind John, Boogie-Woogie, 1930s–1950s, Piano, American
Davis, Rev. Gary, East Coast Blues, 1930s–1970s, Guitar, vocals, American
DeBoeck, Jeff, Traditional Jazz; Swing, 1930s–, Drums, Belgian
Deems, Barrett, Swing, 1930s–1990s, Drums, American
DeKers, Robert, Traditional Jazz; Swing, 1930s–1950s, Trumpet, bandleader, Belgian
Deloof, Gus, Swing, 1930s–1950s, Trumpet, composer, arranger, Belgian
Dennis, Matt, Swing; Big Band, 1930s, Songwriter, vocals, piano, American
Dickenson, Vic, Swing, 1930s–1980s, Trombone, vocals, American
Dillard, Bill, New Orleans; Big Band; Swing; Bebop, 1930s–1980, Trumpet, vocals, American
Donahue, Sam, Swing; Big Band, 1930s–1970s, Saxophone, bandleader, American
Dorsey, Jimmy, Swing; Big Band, 1930s–1950s, Clarinet, saxophone, trumpet, American
Dorsey, Tommy, Swing; Big Band, 1930s–1950s, Trombone, trumpet, American
Douglas, Tommy, Traditional Jazz; Big Band, 1930s–1950s, Clarinet, saxophone, arranger, American
Doyle, Charlie 'Little Buddy', Memphis Blues, 1930s, Vocals, American
Dr Ross, Jump Blues, 1930s–, Harmonica, American
Dunn, Roy, Contemporary Blues; Folk Blues, 1930s–1970s, Guitar, vocals, American
Durst, Lavada 'Dr Hepcat', Texas Blues; Boogie-Woogie, 1930s–1960s, Piano, American
Eldridge, Joe, Swing, 1930s–1940s, Saxophone, violin, American
Eldridge, Roy, Swing, 1930s–1980s, Trumpet, flugelhorn, vocals, American
Ellis, Wilbert 'Big Chief', Country Blues, 1930s–1970s, Piano, American
Elman, Ziggy, Swing; Big Band, 1930s–1980s, Trumpet, American
Estes, Sleepy John, Country Blues, 1930s; 1960s–1970s, Vocals, guitar, American
Evans, Herschel, Swing; Cool Jazz, 1930s, Saxophone, clarinet, American
Farley and Riley, Swing, 1930s, Various instruments, American
Fatool, Nick, Swing; Big Band; Dixieland, 1930s–1990s, Drums, American
Fazola, Irving, New Orleans Jazz; Traditional Jazz, 1930s–1940s, Clarinet, saxophone, American
Feather, Leonard, Swing; Bebop, 1930s–1990s, Author, piano, critic, composer, arranger, British
Featherstonehaugh, Buddy, Swing; British Jazz, 1930s–1960s, Clarinet, saxophones, French
Fields, Ernie, Swing; Big Band, 1930s–1960s, Trombone, bandleader, American
Fitzgerald, Ella, Swing; Bebop, 1930s–1990s, Vocals, American
Foresythe, Reginald, Swing; Big Band, 1930s–1950s, Composer, arranger, piano, British
Fuller, Blind Boy, East Coast Blues, 1930s–1940s, Guitar, vocals, American
Gabler, Milt, Swing, 1930s–2000s, Producer, American
Gaillard, Slim, Swing, 1930s–1950s, Vocals, piano, guitar, composer, American
Gaither, Bill 'Leroy's Buddy', Country Blues, 1930s–1940s, Vocals, guitar, American
Gillum, Bill 'Jazz', Country Blues, 1930s–1940s, Harmonica, American

Girard, Adele, Swing; Dixieland, 1930s–1990s, Harp, American
Gleason, Ralph, All Jazz Styles, 1930s–1970s, Author, critic, American
Glenn, Tyree, Swing; Big Band, 1930s–1970s, Trombone, vibraphone, American
Goodman, Benny, Swing; Big Band, 1930s–1970s, Clarinet, saxophone, bandleader, American
Grace, Terry, Swing, 1930s–1940s, Vocals, American
Grappelli, Stephane, Swing, 1930s–1990s, Violin, American
Gray, Arvella, Chicago Blues, 1930s–1970s, Guitar, American
Griffin, Chris, Swing; Big Band, 1930s–, Trumpet, American
Guarnieri, Johnny, Swing, 1930s–1980s, Piano, composer, American
Guesnon, George, Swing; New Orleans Jazz, 1930s–1960s, Banjo, guitar, vocals, American
Guy, Joe, Swing, 1930s–1940s, Trumpet, American
Guyer, Bobby, Swing; Chicago Jazz, 1930s–1980s, Trumpet, American
Hackett, Bobby, Chicago Jazz; Swing, 1930s–1970s, Cornet, trumpet, guitar, American
Haggart, Bob, Swing; Dixieland, 1930s–1990s, Bass, composer, arranger, American
Hall, Vera, Gospel; Memphis Blues, 1930s–1950s, Vocals, American
Hamilton, John 'Bugs', Swing, 1930s–1940s, Trumpet, American
Hammond, John, All Jazz Styles, 1930s–1980s, Producer, author, critic, American
Hampton, Lionel, Swing; Big Band, 1930s–1990s, Vibraphone, drums, piano, vocals, bandleader, American
Harlem Hamfats, East Coast Blues, 1930s, Various instruments, American
Hart, Clyde, Swing; Bebop, 1930s–1940s, Piano, arranger, American
Hawkins, Erskine, Swing, 1930s–1970s, Trumpet, bandleader, American
Henderson, Horace, Swing; Big Band, 1930s–1950s, Piano, arranger, bandleader, American
Hill, Rosa Lee, Country Blues, 1930s–1960s, Vocals, American
Hines, Earl, Swing; Big Band, 1930s–1980s, Piano, vocals, composer, American
Hinton, Milt, Swing, 1930s–1990s, Bass, American
Hodes, Art, Chicago Jazz, 1930s–1990s, Piano, American
Hodges, Johnny, Swing, 1930s–1960s, Saxophone, composer, American
Holmes, Wright, Texas Blues, 1930s–1950s, Vocals, guitar, American
Homesick James, City Blues, 1930s–1970s, Guitar, American
Hopkins, Claude, Swing, 1930s–1980s, Piano, bandleader, American
Horn, Lena, Swing; Traditional Jazz, 1930s–, Vocals, American
House, Son, Work Songs; Delta Blues, 1930s–1960s, Guitar, vocals, composer, American
Hovington, Frank, Country Blues, 1930s–1940s, Banjo, guitar, American
Howard, Kid, New Orleans Jazz, 1930s–1960s, Trumpet, American
Howard, Rosetta, East Coast Blues, 1930s–1940s, Vocals, American
Hudson, 'Black Bob', Country Blues, 1930s–1940s, Piano, American
Hug, Armand, New Orleans Jazz; Dixieland, 1930s–1970s, Piano, American
Hughes, Spike, Swing, 1930s, Composer, bass, British
Hunter, Ivory Joe, West Coast Blues; Rhythm & Blues, 1930s–1970s, Piano, composer, American
Hurley, Clyde, Dixieland; Swing, 1930s–1950s, Trumpet, American
Hutchenrider, Clarence, Dixieland Revival, 1930s–1980s, Clarinet, American
Jackson, Franz, Swing; Dixieland; Traditional Jazz, 1930s–, Saxophone, clarinet, American
Jackson, Quentin, Swing; Bebop; Hard Bop, 1930s–1970s, Trombone, vocals, bass, American
James, Jesse, Country Blues, 1930s, Piano, vocals, American
James, Skip, Delta Blues; Country Blues, 1930s; 1960s, Guitar, vocals, composer, American
James, Willie Bee, Chicago Blues, 1930s–1980s, Guitar, vocals, American
Jeffery, Robert, Country Blues, 1930s–1970s, Guitar, piano, American
Jeffries, Herb, Swing, 1930s–, Vocals, American
Jenkins, Gordon, Swing; Cool Jazz, 1930s–1990s, Composer, American
Jerome, Jerry, Swing, 1930s–, Saxophone, clarinet, flute, arranger, conductor, American
Jester-Pillars Orchestra, Swing, 1930s, Various instruments, American
Johnson, Budd, Swing; Bebop, 1930s–1980s, Saxophones, clarinet, arranger, American
Johnson, Buddy, Jump Blues; Rhythm & Blues, 1930s–1960s, Pianist, bandleader, composer, American
Johnson, Gus, Swing; Bebop, 1930s–, Drums, American
Johnson, Margaret, Jazz, 1930s, Piano, American
Johnson, Merline, Chicago Blues, 1930s–1940s, Vocals, American
Johnson, Pete, Boogie-Woogie, 1930s–1960s, Piano, American
Johnson, Robert, Delta Blues; Country Blues, 1930s, Guitar, vocals, composer, American
Jones, Albennie, Swing; Classic Blues, 1930s–1950s, Vocals, American
Jones, Curtis, Country Blues, 1930s–1960s, Vocals, piano, American
Jones, Jo, Swing, 1930s–1970s, Drums, American
Jones, Jonah, Swing; Dixieland, 1930s–1990s, Trumpet, bandleader, American
Jordan, Steve, Big Band; Swing, 1930s–1990s, Guitar, American
Jordan, Taft, Big Band; Swing, 1930s–1970s, Trumpet, vocals, American
King Solomon Hill, Country Blues; Texas Blues, 1930s–1940s, Vocals, American
Kirby, John, Swing, 1930s–1950s, Bass, tuba, American
Kirkpatrick, Don, Big Band; Swing, 1930s–1950s, Piano, arranger, American
Knowling, Ransom, Chicago Blues; Country Blues, 1930s–1940s, Bass, American
Krupa, Gene, Swing; Big Band, 1930s–1970s, Drums, American
Kyle, Billy, Swing, 1930s–1960s, Piano, arranger, American
Lavere, Charlie, Swing; Traditional Jazz, 1930s–1980s, Piano, leader, vocals, American

Lawson, Yank, Chicago Jazz; Swing, 1930s–1980s, Trumpet, American
Ledbetter, Huddie 'Leadbelly', Country Blues, 1930s–1940s, Vocals, guitar, American
Letman, Johnny, Big Band; Swing, 1930s–, Trumpet, American
Lewis, Meade 'Lux', Boogie-Woogie, 1930s–1960s, Piano, American
Lewis, Vic, Chicago Jazz; Swing, 1930s–, Guitar, leader, British
Little Son Joe, Memphis Blues, 1930s–1950s, Guitar, vocals, American
Lofton, Cripple Clarence, Country Blues, 1930s–1940s, Vocals, piano, American
Lomax, Alan, Work Songs, 1930s–1990s, Producer, American
Lomax, John A. Sr, Country Blues, 1930s–1940s, Producer, folklorist, American
Lunceford, Jimmie, Swing, 1930s–1940s, Various instruments, arranger, bandleader, American
Manone, Wingy, Chicago Jazz, 1930s–1960s, Trumpet, vocals, American
Marsala, Joe, Chicago Jazz; Swing, 1930s–1940s, Clarinet, saxophones, composer, American
Marsala, Marty, Chicago Jazz; Swing, 1930s–1960s, Trumpet, American
Martin, Carl, East Coast Blues, 1930s–1970s, Guitar, American
Mastren, Carmen, Chicago Jazz; New Orleans Jazz, 1930s–1970s, Guitar, banjo, violin, American
Matlock, Matty, Swing; Dixieland, 1930s–1970s, Saxophone, clarinet, arranger, American
Maxwell, Jimmy, Swing, 1930s–, Trumpet, American
McClennan, Tommy, Delta Blues, 1930s–1940s, Guitar, vocals, American
McCoy, Robert, Boogie-Woogie, 1930s–1940s, Piano, American
McDowell, Mississippi Fred, Delta Blues, 1930s–1970s, Guitar, vocals, American
McEachern, Murray, Swing; Big Band, 1930s–1970s, Trombone, saxophone, trumpet, Canadian
McKinley, Ray, Swing, 1930s–1960s, Drums, vocals, bandleader, American
McMullen, Fred, East Coast Blues, 1930s, Guitar, American
McQuarter, Tommy, Swing; Big Band, 1930s–, Trumpet, flugelhorn, British
Melrose, Lester, Country Blues; Chicago Blues, 1930s–1940s, Producer, American
Memphis Minnie, Country Blues; Chicago Blues, 1930s–1950s, Guitar, vocals, American
Mercer, Johnny, Swing; Chicago Jazz, 1930s–1970s, Vocals, songwriter, American
Merriweather, 'Big Maceo', Chicago Blues, 1930s–1950s, Piano, vocals, American
Miller, Eddie, Swing; Dixieland, 1930s–1990s, Saxophone, clarinet, vocals, American
Millinder, Lucky, Traditional Jazz, 1930s–1950s, Leader, American
Mills Blue Rhythm Band, Swing; Big Band, 1930s, Group, American
Mills Brothers, The, Swing; Traditional Jazz, 1930s–1970s, Various instruments, American
Mills, Irving, Traditional Jazz, 1930s, Composer, bandleader, American
Mince, Johnny, Swing, 1930s–, Clarinet, saxophone, American
Miranda, Carmen, Brazilian Jazz; Latin Jazz, 1930s–1950s, Vocals, Brazilian
Montgomery, Little Brother, Boogie-Woogie, 1930s–1970s, Piano, American
Moore, Russell 'Big Chief', Swing; Chicago Jazz, 1930s–1980s, Trombone, vocals, American
Moss, Buddy, East Coast Blues; Country Blues, 1930s–1940s, Guitar, harmonica, American
Mundy, Jimmy, Swing; Big Band, 1930s–1980s, Saxophone, arranger, American

Murphy, Turk, Chicago Jazz, 1930s–1980s, Trombone, composer, American
Musso, Vido, Swing; Dixieland, 1930s–1970s, Saxophone, clarinet, Italian
Nance, Ray, Swing, 1930s–1970s, Trumpet, cornet, violin, vocals, American
Napoleon, Teddy, Swing; Big Band, 1930s–1960s, Piano, American
Newman, Jack, Country Blues, 1930s, Artist, American
Norvo, Red, Swing; Cool Jazz, 1930s–1980s, Vibraharp, xylophone, American
Oden, 'St Louis' Jimmy, Country Blues, 1930s–1960s, Vocals, composer, piano, American
Page, Hot Lips, Swing, 1930s–1950s, Trumpet, mellophone, American
Page, Walter, Big Band; Swing, 1930s–1950s, Bass, American
Pastor, Tony, Swing, 1930s–1960s, Saxophone, vocals, American
Paul, Les, Swing, 1930s–, Guitar, American
Pecora, Santo, New Orleans Jazz; Dixieland, 1930s–1980s, Trombone, American
Peg Leg Sam, Country Blues, 1930s–1970s, Harmonica, American
Pichon, Walter 'Fats', New Orleans Blues, 1930s–1960s, Bandleader, piano, American
Pickett, Charlie, Country Blues, 1930s, Guitar, American
Pletcher, Stew, Swing, 1930s–1970s, Trumpet, mellophone, American
Powell, Eugene 'Sonny Boy Nelson', Country Blues, 1930s–1990s, Vocals, guitar, American
Prima, Louis, Jump Blues; Rhythm & Blues, 1930s–1970s, Vocals, trumpet, bandleader, American
Privin, Bernie, Swing; Big Band, 1930s–, Trumpet, American
Profit, Clarence, Swing; Traditional Jazz, 1930s, Piano, American
Pullum, Joe, Country Blues, 1930s, Vocals, American
Quintet of the Hot Club of France, Swing, 1930s–1940s, Band, French
Ramirez, Ram, Swing, 1930s–1990s, Piano, organ, composer, Puerto Rican
Randolph, Mouse, New Orleans Jazz; Swing, 1930s–, Trumpet, American

 *see* Introduction pp 90 *see* Sources & Sounds pp 92 *see* Key Artists pp 100 *see* A–Z of Artists pp 120

Rattenbury, Ken, Traditional Jazz; Swing; Big Band, 1930s–, Trumpet, piano, composer, British
Ray, Harmon, Chicago Blues, 1930s–1940s, Vocals, American
Reardon, Casper, Swing; Chicago Jazz, 1930s–1980s, Harp, American
Red Nelson, Delta Blues; Chicago Blues, 1930s–1960s, Vocals, American
Reinhardt, Django, Swing, 1930s–1950s, Guitar, Belgian
Riddle, Leslie, East Coast Blues; Country Blues, 1930s–1970s, Guitar, American
Roland, Walter, Boogie-Woogie; Country Blues, 1930s, Piano, vocals, American
Rose, Wally, Dixieland; Ragtime, 1930s–1990s, Piano, American
Rushing, Jimmy, Swing; East Coast Blues; Jump Blues, 1930s–1970s, Vocals, piano, American
Rushton, Joe, Chicago Jazz, 1930s–1960s, Saxophone, clarinet, American
Russell, Luis, Swing, 1930s–1940s, Piano, bandleader, American
Russell, Pee Wee, Swing; Chicago Jazz, 1930s–1960s, Clarinet, saxophones, American
Russin, Babe, Swing; Big Band, 1930s–1960s, Saxophone, clarinet, American
Sauter, Eddie, Cool Jazz; Hard Bop, 1930s–1970s, Trumpet, arranger, American
Savoy Sultans, Swing, 1930s–1940s, Various instruments, American
Scott, Raymond, Swing; Big Band, 1930s–, Leader, piano, American
Sedric, Gene, Swing, 1930s–1950s, Saxophone, clarinet, American
Shapiro, Art, Chicago Jazz; Swing, 1930s–1940s, Bass, American
Shavers, Charlie, Swing, 1930s–1970s, Trumpet, vocals, composer, American
Shaw, Allen, Memphis Blues, 1930s, Guitar, vocals, American
Shaw, Artie, Swing, 1930s–1950s, Clarinet, saxophones, composer, American
Shaw, Robert, Boogie-Woogie, 1930s; 1960s–1980s, Piano, American
Shaw, Thomas, Country Blues; Texas Blues, 1930s–1970s, Harmonica, guitar, American
Shearing, George, Cool Jazz; Bebop, 1930s–1990s, Piano, British
Shepard, Ollie, Country Blues, 1930s–1940s, Vocals, piano, composer, American
Shirley, Jimmy, Swing; Bebop, 1930s–1980s, Guitar, American
Short, J.D., Country Blues, 1930s–1960s, Piano, guitar, clarinet, American
Showers, 'Little' Hudson, Chicago Blues, 1930s–1950s, Guitar, American
Smith, J.T. 'Funny Paper', Country; Texas Blues, 1930s, Vocals, guitar, American
Smith, Stuff, Swing, 1930s–1960s, Violin, vocals, American
Smith, Willie, Swing, 1930s–1960s, Saxophone, clarinet, American
Smith, Willie 'The Lion', Traditional Jazz, 1930s–1970s, Piano, vocals, composer, American
Spanier, Muggsy, Chicago Jazz, 1930s–1960s, Trumpet, American
Sparks Brothers, Country Blues, 1930s, Various instruments, American
Spirits of Rhythm, The, Swing; Traditional Jazz, 1930s, Various instruments, American
Stacy, Jess, Swing, 1930s–1990s, Piano, American
Staples, Pops, Gospel; Chicago Blues, 1930s–1970s, Guitar, American
Stegmeyer, Bill, Dixieland, 1930s–1960s, Clarinet, saxophone, arranger, American
Stewart, Rex, Chicago Jazz; Swing, 1930s–1960s, Trumpet, American
Strayhorn, Billy, Chicago Jazz, 1930s–1960s, Piano, composer, arranger, American
Sullivan, Joe, Chicago Jazz; Swing, 1930s–1960s, Piano, American
Sullivan, Maxine, Swing, 1930s–1980s, Vocals, American
Sykes, Roosevelt, Chicago Blues, 1930s–1970s, Piano, American
Tampa Red, Chicago Blues, 1930s–1960s, Guitar, American
Tate, Buddy, Swing, 1930s–1990s, Saxophone, American
Tatum, Art, Swing, 1930s–1950s, Piano, American
Teagarden, Jack, Swing; Chicago Jazz, 1920s–1960s, Trombone, vocals, American
Temple, Johnnie 'Geechie', Delta Blues; Chicago Blues, 1930s–1950s, Guitar, bass, American
Tharpe, Sister Rosetta, Jump Blues, 1930s–1960s, Vocals, guitar, American
Thomas, Jesse, Texas Blues, 1930s–1990s, Piano, guitar, American
Thornhill, Claude, Cool Jazz, 1930s–1950s, Piano, arranger, American
Tilton, Martha, Swing, 1930s–1950s, Vocals, American
Tizol, Juan, Swing; Big Band, 1930s–1960s, Valve trombone, arranger, composer, Puerto Rican
Turner, Joe, Boogie-Woogie, 1930s–1990s, Piano, American
VanEps, George, Swing, 1930s–1990s, Guitar, American
Wallace, Sippie, Country Blues, 1930s–1940s; 1960s, Vocals, American
Ward, Helen, Swing, 1930s–1950s, Vocals, American
Warren, Eddie, Swing, 1930s–, Saxophone, clarinet, vocals, American
Washboard Sam, Chicago Blues, 1930s–1950s, Vocals, washboard, American
Watson, Leo, Swing; Big Band, 1930s–1940s, Vocals, drums, trombone, American
Watters, Lu, Chicago Jazz, 1930s–1960s, Trumpet, American
Webb, Chick, Big Band; Swing, 1920s–1930s, Drums, bandleader, American
Webster, Freddie, Swing; Big Band, 1930s–1940s, Trumpet, American
Wells, Viola 'Miss Rhapsody', Gospel, Country Blues, 1930s–1940s, Vocals, American
Wheatstraw, Peetie, Country Blues, 1930s–1940s, Piano, guitar, vocals, American
Whetsol, Artie, Swing, 1930s–1940s, Trumpet, American
White, Bukka, Country Blues, 1930s–1940s; 1960s–1970s, Guitar, piano, vocals, American
White, George, Country Blues; Jump Blues, 1930s–1940s, Vocals, American
White, Georgia, Boogie-Woogie, 1930s–1950s, Vocals, piano, American
White, Josh, Country Blues, 1930s–1960s, Vocals, guitar, composer, American
Wiley, Geechie, Country Blues, 1930s, Vocals, guitar, American
Wiley, Lee, Swing; Modern Jazz, 1930s–1970s, Vocals, American
Wilkins, Dave, Swing, 1930s–1940s, Trumpet, West Indian
Williams, Big Joe, Delta Blues, 1930s–1980s, Guitar, vocals, composer, American
Williams, Blind Connie, Chicago Blues, 1930s, Accordion, guitar, American
Williams, Cootie, Swing, 1930s–1970s, Trumpet, American
Williams, Joe, Swing, 1930s–1990s, Vocals, American
Williams, Rudy, Swing, 1930s–1940s, Saxophone, clarinet, American
Williamson, Homesick James, Chicago Blues, 1930s–1990s, Guitar, American
Williamson, Sonny Boy (I), Chicago Blues, 1930s–1940s, Guitar, harmonica, vocals, American
Wilson, Dick, Modern Jazz, 1930s, Saxophone, American
Wilson, Teddy, Swing, 1930s–1980s, Piano, arranger, American
Wynn, 'Big' Jim, Rhythm & Blues, 1930s–1970s, Saxophone, American
Yancey, Jimmy, Boogie-Woogie, 1930s–1950s, Piano, American
Young, Lee, Swing, 1930s–, Drums, vocals, American
Young, Lester, Swing; Cool Jazz, 1930s–1950s, Saxophone, clarinet, American
Young, Trummy, Swing, 1930s–1960s, Trombone, vocals, American
Zarchy, Zeke, Swing; Big Band, 1930s–1980s, Trumpet, American
Zurke, Bob, Swing; Traditional Jazz; Big Band, 1930s–1940s, Piano, composer, American

see Charlie Christian pp 106 *see* Robert Johnson pp 112 *see* Cab Calloway pp 122 *see* Art Tatum pp 135

THE FORTIES

The 1940s encompassed a wide range of musical art, reflecting extremes of economic hardship and recovery, global war and rebuilding. Empowered by necessarily full-tilt production, US industry recovered from the Depression, though the cream of its youth was siphoned off to fight on distant fronts, and returned to a strange new world. Great Britain suffered air strikes, privations and threat of occupation – traumas which took years to heal. Continental Europe, including Russia and on to the Far East, was gripped by government-sanctioned genocide, military invasion and destruction. At the decade's end, the world was divided by victory and defeat.

Blues and jazz, along with all the other popular musical styles and performance arts, were pressed into service during the Second World War as uplifting propaganda and social balm. Trends of the 1930s did not come to a jolting halt, but nothing was immune from change. The draft thinned the ranks of swing bands, and intense experimentation by ambitious youngsters in smaller ensembles filled the jazz air as uncommonly complicated bebop (simultaneous with a counter-restoration of New Orleans traditionalism). The youngest of the Mississippi Delta blues artists headed for Memphis and Chicago, with newly cheap electric gear; adding soulful balladry and urgent rhythms to their folky older country repertoire, they prepared a path for a whole new brand of pop music called rock'n'roll. Rock, R&B and bebop – they were not even dreamt of when the 1940s began.

Sources & Sounds

KEY ARTISTS

Dizzy Gillespie
Woody Herman
Billie Holiday
John Lee Hooker
Charlie Parker
Big Joe Turner
T-Bone Walker

The 1940s was a decade of wrenching, often violent change in America. War clouds were on the horizon as 1939 turned into 1940. In the autumn of 1940, Franklin Delano Roosevelt was elected to his third term as President of the United States; he created the Fair Employment Practices Committee the following year. The idea was to investigate and report on discrimination in employment. The executive order was largely ignored in the South and where changes were attempted, such as in Mobile, Alabama or Beaumont, Texas, racial violence ensued. The Roosevelt administration offered tepid support and in 1942 the committee was folded into the War Manpower Commission.

'We often talked in the afternoon [at Minton's]. That's how we came to write different chord progressions and the like…. As for those sitters-in that we didn't want, when we started playing these different changes we'd made up, they'd become discouraged after the first chorus….'

Kenny Clarke

America Emerges From The Great Depression

American industry quickly geared up for the war effort. There were no new American automobiles produced between 1942–46 but defence plants were built, modified, adapted and retrofitted with astonishing quickness. Defence plants meant jobs, and the nation was finally ridding itself of the yoke of the Great Depression. Defence jobs in California meant the migration of thousands of black people from Texas and Louisiana, while jobs in the Midwest resulted in new arrivals from Mississippi and Arkansas; much of the nation's manpower was in uniform.

The music industry was also undergoing great changes. The American Society of Composers, Authors and Publishers (ASCAP), the performing rights society, had been challenged by a group of radio-station owners protesting the high fees for on-air musical performances. Broadcast Music Incorporated (BMI) was formed in 1940 as an alternative and presented an opportunity for black songwriters who had been largely ignored by ASCAP.

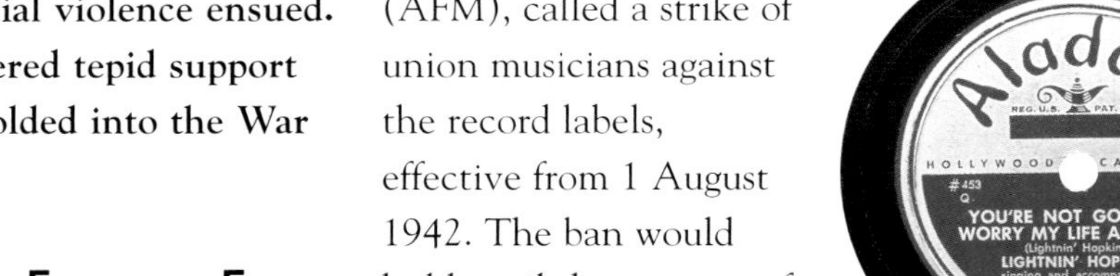

The Record Industry Recovers

James C. Petrillo, the powerful head of the American Federation of Musicians (AFM), called a strike of union musicians against the record labels, effective from 1 August 1942. The ban would hold until the autumn of 1943, when Decca Records settled with the union. RCA and Columbia held out for another 14 months, but Decca's agreement meant that other companies could begin (or resume) recording under the same terms. All of a sudden, new labels began to appear at an astonishing pace in New York, Chicago and Los Angeles. BMI, anxious to stockpile compositions for its catalogue, would advance money to labels with BMI-affiliated publishing companies.

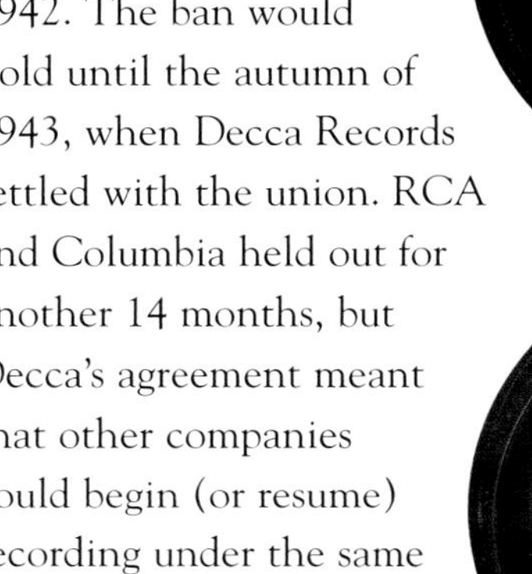

At the height of the swing era, singers had been largely an adjunct to the big bands, but one effect of the strike was that they now made a move to the front of the stage. They were able to record with choirs or small vocal quartets and keep a flow of records coming, with the result that the 1940s saw the growth of the singer as a popular phenomenon in his or her own right, exemplified by the likes of Bing Crosby, Frank Sinatra (1915–98), Nat 'King' Cole (1917–65), Ella Fitzgerald (1917–96), Sarah Vaughan (1924–90),

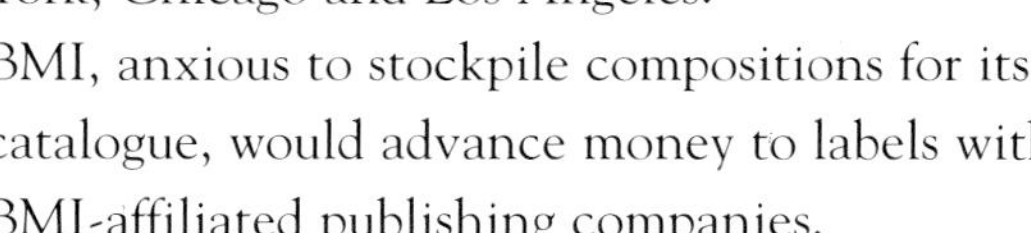

Right
'Landing Blues' by Birmingham Sam (a.k.a. John Lee Hooker) on Savoy; 'You're Not Going To Worry My Life Any More' by Lightnin' Hopkins on Aladdin; John Lee Hooker's 'John L's House Rent Boogie' on Modern.

Dinah Washington (1924–63) and Billie Holiday (1915–59). These figures would now become as well known as the bandleaders that had previously employed them, and they paved the way for the rise of the modern pop star. But the combination of BMI involvement and RCA and Columbia sitting on the sidelines opened the door for jump bands and blues singers as well. Many of the new labels, such as Savoy, Aladdin and Modern, specialized in black jazz, blues and gospel.

Wartime Stringencies Hit The Big Bands

As it happened, the economic upturn generated by the wartime economy did the big bands little good, but their popularity continued through the 1940s, with bandleaders such as Woody Herman (1913–87), Benny Goodman (1909–86), Glenn Miller (1904–44), Stan Kenton (1911–79) and Harry James (1916–83) remaining some of the most admired, recognized and popular personalities of their day.

However, the cultural and music industry developments that took place during the 1940s eventually took their toll on all of these bands, as well as those led by the great African-American leaders such as Duke Ellington (1899–1974) and Count Basie (1904–84). The drafting of musicians in significant numbers, the closure of dance halls around the country, the AFM recording ban, the difficulties of producing records under wartime stringencies, increased transport problems, rationing, inflation – all of these factors combined to make big bands less and less financially viable as the decade progressed. By its end, most of the great bandleaders had disbanded and turned to smaller groups, if only temporarily.

The Country Versus The City

Country blues was still being recorded but more and more artists were moving towards a decidedly urban sound. More roads had been built in the post-Depression era, and this, along with the work opportunities and other factors such as the rise of the jukebox in place of live musicians in many juke joints, further encouraged the continuing influx of musicians from the rural South to the cities, where they

CLASSIC RECORDINGS

1940
Duke Ellington/Blanton-Webster Band: 'Cotton Tail'
Glenn Miller: 'In The Mood'

1941
Billie Holiday: 'God Bless the Child'

1943
Nat 'King' Cole: 'Straighten Up And Fly Right'

1944
Wynonie Harris: 'Who Threw The Whiskey In The Well'

1946
Louis Jordan: 'Choo Choo Ch'Boogie', 'Reet, Petite And Gone'

1947
Amos Milburn: 'Chicken Shack Boogie'

1948
Roy Brown: 'Long About Midnight'
Paul Williams: 'The Hucklebuck'

1949
Jimmy Witherspoon: 'Ain't Nobody's Business If I Do Pt. 2'

Left
Saxophone honker Big Jay McNeely drives the crowd wild with his stage antics.

see Woody Herman pp 154 *see* Nat 'King' Cole pp 172 *see* Stan Kenton pp 177 *see* Dinah Washington pp 185

congregated in the growing communities of areas such as Chicago's South Side or Harlem in New York. Blues music grew louder and more confident; amplification was now being used more frequently by blues artists,

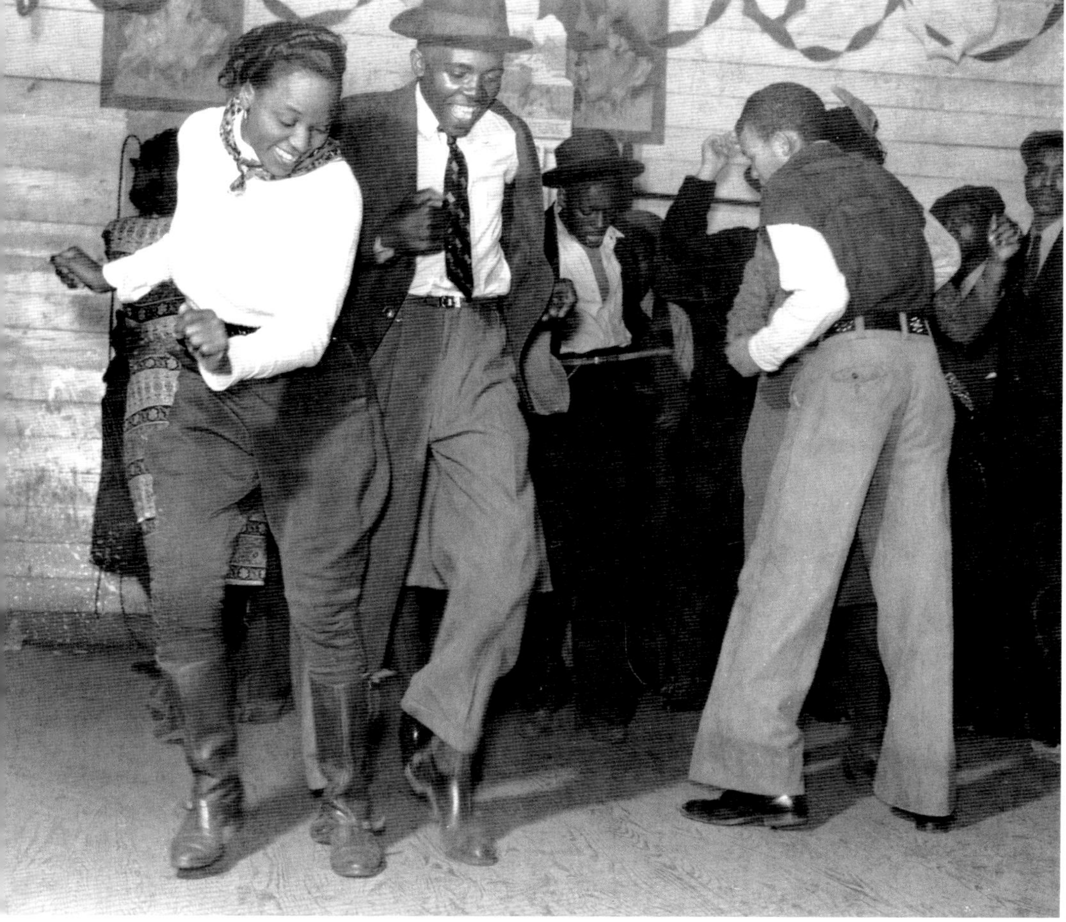

Above
Music fans dance to R&B at a juke joint near Clarksdale, Missouri.

especially to enhance the sounds of the guitar and harmonica, and more blues performers were playing with small bands, which often included percussion.

In Chicago the white record producer, talent spotter and music publisher Lester Melrose was the main point of contact for many musicians wanting to cut a record deal. In the hope of greater record sales and royalties, Melrose would encourage more urban-sounding and crowd-pleasing sides from blues artists; these could involve novelty numbers, or songs with more of a jazz feel. Sometimes, jazz musicians were also invited to play on the records – on Peetie Wheatstraw's (1902–41) sessions recorded in Chicago in 1940–41, he played alongside swing drummer Big Sid Catlett (1910–51) and saxophonist Chu Berry (1980–41).

The Golden Age Of The Saxophone

The saxophone really came into prominence during the 1940s. While its use in jazz big bands and combos was not new, the style introduced by Illinois Jacquet with jazz vibraphonist Lionel Hampton's (1908–2002) band and in early 'Jazz At The Philharmonic' concerts, which emphasized rasping, honking and squealing, was quickly adopted by the jump bands. Recording artists such as Hal Singer (b. 1919) and Big Jay McNeely (b. 1927) found an instrumental road directly to the audience, and saxophone-dominated R&B instrumentals became a growth industry.

Shouters such as Big Joe Turner (1911–85), Wynonie Harris (1913–69), Jimmy Witherspoon (1922–97) and Roy Brown (1925–81) were an important part of the scene, and smooth blues balladeers such as Charles Brown (1922–99) and Amos Milburn (1927–80) added their abilities to the mix. Vocal groups such as the Ravens and Orioles were very much a part of R&B, as were the big bands of Lionel Hampton, Erskine Hawkins, Buddy Johnson and Lucky Millinder – bandleaders who had been able to keep up with the new trend. Artists such as Sonny Terry (1911–86), Brownie McGhee (1915–96), Memphis Slim (1915–88) and Champion Jack Dupree (1910–92)

Right
Wynonie Harris, one of the great blues shouters of the era.

see Introduction pp 142 *see* Key Artists pp 152 *see* A–Z of Artists pp 170 *see* List of Artists pp 186

were also being recorded in an R&B context. In time, things would shake out and these artists would return to their original styles. Others that couldn't keep up would be shunted aside by the industry, some to be rediscovered at a later date and others to disappear for good.

While all this was going on, there were race riots in New York City and Detroit in 1943. President Roosevelt died in 1945 and Vice President Truman ascended to the office. The atom bomb came along in 1945 and while the Axis powers had been defeated, it did not mean that the free world had no enemies. The theft of atomic secrets in 1948 by Soviet spies made the world aware of the growing threat of Communism, and the closing of the defence plants in 1945 sent shockwaves through the US, but a retooling of the domestic economy was immediately ahead.

A New Creative Force In Jazz

While R&B began to infiltrate the big bands and the swing bands fell into decline, the jazz scene was witnessing the emergence of bebop as a major new creative force. Despite its modern and original sound, the music was essentially an evolution from swing rather than a revolutionary departure. Lester Young (1909–59), Coleman Hawkins (1904–69),

Above
Minton's Playhouse, where the bebop style began to take shape (l–r Thelonious Monk, Howard McGhee, Roy Eldridge, Teddy Hill).

Next Page
Dizzy Gillespie on the corner of 52nd Street – the centre of the 1940s New York jazz scene.

see Lionel Hampton pp 125 *see* Peetie Wheatstraw pp 137 *see* Champion Jack Dupree pp 174 *see* Amos Milburn pp 179

Ben Webster (1909–73), Art Tatum (1909–56), Jimmy Blanton and many others had already laid some of the groundwork for the harmonic and rhythmic rethinking that would become central to bebop.

The new music evolved in after-hours jam sessions at clubs such as Minton's Playhouse and Monroe's Uptown House in New York, and later in the jazz clubs of 52nd Street, dubbed 'Swing Street' in its mid-1940s heyday. The recording ban, wartime shortages of shellac and lack of interest from record companies meant that much of it went unrecorded – a fact that can make the transition between swing and bebop seem artificially abrupt, occurring around 1945.

Charlie Parker (1920–55) and Dizzy Gillespie (1917–93) led the way in launching the new sounds, and the arrival of bebop began a new jazz war immediately after the end of the real one. The late 1940s also saw a Dixieland revival centred around Eddie Condon's (1905–73) club on 52nd Street and a slanging match developed between both the practitioners and the fans, polarized along traditionalist vs modernist lines and conducted in a hail of disparaging remarks that did neither side much credit, but generated a lot of publicity for jazz music.

High Art And Low Life

The traditional revival had its counterparts in Europe, notably in England, where jazz groups such as the Crane River Band and Humphrey Lyttelton Band gained ground in the wake of the war. The divisive debates surrounding traditional and modern jazz recurred there, although generally a little later as the impact of bebop percolated through to musicians on the other side of the Atlantic, often through the arrival of American musicians looking for a less stressful and less racist way of life.

Bebop brought new harmonic and rhythmic ideas in to jazz and cemented the role of the virtuoso soloist and improviser at the centre of the music. The seedy club-land in which bebop thrived exacerbated the problems with drugs that were all but endemic in its circles, while pervasive racism and police harassment continued to plague the lives of the musicians. However, the clubs on 52nd Street did allow the development of mixed-race audiences in an America that was still heavily segregated, especially in the southern states.

see Introduction pp 142 *see* Key Artists pp 152 *see* A–Z of Artists pp 170 *see* List of Artists pp 186

The high artistic demands of the music contrasted vividly with the low esteem in which both the artists' work and their lifestyles were held in many quarters. Parker and Gillespie led the way in establishing the principal musical foundations of bebop. Gillespie claimed that the name came from his habit of singing as yet untitled tunes to the other players using nonsense syllables, although other theories exist – for example, Hot Lips Page (1908–54) claimed that Fats Waller (1904–43) provided the name 'bop' one night at Minton's.

The Rise Of Bebop

The bebop musicians took the 4/4 time signature of swing and added a plethora of new rhythmic accents to it, with drummers such as Kenny Clarke (1914–85) and Max Roach (b. 1924) preferring to 'ride' their cymbals and mark strict time with their hi-hats, rather than state a regular beat on the bass drum. That crucial rhythmic development went hand in hand with a new focus on extended harmonies, using much more complex substitute chords and chromatic intervals as the basic building blocks of improvisations. It afforded great scope for melodic, harmonic and rhythmic invention that was fully exploited by musicians such as Parker, Gillespie, Bud Powell (1924–66), Thelonious Monk (1917–82) and others.

That harmonic expansion was a fundamental strength of bebop, but also its built-in weakness. The musicians tended to use chord structures based on standard tunes or blues as the basis for their new melody lines, and bebop evolved as a musical style of great sophistication built on a repetitive and limited structure, which ultimately led to musicians exploring more experimental areas a decade later.

New York City, specifically Harlem and midtown from 42nd Street through to 52nd, was very much the crucible for bebop, and musicians gravitated to the city from all over. Bebop also travelled outwards, notably to the West Coast, where musicians including Dexter Gordon (1923–90), Art Pepper (1925–82), Howard McGhee, Hampton Hawes and Charles Mingus (1922–79) made their own contributions to the evolving form in LA's Central Avenue clubs. As in the swing era, live radio broadcasts from venues such as the Royal Roost in New York remained an important

see Dizzy Gillespie pp 152 *see* Charlie Parker pp 162 *see* Thelonious Monk pp 208 *see* Bud Powell pp 232

element in disseminating the music, and also in leaving a legacy of 'live' recordings to supplement the studio fare, where the musicians still worked under the time restraints of the 78-rpm record.

Bebop also touched the swing bands, its influence discernible in the ensembles of Duke Ellington, Woody Herman, Artie Shaw (1910–2004) and Benny Goodman. By the late 1940s, bebop was the new artistic force in jazz, even if it had not won the populist vote – that remained for the wider public with the eminently more danceable swing, and in the black communities with earthy blues, R&B and jump music.

Previous Page
Drummers such as Kenny Clarke embellished the 4/4 beat of swing to create new rhythms.

Below
Swing devotees dance in the Savoy Club, Harlem.

The Birth Of The Cool

Bebop was hip, with its own look, its own argot and its own rather exclusive set of attitudes. The 1950s would see bop move to a more central position, through the emergence of the related forms of hard bop and soul jazz on the jukeboxes of the African-American community.

The end of the decade also saw the first stirrings of another development that would play a key role in the 1950s; the Nonet sessions of 1949–50 under the leadership of Miles Davis (1926–91), later dubbed the 'Birth Of The Cool', took an alternative approach to the by then well-established mores of bebop, using careful arrangements by the likes of Gerry Mulligan (1927–96) and Gil Evans (1912–88), and a less involved interplay of musical textures that would be taken up in the West Coast and cool jazz movements of the coming decade.

Jazz And Blues Part Ways

So it was that in the 1940s jazz and blues music, which had been so closely linked at the start of the decade, began to pull apart from one another. As far as blues fans were concerned, the Tympany Five, a small jump band led by saxophonist Louis Jordan (1908–75) and playing light, jazz-tinged blues and novelty numbers, was the number one combo in the country. Newly urbanized black communities seized this fresh, rocking music, which represented a welcome move forward from the memories of the rural South. Similar groups led by Roy Milton (1907–83) and Eddie Vinson (1917–88) were also finding an audience. Boogie-woogie, once embraced by jazz bands, was now being abandoned but picked up on by those little blues combos, which utilized the rhythm in very different ways.

Billboard, the record industry trade paper, traced the sales progress of records and its dilemma as to what to call 'black music' was apparent. In 1942 *Billboard* tracked it as the Harlem Hit Parade, changed this name to Race Records in 1945 and in 1949 called it Rhythm & Blues. Finally, they had come up with a term that applied to all secular black music that wasn't bebop or traditional jazz: R&B.

R&B Hits The Airwaves

In 1948 President Truman ordered the desegregation of the US military. Between the battle over civil rights

see Introduction pp 142 *see* Key Artists pp 152 *see* A–Z of Artists pp 170 *see* List of Artists pp 186

and the growing concern with Communism, Truman was challenged by two different factions of his own party when he stood for re-election in the autumn of 1948; he prevailed nonetheless. James C. Petrillo called another strike of the AFM to take effect on 1 January 1948. This one was not as successful, since many of the smaller labels found ways to circumvent the action. Still, there were many small labels, started after the settlement of the 1942 strike, which did not survive 1948. Radio station WDIA in Memphis instituted a black music policy in 1949. It was a huge success and other stations began to play more R&B on the airways. More radio play increased the sales of black records and exposed the music to more people, as it had done in the 1920s.

In December 1948, Detroit bandleader and saxophonist Paul Williams recorded a song called 'The Huckleback'. It was an R&B instrumental that became the biggest black record of 1949. It also started a dance craze and soon people were dancing the hucklebuck in black areas across America. It was the first new dance to come out of the black community during the 1940s. The next decade would have a lot of new dances, a lot more R&B and, right around the corner, rock'n'roll.

Below
The British jazz scene grew following the Second World War. Here Harry Hayes (on clarinet) leads a recording at London's Columbia studios, 1947.

see Louis Jordan pp 176 *see* Eddie 'Cleanhead' Vinson pp 184 *see* Miles Davis pp 200 *see* Gil Evans pp 221

Dizzy Gillespie

CLASSIC RECORDINGS

1945
Dizzy Gillespie Quintet: 'All The Things You Are', 'Dizzy Atmosphere', 'Groovin High'

1945
Dizzy Gillespie & his All-Star Quintet: 'Hot House', 'Salt Peanuts', 'Shaw Nuff'

1947
Dizzy Gillespie & his Orchestra: 'Algo Bueno', 'Manteca', 'Minor Walk', 'Ool-Ya-Koo'

'Musically, he knows what he is doing backwards and forwards…. So the arranging, the chord progressions and things in progressive music, Dizzy is responsible for.'

Billy Eckstine

John Birks 'Dizzy' Gillespie shares the credit for creating bebop with Charlie Parker, but his place in the history of twentieth-century music rests on a considerably wider achievement. He was born in Cheraw, South Carolina in 1917 and acquired his nickname in the 1930s. He moved to New York and worked in big bands with Teddy Hill, Lionel Hampton and Cab Calloway (the latter relationship ending acrimoniously after a notorious altercation over a spitball).

He was a prime mover in the jam sessions at Minton's Playhouse in Harlem, which became the forcing ground for the subsequent evolution of bebop. His speed and facility in the high register reflected the influence of Roy Eldridge, but he quickly displayed an increasingly original musical conception that came to fruition in the seminal group that he led with Charlie Parker in 1946.

Above

Dizzy Gillespie's trumpet had a curious, upright bell made to his specification by the Martin company.

Flying With Bird

The collaboration remains one of the crucial episodes in jazz history and laid the template for the new music that would both illuminate and divide the post-war jazz scene. Bebop demanded formidable technical abilities as well as imagination; Gillespie's pyrotechnic brilliance was the perfect foil for Parker's genius, and was underpinned by a more thorough understanding of harmonic theory than many of his contemporaries routinely possessed. Their partnership, which included further recordings and occasional reunions, such as the famous Massey Hall concert in Toronto in 1953, put bebop on the musical map and assured their joint status as jazz immortals. While Parker burnt himself out and died prematurely, however, Gillespie went on to become a respected elder statesman of the music.

The Cuban Connection

As bebop was coalescing, Dizzy was assembling what would become a celebrated big band – one that made an equally important contribution to the development of modern jazz. Gillespie was a prime mover in the creation of Afro-Cuban jazz (or 'Cubop'), a style that brought Cuban folk and popular idioms into a jazz context. His interest was sparked by Cab Calloway's lead trumpeter Mario Bauzá, who introduced him to percussionist Chano Pozo in 1947. Pozo was fatally shot in a bar in 1948 after contributing to Gillespie's classic Afro-Cuban recordings 'Manteca', 'Guarachi Guaro' and 'Cubana Be,

see Introduction pp 142 *see* Sources & Sounds pp 144 *see* A–Z of Artists pp 170

Above
Gillespie (far left) directs his big band.

Cubana Bop'. Latin tunes were well-established in jazz, but this was the first band to integrate real Afro-Cuban polyrhythms within the new bebop idiom, and others followed suit, including Machito, Tadd Dameron, Charlie Parker and Bud Powell.

The Cuban influence remained a strong element in Gillespie's music. He adopted his trademark upturned trumpet bell in 1953 and broke new ground in 1956 by taking jazz bands on State Department-sponsored tours to Africa, the Near East, Pakistan and South America, as well as Europe.

Politics And People

Gillespie became increasingly aware of his African roots and of the civil rights campaigns in America, even running for President in 1964 under a 'politics ought to be a groovier thing' banner. Astute enough to avoid the pitfalls of involvement with the drugs that plagued the bebop community, Gillespie was a natural showman as well as a brilliant musician, and is one of the select band of jazzmen who became household names.

An attempt to join the fashionable jazz-rock fusion movement in the 1970s was a rare lapse of judgement, and was quickly abandoned. He continued to lead both large and small groups throughout the rest of his career, including the United Nations Orchestra (the use of the singular reflected his adherence to the Baha'i faith and their belief in the unity of peoples), which he led from 1988 until his death from cancer in 1993.

see Charlie Parker pp 162 *see* Mario Bauzá pp 170 *see* Machito pp 178 *see* Chano Pozo pp 182

Woody Herman

CLASSIC RECORDINGS

1936–43
The Band That Plays The Blues: 'Blues In The Night', 'Woodchopper's Ball'

1944–46
Herman's (First) Herd: 'Caldonia', 'I Ain't Got Anything But The Blues', 'I've Got You Under My Skin', 'Summer Sequence'

1947–49
The Second Herd: 'Early Autumn', 'Four Brothers', 'Keen and Peachy', 'Not Really The Blues'

Woodrow 'Woody' Herman (originally Herrmann) led several of the most exciting big bands in jazz history, hitting peaks of achievement in the 1940s that few have equalled. Born in Milwaukee, Wisconsin in 1913 to German immigrants, Herman began his stage career in vaudeville as a child, but his ambition was to lead his own band. He played alto, tenor and baritone saxophone and the clarinet, as well as singing. He worked for a number of bands before joining Isham Jones in 1934.

He fulfilled his ambition to become a bandleader almost by default in 1936, when Jones unexpectedly broke up his band in Knoxville. The players decided to continue as a co-operative band, and Herman was elected as leader of the group. Known as the Band That Plays The Blues, they began to win a big following. 'Woodchoppers Ball' was a huge hit in 1939, selling some five million copies ('It was great,' Herman said later, 'the first thousand times we played it').

'It was marvellous … to work with Bill and Chubby and Flip, Ralph, Pete, and, of course, Sonny and Davey, too. That was an exciting group to be with. Ideas and whole new tunes sprang out of that group like sparks.'

Woody Herman

New Directions For The Herd

In the early 1940s, more sophisticated arrangements gradually began to usurp the less formal 'head' structures that had been the band's staple format. Arrangers such as Dave Matthews, Neal Hefti and Ralph Burns had changed the sound of the band by the time it was officially known as Herman's Herd (later referred to as the First Herd) from 1943. By late 1945 the band was regularly winning popularity polls and setting new box-office records. Igor Stravinsky wrote his *Ebony Concerto* for them, and the concerto was premiered at Carnegie Hall in March 1946, alongside Ralph Burns's 'Summer Sequence', later completed by the famous Stan Getz feature 'Early Autumn'.

The Woodchoppers, a small band drawn from the ranks of the orchestra, also achieved success. The band's notable players included trumpeters Conte Condoli, trombonist Bill Harris, saxophonist Flip Phillips, pianist Ralph Burns, and drummers Dave Tough and then Don Lamond. Herman eventually broke up the First Herd at the height of its popularity in December 1946, for domestic reasons.

Four Brothers

The break-up proved a temporary departure. Herman had formed his Second Herd by October 1947 with a new generation of stars in the making, including the famous 'Four Brothers' saxophone section of Stan Getz, Zoot Sims, Herbie Steward (soon to be replaced by Al Cohn) and Serge Chaloff. Their three-tenors-plus-baritone setup was the Second Herd's distinctive signature sound.

Above
Woody Herman, a fine reedsman and celebrated bandleader.

Far Right
The saxophone section from the Second Herd.

see Introduction pp 142 *see* Sources & Sounds pp 144 *see* A–Z of Artists pp 170

The band reflected a more overt bebop influence than the First Herd, but was also plagued by a less welcome borrowing from bebop – heroin addiction. Moreover, despite the Second Herd's significant musical success, the economies of the music business had turned against big bands and Herman incurred large financial losses. Several key players departed in 1949 and by the end of the year Herman had accepted the inevitable and broken up the band, forming a septet instead.

The Herd Swings On

But Herman could not stay away from big bands for long. The Third Herd ran for much of the 1950s and toured in Europe in 1954 and South America in 1958. The brief Anglo-American Herd made an impact on jazz in the UK in 1959, and the Swinging Herd line-up of the 1960s continued the band's traditions of strong soloists and meaty arrangements. Herman later added soprano saxophone to his roster, dabbled in jazz rock and became involved in the development of formal jazz education, although his bands had been providing a schooling for young musicians from the outset in any case.

His final years were plagued by a long-running dispute with the tax authorities, and eventually all his property and assets were seized by the government. He continued to lead his band until his death in 1987, after which saxophonist Frank Tiberi took over leadership of the Woody Herman Orchestra, which remains active.

see Zoot Sims pp 233 *see* Stan Getz pp 272 *see* Swing pp 384

Billie Holiday

CLASSIC RECORDINGS

1938–39
Billie Holiday & her Orchestra: 'Night And Day', 'Strange Fruit', 'You Go To My Head'

1940–41
'Body And Soul', 'God Bless The Child', 'I Cover The Waterfront'

1944–47
Billie Holiday: 'Don't Explain', 'Easy Living', 'Lover Man', 'My Man'

Billie Holiday was entirely untrained as a singer, but drew on the example of popular recording artists such as Bessie Smith and Louis Armstrong in developing her musical approach. She was able to make much of poor songs as well as great ones. Her phrasing, intonation, attention to the weight and nuance of lyrics, and her lightly inflected, subtly off-the-beat rhythmic placement were all highly individual and became widely influential.

Her early life is confusing. Recent biographical research has confirmed that she was born in Philadelphia in 1915 and was known by several names, the most frequently used being Eleanora Fagan. She was known as Billie from childhood, and took the surname Holiday from her largely absent father, guitarist Clarence Holiday. She was jailed for prostitution in New York in 1930, and began her singing career shortly afterwards in clubs in Brooklyn and then Harlem.

'What comes out is what I feel. I hate straight singing. I have to change a tune to my own way of doing it.'
Billie Holiday

Lady Day And Lester

Producer John Hammond heard her perform and arranged for her to record with Benny Goodman in 1933. She made her professional debut at the Apollo Theater in Harlem in 1934, and in 1935–42, with pianist Teddy Wilson, began the series of recordings that made her name, working alongside major jazz musicians such as trumpeters Buck Clayton and Roy Eldridge and saxophonist Lester Young (who bestowed her with the nickname 'Lady Day'). Young was regarded as her closest musical associate, and there was undoubtedly a special chemistry at work in their collaborations.

Her fame was largely confined to the African-American community at that stage, but spells with Count Basie in 1937 and Artie Shaw in 1938 brought her to wider notice and, in the latter case, helped to break the bar on black musicians working with white bands that was still very much in force. Her standing with intellectuals, leftists and radicals was boosted by her appearances at the interracial Café Society in 1939 and her recording of 'Strange Fruit', a song about southern lynchings that quickly attained cult status.

Success Turns Sour

Trademark ballad performances, including 'God Bless The Child', 'I Cover The Waterfront', 'Gloomy Sunday' (all 1941) and 'Lover Man' (1944), had made her a big name by the mid-1940s. She played her only minor acting role on film in 1946, as a maid opposite Louis Armstrong in *New Orleans*.

Right
Sheet music for Holiday's 1941 hit 'God Bless The Child'.

Far Right
Jazz and blues singer Billie Holiday, whose distinctive voice was filled with emotion, passion and tragedy.

Her drug use led to imprisonment on drug charges in 1947 (recent research has suggested that she may have been set up, although her addiction was real enough). Her relationships with men were rarely to her advantage, emotionally or financially. Her career slipped in the wake of her jail sentence, in large part because she could no longer work in clubs in New York without the Cabaret Card, which was automatically denied to musicians convicted of drug charges.

Hard Times

Her health and her voice began to show the ravages of a hard life and drug abuse, but she was still capable of memorable performances in the 1950s, including a treasured clip made for the television special *The Sound Of Jazz* in 1957, in which she sang her 1939 hit 'Fine And Mellow' with a stellar cast of jazzmen, including Lester Young. Her late recordings and performances were often harrowing, but even her final recordings have the power to move the listener profoundly – in some respects, they may even be heard as more powerful emotional testimonies than her classic but sunnier recordings of the 1930s and 1940s.

She died in New York in 1959, having left an auto-biography, *Lady Sings The Blues* (1956), which has been seen as self-serving. Recently, biographer Stuart Nicholson has suggested that the book – but not the 1972 feature film loosely based on it – may be a more accurate depiction of her life than once seemed likely.

see Count Basie pp 102 *see* Roy Eldridge pp 108 *see* Lester Young pp 118 *see* Artie Shaw pp 133

John Lee Hooker

CLASSIC RECORDINGS

1948
'Boogie Chillen',
'Sally Mae'

1949
'Crawlin' King Snake Blues', 'Devil's Jump', 'Hobo Blues', 'Hoogie Boogie', 'Moaning Blues', 'The Numbers', 'Wandering Blues'

1951
'I'm In The Mood'

John Lee Hooker's sparse blues sound was a major influence on the younger generations of blues musicians dominating the music scene in the 1960s and 1970s. His individual style retained a primitive purity at a time when many of his contemporaries were experimenting with groups and incorporating the influences of other types of music into their blues. Hooker's guitar technique was characterized by a simple drone in the bass, punctuated by sharp, melodic notes played on the upper strings; his music had a loose structure and yet was driven by his rhythms, with constantly repeated figures pushing the beat forward and creating an almost hypnotic effect. This adaptable foundation that Hooker created left room for him to improvise, both musically and lyrically. While his guitar style showed external influences, his rich, heavy vocals were more in the Mississippi tradition that one might expect.

'With one chord, John Lee Hooker could tell you a story as deep as the ocean….'
Carlos Santana

An Informal Musical Education

John Lee Hooker was born on 22 August 1917 near Clarksdale, Mississippi into a family of agricultural labourers. He got his first instrument from singer Tony Hollins, but he was taught how to play by his stepfather, Will Moore. Moore would play weekends at jukes and functions in various Delta locations, often in the company of blues greats such as Charley Patton or Son House. A Louisiana musician, Moore's playing style differed from his Mississippi counterparts and his trademark was a rhythmic pattern that his stepson picked up and made his own; he called it the boogie. The young Hooker was also a regular churchgoer and it was in this environment that he honed his vocal talents, participating and soloing in church choirs and gospel groups.

Above
Hooker's 'Stuttering Blues', which was released on the Rockin' label under the pseudonym John Lee Booker.

In Search Of A Calling

By 1933, John Lee Hooker had left Mississippi and his family for good. He took various menial jobs and played some music in Memphis but soon left for Cincinatti, where he was to stay for several years. At this stage, he had not yet considered the possibility of taking up music as a full-time career, and held down a steady job outside music, although he played at parties and functions on weekends. During his time in Cincinnati, he also sang with several different gospel quartets.

In 1943, Hooker moved to Detroit. He played regularly in clubs and record shops on the east side of the city, around Hastings Street (the centre of the African-American quarter), but still had his basic employment outside music until he was spotted playing by a record-store owner, who introduced him to a local record distributor, Bernie Bessman. As it happened, Bessman was on the lookout for a rhythm & blues act in order to tap into what was then a growing and lucrative market within the music business. Hooker's first recording for Bessman's Sensation label was in September 1948.

'Boogie Chillen' Enters The Chart

The first Hooker record, a stomping, up-tempo boogie called 'Boogie Chillen', featured simply Hooker's vocals, guitar and tapping foot, and was a huge success. Hooker's music had a different quality from the other blues and R&B records of the period; his boogie sound was not based on piano baselines but seemed to hark back to some more ancient voice, with its dark tones, droning bass line and energetic syncopations. The record reached Number One on *Billboard* magazine's Race Records chart and so John Lee Hooker's career as a professional entertainer was launched. Sensation was a subsidiary of Pan American Record Distributors, a local record wholesaler, and Bessman, recognizing his

see Introduction pp 142 *see* Sources & Sounds pp 144 *see* A–Z of Artists pp 170

Above
Boogie guitarist John Lee Hooker relaxes in the studio.

inability to promote a record nationally, licensed 'Boogie Chillen' to Modern Records in Los Angeles.

An astute businessman, Bessman paid Hooker a handsome advance and leased his recordings out to numerous other labels. Thus, within weeks of the Modern release of 'Boogie Chillen', Hooker was recording for a variety of labels under an enormous number of pseudonyms. He was Texas Slim on King, Delta John on Regent, Birmingham Sam on Savoy, Johnny Williams on Prize, Staff and Gotham, the Boogie Man on Acorn and John Lee Booker on Chance and Chess. It did not seem to affect his sales on Modern, where he had solid sellers such as 'Hobo Blues', 'Crawlin' King Snake Blues' and another Number One hit on the *Billboard* R&B charts, 'I'm In The Mood'. For most of his career, Hooker paid little attention to the exclusivity aspect of recording contracts.

Hooker Hits The Road

Throughout the period 1948–51, Hooker worked mostly in Detroit. Usually playing either solo or in a duo, he was very irregular in his patterns, rarely adhering to the 12-bar structure; this informal approach to timing must have made ensemble work difficult for him and the other musicians, which may be one reason why Hooker appeared to prefer solo work rather than delving into jump blues and jazz bands in the manner of Muddy Waters and Howlin' Wolf. While succeeding in keeping the traditional country blues set-up of a bluesman alone with his guitar, there was a certain slickness and sophistication to Hooker's playing and general demeanour that gave his sound a distinctly urban feel.

However, in the city Hooker sometimes performed with a small group he called the Boogie Ramblers, where his work followed the more traditional form. His first major roadwork was done in 1952, with

see Charley Patton pp 23 *see* Son House pp 126 *see* Muddy Waters pp 212 *see* Howlin' Wolf pp 225

Eddie Kirkland on second guitar; they picked up accompanists as needed. Touring the R&B circuit in this way continued to spread his popularity and strengthen his fan base. It wasn't until 1955, when Hooker signed with Vee Jay, that he began recording regularly with a band, as by this time solo blues performances – even in Hooker's capable hands – had started to become an old-fashioned and outdated concept. Hooker invited key blues players such as Jimmy Reed and Eddie Taylor to work as his sidemen and had several hits on Vee Jay, the biggest two being 'Boom Boom' and 'Dimples', both performed and recorded in innumerable versions by blues followers in later years.

Above
John Lee Hooker (left) with his first cousin and fellow blues guitarist, Earl Hooker.

Reaching New Audiences

As the 1950s turned into the 1960s, Hooker's music began to appear on LP. The craze for R&B began to wane, but Hooker's rural roots and stripped-back style meant that he was able to look back to his earlier repertoire and take advantage of the fast-growing interest in folk music. He performed at both the Newport Folk Festival and Newport Jazz Festival in 1960, gaining exposure to large numbers of white college students for the first time; the Rolling Stones and the Animals cited Hooker as a major influence on their early records. Beginning in 1962, Hooker became a regular on the European club and concert circuit, while at home, he spent much of the early 1960s working coffeehouses and folk-music clubs.

He signed a three-year deal with Bluesway in 1966, where he made excellent albums, such as *Live At Café Au Go-Go* with the Muddy Waters' band, until the label folded and was taken over by the parent label, ABC Records, in 1970. He frequently recorded

see Introduction pp 142 *see* Sources & Sounds pp 144 *see* A–Z of Artists pp 170

for European labels while overseas. In the early 1970s Hooker teamed up with a new generation of blues-inspired white musicians, including Steve Miller and a California rock band, Canned Heat; their resultant album, *Hooker 'N Heat* (1971), introduced Hooker to rock'n'roll fans. He had brief roles in the movies *The Blues Brothers* (1980) and *The Color Purple* (1985), and continued to work the festival circuit.

Hooker As Mr. Lucky

While his early recordings were being reissued to remarkable sales figures and critical acclaim, the final glorious chapter in John Lee Hooker's career began with an association with the Rosebud Agency, which handled Hooker's bookings from the mid-1980s. Around that time, Hooker developed a friendship with rock star Carlos Santana and the fruit of that relationship was *The Healer* (1989). The album, which also featured diverse guest musicians including Bonnie Raitt, George Thorogood and Robert Cray, was a huge hit and vaulted Hooker back to stardom. In 1990, he recorded the soundtrack for the film *The Hot Spot*, overdubbing tracks with Taj Mahal and Miles Davis, and 1991 saw the release of *Mr. Lucky*, another star-laden album featuring, among others, Ry Cooder, Van Morrison, Albert Collins and Keith Richards; *Mr. Lucky* reached Number Three in the UK album chart.

Over time Hooker toured less frequently but continued to record and rack up awards until announcing his retirement in 1995. One of the last surviving links to the classic blues era, Hooker sadly died in 2001.

Left
Hooker's playing style was known for its boogie beat.

Below
Hooker's innovation, influence and success continued until his death in 2001.

see Jimmy Reed pp 232 *see* Canned Heat pp 268 *see* Ry Cooder pp 303 *see* Bonnie Raitt pp 337

Charlie Parker

CLASSIC RECORDINGS

1945–46
'Anthropology', 'A Night In Tunisia', 'Koko', 'Ornithology', 'Yardbird Suite'

1947–48
'Bird Feathers', 'Scrapple From The Apple'

1949–52
Charlie Parker with Strings: 'If I Should Lose You', 'Just Friends', 'Summertime'

Right
Parker (left) shares a joke with bebop collaborator Dizzy Gillespie in New York, 1949.

'The way he got from one note to the other and the way he played the rhythm fit what we were trying to do perfectly.... He was the other half of my heartbeat.'

Dizzy Gillespie

Charlie Parker, also known as 'Yardbird' or 'Bird', was a largely self-taught musical genius with acute self-destructive tendencies. His career exemplified both the creative power and the destructive social ethos of bebop. His music burned as brightly as any in jazz, but his lifestyle sent out the wrong message to too many young musicians, despite his frequent warnings to stay away from drugs.

Louis Armstrong had begun the evolution of jazz from an ensemble's to a soloist's music two decades earlier, but bebop brought that process to fruition and Parker was its supreme exponent. His influence was all-pervasive and continues to be so on contemporary musicians, affecting not only saxophonists, but players on every instrument.

Forging The New Sound

Parker was born in Kansas City on 29 August 1920. His was not a musical family, and no one was ever sure of the provenance of his remarkable gift. As a child he was spoilt by his mother, and this would remain evident in his behaviour throughout his brief adult life. Parker was quick-thinking and intelligent, but had little time for his academic studies, often playing truant from high school. However, it so happened that the study of music was greatly encouraged at his school,

see Introduction pp 142 *see* Sources & Sounds pp 144 *see* A–Z of Artists pp 170

and he took up the baritone saxophone, before persuading his mother to scrape enough money together to present him with an alto sax.

Parker preferred the melodic tone and flexibility of the alto, and as his father was barely in the picture and his mother worked long hours, the unsupervised teenaged Charlie began to frequent the Kansas City jazz clubs. He played in the city's famous jam sessions, picking up basic harmony lessons from local musicians such as pianist Bill Channing and saxophonist Tommy Douglas, and made remarkable progress after suffering some early slights from established players. His lack of musical learning meant that, while technically brilliant, he knew little of the surrounding theory, such as the different keys. Moreover, he was apt to bend the rules of what he did know, so that his approach to chord changes and improvisation did not always find favour with the other musicians. Always ahead of his time musically, Parker found this intensely frustrating. Another source of inspiration was Lester Young and Charlie wore out his records, studying Young's eccentric rhythmic experimentation and finely crafted melodic phrasing.

Heading For Harlem

At the age of 15, Parker was married, with his wife expecting their first child; he was already playing professionally and the inevitable wanderlust set in. He left Kansas City for New York in 1937 and found work in the kitchen of a Harlem club where pianist Art Tatum performed; from Tatum he assimilated the creative use of musical quotation. It was around this time that the 'Bird' moniker began to stick. Summoned back to Kansas City for his father's funeral the same year, Parker joined Jay McShann's band, which was basically a blues orchestra, albeit one with vaguely modernist leanings. Continuing to work at various menial jobs at the same time, Parker swiftly became the outstanding soloist in McShann's band, although as ever his remarkably innovative playing was unpredictable and did not always sit happily with the rest of the group.

The Magic Of Mintons

Bird made his recording debut with McShann's band for Decca in 1941. The band also played at New York's Savoy Ballroom, following which the young soloist received favourable reviews. Having endured the rigid structure of big-band arrangements for as long as he could, Parker left McShann and settled in Harlem. There he was sought out by the drummer Kenny Clarke and invited to play at Mintons, a seemingly minor venue that had recently come under the management of forward-thinking musician Teddy Hill and had become a veritable breeding ground of up-and-coming jazz players. In addition to Clarke, the house band included Thelonious Monk (piano), Charlie Christian (guitar), Joe Guy (trumpet) and Nick Fenton (bass). Here, finally, Parker could mix with like-minded musicians who were not intimidated by his innovative improvisations and evident genius. It was at Mintons that the first rumblings of the bebop style could be heard.

Below
Saxophone genius Charlie Parker (third from left) performs among other jazz greats at an All-Stars event organized by *Metronome* magazine.

Parker had encountered Dizzy Gillespie on more than one occasion, but after meeting again at Mintons their friendship and musical partnership really began to take shape. In 1943, the pair joined the big band of Earl Hines, a New Orleans jazz veteran who had participated in Louis Armstrong's legendary Hot Fives sessions. Here, Bird and Diz mischievously introduced

see Lester Young pp 118 *see* Art Tatum pp 135 *see* Kenny Clarke pp 172 *see* Jay McShann pp 179

Above

Parker (second from right) playing at the Birdland Restaurant, New York with (l–r) Max Kaminsky, Lester Young, Hop Lips Page and Lennie Tristano.

modernist elements to the fray, resulting in a thrilling clashing of styles that invigorated not only the music, but also the other musicians and the open-minded Hines. When the Hines band fell apart the following year, Billy Eckstine, one of the group's vocalists, formed his own big band with a more prominent modernist contingent, including Gillespie, Parker and some other former members of Jay McShann's band.

Parker's fluency was attracting attention even then, and his development of a new approach to both rhythmic accents and established melodic-harmonic relationships was bearing fruit. He realized that new and radically different sounding melody lines could be created by avoiding the more obvious notes, and developed his use of the upper 'dissonant' intervals beyond the octave. The effect of these experiments was electrifying. His raw materials were ordinary blues and standard AABA tunes, but he transformed them in spectacular fashion. He had an impeccable musical memory and could translate phrases effortlessly from one instrument or one piece to another.

The Rise Of Bebop And Fall Of Parker

Bird's work with Dizzy Gillespie in 1945–46 and the Savoy recordings of the period formed a benchmark for bebop and seeded the central directions that jazz would explore in the next two decades. He found that the bebop quintet format – trumpet, sax, bass, drums, piano – was the ensemble that best suited his playing style. The Charlie Parker Quintet concentrated mainly on blues and bebop re-workings of classic tunes, which retained the basic harmonic structure of the original but allowed the players to improvise around it. A young Miles Davis played trumpet in the quintet for

see Introduction pp 142 *see* Sources & Sounds pp 144 *see* A–Z of Artists pp 170

Above
Parker practices before his performance at the 1949 International Jazz Festival in Paris.

a while, and although his technical ability was not always up to the standard of his elders, he took inspiration from Parker and would become a similar master of improvisation in the years to come.

Parker had become addicted to heroin sometime in the 1930s and his reliance on the drug is inextricably interwoven with his musical career. He lived in squalor and frequently went for long periods without eating, seeking out his next hit in preference to food. His dependence on heroin would destroy many of Parker's working and personal relationships, not to mention the man himself. An infamous episode in California led to his incarceration in the rehabilitation centre at Camarillo in 1947 (memorialized in his 'Relaxin' at Camarillo'), and tales of his addiction and his heavy drinking are endless. Returning to New York, his self-destructive behaviour continued; he was eventually banned from Birdland, the New York jazz club named in his honour, and the excesses of his life took their predictable toll.

Bird With Strings

He told several people, including the composer Edgar Varese, that he had ambitions to work with more complex musical forms, but never did so. The nearest he got was recording with strings in 1949–52 – sessions that have divided listeners ever since, although they did give him the bestselling 'single' of his career, 'Just Friends'.

Bird Lives!

Prematurely worn out, Parker died on 12 March 1955 while watching Tommy Dorsey's television show in the Manhattan apartment of Baroness Pannonica de Keonigswarter (known as Nica), a rebellious member of the Rothschild family who became a celebrated patroness of jazzmen and a friend to Parker in his final months. Graffiti proclaiming 'Bird Lives!' began to appear in the streets of New York's Greenwich Village almost immediately, posted by anonymous fans, and the legend continued to grow.

He made his great musical discoveries early and never recaptured the glories of his best work of the 1940s, but he was the supreme creative figure of his era and remained the major influence on a generation of jazz players. His astringent and penetrating sonority became the prevailing model and improvisers everywhere studied and practised every nuance of his inventions, just as he had pored over Lester Young's recordings in the late 1930s. His stylistic pre-eminence would only really be challenged with the emergence of modal jazz and free jazz in the late 1950s.

see Earl Hines pp 126 *see* Dizzy Gillespie pp 152 *see* Billy Eckstine pp 174 *see* Miles Davis pp 200

Big Joe Turner

CLASSIC RECORDINGS

1938
Joe Turner: 'Roll 'Em Pete'

1939
Pete Johnson & his Boogie Woogie Boys: 'Cherry Red'

1940
Joe Turner & his Fly Cats: 'Piney Brown Blues'

1941
Big Joe Turner: 'Careless Love', 'Rocks In My Bed'
Art Tatum & his Band: 'Ooh Wee Baby Blues'

1951
Joe Turner: 'Chains Of Love', 'Sweet Sixteen'

1953
'Honey Hush'

1954
'Shake, Rattle & Roll'

'I was sitting up there thinking, "now when is he gonna run out of words?" And then I was thinking "when is he gonna run out of something to play?" But they never ran out of nothing.'

Jay McShann on Big Joe Turner & Pete Johnson

Above
Powerful blues shouter Big Joe Turner, who provided an essential link between the blues and rock'n'roll music.

Joseph Vernon Turner was born on 18 May 1911 in Kansas City, Missouri. He dropped out of school after sixth grade and worked with blind singers on the streets. The blues was in the air in Kansas City and when Turner joined in with the street singers he would make up blues lyrics. Turner was functionally illiterate and never learned to read or write properly.

He studied records in his late teens to learn songs and cited Leroy Carr, Lonnie Johnson, Bessie Smith and Ethel Waters as favourites. By the time he was 17, he had teamed up with Pete Johnson at the Backbiter's Club. There were no microphones at the time and Turner's voice became the stuff of legend as locals told stories of hearing him 10 blocks away. He became the first of a new breed of performer: the blues shouter.

A Fruitful Partnership

In the early 1930s, Turner and Johnson moved to the Black and Tan club, where Turner learned to tend bar. After Prohibition ended in 1933 the pair moved to the Cherry Blossom, a larger spot which had a floor show, including the orchestra of George E. Lee. It was during this time that Johnson and Turner travelled to out-of-town locations such as Omaha, Chicago and St. Louis. In early 1935 the pair moved to the Sunset Café, where they were heard by John Hammond and invited to appear at the Spirituals To Swing concert in New York. A big hit at the concert, Johnson and Turner soon joined forces with Albert Ammons and Meade 'Lux' Lewis, and began a four-year run at a New York nightclub, Café Society, which featured black entertainment. Johnson and Turner made their

see Introduction pp 142 *see* Sources & Sounds pp 144 *see* A–Z of Artists pp 170

recording debut for Vocalion (including 'Roll 'Em Pete') but Joe moved over to Decca in 1940. He was a guest vocalist on jazz dates featuring the Varsity Seven, Benny Carter, Joe Sullivan and Art Tatum, and was paired with artists such as pianists Sammy Price and Willie 'The Lion' Smith on his own recordings.

In the summer of 1941, Turner went to Los Angeles to appear in Duke Ellington's musical *Jump For Joy*. Turner was added to the cast after the show had opened but Ellington had written a blues for Turner to perform in the show, 'Rocks In My Bed'. It became Turner's signature song following the show's close in late September, and his return to New York's Café Society.

In 1945, Joe Turner signed with National Records. He was travelling constantly and National managed to record him in New York, Chicago and Los Angeles, backed by small groups that often included horns. In 1947–48 he recorded sessions in California for Aladdin, Swingtime and MGM. He lived in New Orleans for a time in the late 1940s and early 1950s, and he recorded for Freedom and Imperial during that time, but in 1951 he signed with Atlantic Records; here began the period of his greatest popularity.

Atlantic Years

The Atlantic partners, Ahmet Ertegun and Herb Abrahmson, felt that Turner could thrive in the R&B style that was so popular with black audiences. Turner responded with big hits such as 'Chains Of Love', 'Honey Hush' and 'Shake, Rattle & Roll', forming an important link between the blues and the forthcoming rock'n'roll style. He recorded in Chicago (with electric guitarist Elmore James) and New Orleans, but more often in New York with the arrangements of Jesse Stone. Atlantic also recorded a jazz album, *The Boss Of The Blues* (1956), which reunited Turner with Pete Johnson. The Atlantic association lasted until 1961 and for the next decade Turner freelanced with various different labels. He settled in southern California in the mid-1950s; by the early 1960s he was a regular at European clubs and festivals. In the US, apart from when touring the festivals, he mainly worked in California. His career was revived by an association with Norman Granz and Pablo records, which produced LPs with top jazz stars such as Count Basie on a regular basis, from 1973 until Turner's death. He was prominently featured in the film *Last of the Blue Devils* (1979), a reunion of Kansas City musicians from the 1930s and 1940s. He earned a Grammy nomination for his Muse album *Blues Train* (1982), recorded with the young New England-based band, Roomful of Blues.

Below
Turner appearing in the 1956 film *Shake, Rattle & Rock*, which included footage of Turner and Fats Domino in concert.

see Duke Ellington pp 52 *see* Albert Ammons pp 100 *see* Pete Johnson pp 128 *see* Meade 'Lux' Lewis pp 128

T-Bone Walker

CLASSIC RECORDINGS

1940
Les Hite Orchestra: 'T-Bone Blues'

1942
T-Bone Walker: 'I Got A Break Baby', 'Mean Old World'

1947
'Call It Stormy Monday', 'Hypin' Woman Blues', 'I'm Still In Love With You', 'Prison Blues', 'T-Bone Shuffle'

1950
'Strollin' With Bones'

1951
'Cold, Cold Feeling'

Aaron Thibeaux Walker was born in Linden, Texas on 28 May 1910, the only child of Rance and Movelia Walker. The family moved to Dallas in 1912 and as a pre-teen Walker would lead Blind Lemon Jefferson around the Dallas streets. He taught himself guitar and worked streets and functions until he toured with various travelling shows in the mid- to late 1920s. He made his recording debut for Columbia in 1929 ('Trinity River Blues'/'Wichita Falls Blues') as Oak Cliff T-Bone. The name T-Bone is a phonetic corruption of his middle name.

Walker worked locally with artists as diverse as Cab Calloway and Ma Rainey before moving to the Los Angeles area in 1934, where he worked his own combo at the Little Harlem Club and gradually built a following. He recorded one title ('T-Bone Blues') with the Les Hite orchestra and worked with that band on tours through Chicago and New York for much of 1939–40. He returned to the Little Harlem Club, where he reformed his own group. He played guitar on a record date with Freddie Slack's orchestra in July 1942 and, at the end of the date, recorded two songs ('Mean Old World'/'I Got A Break Baby') for Capitol Records. On the strength of that record he began to tour and to work whites-only clubs in Hollywood. He made frequent stops at the Rhumboogie club in Chicago from 1942–45 and in 1945 he made recordings for the Rhumboogie and Mercury labels.

'I believe that it all comes originally from T-Bone Walker. B.B. King and I were talking about that not long ago and he thinks so, too.'
Freddie King

Above
A versatile musician, Walker (left) is pictured here with jazz greats Dizzy Gillespie (seated) and James Moody.

Black & White

In September 1946, Walker signed an exclusive contract with Black & White Records and worked with producer Ralph Bass. He recorded 49 titles in the next 15 months, among which were all his bestsellers. He had hit records with such well-remembered titles as 'Call It Stormy Monday' and 'T-Bone Shuffle'. He became a national touring attraction and his acrobatic stunts, such as playing the guitar behind his head and doing the splits on stage, helped him to become a major star. Because of the second AFM recording ban, Walker could not make any new recordings during

see Introduction pp 142 *see* Sources & Sounds pp 144 *see* A–Z of Artists pp 170

Left
T-Bone Walker, electric guitar pioneer and great showman.

Below
Walker performing at London's Hammersmith Odeon in December 1970.

1948, but the large stockpile of sides he had recorded provided new releases into 1950. Black & White had gone out of business in 1948 and the masters had been acquired by Capitol.

In the spring of 1950, he signed with Imperial Records. Of the 52 titles he recorded over the next four years there were no national hits, but the music is of a high quality. He signed with Atlantic in 1955 and, once again, there were no big sellers but a considerable amount of memorable music. He continued to tour nationally while headquartered in Los Angeles.

An International Star

In 1962, Walker went to Europe with the American Folk Blues Festival and developed a circuit for himself that led to frequent visits overseas; he was now a part of the American festival scene as well. He freelanced his recording deals and recorded for a variety of labels in a number of countries. His Polydor album *Good Feelin'* (1969) won a Grammy award in 1970. He continued to tour and record until shortly before his death.

Walker was a smooth blues singer with some of the qualities of a crooner, but it was his guitar work that made him such an important artist. He was an influence, to some degree, on almost all of the key guitarists of the post-Second World War generation. His sound, his unhurried phrasing and his self-editing ability are hallmarks of his style. T-Bone Walker certainly never overstayed his welcome.

see Ma Rainey pp 24 *see* Blind Lemon Jefferson pp 56 *see* Cab Calloway pp 122 *see* Dizzy Gillespie pp 152

A-Z of Artists

Far Right
Vocalist and pianist Charles Brown was a legendary performer.

Right
Bandleader Charlie Barnet contributed to the racial integration of jazz music.

Below
Earl Bostic, whose bands included future stars such as John Coltrane.

Charlie Barnet

(Various saxophones, 1913–91)

Charlie Barnet led a successful big band from 1933 until the late 1940s and was one of the earliest white bandleaders to employ black musicians, beginning with Benny Carter as a guest soloist and arranger in 1934. He introduced singer Lena Horne as an unknown in 1941 and featured many notable musicians in his line-ups. His style was based on an energized Basie-like riff formula, but he was also an undisguised admirer of Duke Ellington, and attempted to graft elements of the Ellington band's sophisticated harmonies into his own band arrangements.

He is best remembered for Billy May's arrangement of the much-covered 'Cherokee' in 1939, but enjoyed a number of hits with other riff-based favourites, including 'Pompton Turnpike' and 'Redskin Rhumba', both from 1940. Like Harry James, he attempted to move into acting, and was also involved in the restaurant business, but continued to perform intermittently until the 1970s.

Mario Bauzá

(Trumpet, 1911–93)

Mario Bauzá takes a large amount of credit for bringing music from his native Cuba into jazz. He worked with Noble Sissle and Chick Webb in New York in the 1930s before teaming up with Machito. While with Cab Calloway in 1939–40 he sparked Dizzy Gillespie's interest in Cuban music, which eventually led to 'Cubop'. He was musical director of Machito's Afro-Cubans for 35 years (1940–75), after which he formed his own group.

Earl Bostic

(Alto saxophone, 1913–65)

Earl Bostic was a soulful alto saxophonist from Tulsa who won a wide following in the late 1940s and 1950s for his accessible but technically accomplished style. He served a big band apprenticeship as a player and arranger, but then reinvented himself in more populist mode and made a series of bestselling records in the wake of his big 1951 hit 'Flamingo'. His bands nurtured future stars, including John Coltrane, Benny Golson and Stanley Turrentine.

Charles Brown

(Piano, vocals, 1922–99)

Charles Mose Brown was born in Texas City, Texas and had extensive classical piano training as a youth. He moved to Los Angeles in 1943 and by September 1944 had become the vocalist-pianist in Johnny Moore's Three Blazers. The Blazers had several hits before Brown went solo in 1948 and scored success with songs such as 'Trouble Blues' (1949) and 'Black Night' (1951). As a vocalist, Brown was equally at

see Introduction pp 142 *see* Sources & Sounds pp 144 *see* Key Artists pp 152

home with ballads and blues. He regained international renown later in his life and continued to record up until his death.

Roy Brown

(Vocals, 1925–81)

Roy James Brown was born in New Orleans and raised in Texas and Louisiana. A strong blues shouter, Brown was one of the first stars of New Orleans R&B. He led his own group, Roy Brown & his Mighty, Mighty Men, and wrote most of the material he recorded. He began recording for DeLuxe in 1947 in New Orleans, and had hit records with 'Long About Midnight' (1948), 'Rockin' At Midnight' (1949) and 'Hard Luck Blues' (1950).

Big Sid Catlett

(Drums, 1910–51)

Catlett was one of the most well-respected and versatile jazz drummers of the 1930s and 1940s. He played in a variety of ensembles under such luminaries as Benny Carter, Fletcher Henderson, Benny Goodman and Duke Ellington, before going on to join Louis Armstrong's All-Stars. Catlett's remarkable adaptability enabled him to play in a wide range of styles and he also successfully bridged the gap into bebop, contributing to an early Charlie Parker–Dizzy Gillespie session.

George Chisholm

(Trombone, 1915–97)

Scottish-born George Chisholm made his name as a top-class traditional jazz trombone player, but also played piano and several other brass instruments. He started out in Glasgow dance bands before moving to London, where he became an accomplished bandleader and arranger, and a successful television personality in comedy shows in the 1960s. Notable jazz associations included the RAF's famous wartime band the Squadronaires, Kenny Baker's Dozen, the Alex Welsh Band, and his own Gentlemen of Jazz.

see Duke Ellington pp 52  *see* Benny Carter pp 122 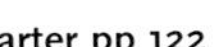 *see* Machito pp 178 *see* John Coltrane pp 250

Kenny Clarke

(Drums, 1914–85)

Kenny 'Klook' Clarke was a native of Pittsburgh, but made his primary contribution to jazz in New York in the early flowerings of bebop. Clarke, who adopted the Muslim faith as Liaquat Ali Salaam in 1946, is widely credited with developing the new rhythmic concepts that fuelled bebop. His work with Dizzy Gillespie and especially Thelonious Monk at Minton's in Harlem in the early 1940s laid the foundation for the move away from the persistently stated two- and four-beat emphasis on the bass drum.

Swing era drummers had already experimented with a lighter and more fluid approach to rhythmic accents, but Clarke developed that concept to new heights, using crisp punctuations on bass drum – known as 'dropping bombs' – to accent his rolling ride cymbal. He was drafted to serve in Europe in 1943–46, and eventually settled in Paris in 1956, where his many associations included the acclaimed Kenny Clarke-Francy Boland Big Band.

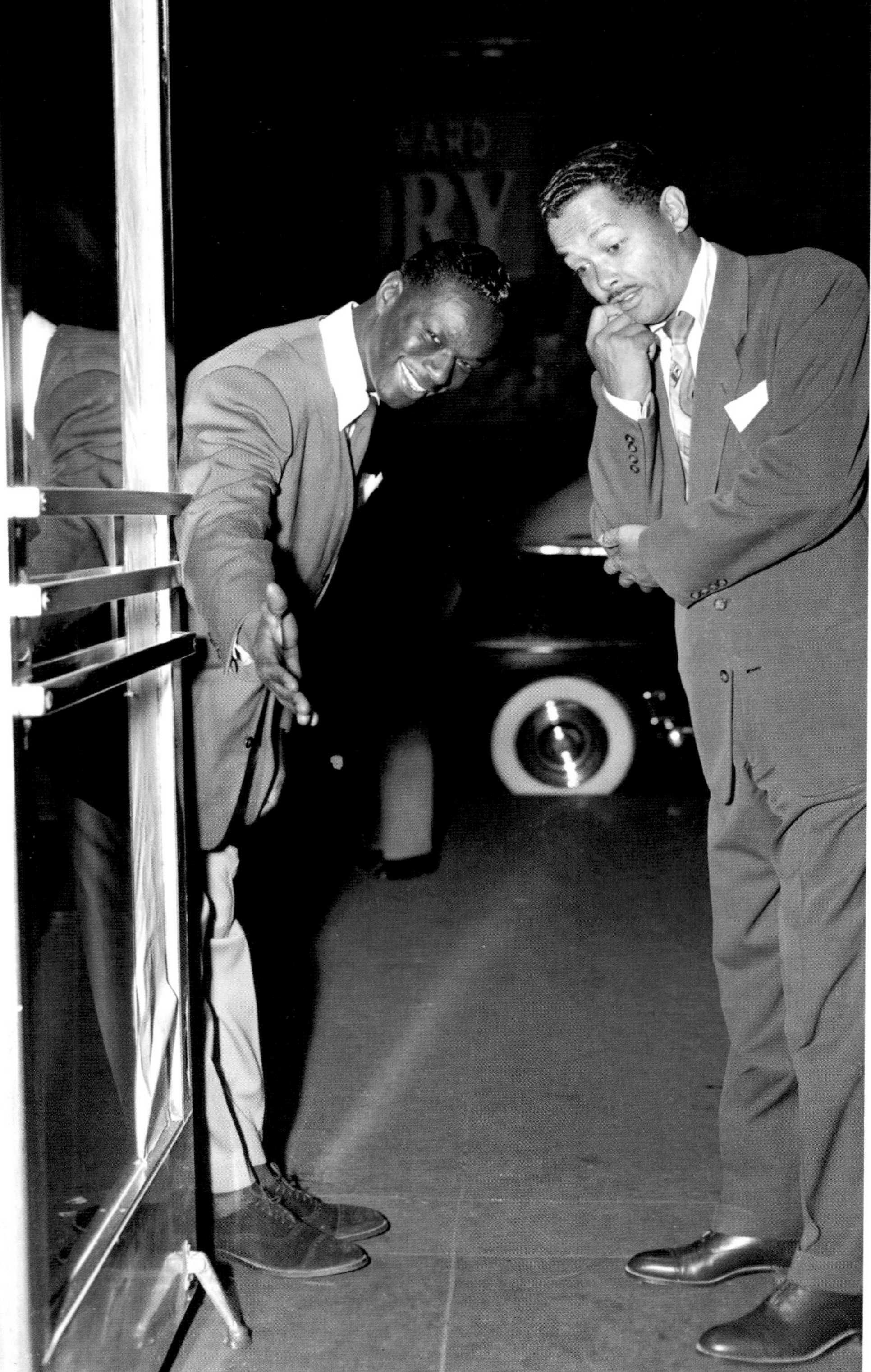

Nat 'King' Cole

(Piano, vocals, 1917–65)

Nat 'King' Cole (real name Coles) was one of the few jazz artists to become a household name as a popular singer, and was one of the first black American artists to have his own radio show (1948–49), and later television show (1956–57). He was born into a musical family in Alabama, but moved to Chicago at the age of four, where he learned piano by ear, before studying music formally as a teenager.

He formed a trio with Oscar Moore (guitar) and Wesley Prince (drums) that became the model for many subsequent groups, including Oscar Peterson's trio. However, a vocal hit with 'Straighten Up And Fly Right' in 1943 set him on a different career path as a sophisticated pop singer. His fame as a vocalist and his later celebrity have tended to overshadow the fact that he was also a very fine and influential jazz pianist in trio and quartet settings.

Arthur 'Big Boy' Crudup

(Guitar, vocals, 1905–74)

Arthur William Crudup was born in Forest, Mississippi and did not learn to play the guitar until his 30s. He worked functions in the Clarksdale area before moving to Chicago in 1940, signing with Bluebird in 1941 and finding considerable popularity on record. He returned to Mississippi after the Second World War and worked locally with Rice Miller and Elmore James. Crudup is

see Introduction pp 142 *see* Sources & Sounds pp 144 *see* Key Artists pp 152

Buddy DeFranco

(Clarinet, b. 1923)

Buddy DeFranco (Boniface Ferdinand Leonardo) became the leading clarinet player of the post-swing era. His liquid sonority and flowing improvisations drew on elements from both swing and bebop, but without settling fully in either camp. He served a big-band apprenticeship with Gene Krupa, Charlie Barnet and Tommy Dorsey in the mid-1940s, but is best known for his work in smaller groups with vibist Terry Gibbs, bands led by George Shearing and Count Basie, and for leading his own groups.

Far Left
Pianist and vocalist Nat 'King' Cole (left) larks about with singer Billy Eckstine.

Left
Arthur 'Big Boy' Crudup, whose compositions were covered to great effect by Elvis Presley.

Below
Rev. Gary Davis's playing style derived from the southeastern Piedmont region.

perhaps best remembered as an outstanding blues songwriter; several of his tunes, such as 'That's All Right' and 'My Baby Left Me', were covered by pop and rock stars, notably Elvis Presley.

Rev. Gary Davis

(Guitar, harmonica, banjo, vocals, 1896–1972)

Gary D. Davis was born in Laurens, South Carolina and was completely blind by the age of 30. He taught himself harmonica, banjo and guitar and played in string bands throughout the teens, going on to work the Carolinas as a street singer in the 1920s. Ordained as a Baptist minister, he performed mostly religious songs after 1937. Davis began recording regularly in the mid-1950s after a move to New York. His unique guitar playing shows traces of ragtime, blues and other early music. He stands with Blind Blake as the finest of Piedmont-area guitar stylists.

see Count Basie pp 102 *see* Gene Krupa pp 128 *see* Thelonious Monk pp 208 *see* Elmore James pp 226

Champion Jack Dupree

(Piano, vocals, 1910–92)

William Thomas Dupree was born in New Orleans. He was raised in the Colored Waifs Home for Boys from infancy. He learned piano at an early age and in the 1920s worked barrelhouses as a soloist, as well as playing with traditional jazz bands. From the early 1930s, he worked as a prizefighter and took occasional music jobs. Dupree was discovered in Chicago and signed to OKeh records in 1940. Among those early sides were the first recordings of 'Junker's Blues' and 'Cabbage Greens'.

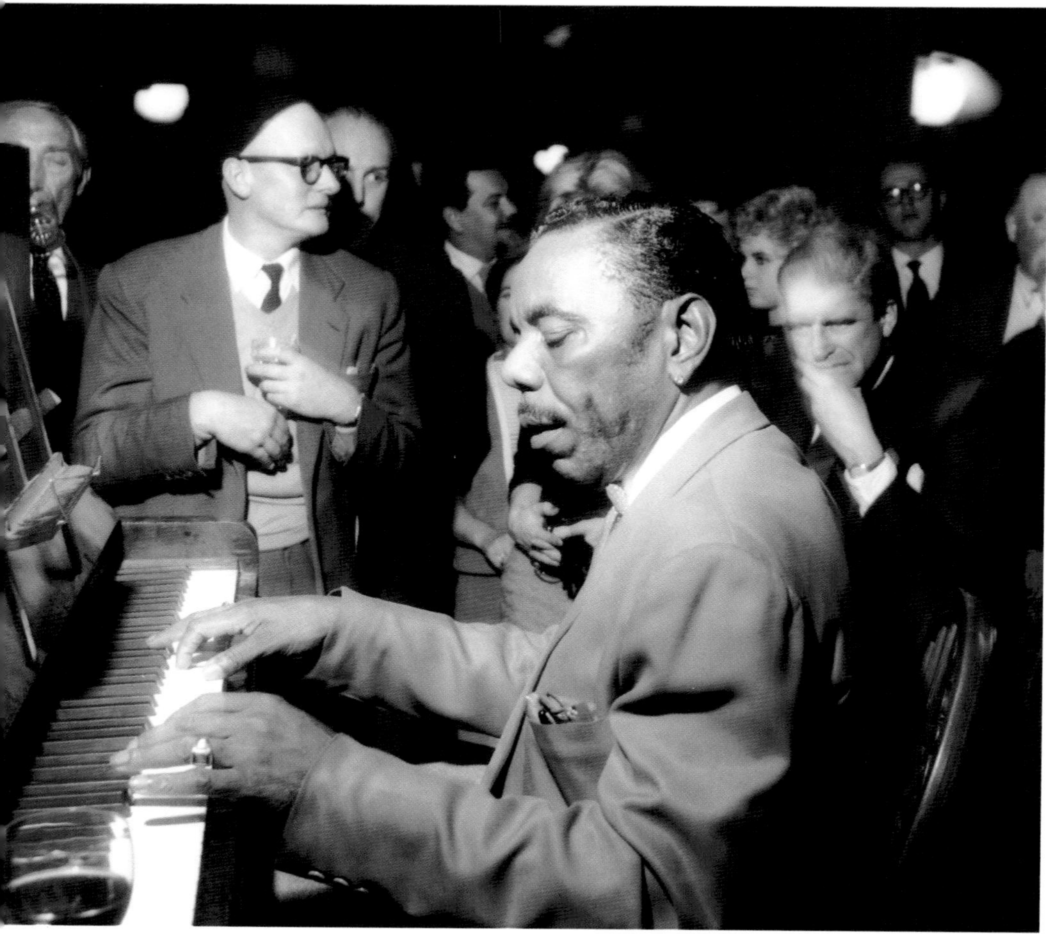

Above
Boxer turned pianist Champion Jack Dupree brought a rowdy and humorous style to the blues scene.

After US Navy service, Dupree settled in New York and recorded for several small labels, including Joe Davis, Continental and Apollo, often in the company of Brownie McGhee. He became known for his strong, two-fisted piano and for his humorous songs and vocals. Dupree settled in Switzerland in 1960 and became one of the most visible blues artists in Europe over the next 30 years.

Billy Eckstine

(Vocals, 1914–93)

Billy Eckstine's smooth baritone voice and suave manner brought his music to a wide audience. He joined pianist Earl Hines in Chicago in 1939 and then led a big band from 1944–47 that many see as the cradle of bebop, although few recordings survive. He was one of the few black singers to be featured on national radio, largely thanks to his beguiling romantic ballads. He remained a draw on the cabaret circuit in later years.

Lloyd Glenn

(Piano, arranger, 1909–85)

Lloyd Colquitt Glenn Sr. was born and raised in San Antonio, Texas. He worked with several southwestern territory bands before joining Don Albert in 1934 in the role of pianist and chief arranger. He moved to California in the early 1940s. Glenn became the prototype of the studio pianist-arranger for blues and R&B record dates while working on sessions for T-Bone Walker, Lowell Fulson and others. A fine blues and boogie-woogie pianist, Glenn recorded hit instrumentals for Swingtime ('Old Time Shuffle Blues' and 'Chica Boo') in 1950–51.

Dexter Gordon

(Tenor and soprano saxophone, 1923–90)

Dexter Gordon is widely credited as the leading figure in the evolution of bebop on his instrument, the tenor saxophone. The Los Angeles native was influenced initially by stars of the swing era, in particular Lester Young, and went on to adapt many of Charlie Parker's alto saxophone innovations to the tenor. He was a notable exponent of the so-called 'chase' form, in which two tenors 'duel' for supremacy; he recorded a famous example with Wardell Gray as 'The Chase' (1947) and was also an inspired interpreter of ballads.

His career took a disastrous drug-induced dip in the 1950s, but he relocated to Europe and returned to music with renewed vigour in the 1960s, in a series of acclaimed recordings for Blue Note Records. He made a triumphal return to America in 1977, and went on to star in Bertrand Tavernier's film *Round Midnight* (1986).

see Introduction pp 142 *see* Sources & Sounds pp 144 *see* Key Artists pp 152

Wardell Gray

(Tenor saxophone, 1921–55)

Wardell Gray died in mysterious, drug-related circumstances without fulfilling his immense potential. His control and invention at fast tempos and fluent, swinging style on the tenor saxophone adapted readily to both swing and bebop settings, while his ballad playing was strong in both emotion and tonal warmth. His sadly underweight recorded legacy is largely derived from live club dates and jam sessions, plus the two volumes of studio recordings issued by Prestige as *Wardell Gray Memorial*. Singer Annie Ross (and later Joni Mitchell) made vocalese hits based on his solos.

Wynonie Harris

(Vocals, 1913–69)

Raised in Omaha, Nebraska, Wynonie Harris first came to prominence in the Lucky Millinder Orchestra of 1944, where he had a number-one Race Chart hit, 'Who Threw The Whiskey In The Well'. A leather-lunged shouter in the Big Joe Turner tradition, Harris had a long successful run on King records (1947–57), which produced huge hits such as 'Good Rockin' Tonight' and 'All She Wants To Do Is Rock' as well as a wealth of other material of a consistently high standard. He specialized in raunchy, risqué songs, but was rarely active in the last few years of his life.

Helen Humes

(Vocals, 1909–81)

Helen Elizabeth Humes was born in Louisville, Kentucky and made her recording debut for OKeh in 1927. She spent 1938–41 in the Count Basie Orchestra, singing mostly ballads. She moved to California in 1945 and recorded for many different labels while working as a solo artist. She had solid hits with 'Be Baba Leba' in 1945 and 'Million Dollar Secret' in 1950. A versatile singer, Humes had a sweet voice and could adapt to almost any material. She returned to her music in the 1970s after a 10-year absence, and remained active until her death.

Bull Moose Jackson

(Tenor saxophone, vocals, 1919–89)

Benjamin Joseph Jackson was born in Cleveland, Ohio and replaced Wynonie Harris as male vocalist with the Lucky Millinder Orchestra in 1945. From 1947 until the late 1950s he toured with his own group, the Buffalo Bearcats. He recorded for Queen/King from 1945; among his biggest hits were 'I Love You, Yes I Do', 'I Can't Go On Without You', 'Little Girl, Don't Cry' and 'Why Don't You Haul Off And Love Me'. Jackson alternated ballads, jump tunes and risqué novelties, as well as occasionally recording instrumentals featuring his saxophone.

Below

Saxophonists Wardell Gray (left) and Dexter Gordon act out their 1947 hit 'The Chase'.

see Earl Hines pp 126 *see* Charlie Parker pp 162 *see* Big Joe Turner pp 166 *see* Brownie McGhee pp 179

Harry James

(Trumpet, 1916–83)

Harry James grew up in a circus and went on to become a media celebrity as a bandleader, a fame that only intensified when he married actress Betty Grable in 1943. James made his initial reputation as a formidable trumpet player with Benny Goodman's band before forming his own group in 1938, but lost some of his credibility with jazz fans when he began to work in a more populist, romantic ballad style in the 1940s.

His playing was admired by his major influences, Louis Armstrong and Bunk Johnson, and his combination of musical invention with bravura technique remained highly impressive throughout his career. He returned to more directly jazz-oriented band arrangements in the 1950s and continued to lead big bands. An inveterate womanizer and compulsive gambler, he worked in Las Vegas for many years from 1963, where his proceeds went straight back into the casinos.

Above

Trumpeter Harry James's admiration of Louis Armstrong and Bunk Johnson was mutual.

J.J. Johnson

(Trombone, arranger, composer, 1924–2001)

J.J. (James Louis) Johnson was the premier bebop trombonist. His speed of execution and fluent, highly inventive approach to both melody and rhythm essentially devised a new language for an instrument that was not obviously made to suit the wide intervals and rapid articulation of the style. He took up trombone in high school in Indianapolis, and honed his craft in swing bands before turning to bebop in the mid-1940s.

He worked with virtually all the great jazz names of the bebop era, including Dizzy Gillespie and Charlie Parker. He was part of Miles Davis's so-called 'Birth Of The Cool' project in 1949–50 and the later 'third stream' experiments initiated by John Lewis and Gunther Schuller in the late 1950s. He co-led a very successful group with Danish trombonist Kai Winding (1954–56). He was a fine composer of film and television music as well as jazz.

Louis Jordan

(Alto saxophone, vocals, bandleader, 1908–75)

Louis Jordan & his Tympany Five were major stars in the 1940s, providing energized recordings and exciting live shows. The alto saxophonist began by playing in

see Introduction pp 142 *see* Sources & Sounds pp 144 *see* Key Artists pp 152

Left
Louis Jordan combined elements of jazz and blues to create a feel-good jump-blues sound.

swing bands, including Chick Webb's, but in 1938 he gambled on the success of his own personality, fronting a small group playing in a more overtly entertaining style. Labelled 'jump blues', this was a precursor of both R&B and rock'n'roll.

He reeled off a succession of jukebox hits through the 1940s, often with novelty titles and lyrics, including 'Five Guys Named Mo', 'Choo Choo Ch'Boogie', 'Ain't Nobody Here But Us Chickens' and 'Saturday Night Fish Fry'. Their appeal, based on melodic good humour and the comic complications of romance, crossed racial boundaries, and his popularity lasted until the early 1950s. Eclipsed by the rise of rock'n'roll, he reverted to more jazz-oriented settings and continued to perform on the cabaret circuit in later years.

Stan Kenton

(Piano, arranger, composer, 1911–79)

Stan Kenton pushed big-band jazz in new directions throughout his career, and in the process divided critical opinion more radically than any other bandleader. He formed his first band in 1940, which became the Artistry in Rhythm Orchestra in 1942. Imaginative arrangements and excellent soloists ensured the band's success. It gave way to the more ambitious Progressive Jazz Orchestra in 1947 and the even more overblown, 43-piece Innovations in Modern Music Orchestra in 1950.

The latter band often featured startling arrangements (notably those by the iconoclastic Bob Graettinger), but fell foul of economic feasibility. Kenton led more standard-sized big bands throughout the 1950s, featuring a galaxy of star players. His expanded groups of the 1960s included the symphonically conceived Los Angeles Neophonic Orchestra. Although uneven in their output, Kenton's bands made a unique contribution to big-band history, and he was also influential as a jazz educator.

Below
Pianist Stan Kenton divided critical opinion with his ambitious big-band innovations.

see Louis Armstrong pp 44 *see* Benny Goodman pp 110 *see* Dizzy Gillespie pp 152 *see* Miles Davis pp 200

Barney Kessel

(Guitar, 1923–2004)

Barney Kessel took inspiration from his fellow Oklahoman, guitarist Charlie Christian, and developed an electric-guitar style that straddled swing and bop in effective fashion. He was featured in the Oscar-nominated short film *Jammin' The Blues* (1944), and recorded with Charlie Parker in 1947. A stint with the Oscar Peterson Trio in 1952–53 led to recordings as a leader from 1953 onwards. Kessel formed Great Guitars with Herb Ellis and Charlie Byrd in 1973; they toured and recorded until his debilitating stroke in 1992.

Below

Esther Phillips, a.k.a. Little Esther, who had several big R&B hits.

Little Esther

(Vocals, 1935–84)

Esther Mae Washington was born in Galveston, Texas. She moved to the Los Angeles area at the age of five and in 1949 was discovered by Johnny Otis. Her first recording with Otis, 'Double Crossing Blues', was a number-one R&B hit in 1950. In that year the pair had two more number ones on the R&B chart, 'Mistrustin' Blues' and 'Cupid's Boogie'. On her own after 1951, Esther continued to record but her career suffered ups and downs due to her narcotics addiction. As Esther Phillips, she returned in 1962 with yet another R&B number-one, 'Release Me', and other hits.

Machito

(Vocals, maracas, c. 1912–84)

Frank Raul Grillo was born in Florida of Cuban extraction and took the name Machito in 1940 when his brother-in-law, trumpet player Mario Bauzá, reorganized his year-old band the Afro-Cubans. Their arrangements clothed Cuban melodies and rhythms in jazz harmonies and instrumental voicings. They were highly influential in the emergence of Afro-Cuban jazz (sometimes known as 'Cubop') in the late 1940s, in the mambo craze of the 1950s and the development of modern salsa and Latin jazz.

Right

Machito, whose band the Afro-Cubans was influential in the 1940s Cubop movement.

see Introduction pp 142 *see* Sources & Sounds pp 144 *see* Key Artists pp 152

Brownie McGhee

(Guitar, vocals, 1915–96)

Walter Brown McGhee was born in Knoxville, Tennessee. He learned to play guitar before his tenth birthday and dropped out of school to play throughout the state in the late 1920s. He met Sonny Terry in 1939 and they joined forces almost immediately. McGhee began recording for OKeh in 1940 and moved to New York.

McGhee recorded on his own (without Terry) for several labels, notably Savoy. He was recorded in an R&B context throughout 1948–58, in addition to his own Piedmont-style acoustic blues and duets with Terry. The duo appeared in the Tennessee Williams Broadway drama *Cat On A Hot Tin Roof* from 1955–57 and toured England in 1958, going on to become regular visitors to Europe. McGhee continued to make his own recordings during the folk-blues revival of the early 1960s and the duo continued into the mid-1970s.

Big Jay McNeely

(Tenor saxophone, b. 1927)

Cecil James McNeely was born and raised in Los Angeles. Inspired by Illinois Jacquet, McNeely played in high school with future jazz stars Sonny Criss and Hampton Hawes. He was discovered by Johnny Otis and made his recording debut in 1948 with a number-one hit, 'Deacon's Hop'. He had another hit in 1959 with 'There Is Something On Your Mind'. A stomping, screaming wildman, McNeely was the quintessential showboating saxophonist of the 1950s.

Jay McShann

(Piano, vocals, 1916–2006)

James Columbus McShann was born in Muskogee, Oklahoma and moved to Kansas City in 1936. He formed a big band in 1940 and recorded for Decca in 1941–43. The band featured vocalist Walter Brown and alto saxophonist Charlie Parker, and had a big hit with 'Confessin' The Blues'. McShann had a hit record on Vee Jay in 1955 with 'Hands Off' and continued to work in the Kansas City area. Prominently featured in the film *Last of the Blue Devils* (1980), McShann was a masterful pianist with equal parts jazz and blues in his style.

Memphis Slim

(Piano, vocals, 1915–88)

John Len Chatman was born in Memphis, Tennessee. He moved to Chicago in 1937, where he worked with Big Bill Broonzy. He began recording in 1940 and formed his band, the House Rockers, after the Second World War. He had several hits on the Miracle label in 1948–49, including 'Messin' Around' and 'Blue And Lonesome'. A prolific recording artist and first-rate blues pianist, Slim was also a songwriter and wrote most of his own material. He went to Europe in 1962 with the American Folk Blues Festival and settled in Paris.

Amos Milburn

(Piano, vocals, 1927–80)

Joseph Amos Milburn Jr. was born in Houston, Texas, and he began recording in 1946 for Aladdin records. Milburn was an exceptionally popular performer between the late 1940s and mid-1950s, with number-one R&B hits such as 'Chicken Shack Boogie', 'Bewildered' and 'Roomin' House Boogie' (all 1948–49). Beginning in 1949, he toured and recorded with his own band, the Aladdin Chickenshackers, and continued his string of hits with 'Bad, Bad Whiskey' and 'One Scotch, One Bourbon, One Beer'. The success of the latter inspired a series of songs with liquor-related themes.

Milburn was a superb pianist, equally at home with slow blues, rolling boogie-woogie, ballad material, novelties and jump blues. He worked frequently with Charles Brown in the late 1950s but became inactive in music after a stroke in 1970.

Below
Amos Milburn, a supremely talented blues pianist and adaptable singer.

see Charlie Christian pp 106 *see* Charlie Parker pp 162 *see* Mario Bauzá pp 170 *see* Sonny Terry pp 183

Glenn Miller

(Trombone, 1904–44)

Glenn Miller was a trombonist of modest accomplishments, but he became one of the most famous big-band leaders in jazz. Although disdained by jazz purists, tunes such as 'In The Mood', 'Moonlight Serenade', 'String Of Pearls' and 'Tuxedo Junction' have remained enduringly popular. Miller's bands played precisely executed riff-based swing tunes and very slow ballads; his signature sound was built on a lead clarinet melody doubled an octave below by tenor saxophone, with the other saxophones, muted trumpets, and trombones all adding soft-focus colour and harmony.

Above

James Moody was one of the first artists to gain kudos for the flute as a jazz instrument.

Miller favoured solid, well-disciplined players who could deliver the exact sound that he required on the arrangements, rather than flamboyant jazz soloists. His catchy melodies, intricate but easy-on-the-ear harmonies and swinging rhythms caught the public imagination; his disappearance in a light aircraft over the English Channel en route to a concert scheduled for his Allied Expeditionary Force Orchestra only added to the mystique.

Roy Milton

(Drums, vocals, 1907–83)

Roy Bunny Milton was born in Wynnewood, Oklahoma. He had his own bands before moving to Los Angeles in 1935, where he formed the Solid Senders combo in 1938 and worked small clubs throughout the city. He began recording in 1945 and had a lengthy relationship with Specialty records throughout 1946–54, which produced such hits as 'R.M. Blues', 'Information Blues' and 'Best Wishes'. The Solid Senders featured pianist Camille Howard and three horns along with the leader's simple yet sincere vocals. The band could handle swing, jump tunes or slow blues.

James Moody

(Tenor and alto saxophone, flute, b. 1925)

James Moody was one of the strongest performers to double on flute in jazz, and was a resourceful and inventive improviser on all his horns. He joined Dizzy Gillespie from the US Air Force in 1946. A recording of 'I'm In The Mood For Love' (1949), made while living in Europe from 1948–51, brought him to a wider audience. He led his own bands in the US from the early 1950s, including a popular septet featuring vocalist Eddie Jefferson (1953–62), in which he often sang a passage of the lyrics in falsetto. Moody continues to tour and record.

Fats Navarro

(Trumpet, 1923–50)

Theodore 'Fats' Navarro died prematurely and left a limited recorded legacy, most of it as a sideman. Nonetheless, he stood alongside Dizzy Gillespie and Miles Davis as one of the most significant trumpeters in bebop. He took over Gillespie's chair in Billy Eckstine's seminal big band in 1945, and enjoyed a brief but creative relationship with pianist and arranger Tadd Dameron in 1948.

Although curtailed, his career saw him work with most of the major bebop artists, including Kenny Clarke, Coleman Hawkins, Dexter Gordon, Bud Powell and Charlie Parker. His conservative approach to rhythm was balanced by carefully sculpted melody lines and a wealth of harmonic invention, while his burnished tone had a sweetness and richness

 *see* Introduction pp 142 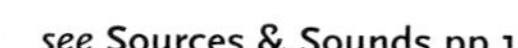 *see* Sources & Sounds pp 144  *see* Key Artists pp 152

Left
Trumpeter Fats Navarro's impressive tonal range was unusual in a bebop player.

unusual among the bebop speed merchants. His recordings for Blue Note as a sideman were gathered in two volumes as *The Fabulous Fats Navarro* (1947). He died of tuberculosis, exacerbated by his heroin addiction.

Robert Nighthawk

(Guitar, vocals, 1909–67)

Robert Lee McCollum was born in Helena, Arkansas. He was taught guitar by his cousin, Houston Stackhouse, in 1930. He moved to St. Louis in 1934, now calling himself Robert McCoy, and first recorded in 1937 on acoustic guitar. He took the name Robert Nighthawk and used it professionally from the early 1940s. Nighthawk had converted to electric guitar by the time he recorded for Aristocrat/Chess from 1948–50. He was a master of the electric slide guitar and his work was influential on future slide stylists such as Muddy Waters and Earl Hooker.

Chico O'Farrill

(Trumpet, composer, arranger, 1921–2001)

Arturo 'Chico' O'Farrill arrived in New York from Havana in 1948 with a self-confessed low opinion of his native Cuban music by comparison with jazz, but found inspiration in the developing Afro-Cuban jazz movement led by Dizzy Gillespie, Machito and Mario Bauzá. He became a key figure in creating what he called the 'very delicate marriage' of Cuban music with jazz. His 'Afro-Cuban Jazz Suite' (1950) is a watershed work and launched a long and successful career. His son, Arturo, is also a major bandleader in Latin jazz.

Sy Oliver

(Trumpet, vocals, arranger, composer, 1910–88)

Sy (Melvin James) Oliver was one of the finest of all big-band arrangers, and a capable instrumentalist and singer as well. His major associations included the bands of Jimmie Lunceford, Benny Goodman and Tommy Dorsey, and he also led his own bands at various times, from the mid-1940s into the 1980s. He worked as music director and arranger for several record companies, as well as filling that role for the New York Jazz Repertory Orchestra in the mid-1970s.

Johnny Otis

(Drums, vibes, vocals, b. 1921)

John Alexander Veliotes, born in Vallejo, California, started as a drummer and formed a big band in 1945. By 1947, Otis had switched to a seven- or eight-piece group. This was one of the earliest R&B combos to tour; the Johnny Otis Rhythm & Blues Caravan included vocalists Little Esther, Mel Walker and the Robins, and scored 10 entries on the R&B charts in 1950 alone. During the 1950s, Otis worked for record labels as an arranger and producer. He introduced Big Mama Thornton, produced vocalist Etta James and recorded with ill-fated singer Johnny Ace.

Below
An elaborate publicity shot for the Johnny Otis Orchestra's single 'The Jelly Roll'.

see Tommy Dorsey pp 123 *see* Dizzy Gillespie pp 152 *see* Billy Eckstine pp 174 *see* Little Esther pp 178

Chano Pozo

(Drums, percussion, 1915–48)

Cuban percussionist Chano Pozo was Dizzy Gillespie's principal collaborator in melding Cuban music with jazz (a.k.a. 'Cubop'). Their historic 1947 recordings 'Manteca' and 'Cubana Be, Cubana Bop' (co-written with George Russell) were the first to integrate real Afro-Cuban polyrhythms within a bop idiom. Their association proved brief; Pozo was shot dead in a bar in Harlem in mysterious circumstances shortly after the recordings were made, but the Afro-Cuban fusion sound remained a significant element in Gillespie's music throughout his career.

Below

Buddy Rich was a virtuoso drummer, equally adept at playing swing and bebop styles.

Sammy Price

(Piano, 1908–92)

Samuel Blythe Price was born in Honey Grove, Texas. His recording debut came in 1929. In 1938 he moved to New York and became the pianist for Decca Records blues sessions. In this capacity – in addition to making his own recordings – he accompanied Blue Lu Barker, Johnny Temple and Sister Rosetta Tharpe, among others. From 1948 Price played in France on a regular basis and made frequent recordings for European labels – as a piano soloist, with jazz bands and with blues singers.

Buddy Rich

(Drums, 1917–87)

Bernard 'Buddy' Rich was a powerhouse drummer with a phenomenal technique, but he was also capable of great delicacy when required. He grew up in the family vaudeville act before joining Joe Marsala's band in 1937. It was the beginning of a series of associations with major swing era bandleaders such as Harry James, Artie Shaw, Tommy Dorsey, Benny Carter and – as a deputy for Jo Jones – Count Basie.

He formed his own band in 1945 and also recorded with major bebop artists Charlie Parker, Dizzy Gillespie and Bud Powell. He worked with James again in the 1950s and 1960s, led a small group, and tried unsuccessfully to establish a career as a singer. He formed a new and much more successful big band of his own from the mid-1960s until 1974, then led a small group and ran his own club. A third big band followed, and Rich enjoyed a high profile, through television appearances, until his death.

Max Roach

(Drums, b. 1924)

Along with Kenny Clarke, Max Roach shares the credit for inventing bebop drumming. When Clarke found himself drafted in 1943, it was Roach who emerged as the leading activist in the search for a drum style to suit the emerging melodic and harmonic complexities of the new music. He developed an approach that was both powerful and flexible enough to match the invention of Charlie Parker or Dizzy Gillespie, while at the same time elevating the drummer to equal status with the front-line soloists for the first time in jazz.

He founded Debut Records with Charles Mingus in 1952 and went on to establish himself as a major bandleader in his own right, beginning in 1954 with a famous group co-led with trumpeter Clifford Brown. He has remained a creative force through decades of stylistic shifts in jazz and has continued to absorb new influences into his ever-evolving music.

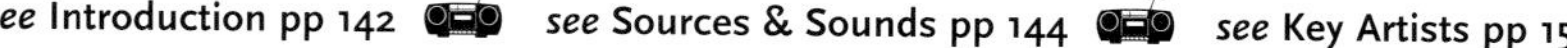
see Introduction pp 142 *see* Sources & Sounds pp 144 *see* Key Artists pp 152

George Russell

(Composer, arranger, b. 1923)

Cincinnati-born George Russell is one of a small number of jazz musicians whose primary reputation was earned as a composer and theoretician rather than as an instrumentalist. Initially a student of drums and later a pianist, Russell ultimately limited his onstage contribution to conducting, albeit in the style of a consummate showman. He framed the basic structure of his lifelong work on *The Lydian Chromatic Concept Of Tonal Organization* while hospitalized in 1945–46, and published the first version of that modally based theory in 1953, with several subsequent revisions. Its influence has been vast.

Russell composed and arranged for Dizzy Gillespie, Buddy DeFranco and Lee Konitz in the late 1940s, and began to record as a leader in 1956. His small-ensemble recordings of 1960–62 were followed by equally impressive big-band projects. He spent 1963–69 in Europe, mentoring Scandinavian musicians, and then accepted a professorship at the New England Conservatory. He won a prestigious MacArthur Fellowship in 1989.

Hal Singer

(Tenor saxophone, b. 1919)

Harold Singer was born in Tulsa, Oklahoma. He worked with territory bands in the late 1930s and went to New York with Roy Eldridge in 1944. Singer worked around New York, playing on sessions for King and Savoy, during 1946–59. His own recording career began in 1948 and he had a number-one hit with 'Cornbread', the first big record of the honking R&B tenor style. He frequently toured with his own groups and with R&B shows during 1948–58, and by the late 1950s he was playing jazz as often as R&B. He relocated to Paris in 1965 and has recorded frequently for European labels.

Sonny Terry

(Harmonica, vocals, 1911–86)

Saunders Terrell was born in Greensboro, Georgia and taught himself to play the harmonica at the age of eight. He lost the sight in one eye, aged 10, and the second eye at 16. Terry played mostly in North Carolina from the late 1920s. He teamed up with Blind Boy Fuller in 1934 and recorded with him from late 1937 until Fuller's death. Sonny Terry was featured at the Spirituals To Swing concerts in New York in 1938 and 1939. He recorded for the Library of Congress in 1938 and made his commercial recording debut a few days later.

Above
Pioneering bebop drummer Max Roach reflects between takes.

He joined forces with Brownie McGhee in 1939 and was present on McGhee's recording of 'The Death Of Blind Boy Fuller' in 1941 – the first time they recorded together. The pair worked in New York with Champion Jack Dupree, Leadbelly and others on the folk-blues circuit of the 1940s, and Terry appeared in the Broadway show *Finian's Rainbow* during 1946–47. The Terry-McGhee team made dozens of duo albums from the mid-1950s through to the mid-1970s.

see Blind Boy Fuller pp 124 *see* Dizzy Gillespie pp 152 *see* Brownie McGhee pp 179 *see* Charles Mingus pp 230

Right
Pianist Lennie Tristano explored a variety of styles and was an important jazz educator.

Lennie Tristano

(Piano, 1919–78)

Lennie Tristano began his career as a performer in promising style in his native Chicago, but later focused much of his time and creative energy on teaching his own musical ideas. He was born weak-sighted and was blind from the age of 10. He gathered a group of important acolytes around him during the late 1940s in New York, including saxophonists Lee Konitz and Warne Marsh and guitarist Billy Bauer, and ran a school of jazz in the city from 1951–56.

He performed and recorded intermittently from the mid-1950s, but continued to teach individual pupils. His musical concept offered an alternative to the prevailing bop orthodoxy of the day, and demanded rigorous discipline and sensitivity to complex nuances of time and tonality. He was an early explorer both of free jazz and of creating multitracked recordings by overdubbing. His own music never found a wide audience and much of it was only released posthumously, but his students ensured that his influence was a significant one.

Below
Sarah Vaughan's extensive vocal range ensured her international success.

Sarah Vaughan

(Vocals, 1924–90)

Sarah Vaughan began her career singing in jazz bands led by Earl Hines and Billy Eckstine, but achieved her greatest fame singing ballads in more commercial settings from the late 1940s onwards. She continued to record in both jazz and popular contexts until 1967, when she took a five-year break. Her striking control and wide vocal range established her as a major international star, and she left an extensive – if sometimes infuriatingly inconsistent – recorded legacy.

Eddie 'Cleanhead' Vinson

(Alto saxophone, vocals, 1917–88)

Edward L. Vinson Jr. was born in Houston, Texas. He studied saxophone in high school and played with the Chester Boone and Milt Larkin Orchestras, before touring with a show featuring Lil Green and Big Bill Broonzy in 1941. He joined the Cootie Williams Orchestra in 1942 and recorded hit vocals on 'Cherry Red Blues' and 'Somebody's Got To Go'. He formed his own group in 1945 and had a number-one Race

see Introduction pp 142 *see* Sources & Sounds pp 144 *see* Key Artists pp 152

Records hit with 'Old Maid Boogie'. Vinson's influences came from modern jazz, and he also had his own influence on the style, penning the Miles Davis hit 'Four'. Vinson continued to tour and record into the 1980s.

Dinah Washington

(Vocals, 1924–63)

Ruth Lee Jones was born in Tuscaloosa, Alabama and raised in Chicago. She joined Lionel Hampton's band in 1943 and made her first recordings that year. Included were the hits 'Salty Papa Blues' and 'Evil Gal Blues'. She left Hampton in 1945 and signed with Mercury records in 1946. Her recorded output included all kinds of material – and she could handle it all. She had a number-one R&B hit in 1949 with 'Baby, Get Lost' – written by jazz critic Leonard Feather – and crossed over into pop music with 'What A Difference A Day Makes', which was a chart hit in 1959.

Ben Webster

(Tenor saxophone, 1909–73)

Ben Webster served an initial apprenticeship in 'territory' bands in the Southwest (including those led by Benny Moten and Andy Kirk) before moving to New York in 1934. He recorded with Billie Holiday and worked with a succession of notable bandleaders before joining Duke Ellington in 1940. He was a key member of Ellington's legendary band of the time, often referred to as 'the Blanton-Webster Band' from the influence exerted by the saxophonist and bassist Jimmy Blanton.

Webster led his own small groups from 1943 and established a reputation for his warm, lyrical approach to ballad playing. He rejoined Ellington in 1948, but problems with alcohol forced him to leave music entirely from 1950–52. He returned to tour with Norman Granz's Jazz at the Philharmonic and recorded extensively as both leader and accompanist. He settled permanently in Europe from 1964, where he remained active on the club and festival circuit.

Jimmy Witherspoon

(Vocals, 1922–97)

Jimmy John Witherspoon was born in Gurdon, Arkansas. He joined the Jay McShann group in California in 1945. He recorded his own records in late 1947 and among them was 'Ain't Nobody's Business Parts 1 & 2', a huge Race Records hit. Witherspoon toured with his own group until 1952 and had another big hit with 'No Rollin' Blues'/'Big Fine Girl'. As a blues shouter, Witherspoon was influenced by Big Joe Turner; later in his life he developed a smoother, jazz-related ballad style.

Below

Versatile R&B and jazz artist Eddie 'Cleanhead' Vinson lays down some vocals in the studio.

see Duke Ellington pp 52 *see* Lionel Hampton pp 125 *see* Earl Hines pp 126 *see* Big Joe Turner pp 166

List of Artists

Entries appear in the following order: name, music style, year(s) of popularity, instruments, country of origin.

Aaron, Alvin, Big Band, 1940s–1950s, Clarinet, saxophones, Canadian
Abadie, Claude, Modern Jazz; Big Band, 1940s–1960s, Clarinet, French
Abney, Don, Swing; Modern Jazz, 1940s–1980s, Piano, American
Adams, J.T., Chicago Blues, 1940s–1960s, Guitar, American
Albam, Manny, Big Band; Cool Jazz; Bebop, 1940s–2000s, Arranger, composer, saxophone, American
Albany, Joe, Modern Jazz; Bebop, 1940s–1970s, Piano, American
Alexander. Mousey, Big Band; Swing, 1940s–1980s, Drums, American
Allen, Lee, Rhythm & Blues, 1940s–1980s, Saxophone, American
Alley, Vernon, Swing, 1940s–1990s, Bass, American
Ambrosetti, Flavio, Bebop, 1940s–, Saxophone, vibraphone, Swedish
Anderson, Cat, Swing; Big Band, 1940s–1970s, Trumpet, American
Anderson, Ernestine, Cool Jazz, 1940s–, Vocals, American
Andrews, Ernie, Bebop; Swing, 1940s–, Vocals, American
Anthony, Ray, Big Band, 1940s–, Trumpet, bandleader, American
Archia, Tom, Bebop, 1940s–1960s, Saxophone, American
Arnold, Harry, Big Band, 1940s–1960s, Saxophone, arranger, bandleader, Swedish
Ashby, Irving, Swing; Bebop, 1940s–1970s, Guitar, American
Babarin, Paul, New Orleans Jazz, 1940s–1960s, Drums, leader, composer, American
Babasin, Harry, Cool Jazz; Bebop; Modern Jazz, 1940s–1980s, Bass, cello, American
Babs, Alice, Swing; Modern Jazz, 1940s–, Vocals, Swedish
Bacsik, Elek, Swing; Traditional Jazz, 1940s–1980s, Guitar, violin, Hungarian
Bailey, Benny, Swing; Big Band; Modern Jazz; Hard Bop, 1940s–, Trumpet, American
Baker, Harold 'Shorty', Swing, 1940s–1960s, Trumpet, American
Baker, Kenny, Traditional Jazz; Swing; Big Band, 1940s–1990s, Trumpet, British
Bales, Burt. Chicago Jazz, 1940s–1980s, Piano, American
Ballen, Ivin, Rhythm & Blues; Down-home Blues, 1940s–1950s, Record label owner, American
Barbarin, Paul, New Orleans Jazz, 1940s–1960s, Drums, American
Barnard, Bob, Traditional Jazz, 1940s–, Trumpet, Australian
Barnet, Charlie, Swing; Big Band, 1940s–1960s, Saxophone, vocals, American
Bass, Ralph, West Coast Blues; Rhythm & Blues; Chicago Blues, 1940s–1970s, Producer, American
Bauer, Billy, Cool Jazz, 1940s–1950s, Guitar, American
Bauzá, Mario, Latin Jazz, 1940s–1990s, Trumpet, saxophone, arranger. Cuban
Bell, Graeme, Traditional Jazz, 1940s–, Piano, bandleader, Australian
Bellson, Louie, Swing; Bebop, 1940s–1990s, Drums, American
Berendt, Joachim-Ernst, All Jazz Styles, 1940s–1990s, Producer, author, concert promoter, German
Berman, Sonny, Swing; Big Band, 1940s, Trumpet, American
Bernhart, Milt, Big Band, 1940s–, Trombone, American
Bert, Eddie, Bebop; Big Band, 1940s–, Trombone, American
Best, Denzil, Swing; Modern Jazz, 1940s–1960s, Drums, American
Betts, Keter, Swing; Bebop; Modern Jazz, 1940s–, Bass, American
Big Maybelle, East Coast Blues; Jump Blues; Rhythm & Blues, 1940s–1960s, Vocals, American
Big Three Trio, The, Chicago Blues, 1940s–1950s, Vocals, guitar, American
Bihari Brothers, Rhythm & Blues, 1940s–1970s, Entrepreneurs, American
Blackwell, Willie '61', Delta Blues, 1940s–1970s, Songwriter, American
Blanchard, Edgar, New Orleans Jazz, 1940s–1960s, Guitar, bandleader, American
Blesh, Rudi. Traditional Jazz; Swing; Ragtime, 1940s–1980s, Producer, author, critic, American
Bolling, Claude, Swing; Big Band, 1940s–, Piano, composer, bandleader, French
Boogie-Woogie Red, Boogie-Woogie, 1940s–1970s, Piano, American
Booker, Charley, Country Blues; Rhythm & Blues, 1940s–1950s, Vocals, guitar, American
Booze, Beatrice, Boogie-Woogie; Jump Blues, 1940s–1960s, Guitar, American
Bostic, Earl, Rhythm & Blues, 1940s–1960s, Saxophone, American
Bowser, Erbie, Texas Blues, 1940s–1990s, Piano, American
Boyd, Eddie, Chicago Blues, 1940s–1980s, Guitar, piano, composer, American
Boze, Calvin, Jump Blues, 1940s–1950s, Vocals, trumpet, American
Braff, Ruby, Dixieland Revival; New Orleans Jazz; Swing, 1940s–2000s, Trumpet, American
Brehm, Simon, Traditional Jazz; Swing, 1940s–1960s, Bass, bandleader, Swedish
Brenston, Jackie, Jump Blues; Rhythm & Blues, 1940s–1960s, Saxophone, American
Brom, Gustav, Modern Jazz; Swing; Dixieland; Big Band, 1940s–1990s, Clarinet, bandleader, Czech
Brooks, Hadda, Boogie-Woogie, 1940s–1960s, Piano, American
Brown, Buster, East Coast Blues, 1940s–1970s, Harmonica, American
Brown, Charles, West Coast Blues, 1940s–1990s, Piano, vocals, American
Brown, Dusty, Chicago Blues, 1940s–, Harmonica, American
Brown, J.T., Chicago Blues, 1940s–1950s, Vocals, saxophone, American
Brown, Ray, Bebop, 1940s–2000s, Bass, cello, American
Brown, Roy, Jump Blues; West Coast Blues, 1940s–1970s, Vocals, composer, American
Brown, Walter, Jump Blues; Rhythm & Blues, 1940s–1950s, Vocals, American
Brunskill, Bill, New Orleans Jazz, 1940s–1980s, Trumpet, leader, British
Buckner, Milt, Big Bands; Swing, 1940s–1970s, Piano, organ, arranger, American
Burbank, Albert, New Orleans Jazz; Dixieland, 1940s–1970s, Clarinet, vocals, American
Burns, Dave, Bebop; Hard Bop, 1940s–, Trumpet, flugelhorn, piano, American
Burns, Ralph, Swing; Bebop; Big Band, 1940s–2000s, Piano, arranger, composer, American
Byard, Jaki, Free Jazz, 1940s–1990s, Piano, saxophones, arranger, American
Cachao, Latin Jazz, 1940s–, Bass, Cuban
Callender, Red, Cool Jazz; Swing; Bebop, 1940s–1980s, Bass, tuba, American
Candoli, Conte, Cool Jazz; Bebop, 1940s–1990s, Trumpet, American
Candoli, Pete, Swing; West Coast Jazz; Big Band, 1940s–, Trumpet, American
Carisi, Johnny, Cool Jazz; Big Band; Jazz Rock, 1940s–1990s, Trumpet, composer, arranger, American
Carle, Frankie, New Orleans Jazz, 1940s–1960s, Piano, bandleader, British
Carolina Slim, Country Blues, 1940s–1950s, Vocals, guitar, American
Carroll, Barbara, Bebop; Modern Jazz, 1940s–, Piano, vocals, American
Carroll, Joe 'Bebop', Bebop, 1940s–1980s, Vocals, American

Carter, Goree, Texas Blues, 1940s–1950s, Guitar, American
Cary, Dick, Traditional Jazz; Swing, 1940s–1990s, Piano, trumpet, arranger, alto horn, American
Caston, Leonard 'Baby Doo', Country Blues; Jump Blues, 1940s–1980s, Vocals, piano, guitar, American
Catlett, 'Big' Sid, Swing, 1940s–1950s, Drums, American
Cesari, Umberto, Swing; Modern Jazz, 1940s–1970s, Piano, Italian
Chaloff, Serge, Bebop, 1940s–1950s, Saxophone, American
Chamblee, Eddie, Swing; Big Band, 1940s–, Saxophone, bandleader, American
Childers, Buddy, Big Band; Swing, 1940s–. Trumpet, American
Chisholm, George, Traditional Jazz; Big Band; British Jazz, 1940s–1990s, Trombone, Scottish
Christie, Keith, Swing; Big Band; Traditional Jazz, 1940s–1970s, Trombone, British
Christy, June, Cool Jazz, 1940s–1980s, Vocals, American
Clark, Gus, Big Band; Swing, 1940s–1950s, Piano, Belgian
Clark, Mahlon, Swing; West Coast Jazz, 1940s–1980s, Clarinet, American
Clarke, Kenny, Bebop, 1940s–1980s, Drums, composer, American
Cleveland, Jimmy, Modern Jazz; Big Band, 1940s–, Trombone, American
Clovers, The, Rhythm & Blues, 1940s–1950s, Vocals, American
Cohn, Al, Bebop; Cool Jazz, 1940s–1980s, Saxophone, American
Cole, Nat 'King', Swing, 1940s–1960s, Piano, vocals, American
Coleman, Earl, Swing; Bebop, 1940s–1990s, Vocals, American
Collins, Dick, Swing; Big Band, 1940–, Trumpet, American
Combe, Stuff, Swing; Bebop, 1940s–1980s, Drums, Swiss
Cook, Willie, Swing; Big Band, 1940s–2000s, Trumpet, American
Cooper, Bob, Cool Jazz; Hard Bop, 1940s–1990s, Saxophone, oboe, American
Cooper, Trenton, Rhythm & Blues, 1940s–1960s, Piano, American
Corb, Morty, Swing; Traditional Jazz, 1940s–1990s, Bass, American
Corcoran, Corky, Big Band, 1940s–1970s, Saxophone, American
Counce, Curtis. Hard Bop, 1940s–1960s, Bass, American
Cousin Joe, Rhythm & Blues; Swing, 1940s–1980s, Vocals, composer, piano, American
Crawford, Ray, Hard Bop; Soul Jazz, 1940s–1990s, Guitar, American
Crayton, Pee Wee, West Coast Blues; Texas Blues, 1940s–1980s, Guitar, American
Criss, Sonny, Hard Bop, 1940s–1970s, Saxophones, American
Crudup, Arthur 'Big Boy', Delta Blues; Rhythm & Blues, 1940s–1970s, Vocals, guitar, American
Crutchfield, James, Boogie-Woogie, 1940s–1980s, Piano, American
Dallas, Leroy, Country Blues, 1940s–1960s. Vocals, guitar, American
Dallwitz, Dave, Traditional Jazz, 1940s–, Piano, trombone, arranger, bandleader, Australian
Dameron, Tadd. Bebop, 1940s–1960s, Piano, composer, arranger, American
Dankworth, John, Bebop; Big Band; British Jazz, 1940s–, Saxophone, arranger, composer, bandleader, British
Darensbourg, Joe, Traditional Jazz; Dixieland; New Orleans Jazz, 1940s–1980s, Clarinet, saxophone, American
Darnell, Larry, Rhythm & Blues, 1940s–1960s, Vocals, American
Davis, Eddie 'Lockjaw', Bebop; Hard Bop, 1940s–1980s, Saxophone, American
Davis, Rev. Gary, Ragtime, 1940s–1970s, Guitar, American
Davis, Lem, Bebop; Swing, 1940s–, Saxophone, American
Davis, Martha, Swing; Bebop, 1940s–1950s, Piano, vocals, American
Davis, Maxwell, Rhythm & Blues, 1940s–1960s, Saxophone, producer, arranger, American
Davis, Tiny, Swing, 1940s–1970s, Trumpet, vocals, American
Davis, Wild Bill, Swing, 1940s–, Organ, piano, arranger, American
DeArango, Bill 'Buddy', Bebop; Hard Bop, 1940s–, Guitar, American
Dedrick, Rusty, Swing; Traditional Jazz, 1940s–, Trumpet, arranger, composer, American
DeFranco, Buddy, Bebop, 1940s–1990s, Clarinet, saxophone, American
Deniz, Frank, Swing; British Jazz, 1940s–, Guitar, bandleader, British
Desmond, Paul, Cool Jazz, 1940s–1970s, Saxophone, American
DiNovi, Gene, Swing; Bebop; Modern Jazz, 1940s–, Piano, American
Domnerus, Arne, Swing; Bebop, 1940s–, Saxophone, clarinet, bandleader, Swedish
Donegan, Dorothy, Swing; Bebop; Boogie-Woogie, 1940s–1990s, Piano, vocals, American
Dorough, Bob, Cool Jazz; Bebop; Swing, 1940s–, Piano, vocals, composer, American
Dukes, 'Little' Laura, Memphis Blues, 1940s–1980s, Vocals, banjo, ukulele, American
Dupree, Champion Jack, Chicago Blues; Rhythm & Blues, 1940s–1990s, Piano, vocals, composer, American
Duskin, Big Joe, Boogie-Woogie, 1940s–1980s, Piano, American
Eager, Allen, Cool Jazz; Bebop, 1940s–2000s, Saxophone, American
Eckstine, Billy, Bebop, 1940s–1980s, Vocals, trumpet, guitar, American
Edelhagen, Kurt, Big Band, 1940s–1980s, Bandleader, piano, German
Edison, Harry 'Sweets', Swing, 1940s–1990s, Trumpet, American
Edwards, David 'Homeyboy', Country Blues, 1940s–, Guitar, harmonica, American
Edwards, Frank, Country Blues, 1940s–2000s, Vocals, guitar, harmonica, American
Edwards, Honeyboy, Modern Electric Blues, 1940s–, Guitar, harmonica, American
Edwards, Teddy, Bebop; Hard Bop, 1940s–2000s, Saxophone, arranger, American
Ellington, Mercer, Swing, 1940s–1990s, Trumpet, arranger, composer, American
Ellis, Herb, Swing; Bebop, 1940s–1990s, Guitar, American
Ericson, Rolf, Swing; Bebop, 1940s–1990s, Trumpet, flugelhorn, Swedish
Evans, Doc, Traditional Jazz; Dixieland, 1940s–1970s, Cornet, American
Ewell, Don, Traditional Jazz; Swing, 1940s–1980s, Piano, American

Fallon, Jack, Big Band; Swing, 1940s–, Bass, Canadian
Fawkes, Wally, British Jazz, 1940s–, Clarinet, saxophone, Canadian
Feld, Morey, Dixieland, 1940s–1960s, Drums, American
Felix, Lennie, Swing, 1940s–1970s, Piano, British
Fields, Herbie, Swing, 1940s–1950s, Clarinet, saxophone, American
Firehouse Fire Plus Two, Dixieland Revival, 1940s–1960s, Various instruments, American
Five Breezes, Jump Blues, 1940s, Various instruments, American
Flanagan, Tommy, Bebop; Hard Bop, 1940s–2000s, Piano, American
Fol, Raymond, Traditional Jazz; Bebop, 1940s–1970s, Piano, French
Forest City Joe, Chicago Blues, 1940s–1950s, Harmonica, composer, American
Forrest, Helen, Swing, 1940s–1980s, Vocals, American
Forrest, Jimmy, Hard Bop, 1940s–1980s, Saxophone, American
Foster, Little Willie, Chicago Blues, 1940s–, Guitar, piano, harmonica, American
Fountain, Pete, Dixieland Revival, 1940s–1990s, Clarinet, saxophones, American
Freeman, Russ, Cool Jazz; Bebop, 1940s–1980s, Piano, American
Frigo, Johnny, Swing, 1940s–, Violin, bass, American
Fuller, Gil, Big Band; Bebop, 1940s–1990s, Arranger, American
Gant, Cecil, West Coast Blues; Rhythm & Blues, 1940s–1950s, Piano, vocals, American
Garner, Erroll, Bebop; Swing, 1940s–1970s, Piano, American
Gaskin, Leonard, Swing, 1940s–, Bass, American
Gaslini, Giorgio, Free Jazz, 1940s–, Piano, composer, Italian
Gayten, Paul, Rhythm & Blues, 1940s–1960s, Vocals, piano, composer, producer, American
Geddins, Bob, Oakland Blues, 1940s–1960s, Entrepreneur, producer, composer, American
Geller, Herb, Hard Bop; Bebop, 1940s–, Saxophone, American
Ghanaba, World Jazz, 1940s–1960s, Drums, percussion, composer, Ghanaian
Gibson, Harry 'The Hipster', Swing, 1940s–1990s, Vocals, piano, American
Gillespie, Dizzy, Bebop, 1940s–1990s, Trumpet, vocals, composer, American

Glenn, Lloyd, West Coast Blues; Jump Blues, 1940s–1950s, Piano, producer, American
Glover, Henry, Rhythm & Blues, 1940s–1960s, Producer, composer, trumpet, American
Gold, Harry, Dixieland, 1940s–, Saxophone, clarinet, leader, arranger, composer, Irish
Gonzales, Babs, Bebop, 1940s–1970s, Vocals, American
Goode, Coleridge, Swing, 1940s–, Violin, bass, Jamaican
Gordon, Bob, Cool Jazz, 1940s–1950s, Saxophone, American
Gordon, Dexter, Bebop; Hard Bop, 1940s–1980s, Saxophones, American
Gordon, Joe, Hard Bop, 1940s–1960s, Trumpet, American
Graham, Kenny, World Jazz, 1940s–, Saxophone, keyboards, composer, arranger, British
Granz, Norman, Bebop, 1940s–1990s, Producer, American
Gray, Wardell, Bebop; Swing, 1940s–1950s, Saxophone, American
Green, Bunky, Hard Bop, 1940s–1980s, Saxophone, American
Green, Freddie, Swing, 1940s–1980s, Guitar, American
Green, Lil, Country Blues, 1940s–1950s, Vocals, American
Green, Urbie, Swing; Bebop, 1940s–, Trombone, American
Greer, Big John, East Coast Blues, 1940s–1950s, Vocals, saxophone, American
Grey, Al, Bebop; Swing, 1940s–1990s, Trombone, American
Griffin, Johnny, Bebop; Hard Bop, 1940s–, Saxophone, American
Grimes, Tiny, Bebop, 1940s–1970s, Guitar, vocals, American
Grimes, Tiny, Jump Blues, 1940s–1970s, Guitar, American
Gwaltney, Tommy, Traditional Jazz, 1940s–1970s, Saxophone, clarinet, vibraphone, xylophone, American
Hafer, Dick, Cool Jazz, 1940s–1990s, Saxophone, American
Haig, Al, Bebop, 1940s–1980s, Piano, American
Haim, John, British Jazz, 1940s, Cornet, leader, British
Hakim, Sadik, Bebop, 1940s–1980s, Piano, American
Harding, Buster, Swing, 1940s–1960s, Arranger, piano, Canadian
Harewood, Al, Bebop, 1940s–1960s, Drums, American
Harris, Bill, Swing; Bebop, 1940s–1970s, Trombone, American
Harris, Peppermint, Jump Blues; West Coast Blues, 1940s–1970s, Vocals, American
Harris, Wynonie, Jump Blues; Rhythm & Blues, 1940s–1960s, Vocals, drums, American
Harrison, Lou, World Fusion, 1940s–1990s, Composer, American
Hartman, Johnny, Modern Jazz, 1940s–1980s, Vocals, American
Harvey, Eddie, Traditional Jazz; Modern Jazz, 1940s–1980s, Trombone, piano, composer, arranger, educator, British
Hasselgard, Stan, Swing; Bebop, 1940s, Clarinet, Swiss
Hawkins, Roy, West Coast Blues; Rhythm & Blues, 1940s–1950s, Piano, vocals, American
Haymes, Dick, Swing, 1940s–1970s, Vocals, Argentinian
Heard, J.C., Swing; Bebop, 1940s–1980s, Drums, American
Heath, Albert 'Tootie', Hard Bop, 1940s–1990s, Drums, American
Heath, Percy, Bebop; Hard Bop; Cool Jazz, 1940s–1990s, Bass, American
Heath, Ted, Big Band; Swing, 1940s–1960s, Trombone, bandleader, British
Hefti, Neal, Swing; Big Band, 1940s–1990s, Trumpet, arranger, composer, American
Helm, Bob, Dixieland Revival, 1940s–1990s, Clarinet, American
Hemphill, Sid, Memphis Blues, 1940s–1950s, Fife, violin, guitar, drums, mandolin, banjo, harmonica, American
Henderson, Duke, West Coast Blues, 1940s–1950s, Vocals, American
Hendricks, Jon, Bebop, 1940s–, Vocals, American
Henley, John Lee, Country Blues, 1940s–, Harmonica, American

Henry, Big Boy, Country Blues, 1940s–, Guitar, American
Henry, Ernie, Hard Bop, 1940s–1950s, Saxophone, American
Hentoff, Nat, All Jazz Styles, 1940s–, Author, critic, American
Herman, Woody, Swing; Big Band; Cool Jazz, 1940s–1980s, Clarinet, saxophone, vocals, bandleader, American
Hibbler, Al, Jump Blues, 1940s–1990s, Vocals, American
Hogg, John, Country Blues; Rhythm & Blues, 1940s–1950s, Guitar, American
Hogg, Smokey, Country Blues; Rhythm & Blues, 1940s–1950s, Vocals, guitar, American
Holiday, Billie, Swing, 1940s–1950s, Vocals, American
Hollis, Tony, Country Blues, 1940s, Vocals, guitar, American
Hooker, John Lee, Delta Blues; Country Blues, 1940s–1990s, Guitar, composer, American
Hope, Elmo, Hard Bop; Bebop, 1940s–1960s, Piano, composer, American
Hope, Stan, Hard Bop; Big Band, 1940s–1990s, Piano, American
Houston, Cisco, Folk Blues, 1940s–1960s, Guitar, vocals, American
Howard, Camille, Boogie-Woogie; Rhythm & Blues, 1940s–1950s, Piano, vocals, American
Hubble, Eddie, Dixieland Revival, 1940s–, Trombone, American
Hucko, Peanuts, Chicago Jazz; Swing, 1940s–1990s, Clarinet, saxophone, American
Humes, Helen, Country Blues; Jump Blues, 1940s–1970s, Vocals, American
Hyams, Margie, Swing; Bebop, 1940s–1950s, Vibraphone, American
Hyman, Dick, Swing, 1940s–, Piano, composer, American
Jackie & Roy, Bebop; Modern Jazz, 1940s–2000s, Vocals, American
Jackson, Armand 'Jump', Chicago Blues, 1940s–1980s, Bandleader, drums, American
Jackson, Bull Moose, Jump Blues; Rhythm & Blues, 1940s–1950s, Saxophone, American
Jackson, Chubby, Swing; Bebop, 1940s–2000s, Bass, American
Jackson, Melvin 'Lil' Son', Texas Blues, 1940s–1960s, Guitar, vocals, American
Jackson, Willis 'Gator', Soul Jazz; Hard Bop, 1940s–1980s, Saxophone, American
Jacquet, Illinois, Swing; Bebop, 1940s–1990s, Saxophone, American
James, Harry, Swing, 1940s–1970s, Trumpet, American
Jazz at the Philharmonic, Swing; Bebop, 1940s–1980s, Various instruments, American
Johnson, Alfred 'Snuff', Texas Blues, 1940s–1980s, Guitar, American
Johnson, Dink, New Orleans Jazz, 1940s–1950s, Piano, clarinet, drums, American
Johnson, Ella, Jump Blues; Rhythm & Blues, 1940s–1950s, Vocals, American
Johnson, J.J., Bebop; Hard Bop, 1940s–1990s, Trombone, arranger, composer, American
Jones, Dill, Swing; Bebop; Modern Jazz, 1940s–1980s, Piano, British
Jones, Etta, Modern Jazz, 1940s–2000s, Vocals, American
Jones, Jimmy, Swing, 1940s–1980s, Piano, arranger, composer, American
Jones, Little Johnny, Chicago Blues; Boogie-Woogie, 1940s–1960s, Piano, American
Jones, Max, All Jazz Styles, 1940s–1990s, Author, critic, British
Jones, Nyles, Texas Blues, 1940s–1990s, Guitar, American
Jordan, Duke, Bebop; Hard Bop, 1940s–1990s, Piano, composer, American
Jordan, Louis, Swing; East Coast Blues; Jump Blues, 1940s–1970s, Saxophone, vocals, bandleader, American
Kaminsky, Max, Dixieland, 1940s–1990s, Trumpet, American
Kansas City Red, Chicago Blues, 1940s–1990s, Drums, vocals, bandleader, American
Kay, Connie, Cool Jazz, 1940s–1990s, Drums, American
Kelly, George, Swing; Big Band, 1940s–, Saxophone, vocals, arranger, American
Kenton, Stan, Big Band, 1940s–1970s, Piano, composer, American
Kessel, Barney, Bebop; Cool Jazz, 1940s–1990s, Guitar, American
King, Saunders, Jump Blues, 1940s–1960s, Vocals, guitar, American
Klink, Al, Swing; Big Band, 1940s–, Saxophone, American
Knepper, Jimmy, Hard Bop; Big Band, 1940s–, Trombone, American
Koller, Hans, Modern Jazz; Cool Jazz, 1940s–, Saxophone, clarinet, sopranino, Austrian
Konitz, Lee, Cool Jazz, 1940s–, Saxophones, American
Lanphere, Don, Modern Jazz; Bebop, 1940s–2000s, Saxophone, American
LaPorta, John, Cool Jazz, 1940s–2000s, Saxophone, clarinet, American
Lawrence, Elliot, Swing; Cool Jazz; Big Band, 1940s–, Piano, composer, bandleader, American
Lee, John, Country Blues, 1940s–1960s, Guitar, American
Lee, Julia, Jump Blues, 1940s–1950s, Vocals, piano, American
Lee, Peggy, Swing, 1940s–1990s, Vocals, American
Leeman, Cliff, Swing, 1940s–1980s, Drums, American
Lees, Gene, All Jazz Styles, 1940s–, Author, critic, composer, Canadian
LeSage, Bill, Bebop; Big Band; British Jazz, 1940s–, Piano, accordion, vibraphone, percussion, British
Lesberg, Jack, Swing; Chicago Jazz, 1940s–, Bass, American
Levy, Lou, Cool Jazz; Bebop, 1940s–1990s, Piano, American
Lewis, Mel, Bebop, 1940s–1980s, Drums, American
Lewis, Smiley, Rhythm & Blues, 1940s–1960s, Piano, vocals, American
Liggins, Jimmy, Jump Blues; Rhythm & Blues, 1940s–1950s, Guitar, American
Liggins, Joe, Jump Blues; Rhythm & Blues, 1940s–1950s, Piano, arranger, American
Liston, Melba, Hard Bop; Bebop, 1940s–1990s, Trombone, arranger, American
Little Hatch, Chicago Blues, 1940s–1970s, Harmonica, American
Little Miss Cornshucks, Rhythm & Blues, 1940s–1950s, Vocals, American
Littlefield, Little Willie, Jump Blues; West Coast Blues; Boogie-Woogie; Rhythm & Blues, 1940s–1990s, Piano, vocals, American
Louis, Joe Hill, Delta Blues, 1940s–1950s, Guitar, harmonica, American
Lutcher, Joe, Rhythm & Blues, 1940s–1950s, Saxophone, American
Machito, Latin Jazz, 1940s–1980s, Vocals, percussion, bandleader, Cuban
Mackel, Billy, Swing; Big Band, 1940s–, Guitar, American
Maiden, Sidney, Chicago Blues; Delta Blues, 1940s–1960s, Harmonica, American
Manne, Shelley, Bebop; Cool Jazz, 1940s–1980s, Drums, composer, American
Marmarosa, Dodo, Bebop, 1940s–1960s, Piano, American
Marsh, Warne, Cool Jazz, 1940s–1980s, Saxophone, reeds, American
Marshall, Wendell, Swing; Soul Jazz; Hard Bop; Modern Jazz, 1940s–2000s, Bass, American
Martin, Fiddlin' Joe, Delta Blues, 1940s–1970s, Drums, American
Martinez, Sabú, Latin Jazz, 1940s–1970s, Percussion, Cuban
Massey, Cal, Free Jazz; Swing, 1940s–1970s, Composer, trumpet, American
Masso, George, Dixieland Revival, 1940s–, Trombone, composer, leader, piano, vibraphone, American
May, Billy, Big Band; Swing, 1940s–1970s, Trumpet, bandleader, arranger, composer, American
Mayfield, Percy, West Coast Blues; Rhythm & Blues, 1940s–1970s, Vocals, composer, American
McCarthy, Albert, All Jazz Styles, 1940s–1980s, Author, British
McGarity, Lou, Chicago Jazz; Swing; Dixieland Revival, 1940s–1970s, Trombone, violin, vocals, American
McGhee, Brownie, East Coast Blues; Country Blues, 1940s–1990s, Guitar, American

see Introduction pp 142 *see* Sources & Sounds pp 144 *see* Key Artists pp 152 *see* A–Z of Artists pp 170

McGhee, Howard, Bebop; Hard Bop, 1940s–1980s, Trumpet, American
McKibbon, Al, Bebop; Hard Bop, 1940s–1990s, Bass, American
McKinley, L.G., Chicago Blues, 1940s–1950s, Guitar, American
McNeely, Big Jay, Jump Blues; Rhythm & Blues; West Coast Blues, 1940s–1990s, Saxophone, American
McShann, Jay, Swing; Big Band; Jump Blues, 1940s–, Piano, vocals, American
McVea, Jack, Jump Blues, 1940s–1960s, Saxophone, clarinet, American
Memphis Slim, Boogie-Woogie, 1940s–1980s, Piano, vocals, American
Mercy Dee, Rhythm & Blues, 1940s–1960s, Piano, American
Merseysippi Jazz Band, British Jazz, 1940s–1950s, Various instruments, British
Middleton, Velma, Swing, 1940s–1960s, Vocals, American
Milburn, Amos, Jump Blues; West Coast Blues; Rhythm & Blues, 1940s–1960s, Piano, vocals, American
Miller, Big, Swing; Big Band; Jump Blues, 1940s–, Vocals, American
Miller, Glenn, Swing; Big Band, 1940s, Trombone, arranger, composer, bandleader, American
Milton, Roy, Jump Blues; West Coast Blues; Rhythm & Blues, 1940s–1980s, Vocals, drums, American
Mitchell, Billy, Swing; Bebop, 1940s–, Reed, American
Mitchell, Walter, Boogie-Woogie, 1940s–, Harmonica, American
Molton, Flora, Jump Blues, 1940s–1980s, Guitar, American
Montgomery, Marian, Bebop; Big Band; Modern Jazz, 1940s–1960s, Guitar, American
Moody, James, Bebop; Hard Bop, 1940s–, Saxophone, flute, vocals, American
Moore, Arnold 'Gatemouth', Rhythm & Blues; Jump Blues, 1940s–2000s, Vocals, American
Moore, Johnny & the Three Blazers, Jump Blues, 1940s–1950s, Various instruments, American
Moore, Oscar, Cool Blues; Jump Blues, 1940s–1980s, Guitar, American
Moraes, Vinícius de, Latin Jazz, 1940s–1980s, Composer, Brazilian
Morse, Ella Mae, Country Blues, 1940s–1980s, Vocals, American
Moss, Danny, Big Band; Swing, 1940s–, Saxophone, reeds, British
Mulligan, Mick, Traditional Jazz, 1940s–1960s, Trumpet, leader, British
Murphy, Rose, Swing, 1940s–1980s, Piano, vocals, American
Napoleon, Marty, Swing; Big Band, 1940s–, Piano, American
Navarro, Fats, Bebop, 1940s–1950s, Trumpet, American
Nelson, Louis, New Orleans Jazz, 1940s–, Trombone, American
Newman, Joe, Swing, 1940s–1990s, Trumpet, American
Nicholson, J.D., West Coast Blues; Rhythm & Blues, 1940s–1960s, Piano, American
Nighthawk, Robert, Chicago Blues, 1940s–1960s, Guitar, vocals, American
Nix, Willie, Chicago Blues, 1940s–1970s, Vocals, drums, American
O'Day, Anita, Swing; Bebop, 1940s–1990s, Vocals, American
O'Farrill, Chico, Latin Jazz; Bebop, 1940s–1970s, Trumpet, arranger, Cuban
O'Connell, Helen, Swing; Big Band, 1940s–1940s, Vocals, American
Oliver, Sy, Swing, 1940s–1980s, Trumpet, arranger, vocals, bandleader, American
Orioles, The, Rhythm & Blues, 1940s–1960s. Vocals, American
Osborne, Mary, Swing, 1940s–1990s, Guitar, American
Otis, Johnny, Jump Blues; West Coast Blues; Rhythm & Blues, 1940s–1990s, Producer, songwriter, drums, American
Owens, Calvin, Rhythm & Blues; Modern Electric Blues, 1940s–, Trumpet, bandleader, American
Paris, Jackie, Bebop; Big Band, 1940s–, Vocals, American
Parker, Charlie, Bebop; Big Band, 1940s–1950s, Saxophones, American
Parker, Leo, Hard Bop; Bebop, 1940s–1960s, Saxophone, American
Parker, Sonny, Jump Blues; Rhythm & Blues, 1940s–1950s, Vocals, American
Pavageau, Alcide 'Slow Drag', New Orleans Jazz, 1940s–1960s, Bass, American
Payne, Sonny, Bebop, 1940s–1970s, Drums, American
Payton, Earlee, Rhythm & Blues, 1940s–1960s, Harmonica, American
Pettiford, Oscar, Bebop, 1940s–1950s, Bass, cello, American
Petway, Robert, Country Blues, 1940s, Vocals, guitar, American
Phillips, Flip, Swing; Bebop, 1940s–2000s, Saxophone, clarinet, American
Phillips, Gene, West Coast Blues; Jump Blues, 1940s–1950s, Guitar, American
Phillips, Esther, Rhythm & Blues, 1940s–1960s, Vocals, American
Piano Slim, Boogie-Woogie; Jump Blues, 1940s–, Vocals, saxophone, drums, American
Piazzolla, Astor, Latin Jazz, 1940s–1990s, Piano, bandleader, composer, arranger, Argentinian
Pickett, Dan, Country Blues, 1940s–1950s, Vocals, guitar, American
Pierce, Nat, Swing; Big Band, 1940s–1990s, Piano, arranger, bandleader, American
Pomus, Doc, Rhythm & Blues, 1940s–1990s, Vocals, composer, American
Potter, Tommy, Bebop, 1940s–1950s, Bass, American
Powell, Mel, Swing, 1940s–1960s, Piano, composer, American
Pozo, Chano, Latin Jazz, 1940s, Percussion, vocals, Cuban
Previn, André, Cool Jazz; Bebop, 1940s–, Piano, French
Price, Sammy, Boogie-Woogie; Jump Blues, 1940s–1980s, Piano, bandleader, American
Prysock, Arthur, Rhythm & Blues, 1940s–1990s, Vocals, American
Puente, Tito, Latin Jazz, 1940s–1990s, Percussion, vibraphone, American
Pugh, Joe Bennie, Delta Blues; Chicago Blues, 1940s–1950s, Harmonica, American
Puma, Joe, Modern Jazz, 1940s–2000s, Guitar, American
Purnell, Alton, New Orleans Jazz, 1940s–1980s, Piano, vocals, American
Quebec, Ike, Hard Bop; Soul Jazz; Swing, 1940s–1960s, Saxophone, American
Quinichette, Paul, Swing, 1940s–1980s, Saxophone, American
Raeburn, Boyd, Bebop, 1940s–1950s, Saxophones, American
Ramey, Gene, Swing; Big Band; Jump Blues, 1940s–1980s, Bass, American
Rich, Buddy, Swing; Bebop; Big Band, 1940s–1980s, Drums, vocals, American
Richards, Johnny, Latin Jazz, 1940s–1960s, Composer, Brazilian
Richman, Boomie, Swing; Dixieland, 1940s–, Saxophone, clarinet, flute, American
Roach, Max, Bebop; Hard Bop, 1940s–1990s, Drums, composer, American
Robins, The, Rhythm & Blues, 1940s–1950s, Vocals, American
Rodney, Red, Bebop; Hard Bop, 1940s–1990s, Trumpet, American
Rosolino, Frank, Bebop; Big Band, 1940s–1970s, Trombone, American
Rouse, Charlie, Hard Bop, 1940s–1980s, Saxophone, American
Royal, Ernie, Bebop; Swing; Big Band, 1940s–1980s, Trumpet, American
Royal, Marshal, Swing, 1940s–1990s, Saxophone, clarinet, American
Russell, Curly, Bebop, 1940s–1950s, Bass, American
Russell, George, Free Jazz; Modern Jazz; Big Band, 1940s–, Piano, composer, arranger, American
Safranski, Eddie, Swing; Bebop; Big Band, 1940s–1970s, Bass, American
Sangster, John, Traditional Jazz, 1940s–, Composer, arranger, multi-instrumentalist, Australian
Schneider, Moe, Dixieland, 1940s–, Trombone, American
Schroeder, Gene, Chicago Jazz; Swing; Big Band, 1940s–1960s, Piano, American
Scott, Clifford, Swing, 1940s–1990s, Saxophone, flute, American
Scott, Hazel, Cool Jazz, 1940s–1950s, Piano, American
Scott, Jimmy Little, Rhythm & Blues, 1940s–, Vocals, American
Scott, Ronnie, Bebop; Big Band; Modern Jazz, 1940s–1990s, Saxophone, bandleader, British
Sealey, Paul, New Orleans Jazz; Traditional Jazz, 1940s–1960s, Guitar, banjo, bass, British
Sellers, John 'Brother', Country Blues; Folk Blues, 1940s–1960s, Vocals, guitar, American
Severinsen, Doc, Swing; Big Band, 1940s–, Trumpet, bandleader, American
Shakey Jake, Chicago Blues, 1940s–1980s, Harmonica, American
Silk, Eric, New Orleans Jazz, 1940s–1970s, Banjo, leader, British
Sims, Frankie Lee, Country Blues, 1940s–1960s, Guitar, American
Singer, Hal, Jump Blues; Rhythm & Blues, 1940s–, Saxophone, American
Skrimshire, Nevil, British Jazz, 1940s–, Guitar, British
Slack, Freddie, Boogie-Woogie, 1940s–1950s, Piano, bandleader, American
Slim, Harpo, Country Blues; Rhythm & Blues, 1940s–1960s, Vocals, American
Smalls, Cliff, Rhythm & Blues; Swing, 1940s–, Piano, trombone, arranger, American
Smith, George 'Harmonica', Modern Electric Blues, 1940s–1980s, Harmonica, American
Smith, Paul, Swing; Cool Jazz; Bebop, 1940s–, Piano, arranger, American
Smith, Tab, Swing, 1940s–1950s, Saxophones, American
Spires, Arthur 'Big Boy', Texas Blues, 1940s–1950s, Guitar, American
Stein, Lou, Swing; Bebop, 1940s–, Piano, American
Stewart, Slam, Swing, 1940s–1980s, Bass, vocals, American
Stidham, Arbee, Jump Blues, 1940s–1960s, Vocals, guitar, American
Stobart, Kathy, Modern Jazz, 1940s–, Saxophone, British
Stone, Jesse, Rhythm & Blues, 1940s–1950s, Producer, composer, piano, American
Sulieman, Idress, Hard Bop; Bebop, 1940s–2000s, Trumpet, flugelhorn, American
Sutton, Ralph, Traditional Jazz, 1940s–2000s, Piano, American
Tarrant, Rabon, Jump Blues, 1940s–1950s, Vocals, drums, American
Taylor, Billy, Bebop; Hard Bop; Swing, 1940s–, Piano, American
Terry, Sonny, East Coast Blues; Country Blues, 1940s–1980s, Harmonica, vocals, American
Thomas, Kid, Chicago Blues, 1940s–1950s, Harmonica, vocals, American
Thompson, Eddie, Bebop; Modern Jazz, 1940s–1980s, Piano, British
Thompson, Lucky, Bebop; Hard Bop, 1940s–1970s, Saxophones, American
Thompson, Sir Charles, Swing; Bebop, 1940s–, Piano, organ, composer, American
Tibbs, Andrew, Chicago Blues, 1940s–1960s, Vocals, American
Tinsley, John, Country Blues, 1940s–1950s, Guitar, composer, American
Tormé, Mel, Swing; Bebop, 1940s–1990s, Vocals, percussion, American
Treniers, The, Jump Blues; Rhythm & Blues, 1940s–1980s, Various instruments, American
Trice, Richard & Willie, Country Blues, 1940s–1960s, Vocals, guitar, American
Tristano, Lennie, Cool Jazz; Bebop, 1940s–1960s, Piano, composer, American
Turner, Big Joe, Jump Blues; Rhythm & Blues; Boogie-Woogie, 1940s–1980s, Vocals, artist, American
Turner, Ike, Rhythm & Blues, 1940s–, Piano, guitar, vocals, bandleader, producer, American
Turner, Zeb, Boogie-Woogie, 1940s–1950s, Guitar, American
Turney, Norris, Swing, 1940s–2000s, Saxophone, flute, American
Van Walls, Harry 'Piano Man', Rhythm & Blues, 1940s–1990s, Piano, American
Vaughan, Sarah, Bebop; Cool Jazz, 1940s–1980s, Vocals, American
Ventura, Charlie, Swing; Bebop, 1940s–1990s, Saxophone, bandleader, American
Vinson, Eddie 'Cleanhead', Bebop; Jump Blues; West Coast Blues; Rhythm & Blues, 1940s–1980s, Saxophone, vocals, composer, American
Vinson, Mose, Boogie-Woogie, 1940s–1950s, Piano, American
Walker, T-Bone, Texas Blues, 1940s–1970s, Guitar, vocals, composer, American
Wallington, George, Bebop, 1940s–1960s, Piano, composer, American
Walton, Mercy Dee, West Coast Blues, 1940s–1960s, Piano, American
Washboard Willie, Jump Blues, 1940s–1980s, Washboard, American
Washington, Dinah, Rhythm & Blues; Swing, 1940s–1960s, Vocals, American
Waterford, Charles 'Crown Prince', Rhythm & Blues, 1940s–, Vocals, American
Waters, Benny, Swing, 1940s–1990s, Saxophones, clarinet, arranger, American
Wayne, Chuck, Swing; Modern Jazz, 1940s–1990s, Guitar, American
Webb, George, Dixieland Revival; British Jazz, 1940s–1970s, Piano, leader, British
Webster, Ben, Swing, 1940s–1970s, Saxophones, arranger, American
Wess, Frank, Cool Jazz; Swing; Bebop, 1940s–, Saxophones, flute, American
Whittle, Tommy, Big Band; Swing, 1940s–, Saxophone, reeds, British
Wilber, Bob, Traditional Jazz, 1940s–, Clarinet, soprano saxophone, arranger, composer, American
Wilder, Joe, Swing, 1940s–, Trumpet, flugelhorn, American
Williams, Joe, Jump Blues, 1940s–1990s, Vocals, American
Williams, John, Swing, 1940s–1960s, Saxophone, American
Williams, L.C., Texas Blues, 1940s–1950s, Vocals, drums, American
Williams, Lester, Rhythm & Blues, 1940s–1950s, Guitar, American
Williams, Paul 'Hucklebuck', Jump Blues; Rhythm & Blues, 1940s–1960s, Saxophone, bandleader, American
Willis, Ralph, Country Blues, 1940s–1950s, Guitar, American
Wilson, Gerald, Bebop, 1940s–1990s, Trumpet, arranger, composer, American
Wilson, Gerald, Dixieland, 1940s–, Trumpet, arranger, American
Wilson, Shadow, Bebop; Swing, 1940s–1950s, Drums, American
Windhurst, Johnny, Chicago Jazz; Swing; Big Band, 1940s–1970s, Trumpet, American
Winding, Kai, Bebop, 1940s–1970s, Trombone, American
Witherspoon, Jimmy, Jump Blues, 1940s–1990s, Vocals, guitar, American
Woodman, Britt, Swing; West Coast Jazz, 1940s–2000s, Trombone, American
Woods, Oscar 'Buddy', Country Blues, 1940s, Vocals, guitar, American
Wright, Billy, Jump Blues, 1940s–1950s, Vocals, American
Wright, Denny, Swing; Bebop, 1940s–1990s, Guitar, composer, arranger, conductor, British
Yancey, Mama, Boogie-Woogie, 1940s, Vocals, American
Young, Johnny, Modern Electric Blues; Chicago Blues, 1940s–1960s, Vocals, mandolin, guitar, American
Zentner, Si, Swing; Big Band, 1940s–2000s, Trombone, bandleader, American

see Billie Holiday pp 156 *see* T-Bone Walker pp 168 *see* Champion Jack Dupree pp 174 *see* Louis Jordan pp 176

THE FIFTIES

The 1950s was a big decade for blues and jazz – arguably, the biggest. In the wake of international triumph and the stirrings of empire, the US enjoyed a boom of babies, cars, television, and urban and suburban development, that trickled down to embolden a stronger movement for civil rights for black people, inspired immigration from Cuba, Puerto Rico and other Caribbean ports, and normalized the spread of its cultural products worldwide. Europe, so much harder hit by the previous decade's war, was in a period of renewal, with the emergence of its first generation since the 1920s that could even imagine itself carefree. There were still conflicts, threats and dangers. The US brewed itself a Cold War with Communism as the bogeyman, Europe was divided by the Iron Curtain, and modernization had not yet arrived fully in Spain, Portugal, Greece and southern Italy as it had in Great Britain, France, Scandinavia, West Germany and the Netherlands.

What did this mean to music? Blues players, backing themselves with loud combos and staunch beats, raised a shout that echoed through the songs of Bo Diddley, Chuck Berry, Ray Charles and Fats Domino to be taken up by white teenagers, including one hip-shaking Elvis Presley. Jazz singers and instrumentalists, ever-more highly regarded for their swinging sophistication and lionized for their bohemian lifestyles, gained self-esteem as well as eager acolytes wherever their newly long-playing records were heard. Blues and jazz had spread wildly and widely since their first recordings in the teens and twenties. In the fifties, blues and jazz stepped out as ambassadors – and wherever they went, their call met with eager, imitative response.

ROCK

Sources & Sounds

KEY ARTISTS

Ray Charles
Miles Davis
Fats Domino
Bill Evans
Thelonious Monk
Gerry Mulligan
Muddy Waters

The 1950s was a period of sharp social and political contrasts. The decade is often regarded as a stultifyingly conservative and rather monochrome one, but the suburbanization and the solidification of middle-class values took place under the looming shadow of the Cold War in America and the physical separation of East and West in Europe. The threat of atomic weapons loomed large, and the 'space race' added further tensions to what were already fraught international relations. In Europe, wartime austerity carried on well into the 1950s, and the domination of US culture on a global basis became increasingly apparent – transmitted through media including films, music, Broadway musicals, radio and eventually television.

The US was at war in 1950, although the Truman administration referred to Korea as a 'police action'. Dwight Eisenhower was elected President in 1952, partly on his promise to 'go to Korea'. He fulfilled this promise and a truce was negotiated, which remains in place more than 50 years later. Eisenhower embarked on a programme of highway development so that the country became more accessible by car, making it much easier for bands to travel. Vast super-highways such as Routes 80, 40 and 10 now went from coast to coast. He also worked to abolish segregation in Washington, DC; this proved slightly more difficult.

'In New Orleans … there was the African influence … from Western Europe came the harmonic sense, the tonal structure, the instruments employed. Today … there are the newer influences of contemporary serious composers: Bartok, Stravinsky, Milhaud, and others.'

Dave Brubeck

Right
African-American jazz artists such as Charles Mingus promoted civil rights in their music.

Separate But Not Equal

America was still largely segregated and the majority white population seemed worryingly comfortable with its racial separation. In 1954 the United States Supreme Court voted to overturn Plessy vs Ferguson, an 1896 ruling that 'segregation was in the natural order of things' and that 'separate but equal' was the law of the land. The Court, in a unanimous verdict, ruled that 'In the field of public education, the doctrine of separate but equal has no place'; this destroyed the legal basis for segregation. A period of intensifying campaigns was launched, attempting to secure civil rights for the African-American population, and the seeds were sown for the removal of segregationist legislation that would occur during the 1960s. These cultural events were directly reflected in the music of several major jazz musicians, including Sonny Rollins (b. 1930), Max Roach (b. 1924) and Charles Mingus (1922–79).

see Introduction pp 188 *see* Key Artists pp 198 *see* A–Z of Artists pp 216 *see* List of Artists pp 236

colour-blind and was accessible to all; white teenagers were finding black radio stations in ever-increasing numbers. Record labels saw the potential in these songs and began to produce cover records, with white artists duplicating or sanitizing the arrangements of hit R&B records.

Rock'N'Roll Revolution

However, in the 1950s jazz and blues faced a major new competitor in the quest for listeners – one that was to dominate almost from the outset. Rock'n'roll exploded on to the music scene – the convenient launch point is usually taken to be Bill Haley's 'Rock Around The Clock' in 1954, but the groundwork had already been laid by jazz, blues, gospel, R&B and country music. Rockabilly music, which took elements from white hillbilly and black R&B influences, found a home at Sam Phillips' Sun Records in Memphis and for a while its frantic reverberations dominated the pop music market. The rise of the teenager as a distinct – and increasingly independent – consumer group was also a new 'invention' of the decade, and the new music forms that were developing around this time fed directly into the new teen-oriented market.

However, winning over the hearts and minds of many US citizens would take a little longer.

It is significant that these developments came during a time of great glory for the blues. In 1954 Muddy Waters (1915–83) recorded his full band for the first time. The modern Chicago blues sound was now fully established and artists such as Howlin' Wolf (1910–76), Sonny Boy Williamson II (Rice Miller, c. 1912–65), Jimmy Reed (1925–76) and Little Walter (1930–68) were beginning to have big hit records and reach a broader public. R&B, that sprawling, inclusive idiom that covered blues shouters, saxophone honkers, jump blues and crooning, gospel-inspired vocal groups, was peaking. The biggest selling record of the year was by Guitar Slim (1925–59), and one by Big Joe Turner (1911–85) was fifth. Their success was largely driven by radio play; in every major city there was now at least one radio station where black music was played every day. Stations such as WLAC in Nashville, with a clear channel signal, could reach as many as 38 states. Radio was

The Role Of The DJ

Celebrity disc jockeys were the key communicators in the world of rock'n'roll radio. One of the most famous was Alan Freed in New York, who insisted on playing the original versions of hit songs. He also insisted on calling the music that he played – whether by black or white artists – rock'n'roll, and is widely credited with coining the term. The small labels that emerged from the

CLASSIC RECORDINGS

1951
Howlin' Wolf: 'How Many More Years'

1953
Guitar Slim: 'Things That I Used To Do'
Muddy Waters: 'Evil'

1954
Clarence 'Gatemouth' Brown: 'Okie Dokie Stomp'
Etta James: 'The Wallflower'

1955
Horace Silver: 'The Preacher'

1956
Sonny Rollins: 'St. Thomas'

1959
Dave Brubeck Quartet: 'Take Five'
Ray Charles: *The Genius Of Ray Charles*
Miles Davis: *Kind Of Blue*

Above
Black students enter a racially mixed school in Little Rock, Arkansas under armed escort.

Left
Muddy Waters backstage in London; Waters' 1950s UK tours paved the way for the blues tours of the next decade.

see Muddy Waters pp 212 *see* Charles Mingus pp 230 *see* Sonny Rollins pp 233 *see* Sonny Boy Williamson II pp 235

carnage of the recording bans of the 1940s were now an industry unto themselves and they were flexing their muscles. Disc jockeys were paid by labels to play specific songs on the air, and black records began to cross over to the pop charts with greater frequency. Rock'n'roll allowed white artists such as and Jerry Lee Lewis to flourish and be accepted into what had been a blacks-only idiom, while at the same time giving black, R&B-schooled performers like Little Richard a chance to infiltrate a wider market. It was rebellious, fresh and sexy, and it outraged the authorities; audiences, black and white, loved it.

The less enthusiastic attitude of the establishment, while reinforcing rock'n'roll's popularity among the young, meant that the new music was attacked everywhere in the press. The old ASCAP-BMI wars were rekindled and the big record labels began to lose their dominance in the pop field. Before the end of the decade, the establishment seemed to be getting its way; rock'n'roll music, which had at first been so shocking, became bland and commercialized. The blues element, which had been such a key component of the early style, was receding (although it was still evident in the music of artists such as Chuck Berry and Bo Diddley) and R&B was more or less finished. Furthermore, in one of the biggest scandals of the decade, a number of the disc jockeys that had championed R&B records – Alan Freed among them – were charged with accepting 'payola'.

Above
Hysterical teenagers cheer Elvis Presley as rock'n'roll fever sweeps the US.

Right
'Rock Around The Clock' introduced rock'n'roll.

Far Right
Alan Freed, one of the first broadcasters to grant both black and white artists airplay.

Jazz Music Loses Its Crown

Jazz had enjoyed a brief tenure as the principal popular music of America from the 1920s to the early 1940s, but would never regain that position. In the 1950s, though, hard-bop artists enjoyed wide popularity within African-American communities, and jazz was still a mainstay of the neighbourhood jukeboxes and clubs. In Europe, bop began to generate its own adherents, led by the likes of John Dankworth, Ronnie Scott and Tubby Hayes in England; the divisive arguments of the 1940s in America were replicated on the jazz scenes there. As in Hitler's Germany, jazz also came to be seen as an underground symbol of freedom within the Communist bloc, and spawned a clandestine music scene in later decades.

The Dixieland revival that had begun in the previous decade also continued to thrive throughout the 1950s, both in the clubs and on wax, in the hands of musicians such as guitarist Eddie Condon (1905–73) and saxophonist Adolphus 'Doc' Cheatham (1905–97) in the US, Ken Colyer (1928–88) and Chris Barber (b. 1930) in the UK and New Orleans veteran Louis Armstrong (1901–71), whose All Star band toured internationally, bringing Dixieland-flavoured jazz to audiences across the globe.

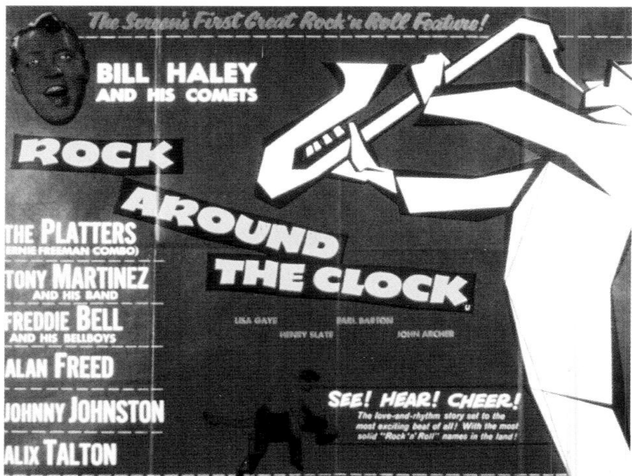

Hard Bop Takes Centre Stage

Hard bop became the 'mainstream' jazz form of the 1950s. It grew out of the new direction pioneered by the bebop artists of the late 1940s, but introduced an earthier feel that drew more overtly on blues and gospel. Art Blakey (1919–90) and Horace Silver (b. 1928) led the way in establishing the genre, while Jimmy Smith (1925–2005) laid down the ground rules for the related form of soul jazz, and paved the way for an eruption of Hammond organ trios.

see Introduction pp 188 *see* Key Artists pp 198 *see* A–Z of Artists pp 216 *see* List of Artists pp 236

The music associated with hard bop draws on the rhythmic and harmonic principles laid down in bebop, but with simpler motifs, a greater rigidity in the theme-solos-theme structure and a heavier reliance on 'running' the chord changes. The music had a heavier feel in both instrumental expression and rhythm than the airier registers of bebop, and its more obvious use of blues, gospel and R&B antecedents prompted the 'soul' and 'funk' tags, which quickly became attached to the music. It had a visceral, exciting sound with a distinctly urban ambiance, and it is no accident that many of its principal creators came from the big cities of the Northeast and Midwest – places such as New York, Chicago, Pittsburgh, Detroit and Philadelphia.

Gospel Meets The Blues

Meanwhile, Ray Charles was on to something different: he was beginning to secularize gospel music. Gospel performers, who had previously been shunned by their fans when they attempted to record 'the devil's music', were now routinely venturing into the blues and pop styles. Sam Cooke was one of the first performers to make the move; Johnny Taylor, Aretha Franklin and Lou Rawls would follow. The soul music that flourished in the next decade came alive in the mid-1950s, championed by specialist labels such as Atlantic Records, and was gradually forging a place for itself.

Country blues artists had been shunted aside in the onrushing march of everything else. With the increasing popularity of amplified, electric blues, many acoustic and solo performers found that their music was considered old-fashioned and outdated. Lightnin' Hopkins (1911–82) went almost five years without recording, and a large number of similar performers had to find ways of earning a living outside the music industry. From 1958, however,

see Eddie Condon pp 71 *see* Ray Charles pp 198 *see* Horace Silver pp 233 *see* Jimmy Smith pp 234

Above
Art Blakey helped to form the new hard-bop sound.

there was a revival of interest in folk music in the US, which included country blues artists. By the middle of the next decade, many black blues artists who had recorded in the 1920s were being tracked down, 'rediscovered', recorded and made into international stars.

A Complex Mosaic

Jazz music continued to explore new territory as the 1950s drew to a close. By the end of the decade, the perceived limitations of the hard-bop format were pushing some musicians into more experimental directions. The emergence of pianist Cecil Taylor (b. 1929) and the arrival of saxophonist Ornette Coleman (b. 1930) in New York in 1959 were crucial turning points in the move towards free jazz in the 1960s, but bop did not relinquish its position immediately and continued to thrive in the hands of young musicians such as Lee Morgan (1938–72), Wes Montgomery (1925–68), Cannonball Adderley (1928–75) and Hank Mobley.

If hard bop was the signature jazz sound of the 1950s, it was only part of an increasingly complex

see Introduction pp 188 *see* Key Artists pp 198 *see* A–Z of Artists pp 216 *see* List of Artists pp 236

mosaic within the broad parameters of the music. While Louis Armstrong was consolidating his position as the most famous of all jazz names, many of the big-band leaders had reformed their groups (or never actually halted), including Duke Ellington (1899–1974), Count Basie (1904–84), Woody Herman (1913–87), Benny Goodman (1909–86), Stan Kenton (1912–79), Buddy Rich (1917–87) and Harry James (1916–83).

Following the developments in popular music since the late 1930s, jazz-oriented singers including Frank Sinatra (1915–98), Ella Fitzgerald (1917–96), Sarah Vaughan (1924–90) and Nat 'King' Cole (1917–65) had by now become international stars, crossing over to pop audiences with ease. The major names in modern jazz were all musicians who had launched their careers in bebop (or had been strongly influenced by it), but had moved off in diverse directions. They included Miles Davis (1926–91), Thelonious Monk (1917–82), Dizzy Gillespie (1917–93), Charles Mingus, Sonny Rollins and John Coltrane (1926–67) – all of whom helped to shape the development of jazz in different ways.

Playing It Cool

Modal jazz was well established by the end of the decade, reflected in the success of Miles Davis's album *Kind Of Blue* (1959). Cool jazz was also a key contributor to the mix. Often seen as a largely white reaction to the mainly black hard-bop mainstream, cool jazz grew out of the arranging experiments of Gerry Mulligan (1927–96) and Gil Evans (1912–88), exemplified in Miles Davis's Nonet recordings of 1949–50 (later dubbed the 'Birth Of The Cool' on their LP release). As the name implies, cool jazz adopted a less frenetic and more arrangement-oriented approach than hard bop, although the forms are clearly related; indeed, they are effectively a parallel development from the same harmonic and rhythmic foundations in bebop.

Mulligan's subsequent quartet in Los Angeles with trumpeter Chet Baker (1929–88) proved very popular, and the West Coast became the centre of the cool movement (it is sometimes referred to as 'West Coast' jazz) in the work of artists such as Shorty Rogers, Bud Shank, Shelly Manne, Chico Hamilton and Teddy Edwards. Major names like Dave Brubeck (b. 1920), Stan Getz (1927–91) and Art Pepper (1925–82) often reflected a cooler approach, while Lennie Tristano (1919–78) acolytes Lee Konitz and Warne Marsh also explored related ground.

The Blues Spreads Overseas

While the jazz movements of the 1950s took hold in particular areas across the US, overseas markets were

Below
Singer and songwriter Sam Cooke was one of the first gospel performers to infuriate his fans by moving into secular music.

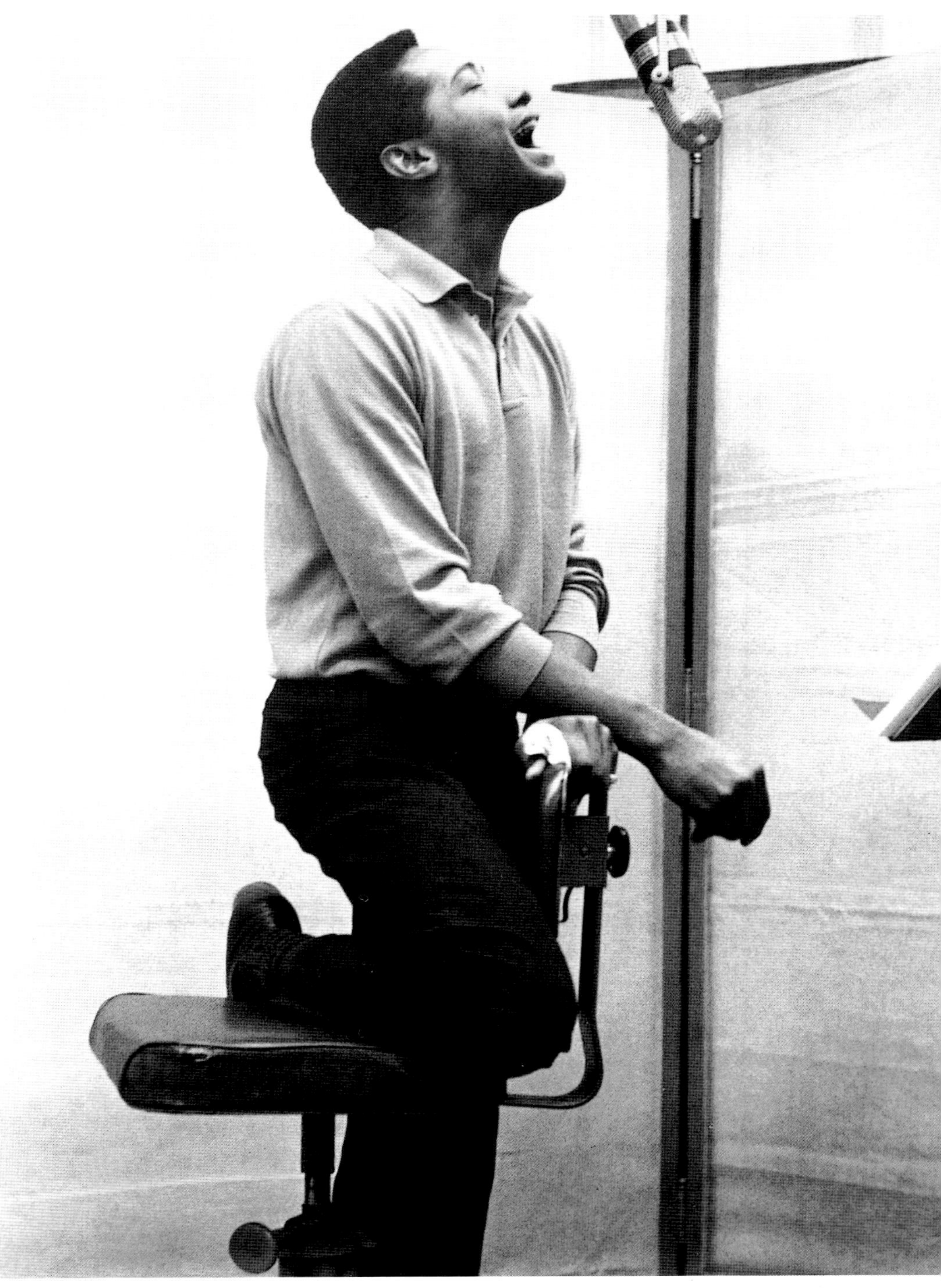

see Louis Armstrong pp 44 see Miles Davis pp 200 see Gerry Mulligan pp 210 see Cecil Taylor pp 280

Above
Vocalist Frank Sinatra.

becoming more important for blues artists. The European tours of Big Bill Broonzy (1893–1958) and Muddy Waters in the 1950s would lead to the fully fledged, multi-artist tours of the 1960s. Champion Jack Dupree (1910–92) had settled in Europe; Mickey Baker (b. 1925) and Memphis Slim (1915–88) would follow. Blues artists were welcome all over the globe and this was a trend that would only increase over time. European labels began to produce their own blues recordings, no longer content to license masters from the US.

B.B. King (b. 1925) kept working, averaging more than 300 dates a year from the mid-1950s. He was an artist whose popularity at this time was almost unknown to white audiences, but a steady stream of hit singles and budget-priced LPs kept his name in front of the black public, especially in the South, during the entire decade. Bobby Bland (b. 1930) made a breakthrough in 1957, while some stars from the early 1950s, such as Amos Milburn (1927–80) and Charles Brown (1922–99), dropped out of sight. Saxophone honkers such as Hal Singer (b. 1919), Sam 'The Man' Taylor and Big Al Sears were replaced by King Curtis, who in the rock'n'roll years assumed much of the New York studio work all by himself. Producers such as Jerry Leiber and Mike Stoller, who also wrote songs for artists including the Coasters, became at least as important as the 'professors' such as Jesse Stone and Howard Biggs in guiding record dates.

Above
Trumpeter Chet Baker.

The Advent Of The LP

The revival of the blues' popularity in the 1950s resulted in part from the introduction of the long-playing record. In 1950, 78 rpm was the dominant speed of records. The 45- and 331/3-rpm speeds, introduced in 1948, were slow to gain ground. Atlantic issued its first 45 single in 1951, while Chess did not have any blues LPs until 1958. By the end of the decade, however, 78 rpm had faded completely away and LPs were becoming more important. New country blues recordings were issued in this format.

The arrival the LP was also significant to the developments in jazz; as jazz was largely based around improvisation and solos, musicians often played at very extended lengths in live performance, even before the bebop era – especially in club sets or jam sessions. Broadcasts permitted the players to stretch out, but it was only with the advent of the longer playing time of the LP that jazz musicians were able to begin reflecting their live work more accurately in the recording studio. That could be a mixed blessing, and many 1950s recordings were little more than loose blowing sessions, but it did allow a more faithful record of a musician's style and abilities to be preserved in the studio environment.

The 1950s, then, turned out to be a complex decade, both within jazz and blues and in the wider world, rather than – as they are sometimes depicted – simply the dull, hidebound prelude to the new freedoms and excesses of the 1960s. There was change aplenty in the music of the era, and many of the new developments would be widely influential to the musicians of the next generation, just as in a broader sense many of the political and cultural decisions made during the decade would continue to ripple through history. The best music of the period has proved to be exceptionally durable and many of the artists who developed at this time went on to even greater achievements in the decades to come.

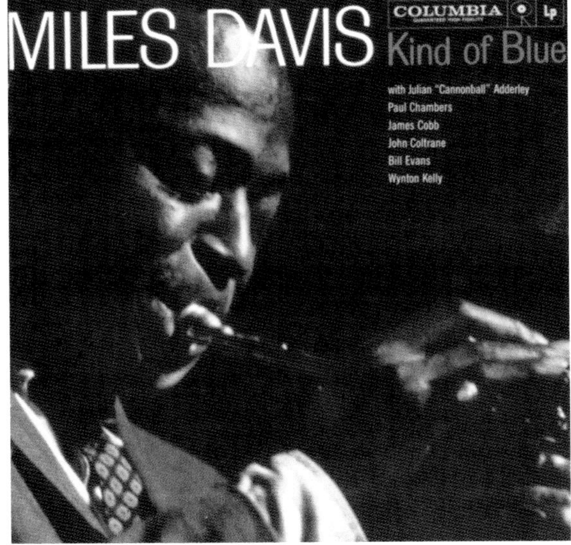

Left
Miles Davis's *Kind Of Blue*.

see Big Bill Broonzy pp 104 *see* Chet Baker pp 216 *see* Bobby 'Blue' Bland pp 218 *see* B.B. King pp 260

Ray Charles

CLASSIC RECORDINGS

1954
'I Got A Woman'

1955
'A Fool For You', 'Drown In My Own Tears', 'Hallelujah, I Love Her So'

1959
'What'd I Say'
The Genius Of Ray Charles, 'Just For A Thrill', 'Let The Good Times Roll'

1960
'Georgia On My Mind'

1961
'Hit The Road Jack', 'Unchain My Heart'

Ray Charles Robinson was born on 23 September 1930 in Albany, Georgia. Blind by the age of seven, he was educated at the Florida School for the Deaf and Blind in St. Augustine, where he studied piano and learned to read music in braille.

A Musical Education

Shortly after his fifteenth birthday, he was expelled and left for Jacksonville, Florida to try to make a living from music. Ray continued his music education at the local union hall in Jacksonville. Within a few months, he was starting to play little jobs around the city. When he was at home, Ray would listen to country music, spirituals and blues on the radio; on his jobs, he heard singers such as Nat 'King' Cole and Charles Brown on the jukebox. Ray listened closely to these two singers and began to use them as his vocal models.

Over the next two years, Ray worked with a variety of different bands. In some cases he wrote arrangements, at other times he played alto sax or wrote songs. He travelled throughout Florida and got his first featured gig in Tampa, playing piano and singing with a combo modelled after that of Nat 'King' Cole.

'I do jazz, blues, country music and so forth. I do them all, like a good utility man.'
Ray Charles

In March 1948 Ray moved to Seattle, Washington on the advice of G.D. McKee, a guitarist with whom Ray had been working in Tampa. The pair quickly found plenty of work in their new surroundings, and within a few months had been signed by Downbeat Records. 'Confession Blues', one of Ray's tunes, became a hit in the spring of 1949. At this point Ray – who had been known as R.C. Robinson – became Ray Charles. The owner of Downbeat Records (now Swingtime), Jack Lauderdale, teamed Ray with his number-one act, Lowell Fulson and Ray became a part of Fulson's show, playing piano and singing in the band between 1950–52. The hit 'Baby, Let Me Hold Your Hand' brought Ray more attention, but Lauderdale had entered a dry spell and Charles's contract was sold to Atlantic Records.

A Shaky Start

Ray Charles's first recording session in his own name, in September 1952, was uneventful and follow-ups yielded only one minor hit ('It Should've Been Me'). Meanwhile, Charles was working as a solo artist, picking up musicians along the way. In the summer of 1954 he organized a band to back Ruth Brown on tour, after which the band continued on its own. In November, Ray was ready to call Atlantic Records.

'I Got A Woman', recorded on 18 November 1954, changed everything. The tune was based on a gospel song and, for the first time, all Charles's passion and fervour was captured on record. It was an R&B number one and Ray's biggest hit of the 1950s. His next session produced another number one, 'A Fool For You'. Ray Charles had arrived.

Ray Charles: 'The Genius'

Towards the end of the decade, Ray Charles spread his wings. He recorded jazz instrumentals, blues,

Right
Gifted pianist and entertainer Ray Charles.

Far Right Top
Charles in the 1980 film *The Blues Brothers*.

Far Right Bottom
Downbeat Records star Lowell Fulson.

see Introduction pp 188 *see* Sources & Sounds pp 190 *see* A–Z of Artists pp 216

gospel-inspired material and an album with a large orchestra, *The Genius Of Ray Charles* (1959). At the end of the decade, after more number ones with 'Drown In My Own Tears' and 'What'd I Say', Charles signed with ABC-Paramount. The deal included Ray's ownership of his own masters and complete artistic control.

From this point, Ray Charles rarely looked back. He formed a big band, founded his own record label, Tangerine, and continued to have hits. He recorded a variety of jazz, pop, R&B, soul, and country & western material throughout the 1960s and 1970s, to varying degrees of success, but came back to prominence in the 1980s with a cameo in *The Blues Brothers* (1980) and a USA For Africa single 'We Are The World'. Charles, winner of 12 Grammys and a Lifetime Achievement Award, died on 10 June 2004. His album *Genius Loves Company* (2004), featuring duets with a variety of artists, was released posthumously to huge sales and recieved multiple awards, simultaneous with an Oscar-winning Hollywood biopic, *Ray* (2004).

see **Charles Brown pp 170** *see* **Nat 'King' Cole pp 172** *see* **Ruth Brown pp 219** *see* **Lowell Fulson pp 222**

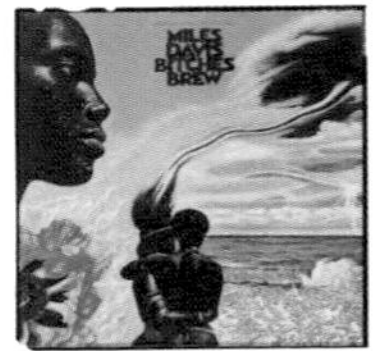

Miles Davis

CLASSIC RECORDINGS

1949–50
Birth Of The Cool, 'Darn That Dream', 'Deception', 'Venus De Milo'

1954
Miles Davis And The Modern Jazz Giants, 'Bemsha Swing', 'The Man I Love'

1958
Milestones, 'Milestones', 'Straight No Chaser'

1958
Porgy And Bess, 'I Loves You Porgy', 'Summertime'

1959
Kind Of Blue, 'So What'

The history of post-war jazz tracked the musical development of Miles Dewey Davis III so closely that it is tempting to see the trumpeter as the orchestrator of each of the most significant stylistic shifts of the era. With the notable exception of free jazz, Miles seemed to trigger a new seismic shift in the music with each passing decade. The reality is inevitably less simple, but there is no question that if Miles did not initiate successive revolutions, he was consistently in the frontline of their development and popularization.

Davis's playing style, often described as 'cool', was unique in the hotbed of 1940s New York bebop. His tone was pensive and soft, with little attack, vibrato or other ornamentation. His frequent use of a mute further created a sense of intimacy, drawing the listener into the music. While his solos may have been expressed simply, they were at the same time highly sophisticated, and his modal improvisation technique helped to lay the foundations for the free-jazz movement of the 1960s.

'Don't play what's there, play what's not there.'
Miles Davis

Right
Miles Davis (far right) with Sidney Bechet (far left) at the 1949 Jazz Fair in Paris, France.

Early Heroes

Born into a black, bourgeois family in Alton, Illinois in 1926, Miles was brought up in St. Louis and first played music professionally in that city. His parents were musical and encouraged their son's interests, while his father had a love of jazz music and presented Miles with a trumpet for his thirteenth birthday. Miles played in his high school band and through his teacher was privileged enough to meet one of his heroes, Clark Terry, on whom he modelled his playing style. Another lucky break came when Billy Eckstein's band came to St. Louis, featuring Dizzy Gillespie and Charlie Parker, with whose work Davis was familiar from records. During the performance the third trumpet player was taken ill, and Davis stepped in.

Moving to New York in 1945 to study at the Juilliard School of Music, Davis was in time to catch the flowering of bebop and determined to find Parker and play with him again; he succeeded and soon became Parker's regular trumpet player at the Three Deuces in 52nd Street. He also played with Parker's quintet on the keystone bebop recordings with Savoy, although his technical dexterity was not quite up to Parker's and Gillespie's standards, and he gave way to

see Introduction pp 188 *see* Sources & Sounds pp 190 *see* A–Z of Artists pp 216

Gillespie on some of the more up-tempo numbers. After brief sojourns with Benny Carter's and Billy Eckstein's Bands, Miles was back playing with Parker in New York. During this time, he honed his playing skills and solo technique, striking out on his own in 1947 after growing weary of Parker's unpredictable behaviour.

Above
The classic quintet of the 1960s: (l–r) Herbie Hancock, Davis, Ron Carter, Wayne Shorter, Tony Williams.

Miles Ahead

Although Davis knew that bebop was currently where it was at, the frenetic style of the new music was not his real forte. Davis preferred a more detached, lyrical style in the manner of Lester Young. One who knew Young was the pianist, composer and arranger Gil Evans; Davis admired Evans' ability to move away subtly from the basic beat in his arrangements, and the way in which his compositions favoured soloing and improvisation. Davis formed an ensemble and enlisted Evans as arranger, and 1948 saw the beginning of a successful working relationship that would open new avenues in jazz music. Evans was able to work Davis's musical vision into an orchestral setting, and both the curious instrumentation and the arrangements themselves showed originality, as did the sense of tranquillity created by the lack of range in dynamics and tempo. Further arrangements by Evans and Gerry Mulligan resulted in the landmark 1949–50 sessions, later dubbed the 'Birth Of The Cool', which paved the way for cool jazz. That new style, which took off on the West Coast jazz scene quickly came to be seen, despite Miles, as a largely white response to bebop.

A Successful Quintet

Davis spent the early 1950s playing in small groups, with varying degrees of success, alongside such luminaries as Sonny Rollins, Thelonious Monk and Davis's erstwhile hero, Charlie Parker. In 1954 Davis kicked his heroin addiction and re-launched his flagging career. His use of a Harmon Mute with its stem removed gave him a lyrical, instantly recognizable sound, and perhaps helped him to work around the fact that, by jazz standards, he was not a dazzling virtuoso. The latter half of the 1950s witnessed outstanding peaks of Davis's achievement. In those years, he led his great quintet with pianist Red Garland, bassist Paul Chambers and drummer Philly Jo Jones, and featuring on saxophone at various times John Coltrane, Sonny Rollins and Cannonball Adderley.

An appearance at the 1955 Newport Jazz Festival established Davis's role as a key player in contemporary jazz, and resulted in a recording contract with Columbia. Within this band, Miles also worked at and perfected the art of the understated solo, which would be an inspiration to many.

Reuniting with Evans towards the end of the decade and returning to their ensemble work, Davis recorded some of his best known albums, including *Miles Ahead* (1957), which featured a nineteen-piece

see Lester Young pp 118 *see* Dizzy Gillespie pp 152 *see* Charles Parker pp 162 *see* Gil Evans pp 221

orchestra and Davis playing a melancholy flugelhorn. Evans' ingenious arrangement of Gershwin's *Porgy and Bess* followed in 1958, and then *Sketches Of Spain* (1959–60), which drew from Spanish influences and opened up the possibilities for mingling jazz with music from other parts of the world, which would become more commonplace in the 1960s and 1970s. Another recording of note at this time was Davis's beautiful, brooding soundtrack for a Louis Malle *film noir*, *L'Ascenseur pour l'échafaud* (1948), which served to introduce his music to a new audience.

Mastering The Modes

The influence of George Russell led Davis towards a modal theory of jazz, in which improvisation was based on a set of scales (modes were originally part of early Greek music) rather than on the chord-based structures of bop. Miles brought these ideas to a wide audience, notably in *Milestones* (1958) and the classic *Kind Of Blue* (1959), featuring the masterful Bill Evans on piano and energetic solos from Cannonball Adderley and John Coltrane that contrasted effectively with Davis's more reserved playing.

Typically, though, a new decade brought another change of direction. Avoiding the trappings of free jazz, as pioneered by Ornette Coleman, Davis's classic 1960s quintet with saxophonist Wayne Shorter, pianist Herbie Hancock and the rhythm section of Ron Carter (bass) and Tony Williams (drums) was one of the great units in jazz history. In 1969, he recorded *In A Silent Way* with an electrically enhanced line-up that included Chick Corea and Joe Zawinul (keyboards), John Mclaughlin (guitar) and Dave

see Introduction pp 188 *see* Sources & Sounds pp 190 *see* A–Z of Artists pp 216

Holland (bass). This was followed by the landmark *Bitches Brew* (1969), Davis's bestselling record and generally regarded as the cornerstone of the jazz-rock wave of the 1970s. Many older jazz fans parted company with his music at this point, but Miles was unrepentant in seeking a new, rock-oriented audience.

The textural mass of his music grew increasingly dense with guitars and keyboards, and he himself became progressively more distant from his audience, a move exacerbated by poor health and drug use. He was in the habit of playing with his back to the house, using a trumpet fitted with a modified wah-wah pedal.

Back In Business

He stopped playing altogether throughout 1975–80, but resumed his performing and recording career with a series of pop-funk-oriented bands in the 1980s, also working again with Gil Evans in 1983 on *Star People*. A well-received album from 1988, *Tutu*, suggested to many that Davis had still not lost his touch. Out-of-character reunions in the summer of 1991 with some of his eminent former sidemen at Montreux and in France, and the revisiting of nostalgic numbers from his early albums in live performances suggested that he was aware his death in September was imminent.

For four decades Miles had launched the careers of musicians including John Coltrane and Bill Evans in the 1950s, Ron Carter, Wayne Shorter and Herbie Hancock in the 1960s, John McLaughlin, Chick Corea, Jack DeJohnette and Dave Holland in the 1970s, and John Scofield, Mike Stern and Kenny Garrett in the 1980s. He was always open to experiments and brought together diverse influences, ranging from Stockhausen's electronic textures to soul, funk, hip hop and ethnic instruments.

The connecting thread in all of this was Miles himself. His own sound and approach remained largely a constant at the centre of all these changing musical contexts. The abrasive personality, menacing aloofness, foul language and arrogant demeanour that saw him dubbed the 'Prince of Darkness' seemed only to add to his charisma.

Above
Davis often either initiated or championed successive jazz revolutions.

Far Left
Davis relaxes between takes in the recording studios of Fontana Records.

see George Russell pp 183 *see* Wayne Shorter pp 279 *see* Herbie Hancock pp 305 *see* Dave Holland pp 306

Fats Domino

CLASSIC RECORDINGS

1949
'The Fat Man'

1952
'Goin' Home'

1953
'Goin' To The River', 'Please Don't Leave Me'

1955
'Ain't That A Shame', 'All By Myself', 'Poor Me'

1956
'Blueberry Hill', 'I'm In Love Again'

1957
'I'm Walkin''

1959
'I Want To Walk You Home'

Antoine Domino Jr. was born on 26 February 1928 in New Orleans, Louisiana, the youngest of eight children. His father played violin and worked at the Fair Grounds Race Track in New Orleans. Young Antoine studied piano and credits Harrison Varrett, a former member of Papa Celestin's band, with giving him the advice and encouragement to keep going. He practiced assiduously in his teens and was attracted to the music of boogie-woogie giants Meade 'Lux' Lewis and Albert Ammons, which he heard on jukeboxes, as well as the work of pianist/vocalists such as Charles Brown and Amos Milburn.

'When Fats plays that it's magic.... It's something just a little bigger than life, just the way Fats is.'

Allen Toussaint, on the introduction to 'Goin' Home'

Domino Signs With Imperial

He began playing parties and social functions at the age of 16 and the following year joined the combo of Billy Diamond, who christened him 'Fats'. In 1949, he began a regular gig at the Hideaway Club and started to draw crowds and get noticed. New Orleans bandleader Dave Bartholomew, who was serving as a talent scout for Imperial Records, brought the label's owner Lew Chudd to hear Fats at the Hideaway. Domino was signed; Bartholomew worked as producer and the two co-wrote songs together. In the first session, cut on 10 December 1949, Fats and

Right
Dave Bartholomew – bandleader, producer, composer, talent scout, trumpeter and Domino's mentor in the early days.

see Introduction pp 188 see Sources & Sounds pp 190 see A–Z of Artists pp 216

Bartholomew's band recorded 'The Fat Man' – basically Champion Jack Dupree's 'Junker's Blues', dressed up with a new lyric from Bartholomew. It became a smash hit and climbed as high as number two on the *Billboard* magazine Race Records chart.

A Signature Sound

Fats then formed a band modelled on Bartholomew's, which even included some of the same personnel. Much of Fats Domino's sound is based on his vocals and piano, plus tenor saxophone solos; the arrangements on his early records do not differ greatly from those of other blues bands, but the piano's distinctive sound and use of triplets became a Domino trademark after first appearing on 'Every Night About This Time' in 1950.

'Goin' Home' hit number one in 1952 and Fats continued his streak of bestselling singles. He was still working around New Orleans for the most part and recording with the same nucleus of players. He took time out to play piano on 'Lawdy Miss Clawdy' by Lloyd Price, another number-one hit (and yet another lyric grafted on to the 'Junker's Blues' melody). The R&B coming out of New Orleans was beginning to sweep the country and Fats Domino was leading the way. The year 1953 found more hits with 'Please Don't Leave Me' and 'Goin' To The River', which infiltrated the pop chart. Herb Hardesty took most of the tenor sax solos with Fats and began to tour with him, although later on Hardesty tended to split the solos with Lee Allen.

Rock'N'Roll?

Rock'n'roll really arrived in 1955 and Fats was at the head of the pack. He had three consecutive number-one hits with 'Ain't That A Shame', 'All By Myself' and 'Poor Me'. In 1956 he delivered three more: 'I'm In Love Again', 'Blueberry Hill' and 'Blue Monday'. The sound of Fats Domino's band changed little during this period; when people asked him about rock'n'roll, he would tell them that he called it R&B and that he had been playing it for years. Indeed, he still plays that way – complete with triplet rhythms and a large saxophone section – and little has changed in the 50 years since Fats Domino was the talk of the town. He has enjoyed so many successful hit records that he is unable to play them all in any one show.

Above
New Orleans pianist and rock'n'roll superstar Fats Domino.

see Meade 'Lux' Lewis pp 128 *see* Charles Brown pp 170 *see* Amos Milburn pp 179 *see* Dave Bartholomew pp 217

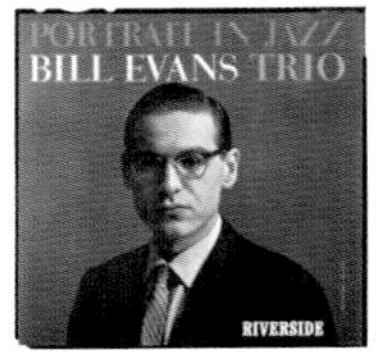

Bill Evans

CLASSIC RECORDINGS

1956
New Jazz Conceptions, 'Speak Low'

1958
Everybody Digs Bill Evans, 'Peace Piece'

1959
Portrait in Jazz, 'Autumn Leaves', 'Come Rain Or Come Shine'

1961
Sunday At The Village Vanguard/Waltz For Debby, 'Detour Ahead', 'My Foolish Heart', 'Waltz For Debby'

1962
How My Heart Sings, 'How My Heart Sings', 'Summertime'

1963
Conversations With Myself, 'How About You'

Bill Evans was one of the most lyrical and romantic of all jazz pianists. His distinctive lightness of touch and singing tone on the piano shone most brightly in his favoured trio settings with compatible bass players and drummers, including famous line-ups that featured Scott LaFaro and Paul Motian, and later Eddie Gomez and Marty Morrell.

Evans was born in Plainfield, New Jersey in 1929 and studied classical piano (and also violin) from the age of six (the trademark hunched position that he later adopted at the keyboard would doubtless have horrified his teacher!). He turned to jazz in his teens and began working professionally in New York in the early 1950s. He came to wider notice through associations with George Russell, Cannonball Adderley and – most significantly – the Miles Davis Sextet of the late 1950s.

Rethinking The Piano Trio

Evans' contributions as pianist or composer to all but one track on the classic *Kind Of Blue* was as crucial as anyone's to the success of that famous session. His own recording career as a leader began with *New Jazz Conceptions* (1956). His influences included Bud Powell and Horace Silver, but while his style remained rooted in bop, he developed his approach in an individual fashion that laid heavy stress on the lyrical facets of his music and on original harmonic thinking.

'He changed forever the way the piano was approached. He opened up so many different possibilities in terms of harmony and rhythm.... He was creating all the time.'

Joe La Barbera

His famous trio with bassist Scott LaFaro and drummer Paul Motian brought a new lustre to one of jazz's most established formats, but the tragic death of LaFaro in a road accident in 1961 brought the group to a premature end. The live recordings that they made at the Village Vanguard in New York are among the highest accomplishments of the trio repertoire in jazz. LaFaro was well-equipped to adopt the kind of interactive accompanying role that Evans favoured, and set a benchmark that the pianist always sought to emulate in his choice of bassists. Later incumbents of that key position included Gary Peacock and Eddie Gomez.

Above
Bill Evans played in a small group in the 1970s, a period in which he also experimented with the sound of a Fender Rhodes electric piano.

A Pervasive Influence

The pianist's refined sense of melodic inflection and harmonic subtlety proved very influential, not only on his peers but also on a subsequent generation of great jazz pianists, including Herbie Hancock, Chick Corea and Keith Jarrett. That influence remains equally pervasive today. If the trio was his principal vehicle, Evans also explored the use of overdubbing to create multitracked 'solo' piano recordings, as on *Conversations With Myself* (1963). He recorded duo albums with guitarist Jim Hall and singer Tony Bennett, as well as with Eddie Gomez, and sometimes worked with horn players added to his trio. He also recorded with a symphony orchestra in 1965.

see Introduction pp 188 *see* Sources & Sounds pp 190 *see* A–Z of Artists pp 216

Making The Piano Sing

Evans' ability to radically remake standard tunes by the most deft and subtle of alterations was legendary, and his own compositions have stood the test of time. His best-known originals include 'Blue In Green' (jointly credited to Miles Davis), 'Waltz For Debby', 'Comrad Conrad', 'Peace Piece', 'Detour Ahead', 'Funkallero', 'Interplay', 'NYC's No Lark' (an anagram of the name of pianist Sonny Clark, and a tribute to his memory), 'Laurie', 'Re: Person I Knew' (another anagram, of producer Orrin Keepnews), 'Song For Helen', 'Time Remembered' and 'We Will Meet Again'.

He experimented with a Fender Rhodes electric piano in the 1970s, but his music is inextricably welded to the sonority of the acoustic piano, and his ability to make that instrument sing lay at the heart of his achievement. He acquired a heroin addiction while serving in the US Army, and was plagued with drug problems and ill-health at various times in his career. He died in New York in September 1980, having done much to redefine the art of the piano trio.

Below

Pianist Bill Evans, whose classical training gave him a romantic sensitivity unusual in jazz performers.

see Miles Davis pp 200 *see* Bud Powell pp 232 *see* Cannonball Adderley pp 266 *see* Keith Jarrett pp 307

Thelonious Monk

CLASSIC RECORDINGS

1947–52
Complete Blue Note Recordings, 'Crepescule With Nellie', 'Epistrophy', 'Evidence', 'In Walked Bud', ''Round Midnight', 'Straight No Chaser', 'Well You Needn't'

1952–54
Complete Prestige Recordings, 'Bemsha Swing', 'Blue Monk'

1957
Monk's Music, 'Ruby My Dear'

Thelonious Monk was one of the most original and idiosyncratic figures in jazz history. Almost from the start of his long career, the pianist and composer pursued a singular but relentlessly focused path through jazz, playing his own music in his own instantly identifiable way, with a seeming disregard for popular acceptance that was extreme even by jazz standards.

Thelonious Sphere Monk Jr. was born in Rocky Mount, North Carolina on 10 October 1917, but lived in New York from the age of six. The Harlem stride pianists of the 1920s became a sublimated but palpable influence on his rhythmic style.

His idiosyncratic approach extended to every element of his music. His angular melodies, unconventional dissonant harmonies and oblique rhythmic patterns all bore his stamp, as did his touch at the keyboard (not to mention his penchant for using his elbow and forearm to crash out huge clusters of notes, or breaking into a little dance around the instrument).

Right
A US Post Office stamp featuring Thelonious Monk, from the Jazz Series.

'He'll come in [Minton's] any time and play for hours with only a dim light and the funny thing is he'll never play a complete tune. You never know what he's playing.'
Teddy Hill

A Unique Artistic Vision

Monk recycled his compositions endlessly in concert and on records, often in rather rigidly demarcated fashion. He was an introverted, eccentric figure in the colourful world of jazz, but he had a unique artistic vision and a single-minded determination to realize that vision. He was at the centre of the group of musicians who forged the framework for bebop at Minton's Playhouse in the mid-1940s, but even there his highly individual style placed him a little to the side of the central flow of the music (Bud Powell, a friend of Monk's, provided the more canonical example of the bebop pianist).

He worked with Coleman Hawkins, Lucky Millinder, Cootie Williams and Dizzy Gillespie in the mid-1940s, and began recording as a leader for Blue Note Records in 1947. His recordings for that label (until 1952), Prestige (1952–54) and Riverside (1954–60) comprise the bulk of his classic music. He signed to Columbia in 1960 and recorded in solo and big-band settings with the label – as well as in the familiar quartet format – but added only 11 new compositions in that time, preferring to rework his classic canon of the 1950s until his departure from the label, and start of total withdrawal, in 1969.

Right
Innovative bebop pianist Thelonious Monk.

see Introduction pp 188 see Sources & Sounds pp 190 see A–Z of Artists pp 216

Above
Monk at New York's Carnegie Hall in his last live appearance, 1976.

No Compromises Accepted

Monk's music rarely diverged from the structures of the standard 12-bar and 32-bar forms that dominated the era, but they were recast in strange new harmonies and rhythms. He brooked no compromises with his music, and many musicians baulked at the discipline his music required, although others – John Coltrane, Clark Terry, Steve Lacy and Charlie Rouse among them – embraced its spiky demands. Many of his tunes have entered the jazz repertoire, including ''Round Midnight', 'Blue Monk', 'In Walked Bud', 'Rhythm-A-Ning', 'Misterioso', 'Straight No Chaser', 'Well You Needn't' and 'Evidence'.

His increased profile led to his making a tour of Europe in 1961, and being featured on the cover of *Time* magazine in 1964. It had been a long time coming, but he went on to tour abroad regularly throughout the 1960s, mainly with his quartet but also with a nine-piece group in 1969; there are numerous live recordings from Europe and Japan as well as America in that decade.

A Timeless Legacy

His public appearances became increasingly rare in the early 1970s. He made his final studio recordings in London in 1971, and played his last concert at the Newport in New York jazz festival in 1976. His often-troubled psychological state and bizarre personal life were overseen by three protective women – his mother, his wife Nellie and his patron the Baroness Pannonica de Koenigswarter. He retired to the Baroness's home in Weehawken, New Jersey in 1976, and there he lived the rest of his life in self-imposed seclusion. He died of a cerebral haemorrhage in February 1982, leaving behind a mysterious, near-mythic reputation and a timeless, unique and endlessly challenging contribution to jazz.

see Coleman Hawkins pp 74 *see* Bud Powell pp 232 *see* John Coltrane pp 250 *see* Steve Lacy pp 308

Gerry Mulligan

CLASSIC RECORDINGS

1949–50
'Jeru', 'Venus De Milo'

1952–53
Gerry Mulligan Quartet: 'My Funny Valentine', 'The Lady Is A Tramp'

1954
California Concerts, 'Blues Going Up', 'Yardbird Suite'

1957
Mulligan Meets Monk, 'I Mean You', ''Round Midnight'

1959
Gerry Mulligan Meets Ben Webster, 'Chelsea Bridge', 'In A Mellotone'

Gerry Mulligan was the leading exponent of the baritone saxophone in jazz, and one of the key instigators of the style that came to be known as cool jazz. Along with trumpeter Chet Baker, Mulligan came to exemplify the cool ethos in the 1950s; he returned to the roots of that style with his *Re-Birth Of The Cool* (1992).

The title and the concept echoed the groundbreaking Nonet sessions of 1949–50, which were led by Miles Davis but fuelled by the arrangements of Mulligan and Gil Evans. The use of French horn and the intricate weave of timbre and texture in the music foreshadowed the later developments of the 'third stream' (the movement's main progenitors, pianist John Lewis and composer Gunther Schuller, were both involved in the sessions), as well as the cool school.

'Mulligan's main contribution was to bring jazz dynamics down to the dynamic range of a string bass – and then to use counterpoint in a natural, unschooled way.'

John Graas

Birth Of The Cool

Mulligan was born in New York City in April 1927 and grew up in Philadelphia. He began arranging music in his teens, inspired by the example of the great swing band arrangers such as Duke Ellington, Jimmy Mundy, Fletcher Henderson, Sy Oliver and Gil Evans.

Above
A performance at the 1955 Newport Jazz Festival featuring (l–r) Percy Heath, Miles Davis and Mulligan.

Right
Baritone saxophonist Gerry Mulligan was an important figure in cool jazz, as well as a gifted composer and arranger.

Mulligan wrote arrangements for the Claude Thornhill band in New York in 1946, and was introduced to the textural possibilities of twentieth-century classical music by Evans and drummer Gene Krupa, a devotee of Ravel. Mulligan was an eager learner and quickly began to develop a style that built on his roots in swing but displayed a more contemporary idiom and personal voice.

The 'Birth Of The Cool' recordings of 1949–50 featured his compositions ('Jeru', 'Venus De Milo', 'Rocker') and arrangements. The clarity, control, swing, and rhythmic and harmonic invention of the music were all less frenetic than the bop model, and the cooler approach was ideal for Mulligan.

Quartet And Big Band

Mulligan formed the first of his 'pianoless' quartets in Los Angeles in 1951, featuring Chet Baker's romantic trumpet. The contrapuntal possibilities of two (or more) horns, bass and drums would preoccupy him throughout the 1950s. His collaborators included trumpeters Jon Eardley and Art Farmer, valve trombonist Bob Brookmeyer and saxophonist Zoot Sims.

see Introduction pp 188 *see* Sources & Sounds pp 190 *see* A–Z of Artists pp 216

Mulligan began touring with his Concert Jazz Band in 1960, and continued to work on and off in that format throughout the rest of his career. While he made his greatest impact with his smaller groups, where improvisation was the primary element of the music, the large ensemble lent itself well to his particular style of writing and arranging. He revelled in the greater textural possibilities that the big band offered, and he went on to experiment with composing for orchestral ensembles as well, albeit less successfully.

Exploring The Big Horn

Mulligan's interest in musical textures extended to his choice of instrument. He began playing tenor saxophone but was seduced very quickly by the deeper sonorities and extended textural possibilities offered by the baritone register. Although he also played soprano saxophone and piano, he was best known for his finely burnished sound on baritone saxophone, and was one of the small group of players who have evolved a genuinely distinctive soloist's voice on that instrument.

The stamp of the swing era never left Mulligan's music, both as player and writer. He favoured a lightly textured, flowing style that relied on grace rather than volume, with a special liking for the whispered effects that can be achieved by players who understand the virtues of playing *pianissimo*, but without any sacrifice of intensity.

Given his close link with the cool approach, it is a useful corrective to the typecasting impulse to remember that he also collaborated with the likes of Thelonious Monk and Charles Mingus, and proved himself adaptable to the demands of these two idiosyncratic giants. Despite a long illness, he continued to perform until shortly before his death in January 1996.

Below

Mulligan with his band at the Capital Jazz Festival in 1982.

see Chet Baker pp 216 *see* Gil Evans pp 221 *see* Zoot Sims pp 233 *see* Art Farmer pp 271

Muddy Waters

CLASSIC RECORDINGS

1948
'I Can't Be Satisfied'

1950
'Louisiana Blues', 'Rollin' Stone'

1951
'Honey Bee', 'Long Distance Call'

1953
'Mad Love'

1954
'I'm Your Hoochie Coochie Man', 'Just Make Love To Me'

1959
Muddy Waters Sings Big Bill Broonzy, 'I Feel So Good'

1960
Muddy Waters at Newport, 'Got My Mojo Working'

Muddy Waters was without question the creator of the Chicago blues sound, the most important figure in post-war blues and the greatest influence on the British blues movement that followed. The Rolling Stones even went as far as to name themselves after a Muddy song.

Muddy's music blended the downhome essence of Mississippi Delta blues with the sophistication of Chicago's more urbanized sound, transforming blues music from a relatively self-contained genre into a worldwide phenomenon. His voice was rich, passionate and fiery, while his guitar style employed a refined slide technique that cut confidently through his vocals with a stinging yet soulful tone. Muddy's tendency to sing slightly behind the beat gave his blues a laid-back feel, while his bending of notes and variations in pitch to match the emotional intensity of phrase enhanced the sincerity of his music.

McKinley Becomes Muddy

McKinley Morganfield was born in April 1915 in Rolling Fork, Mississippi and was raised by his grandmother Della Jones, a sharecropper on Stovall Plantation near Clarksdale. It was Della who gave him the name Muddy, in reference to his tendency as a child to play in the dirt. His education ended with the third grade and he remained illiterate throughout his life. Muddy was working on the plantation by the time he was 10.

'Muddy can really sing the blues … hollering, shouting, crying, getting mad – that's the blues.'

Big Bill Broonzy

Initially, young Muddy took up Jew's harp, moving on to harmonica when he was around seven years old. He was a regular churchgoer throughout his childhood, which is where he gained much of his early exposure to music. On weekends, he was also able to hear music in local juke joints and on his grandmother's phonograph. He was 13 when he heard Leroy Carr's 'How Long Blues' and began to play along. He heard Charley Patton, in person and on record, and also caught Big Joe Williams and the Mississippi Sheiks in Clarksdale. Within a few months, he was playing functions in the area.

In 1932, Muddy bought his first guitar and taught himself to play, performing at picnics and fish fries with a guitarist friend. He became fascinated with Son House, who appeared frequently at area juke joints, and House showed the youngster how to fashion his first slide. Muddy also learned from Patton and his

Right
Muddy Waters, 'the Father of Chicago Blues'.

see Introduction pp 188 *see* Sources & Sounds pp 190 *see* A–Z of Artists pp 216

good friend Robert Lee McCollum, later Robert Nighthawk, and saw Robert Johnson play in 1937. Much later, Muddy would declare that his style was a mixture of House and Johnson influences, along with his own innovations.

From Stovall To Chicago

When folk music collector Alan Lomax came to Mississippi in 1941 in search of Robert Johnson, unaware that he had died three years previously, he encountered Muddy Waters and was impressed enough to record him, playing a steel-bodied guitar and using an actual bottleneck as a slide, for the Library of Congress. Lomax returned the following year to make some further recordings with Muddy; on some of these later tracks he was joined by Son Sims or Charles Berry on second guitar, and occasionally Sims' small string band.

Following a touring job playing harmonica with a New Orleans band, in May 1943 Muddy left Mississippi for Chicago. His name was already known there through the recommendation of other Mississippi musicians, and he found openings playing at house parties. Encouraged by Big Bill Broonzy, Muddy began to work with guitarist Jimmy Rogers. The noisy, busy city clubs were not best suited to performing acoustic blues, and Muddy acquired his first electric guitar in 1945, developing an amplified bottleneck sound that gave his intricate playing more clarity and added delicate harmonics. Muddy was one of the first blues musicians to use electrification as a tool to add intensity and rawness to his music, rather than simply as a means to play more loudly.

In April 1947 he recorded for Aristocrat Records; 'Gypsy Woman'/'Little Anna Mae', Muddy's first record, featured his vocal and guitar with Sunnyland Slim on piano and Big Crawford on bass. A second session in April 1948 produced 'I Can't Be Satisfied'/'I Feel Like Goin' Home', which was only a minor hit but helped Muddy to realize that he could be a successful entertainer. Leonard Chess, Muddy's producer and owner of Aristocrat (soon to become Chess Records), was rather conservative in choosing the supporting cast; Muddy was accompanied only by Crawford up until 1950 and it was December 1951 before Little Walter, Rogers and Muddy were recorded together. The band took up a residency at a Chicago club called Smitty's Corner, where Indiana Avenue met 35th Street, and the modern sound of the Chicago blues began to take shape.

Above
Blues great Muddy Waters, whose illustrious recording career was an inspiration to countless blues artists.

see Big Bill Broonzy pp 104 *see* Robert Johnson pp 112 *see* Son House pp 126 *see* Chicago Blues pp 423

A Successful Line-Up

Otis Spann was introduced to Muddy by Rogers in 1952 and in January 1954 Muddy, Walter, Rogers, Spann, Willie Dixon and drummer Fred Below went into the studio. The session produced 'I'm Your Hoochie Coochie Man', Muddy's biggest single, and 'Just Make Love To Me', 'I'm Ready' and 'Mannish Boy' followed in quick succession. The catchy, stop-time blues riff, which Waters and band created, served to punctuate the songs and was picked up on and used by numerous other musicians. The personnel in the band turned over with some regularity: Walter left in 1952, although he made most of the record dates; Pat Hare replaced Rogers in 1957; Dixon was used only on record dates, and there were several different drummers. Yet somehow the sound of the Muddy Waters band remained remarkably consistent – he was an exceptional bandleader. The band was Chicago's most renowned and influential, and many important blues artists played in its ranks. The winning combination of Dixon's classic compositions and Muddy's commanding personality meant that Muddy Waters soon became a big star.

Below
Waters' live performances boosted his popularity with black and white audiences.

Muddy Reaches New Audiences

In 1958 Muddy Waters was encouraged by British bandleader Chris Barber to tour England. It was his first opportunity to play before large white audiences – at home, his fans were mainly black and were dwindling in numbers due to the popularity of rock'n'roll. Ironically, Muddy had played his own role in the flowering of this R&B-rooted genre, by introducing Chuck Berry to Chess Records in 1955. Despite some criticism for his use of amplification, Muddy's shows rocked skiffle-mad 1950s England and inspired Cyril Davis and Alexis Korner to branch out into the blues, thereby jump-starting the 1960s blues revival.

Muddy played New York's Carnegie Hall in 1959, and the following year he played the Newport Jazz Festival and was recorded live by Chess. The album was enormously important for Muddy's career – you can hear the largely white, college-age kids responding to Muddy's band. The song 'Got My Mojo Working' gained popularity through this performance and became his signature track. In the 1960s he continued to perform around Europe at folk festivals and package tours and remained in the public eye. Although Muddy's popularity began to wane slightly as a result of the rise of soul music in the mid- to late 1960s, he moved with the times and absorbed elements of psychedelic rock into his music. It had taken him just under 20 years to go from McKinley Morganfield, on Stovall's Plantation in Mississippi, to Muddy Waters, world-famous bandleader and recording artist.

see Introduction pp 188 *see* Sources & Sounds pp 190 *see* A–Z of Artists pp 216

Above
Muddy Waters' old home on Stovall Plantation, Clarksdale, Mississippi.

Muddy In The Movies

The 1970s saw Muddy continuing to work mainly on the festival and college circuits, with members of his band in this period including pianist Pinetop Perkins and guitar player Luther Johnson Jnr. He recorded *The London Sessions* in 1971, with guest musicians Rory Gallagher, Steve Winwood and Georgie Fame. An appearance in Martin Scorsese's 1978 film *The Last Waltz*, which documented the farewell concert of the band, treated audiences to an impassioned performance of 'Mannish Boy', enhanced by the wailing harmonica of Paul Butterfield. Allegedly, budgetary constraints had at one stage cast doubt over whether Muddy would appear, but Levon Helm, the Band's Mississippi Delta-rooted drummer, was insistent.

A tour with Texan blues guitarist Johnny Winter led to a successful partnership that resulted in the two bluesmen collaborating on four albums, with Winter also acting as producer and arranger. These records, which included *Hard Again* (1977) and *King Bee* (1981), represented a kind of renaissance for Muddy, showing a return to the passion and drive of his early career, that had been less apparent in his work since the 1960s. He continued to record, tour and collaborate throughout the rest of his life, which was filled with acknowledgements and awards befitting the man who was the source and inspiration of the modern blues sound. He died from heart failure on 30 April 1983.

Left
Muddy's single 'Evil', recorded for the legendary Chess label.

see Willie Dixon pp 221 *see* Pinetop Perkins pp 278 *see* Otis Spann pp 279 *see* Johnny Winter pp 311

A–Z of Artists

Above
Gene Ammons, big-toned tenor saxophonist and son of boogie-woogie great Albert Ammons.

Gene Ammons

(Tenor saxophone, 1925–74)

The son of pianist Albert Ammons, Gene was equally at home in jazz and R&B settings. He was a prolific recording artist and his hard-hitting, emotionally direct blowing in a blues and funk vein also featured in a popular two-tenor band, co-led by Sonny Stitt. His work in a soul-jazz idiom with organists such as Jack McDuff and Johnny Smith added to his popularity. He served a harsh prison sentence for marijuana possession from 1962–69, resuming his recording career upon his release.

Chet Baker

(Trumpet, 1929–88)

Chet Baker was an icon of cool at the height of his fame in the 1950s. His recording of 'My Funny Valentine' with Gerry Mulligan in 1952 established him as a star of the emerging cool jazz genre; his boyish, film-star looks (later ravaged by drug abuse) and a light, seductively lyrical trumpet style assured his popularity for much of the decade. Baker was born in Yale, Oklahoma but moved to Los Angeles at a young age. He led his own quartet on the West Coast from 1953.

Drugs, imprisonment in both the US and Europe, and poor health took a heavy toll from the late 1950s; he also lost some teeth in an assault in 1968, which kept him off the stage until 1973. He worked mainly in Europe from 1975, where he was in demand as a soloist in both small group and orchestral settings, and remained an artful improviser throughout the many vicissitudes of his career. He died after falling from a hotel window in Amsterdam.

Mickey Baker

(Guitar, b. 1925)

McHouston Baker was born in Louisville, Kentucky. Originally a jazz player, he switched to blues after seeing guitarist Pee Wee Crayton. He began his recording career at Savoy in 1952 and became the first-call guitarist for R&B session work in New York. He teamed with vocalist Sylvia Vanderpool and, as Mickey & Sylvia, they had a huge hit with 'Love Is Strange' in 1956–57. Baker has published several books on guitar instruction. He settled in Paris, France in 1961.

Chris Barber

(Trombone, b. 1930)

Chris Barber has been a key figure on the British traditional jazz scene since he broke away from Ken Colyer's band to lead his own group in 1954. The band was one of the leading names in the so-called 'trad boom' of the late 1950s. It became the Chris Barber Jazz & Blues Band – with the addition of electric guitar – in 1968, and brought fresh arrangements and cogent soloing to their venerable traditional jazz and blues repertoire. Barber now tours with his Big Band.

Right
Chris Barber (far right) with his traditional-style jazz band.

see Introduction pp 188 *see* Sources & Sounds pp 190 *see* Key Artists pp 198

Above

Clarinetist Acker Bilk and his Paramount Jazz Band were influential in the traditional jazz boom.

Dave Bartholomew

(Trumpet, producer, composer, b. 1918)

Davis Louis Bartholomew was born in Edgard, Louisiana. He was one of the most prominent bandleaders in New Orleans in the mid-1940s. He recorded for DeLuxe, King and Imperial during the 1940s and 1950s, but is best known as the producer, bandleader and songwriting partner of Fats Domino, whom he produced at Imperial from 1949 into the 1960s. He also produced Smiley Lewis, the Spiders, Snooks Eaglin and dozens of other New Orleans R&B greats.

Acker Bilk

(Clarinet, b. 1929)

Acker Bilk was born in Somerset, England. He took up clarinet in the Army and formed his first band in 1950. His Paramount Jazz Band adopted trademark uniforms of striped waistcoats and bowler hats and was very successful in the UK's trad boom of the late 1950s. Bilk enjoyed a major pop hit with his own 'Stranger On The Shore' in 1961 and remained a popular draw on the international traditional jazz circuit in subsequent decades.

see Fats Domino pp 204 *see* Gerry Mulligan pp 210 *see* Sonny Stitt pp 234 *see* Snooks Eaglin pp 271

Art Blakey

(Drums, 1919–90)

Art Blakey (also later known as Buhaina or simply Bu after he converted to Islam) led the quintessential hard bop group the Jazz Messengers across four decades from the late 1940s, and was a fervent advocate of the music he loved. He formed his first band in his native Pittsburgh, but moved to New York and played in Billy Eckstine's seminal big band in 1944–47, before relaunching his career as a bandleader with the Seventeen Messengers.

Blakey first used the Jazz Messengers' name in collaboration with Horace Silver from 1956. The band had a horns-plus-rhythm set-up in quintet and sextet forms and defined hard bop, spicing bebop with the earthy urgency of blues, gospel and R&B. Blakey's propulsive drumming drove a band whose changing personnel – including trumpeters Lee Morgan, Freddie Hubbard and Wynton Marsalis, saxophonist Wayne Shorter, trombonist Curtis Fuller and pianist Bobby Timmons – was remarkable.

Below
Bobby 'Blue' Bland performs a slow number at a crowded dance.

Bobby 'Blue' Bland

(Vocals, b. 1930)

Robert Calvin Brooks was born in Rosemark, Tennessee. He began recording in 1951 and was associated with B.B. King, Junior Parker, Johnny Ace and others in Memphis. A suave, deep-voiced blues romantic, he signed with Duke Records in 1952 and was one of the most consistent hitmakers in the soul blues idiom from the late 1950s to the 1970s. He had R&B number ones with 'Further On Up The Road' (1957), 'I Pity The Fool' (1961) and 'That's The Way Love Is' (1963).

James Booker

(Piano, organ, vocals, 1939–83)

James Carroll Booker III was born in New Orleans, Louisiana. He studied classical piano from the age of four and made his recording debut for Imperial at 14. He worked as a session musician in New Orleans from the mid-1950s and recorded for many different labels, as well as playing and arranging for the Lloyd Price big band in the early 1960s. Despite some successful European tours, a narcotics addiction slowed his career development, but he is still remembered with deep admiration in his home town.

Clarence 'Gatemouth' Brown

(Guitar, violin, vocals, 1924–2005)

Clarence Brown Jr. was born in Vinton, Louisiana and raised in Orange, Texas. By the age of 10 he had learned guitar and violin. After the Second World War he settled in the Houston, Texas area. He made his recording debut in 1947 for Aladdin and signed with Peacock Records in 1949. Brown formed his own group, Gate's Express, in 1953, which continued on until his death in 2005. He toured Europe in 1971 and became a frequent overseas traveller.

Brown began to freelance his recording opportunities in the 1960s. He expanded his musical palette by adding country, jazz and Cajun material to his repertoire. On guitar, his signature tune 'Okie Dokie Stomp' exemplified his style of rapid, single notes. He used his violin more when playing other styles but it was also very effective on slow blues. Brown was first known as an instrumentalist, although his recordings of recent years have been mostly vocals. He was one of the great modern Texas guitarists, along with T-Bone Walker and Albert Collins.

Clifford Brown

(Trumpet, 1930–56)

The tragic death of Clifford Brown in a road accident robbed jazz of one of its brightest young stars, but even

see Introduction pp 188 *see* Sources & Sounds pp 190 *see* Key Artists pp 198

his truncated legacy has established his standing as a major figure and profound influence. He took up the trumpet at the age of 13, drawing on the influence of bebop stars Dizzy Gillespie and Fats Navarro. The latter's rich sonority and melodic lyricism made a particularly telling impact on the development of Brown's own style.

He recorded with Lou Donaldson, J.J. Johnson and Art Blakey for Blue Note, and cut his own sessions for Pacific Jazz, but his best-known work was recorded in 1954–56, with the quintet he co-led with drummer Max Roach. His technical virtuosity and improvisational flair marked him out as a potential giant. He contributed several much-played compositions to the jazz repertoire, notably 'Joy Spring' and 'Daahoud'.

Above
Dave Brubeck (right) with Paul Desmond, the composer of the quartet's biggest hit 'Take Five'.

Left
Trumpet star Clifford Brown, who died tragically young in 1956.

Nappy Brown

(Vocals, b. 1929)

Napoleon Brown Goodson Culp was born in Charlotte, North Carolina. He sang with a gospel group, the Heavenly Lights, which recorded for Savoy, but was convinced to try blues material in 1954 and had several hits, including 'Don't Be Angry'. He returned to singing gospel in the 1960s but was rediscovered in the late 1970s by the blues community. He recorded several CDs for various labels in the 1980s and 1990s. He continues to tour and record.

Ruth Brown

(Vocals, b. 1928)

Ruth Alston Weston was born in Portsmouth, Virginia. She was heard performing in Washington, DC, where she was recommended to Atlantic Records. Her 1950 R&B number one 'Teardrops From Your Eyes' was followed by four more, including '(Mama) He Treats Your Daughter Mean', and she was so successful that the fledgeling label became known as 'the house that Ruth built'. After a period away from music in the 1960s and 1970s, Brown re-emerged to great acclaim for work on radio, TV, stage and film.

Dave Brubeck

(Piano, b. 1920)

The Dave Brubeck Quartet was one of the most successful jazz groups of all time; Brubeck's fascination with unusual time signatures brought major hits with 'Take Five' (written by saxophonist Paul Desmond) and 'Blue Rondo À La Turk' in 1959. His recording of 'Dialogues For Jazz Combo And Orchestra', composed by his brother Howard, appeared the same year, and the writing of large-scale works became increasingly central to Brubeck's compositions. He has continued to tour with small groups.

see Fats Navarro pp 180 *see* Max Roach pp 182 *see* Albert Collins pp 270 *see* Lee Morgan pp 277

Above

Co-founder of the Crane River Band, Ken Colyer was influential in the revival of traditional jazz.

Ken Colyer

(Cornet, trumpet, guitar, 1928–88)

Ken Colyer was a key figure in the UK revivalist movement. He took an infamously purist stance on the New Orleans style of ensemble playing, brooking no departures from orthodoxy. He co-founded the influential Crane River Band in 1949 and formed his own Jazzmen after a visit to New Orleans in 1953, but was ousted when Chris Barber assumed leadership the following year. Colyer formed an influential new band, and then continued to lead his own groups.

James Cotton

(Harmonica, vocals, b. 1935)

James Henry Cotton was born in Tunica, Mississippi and was inspired by hearing Sonny Boy Williamson II (Rice Miller) on the radio. He worked with his mentor from the late 1940s until 1953, when he made his recording debut for Sun Records. He joined Muddy Waters in 1954 and played with him, on and off, until 1966. He toured Europe with Muddy Waters in 1961 and has been a frequent international traveller. He formed his own group in 1966 and continues to tour and record.

Floyd Dixon

(Piano, vocals, 1928–2006)

Floyd Dixon was born in Marshall, Texas and was raised in Los Angeles from the age of 13. He made his recording debut aged 18 for Supreme Records and also

see Introduction pp 188 *see* Sources & Sounds pp 190 *see* Key Artists pp 198

Left
Bassist, songwriter and producer Willie Dixon (centre) plays on a session at Chess Studios with J.B. Lenoir (far left).

recorded for Modern and Peacock before switching to Aladdin in 1950 and releasing his biggest record, 'Call Operator 210'. He continued to record while working primarily on the West Coast. Dixon was a pianist and vocalist in the Charles Brown tradition.

Willie Dixon

(Bass, vocals, songwriter, 1915–92)

Willie James Dixon was born in Vicksburg, Mississippi and moved to Chicago at the age of 11. He learned bass and made his recording debut with the Five Breezes in 1940. After the Second World War he formed the Big Three trio, with whom he worked and recorded until 1952. He began a lengthy working relationship with Chess Records as a studio bassist, talent scout and songwriter, and wrote songs associated with Muddy Waters, Howlin' Wolf, Koko Taylor and Cream, among others. He joined forces with Memphis Slim in 1959 and toured internationally, and later formed his own band, the Chicago Blues All-Stars.

Bill Doggett

(Organ, piano, arranger, 1916–96)

William Ballard Doggett was born in Philadelphia, Pennsylvania. The band he led was taken over by Lucky Millinder in 1940 and Doggett stayed on as pianist and arranger. After working with the Ink Spots, he played with Louis Jordan's band from 1947–51. He was active as a studio pianist, organist and arranger until 1953, when he formed the first organ/tenor sax combo. His biggest hit, 'Honky Tonk', was recorded in 1956 for King and was an R&B number one.

He continued to tour and record until his death and performed regularly on the festival circuit, often using his concerts to promote civil rights issues.

Gil Evans

(Arranger, composer, piano, 1912–88)

Gil Evans (born Ian Green) achieved fame through his work with Miles Davis on the seminal recordings *Miles Ahead* (1957), *Porgy And Bess* (1959) and *Sketches Of Spain* (1960). His own output was relatively small, but his influence was much larger. His greatest gift lay in arranging – or more accurately, re-composing – the music of others, elaborately cloaked in his own distinctive manipulations of timbre, colour, texture and shape.

Working with Claude Thornhill in the 1940s allowed him to experiment with unusual instrumentation and distinctive ideas, which came to fruition in the projects with Miles, including his contribution to the 'Birth of the Cool' sessions (1949–50). His own recordings included *Out Of The Cool* (1960) and *The Individualism Of Gil Evans* (1964). His orchestra became an attraction on the international circuit from the mid-1970s; his later music was notably more improvisational in content and allowed the players considerable freedom within looser, sometimes electric and rock-referent structures.

Below
Gil Evans (right) and Miles Davis, who worked together on the 1949–50 Nonet 'Birth Of The Cool' sessions, among various other projects.

see Louis Jordan pp 176 *see* Memphis Slim pp 179 *see* Miles Davis pp 200 *see* Sonny Boy Williamson II pp 235

Panama Francis

(Drums, 1918–2001)

David Albert Francis was born in Miami, Florida. He worked around Florida with saxophonist George Kelly before going to New York in 1938. The following year he made his recording debut with Roy Eldridge, who named him after his choice of hats. Francis worked with Lucky Millinder from 1940–46 and Cab Calloway from 1947–52 but his reputation dates mainly from his session work in New York. He was the first-call drummer on R&B sessions throughout the 1950s and early 1960s, and was an important figure in changing the black swing beat to R&B.

Below
João Gilberto's vocalist collaborator Astrud Gilberto performs with two other important figures in the bossa nova movement, Antonio Carlos Jobim (centre) and Stan Getz.

Lowell Fulson

(Guitar, vocals, 1921–99)

Lowell Fulson was born in Tulsa, Oklahoma and began his professional career in Oakland, California. He made his recording debut in 1946 and by 1950 he was a hitmaker for Swingtime Records with such songs as 'Every Day I Have The Blues' and 'Blue Shadows'. His band at this time featured a relatively unknown Ray Charles on piano. He switched to Chess in 1945 and had another hit with 'Reconsider Baby'; his final big record came in 1967 with 'Tramp'. Originally inspired by T-Bone Walker, Fulson managed to stay current with changing blues trends throughout his career.

João Gilberto

(Vocals, guitar, b. 1931)

João Gilberto came to the notice of the wider jazz public in the wake of saxophonist's Stan Getz's successful *Jazz Samba* (1962). Gilberto had earlier been working with composer Antonio Carlos Jobim on a development of the samba known as 'bossa nova', and Getz translated that form into a popular success. The subsequent *Getz/Gilberto* (1963) album included vocals by his companion, Astrud Gilberto, and spawned a famous hit version of 'The Girl From Ipanema'. Gilberto is a successful international performing artist as well as composer.

Jimmy Giuffre

(Clarinet, baritone, tenor and soprano saxophones, b. 1921)

Jimmy Giuffre composed 'Four Brothers' for Woody Herman's saxophone section in 1947 and later joined the Second Herd. He formed his important trio with Jim Hall (guitar) and Ralph Peña (bass) in 1957, then replaced bass with Bob Brookmeyer's trombone in 1958. A subsequent trio with Paul Bley (piano) and Steve Swallow (bass) in 1961–62 was influential in the rise of free jazz. He remained open to new directions and experimented with electric instruments in the 1980s.

Rosco Gordon

(Piano, vocals, 1928–2002)

Rosco Gordon was born in Memphis, Tennessee. He won an amateur contest in 1950 and was soon appearing on WDIA radio with his own show. He began recording with Sam Phillips in 1951; Phillips sold the master of 'Booted' to Chess Records and the

see Introduction pp 188 *see* Sources & Sounds pp 190 *see* Key Artists pp 198

Slim was a flamboyant performer, noted for the wild colours of his suits and hair. He was famous for his 'walks': using a lengthy extension cord he would parade around a room or even out into the street, playing his guitar all the while as the sound continued to come out of his amplifier on stage.

Left
Eccentric blues pianist Rosco Gordon, whose music influenced early ska and reggae.

Eddie Harris

(Tenor saxophone, vocals, 1934–96)
Eddie Harris was one of the few jazz musicians to achieve the distinction of a million-selling hit single with his version of the theme from the film *Exodus* (1960). A funky, hard-blowing saxophonist from Chicago, he pioneered the use of electronics with tenor saxophone through the Varitone signal processor and similar devices from the mid-1960s. Harris also played several other instruments and sang; he had an expressive sound and polished technique in straight and exploratory jazz, as well as in crossover settings.

Below
Innovative saxophonist Eddie Harris sold a million copies of his adaptation of the *Exodus* film theme.

master of 'No More Doggin'' to Modern. Gordon had two hits, on two different labels, at the same time in 1952. He had a further hit with 'Just A Little Bit' on Vee Jay in 1959.

Gordon was out of music full-time after the 1960s. He moved to New York and operated a dry-cleaning business, before forming his own record label and issuing 45-rpm singles during the 1980s. He was recorded by Stony Plain in 2000 and toured again for the last two years of his life. The idiosyncratic, loping rhythms of Gordon's music was influential on the development of ska and reggae music in Jamaica.

Guitar Slim

(Guitar, vocals, 1925–59)
Eddie Lee Jones was born in Greenwood, Mississippi. He sang in church as a child but had relocated to New Orleans by the age of 17, where he worked with Huey 'Piano' Smith in a small group until 1953. His recording debut was on Imperial in 1951, but his most important recordings were for Specialty during 1954–55 and Atlantic in 1956–58. Guitar Slim had only one hit, but it was an R&B number one: 'Things That I Used To Do', arranged by the pianist on the session, Ray Charles.

see Roy Eldridge pp 108 *see* Ray Charles pp 198 *see* Antonio Carlos Jobim pp 227 *see* Stan Getz pp 272

Roy Haynes

(Drums, b. 1925)

Roy Haynes is a major jazz drummer in settings ranging from swing to jazz rock, taking in most genres of the music including free jazz. He spent three years with Charlie Parker (1949–52) and five with Sarah Vaughan (1953–58), and by the mid-1960s had also worked with Bud Powell, Miles Davis, Thelonious Monk, Eric Dolphy and John Coltrane. Later associations include Gary Burton, Chick Corea and Pat Metheny. He has continued to lead his own groups.

Jimmy Heath

(Tenor and soprano saxophone, flute, b. 1926)

Jimmy Heath's early devotion to Charlie Parker saw him nicknamed 'Little Bird', but he switched from alto to tenor saxophone and developed his own voice. He honed his writing skills with the Dizzy Gillespie Orchestra throughout 1949–50. He spent 1955–59 in prison, but rebuilt his career with a series of recordings for Riverside. Later, he performed with bassist Percy Heath and drummer Albert 'Tootie' Heath in the Heath Brothers. He remains an influential jazz arranger and educator.

Earl Hooker

(Guitar, vocals, 1930–70)

Earl Zebedee Hooker Jr., a cousin of John Lee Hooker, was born in Clarksdale, Mississippi. He learned guitar by the age of 10 and moved to Chicago in 1941. Hooker was inspired by Robert Nighthawk and at the end of 1940s returned south, where he played with Rice Miller and Ike Turner. He first recorded in 1952, and from 1959 recorded a series of singles for small Chicago labels. He recorded and toured internationally in 1965 and 1969. Hooker was a slide guitar player of great originality but was slowed by tuberculosis, which eventually killed him.

Lightnin' Hopkins

(Guitar, vocals, 1911–82)

Sam Hopkins was born in Centerville, Texas. His father and two brothers were musicians and he learned guitar from an early age. He met and played with Blind Lemon Jefferson at the age of eight. He accompanied his cousin, Texas Alexander, for much of the 1930s, drifting through Texas. He was discovered in Houston by Lola Cullum in 1946 and signed with Aladdin Records. His first record featured pianist Thunder Smith and with that release he became Lightnin' Hopkins. He recorded hundreds of songs from 1948–54, for a variety of different labels.

After a dry patch, Hopkins was 'rediscovered' during the folk blues revival of the late 1950s and from 1959 recorded dozens of albums for various labels. He toured constantly, became a regular on the festival circuit in North America and did considerable film

see Introduction pp 188 *see* Sources & Sounds pp 190 *see* Key Artists pp 198

and TV work. Lightnin' Hopkins' great gift was his ability to create songs from the flimsiest suggestion, and to play exquisite country blues guitar even though he lived in a big city for most of his life. He also had an extraordinarily fluid sense of song structure and time.

Big Walter Horton

(Harmonica, vocals, 1918–61)

Walter Horton was born in Horn Lake, Mississippi. He taught himself harmonica at the age of five and was working the streets shortly thereafter. He moved to Chicago in 1940 but it wasn't until later in the decade that he began to be more active professionally. Horton replaced Junior Wells in the Muddy Waters Band in 1953 and worked with Muddy for about a year. One of Chicago's finest harmonica players, he recorded with a variety of different musicians, but was particularly associated with Johnny Shines and Jimmy Rogers.

Howlin' Wolf

(Guitar, harmonica, vocals, 1910–76)

Chester Arthur Burnett was born in White Station, Mississippi. Inspired by Charley Patton, Wolf earned his living as a farmer in the West Memphis, Arkansas area and was strictly a weekend performer until he was almost 40 years old. He got a radio spot in 1948 and the sound of that band, which was electric rather than acoustic, heightened interest in his work. He began to record in 1951 for Sam Phillips, who sold his masters to both Modern Records and Chess Records. Ultimately, Chess won out and Howlin' Wolf recorded for the label from 1952 until his death.

While Wolf was a capable guitarist and harmonica player, it was his intense, growling voice that dominated his performances – it was one of the great blues voices of all time. Unlike many of his blues peers, Wolf was a flamboyant entertainer who could rock the house. He was considered a leading light of the Chicago blues scene for many years.

Above
Texan blues legend Lightnin' Hopkins enjoys a cigarette in the studio.

Far Left
Slide guitarist Earl Hooker, who played with Rice Miller and Ike Turner, among others.

Left
The inimitable Howlin' Wolf, owner of one of the most distinctive voices in the blues, blows a solo on the harmonica.

see Charley Patton pp 23 *see* Dizzy Gillespie pp 152 *see* Robert Nighthawk pp 181 *see* Sarah Vaughan pp 184

Milt Jackson

(Vibraphone, 1923–99)

Milt Jackson diverged from his two great predecessors on vibes, Lionel Hampton and Red Norvo, by developing a linear, rhythmically inflected approach rooted in bebop rather than swing. He preferred the slightly larger vibraharp to the more familiar vibraphone, and adjusted the oscillator to give a trademark rich, warm sound.

Right
Milt Jackson (right) and Percy Heath perform in the long-lived Modern Jazz Quartet.

He recorded as a leader and worked with many major names, including Coleman Hawkins, John Coltrane, Oscar Peterson and Ray Charles, but was best known as part of the long-running Modern Jazz Quartet, one of the most successful groups in jazz history. That band began as the Milt Jackson Quartet but ran as the MJQ from 1952–74, and occasionally thereafter. Jackson was a gifted soloist, steeped in the earthy pragmatism of gospel and blues; his playing provided a counterweight to the intricate classicism of pianist John Lewis's compositions and arrangements for the group, but without upsetting the balance of the music.

Below
Ahmad Jamal, an inventive improviser who mainly works in jazz trios.

Ahmad Jamal

(Piano, b. 1930)

Ahmad Jamal made his name with his very successful trio of the late 1950s and had a hit with his version of 'Poinciana' in 1958. His light touch and use of space has led some to hear too much of the cocktail lounge in his playing, but he is an inventive and influential musician and composer. He experimented with more avant-garde approaches after a break from performing in the early 1960s, and later with electric instruments and symphonic settings; however, he has mostly worked in trios.

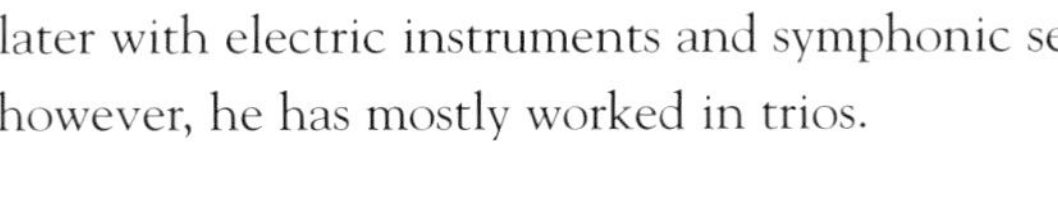

Elmore James

(Guitar, vocals, 1918–63)

Elmore Brooks was born in Richland, Mississippi. He learned guitar at an early age and was playing functions by the age of 14. He often worked with Rice Miller from the late 1930s until he was drafted into the Navy in 1943. He rejoined Miller after the war and was headquartered in West Memphis, Arkansas. James recorded 'Dust My Broom' at the tail end of a Rice Miller session for Trumpet Records in 1951, and it became a surprise hit.

James moved to Chicago, where he formed his own group, the Broomdusters, and recorded for Modern/Flair/ Meteor from 1952–56 and Fire/Fury/Enjoy in 1959–62. He was the premier electric slide guitarist of his era and his signature riff, used on 'Dust My Broom', was heard on many of his recordings and copied by countless imitators.

see Introduction pp 188 *see* Sources & Sounds pp 190 *see* Key Artists pp 198

Etta James

(Vocals, b. 1938)

Jamesetta Hawkins was born in Los Angeles, California. She moved to the San Francisco area, where she was discovered by Johnny Otis. She made her recording debut at the age of 16 for Modern, and had a number-one R&B hit with her first record, 'The Wallflower' (a.k.a. 'Roll With Me Henry'). She worked in rock'n'roll package tours throughout the 1950s before signing with Chess Records in 1960 and scoring another big record with 'At Last'. A versatile performer, Etta James can deliver the goods on low-down blues, rockers and tender ballads, and won a blues Grammy in 2005.

Antonio Carlos Jobim

(Composer, piano, guitar, 1927–94)

Jobim was the best known of the Brazilian composers who made an impact on jazz. His international reputation blossomed due to his songs in the film *Black Orpheus* (1959) and with João Gilberto he sparked a bossa nova craze, boosted by Stan Getz and Charlie Byrd's *Jazz Samba* (1962). He led his own band on international tours, and his songs – including 'Girl From Ipamena', 'Desifinado' and 'One Note Stand' – with original lyrics in Portuguese and light, sophisticated harmonies, remain jazz staples.

Quincy Jones

(Trumpet, arranger, b. 1933)

Quincy Jones started out as a trumpet player but first achieved public acclaim as an arranger and subsequently went on to earn an even greater reputation as a record producer for artists including Aretha Franklin and Michael Jackson. He began arranging with Lionel Hampton in 1951 and toured as music director of Dizzy Gillespie's big band in 1956. He wrote for Ray Charles and Frank Sinatra among many others, and produced USA For Africa's 'We Are The World' (1985). He is also a successful film composer and record-company executive.

Earl King

(Guitar, vocals, 1934–2003)

Earl Silas Johnson IV was born in New Orleans, Louisiana. He was influenced by Guitar Slim and made his recording debut for Savoy, as Earl Johnson, in 1953. Upon switching to Specialty in 1954, he became Earl King. Often associated with New Orleans blues pianist Huey 'Piano' Smith in the 1950s, King scored his biggest hit with 'Those Lonely, Lonely Nights' for Ace Records in 1955. A favoured songwriter among New Orleans R&B artists, King recorded for many small New Orleans labels over the years. He remained an active performer until shortly before his death.

Below

Trumpeter Quincy Jones is also a successful composer, arranger and record producer.

see Lionel Hampton pp 125 *see* João Gilberto pp 222 *see* Huey 'Piano' Smith pp 234 *see* Sonny Boy Williamson II pp 235

Above
J.B. Lenoir performs in the UK during the 1965 American Folk Blues Festival tour.

Steve Lacy

(Soprano saxophone, 1934–2004)

Steve Lacy began his career in Dixieland jazz, sitting in with Henry 'Red' Allen, Rex Stewart and Herbie Nichols, among others, at New York's Café Metronome. However, he quickly shifted tack and became one of the leading figures in the jazz avant-garde. Soprano saxophone is now widely played, but Lacy concentrated on the then-neglected horn from the outset with single-minded focus.

He worked with Cecil Taylor and Thelonious Monk in the late 1950s and Monk's music remained a constant artistic preoccupation, including in later projects with trombonist Roswell Rudd and pianist Mal Waldron. Lacy also began a long musical relationship with Gil Evans at that time and became involved with free jazz in the early 1960s. He began to perform in Europe in 1965 and lived in France from 1970–2002, where he continued to pursue new and experimental musical ideas in a wide variety of contexts. These included his long-running sextet; electronic music; projects involving his wife (singer Irène Aebi); collaborations with poets, dancers and visual artists; and an ambitious improvisational 'opera', *The Cry*.

J.B. Lenoir

(Guitar, vocals, 1929–67)

J.B. Lenoir was born in Monticello, Mississippi; his parents were farmers as well as musicians. He learned to play the guitar at the age of eight and left home in the early 1940s to work with Rice Miller and Elmore James, before settling in Chicago in 1949 and making his recording debut in 1951 for Chess Records. He worked around Chicago for most of the decade and recorded for a number of different labels. Lenoir toured Europe with the American Folk Blues Festival in 1965. He is best remembered for his original compositions – many of which explored topical themes – and his distinctive, keening falsetto vocals.

see Introduction pp 188 *see* Sources & Sounds pp 190 *see* Key Artists pp 198

John Lewis

(Piano, 1920–2001)

John Lewis was an important pianist, composer and educator, but was best known as the musical director of the most successful jazz group of the era, the Modern Jazz Quartet. Over five decades, Lewis was the architect of the group's characteristic fusion of jazz and classical music. The MJQ's light, spacious, swinging arrangements established them as an international concert draw, while Lewis's compositions amounted to a substantial canon.

His work away from the group was also significant. He worked with Dizzy Gillespie, Charlie Parker and Miles Davis (on the 'Birth Of The Cool' sessions) in the late 1940s and co-founded the jazz-classical fusion movement known as 'third stream' with Gunther Schuller in the late 1950s. He was musical director of the Monterey Jazz Festival from 1958–82, and was leader and director of two ensembles: Orchestra USA (1962–65) and the American Jazz Orchestra (1985–92). Lewis's acclaimed solo album, *Evolution II* (2001), was issued shortly before his death.

Little Walter

(Harmonica, vocals, 1930–68)

Marion Walter Jacobs was born in Marksville, Louisiana. He taught himself harmonica at the age of eight and was working the New Orleans streets by the time he was 12. He worked in Helena, Arkansas (where he met Rice Miller) and St. Louis before arriving in Chicago in 1946. He was encouraged by guitarists Tampa Red and Big Bill Broonzy and also met Jimmy Rogers. He made his recording debut in 1947 and joined forces with Muddy Waters the following year. He worked with Muddy until 1952 when his own Checker record, 'Juke', became an R&B number one.

Walter formed his own group with the Aces (David Meyers, Louis Meyers and Fred Below), and toured clubs and concert halls on R&B package tours. He continued to have hit records (including a second number-one R&B hit, 'My Babe') throughout the decade. He toured England in 1962 and 1964. Little Walter was an innovative superstar on harmonica, able to create unusually swinging, melodic single-note solos.

Professor Longhair

(Piano, vocals, 1918–80)

Henry Roeland Byrd was born in Bogalusa, Louisiana and formed his first combo, Professor Longhair and the Four Hairs, shortly after the Second World War. His Atlantic sessions in 1949 and 1953 produced his signature songs 'Mardi Gras in New Orleans' and 'Tipitina'. As an ebullient and racy vocalist, and a pianist who employed a characteristic rhumba-boogie, Longhair is the link between older New Orleans pianists and the new arrivals of the 1950s. He enjoyed a comeback after appearing at the 1971 New Orleans Jazz & Heritage Festival, and returned to touring and recording until his death.

Humphrey Lyttelton

(Trumpet, clarinet, b. 1921)

Humphrey Lyttelton acquired a passion for jazz as a schoolboy at Eton and developed it in the Grenadier Guards – not a standard jazz background. His professional career began with George Webb's Dixielanders in 1947. He led his own bands from 1948, and courted controversy in the 1950s by bringing bop musicians into his group, to the immense chagrin of traditional purists. His contribution to British jazz as a player, composer, bandleader, historian, broadcaster and writer has been a substantial one.

Below
British trumpeter Humphrey Lyttelton blows his horn while guitarist Eddie Condon operates the valves.

see Tampa Red pp 135 *see* Thelonious Monk pp 208 *see* Elmore James pp 226 *see* Cecil Taylor pp 280

Jackie McLean

(Alto saxophone, 1931–2006)

Jackie McLean worked with Sonny Rollins and practised with Bud Powell as a teenager. His invention and passionate delivery on alto saxophone attracted collaborations with Miles Davis (1951–52), Charles Mingus (1956, 1958–59) and Art Blakey (1956–57). He recorded a series of albums for Prestige and acted in Jack Gelber's play *The Connection* (1959–61). His powerful recordings for Blue Note in the early 1960s were more experimental. He became an eminent jazz educator in later decades.

Right
Jackie McLean's saxophone playing had a distinctive, passionate and powerful sound.

Charles Mingus

(Bass, piano, composer, 1922–79)

Charles Mingus had a tempestuous, multi-faceted personality, which is reflected in the almost schizophrenic extremes of his music and the sheer magnitude of his creative aspirations. Early work with Lionel Hampton and Red Norvo brought him in 1951 from California to York, where he worked with Miles Davis, Duke Ellington, Charlie Parker and others.

Mingus formed Debut Records with Max Roach and issued some of his early Jazz Workshop recordings on the label (along with the famous concert from Massey Hall in 1953 with Parker, Gillespie, Powell and Roach). His radical style of ensemble improvisation and his enduring compositions are captured in groundbreaking discs such as *Pithecanthropus Erectus* (1956), *Ah Um* (1959) and the big band album *The Black Saint and the Sinner Lady* (1963). His large-scale work *Epitaph* was only performed in complete form in 1989, a decade after his death.

Below
The sometimes difficult Charles Mingus is remembered for his radical style and enduring compositions.

Earl Palmer

(Drums, b. 1924)

Earl Cyril Palmer was born in New Orleans, Louisiana. As a member of Dave Bartholomew's band, he played drums on the first Fats Domino session in 1949. He soon became the first – and sometimes only – call drummer for New Orleans R&B record dates, recording with a variety of artists that included Little Richard,

 *see* Introduction pp 188 *see* Sources & Sounds pp 190 *see* Key Artists pp 198

Smiley Lewis, Bobby Mitchell, the Spiders and Shirley & Lee, and he is generally credited with bringing the New Orleans street beat into the studio. He moved to Los Angeles in 1957 and continued to be a top studio drummer for many years.

Little Junior Parker

(Harmonica, vocals, 1932–71)

Herman Parker Jr. was born in Bobo, Mississippi and worked with Howlin' Wolf as early as 1949 in West Memphis. Parker was associated with B.B. King, Bobby Bland and Johnny Ace in the Memphis scene of the early 1950s. He recorded for Sun with his own group, the Blue Flames, in 1953 ('Mystery Train') and signed with Duke Records in December of that year, where he stayed until 1966. Parker was a first-rate harmonica player but an even better singer. He was more of a crooner than a shouter and, as such, his blues ballads were always outstanding.

Art Pepper

(Alto and tenor saxophones, 1925–82)

Art Pepper was a soloist with Stan Kenton (1947–52) and took part in trumpeter Shorty Rogers's first so-called West Coast jazz recordings in 1951. He made a series of classic records for the California-based Contemporary label (1957–60), but was imprisoned at various times for heroin-related offences, culminating in three years' voluntary rehabilitation in Synanon from 1969. He played with the Don Ellis Orchestra in 1975 and enjoyed a triumphant finale to his career as a leader from 1977.

Oscar Peterson

(Piano, b. 1925)

Canadian pianist Oscar Peterson made his name on 'Jazz At The Philharmonic' (JATP) tours in the early 1950s, and formed his own trio in 1952. His most famous line-up (1953–58) featured Herb Ellis (guitar) and Ray Brown (bass); he replaced the guitar with more conventional drums from 1958. His extravagant improvisations combined pre-bop and bop elements. He was a virtuoso technician until illness restricted his playing in the 1990s; he recorded voluminously, produced most often by his champion, JATP founder Norman Granz.

Oscar Pettiford

(Bass, cello, composer, 1922–60)

Oscar Pettiford was the first bass player to develop the new melodic and rhythmic concepts of bebop on his instrument and was an accomplished cellist and composer. He was of mixed African-American and Native American extraction and had a famously irascible temperament, frequently falling out with his many collaborators. He worked with Duke Ellington and Woody Herman, and led his own small groups and a big band (1956–57). He spent his final two years in Europe.

Piano Red

(Piano, vocals, 1911–85)

Willie Lee Perryman was born in Hampton, Georgia. Perryman was sometimes known as Dr. Feelgood, and his older brother, Rufus, was known as Speckled Red. He worked mainly as a soloist in the Atlanta area before signing with RCA in 1950. His first record, 'Rockin' With Red'/'Red's Boogie' was a two-sided hit. His early records emphasized his piano, but later sessions were in more of an R&B groove, with horns and vocal groups. He continued to tour mostly in Europe, under the name Dr. Feelgood, until his death.

Below
Oscar Peterson puts his all into a solo during a 1957 performance.

see Duke Ellington pp 52 *see* Max Roach pp 182 *see* Dave Bartholomew pp 217 *see* Howlin' Wolf pp 225

Above
Highly influential bebop pianist Bud Powell takes a break.

Bud Powell

(Piano, 1924–66)

Bud Powell was the pre-eminent bebop pianist. His spare chords and asymmetric accents in the left hand combined with fluid linear inventions in the right hand to establish the foundation of the standard approach to bop piano playing. The mental instability and introverted character that dogged his life are often ascribed to a beating by the police in 1945 but may have preceded it.

He was part of Dizzy Gillespie's seminal bebop quintet in 1945, recorded with Charlie Parker in 1947 and made a series of classic trio recordings from 1949–56 that are his primary legacy. He also took part in the famous Massey Hall concert in 1953 with Parker, Gillespie, Mingus and Roach. He moved to Paris, France in 1959 and continued to perform there (albeit erratically) until 1964, when he made an unsuccessful return to the US. His troubled life in Paris was the major inspiration for the film *Round Midnight* (1986).

Snooky Pryor

(Harmonica, vocals, b. 1921)

James Edward Pryor was born in Lambert, Mississippi. He learned harmonica at the age of 14 and left home in 1937 to work as an itinerant musician. He settled in Chicago in 1940. After Army service during the Second World War he got the idea of amplifying his harmonica, and was the first to develop that sound. He recorded for small Chicago labels throughout the 1950s but left music in the early 1960s, only to be 'rediscovered' in the early 1970s.

Jimmy Reed

(Guitar, harmonica, vocals, 1925–76)

Mathis James Reed was born in Dunleith, Mississippi. His friend Eddie Taylor taught him guitar and harmonica, but he rarely played professionally until he moved to Gary, Indiana in 1948 and gradually worked himself into the Chicago blues scene. He recorded on harmonica with John Brim and, after failing an audition for Chess Records, recorded his own session for Chance Records in 1953. At this point, he reunited with Eddie Taylor.

Reed recorded for Vee Jay from 1953 until the label folded in 1965. His most successful period was 1955–61, when he had seven top 10 R&B hits ('Big Boss Man', 'Bright Lights, Big City' etc.). Reed's formula was simple: a lazy tempo with a boogie figure on the bottom, harmonica solos and his slurred, almost unintelligible vocals. He was the most consistently popular Chicago bluesman, his records routinely making the pop chart, but credit must also go to his faithful guitarist Taylor and his wife, Mama Reed, who helped to write many of his songs.

Dannie Richmond

(Drums, 1935–88)

Dannie Richmond's career is inextricably linked with that of Charles Mingus. He played saxophone and piano before taking up drums in 1956, working closely with Mingus until 1979. Richmond's energetic, versatile style was also well-suited to jazz rock;

see Introduction pp 188 *see* Sources & Sounds pp 190 *see* Key Artists pp 198

he played with the UK band Mark-Almond (1970–73) and worked with Joe Cocker and Elton John. He co-founded Mingus Dynasty in 1979, and played with bassist Cameron Brown, saxophonist George Adams and pianist Don Pullen until his death.

Sonny Rollins

(Tenor and soprano saxophone, b. 1930)

Sonny Rollins stands alongside John Coltrane as the major bop-rooted stylist on tenor saxophone. He cut his teeth in New York with bop giants including Charlie Parker, Bud Powell, Thelonious Monk and Miles Davis. He was a member of the Clifford Brown–Max Roach Quintet (1955–57), and has led his own bands since then. His late 1950s recordings confirmed his standing as one of the great talents in the music; calypso-based tunes have been a recurring motif since 'St. Thomas' (1956).

He stopped performing to recharge creatively between 1959–61, then recorded with an early hero, Coleman Hawkins (1963), and flirted with the emerging free jazz avant-garde (1965–66). He took his long and discursive soloing to its logical conclusion in *The Solo Album* (1985) and experimented with soprano saxophone, also adding various electric instruments to his group. Rollins is capable of a power and invention that few musicians in jazz have been able to match.

Horace Silver

(Piano, b. 1928)

Horace Silver stands with Art Blakey as the progenitor of the earthier development of bebop, known as hard bop. His Hartford-based trio was hired by Stan Getz in 1950 and he moved to New York the following year. He began recording for Blue Note in 1952, a relationship that would last for 28 years. He formed a band with Art Blakey that became the latter's Jazz Messengers when the pianist left in 1956.

Like the Jazz Messengers, Silver's quintets became a nursery for new talent as well as a vehicle for his own compositions; many of his tunes became part of the standard jazz repertoire. He incorporated the influence of his father's native Cape Verdean folk music, most famously on 'Song For My Father'. His more experimental music of the 1970s was less well-received, but he returned to hard bop from the early 1980s and remains a successful artist, although increasingly hampered by arthritis.

Zoot Sims

(Tenor, soprano and alto saxophones, 1925–85)

John 'Zoot' Sims performed in the family vaudeville act as a child and was a professional musician at 15. His Lester Young-derived tenor sound and artful improvisations were heard to advantage in large and small bands. He worked with Benny Goodman intermittently over four decades, and was part of Woody Herman's famous 'Four Brothers' saxophone section (1947–49). His small groups included stints with Gerry Mulligan (1954–56) and tenor saxophonist Al Cohn, a partnership resumed on many occasions.

Left
Sonny Rollins, one of the most inventive voices on the saxophone since Charlie Parker.

Below
Saxophonist Zoot Sims recording material for the *Jutta Hipp With Zoot Sims* album in 1956.

see Charlie Parker pp 162 *see* Art Blakey pp 218 *see* Charles Mingus pp 230 *see* John Coltrane pp 250

Frank Sinatra

(Vocals, 1915–98)

Frank Sinatra was best known as a popular singer and film actor but established his jazz credentials early in his career. He combined the smooth, Italian *bel canto* style with a sure sense of swing, toured with Harry James and learned about breath control from Tommy Dorsey (1940–42). He worked with arrangers Billy May, Gordon Jenkins and Nelson Riddle in his classic years (1953–61). Later projects included collaborations with Count Basie (1962–66) and Duke Ellington (1967).

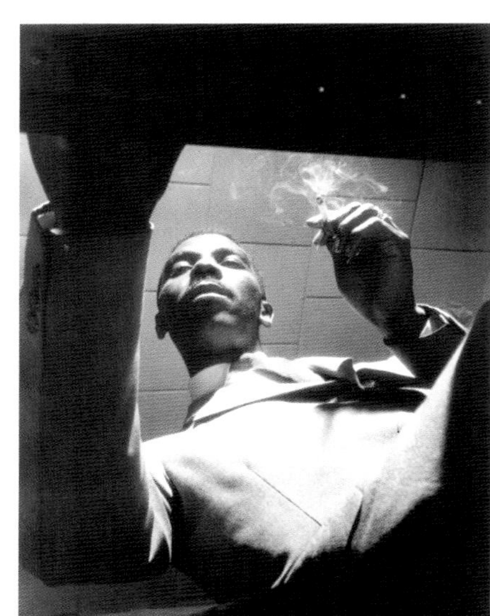

Above

Soul jazz organist Jimmy Smith, who recorded for Blue Note in the 1950s.

Huey 'Piano' Smith

(Piano, vocals, b. 1934)

Huey P. Smith was born in New Orleans, Louisiana and worked with Earl King and Guitar Slim in the early 1950s. He made his recording debut for Savoy in 1953 but his on-off tenure with Ace Records from 1955–64 was his most important. His group the Clowns had two huge R&B records in 'Rockin' Pneumonia And The Boogie-Woogie Flu' and 'Don't You Just Know It' in 1957–58. Smith was a fine songwriter, pianist and vocalist, and one of the bright stars of the New Orleans R&B scene of the late 1950s and early 1960s.

Jimmy Smith

(Organ, piano, 1925–2005)

Jimmy Smith, a fluent and inventive jazz improviser, is regarded as the greatest of the soul jazz organists; he essentially defined the form in his performances and recordings for Blue Note in the 1950s. His adoption of the Hammond organ to soul jazz's combination of jazz improvisation over blues-rooted grooves opened up a new field. Smith was the genre's most eminent practitioner, although he spawned dozens of imitators and a generation of younger players such as Joey DeFrancesco.

Sonny Stitt

(Alto, tenor and baritone saxophones, 1924–82)

Edward 'Sonny' Stitt was equally proficient on the alto and tenor saxophones. Initially a devotee of Charlie Parker, he developed into a hard-hitting and fluid improviser with a reputation for extreme toughness in 'cutting' contests. He worked with Dizzy Gillespie, Bud Powell, J.J. Johnson and Oscar Peterson, but is best known for his collaborations with fellow tenormen Sonny Rollins, Dexter Gordon, Eddie 'Lockjaw' Davis and Gene Ammons. His prolific discography is uneven, but often brilliant.

Sunnyland Slim

(Piano, vocals, 1906–95)

Albert Luandrew was born in Vance, Mississippi. He was self-taught as a pianist and spent the period 1925–39 in Memphis, playing functions and small clubs. He went to Chicago to find work outside music, but instead fell in with the local blues crowd and worked with Tampa Red, Jump Jackson and Muddy Waters. He began recording in 1947 and recorded for more than two dozen small labels around Chicago. A solid, workman-like performer, Slim was the patriarch of the Chicago blues scene in his later years.

Rufus Thomas

(Vocals, 1917–2001)

Rufus Thomas Jr. was born in Cayce, Mississippi and raised in Memphis, Tennessee. He worked with tent and minstrel shows throughout the 1930s. He recorded for Sun Records in the early 1950s and had the label's first hit with 'Bear Cat' in 1953; he also worked as a disc jockey at WDIA, Memphis. He began recording for Stax in 1959 and had big R&B hits with humorous dance songs such as 'Walkin' The Dog' and 'Do The Funky Chicken'. Billed as the 'World's Oldest Teenager', Rufus Thomas was an ambassador for Memphis blues and is the father of 1960s soul siren Carla Thomas.

see Introduction pp 188 *see* Sources & Sounds pp 190 *see* Key Artists pp 198

Big Mama Thornton

(Harmonica, vocals, 1926–84)

Willie Mae Thornton was born in Montgomery, Alabama. She settled in Houston, Texas in 1948 and began recording for the Peacock label in 1951. She toured with Johnny Otis in 1952–53 and recorded her number-one R&B hit, 'Hound Dog', with his band. The record, famously covered by Elvis Presley, enabled her to branch out on her own. After leaving Peacock in 1957, she settled in the San Francisco area and worked as a solo artist. She recorded albums for Arhoolie, Mercury and Vanguard in the 1960s and 1970s.

Sonny Boy Williamson II (Rice Miller)

(Harmonica, vocals, c. 1912–65)

Alex Ford 'Rice' Miller was born in Glendora, Mississippi. He taught himself the harmonica at the age of five and by his early teens had left home to sing and play as 'Little Boy Blue'. He worked streets, clubs and functions through Mississippi and Arkansas during the 1930s, often playing with Robert Johnson, Elmore James and Robert Lockwood Jr. In 1941 he began a radio programme, *King Biscuit Time*, on KFFA in Helena, Arkansas and billed himself as Sonny Boy Williamson.

Sonny Boy started recording for Trumpet in 1951. He switched to Checker in 1955 and had a big R&B hit with 'Don't Start Me To Talkin''. He toured Europe with the American Folk Blues Festival in 1963 and recorded with the Yardbirds. Rice Miller was an outstanding harmonica player and also had a fantastic blues voice; he was one of the great blues personalities of the 1950s and 1960s.

Above

Saxophonist Sonny Stitt (left of standing group) with Thelonious Monk (seated far left) and (l–r) Clark Terry, Roy Eldridge and Al McGibbon, performing at Monterey, 1971.

Far Left

Sonny Boy Williamson II (Rice Miller) tours with the 1963 American Folk Blues Festival.

see Johnny Otis pp 181 *see* Guitar Slim pp 223 *see* Sonny Rollins pp 233 *see* Joey DeFrancesco pp 356

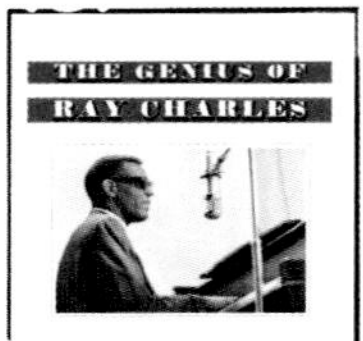

List of Artists

Entries appear in the following order: name, music style, year(s) of popularity, instruments, country of origin.

Aaltonen, Juhani, Modern Jazz; Jazz Rock, 1950s–, Flute, saxophones, Finnish
Aarons, Al, Modern Jazz; Bebop, 1950s–1980s, Flugelhorn, trumpet, American
Abdul-Malik, Ahmed, Bebop; Hard Bop; World Fusion, 1950s–1980s, Bass, American
Abene, Mik, Modern Jazz, 1950s–1990s, Piano, American
Ace, Johnny, Rhythm & Blues, 1950s, Guitar, vocals, American
Aces, Chicago Blues, 1950s–1970s, Various instruments, American
Adams, Alberta, Rhythm & Blues, 1950s–, Vocals, American
Adams, Faye, East Coast Blues; Jump Blues; Rhythm & Blues, 1950s–1960s, Vocals, American
Adams, Johnny, Rhythm & Blues, 1950s–1990s, Vocals, American
Adams, Marie, Rhythm & Blues, 1950s–1990s, Vocals, American
Adams, Pepper, Hard Bop, 1950s–1980s, Saxophone, American
Adams, Woodrow, Delta Blues, 1950s–1960s, Guitar, harmonica, American
Adderley, Nat, Hard Bop; Soul Jazz, 1950s–1990s, Trumpet, American
Agee, Ray, West Coast Blues, 1950s–1970s, Vocals, American
Akiyoshi, Toshiko, Big Band; Modern Jazz; Hard Bop, 1950s–, Piano, composer, bandleader, Chinese
Alcorn, Alvin, New Orleans Jazz, 1950s–1970s, Trumpet, American
Alexander, Dave, Boogie-Woogie; West Coast Blues, 1950s–, Piano, American
Alexandria, Lorez, Swing; Bebop, 1950s–1990s, Vocals, American
Allan, Jan, Modern Jazz; Free Jazz, 1950s–, Trumpet, Swedish
Allen, Annisteen, Jump Blues, 1950s–1960s, Vocals, American
Allen, Marshall, Free Jazz, 1950s–, Saxophone, flute, American
Allison, Mose, Hard Bop; Country Blues, 1950s–, Piano, vocals, composer, American
Almeida, Laurindo, Brazilian Jazz; Latin Jazz, 1950s–1990s, Guitar, Brazilian
Alphonso, Roland, Swing; Jamaican Jazz, 1950s–1990s, Saxophone, Cuban
Amram, David, World Fusion; Latin Jazz; Bebop, 1950s–1990s, French horn, composer, American
Andrews, Ernie, West Coast Blues, 1950s; 1980s–, Vocals, American
Antolini, Charley, Big Band; Swing, 1950s–, Drums, Swedish
Appleyard, Peter, Cool Jazz, 1950s–, Vibraphone, British
Arnold, Billy Boy, Chicago Blues, 1950s–, Harmonica, vocals, American
Arnold, Horace, Modern Jazz, 1950s–, Drums, American
Ashby, Dorothy, Bebop, 1950s–, Harp, American
Ashby, Harold, Swing; Traditional Jazz, 1950s–1990s, Saxophone, American
Attenoux, Michel, Traditional Jazz; Swing, 1950s–1980s, Saxophone, French
August, Joseph 'Mr. Google' 'Mr. G', Rhythm & Blues, 1950s–1990s, Vocals, American
Austin, Claire, Swing; Dixieland; Traditional Jazz, 1950s–1980s, Vocals, American
Austin, Sil, East Coast Blues; Jump Blues, 1950s–1970s, Saxophone, American
Avon Cities Jazz Band, New Orleans Jazz; Rhythm & Blues, 1950s–, Various instruments, British
Badini, Gerard, Swing; Modern Jazz, 1950s–, Saxophone, clarinet, piano, composer, bandleader, French
Bailey, Dave, Modern Jazz, 1950s–, Drums, American
Bailey, Donald, Modern Jazz, 1950s–, Drums, American
Baker, Chet, Cool Jazz, 1950s–1980s, Trumpet, vocals, flugelhorn, American
Baker, David, Big Band; Modern Jazz, 1950s–, Trombone, cello, composer, American
Baker, Etta, Country Blues, 1950s; 1980s–1990s, Guitar, American
Baker, Lavern, Rhythm & Blues; Jump Blues, 1950s–1960s; 1980s–1990s, Vocals, American
Baker, Mickey, Rhythm & Blues; East Coast Blues, 1950s–1970s, Guitar, American
Baldry, Long John, British Blues; Blues Rock, 1950s–, Vocals, British
Ball, Kenny, New Orleans Jazz; Chicago Jazz; Dixieland, 1950s–1990s, Trumpet, vocals, bandleader, British
Ballard, Hank, Rhythm & Blues, 1950s–1990s, Vocals, composer, American
Balliett, Whitney, All Jazz Styles, 1950s–, Author, critic, American
Barber, Chris, New Orleans Jazz; Chicago Jazz; Dixieland, 1950s–1990s, Trombone, vocals, bandleader, British
Barnes, John, Modern Jazz, 1950s–, Clarinet, flugelhorn, British
Barretto, Ray, Latin Jazz, 1950s–, Percussion, American
Barron, Bill, Hard Bop; Modern Jazz, 1950s–1980s, Saxophone, American
Barron, Kenny, Hard Bop; Modern Jazz, 1950s–, Piano, American
Bartholomew, Dave, Rhythm & Blues, 1950s–1990s, Producer, composer, bandleader, trumpet, American
Batiste, Alvin, Free Jazz, 1950s–, Clarinet, American
Bean, Billy, Modern Jazz, 1950s–1960s, Guitar, American
Beasley, Jimmy, Rhythm & Blues, 1950s, Vocals, piano, American
Beck, Joe, Fusion, 1950s–, Guitar, American
Belgrave, Marcus, Modern Jazz; Big Band, 1950s–, Trumpet, American
Below, Fred, Chicago Blues, 1950s–1960s, Drums, American
Belvin, Jesse, Rhythm & Blues, 1950s, Vocals, composer, American
Bennett, Max, Swing; Big Band, 1950s–, Bass, composer, American
Bennett, Tony, Swing; Cool Jazz, 1950s–, Vocals, American
Benton, Brook, Rhythm & Blues, 1950s–1970s, Vocals, American
Berry, Bill, Swing; Big Band, 1950s–, Trumpet, cornet, bandleader, American
Berry, Chuck, Rhythm & Blues, 1950s–1990s, Vocals, guitar, composer, American
Berry, Richard, Rhythm & Blues, 1950s–1960s, Vocals, composer, American
Bey, Andy, Hard Bop; Soul Jazz; Modern Jazz, 1950s–, Vocals, American
Bickert, Ed, Cool Jazz; Modern Jazz, 1950s–, Guitar, Canadian
Bilk, Acker, New Orleans Jazz; Traditional Jazz, 1950s–1990s, Clarinet, vocals, bandleader, British
Billbeg, Rolf, Modern Jazz; Big Band, 1950s–1960s, Saxophone, Swedish
Bjorksten, Hacke, Modern Jazz, 1950s–, Saxophone, bandleader, Finnish
Blackburn, Lou, World Fusion; Big Band, 1950s–1990s, Trombone, American
Blackwell, Ed, Free Jazz, 1950s–1990s, Drums, American
Blackwell, Francis 'Bumps', Rhythm & Blues, 1950s–1960s, Producer, arranger, American
Blackwell, Otis, East Coast Blues, 1950s–1970s, Vocals, piano, composer, American
Blakey, Art, Hard Bop, 1950s–1990s, Drums, American
Bland, Bobby 'Blue', Texas Blues; Rhythm & Blues, 1950s–, Vocals, American
Blue, Little Joe, West Coast Blues; Modern Electric Blues, 1950s–1980s, Vocals, American
Bo, Eddie, Rhythm & Blues, 1950s–, Piano, vocals, American
Bobo, Willie, Latin Jazz, 1950s–1980s, Percussion, Spanish
Boland, Francy, Big Band; Swing; Bebop, 1950s–, Piano, arranger, composer, bandleader, Belgian
Bond, Jimmy, Modern Jazz; Bebop, 1950s–, Bass, composer, American
Bonfá, Luiz, Brazilian Jazz, 1950s–1990s, Guitar, composer, Brazilian
Bonner, Juke Boy, West Coast Blues; Texas Blues, 1950s–1970s, Guitar, vocals, American
Booker, James, Boogie-Woogie; Rhythm & Blues, 1950s–1980s, Piano, American
Botschinsky, Allan, Big Band; Fusion Jazz, 1950s–, Trumpet, flugelhorn, arranger, composer, Danish
Boykins, Ronnie, Free Jazz; Big Band, 1950s–1970s, Bass, American
Bradford, Bobby, Free Jazz; Modern Jazz, 1950s–, Cornet, trumpet, composer, American
Bradshaw, Sonny, Jamaican Jazz; Big Band, 1950s–, Trumpet, flugelhorn, arranger, bandleader, Jamaican
Bregman, Buddy, Big Band, 1950s–1960s, Producer, American
Brewer, Teresa, Swing; Big Band, 1950s–, Vocals, American
Bright, Ronnell, Modern Jazz; Big Band, 1950s–, Piano, composer, American
Brignola, Nick, Hard Bop; Modern Jazz; Big Band, 1950s–2000s, Saxophone, flute, American
Brim, Grace, Chicago Blues, 1950s–1970s, Vocals, harmonica, drums, American
Brim, John, Chicago Blues, 1950s–1960s; 1990s, Guitar, American
Brisker, Gordon, Modern Jazz; Big Band; Australian Jazz, 1950s–, Saxophone, arranger, American
Brock, 'Big' George, Chicago Blues; Rhythm & Blues, 1950s–, Bandleader, harmonica, American
Brodie, Hugh, Modern Jazz, 1950s–, Saxophone, American
Brookmeyer, Bob, Cool Jazz, 1950s–, Valve trombone, piano, arranger, American
Brooks, Bubba, Swing, 1950s–2000s, Saxophone, American
Brooks, Lonnie, Modern Electric Blues, 1950s–1990s, Guitar, American
Brooks, Tina, Hard Bop, 1950s–1960s, Saxophone, American
Brown, Brian, Free Jazz; World Fusion, 1950s–, Saxophone, composer, bandleader, American
Brown, Clarence 'Gatemouth', Texas Blues; Country Blues, 1950s–, Guitar, American
Brown, Clifford, Hard Bop; Bebop, 1950s, Trumpet, American
Brown, James, Rhythm & Blues, 1950s–, Vocals, composer, American
Brown, Marshall, Swing; Big Band; Modern Jazz, 1950s–1980s, Trombone, bandleader, American
Brown, Nappy, Jump Blues; Rhythm & Blues, 1950s–1960s; 1980s–1990s, Vocals, American
Brown, Oscar Jr, Modern Jazz; Soul Jazz, 1950s–, Vocals, composer, American
Brown, Ruth, Jump Blues; Rhythm & Blues, 1950s–1960s; 1980s–1990s, Vocals, American
Brown, Sandy, Traditional Jazz; Swing; Jazz Rock, 1950s–1970s, Clarinet, vocals, composer, leader, British
Brubeck, Dave, Cool Jazz; West Coast Jazz, 1950s–, Piano, composer, American
Bryant, Ray, Soul Jazz; Swing; Bebop, 1950s–, Piano, American
Bryant, Rusty, Soul Jazz; Hard Bop, 1950s–1980s, Saxophone, American
Bryce, Owen, Dixieland, 1950s–1990s, Trumpet, bandleader, British
Bryden, Beryl, Traditional Jazz, 1950s–1990s, Vocals, washboard, British
Buddle, Errol, Modern Jazz; Big Band, 1950s–, Bassoon, saxophone, Australian
Budimir, Dennis, Big Band; Modern Jazz, 1950s–, Guitar, American
Budwig, Monty, Cool Jazz; Bebop, 1950s–1990s, Bass, American
Bunch, John, Swing, 1950s–, Piano, American
Burns, Eddie, Chicago Blues; Detroit Blues, 1950s–, Vocals, guitar, harmonica, American
Burns, Roy, Swing; Modern Jazz, 1950s–, Drums, American
Burrage, Howard, Rhythm & Blues; Chicago Blues, 1950s–1960s, Vocals, composer, producer, American
Burrell, Kenny, Bebop; Hard Bop; Cool Jazz, 1950s–, Guitar, vocals, American
Burrows, Don, Modern Jazz; Swing; Cool Jazz, 1950s–, Clarinet, saxophone, flute, Australian
Butler, Billy, Jump Blues; Rhythm & Blues, 1950s–1980s, Guitar, American
Butler, Frank, Bebop; West Coast Jazz; Hard Bop, 1950s–1980s, Drums, American
Butler, Jerry, Rhythm & Blues, 1950s–1990s, Vocals, American
Byers, Billy, Big Band, 1950s–1990s, Trombone, arranger, American
Byrd, Charlie, Brazilian Jazz; Latin Jazz, 1950s–1990s, Guitar, American
Byrd, Donald, Fusion; Hard Bop, 1950s–, Trumpet, flugelhorn, American
Cadets, The, Rhythm & Blues, 1950s–1960s, Various instruments, American
Caesar, Harry 'Little', Rhythm & Blues, 1950s, Vocals, American
Cameron, Jay, Swing; Modern Jazz, 1950s–, Saxophone, American
Candido, Latin Jazz, 1950s–, Drums, Cuban
Capp, Frank, Modern Jazz; Swing; Big Band, 1950s–, Drums, bandleader, American
Carr, Sister Wynona, Jump Blues; Rhythm & Blues, 1950s, Vocals, composer, American
Carson, Ernie, Dixieland Revival, 1950s–1990s, Cornet, American
Carter, Betty, Bebop, 1950s–1990s, Vocals, American
Carter, Joe, Chicago Blues, 1950s–, Guitar, American
Castro, Joe, Swing; Hard Bop; Bebop, 1950s–, Piano, bandleader, American
Castro-Neves, Oscar, Brazilian Jazz; Modern Jazz, 1950s–, Guitar, composer, arranger, Brazilian
Cathcart, Dick, Swing, 1950s–1980s, Trumpet, vocals, American
Cerri, Franco, Modern Jazz; Swing; Bebop, 1950s–, Guitar, bass, Italian
Chambers, Paul, Hard Bop, 1950s–1960s, Bass, American
Charles, Dennis, Free Jazz, 1950s–1990s, Drums, American
Charles, Ray, Rhythm & Blues, 1950s–2000s, Vocals, piano, composer, American
Charles, Teddy, Cool Jazz, 1950s–1990s, Vibraphone, composer, American
Charlesworth, Dick, Traditional Jazz, 1950s–1970s, Clarinet, saxophone, British
Chase, Bill, Swing; Jazz Rock; Big Band, 1950s–1970s, Trumpet, American
Chavis, Wilson 'Boozoo', Zydeco, 1950s–, Accordion, harmonica, American
Chescoe, Laurie, Dixieland, 1950s–1990s, Drums, bandleader, British
Chilton, John, Swing; Traditional Jazz, 1950s–, Trumpet, flugelhorn, composer, bandleader, author, British
Christian, Little Johnny, Chicago Blues, 1950s–, Vocals, bass, American
Christie Brothers Stompers, New Orleans Jazz; Chicago Jazz, 1950s, Various instruments, British
Cirillo, Wally, Modern Jazz, 1950s–1970s, Piano, composer, American
Clare, Kenny, Big Band, 1950s–1980s, Drums, British
Clark, Buddy, Modern Jazz; Bebop; Big Band, 1950s–, Bass, arranger, American
Clark, Dave, Rhythm & Blues, 1950s–1980s, Producer, composer, American
Clark, Dee, Rhythm & Blues, 1950s–1980s, Vocals, American
Clark, Sonny, Bebop; Hard Bop, 1950s–1960s, Piano, American
Clay, James, Hard Bop, 1950s–1990s, Saxophone, flute, American
Clooney, Rosemary, Traditional Jazz; Swing, 1950s–, Vocals, American
Clyne, Jeff, Swing; Big Band; Modern Jazz, 1950s–, Bass, American
Coasters, The, Rhythm & Blues, 1950s–1970s, Vocals, American
Coates, John Jr, Cool Jazz, 1950s–, Piano, American
Cobb, Jimmy, Hard Bop, 1950s–, Drums, American
Cobbs, Willie, Country Blues; Modern Electric Blues, 1950s–, Vocals, harmonica, guitar, American
Coe, Tony, Hard Bop; Modern Jazz, 1950s–, Saxophone, clarinet, British
Coggins, Gil, Modern Jazz, 1950s–2000s, Piano, American
Coker, Dolo, Bebop, 1950s–1980s, Piano, American
Cole, Ann, Rhythm & Blues, 1950s–1960s, Vocals, American
Cole, Freddy, Swing, 1950s–, Vocals, piano, American
Coleman, George, Hard Bop, 1950s–, Saxophones, American
Coles, Johnny, Hard Bop, 1950s–1990s, Trumpet, flugelhorn, American
Collette, Buddy, Cool Jazz, 1950s–, Saxophone, clarinet, flute, American
Collie, Max, New Orleans Jazz, 1950s–, Trombone, vocals, Australian
Collier, James Lincoln, All Jazz Styles, 1950s–, Author, American
Collins, Joyce, Hard Bop, 1950s–, Piano, vocals, American
Colyer, Ken, New Orleans Jazz, 1950s–1980s, Trumpet, vocals, bandleader, British
Connor, Chris, Cool Jazz, 1950s–, Vocals, American
Cook, Junior, Hard Bop, 1950s–1990s, Saxophone, American
Cooke, Sam, Rhythm & Blues, 1950s–1960s, Vocals, composer, American
Coon, Jackie, Traditional Jazz, 1950s–, Flugelhorn, American
Cooper, Buster, Swing, 1950s–, Trombone, American
Costa, Eddie, Bebop, 1950s–1960s, Piano, vibraphone, American
Costa, John, Swing, 1950s–1990s, Piano, American
Cotten, Elizabeth, Rhythm & Blues, 1950s–1980s, Guitar, vocals, composer, American
Cotton, James, Modern Electric Blues; Chicago Blues, 1950s, Guitar, harmonica, American
Crawford, Hank, Soul Jazz; Hard Bop, 1950s, Saxophone, piano, American
Crawford, James 'Sugar Boy', Rhythm & Blues, 1950s–1960s, Vocals, piano, American
Creach, John 'Papa', Jump Blues, 1950s–1990s, Vocals, violin, American
Crimmins, Roy, Dixieland Revival; Chicago Jazz, 1950s–1980s, Trombone, British
Crombie, Tony, Swing; Jazz Rock; Bebop, 1950s–1990s, Drums, composer, British
Cruz, Celia, Latin Jazz, 1950s–, Vocals, Cuban
Cuba, Joe, Latin Jazz, 1950s–1970s, Percussion, American
Cuppini, Gil, Swing; Big Bands, 1950s–1990s, Drums, bandleader, Italian
Curtis, King, Rhythm & Blues, 1950s–1960s, Saxophones, American
Dahlander, Bert, Modern Jazz; Swing, 1950s–, Drums, Swedish
Dale, Larry, East Coast Blues; Rhythm & Blues, 1950s–1960s, Guitar, American
Dane, Barbara, Folk Blues, 1950s–, Vocals, guitar, piano, American
Daniels, Maxine, Modern Jazz, 1950s–, Vocals, British
Daniels, Mike, Big Band, 1950s–, Trumpet, leader, British
Davenport, Lester, Chicago Blues, 1950s–, Harmonica, drums, bass, American
Davenport, Wallace, Swing; Bebop, 1950s–2000s, Trumpet, bandleader, American
Davern, Kevin, Dixieland Revival; Swing, 1950s–, Clarinet, saxophones, American
Davies, John R.T., Traditional Jazz, 1950s–2000s, Saxophones, guitar, banjo, drums, producer, discographer, British
Davis, Art, Hard Bop; Modern Jazz, 1950s–, Bass, American
Davis, Charles, Hard Bop, 1950s–, Saxophone, American
Davis, Jackie, Soul Jazz, 1950s–, Organ, American
Davis, James 'Thunderbird', Modern Electric Blues, 1950s–1980s, Vocals, American
Davis, Jimmy, Delta Blues; Country Blues, 1950s–1990s, Vocals, guitar, American
Davis, Larry, Texas Blues, 1950s–1990s, Drums, guitar, American
Davis, Miles, Bebop; Hard Bop; Cool Jazz; Jazz Rock; Fusion, 1950s–1990s, Trumpet, flugelhorn, composer, American
Davis, Richard, Hard Bop, 1950s–, Bass, American
Davis, Walter Jr, Bebop; Hard Bop, 1950s; 1970s–1980s, Piano, American
Dawson, Alan, Hard Bop, 1950s–1990s, Drums, American
Dearie, Blossom, Bebop, 1950s–, Vocals, piano, American
Dennis, Willie, Big Band, 1950s–1960s, Trombone, American
Deuchar, Jimmy, Bebop; British Jazz, 1950s–1990s, Trumpet, flugelhorn, Scottish
Diddley, Bo, Rhythm & Blues; Chicago Blues, 1950s–, Guitar, vocals, composer, American
Dillard, Varetta, Rhythm & Blues, 1950s–1960s, Vocals, American
Disley, Diz, Swing, 1950s–, Guitar, bandleader, Canadian
Distel, Sacha, Modern Jazz; Bebop, 1950s–2000s, Guitar, vocals, French
Dixon, Eric, Big Band; Bebop; Hard Bop, 1950s–1980s, Saxophone, American
Dixon, Floyd, Jump Blues; Rhythm & Blues; West Coast Blues, 1540s–1970s; 1990s, Guitar, vocals, American
Dixon, Willie, Jump Blues; Chicago Blues, 1950s–1990s, Bass, composer, producer, American
Doctor Ross, Delta Blues, 1950s–1990s, Guitar, vocals, harmonica, American
Doggett, Bill, Rhythm & Blues, 1950s–1990s, Piano, organ, composer, American
Domino, Fats, Rhythm & Blues, 1950s–1980s, Piano, vocals, American
Dominoes, The, Rhythm & Blues, 1950s–1960s, Vocals, American
Don & Dewey, Rhythm & Blues, 1950s–1960s, Vocals, American
Donaldson, Bobby, Swing; Bebop, 1950s–1970s, Drums, American
Donaldson, Lou, Bebop; Hard Bop, 1950s–, Saxophone, American
Donegan, Lonnie, Traditional Jazz, 1950s–2000s, Vocals, guitar, banjo, Scottish
Douglas, K.C., Delta Blues, 1950s–1970s, Guitar, composer, American
Draper, Ray, Hard Bop, 1950s–1980s, Tuba, American
Drew, Kenny, Hard Bop, 1950s–1990s, Piano, American
Drifters, The, Rhythm & Blues, 1950s–1990s, Vocals, American
Drifting Slim, Memphis Blues, 1950s–1970s, Harmonica, guitar, drums, American
Drootin, Buzzy, Swing; Dixieland, 1950s–, Drums, Russian
Du Droppers, The, Rhythm & Blues, 1950s, Vocals, American
Dukes of Dixieland, Dixieland Revival, 1950s–, Various instruments, American
Duran, Eddie, Cool Jazz, 1950s–, Guitar, bandleader, American
Dutch Swing College Band, Dixieland; Swing; Big Band, 1950s–, Various instruments, Dutch
Duvivier, George, Swing; Big Band; Bebop, 1950s–1990s, Bass, arranger, American
Dyer, Johnny, Delta Blues; Chicago Blues; West Coast Blues, 1950s–2000s, Vocals, harmonica, American
Eardley, Jon, Cool Jazz; Bebop, 1950s–1970s, Trumpet, American
Easy Baby, Rhythm & Blues; Modern Electric Blues, 1950s–1960s, Vocals, harmonica, American
Edwards, Clarence, Chicago Blues, 1950s–, Guitar, American
Egan, Willie, Boogie-Woogie, 1950s, Piano, vocals, American
Elliott, Don, Cool Jazz; Swing; Fusion, 1950s–1970s, Mellophone, vibraphone, vocals, composer, American
Elsdon, Alan, Traditional Jazz, 1950s–, Trumpet, flugelhorn, vocals, leader, British
Emerson, Billy 'The Kid', Memphis Blues, 1950s–, Piano, American
Enevoldsen, Bob, Cool Jazz; West Coast Jazz, 1950s–, Trombone, saxophone, bass, American
Ervin, Booker, Hard Bop, 1950s–1960s, Saxophone, composer, American
Erwin, Pee Wee, Swing, 1950s–1980s, Trumpet, American
Esquerita, Rhythm & Blues, 1950s, Vocals, piano, American
Evans, Bill, Cool Jazz; Modal Jazz, 1950s–1980s, Piano, composer, American
Evans, Gil, Cool Jazz; Fusion, 1950s–1980s, Piano, arranger, composer, Canadian
Evans, Lucky, Chicago Blues, 1950s–, Vocals, American
Everett, Betty, Rhythm & Blues, 1950s–1970s, Vocals, American
Fagerquist, Don, Cool Jazz; Bebop, 1950s–2000s, Trumpet, American
Fahey, John, Country Blues; Delta Blues, 1950s–1990s, Guitar, composer, author, American
Fairweather, Al, Traditional Jazz; Jazz Fusion, 1950s–1990s, Trumpet, arranger, composer, leader, British
Falay, Maffy, Bebop; World Fusion, 1950s–, Trumpet, Turkish
Farlow, Tal, Bebop; Cool Jazz, 1950s–1990s, Guitar, American
Farlowe, Chris, Rhythm & Blues, 1950s–, Vocals, British
Feldman, Victor, Cool Jazz, 1950s–1980s, Vibraharp, percussion, British
Ferguson, Maynard, Hard Bop, 1950s–1990s, Trumpet, flugelhorn, bandleader, Canadian
Ferguson, Robert 'H-Bomb', Rhythm & Blues; Jump Blues, 1950s–1990s, Vocals, piano, American
Five Keys, The, East Coast Blues; Rhythm & Blues, 1950s–1960s, Vocals, American
Five Royales, The, Rhythm & Blues, 1950s–1960s, Vocals, American
Florence, Bob, Modern Jazz, 1950s–, Piano, arranger, composer, bandleader, American
Flores, Chuck, Swing; Modern Jazz; Big Band, 1950s–, Drums, bandleader, American
Flory, Med, Big Band; Bebop; Swing, 1950s–, Saxophone, arranger, bandleader, American
Floyd, Frank, Country Blues, 1950s–1970s, Guitar, harmonica, American
Fonatana, Carl, Cool Jazz; Bebop, 1950s–1990s, Trombone, American
Fonseque, Raymond, Traditional Jazz, 1950s–, Trombone, arranger, bandleader, French
Ford, Frankie, Rhythm & Blues, 1950s–, Piano, vocals, American
Foster, 'Baby Face' Leroy, Chicago Blues, 1950s, Vocals, drums, guitar, American
Foster, Frank, Hard Bop; Swing, 1950s–1990s, Saxophone, arranger, American
Four Freshman, Swing, 1950s–1990s, Various instruments, American
Fowler, T.J., Jump Blues, 1950s, Piano, bandleader, American
Fowlkes, Charlie, Swing; Big Band, 1950s–1970s, Saxophone, American
Fran, Carol, Rhythm & Blues, 1950s–, Vocals, piano, American
Francis, Panama, Rhythm & Blues; Swing, 1950s–1980s, Drums, bandleader, American
Frank, Edward, Rhythm & Blues, 1950s–1990s, Piano, American
Frankenfield, Parke, Dixieland; Big Band; Swing, 1950s–, Multi-instrumentalist, vocals, arranger, bandleader, American
Frazier, Calvin, Jump Blues, 1950s, Vocals, guitar, American
Freeman, Stan, Cool Jazz; Swing; Bebop, 1950s–1960s, Piano, composer, American
Friedman, Don, Hard Bop; Modern Jazz, 1950s–, Piano, American
Frost, Frank, Modern Electric Blues, 1950s–1990s, Keyboards, guitar, American
Fruscella, Tony, Cool Jazz, 1950s–1960s, Trumpet, American
Fuller, Curtis, Hard Bop, 1950s–1990s, Trombone, American
Fuller, Jesse, Country Blues; West Coast Blues, 1950s–1960s, Bass, guitar, harmonica, American
Fuller, Johnny, Rhythm & Blues; West Coast Blues, 1950s–1980s, Guitar, American
Fulson, Lowell, West Coast Blues; Texas Blues, 1950s–1990s, Guitar, vocals, American
Gaddy, Bob, Rhythm & Blues, 1950s–1990s, Vocals, piano, American
Gaines, Earl, Rhythm & Blues, 1950s, Vocals, American
Gaines, Grady, Jump Blues; Texas Blues; Rhythm & Blues, 1950s–, Saxophone, American
Galbraith, Barry, Swing; Soul Jazz; Hard Bop, 1950s–, Guitar, American
Galbraith, Charlies, Dixieland; British Jazz, 1950s–, Trombone, leader, British
Ganley, Allan, Bebop; Big Band; British Jazz, 1950s–, Drums, composer, arranger, British
Garland, Red, Hard Bop, 1950s–1980s, Piano, American
Garlow, Clarence 'Bon Ton', Rhythm & Blues, 1950s, Vocals, guitar, American
Garrick, Michael, Free Jazz, 1950s–, Piano, organ, composer, British
Gayles, Billy, Jump Blues; Rhythm & Blues, 1950s–1990s, Vocals, drums, American
Gaynair, Wilton 'Bogey', Modern Jazz; Hard Bop, 1950s–1990s, Saxophone, Jamaican
Gibbs, Terry, Bebop, 1950s–1990s, Vibraphone, drums, American
Gilberto, João, Brazilian Jazz, 1950s–, Vocals, guitar, Brazilian
Gilmore, Boyd, Country Blues, 1950s, Vocals, guitar, American
Gilmore, John, Free Jazz; Bebop, 1950s–1990s, Saxophone, drums, American
Girard, George, Chicago Jazz, 1950s, Trumpet, vocals, American
Gitler, Ira, All Jazz Styles, 1950s–, Author, critic, American
Giuffre, Jimmy, Bebop; Cool Jazz, 1950s–, Clarinet, saxophones, flute, American
Gleason, Jackie, Swing, 1950s–1960s, Musical director, American
Goldie, Don, Dixieland, 1950s–1990s, Trumpet, American
Golson, Benny, Hard Bop, 1950s–, Saxophone, arranger, composer, American
Gonsalves, Paul, Swing; Bebop, 1950s–1970s, Saxophone, guitar, American
Gordon, Rosco, Rhythm & Blues, 1950s–1990s, Vocals, piano, composer, American
Gourley, Jimmy, Bebop; Hard Bop; Modern Jazz, 1950s–, Bass, author, American
Graas, John, Cool Jazz, 1950s–, French horn, American
Gray, Henry, Chicago Blues, 1950s–1990s, Vocals, piano, American
Great Gates, Jump Blues; Rhythm & Blues, 1950s, Vocals, piano, organ, American
Green, Bennie, Swing; Bebop, 1950s–1960s, Trombone, American
Green, Clarence, Texas Blues, 1950s–1990s, Piano, American
Green, Grant, Hard Bop, 1950s–1970s, Guitar, American
Green, L.C., Detroit Blues, 1950s, Vocals, guitar, American
Greene, Rudy, Rhythm & Blues, 1950s–1960s, Vocals, American
Greig, Stan, Traditional Jazz; Boogie-Woogie, 1950s–, Piano, drums, bandleader, British
Griffin Brothers, Chicago Blues, 1950s, Various instruments, American
Grosz, Marty, Dixieland Revival, 1950s–1990s, Guitar, banjo, vocals, American
Gryce, Gigi, Hard Bop, 1950s–1970s, Saxophone, flute, composer, American
Guaraldi, Vince, Cool Jazz, 1950s–1970s, Piano, composer, American
Guitar Gable, Rhythm & Blues; New Orleans Blues, 1950s, Guitar, American
Guitar Shorty, Modern Electric Blues, 1950s–, Guitar, American
Guitar Slim, Rhythm & Blues, 1950s, Guitar, American
Gulda, Friedrich, Free Jazz, 1950s–1990s, Piano, flute, saxophone, composer, vocals, Austrian
Gullin, Lars, Cool Jazz; Bebop, 1950s–1970s, Saxophone, composer, arranger, Swedish
Gunter, Arthur, Rhythm & Blues, 1950s, Vocals, guitar, American
Hadi, Shafi, Rhythm & Blues, 1950s–1960s, Saxophone, American
Halcox, Pat, New Orleans Jazz, 1950s–, Trumpet, flugelhorn, cornet, arranger, leader, British
Hall, Jim, Cool Jazz, 1950s–, Guitar, American
Hall, Rene, Rhythm & Blues; Jump Blues, 1950s–1970s, Guitar, producer, arranger, American
Hallberg, Bengt, Bebop; Cool Jazz, 1950s–, Piano, composer, arranger, Swedish
Hamilton, Andy, Free Jazz, 1950s–1990s, Saxophone, composer, Jamaican
Hamilton, Chico, Cool Jazz; Hard Bop, 1950s–, Drums, American
Hamilton, Jimmy, Bebop; Swing, 1950s–1990s, Clarinet, saxophone, arranger, American
Hampton, Slide, Bebop; Hard Bop, 1950s–, Trombone, arranger, composer, American
Handy, John, Modern Jazz, 1950s–, Saxophone, American
Hanna, Jake, Swing, 1950s–, Drums, American
Hanna, Roland 'Sir', Swing; Hard Bop; Modern Jazz, 1950s–2000s, Piano, American
Harden, Wilbur, Hard Bop, 1950s–1960s, Trumpet, flugelhorn, American
Hardman, Bill, Hard Bop, 1950s–1990s, Trumpet, flugelhorn, American
Hare, Pat, Modern Electric Blues, 1950s–1960s, Guitar, American
Harmonica Fats, Modern Blues; Modern Electric Blues, 1950s–, Harmonica, vocals, American
Harmonica Slim, West Coast Blues, 1950s–1960s, Harmonica, American
Harper, Toni, Boogie-Woogie; Rhythm & Blues, 1950s–1960s, Vocals, American
Harriott, Joe, Free Jazz; Modern Jazz; World Fusion, 1950s–1970s, Saxophone, Jamaican
Harris, Alfred, Down-home Blues, 1950s, Harmonica, vocals, American
Harris, Barry, Bebop, 1950s–, Piano, American
Harris, Benny, Bebop, 1950s–, Trumpet, American
Harris, Don 'Sugarcane', Rhythm & Blues, 1950s–1990s, Vocals, violin, guitar, American
Harris, Eddie, Soul Jazz; Hard Bop, 1950s–1990s, Saxophone, keyboards, vocals, American
Harris, Gene, Soul Jazz; Hard Bop; Fusion, 1950s–1990s, Piano, keyboards, American
Harrison, Vernon 'Boogie-Woogie Red', Boogie-Woogie, 1950s–1980s, Piano, American
Harrison, Wilbert, Rhythm & Blues, 1950s–1970s, Vocals, American
Hastings, Lennie, Modern Jazz, 1950s–1970s, Drums, piano, bandleader, British
Havens, Bob, Dixieland Revival, 1950s–, Trombone, vibraphone, American

see Introduction pp 188 *see* Sources & Sounds pp 190 *see* Key Artists pp 198 *see* A–Z of Artists pp 216

Hawdon, Dick, Modern Jazz, 1950s–, Trumpet, flugelhorn, bass, mellophone, British
Hawes, Hampton, Bebop; Hard Bop, 1950s–1970s, Piano, American
Hawkins, Screamin' Jay, Rhythm & Blues, 1950s–1990s, Vocals, piano, saxophone, American
Hayes, Louis, Hard Bop, 1950s–, Drums, American
Hayes, Tubby, Big Band; Hard Bop; Modern Jazz, 1950s–1970s, Saxophone, flute, vibraphone, arranger, composer, British
Haynes, Roy, Bebop; Hard Bop, 1950s–, Drums, American
Heartsman, Johnny, Rhythm & Blues; Modern Electric Blues, 1950s–1990s, Vocals, guitar, flute, American
Heath, Jimmy, Hard Bop, 1950s–1990s, Saxophone, flute, composer, American
Henderson, Bill, Modern Jazz, 1950s–, Vocals, American
Henry, Clarence 'Frogman', Rhythm & Blues, 1950s–1960s, Piano, trombone, American
Herbolzheimer, Peter, Bebop; Swing, 1950s–, Trombone, composer, arranger, Romanian
Higgins, Billy, Hard Bop; Free Jazz, 1950s–1990s, Drums, American
Higgins, Chuck, Jump Blues, 1950s, Saxophone, American
Higgins, Eddie, Hard Bop; Modern Jazz, 1950s–, Piano, American
Hill, Andrew, Modal Jazz, 1950s–, Piano, composer, American
Hill, Buck, Hard Bop, 1950s; 1970s–, Saxophone, American
Hi-Los, The, Swing, 1950s–1960s, Various instruments, American
Hipp, Jutta, Hard Bop; Cool Jazz; Bebop, 1950s, Piano, German
Hirt, Al, Dixieland Revival, 1950s–1990s, Trumpet, American
Holley, Major 'Mule', Swing; Bebop, 1950s–1990s, Bass, American
Holloway, Red, Soul Jazz; Swing; Bebop, 1950s–, Saxophones, American
Holman, Bill, Hard Bop; Modern Jazz; Big Band, 1950s–, Saxophone, arranger, composer, bandleader, American
Holmes, Richard 'Groove', Soul Jazz; Hard Bop, 1950s–1990s, Organ, American
Holts, Roosevelt, Country Blues, 1950s–1960s, Vocals, guitar, American
Hooker, Earl, Delta Blues; Chicago Blues, 1950s–1970s, Guitar, American
Hopkins, Lightnin', Texas Blues, 1950s–1970s, Vocals, guitar, American
Hopkins, Linda, East Coast Blues; Jump Blues, 1950s–1980s, Vocals, American
Horn, Paul, World Fusion; Hard Bop, 1950s–, Flute, saxophone, clarinet, American
Horton, Big Walter, Chicago Blues, 1950s–1980s, Harmonica, American
Houston, Bee, Texas Blues, 1950s–1980s, Guitar, American
Houston, Joe, Jump Blues, 1950s–, Vocals, saxophone, American
Howlin' Wolf, Chicago Blues, 1950s–1970s, Vocals, guitar, American
Huff, Luther, Delta Blues, 1950s, Guitar, mandolin, American
Hughes, Joe 'Guitar', Texas Blues; Modern Electric Blues, 1950s–, Guitar, American
Humair, Daniel, Bebop; Hard Bop, 1950s–, Drums, composer, Swiss
Humble, Derek, Bebop; Big Band; Modern Jazz, 1950s–1970s, Saxophone, clarinet, British
Humphrey, Percy, New Orleans Jazz; Dixieland, 1950s–1990s, Trumpet, American
Hunt, Fred, Dixieland Revival, 1950s–1980s, Piano, bandleader, British
Ind, Peter, Cool Jazz; Bebop, 1950s–, Bass, British
Isaacs, Ike, Big Band; Swing, 1950s–, Guitar, Burmese
Isley Brothers, The, Rhythm & Blues, 1950s–, Vocals, American
Israels, Chuck, Cool Jazz; Modern Jazz, 1950s–, Bass, American
Jacks, The, Rhythm & Blues, 1950s–1960s, Various instruments, American
Jackson Jr., Oliver, Rhythm & Blues; Swing; Dixieland, 1950s–, Drums, American
Jackson, Grady 'Fats', Rhythm & Blues, 1950s–1990s, Vocals, saxophone, American
Jackson, Milt, Bebop; Hard Bop, 1950s–1990s, Vibraphone, piano, American
Jacobs, 'Boogie Jake', Electric Blues; Chicago Blues, 1950s–1970s, Guitar, American
Jamal, Ahmad, Cool Jazz, 1950s–, Piano, American
James, Elmore, Chicago Blues, 1950s–1960s, Guitar, vocals, composer, American
James, Etta, Rhythm & Blues, 1950s–, Vocals, American
Jasper, Bobby, Hard Bop; Cool Jazz, 1950s–1960s, Saxophone, flute, Belgian
Jefferson, Eddie, Bebop, 1950s–1970s, Vocals, composer, American
Jeffrey, Paul, Rhythm & Blues, 1950s–, Saxophone, arranger, American
Jenkins, Bobo, Modern Electric Blues; Detroit Blues, 1950s–1960s, Vocals, guitar, American
Jenkins, Gus, Rhythm & Blues, 1950s, Vocals, piano, American
Jenkins, John, Hard Bop, 1950s–, Saxophone, American
Jensen, Arne Papa Bue, New Orleans Jazz; Dixieland, 1950s–, Trombone, Dutch
Jobim, Antonio Carlos, Brazilian Jazz; World Fusion; Latin Jazz, 1950s–1990s, Guitar, piano, composer, Brazilian
Johnson, Conrad, Jump Blues; Texas Blues, 1950s–2000s, Saxophone, bandleader, American
Johnson, Johnnie, Boogie-Woogie; Rhythm & Blues, 1950s–1990s, Piano, American
Johnson, Marv, Rhythm & Blues, 1950s–1960s, Vocals, composer, American
Johnson, Plas, Swing; Hard Bop; Soul Jazz; Jump Blues; Rhythm & Blues, 1950s–, Saxophone, American
Johnson, Willie, Chicago Blues, 1950s–1990s, Guitar, American
Jolly, Pete, Cool Jazz; Bebop, 1950s–2000s, Piano, American
Jones, Birmingham, Chicago Blues, 1950s–1970s, Saxophone, guitar, American
Jones, Dave, British Dixieland, 1950s–, Clarinet, saxophone, British
Jones, Floyd, Chicago Blues, 1950s–1960s, Guitar, composer, American
Jones, Hank, Swing; Bebop, 1950s–1990s, Piano, American
Jones, Philly Joe, Hard Bop, 1950s–1980s, Drums, piano, American
Jones, Quincy, Swing; Bebop, 1950s–, Trumpet, arranger, composer, American
Jones, Sam, Hard Bop, 1950s–1980s, Bass, cello, American
Jordan, Clifford, Hard Bop, 1950s–1990s, Saxophone, American
Julian, Don, Rhythm & Blues, 1950s–1970s, Vocals, American
Kamuca, Richie, Cool Jazz, 1950s–1970s, Saxophone, American
Katz, Dick, Swing; Modern Jazz, 1950s–, Piano, arranger, American
Keane, Shake, Free Jazz; Modern Jazz; World Fusion, 1950s–, Trumpet, flugelhorn, West Indian
Keepnews, Orrin, Modern Jazz, 1950s–, Producer, author, American
Kelley, Peck, Traditional Jazz, 1950s, Piano, American
Kelly, Arthur Lee, Louisiana Blues, 1950s–, Vocals, American
Kelly, Wynton, Hard Bop, 1950s–1970s, Piano, American
Kennedy, Tiny, East Coast Blues; Jump Blues, 1950s, Vocals, American
Kenner, Chris, New Orleans Blues, 1950s–1960s, Vocals, composer, American
Key, Troyce, Texas Blues; Modern Electric Blues, 1950s–1990s, Guitar, American
King Curtis, Rhythm & Blues; East Coast Blues, 1950s–1970s, Saxophone, American
King Pleasure, Bebop, 1950s–, Vocals, American
King, Earl, Rhythm & Blues, 1950s–, Vocals, guitar, American
Kinsey, Tony, Bebop; Big Band; British Jazz, 1950s–, Percussion, piano, composer, arranger, British
Kittrell, Christine, Rhythm & Blues, 1950s–1960s, Vocals, piano, American
Klein, Oscar, New Orleans Jazz; Dixieland, 1950s–, Trumpet, guitar, Austrian
Koffman, Moe, Bebop; Jazz Pop, 1950s–2000s, Saxophone, flute, Canadian
Kolax, King, Jump Blues, 1950s–1960s, Trumpet, bandleader, American
Kotick, Teddy, Bebop; Big Band; Cool Jazz, 1950s–, Bass, American
Kral, Irene, Modern Jazz, 1950s–1970s, Vocals, American
Kuhn, Rolf, Swing, Modern Jazz, 1950s–, Clarinet, bandleader, German
LaFaro, Scott, Rhythm & Blues, 1950s–, Bass, American
Lafitte, Guy, Swing; Bebop, 1950s–, Saxophone, French
Laine, Cleo, Bebop; Big Band; British Jazz, 1950s–, Vocals, British
Lamb, Joseph, Ragtime, 1950s, Piano, composer, American
Lambert, Henricks & Ross, Bebop, 1950s–1960s, Vocals, American
Land, Harold, Hard Bop, 1950s–2000s, Saxophone, flute, American
Larkins, Ellis, Swing, 1950s–2000s, Piano, American
LaRoca, Pete, Hard Bop; Latin Jazz, 1950s–, Drums, American
Lateef, Yusef, Hard Bop, 1950s–, Saxophone, flute, reeds, American
Laurie, Cy, Dixieland Revival; New Orleans Jazz, 1950s–, Clarinet, vocals, leader, British
Laws, Hubert, Hard Bop; Fusion; Soul Jazz, 1950s–1990s, Flute, saxophone, guitar, composer, American
Lawson, Hugh, Hard Bop, 1950s–1990s, Piano, American
Lazy Lester, Modern Electric Blues, 1950s–, Vocals, harmonica, American
Lea, Barbara, Dixieland, 1950s–, Vocals, American
Left Hand Frank, Chicago Blues, 1950s–, Guitar, vocals, American
Lefty Dizz, Chicago Blues, 1950s–, Guitar, American
Legrand, Michel, Hard Bop, 1950s–, Piano, composer, arranger, French
Lemon, Brian, Dixieland Revival; Post-Bop; British Jazz, 1950s–, Piano, arranger, British
Lenoir, J.B., Chicago Blues, 1950s–1960s, Guitar, American
Levey, Stan, Cool Jazz; Bebop, 1950s, Drums, American
Levine, Bobby 'Lips', Big Band; Swing, 1950s–, Clarinet, saxophone, American
Levitt, Rod, Bebop, 1950s–, Trombone, composer, arranger, American
Lewis, John, Bebop; Cool Jazz, 1950s–2000s, Piano, arranger, composer, American
Lewis, Pete 'Guitar', Jump Blues; Rhythm & Blues, 1950s, Vocals, guitar, American
Lewis, Ramsey, Soul Jazz, 1950s–1990s, Piano, keyboards, American
Ley, Eggy, Dixieland, 1950s–1980s, Saxophone, vocals, leader, British
Lightfoot, Alexander 'Papa George', Rhythm & Blues, 1950s, Vocals, harmonica, American
Lightfoot, Terry, British Jazz; Traditional Jazz, 1950s–, Clarinet, saxophone, vocals, leader, British
Lighthouse All-Stars, The, Cool Jazz; Bebop, 1950s, Various instruments, American
Lightnin' Slim, Chicago Blues, 1950s–1970s, Guitar, American
Linkchain, Hip, Chicago Blues, 1950s–1980s, Guitar, songwriter, vocals, American
Lipscomb, Mance, Country Blues, 1950s–1970s, Guitar, vocals, American
Little Anthony & the Imperials, Rhythm & Blues, 1950s–1960s, Vocals, American
Little Richard, Rhythm & Blues, 1950s–1990s, Vocals, piano, American
Little Walter, Chicago Blues, 1950s–1960s, Harmonica, vocals, composer, American
Little Willie John, Rhythm & Blues, 1950s–1960s, Vocals, American
Little, Booker, Hard Bop, 1950s–1960s, Trumpet, American
Lonesome Sundown, Chicago Blues, 1950s–1970s, Piano, guitar, American
Love, Billy, Delta Blues, 1950s, Vocals, American
Love, Clayton, Rhythm & Blues, 1950s–, Vocals, piano, American
Love, Preston, Jump Blues, 1950s–2000s, Saxophone, producer, American
Love, Willie, Delta Blues; Rhythm & Blues, 1950s, Vocals, piano, American
Lowe, Mundell, Cool Jazz; Swing, 1950s–, Guitar, American
Lucas, Bill 'Lazy', Chicago Blues, 1950s–1980s, Vocals, piano, American
Lusher, Don, Swing; Big Band, 1950s–, Trombone, British
Lutcher, Nellie, Jump Blues, 1950s–1960s, Vocals, piano, American
Lyons, Willie James, Chicago Blues, 1950s–1970s, Guitar, vocals, American
Lyttelton, Humphrey, New Orleans Jazz; Chicago Jazz, 1950s–, Trumpet, clarinet, bandleader, author, British
Mabern, Harold, Hard Bop; Soul Jazz, 1950s–, Piano, composer, American
Mabon, Willie, Chicago Blues; Rhythm & Blues, 1950s–1980s, Vocals, piano, harmonica, American
Macero, Ted, Free Jazz, 1950s–, Saxophone, producer, American
Mainieri, Mike, Free Jazz; Jazz–Rock, 1950s–, Vibraphone, keyboards, arranger, composer, producer, bandleader, American
Mance, Junior, Soul Jazz; Bebop, 1950s–, Piano, American
Margolis, Sam, Swing, 1950s–, Clarinet, saxophone, American
Mariano, Charlie, Bebop, 1950s–, Saxophones, flute, American
Mayes, Pete, Texas Blues, 1950s–1980s, Guitar, American
Mayfield, Curtis, Rhythm & Blues, 1950s–1990s, Vocals, guitar, composer, American
Mays, Curley, Rhythm & Blues, 1950s–1960s, Guitar, American
Mayweather, George 'Earring', Chicago Blues, 1950s–1990s, Vocals, harmonica, American
McCain, Jerry 'Boogie', Modern Electric Blues, 1950s–1960s; 1980s–, Harmonica, composer, American
McCracklin, Jimmy, West Coast Blues; Rhythm & Blues, 1950s–1990s, Vocals, American
McDuff, Jack, Soul Jazz; Hard Bop, 1950s–1990s, Organ, piano, American
McFarland, Gary, Hard Bop, 1950s–1990s, Vibraphone, composer, arranger, producer, American
McGhee, Sticks, Country Blues; East Coast Blues, 1950s–1960s, Vocals, guitar, American
McKenna, Dave, Swing, 1950s–, Piano, American
McKusick, Hal, Cool Jazz, 1950s–1990s, Saxophone, American
McLean, Jackie, Hard Bop, 1950s–, Saxophone, composer, American
McMahon, Andrew 'Blueblood', Chicago Blues, 1950s–1980s, Bass, American
McPartland, Marian, Swing; Bebop, 1950s–, Piano, bandleader, British
McPhatter, Clyde, Rhythm & Blues, 1950s–1960s, Vocals, American
McPherson, Charles, Bebop; Hard Bop, 1950s–1990s, Saxophone, American
McRae, Carmen, Modern Jazz, 1950s–1990s, Vocals, piano, American
Melle, Gil, Hard Bop; Bebop; Cool Jazz, 1950s–1990s, Saxophone, composer, American
Melly, George, British Jazz, 1950s–, Vocals, author, British
Merrill, Helen, Modern Jazz; Cool Jazz; Bebop, 1950s–, Vocals, American
Michelot, Pierre, Swing; Bebop, 1950s–, Bass, arranger, French
Mickey & Sylvia, Rhythm & Blues, 1950s–1960s, Guitar, vocals, American
Mikkelborg, Palle, Free Jazz, 1950s–, Trumpet, composer, conductor, Danish
Miles, Luke, Modern Electric Blues, 1950s–1980s, Vocals, American
Miller, Jay D., Jump Blues; Swamp Blues, 1950s–1960s, Producer, composer, American
Mingus, Charles, Bebop; Hard Bop, 1950s–1970s, Bass, composer, American
Minton, Phil, Jazz Rock; Free Jazz, 1950s–, Vocals, trumpet, British
Mitchell, Blue, Hard Bop, 1950s–1970s, Trumpet, American
Mitchell, Red, Cool Jazz; Hard Bop, 1950s–1990s, Bass, piano, vocals, American
Mobley, Hank, Hard Bop, 1950s–1970s, Saxophone, American
Modern Jazz Quartet, The, Cool Jazz, 1950s–, Various instruments, American
Moholo, Louis, Free Jazz, 1950s–, Drums, vocals, cello, percussion, South African
Monk, Thelonious, Bebop; Modal Jazz; Hard Bop, 1950s–1970s, Piano, composer, American
Monterose, J.R., Hard Bop, 1950s–1980s, Saxophone, arranger, composer, American
Montgomery Brothers, The, Soul Jazz, 1950s–1960s, Various instruments, American
Montoliu, Tete, Hard Bop, 1950s–1990s, Piano, Spanish
Montrose, Jack, Cool Jazz, 1950s–1990s, Saxophone, composer, arranger, American
Moonglows, The, Rhythm & Blues, 1950s, Vocals, American
Moore, Brew, Cool Jazz, 1950s–1970s, Saxophone, American
Moore, Merrill, Boogie-Woogie; Rhythm & Blues, 1950s–1970s, Piano, vocals, American
Morello, Joe, Cool Jazz; Hard Bop, 1950s–, Drums, American
Morgan, Alun, All Jazz Styles, 1950s–, Author, critic, Welsh
Morgan, Frank, Hard Bop; Bebop, 1950s–1990s, Saxophone, American
Morgenstern, Dan, All Jazz Styles, 1950s–, Author, German
Mosca, Sal, Cool Jazz, 1950s–1990s, Piano, American
Most, Sam, Cool Jazz; Bebop, 1950s–, Saxophone, flute, American
Muddy Waters, Chicago Blues, 1950s–1980s, Guitar, vocals, American
Mulligan, Gerry, Cool Jazz, 1950s–1990s, Saxophone, arranger, composer, American
Muranyi, Joe, Swing; New Orleans Jazz, 1950s–, Clarinet, saxophone, vocals, American
Murphy, Mark, Modern Jazz, 1950s–, Vocals, American
Myers, Louis, Modern Electric Blues, 1950s–1990s, Vocals, guitar, harmonica, American
Myers, Sam, Modern Electric Blues, 1950s–, Vocals, harmonica, American
Naura, Michael, Bebop; Fusion, 1950s–, Piano, flute, composer, Lithuanian
Neal, Raful, Modern Electric Blues, 1950s–1960s, Harmonica, American
Neidlinger, Buell, Free Jazz, 1950s–1990s, Bass, cello, American
Nelson, Jimmy, Jump Blues; Rhythm & Blues, 1950s–1960s, Vocals, American
Nelson, Oliver, Hard Bop, 1950s–1970s, Saxophones, composer, American
Newborn, Calvin, Rhythm & Blues, 1950s–1990s, Guitar, American
Newborn, Phineas Jr, Hard Bop, 1950s–1980s, Piano, American
Newman, David 'Fathead', Soul Jazz; Hard Bop, 1950s–, Saxophone, American
Newsom, Tommy, Cool Jazz; Bebop, 1950s–, Saxophone, American
Nichols, Herbie, Dixieland Revival; Swing; Bebop, 1950s, Piano, composer, American
Niehaus, Lennie, Cool Jazz; Bebop, 1950s–1990s, Saxophone, American
Nistico, Sal, Hard Bop; Bebop, 1950s–1990s, Saxophone, American
Nixon, Elmore, Jump Blues, 1950s–1970s, Piano, American
Nolen, Jimmy, Funk, 1950s–1980s, Guitar, American
Noto, Sam, Bebop, 1950s–, Flugelhorn, trumpet, American
Odetta, Country Blues, 1950s–, Vocals, guitar, American
Offitt, Lillian, Chicago Blues, 1950s–1960s, Vocals, American
Oliver, Paul, Country Blues; Delta Blues, 1950s–1990s, Author, producer, folklorist, British
Olympics, The, Rhythm & Blues, 1950s–1960s, Vocals, American
Ortega, Anthony, Big Band; Bebop, 1950s–, Saxophone, clarinet, flute, American
Owens, Jay, Rhythm & Blues; Soul Blues, 1950s–, Vocals, guitar, American
Paich, Marty, Bebop; Cool Jazz, 1950s–1990s, Piano, arranger, American
Palmer, Earl, Rhythm & Blues, 1950s–, Drums, American
Palmieri, Charlie, Latin Jazz, 1950s–1980s, Piano, American
Parker, Bobby 'Barber', Rhythm & Blues, 1950s–, Vocals, guitar, American
Parker, Junior, Rhythm & Blues, 1950s–1970s, Vocals, American
Patrick, Pat, Free Jazz, 1950s–1990s, Saxophone, American
Patt, Frank 'Honeyboy', Rhythm & Blues, 1950s–1970s, Guitar, American
Payne, Cecil, Bebop; Hard Bop, 1950s–, Saxophones, American
Peagler, Curtis, Swing; Modern Jazz; Big Band, 1950s–, Saxophone, American
Pearson, Duke, Hard Bop, 1950s–1970s, Piano, producer, American
Pepper, Art, Bebop; Hard Bop; Cool Jazz, 1950s–1980s, Saxophones, clarinet, American
Perkins, Bill, Cool Jazz; Hard Bop, 1950s–, Saxophones, flute, clarinet, American
Perkins, Carl, Bebop; Hard Bop, 1950s, Piano, American
Persip, Charlie, Hard Bop, 1950s–, Drums, American
Persson, Aake, Swing; Bebop, 1950s–1970s, Trombone, Swedish
Peterson, Oscar, Swing; Bebop, 1950s–, Piano, Canadian
Petrowsky, Ernst-Ludwig, Free Jazz, 1950s–, Reeds, flute, German
Pettis, 'Alabama' Junior, Chicago Blues, 1950s–1980s, Guitar, American
Piano Red, Boogie-Woogie, 1950s–1960s, Piano, keyboards, American
Picard, John, Modern Jazz, 1950s–, Trombone, piano, British
Pickens, Edwin 'Buster', Country Blues, 1950s–1960s, Vocals, piano, American
Pisano, John, Bebop, 1950s–, Guitar, American
Pizzarelli, Bucky, Swing, 1950s–, Guitar, American
Pleasure, King, Bebop, 1950s–1970s, Vocals, American
Pomeroy, Herb, Bebop, 1950s–, Composer, trumpet, educator, American
Powell, Bud, Bebop, 1950s–1960s, Piano, composer, American
Powell, Richie, Hard Bop, 1950s, Piano, arranger, American
Prado, Perez, Latin Jazz, 1950s–1980s, Piano, composer, Cuban
Preservation Hall Jazz Band, Dixieland Revival, 1950s–, Various instruments, American
Presley, Elvis, Rhythm & Blues, 1950s–1970s, Vocals, piano, guitar, American
Prevost, Eddie, Free Jazz; Bebop; Hard Bop, 1950s, Drums, percussion, British
Price, Big Walter, Rhythm & Blues, 1950s–, Vocals, piano, American
Price, Lloyd, Rhythm & Blues, 1950s–1960s; 1980s, Piano, vocals, producer, American
Priester, Julian, Free Jazz; Modern Jazz, 1950s–, Trombone, American
Professor Longhair, Rhythm & Blues, 1950s–1980s, Piano, vocals, composer, American
Pryor, Snooky, Chicago Blues, 1950s–1990s, Vocals, harmonica, American
Prysock, Red, Jump Blues; Rhythm & Blues, 1950s–1960s, Saxophone, American
Quattlebaum, Doug, East Coast Blues, 1950s–1960s, Guitar, American
Randall, Freddy, Dixieland Revival; Traditional Jazz, 1950s–, Trumpet, British
Raney, Jimmy, Cool Jazz, 1950s–1990s, Guitar, American
Rawls, Lou, Rhythm & Blues, 1950s–, Vocals, American
Red, Sonny, Hard Bop, 1950s–1970s, Saxophone, American
Redd, Freddie, Hard Bop, 1950s–1990s, Piano, composer, American
Reece, Dizzy, Hard Bop, 1950s–, Trumpet, Jamaican
Reed, Jimmy, Chicago Blues; Rhythm & Blues, 1950s–1970s, Vocals, guitar, composer, American
Renaud, Henri, Hard Bop; Bebop, 1950s–, Piano, French
Rendell, Don, Bebop; Big Band; British Jazz, 1950s–, Saxophone, clarinet, flute, British
Rhodes, Todd, Jump Blues, 1950s, Piano, bandleader, American
Rice, Sir Mac, Rhythm & Blues, 1950s–, Vocals, composer, American
Richards, Red, Chicago Jazz; Swing, 1950s–, Piano, vocals, American
Richardson, Jerome, Cool Jazz; Hard Bop, 1950s–1990s, Saxophones, flute, American
Richardson, John, Dixieland Revival; Traditional Jazz, 1950s–, Drums, British
Richmond, Dannie, Modern Jazz, 1950s–1980s, Drums, American
Ridgley, Tommy, New Orleans Blues; Rhythm & Blues, 1950s–1990s, Vocals, piano, American
Roberts, Howard, Cool Jazz, 1950s–1990s, Guitar, American
Robinson, Freddie, Modern Electric Blues, 1950s–1980s, Guitar, arranger, American
Robinson, L.C. 'Good Rockin'', Modern Electric Blues, 1950s–1970s, Vocals, guitar, violin, American
Robinson, Prince, Big Band; Swing, 1950s, Clarinet, saxophone, American
Roca, Pete la, Latin Jazz; Hard Bop, 1950s–1990s, Drums, American
Rockin' Dopsie, Zydeco, 1950s–1990s, Accordion, American
Rodgers, Sonny, Delta Blues; Chicago Blues, 1950s–, Guitar, American
Rogers, Jimmy, Chicago Blues, 1950s–1990s, Drums, American
Rogers, Shorty, Cool Jazz, 1950s–1990s, Trumpet, flugelhorn, American
Rollins, Sonny, Bebop; Hard Bop, 1950s–, Saxophones, composer, American
Ross, Annie, Bebop, 1950s–, Vocals, songwriter, actress, British
Ross, Ronnie, Modern Jazz, 1950s–1980s, Saxophone, clarinet, flute, Indian
Rowles, Jimmy, Bebop; Swing, 1950s–1990s, Piano, vocals, American
Rudd, Roswell, Free Jazz, 1950s–, Trombone, composer, American
Ruff, Willie, Hard Bop; Bebop, 1950s–1990s, Bass, french horn, American
Rugolo, Pete, Swing, 1950s–1990s, Arranger, bandleader, American
Rumsey, Howard, Cool Jazz; Bebop, 1950s–1960s, Bass, bandleader, American
Russell, Hal, Free Jazz, 1950s–1990s, Saxophone, trumpet, vibraphone, drums, bandleader, American
Russo, Bill, Big Band, 1950s–, Arranger, composer, trombone, American
Sahm, Doug, Country Rock; Blues Rock, 1950s–1990s, Guitar, arranger, composer, American
Sain, Oliver, Rhythm & Blues, 1950s–2000s, Saxophone, composer, producer, bandleader, American
Salvador, Sal, Cool Jazz; Bebop, 1950s–1990s, Guitar, American
Santamaria, Mongo, Latin Jazz, 1950s–1990s, Percussion, Cuban
Sathe, Keshav, World Fusion, 1950s–, Tabla, Indian
Saunders, Red, Rhythm & Blues; Jump Blues, 1950s–1960s, Drums, bandleader, American
Schifrin, Lalo, Bebop, 1950s–, Piano, composer, Argentinian
Schweizer, Irene, Free Jazz, 1950s–, Piano, bandleader, Swiss
Scobey, Bob, Chicago Jazz, 1950s–1960s, Trumpet, American
Scott, Buddy, Modern Electric Blues; Chicago Blues, 1950s–1990s, Vocals, guitar, American
Scott, Joe, Rhythm & Blues, 1950s–1970s, Trumpet, arranger, composer, American
Scott, Shirley, Soul Jazz; Hard Bop, 1950s–1990s, Organ, American
Scott, Tony, Cool Jazz, 1950s–1990s, Clarinet, saxophones, piano, arranger, American
Sears, Big Al, Jump Blues; Rhythm & Blues, 1950s–1960s, Saxophone, American
Semien, 'Ivory' Lee, Texas Blues, 1950s–, Vocals, drums, American
Semple, Archie, Swing; Chicago Jazz, 1950s–1960s, Clarinet, British
Shank, Bud, Cool Jazz; Hard Bop, 1950s–, Saxophones, flute, American
Sharpe, Ray, Texas Blues, 1950s, Guitar, vocals, American
Shaw, Arvell, New Orleans Jazz; Swing, 1950s–, Bass, American
Shaw, Clarence, Bebop, 1950s–1960s, Trumpet, American
Sheldon, Jack, Bebop, 1950s–, Trumpet, American
Shepherd, Dave, Dixieland Revival; British Jazz, 1950s–, Clarinet, bandleader, British
Shihab, Sahib, Bebop; Hard Bop, 1950s–1990s, Saxophone, flute, American
Shirley & Lee, Rhythm & Blues, 1950s–1960s, Vocals, American
Shirley, Don, Cool Jazz, 1950s–1970s, Piano, arranger, composer, Jamaican
Silver, Horace, Hard Bop; Fusion, 1950s–, Piano, composer, American
Simone, Nina, Smooth Jazz, 1950s–2000s, Vocals, piano, American
Sims, Clarence 'Guitar', West Coast Blues, 1950s–1980s, Vocals, American
Sims, Zoot, Bebop; Cool Jazz, 1950s–1980s, Saxophones, American
Sinatra, Frank, Swing, 1950s–1990s, Vocals, American
Skidmore, Jimmy, New Orleans Jazz; Chicago Jazz; Bebop, 1950s–, Saxophone, British
Slim, Sunnyland, Chicago Blues, 1950s–1980s, Piano, American
Slim, T.V., Country Blues; Rhythm & Blues, 1950s–1960s, Guitar, American
Slim, Tarheel, Rhythm & Blues, 1950s–1970s, Guitar, vocals, American
Small, Drink, Folk Blues; Disco Blues, 1950s–, Guitar, American
Smith, Betty, Swing, 1950s–1990s, Saxophone, vocals, leader, British
Smith, Huey 'Piano', Rhythm & Blues, 1950s–1960s, Piano, American
Smith, Jimmy, Hard Bop, 1950s–2000s, Organ, piano, vocals, American
Smith, Johnny, Cool Jazz, 1950s–1990s, Guitar, American
Smith, Johnny 'Hammond', Hard Bop; Soul Jazz, 1950s–1990s, Organ, American
Smith, Keely, Swing, 1950s–, Vocals, American
Smith, Louis, Hard Bop, 1950s–, Trumpet, American
Solal, Martial, Modern Jazz, 1950s–, Piano, composer, arranger, bandleader, North African
Solomon, Clifford, Jump Blues; West Coast Blues, 1950s–2000s, Saxophone, American
Solomon, King, Modern Electric Blues; Rhythm & Blues, 1950s–, Vocals, American
South Frisco Jazz Band, Dixieland Revival, 1950s–1990s, Various instruments, American
Southern, Jeri, Cool Jazz, 1950s–1960s, Vocals, American
Spaniels, The, Rhythm & Blues, 1950s–1970s, Vocals, American
Spaulding, James, Hard Bop; Modern Jazz, 1950s–, Saxophone, flute, American
Staton, Dakota, Modern Jazz, 1950s–, Vocals, American
Stitt, Sonny, Bebop, 1950s–1980s, Saxophone, American
Stovall, Jewell 'Babe', Folk Blues; New Orleans Jazz, 1950s–1970s, Guitar, American
Strange, Pete, British Jazz; New Orleans Jazz; Chicago Jazz, 1950s–, Trombone, arranger, British
Strong, Nolan, Rhythm & Blues, 1950s–1960s, Vocals, American
Strozier, Frank, Hard Bop; Modern Jazz, 1950s–, Saxophone, flute, clarinet, piano, American
Sullivan, Ira, Modern Jazz; Bebop, 1950s–, Saxophone, trumpet, flute, American
Tate, Grady, Hard Bop, 1950s–1990s, Drums, vocals, American
Taylor, Art, Bebop; Hard Bop, 1950s–1990s, Drums, American
Taylor, Creed, American Jazz, 1950s–, Producer, American
Taylor, Eddie, Modern Electric Blues; Rhythm & Blues, 1950s–1980s, Guitar, American
Taylor, Johnnie, Rhythm & Blues, 1950s–2000s, Vocals, American
Taylor, Ted, Rhythm & Blues, 1950s–1980s, Vocals, American
Temperley, Joe, Swing; Hard Bop, 1950s–, Saxophone, clarinet, flute, Scottish
Terry, Clark, Bebop; Swing, 1950s–, Trumpet, flugelhorn, American
Thielemans, Toots, Brazilian Jazz; Latin Jazz; Swing; Bebop, 1950s–, Harmonica, guitar, composer, Belgian
Thigpen, Ed, Bebop; Hard Bop, 1950s–1990s, Drums, American
Thomas, Lafayette 'Thing', Modern Electric Blues; West Coast Blues, 1950s–1960s, Vocals, guitar, American
Thomas, René, Hard Bop; Cool Jazz, 1950s–1970s, Guitar, Belgian
Thomas, Rockin' Tabby, Chicago Blues, 1950s–1990s, Guitar, vocals, American
Thomas, Rufus, Rhythm & Blues, 1950s–1990s, Vocals, composer, American
Thompson, Sonny, Jump Blues, 1950s–1960s, Piano, composer, bandleader, American
Thornton, Big Mama, Texas Blues; Rhythm & Blues, 1950s–1970s, Vocals, American
Three Sounds, The, Soul Jazz; Hard Bop, 1950s–1960s, Various instruments, American
Timmons, Bobby, Soul Jazz; Hard Bop, 1950s–1960s, Piano, vibraphone, composer, American
Tjader, Cal, Cool Jazz; Latin Jazz, 1950s–1980s, Vibraphone, percussion, American
Toussaint, Allen, Rhythm & Blues, 1950s–1990s, Artist, American
Turner, Bruce, New Orleans Jazz; Chicago Jazz, 1950s–1980s, Saxophone, clarinet, composer, leader, British
Turner, Titus, East Coast Blues; Jump Blues; Rhythm & Blues, 1950s–1970s, Vocals, composer, American
Twardzik, Dick, Swing; Cool Jazz, 1950s, Piano, composer, American
Tyler, Alvin 'Red', Rhythm & Blues, 1950s–1990s, Saxophone, American
Ulanov, Barry, All Jazz Styles, 1950s–2000s, Author, American
Upchurch, Phil, Rhythm & Blues, 1950s–, Guitar, American
Valdes, Carlos 'Patato', Latin Jazz, 1950s–, Percussion, Cuban
Valentine, Cal, Texas Blues, 1950s–1990s, Guitar, American
Van Ronk, Dave, Folk Blues, 1950s–2000s, Vocals, guitar, American
VanGelder, Rudy, Modern Jazz, 1950s–, Recording engineer, American
VanRooyen, Ack, Cool Jazz, 1950s–, Trumpet, flugelhorn, Dutch
Vincent, Monroe, Louisiana Blues, 1950s–1960s, Harmonica, vocals, American
Vinnegar, Leroy, Cool Jazz, 1950s–1990s, Bass, American
Waldron, Mal, Hard Bop, 1950s–2000s, Piano, composer, American
Walker, Johnny 'Big Moose', Chicago Blues, 1950s–1990s, Vocals, piano, American
Walker, Jr. & The All-Stars, Rhythm & Blues, 1950s–1990s, Vocals, saxophone, American
Walton, Cedar, Hard Bop, 1950s–, Piano, composer, American
Ward, Billy, Rhythm & Blues, 1950s, Vocals, American
Ware, Wilbur, Hard Bop, 1950s–1970s, Bass, American
Warren, Baby Boy, Detroit Blues, 1950s–1960s, Vocals, guitar, American
Washington, Tuts, Boogie-Woogie, 1950s–1980s, Piano, American
Watkins, Doug, Bebop; Hard Bop, 1950s–1960s, Bass, American
Watkins, Julius, Hard Bop, 1950s–1970s, French horn, American
Watts, Noble, East Coast Blues; Jump Blues, 1950s–1990s, Saxophone, American
Wayne, Wee Willie, New Orleans Blues, 1950s, Vocals, American
Webb, Boogie Bill, Rhythm & Blues; Country Blues, 1950s–1980s, Guitar, American
Wein, George, Dixieland; Traditional Jazz, 1950s–, Piano, vocals, promoter, American
Wellins, Bobby, Free Jazz, 1950s–, Saxophone, British
Wellstood, Dick, Traditional Jazz; Ragtime, 1950s–1980s, Piano, American
Welsh, Alex, Traditional Jazz; Chicago Jazz; Dixieland Revival, 1950s–1970s, Cornet, vocals, leader, British
Weston, Randy, Hard Bop, 1950s–1990s, Piano, composer, American
Wheeler, Big, Chicago Blues, 1950s–, Harmonica, vocals, American
Wheeler, Golden, Chicago Blues, 1950s–, Harmonica, American
White, Lavelle, Rhythm & Blues, 1950s–, Vocals, songwriter, American
Wiggins, Gerald, Swing; Bebop, 1950s–1990s, Piano, American
Wilen, Barney, Free Jazz, 1950s–, Saxophone, French
Wilkins, Ernie, Bebop; Swing, 1950s–1990s, Saxophones, American
Wilkins, Joe Willie, Country Blues; Delta Blues, 1950s–1970s, Vocals, guitar, American
Williams, Andre, Rhythm & Blues, 1950s–1970s; 1990s–, Vocals, American
Williams, Jody, Rhythm & Blues; Chicago Blues, 1950s–1960; 2000s, Vocals, guitar, American
Williams, Joseph 'Jo Jo', Delta Blues; Chicago Blues, 1950s–1970s, Guitar, American
Williams, Larry, Rhythm & Blues, 1950s–1970s, Vocals, piano, composer, American
Williams, Martin, All Jazz Styles, 1950s–1990s, Author, critic, American
Williams, Richard, Modern Jazz; Swing, 1950s–, Trumpet, piano, saxophone, composer, American
Williams, Robert Pete, Country Blues, 1950s–1970s, Guitar, vocals, American
Williamson, Claude, Cool Jazz; Bebop, 1950s–1990s, Piano, American
Williamson, Sonny Boy (II), Delta Blues; Chicago Blues, 1950s–1960s, Harmonica, vocals, American
Williamson, Stu, Cool Jazz, 1950s–1990s, Trumpet, trombone, American
Willis, Chuck, Rhythm & Blues, 1950s, Vocals, American
Wilson, Hop, Texas Blues, 1950s–1970s, Guitar, American
Wilson, Jackie, Rhythm & Blues, 1950s–1970s, Vocals, American
Wilson, Jimmy, Rhythm & Blues; West Coast Blues, 1950s, Vocals, American
Woode, Jimmy, Modern Jazz; Hard Bop; Bebop, 1950s–, Bass, American
Woods, Phil, Bebop; Hard Bop, 1950s–, Saxophone, clarinet, American
Woodyard, Sam, Swing, 1950s–1980s, Drums, American
Workman, Reggie, Hard Bop; Free Jazz, 1950s–, Bass, American
Wright, Eugene, Cool Jazz; Swing, 1950s–1970s, Bass, American
Wright, O.V., Rhythm & Blues, 1950s–1970s, Vocals, American
Wyands, Richard, Hard Bop; Modern Jazz, 1950s–, Piano, American
Young, Snooky, Swing, 1950s–1990s, Trumpet, American
Young, Webster, Cool Jazz, 1950s–1960s, Trumpet, American
Zwerin, Mike, Bebop; Hard Bop, 1950s–1960s, Trombone, trumpet, author, American

see Muddy Waters pp 212 *see* Earl Hooker pp 224 *see* Art Pepper pp 231 *see* Horace Silver pp 233

THE SIXTIES

The cultural momentum of the 1950s spilled directly into the 1960s – arguably, the change of the decade (and century) in jazz was 1959, when Dave Brubeck, Miles Davis, Ornette Coleman, John Coltrane, Gil Evans, Lambert, Hendricks & Ross, Jackie McLean, Charles Mingus, Thelonious Monk, Wes Montgomery, Sun Ra, Sonny Rollins, George Russell, Dinah Washington and Cecil Taylor all issued or recorded significant and redefining work. In 1960 most blues was issued as disposable 45-rpm singles, but that changed mid-decade, after Columbia Records released the first collection of Robert Johnson recordings from the 1930s, and Chess Records put out LP compilations of hits by Muddy Waters, Howlin' Wolf, Sonny Boy Williamson, Little Walter et al.

In that format, the blues hit the UK with a bang, resulting in the birth of the Beatles, the Rolling Stones and the Yardbirds, bands that made the US listen to itself again. Between the British Invasion and the folk-music movement, interest in blues of all eras was rekindled, and rock'n'roll was soon stretching the traditional form into psychedelic shape. In parallel, jazz mainstreamers began to adopt the freedoms, or move towards the market preferences, of younger, larger audiences. Transformation was again the cultural watchword, as assassinations shook the US, civil rights became undeniable and a war in Asia provoked unrivalled discontent. The music of Brazil had its first profound influence, new instruments and studio techniques allowed musicians options beyond imagination and fusions of all styles, from anywhere and everywhere, foreshadowed the shape of things to come.

ES
N MAYALL
H ERIC CLAPTON
I AM A
GUITAR
NAMED
LUCILLE
PLEASE
HANDLE
WITH CARE

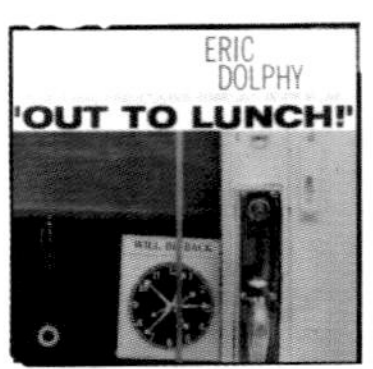

Sources & Sounds

KEY ARTISTS

Ornette Coleman
John Coltrane
Buddy Guy
Freddie Hubbard
Albert King
B.B. King
Sun Ra

Although the 1960s was an era of relative prosperity, it brought great cultural upheaval. Teenagers and twenty-somethings grew their hair long, donned psychedelic togs, took an interest in Eastern religions, and increased their sexual liberation and consumption of drugs. In America the accelerating Vietnam War caused a rift between generations, while social revolution was also rearing its head in Europe. Embracing the music of a cultural group that was actively protesting for civil rights – African-Americans – was part of the package. It was not much of a leap to also embrace the people who made that music, and jazz and blues inadvertently became a bridge between races that led to common ground. When the Paul Butterfield Blues Band emerged with an integrated cast in 1965 and when Muddy Waters hired his first white sideman (harmonica player Paul Oscher), these bands sent a message – intentional or not – in support of both youth and racial integration.

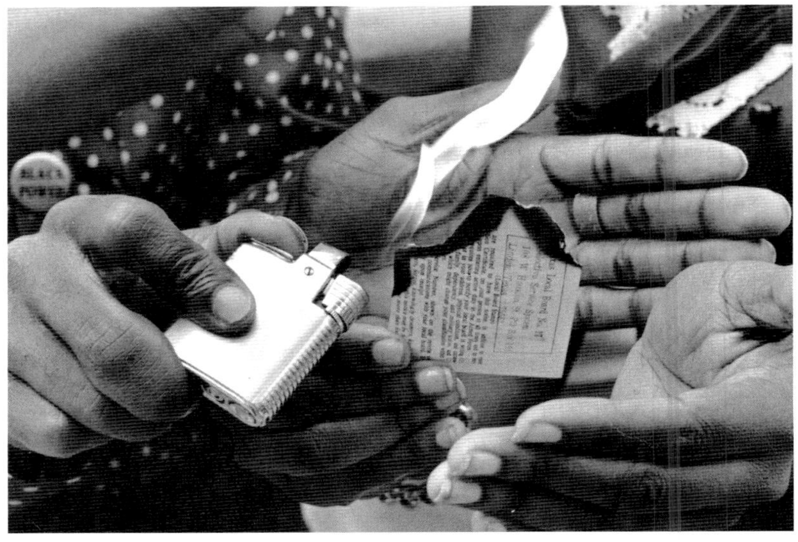

'Wolf loved it when he heard the Rolling Stones and Eric Clapton play his songs…. He said, "Hubert, them white boys is gonna make me famous. Then maybe we can make us some money."'

Hubert Sumlin

The Blues Is Reborn

The foundations for the blues explosion of the 1960s had been laid in the previous decade with the immense popularity of rock'n'roll. While the rock'n'roll revolution did not win everyone over, an older generation of folk enthusiasts still pursued their acoustic passions, while some curious younger listeners began to investigate the roots of the new music, and on both sides of the Atlantic these fans played a crucial role in launching the decade's blues revival. Collectors of 78-rpm discs, such as Gayle Dean Wardlow, travelled to rural southern towns looking for prized acetate recordings by bluesmen of the 1920s and 1930s, and began to turn up surprising bonuses in the form of the artists themselves. Musicologist Alan Lomax (1915–2002), musician John Fahey and Bob Jones, a young hand at the Newport Folk Festival, were all in the thick of rediscovering a whole host of bluesmen and -women previously only embodied by scratched discs. Thus the blues boom of the 1960s truly began.

The old records were reissued as vinyl LPs. The old musicians were dusted off and began to tour. Some, including Son House (1902–88), hadn't held a guitar in years and had to be re-taught some of their own numbers. Others, such as Mississippi John Hurt (1893–1966) and Rev. Gary Davis (1896–1972), emerged with their virtuosity intact. Although Robert Johnson (1911–38) had long been dead, his *King Of The Delta Blues Singers* collection was issued in 1961, and his razor-edged guitar virtuosity and keening vocal style fired the imaginations of many budding guitarists – Eric Clapton and Keith Richards included, who both went on to cover Johnson songs ('Cross Road Blues' and 'Love In Vain', respectively).

Running Free

The blues music may have been finally finding its feet, but for jazz music the 1960s was as turbulent a time as

Above

Vietnam War protesters burn draft cards. Social issues such as the war began to divide the generations in the 1960s.

see Introduction pp 238 *see* Key Artists pp 248 *see* A–Z of Artists pp 266 *see* List of Artists pp 282

it was for the world's socio-political climate. Several major movements arose during the decade, generating balanced waves of controversy and mass popularity. Perhaps the most divisive development of the 1960s was the rise of free jazz, the roots of which had been planted several years before by renegades such as Cecil Taylor (b. 1929), Ornette Coleman (b. 1930) and Sun Ra (1914–93), who had bold new visions about how jazz could evolve in order to stay fresh and relevant. In December 1960 the movement received its name and philosophy from the Atlantic album *Free Jazz: A Collective Improvisation By The Ornette Coleman Double Quartet*. Coleman and seven creative peers improvised with the barest of guidelines, one-upping each other continually until the final climax of a wild, polyphonic performance unlike anything that had been heard before. *Free Jazz* was the match that lit a searing flame in the musical world for years to come.

Free jazz was an artistic translation of the American civil rights struggle. As black playwrights, poets and authors had spoken their minds about the injustices being inflicted upon their people a century after the Emancipation Proclamation, jazz musicians also took up the call to arms. The music they created was a mirror image of the anguish, bitterness, yearning, resistance, sarcasm and faith inside their collective heart. Their jazz raged, or was introspective and lamenting, or was raw, or, perhaps, free.

CLASSIC RECORDINGS

1961
Little Milton: 'Feel So Bad'

1964
John Coltrane: *A Love Supreme*
Eric Dolphy: *Out To Lunch*
Horace Silver: 'Song For My Father'

1966
Canonball Adderley: 'Mercy, Mercy, Mercy'
John Mayall with Eric Clapton: *Blues Breakers*

1967
Jimi Hendrix Experience: *Are You Experienced?*

1968
Cream: 'Crossroads'

1969
Miles Davis: *Bitches Brew*
Fleetwood Mac: 'I Need Your Love So Bad'

Above
Keith Richards (far right) of the Rolling Stones was among the many to be influenced by the 1961 release of Robert Johnson's *King Of The Delta Blues*.

Left
Cecil Taylor is a great innovator of free jazz and has a distinctive, percussive piano style.

see **Robert Johnson pp 112** *see* **Ornette Coleman pp 248** *see* **Cecil Taylor pp 280** *see* **Free Jazz pp 394**

Above
Saxophonist Albert Ayler, who influenced John Coltrane, led his ensembles through several distinct, ecstatic musical styles.

Far Right
Lee Morgan had a 1964 hit with 'The Sidewinder'.

A Spiritual Side To Jazz

Coleman was an essential spokesman for the new music, his alto sax a voice crying out for humanity. Cecil Taylor, who reconceived the piano for its percussive potential, was similarly emotional, intellectual and articulate. Bandleader Sun Ra built a complex fantasy world about himself, claiming to be a visitor from Saturn who was seeking a new home in the cosmos for the black race. Ra appealed to both a sense of tradition and community and jazz's self-referential, experimental streak, operating independently almost beyond commercial society. John Coltrane (1926–67) and Albert Ayler (1936–70) took a different spiritual tack, actively seeking God through free musical expression.

Coltrane made a lasting impression with his 1964 devotional suite *A Love Supreme*, his greatest popular achievement, before heading further into extreme freedom. Many critics (especially older and politically conservative ones) hated the new music and labelled it 'anti-jazz'. Although free jazz was a novel, exciting and honest form of music that

see Introduction pp 238 *see* Key Artists pp 248 *see* A–Z of Artists pp 266 *see* List of Artists pp 282

reflected the turmoil of the era, it never won over the majority of jazz listeners. It has since, however, had a continuing impact on jazz and its major proponents have become revered by critics and honoured with international awards.

Blue Notes And Bossas

While free jazz may have barely made a dent in the music market, hard bop was the sound of the times for most jazz listeners. The soulful, blues-drenched, rhythmically rich style was all the rage on jazz radio and in clubs. A dozen record labels capitalized upon hard bop, none with more success than Blue Note. Founded in the 1930s, Blue Note embraced the hard-bop aesthetic and promoted it with vigour, making stars out of Art Blakey (1919–90), Dexter Gordon (1923–90), Jackie McLean (1931–2006), Horace Silver (b. 1928), Joe Henderson, Lee Morgan (1938–72), Kenny Dorham (1924–72), Wayne Shorter (b. 1933), Herbie Hancock (b. 1940), Freddie Hubbard (b. 1938) and a host of other young jazzmen. Occasionally a Top 10 victory was chalked up, as with Lee Morgan's 1964 crossover hit 'The Sidewinder'. For several years Blue Note was the premier label for jazz in the US.

More short-lived, but just as lucrative for a time, was the bossa nova craze. Tenor saxophonist Stan Getz (1927–91), a former member of the Woody Herman Orchestra and star of the 'cool school', collaborated first with guitarist Charlie Byrd and then with the Brazilian musicians João Gilberto (b. 1931) and Antonio Carlos Jobim (1927–94) on a series of albums which brought jazz and Brazilian musical styles together into a captivating new sound. 'The Girl From Ipanema', featuring the warm, distingué singing of the woman who became known as Astrud Gilberto, was a huge US hit in 1963 and guaranteed the bossa nova a place in jazz history.

The Great Festivals

As jazz music continued to look forward, blues music was enjoying a revival of its rural roots. The Newport Folk Festival, established in 1959, helped to propel many of the now-forgotten early blues artists back into the public eye and also drew more contemporary figures such as John Lee Hooker (1917–2001) and Muddy Waters (1915–83). However, the watershed year for

see John Coltrane pp 250  see Sun Ra pp 264  see Stan Getz pp 272 see Lee Morgan pp 277

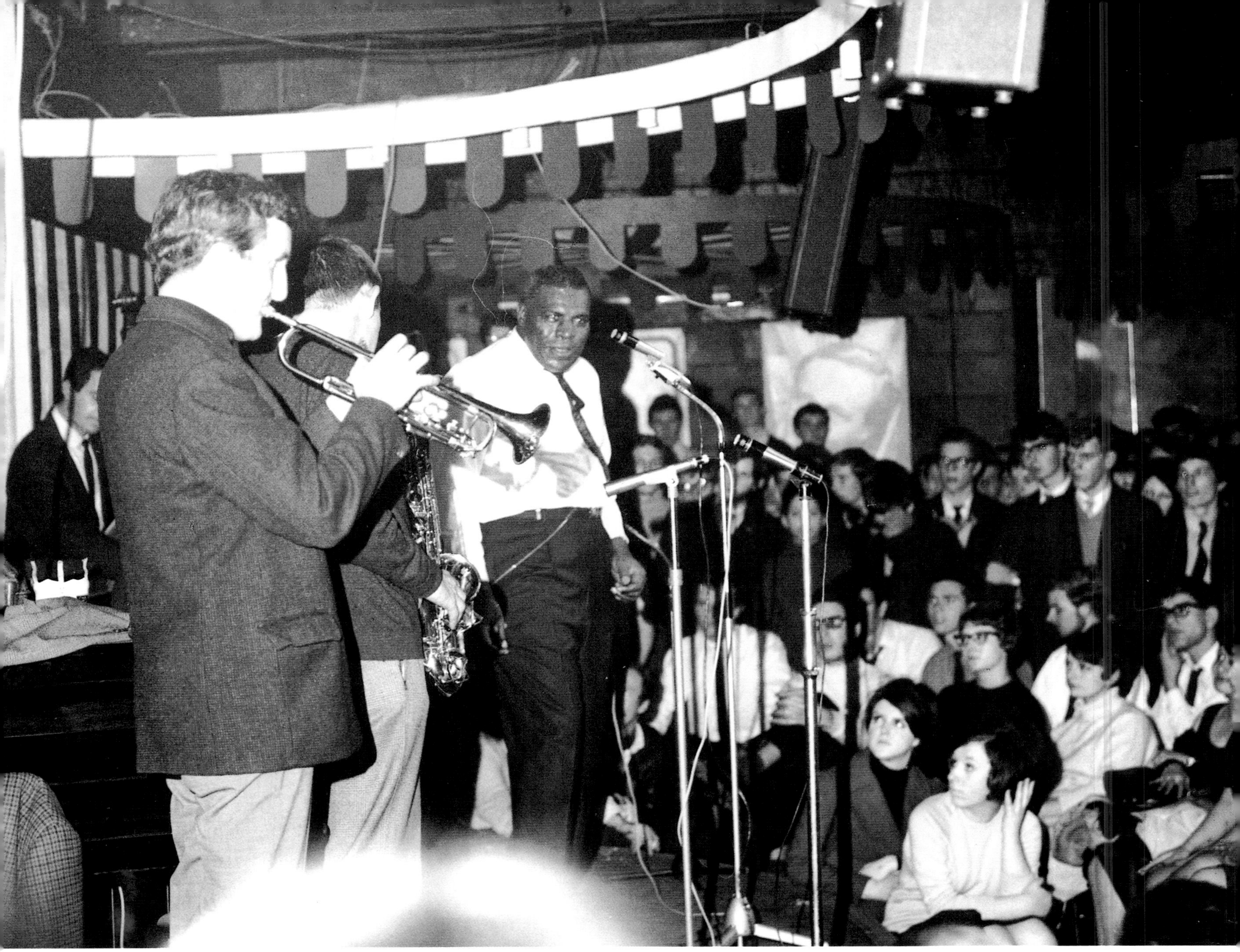

Above
Howlin' Wolf performs at London's Marquee Club with Chris Barber's band in 1964.

blues at Newport was 1966, when Lomax organized a bill that featured Howlin' Wolf (1910–76), Son House, Skip James (1902–69), Bukka White (1906–77) and others. Newport was the catalyst for the cross-pollination of blues and the singer-songwriter-based original music that was beginning to redefine the folk idiom. Bob Dylan, who had started out with traditional blues numbers, began to take on increasingly modern elements of the genre, culminating in 1965's *Highway 61 Revisited*. Dylan's controversial electric performance that summer at Newport ensured that folk music was no longer a purely acoustic medium; contemporary blues had been given a toe-hold in rock and pop.

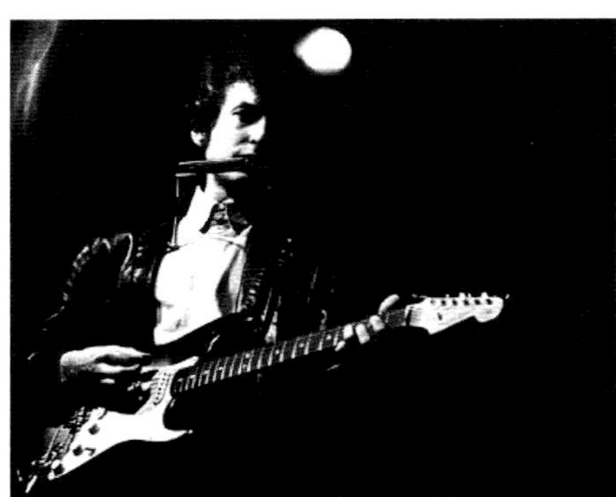

Europe also caught festival fever. In 1962, German fans Horst Lippmann and Fritz Rau organized the American Folk Blues Festival. Between the initial tour – which travelled around Europe – and 1964, a veritable who's who of blues stars had appeared on the bill. The main difference between the American Folk Blues Festival and Newport was electricity. Although Waters and Wolf played amplified sets at Newport, traditionalists such as Pete Seeger and Lomax booked mostly acoustic acts – hence why Dylan's electric debut caused such a stir. The travelling European festival

see Introduction pp 238 *see* Key Artists pp 248 *see* A–Z of Artists pp 266 *see* List of Artists pp 282

offered performances that were not only electric, but often electrifying. Waters had met resistance when he first travelled abroad with his electric guitar in 1958; then, blues audiences comprised vintage recording fans and jazz aficionados. But by 1962 there was a new, younger audience emerging that would permanently change the face of blues music.

A New Generation

Jazz and skiffle guitarist Alexis Korner (1928–84) saw Muddy's 1958 UK tour and became the first white British musician to really seize electrified blues and make it his own. He couldn't find a club in London that would book his group Blues Incorporated, so he opened one himself. It became a magnet for future English blues players – Mick Jagger, Charlie Watts, Keith Richards, John Mayall and Eric Clapton were among those who haunted the Ealing establishment. When the Rolling Stones, the Yardbirds and the Animals began to make hits, the sound of the blues – albeit filtered through rock'n'roll – echoed back across the Atlantic.

For many young Americans this music seemed novel – but not all. In Chicago, Mike Bloomfield (1943–81), Paul Butterfield (1942–87) and Charlie Musselwhite (b. 1944) had absorbed the blues in the ghetto clubs where black artists reigned seven nights a week. In New York City, Al Kooper and his cohorts in the Blues Project, as well as members of the Lovin' Spoonful, the Young Rascals and other groups, developed their own variations on the blues. Meanwhile, Jimi James & the Blue Flames were holding down a residency at Greenwich Village's Café Wha? that attracted musicians such as Dylan, Bloomfield and John Hammond Jr. (b. 1942); here audiences could catch the group's incendiary guitarist and frontman before he was swept off to England by former Animals bassist Chas Chandler and renamed Jimi Hendrix.

New York was also home to the seminal R&B label Atlantic Records, which – like Chess and other independent blues recording companies – fuelled the imaginations of young white players and listeners with its releases by African-American artists. Although Atlantic had nurtured R&B, it also released sides by blues musicians including T-Bone Walker (1910–75), Jimmy Yancey (1898–1951), Guitar Slim (1926–59), Professor Longhair (1918–80), Otis Rush (b. 1934) and Freddie King (1934–76). More importantly, Atlantic was the distributor of Stax Records, which produced classics by Albert King (1923–92) and Booker T. and the MGs, and was in the vanguard of soul music.

Demise Of The Cool

The developments in blues music enhanced the popularity of the various styles that had come earlier; however, this was not the case with jazz. The 1960s saw the dwindling of cool jazz in the face of the more passionate and experimental strains that now dominated the scene. Pianist Lennie Tristano (1919–78), who had built a cult following of fanatically devoted young musicians, spent less time onstage and more time teaching at his home. On the West Coast, cool icons such as Shorty Rogers and Bud Shank were fortunate enough to find work in Hollywood's film and television studios as their sounds went out of vogue. Jimmy Giuffre (b. 1921) and Gerry Mulligan (1927–96), who had made names for themselves in Los Angeles, found more fertile ground in New York City and abandoned much of their cool-jazz interest. Even the Modern Jazz Quartet, mixing hard bop and cool jazz, took frequent hiatuses. One legacy of cool jazz was the so-called 'third stream' of jazz and classical hybrids, in which both Giuffre and the MJQ's John Lewis (1920–2001) took part.

Below
A publicity poster for the 1965 American Folk Blues Festival.

Miles Davis, Revolutionary

The most prominent of the cool jazz pioneers, Miles Davis (1926–91), was perhaps the key innovator of

Far Left
Bob Dylan in his revolutionary electric performance at the 1965 Newport Folk Festival.

see Howlin' Wolf pp 225 see Mike Bloomfield pp 267 see Jimi Hendrix pp 273 see Alexis Korner's Blues Incorporated pp 275

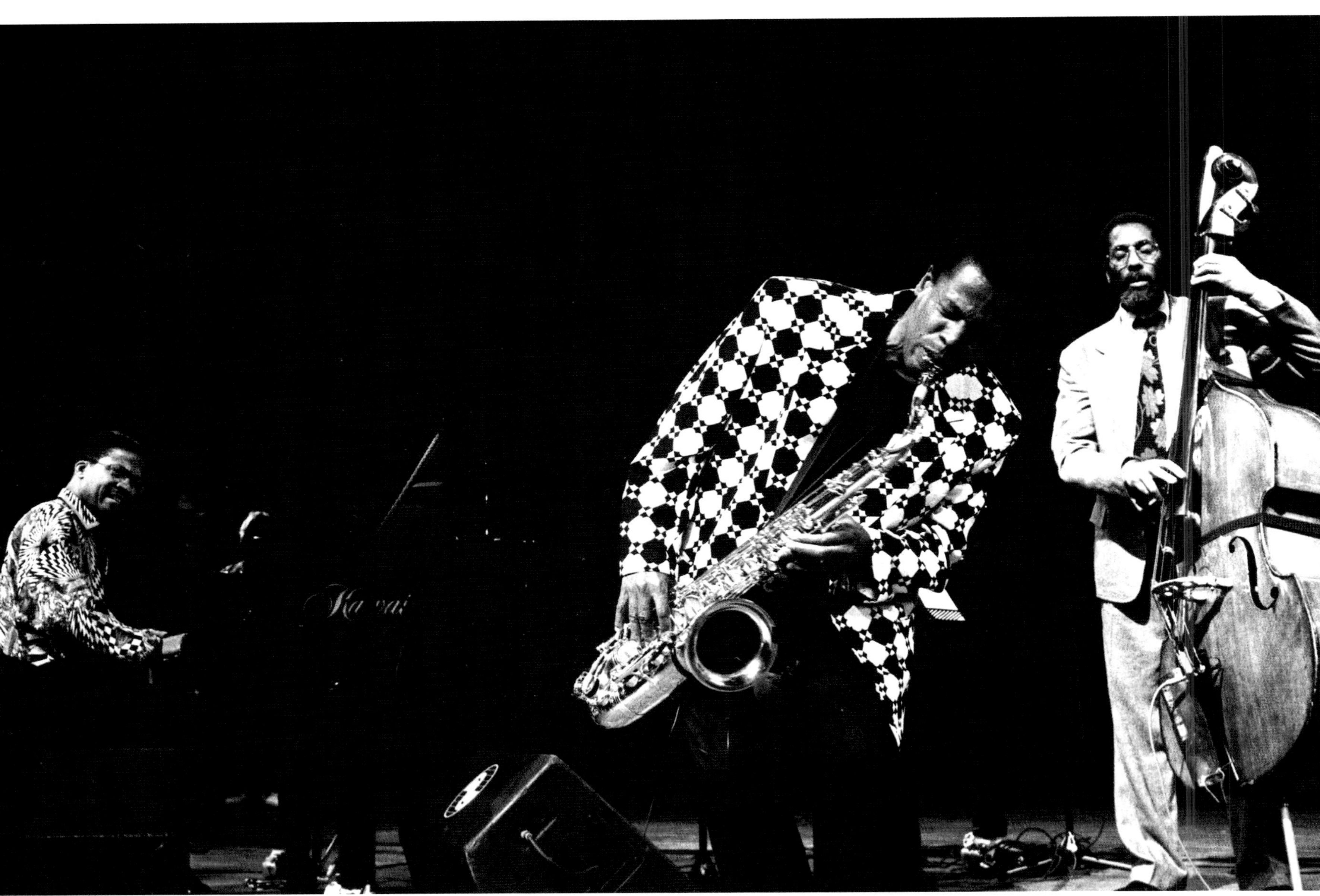

Above
(l–r) Herbie Hancock, Wayne Shorter and Ron Carter.

the 1960s. He ushered in the decade with an extension of the modal jazz studies he had championed in 1959's *Kind Of Blue*. Davis's partnership with arranger Gil Evans (1912–88) continued with the triumphant *Sketches Of Spain* (1959–60), including a long, introspective version of the Spanish guitar opus 'Concierto de Aranjuez', and the less accomplished bossa nova venture *Quiet Nights* (1962). With the latter album Davis felt that his experiments with Evans had run their course, so he abruptly changed direction from their orchestral works.

In 1963 Davis gathered what would become the greatest rhythm section of his career. Drummer Tony Williams (1945–97), already a jazz veteran at the age of 18, joined pianist Herbie Hancock and bassist Ron Carter (b. 1937) in backing Davis and a series of tenor saxophonists: first George Coleman, then Sam Rivers (b. 1923) and finally Wayne Shorter, whose innovative compositions gave a bold new sound to the Davis quintet. The trumpeter's modal jazz excursions had been pulling away from the rigour of set chord patterns and now Davis took it one step further. In the quintet's repertoire, chords and traditional improvisation were often abandoned altogether. There were no up-front solos in pieces such as Shorter's 'Nefertiti' – only fully composed passages. At other times, the rhythm section would play ostinatos – repetitive patterns over which Davis would improvise. Hancock, Carter and Williams became masters of subtle

see Introduction pp 238 *see* Key Artists pp 248 *see* A–Z of Artists pp 266 *see* List of Artists pp 282

variation, altering the mood and feeling of tunes almost imperceptibly over the course of several minutes, while the horns had their say in the foreground. This kind of rhythmic and harmonic play was about as close as Davis ever got to free jazz until his 1970s electric works.

Jazz Goes Electric

Later in the decade Davis brought in more young musicians and explored the concept of electric jazz. He initially encouraged Chick Corea, Keith Jarrett (b. 1945) and Joe Zawinul (b. 1932) to play electric piano and organ in a brave first step towards what became known as 'fusion', the union of jazz and rock elements. British electric guitarist John McLaughlin (b. 1942) pushed the envelope further outward with his unprecedented performances. Eventually Davis plugged his trumpet into a wah-wah pedal to emulate the guitar of Jimi Hendrix (1942–70). Record producer Teo Macero was also a primary factor in the new sound, manipulating the band's tapes into exhilarating collages of music. In 1969 Davis and his troupe made two groundbreaking albums for Columbia, *In A Silent Way* and *Bitches Brew*, which announced the arrival of a fresh new form of jazz. As he had 10 years before with *Kind Of Blue* (1959), Miles Davis had forever altered the course of music.

The Blues Meets Rock Music

From the middle of the decade, electricity was also taking over blues music, as the English bluesmen fused traditional blues with their increasingly sophisticated equipment, and sent out their own message. Much of the success of *Blues Breakers* (1966), the debut album from John Mayall's band, hung on the dazzling playing of guitarist Eric Clapton; this indicated that audiences were ready to listen to blues in a different way. Until then, the style – despite its legacy of great musicians – had been primarily a vocal music. Clapton adopted the techniques of Buddy Guy (b. 1936), Freddie King, B.B. King (b. 1925) and Albert King, and pushed them to a new level of virtuosity. After Clapton, who went on to form the improvisational blues rock supergroup Cream, the blues became associated with the sound of the guitar – particularly that of flattened blue notes and bent, vibrato-coloured strings, teased from an electric instrument.

In 1967 talented blues guitarist Peter Green formed Fleetwood Mac, a group of hardcore blues enthusiasts who gradually developed their own musical style. The early three-guitar line-up cycled through different hues of blues: Green loved stylists such as Elmore James, Jeremy Spencer emulated Chuck Berry and Elvis Presley, and Danny Kirwan leaned towards psychedelia. By 1973 all three had left the band due to personal conflicts and there followed a progressive movement away from the blues.

If Clapton did not seal the deal as far as virtuoso electric blues guitarists were concerned, the arrival of Jimi Hendrix did. Hendrix was the musical embodiment of the 1960s – a young black man who became a cultural superstar by pushing the limits of musical freedom. Established bluesmen, including B.B. King and Albert King, suddenly found themselves playing alongside rock stars before racially mixed audiences at large festivals and important venues. The blues seeped throughout the cultural terrain, making the 1960s the greatest period of growth and popularity the genre had experienced since it first emerged on recordings in the 1920s and 1930s.

Left
Rahsaan Roland Kirk played multiple horns.

see Miles Davis pp 200 *see* Fleetwood Mac pp 272 *see* Tony Williams pp 281 *see* John McLaughlin pp 300

Ornette Coleman

CLASSIC RECORDINGS

1958
Something Else!, 'Invisible', 'The Blessing', 'When Will The Blues Leave?'

1959
Change Of The Century, 'Free', 'Ramblin'', 'The Face Of The Bass', 'Una Muy Bonita'

1960
This Is Our Music, 'Blues Connotation', 'Embraceable You', *Free Jazz: A Collective Improvisation By The Ornette Coleman Double Quartet*, 'Free Jazz'

Since his emergence in the mid-1950s, alto saxophonist and creative composer Ornette Coleman has risen above controversy to become a respected elder statesman of jazz. Born in 1930 in Fort Worth, Texas, Coleman taught himself the saxophone through trial and error. By avoiding chord structures and set rhythms in favour of melodic experimentation, he developed the new style of 'free jazz'. He dubbed his controversial theory 'harmolodics' – a combination of harmony, motion and melody. Coleman's characteristic tone and his variety of intonation effects often recall a plaintive human voice, touched by the blues.

Breaking New Ground

Coleman received his first saxophone at the age of seven. As he found his way around the horn, Coleman developed notions about music that clashed with traditional practices but remained permanent parts of his artistic philosophy. Four years after beginning his career at the age of 15 with an R&B group, Coleman took to the road and encountered hostility from musicians and audiences who appreciated neither his bebop alterations nor his unkempt appearance. However, bandleaders admired his songwriting abilities and assigned him to refresh their books of blues-related pieces.

'Musicians tell me, if what I'm doing is right, they should never have gone to school.'
Ornette Coleman

In 1956 Coleman found himself unemployed in Los Angeles, where he met some like-minded musicians who were interested in his new concepts. His circle included trumpeters Don Cherry and Bobby Bradford, bassist Don Payne, drummer Billy Higgins and Canadian-born pianist Paul Bley, under whose name they performed at the Hillcrest Club. Recordings of those exciting gigs were released years later by Bley's IAI record label.

In 1958 bassist Red Mitchell brought one of Coleman's compositions to Contemporary Records boss Lester Koenig, who signed Coleman to a contract. Coleman and Cherry had developed a loose, intuitive ensemble sound, evident on several Coleman compositions such as 'When Will The Blues Leave' and 'The Blessing', backed somewhat uneasily by Payne and Higgins. Coleman's second Contemporary release featured another sheaf of originals, including 'Tears Inside' and 'Rejoicing'. The session's drummer was big-band veteran and LA jazz-club operator Shelly Manne. Open-minded, responsive pianist Walter Norris interpreted Coleman's compositions creatively, but the altoist later remarked that the piano's chordal, tempered nature was incompatible with the melody-driven freedom that he sought.

The Birth Of Free Jazz

In 1959 Coleman, Cherry, bassist Charlie Haden and drummer Ed Blackwell moved to New York, where they impressed composer-conductor Leonard Bernstein. Coleman continued to experiment with different ensembles and ideas, few as well-received as his famous quartet. In 1960 he recorded the landmark *Free Jazz:*

Right
Alto saxophonist and composer Ornette Coleman, one of the chief exponents of free jazz.

see Introduction pp 238 *see* Sources & Sounds pp 240 *see* A–Z of Artists pp 266

A Collective Improvisation By The Ornette Coleman Double Quartet for Atlantic Records. It consisted of one long group improvisation, punctuated by a few composed reference points. The performers – Coleman, Cherry, Haden, Blackwell, Higgins, trumpeter Freddie Hubbard, Eric Dolphy on bass clarinet and second bassist Scott LaFaro (who died prematurely in a car accident seven months after the session) – interacted continuously, as individuals and also as an ensemble.

Above
Coleman (centre) performs at Newport in 1977 with Don Cherry (left) and Dewey Redman.

Further Innovations

Following *Free Jazz*, Coleman experimented with a new trio. He took up the violin and trumpet, although these instruments have never been more than ornaments in his overall conception. He dabbled in chamber music, wrote some film scores and arrangements for a posthumous John Coltrane release and often reunited with his former sidemen. Tenorman Dewey Redman became a key associate in that period. In 1966 Coleman controversially began using his 10-year-old son Denardo as his regular drummer. Denardo has since continued to play drums and act as a producer for both his father and his mother, poet-vocalist Jayne Cortez.

In 1972 Coleman premiered his mammoth *Skies Of America*, a *concerto grosso* in which his ensemble improvised with a symphony orchestra. After collaborating with Yoko Ono and Morocco's Master Musicians of Jajouka, Coleman assembled the electric band Prime Time and recorded *Dancing In Your Head* in 1976. The group included two drummers (one of them often tabla player Badal Roy), two electric guitarists and electric bass. Later, multi-keyboardist David Bryant further widened Prime Time's scope, culminating in *Tone Dialing* (1995).

Since the late 1990s, Coleman has returned to acoustic groups with pianists. He has also led a quartet with two bassists and his son Denardo. Coleman, who remains a unique saxophone melodicist, an inspiring and world-renowned artist and an enduring composer, has also recorded with Pat Metheny, Jerry Garcia (of the Grateful Dead) and an esoteric range of other musicians.

see Paul Bley pp 267 *see* Don Cherry pp 269 *see* Eric Dolphy pp 271 *see* Charlie Haden pp 272

John Coltrane

CLASSIC RECORDINGS

1959
Giant Steps, 'Countdown', 'Naima'

1960
My Favorite Things, 'My Favorite Things', 'Summertime'

1961
Africa/Brass, 'Africa', 'Blues Minor'

1962
Duke Ellington and John Coltrane, 'Big Nick', 'In A Sentimental Mood'

1964
A Love Supreme, 'A Love Supreme' Parts 1–4'

1965
Ascension, 'Ascension'

Right
The controversial and endlessly experimental avant-garde saxophonist John Coltrane.

By the time John Coltrane died in 1967 at the age of 40, he had experienced one of the most remarkable careers in music. 'Trane' was a compelling voice who contributed to some of jazz's greatest innovations, from bebop to free jazz, resulting in both controversy and enduring success through critical and popular acclaim. Revered during his lifetime almost as a saint by many, Coltrane continued to push musical boundaries throughout his short life and influenced and inspired countless musicians even beyond the field of jazz.

> *'He contributed a whole different kind of openness to the music and added a spiritual essence to the music scene.'*
> Herbie Hancock

Coltrane was a relatively shy, reserved man, which marked him out among the many more flamboyant characters that populated the jazz world in which he matured. An unwilling leader, he was nevertheless driven by a desire to be a recognized figure with influence. He certainly achieved this aim.

From R&B To Bebop

Coltrane was born in 1926 in Hamlet, North Carolina and enjoyed a musical education from an early age, playing alto saxophone in high school and church bands. Johnny Hodges and Lester Young were among his early influences. In 1943 he moved to Philadelphia, where he continued his studies at the Ornstein School of Music. He made his first recordings while in the Army and switched to tenor sax at the encouragement of Eddie 'Cleanhead' Vinson.

After beginning to take inspiration from rising stars Charlie Parker and Dexter Gordon, Coltrane's work in R&B bands led to bebop gigs, and in 1949 Coltrane joined Dizzy Gillespie's big band. In the post-war period, running a big band was an expensive business and therefore a difficult way to make a living; Gillespie was forced to downsize to a quintet, in which Coltrane also played. By this stage, Coltrane's interest in unusual musical forms was already becoming apparent.

see Introduction pp 238 *see* Sources & Sounds pp 240 *see* A–Z of Artists pp 266

He returned to his studies, this time at the Granoff School of Music and continued to grow musically, although unfortunately, like many of his jazz contemporaries, Coltrane became addicted to heroin.

Playing With The Greats

In 1952 Coltrane joined Earl Bostic's band, a swing and R&B outfit led by a very accomplished sax player; Coltrane continued to hone his playing style in Bostic's employ. He was also privileged to play from 1953–54 with one of his early heroes, Johnny Hodges, who had formed his own band after leaving the great Duke Ellington. However, by this stage Coltrane was experiencing a number of physical and mental problems and Hodges was obliged to fire him. In addition to his heroin dependence, an addiction to sweets was causing Trane's teeth to become extremely painful, and the inevitable drinking and weight gain ensued.

In 1955 Coltrane met Miles Davis and joined his legendary Quintet, which included pianist Red Garland, bassist Paul Chambers and drummer Philly Joe Jones and was among the most popular jazz groups of the day. The band cut several albums for Prestige in the mid-1950s, with Davis and Coltrane on the front line. Coltrane played in a choppy, hard-bop style, which contrasted beautifully with Davis's more reserved sound. Around this time Coltrane also married Naima, a muslim, who furthered his interest in spirituality and eastern cultures. Davis fired the tenorman in 1957, allegedly because of his drug problems, but Coltrane was able to take with him the modal style inherent in Davis's improvisations – based around scales rather than chords – which would become important in his later work.

Coltrane returned home to Philadelphia, where he overcame his addictions, had a spiritual awakening (which involved an interest in religions from many different cultures) and returned to jazz a new man. He worked with Thelonious Monk at the Five Spot club in New York before landing his own recording contract with Prestige. Working with Monk not only widened Coltrane's audience, but also proved another stage in his musical development; although they had very different playing styles, both musicians liked to stray from the beaten track and relished experimenting with irregularity in harmony and rhythm.

'Sheets Of Sound'

By the time Coltrane rejoined Davis to fill Sonny Rollins' place in 1958, he had developed a technique of playing lengthy cascades of notes in propulsive harmonic extrapolations of complicated chord changes, termed 'sheets of sound' by writer Ira Gitler. He would attempt to recreate the notes from four separate chords in the space of one chord change, sometimes playing at a speed of up to 1,000 notes a minute. This affected not only the harmonic content of the music, but also the rhythm, as the inability to define the length of the individual notes disjointed the sound from the beat and undermined that fundamental musical relationship. The saxophonist joined Davis, altoman Julian 'Cannonball' Adderley and pianist Bill Evans on the classic *Kind Of Blue*, another work based around modal scales instead of chords. Coltrane responded with his own harmonically complicated *Giant Steps* (1959–60) for Atlantic Records; the title composition remains a test for any jazz musician. Coltrane's interest in modal music, both from Davis and his interest in Eastern

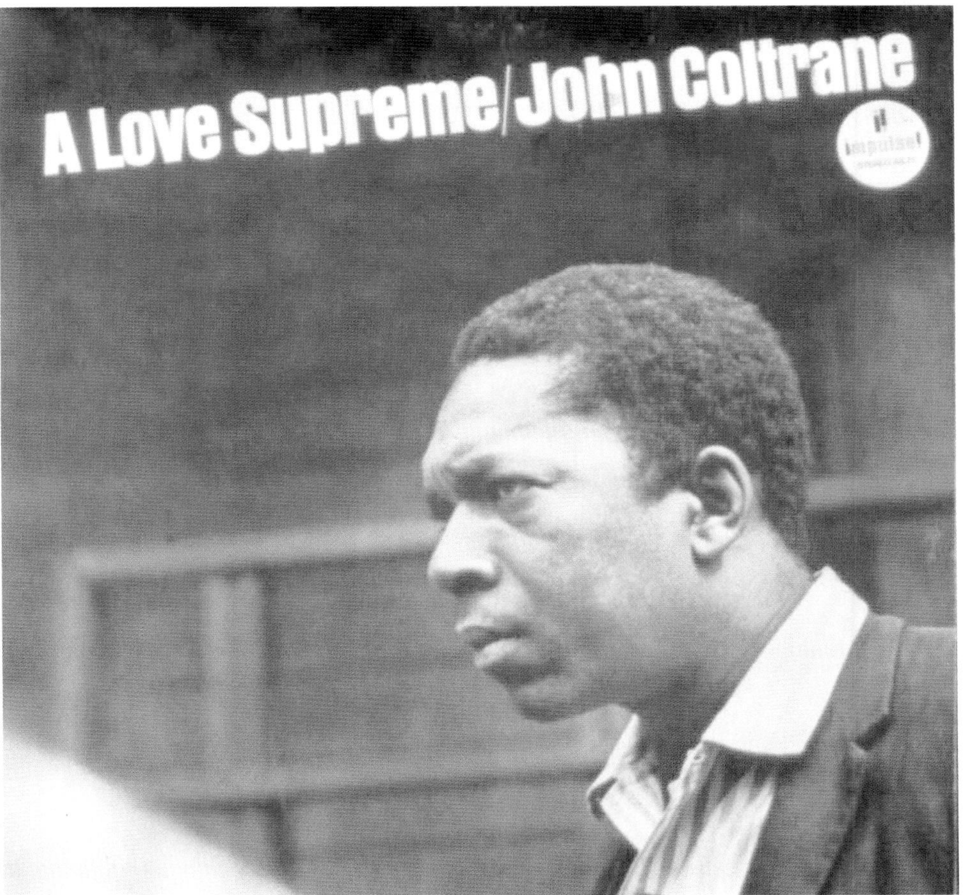

Above

One of Coltrane's best known albums, 1964's *A Love Supreme*.

see Johnny Hodges pp 126 see Dizzy Gillespie pp 152 see Bill Evans pp 206 see Thelonious Monk pp 208

Above
(l–r) Johnny Griffin, Coltrane and Hank Mobley during a recording session for Griffin's *Blowing Session* album.

music, led to his exploration of polytonality, which characterizes this phase of his career and was very influential on musicians from a wide range of genres.

An Eastern Influence

Partly inspired by the reissue of Sidney Bechet's records, following the New Orleans veteran's death in 1959, Coltrane began to play the soprano saxophone, concentrating more on sweeping melodies than the 'sheets of sound' effect. The soprano sax lent itself well to Islamic, Indian and African sounds, which Coltrane began to blend into his music. In 1960 he scored a big hit with *My Favorite Things*, which established him as a major star. Based on the saccharine Richard Rogers composition from *The Sound of Music*, the piece featured a shifting, modal backing embellished with improvised variations on the melody, and showed influences of Arabic music.

Bassist Jimmy Garrison, pianist McCoy Tyner and drummer Elvin Jones formed the core of Coltrane's early 1960s quartet, which soon became one of the most lauded ensembles in jazz. However, as his career progressed, the artistically restless Coltrane continued to develop his instrumental technique, grounded in what became a deeply spiritual and personal vision. He collaborated with his long-term acquaintance and gifted reedman Eric Dolphy, recording dates at New York's Village Vanguard that were later edited into an array of albums, as well as with Duke Ellington, cornettist Don Cherry, vibist Milt Jackson and vocalist

see Introduction pp 238 *see* Sources & Sounds pp 240 *see* A–Z of Artists pp 266

Left
Coltrane had an almost religious commitment to jazz.

Johnny Hartman. In 1961 Coltrane moved to Impulse Records, where his open-minded recording manager Bob Thiele fully supported Coltrane's spiritualism and avant-garde approach to jazz music, defending him when necessary against corporate intervention.

In December 1964 Coltrane's basic quartet recorded *A Love Supreme*. The album-length devotional suite offered jazz more exotic than most fans had ever heard. The work was based around a simple, four-note phrase; a continuous drone and steady rhythm formed the backdrop for Coltrane's inventive polytonality in the upper layers of the music. *A Love Supreme* was the culmination of Coltrane's diverse religious and cultural beliefs and had a redemptive quality, as if he were expressing his gratitude to the spiritual forces that had saved him from his addictions in the previous decade. The public embraced the work readily, and it became another of the era's hallmark jazz albums. The spiritualist and sonically futuristic nature of *A Love Supreme* meant that it succeeded in transcending the confines of jazz audiences, also appealing to the San Francisco, flower-power generation.

Ascending To Freedom

Having been inspired by the work of Ornette Coleman for some time, Coltrane moved further into free jazz in June 1965, assembling a large ensemble that included trumpeter Freddie Hubbard and saxophonists Pharoah Sanders and Archie Shepp. They recorded *Ascension* (1965), two album-length versions of thematically and harmonically unbridled, dense and extremely high-energy improvisation. A few days later Coltrane and Shepp unveiled their somewhat more muted but nonetheless radical new directions at the Newport Jazz Festival.

Although Jones and Tyner followed Coltrane's fearless explorations through frequent sessions that resulted in albums such as *Transition* (1965) and *Meditations* (1966), they were uncomfortable with some of his more free-form, polyphonic and polyrhythmic directions. In 1965 Alice Coltrane, the saxophonist's second wife, became the pianist, and drummer Rashied Ali emerged as a significant player, especially on duet recordings preserved as *Interstellar Space* (1967). John Coltrane continued to explore intense, abstract, progressive and uncompromising jazz until his death from liver disease in July 1967. He stands as a jazz saint to the modern world, a model of musical devotion, authentic discovery and enduring art.

Below
Pianist McCoy Tyner played in Coltrane's hugely popular quartet of the early 1960s.

see Milt Jackson pp 226 *see* Freddie Hubbard pp 256 *see* Elvin Jones pp 274 *see* McCoy Tyner pp 280

Buddy Guy

CLASSIC RECORDINGS

1960–67
The Complete Chess Studio Recordings, 'Broken Hearted Blues', 'First Time I Met The Blues', 'Let Me Love You Baby', 'My Time After Awhile', 'Stone Crazy'

1965
Hoodoo Man Blues by Junior Wells' Chicago Blues Band, featuring Buddy Guy, 'Chittlin Con Carne', 'Hoodoo Man Blues'

1967
A Man And The Blues, 'Jam On A Monday Morning', 'One Room Country Shack', 'Sweet Little Angel'

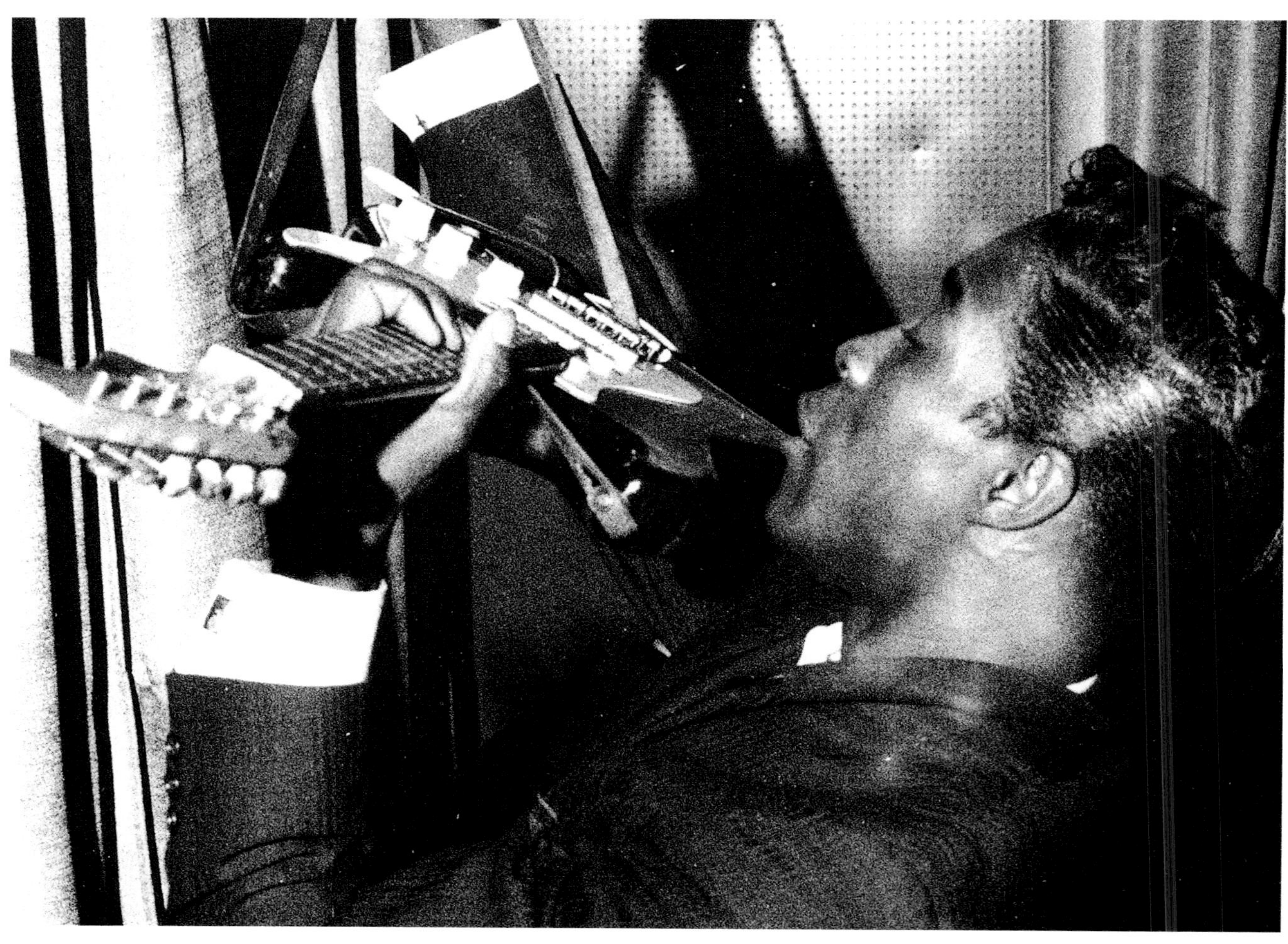

Above
Electric blues star Buddy Guy performs at London's Marquee Club in 1965.

'He is a consummate blues musician. He's living history.'
Eric Clapton

'When I first heard of the electric guitar, I thought somebody was bullshittin' me,' says George 'Buddy' Guy. 'We lived so far in the country I didn't even know what an acoustic guitar was until my mother started getting mail-order catalogs'. In 2005, Guy, who was born in Lettsworth, Louisiana on 30 July 1936, stands at the pinnacle of modern electric blues. Guy's first instruments were one-stringed contraptions that he made from screen wire, nails and paint cans, before he graduated to a battered acoustic bartered for by his father. He first heard an electric six-string played by Lightnin' Slim at a general store near the plantation where his family sharecropped, and the sound took root. After witnessing Guitar Slim's fiery live act in a Baton Rouge club, Guy's interest in becoming a baseball player vanished. He moved to Baton Rouge himself and began playing professionally, until he earned enough money for a bus ticket to Chicago in 1957.

Chicago Blues

The Windy City was less than welcoming. Guy failed to find work on the bandstand or elsewhere, although Chicago's blues scene was at its peak, heightened by Howlin' Wolf, Muddy Waters and many other stars and journeymen, as well as the presence of the Chess, United and Cobra labels. Frustrated and starving, Guy resolved to return home, but Waters intervened and took the young musician under his wing. Guy then became a regular session player at Chess and recorded singles for Chess and Cobra. He supported Waters on

see Introduction pp 238 *see* Sources & Sounds pp 240 *see* A–Z of Artists pp 266

Left
Musicologist Sam Charters, who produced Guy's early albums.

the 1963 classic *Folk Singer* and fell into a partnership with vocalist and harmonica player Junior Wells, with whom he recorded *Hoodoo Man Blues* (1965) and *Southside Blues Jam* (1967) on Delmark. Although he could not break out of the Chicago scene, Guy became known for his great live delivery (hanging from rafters and playing with his teeth), his gospel-style testifying and a guitar vocabulary built on explosive dynamics, off-the-neck bends, subtle chromatic lines and uninhibited improvisation.

His Reputation Spreads And Wanes

Guy's reputation reached further than he imagined. His playing influenced guitarists as widespread as Eric Clapton and Jimi Hendrix. Equally impressed, musicologist Samuel Charters produced Guy's first solo albums for the Vanguard label, including the brilliant *A Man & The Blues* (1968), still widely considered to be Guy's masterpiece. In 1970 Guy and Wells were invited to tour with the Rolling Stones; they then found themselves on the international festival circuit, together and with their bands, but their fame was fleeting. Guy spent the 1980s without a contract, playing clubs including his own, the Checker-board Lounge. He later opened Legends in downtown Chicago.

At The Zenith

It took another acolyte, Texan guitarslinger Stevie Ray Vaughan, to propel Guy to the top of the contemporary blues world, where he remains, second only to B.B. King. Vaughan's tireless support won Guy a contract with Silvertone Records, resulting in 1991's *Damn Right, I've Got The Blues* – which was also the title of Guy's 1993 autobiography, co-written by Donald E. Wilcock. The disc, which includes cameos by Jeff Beck, Mark Knopfler and Eric Clapton, received significant airplay and thrust Guy back to the festival and outdoor amphitheatre circuit, where he continues to play today. Several subsequent CDs found Guy aiming for pop crossover breakthroughs, but their diminishing sales figures indicated that they were eroding his standing among his listeners.

Once again, a prominent fan interceded. Producer Dennis Herring took the reins for 2001's *Sweet Tea*, using vintage amplifier tones and songs culled primarily from the catalogue of modern Mississippi juke blues master Junior Kimbrough. The raw-sounding venture restored Guy's momentum, which he maintained by joining Herring again for 2003's *Blues Singer*, an acoustic country blues homage to Muddy Waters' *Folk Singer* (1964) that returned Guy to his rural roots.

Below
Guy sporting a Stevie Ray Vaughan T-shirt at the launch of his 1991 album *Damn Right I've Got The Blues*.

see Muddy Waters pp 212 *see* Guitar Slim pp 223 *see* Junior Wells pp 281 *see* Junior Kimbrough pp 358

Freddie Hubbard

CLASSIC RECORDINGS

1960
Open Sesame, 'All Or Nothing At All', 'Gypsy Blue'

1961
Mosaic by Art Blakey and the Jazz Messengers, 'Arabia', 'Crisis'

1961
Hub Cap, 'Plexus'

1962
Hub-Tones, 'Hub-Tones', 'You're My Everything'

1966
Backlash, 'Little Sunflower'

1967
High Blues Pressure, 'Can't Let Her Go'

1970
Red Clay, 'Red Clay'

In the 1960s and early 1970s, trumpeter Freddie Hubbard was the primary alternative to Miles Davis's domination of the field. Hubbard came up in the hard-bop era, blew free jazz with Ornette Coleman and John Coltrane, and established a body of exemplary compositions, recordings and improvisations with the best of the 1960s Blue Note artists: Art Blakey, Herbie Hancock, Wayne Shorter, Andrew Hill, Eric Dolphy, Lee Morgan, Tony Williams, Sam Rivers and many others.

Outward Bound

Born in Indianapolis in 1938, Hubbard drew inspiration from the bebop trumpeters of the early 1950s, particularly Clifford Brown. The Montgomery brothers, guitarist Wes, vibist Buddy and bassist Monk, were quick to hire the young trumpeter because of his stylistic resemblance to Brown. At the age of 20 Hubbard moved to New York City, where he roomed and formed a working relationship with reedsman Eric Dolphy. Hubbard played in the bebop-oriented bands of Sonny Rollins, Philly Joe Jones and J.J. Johnson.

1960 was a banner year: Hubbard made his first album for Blue Note – *Open Sesame* – performed on Dolphy's *Outward Bound* and Ornette Coleman's landmark *Free Jazz* and then went on tour with Quincy Jones.

'He had the biggest sound and the most powerful swing out there, on almost any instrument. It was pretty amazing.'
Don Braden

In 1961 Hubbard made another lasting impression with Oliver Nelson on *Blues And The Abstract Truth*, which resulted in the classic 'Stolen Moments'. That same year he joined tenorman Wayne Shorter and trombonist Curtis Fuller on the front line of Art Blakey's Jazz Messengers, the premier hard-bop ensemble. He remained a Messenger for three years, appearing on some of the band's finest recordings. In 1964 he left the group and contributed to two more enduring sessions, Dolphy's *Out To Lunch* and Herbie Hancock's *Maiden Voyage*. The following year Hubbard ventured deeper into free jazz on John Coltrane's *Ascension*, before joining Max Roach's band.

Above
Trumpeter Freddie Hubbard was inspired by Clifford Brown and played with the Montgomery brothers from a young age.

Rising Star

In 1966 Hubbard took steps to broaden his profile, putting together a quintet that featured alto saxophonist James Spaulding. His next two recordings, *Backlash* – which included his perennially popular composition 'Little Sunflower' (1966) – and *High Blues Pressure* (1967), both for the Atlantic label, garnered more critical acclaim for Hubbard. His subsequent albums included the politically themed, abstract electronic composition *Sing Me A Song Of Songmy* (1971), and in 1970 he broke new ground on producer Creed Taylor's CTI label. Taylor was a master at

see Introduction pp 238 *see* Sources & Sounds pp 240 *see* A–Z of Artists pp 266

reshaping jazz with more popular flourishes such as electric instruments and strings, and Hubbard benefitted greatly from his touch. The soulful albums *Red Clay* (1970), *Straight Life* (1970) and *First Light* (1972) all propelled Hubbard to the top of the jazz record and radio charts.

His triumphs on CTI collapsed when Hubbard signed with Columbia Records in 1972. The label pushed the 'contemporary' angle, dragging the trumpeter into one shallow, poorly conceived session after another. By the mid-1970s Hubbard seemed destined for has-been status. Herbie Hancock helped to rescue Hubbard's career by hiring him for the VSOP repertory group in 1977. The quintet revisited the musicians' 1960s Blue Note accomplishments and proved that an acoustic setting was where Hubbard shone the brightest.

Welcome Return

Rejuvenated as a player and composer, Freddie Hubbard resumed his climb up the jazz echelon with a triumphant appearance at the 1980 North Sea Jazz Festival in Holland. New records for Pablo, Prestige and Enja led fans to embrace the trumpeter once more, although his stardom was still long past. In 1985 he signed back with the rejuvenated Blue Note, working with the brilliant trumpeter Woody Shaw on a few projects. Unfortunately, Hubbard soon became plagued by lip trouble that ruined his embouchure and required surgery. It took him several more years to return to a point where he could play comfortably again, but he remains on the scene and has recorded with David Weiss's New Jazz Composers Octet.

Above
Pianist Herbie Hancock (left), shown here with Ron Carter, helped to resurrect Hubbard's career in the late 1970s.

see Art Blakey pp 218 *see* Clifford Brown pp 218 *see* Herbie Hancock pp 305 *see* Woody Shaw pp 310

Albert King

CLASSIC RECORDINGS

1953–66
The Big Blues, 'Don't Throw Your Love On Me So Strong', 'Let's Have A Natural Ball'

1967
'Born Under A Bad Sign'

1968
Years Gone By, 'Killing Floor', 'The Sky Is Falling'

1968
Live Wire/Blues Power, 'Blues Power'

1972
I'll Play The Blues For You, 'Breaking Up Somebody's Home', 'I'll Play The Blues For You'

1977
Albert Live, 'Blues At Sunrise', 'Jam In A Flat'

Right
Albert King, whose clear, sparse sound was a welcome departure.

'He wasn't my brother in blood, but he sure was my brother in blues.'
B.B. King

Albert King's late 1960s and early 1970s recordings for the Stax label remain cornerstones of modern blues. Tunes like 'Born Under A Bad Sign', 'Crosscut Saw' and 'I'll Play the Blues For You' are also an antidote to the over-the-top playing indulged in by so many contemporary blues guitarists. For King, a six-foot-four, 250-pound man possessed of a big, mellow voice and an equally proportional guitar tone, each carefully chiselled note took on the resonance of a life experience.

Born Albert Nelson on 25 April 1923 in Indianola, Mississippi, near the birthplace of B.B. King, Albert King was raised on a plantation in Arkansas, where he occasionally heard Howlin' Wolf perform at parties and roadhouses. He taught himself guitar and began playing local juke joints in 1939. King travelled north and sang lead tenor with the Harmony Kings gospel quartet around South Bend, Indiana for several years before arriving in Chicago, where he played drums with Jimmy Reed, Jackie Wilson, Brook Benton and others.

Far Right
King, still brandishing a trademark Gibson Flying V guitar, performs at the Hammersmith Odeon, London in 1983.

Guitar Prowess

As a guitarist, King's technique was evolving. He graduated from acoustic to electric guitar, playing in a single-note style based on that of B.B. King, whose surname he also borrowed. These B.B. approximations can be heard on his early singles for the Parrot and Bobbin labels, including his first national hit, 'Don't Throw Your Love On Me So Strong', from 1961. By the time King signed to Stax Records in Memphis

see Introduction pp 238 *see* Sources & Sounds pp 240 *see* A–Z of Artists pp 266

in 1966, he had developed his own brawny style. In the late 1950s he had purchased the Gibson Flying V guitar that became his signature instrument. The left-handed musician turned it upside down, tuned it to an open E-minor chord and turned his amplifier's volume up. The resulting sound – round-toned, deliberately squeezed from each string and full of melismatic bent notes – was the soulful equivalent of his gospel-honed voice.

The Stax Years

Featuring a roster of artists and session players that included Booker T. & the MGs, Isaac Hayes and the Memphis Horns, King's Stax singles and albums brought blues into the soul era. The spread of FM radio, along with Eric Clapton's incorporation of King's licks and a cover of his 'Born Under A Bad Sign' into Cream's repertoire, introduced King to white listeners. In 1964 King was invited to open a series of shows for Janis Joplin and Jimi Hendrix at San Francisco's Fillmore Auditorium, which solidified his reputation with the rock audience.

King's popularity remained strong until the late 1970s, which was an especially difficult time for blues, as arena rock captured the commercial airwaves and disco claimed clubs that had patronized live music. However, thanks to an association he made with a young guitarist and fan named Stevie Ray Vaughan at the Austin, Texas club Armadillo World Headquarters, King would again experience something of a renaissance. Vaughan continually sang King's praises after his own ascent to blues and rock stardom in the early 1980s, and invited King to open many important shows. In 1983 they appeared together on Hamilton, Ontario television station CHCH. The ensuing jam and conversation eventually became the CD *Albert King With Stevie Ray Vaughan* (1999).

In Paradise

Although King never regained the level of commercial success he'd achieved with Stax in the 1960s, he toured regularly, playing clubs and blues festivals until he suffered a fatal heart attack in Memphis on 21 December 1992. His body lies beneath a large tombstone at the Paradise Gardens Cemetery in Edmonson, Arkansas bearing a bronze plaque with the epitaph 'I'll play the blues for you'.

see Jimmy Reed pp 232 *see* B.B. King pp 260 *see* Janis Joplin pp 274 *see* Stevie Ray Vaughan pp 330

B.B. King

CLASSIC RECORDINGS

1952–56
Do The Boogie! Early 50s Classics, 'Everyday I Have The Blues', 'Please Love Me', 'Why I Sing The Blues'

1964
Live At The Regal, 'Help The Poor', 'You Upset Me Baby', 'Rock Me Baby'

1970
Live In Cook County Jail, 'How Blue Can You Get', 'The Thrill Is Gone', 'Worry, Worry'

2000
Riding With The King, 'Three O'Clock Blues'

When the great Mississippi musician Riley King left the cotton fields to seek his fortune in Memphis in 1946, he had $2.50 in his pocket and a battered guitar in his hand. Today, his name is synonymous with blues music itself, yet his ascendance to the zenith of the blues world has never altered his friendly, downhome nature. King is one of the most influential guitarists of the past 50 years, with a lush, sustained yet punchy tone and singing vibrato that has had a vast impact on generations of players across all genres. The soaring phrases of his warm, Delta-accented voice cut right to the emotional core of the blues.

King combined the urban Chicago sound with the more refined blues of the East Coast, while also adding elements of his own, Memphis-influenced style. He took inspiration from a number of jazz musicians, including guitarists Charlie Christian and Django Reinhardt and saxophonist Lester Young, as well as blues artists such as T-Bone Walker, Lonnie Johnson and Blind Lemon Jefferson. King's diverse influences gave him an original approach to harmony and phrasing; he played slightly off the beat and preferred to use vibrato in the place of a slide to colour his improvisations.

'Well B.B. was like a hero. You listen to the way that band swings on Live At The Regal, *it's just like a steam roller.'*

Mick Fleetwood

Blues Boy

King was born on a plantation near Indianola on 16 September 1925. He had a difficult childhood, with the intimidations of jim crow compounded by his mother's death when he was 10 years old. Like many of his blues contemporaries, King grew up working in the cotton fields. His parents and grandparents were musical, and although King never received any formal music education, he sang in gospel groups and church choirs from an early age and by 16 had taught himself to play the guitar and could be seen busking on the Delta streets.

King was singing regularly in a gospel quartet when he left for Memphis to stay for a time with his cousin, bluesman Bukka White. With his bold voice and charisma, betraying the influence of R&B showmen such as Roy Brown (albeit tempered by more gentle gospel inflections), and a distinctive guitar style, King began to enter and frequently win talent shows. One such contest, held weekly at Beale Street's Palace Theater, was compered by the comedian, entertainer and future star of Sun Records, Rufus Thomas, and was also a significant starting point for the careers of other R&B musicians including Ike Turner and Roscoe Gordon.

In 1948, after an enforced return to the Mississippi plantation, King secured a daily 10-minute

Right
Dynamic guitarist B.B. King, perhaps the most influential blues artist of the post-war era.

see Introduction pp 238 *see* Sources & Sounds pp 240 *see* A–Z of Artists pp 266

Above

King in London with his trusty guitar Lucille.

spot on radio station WDIA. He used it to sell patent medicines like Pepticon while also plugging his area gigs. King chose 'The Beale Street Blues Boy' as his radio moniker, which was then abbreviated to 'B.B.' for 'Blues Boy'. This show led King to a more prestigious role presenting *Sepia Swing Show*, on which he spun discs by mainly R&B and jump blues artists, including Amos Milburn, T-Bone Walker, Lowell Fulson and Louis Jordan, while constantly absorbing elements from their music. The next year he made his debut recordings for the local Bullet label, then signed with Los Angeles-based Modern Records. King's first hit was 'Three O'Clock Blues' (1951), which was based on a song by Lowell Fulson. It remained at Number One in the R&B chart for 15 weeks and is still a staple of the nearly 200 shows he plays each year.

Playing The Chitlin Circuit

King spent most of the 1950s and 1960s expanding his touring base. Initially, he worked at roadhouses within a few hours of Memphis. At a show in Twist, Arkansas in December 1949, he nearly lost his life when he rushed into a burning club to rescue his Gibson L-30 guitar. From that day he has named each of his guitars 'Lucille', after the woman who allegedly started the fire.

When more hit records, including 'You Upset Me Baby' and 'Please Love Me', allowed King to demand $800 a show, he began touring widely in the South. At first he was supported by Memphis bandleader Bill Harvey's group, travelling in a Cadillac and two station wagons to the small theatres and auditoriums where the New York City-based booking agency Universal Attractions had arranged

see Django Reinhardt pp 132 *see* Bukka White pp 138 *see* T-Bone Walker pp 168 *see* Lowell Fulson pp 222

Above
Legendary blues singer and guitarist B.B. King during a performance at London's Alexandra Palace.

his shows. In 1955, King assembled his own B.B. King Orchestra and got a loan for his first bus – a used Aero that he dubbed 'Big Red'. His touring route began to include northern African-American population centres, such as Chicago, Los Angeles and Harlem, and he even appeared at mainstream venues such as the Apollo Theater.

Blues Enters The Pop Charts

King cut many of his finest numbers during this period, 'Sweet Sixteen', 'Rock Me Baby' and 'How Blue Can You Get' among them. The jump blues influence of Louis Jordan can be heard on many of these sides. King also attempted to run his own record label, although it was not successful. In 1962, he switched to ABC-Paramount Records and made the concert album *Live At The Regal* (1964), recorded in a Chicago theatre before a wildly enthusiastic crowd. Although most white fans were listening to acoustic blues at the time, a new generation of musicians began to sing his praises. King's 1967 album *Blues Is King* (1967) launched ABC's successful Bluesway series.

see Introduction pp 238 *see* Sources & Sounds pp 240 *see* A–Z of Artists pp 266

Under the management of Sidney A. Seidenberg, King was able to secure gigs at important venues such as the Fillmores East and West, while high-profile admirers such as Eric Clapton, Mike Bloomfield, Jimi Hendrix and Johnny Winter helped King to reach the rock audience. His star rose, and then soared when the song that would become his signature tune, 'The Thrill Is Gone', hit Number 3 on the R&B charts and Number 15 on the American pop charts in January 1970. The use of a string arrangement and the overall accessibility of the record resulted in its appeal to a wider audience and catapulted blues music into the pop mainstream.

Recognition Is Achieved

Since then King has been the blues' top traditional performer, recording several excellent and star-studded albums including *Indianola Mississippi Seeds* (1970) with musicians including Leon Russell and Carole King; *Live In Cook County Jail* (1971); *Live In London* (1971) with Alexis Korner, Steve Winwood and Ringo Starr; *LA Midnight* (1972), which featured two jazz saxophonists as well as rock and blues artists such as Taj Mahal; and *Now Appearing At Ole Miss* (1980). King continued to tour throughout the 1970s and signed with MCA in 1979, recording an album, *Take It Home*, with the jazz funk group the Crusaders. An album recorded in 1983, *Blues'n'Jazz*, (1983) again saw him recording with jazz musicians while continuing to explore and augment blues music traditions.

King made his home in Las Vegas, which remains his base, but graduated to international touring and travelled widely, playing in dozens of countries. He was inducted into the Blues Foundation's Hall Of Fame in 1984 and the Rock And Roll Hall Of Fame in 1987. He also received a Grammy Award for Lifetime Achievement that year. In 1989 he recorded the smash 'When Loves Comes To Town' with U2, which introduced King to a new generation of rock fans. His B.B. King's Blues Club operates nightly on 42nd Street in New York.

Life At The Top

King penned his autobiography, *Blues All Around Me*, with journalist David Ritz in 1996. Although he has been afflicted by diabetes and arthritis, he remains a gracious and compelling performer and has grown as a guitarist, incorporating more jazz chords and scales into his live improvisations. Since 1991, he has headlined the travelling B.B. King Blues Festival each summer. Although recent albums such as *Blues On The Bayou* (1998) and *Makin' Love Is Good For You* (2000) are not among his best, *Riding With The King* (2000), a collaboration with his apostle Eric Clapton, won a Grammy Award and hit the top of the pop charts.

King's inventive blues style has inspired countless musicians over the decades, with some of the more obvious examples including Buddy Guy, Freddie King and Albert King. His influence has also penetrated the rock genre, in particular his penchant for extended and often largely improvised guitar solos. In recent years, King has played a 'global ambassador' role for blues music that recalls Louis Armstrong's jazz equivalent in the 1960s; both men have been considered to be successful entertainers and show-business figures, in addition to their achievements as great innovators, performers and promoters of black music.

Below
King's emotional but warm guitar playing places him among the blues greats.

see Louis Jordan pp 176 *see* Buddy Guy pp 254 *see* Freddie King pp 274 *see* Taj Mahal pp 280

Sun Ra

CLASSIC RECORDINGS

1958
Jazz In Silhouette, 'Ancient Aiethiopia', 'Blues At Midnight', 'Saturn'

1958–60
Sound Sun Pleasure, 'Enlightenment', 'You Never Told Me That You Care'

1960
Holiday For Soul Dance, 'Body And Soul', 'But Not For Me', 'Early Autumn'

1965
The Heliocentric Worlds Of Sun Ra, Volumes 1 & 2, 'Other Worlds', 'Sun Myth'

Above
Eccentric keyboard player Sun Ra.

From the 1950s through to the 1990s there was rarely a stranger experience for jazz audiences than witnessing the stage shows of Sun Ra and his Solar-Myth Arkestra. The mysterious, robed keyboardist and his exotic big band blended theatrics with pure jazz and free exploration, crafting a unique brand of 'space jazz' that reflected the mid-century's curiosity about exploring the unknown universe.

'The outer space beings are my brothers. They sent me here. They already know my music.'
Sun Ra

Swinging Beginnings

Although Sun Ra claimed to have come to Earth from Saturn, he was in fact born Herman 'Sonny' Blount in Birmingham, Alabama in 1914. He was mostly self-taught as a pianist and performed with his own bands from the age of 20. Later, at Alabama State College, Blount proved to be such an exceptional student that he was permitted to teach from time to time.

Acclaimed as a creative, knowledgeable pianist, young Blount was also an inventive arranger. In 1946 he was hired by bandleader Fletcher Henderson, but his arrangements were so difficult and unusual that the musicians' complaints got him fired within a year. Around this time, Blount had been discussing Egyptian cosmology and science fiction with record producer Alton Abraham. The pair decided to put together a band that combined jazz, mythology, black pride and pulp science fiction. At the helm would be Blount, who assumed the persona of 'Sun Ra, Traveler of the Spaceways'. They built up a fantastic backstory for Ra as a sojourner from Saturn who searched the galaxy to find a new home for the mistreated black race on Earth.

Space Is The Place

By the mid-1950s Sun Ra was leading the first incarnation of his big band, called the Arkestra (sometimes augmented with spacy appellations such as 'Solar-Myth' or 'Myth-Science'). Blount's expansive knowledge of jazz history, from Jelly Roll Morton to the modern day, was filtered into his arrangements and compositions for the Arkestra. The band boasted

see Introduction pp 238 *see* Sources & Sounds pp 240 *see* A–Z of Artists pp 266

several excellent musicians, among them trombonist Julian Priester, bassist Ronnie Boykins and saxophonists John Gilmore, Marshall Allen and Pat Patrick. Sun Ra used a number of keyboards, including Wurlitzer organ, clavinet and Moog synthesizer. The Arkestra's unusual sonic palette added to the other-worldliness of its music. Ra was a strict enforcer of rules, leading the band as a sort of commune and counselling its members against drug abuse and other unwelcome excesses.

The Arkestra debuted on record in 1957 with *Jazz By Sun Ra* (reissued on Delmark as *Sun Song*). The combination of straight jazz, heavy percussion and far-reaching improvisation heralded a new direction for jazz, but the album received scant distribution and little notice. That same year Ra formed his own record label, Saturn, which issued new Arkestra albums in haphazard form with hand-painted covers and unreliable sound quality. Saturn was one of the earliest labels run completely by musicians, and the enterprise endured even after Ra's death.

Other Worlds Of Sound

However, taut musicianship and consistently interesting music were not sufficient for the Arkestra to be taken seriously by many audiences or music critics, due in part to its outlandish stage costumes and cosmic pretensions. Still, Sun Ra became one of the most recognized, if begrudgingly respected, performers in modern jazz. The psychedelic era was a boon to the bandleader, whose spacey aesthetic was easy for the hippie generation to embrace. In 1972 the band made the movie *Space Is The Place*, based upon Sun Ra's invented mythology.

In the 1980s Sun Ra began to back away from writing original material, preferring to interpret past masters such as Duke Ellington and Fletcher Henderson. In the 1990s he became wheelchair-bound following a series of strokes and died on 30 May 1993, having schooled a further generation of players (including violinist Billy Bang and trombonist Craig Harris). After his death, Evidence Records initiated a reissue programme of Sun Ra's Saturn recordings.

Below
Duke Ellington (left), a key influence on Sun Ra's later compositions, 1969.

see Duke Ellington pp 52 *see* Jelly Roll Morton pp 60 *see* Fletcher Henderson pp 74 *see* Free Jazz pp 394

A–Z of Artists

Muhal Richard Abrams

(Piano, b. 1930)

Muhal Richard Abrams was one of the principal architects of free jazz in Chicago. After playing with Eddie Harris and the MJT+3, Abrams founded his Experimental Band in 1961 to explore original composition and new directions. In 1965 he founded the Association for the Advancement of Creative Musicians (AACM), which emphasizes creativity, professionalism and social responsibility. Abrams is a gifted composer and bandleader, having recorded many excellent albums with some of Chicago's – and later New York's – finest musicians.

Cannonball Adderley

(Alto saxophone, 1928–75)

Julian 'Cannonball' Adderley and his brother, trumpeter Nat, presided over one of the 1960s' hippest hard-bop outfits with pianist Joe Zawinul; 'Mercy, Mercy, Mercy' was one of their crossover hits. Adderley had been employed as a Florida school band director when he was overheard at a New York gig and was encouraged by musicans. Besides his own popular groups, Adderley recorded impressively with Miles Davis, John Coltrane, Bill Evans and Gil Evans' Orchestra.

Below

(l–r) Joe Zawinul, Nat Adderley, Sam Jones, Cannonball Adderley and Louis Hayes perform on BBC2's *Jazz 625* in 1964.

The Animals

(Vocal/instrumental group, 1962–68)

This R&B-influenced UK rock group from Newcastle comprised powerful blues singer Eric Burdon (vocals), Hilton Valentine (guitar), Chas Chandler (bass), Alan Price (keyboards) and John Steel (drums). They backed visiting US bluesmen before releasing their US and UK number-one hit 'House of the Rising Sun' in 1964. A string of blues- and R&B-influenced smashes followed. After the band split, Chandler went on to manage Jimi Hendrix while Burdon moved to California and recorded with War and Night Shift.

Albert Ayler

(Various saxophones, 1936–70)

Albert Ayler was one of the most controversial free-jazz performers. Eccentric and tirelessly inventive, he shifted ensemble roles in his music so that drummers and bassists were on equal ground with the horns. Ayler influenced John Coltrane and many younger saxophonists, and his recordings gradually moved from free jazz towards rock and soul themes. *Spiritual Unity* (1964) remains one of his most acclaimed albums. Ayler died in mysterious circumstances at the age of 34.

Carla Bley

(Piano, organ, arranger, b. 1938)

Self-taught, Carla Bley is as respected for her compositions and arrangements as for her excellent piano and organ playing. In the 1950s she was briefly married to pianist Paul Bley, who championed her works. In 1965, with her second husband, trumpeter Michael Mantler, Bley co-founded the Jazz Composers

see Introduction pp 238 *see* Sources & Sounds pp 240 *see* Key Artists pp 248

Orchestra Association to encourage the creation and distribution of new music in New York. Bley continues to lead a big band and smaller ensembles, often featuring electric bassist Steve Swallow.

Paul Bley

(Piano, synthesizer, b. 1932)

Paul Bley came from Montreal to New York in the early 1950s and worked with Jackie McLean. Later, in Los Angeles, he pioneered free jazz with Ornette Coleman. Throughout his career Bley has performed the compositions of his ex-wives – keyboardist Carla Bley and singer/pianist Annette Peacock – and his own pieces, often ruminative improvisations. Bley helped to popularize the new Moog synthesizer in the early 1970s and has collaborated with Gary Burton, Barre Phillips, Evan Parker, Pat Metheny, Jaco Pastorius, and many others.

Above

The Animals' albums were largely R&B, lacking the pop of their hit singles

Mike Bloomfield

(Guitar, vocals, 1943–81)

Bloomfield apprenticed in Chicago with legends such as Muddy Waters and Howlin' Wolf, as well as among his peers Paul Butterfield, Charlie Musselwhite and Elvin Bishop. He played on classics with the Paul Butterfield Blues Band (1966's *East-West*), Bob Dylan (1965's *Highway 61 Revisited*) and organist Al Kooper (1968's *Super Session*). He helped to form Electric Flag and briefly played in KGB, but then took refuge in acoustic blues in the late 1970s, making virtuoso, instructive recordings until his death from an overdose in 1981.

The Blues Project

(Vocal/instrumental group, 1965–71)

The Blues Project was formed around respected session musicians Tommy Flanders (vocals), Danny Kalb (guitar), Steve Katz (guitar, vocals), Al Kooper (organ, vocals), Andy Kulberg (bass, flute) and Roy Blumenfeld (drums). This experimental band, with a love of urban and country blues, quickly rose to the apex of the New York City music scene. By 1967 it had played huge outdoor concerts in Central Park and toured the US, spreading its influence. They recorded three albums, including the excellent debut *Live At The Café Au Go Go* (1966), before Kooper and Katz departed to form Blood, Sweat & Tears.

Gary Burton

(Vibraphone, b. 1943)

Gary Burton is one of the most impressive vibists in jazz, at times using four mallets in order to harmonize with himself. He began his career in country music with guitarist Hank Garland, played jazz with George Shearing and Stan Getz, and then helped to instigate the jazz-rock fusion movement through his group with guitarist Larry Coryell and drummer Roy Haynes. Burton has made marvellous duet albums with Chick Corea and Paul Bley, and taught at Berklee College of Music from 1971–2002.

see John Coltrane pp 250 *see* Larry Coryell pp 270 *see* Steve Swallow pp 310 *see* Joe Zawinul pp 311

Above
Los Angeles band Canned Heat covered a selection of 1920s and 1930s blues tracks.

Paul Butterfield Blues Band

(Vocal/instrumental group, 1963–67)

Harmonica player and singer Butterfield conditioned his band – Jerome Arnold (bass), Elvin Bishop and Mike Bloomfield (guitars), Sam Lay (drums, vocals) and Mark Naftalin (keyboards) – in black Chicago clubs. They backed Dylan's electric debut at the 1965 Newport Folk Festival and helped to usher blues into the psychedelic era, with the groundbreaking *East-West* (1966). After the departure of Bloomfield, Butterfield changed his sound and added a horn section for *The Resurrection Of Pigboy Crabshaw* (1967), considered to be the band's last blues album.

Canned Heat

(Vocal/instrumental group, 1966–present)

Comprising Bob Hite (vocals, harmonica), Al Wilson (guitar, harmonica, vocals), Henry Vestine (guitar), Larry Taylor (bass) and Fito De La Perra (drums), this Los Angeles band's heyday was between 1966–70, when covers of the Memphis Jug Band's 'On The Road Again' and Henry Thomas's 'Goin' Up The Country' propelled them up the charts. A teaming with John Lee Hooker, *Hooker 'N Heat* (1971), is a highlight in a long slide to the oldies circuit, which began with the fatal overdose of Wilson in 1970 and included the death of Hite in 1981.

Ron Carter

(Bass, piccolo bass, b. 1937)

A consummately professional bassist, Ron Carter possesses a distinctive tone and phenomenal dexterity that place him at the upper level of jazz rhythmists. In the early 1960s Carter joined drummer Chico Hamilton's popular quintet, then worked with Eric Dolphy, Don Ellis, Thelonious Monk, Cannonball Adderley and Art Farmer. From 1963–68 Carter played in Miles Davis's immortal rhythm section with Herbie Hancock and Tony Williams. He has an equally sturdy background in classical music.

Right
Bassist Ron Carter has played in some of jazz's most influential and popular ensembles.

see Introduction pp 238 *see* Sources & Sounds pp 240 *see* Key Artists pp 248

Clifton Chenier

(Accordion, vocals, 1925–87)

This Opelousas, Louisiana native cut his teeth on French dance tunes flavoured by Creole blues, as played by his musical forebear Amédée Ardoin. Chenier invented the zydeco style by adding elements of R&B, country and rock'n'roll, combined with a swinging beat. He enjoyed a string of hit singles, including his career-making 1955 US hit 'Eh, Petit Fille'. Chenier's son C.J. joined his band in 1978, and today C.J. carries on his father's musical tradition, updated with a twist of funk. Clifton's blues guitarist cousin Roscoe Chenier also regularly tours.

Don Cherry

(Cornet, 1936–95)

Besides serving as the perfect complement for Ornette Coleman in the saxophonist's early quartet, cornettist Don Cherry was a pioneer of the now-popular 'world music' movement. His musician father brought the family to Los Angeles from Cherry's birthplace in Oklahoma, where Cherry played in the Jazz Messiahs before meeting Coleman. After leaving the Coleman group and moving to New York, Cherry co-led the New York Contemporary Five with Archie Shepp and then earned a recording contract with Blue Note, resulting in the classic albums *Complete Communion* (1965) and *Symphony for Improvisers* (1966).

In 1968 he gathered artists from Europe and America, performing music inspired by the Balinese gamelan and Middle Eastern sounds. *Eternal Rhythm*, recorded that year, is a fine early document of his jazz-world music fusions. Cherry continued to investigate sounds inside and outside jazz, working with Turkish musicians, the cross-cultural trio Codona, more mainstream jazz groups, a Coleman repertory quartet called Old and New Dreams, and Coleman himself on occasion. He is the father of pop singers Neneh and Eagle Eye Cherry.

Below

Cornettist Don Cherry, here playing an African hunter's harp, helped to introduce music from other cultures into the western world.

see John Lee Hooker pp 158 see Ornette Coleman pp 248 see Mike Bloomfield pp 267 see Archie Shepp pp 279

Albert Collins

(Guitar, vocals, 1932–93)

Collins's highly original and bold, chiselled tone – achieved through an idiosyncratic tuning and high volume – earned the Texan his nickname 'The Iceman'. The moniker was abetted by a string of chilly-themed, early 1960s instrumental hits that incorporated R&B rhythms, including the million-selling 'Frosty', 'Sno Cone' and 'Thaw Out'.

Above
Texan guitarist Albert Collins, whose hard, cold tone earned him the nickname 'The Iceman'.

Although his cousin was Lightnin' Hopkins, Collins's agressive playing style was primarily influenced by T-Bone Walker and Gatemouth Brown. He played almost exclusively on the so-called 'crawfish circuit' in Louisiana and Texas, reaching mostly black audiences.

He crossed over to the mainstream in the late 1960s, when he moved to California and was adopted by San Francisco's psychedelic rock scene. Nonetheless, he achieved his greatest popularity after signing with Chicago-based Alligator Records in 1978, playing the Montreux Jazz Festival and winning a Grammy for 1985's *Showdown!*, a collaboration with Robert Cray and Johnny Copeland. Collins was still among the top attractions in blues when he died from cancer in 1993.

Larry Coryell

(Guitar, b. 1943)

Guitarist Larry Coryell got his start in New York with Chico Hamilton. He was a trailblazer of both free jazz and jazz-rock fusion in groups such as the Free Spirits – with saxophonist Jim Pepper and drummer Bob Moses – and in vibist Gary Burton's band. A remarkable technician, Coryell also ventured into free-jazz territory with the Jazz Composers Orchestra Association, dug deeper in to pyrotechnic fusion with the Eleventh House and performed crystalline acoustic jazz in the mid-1970s.

Cream

(Vocal/instrumental group, 1966–68)

In 1966, Eric Clapton (guitar) joined Jack Bruce (bass, vocals, harmonica) and Ginger Baker (drums) to form Cream, the first rock supergroup. These virtuosos fused blues, rock and jazz-like improvisation into a sound that became so popular it altered modern blues from a primarily vocal style into a music dominated by the electric guitar. Their albums *Fresh Cream* (1966), *Disraeli Gears* (1967) and *Wheels Of Fire* (1968) remain dramatic examples of modern blues reinterpretation.

Jack DeJohnette

(Drums, piano, b. 1942)

Few drummers successfully bridge the gap between free jazz and bebop to the same extent as Jack DeJohnette. An intensely intuitive player, young DeJohnette played early on with Jackie McLean and Charles Lloyd. In 1969 he replaced Tony Williams in Miles Davis's electric ensemble, appearing on the essential *Bitches Brew* (1969). After leaving Davis he led the fusion ensemble Compost and the expansive, compositional groups New Directions and Special Edition. He has also recorded many albums in trio with Keith Jarrett and bassist Gary Peacock.

see Introduction pp 238 *see* Sources & Sounds pp 240 *see* Key Artists pp 248

Eric Dolphy

(Alto saxophone, bass clarinet, flute, 1928–64)

In the six years before his untimely death, Eric Dolphy became one of the most beloved and influential

musicians in jazz. Brilliant on alto saxophone, he also helped to legitimize the flute and bass clarinet as viable jazz horns. Dolphy worked in relative obscurity until 1958, when he was discovered and hired by popular drummer Chico Hamilton.

He earned positive attention from the jazz press and moved on to work with Charles Mingus in 1960. Dolphy also looked into 'third stream' fusions of jazz and classical music with John Lewis and Gunther Schuller, as well as intense music with Ornette Coleman, John Coltrane and his own groups. Oliver Nelson's 1961 album *Blues And The Abstract Truth* featured the imposing front line of Dolphy and Freddie Hubbard. *Out To Lunch*, recorded in February 1964, is perhaps his most fully realized work. Not long after touring Europe with Mingus, Dolphy died suddenly in Berlin.

Kenny Dorham

(Trumpet, 1924–72)

The star of fame never shone brightly enough upon trumpeter Kenny Dorham, who too often took a back seat to his peers. He played with Dizzy Gillespie, Billy Eckstine and Lionel Hampton before joining Charlie Parker's bebop band in 1948. Dorham was a founding member of Art Blakey's Jazz Messengers in 1954, then replaced Clifford Brown in Max Roach's quartet. He led several fine sessions for Blue Note and Riverside before dying of kidney disease.

Snooks Eaglin

(Guitar, vocals, b. 1936)

Glaucoma and a brain tumour left Eaglin blind at the age of 19 months, but his unorthodox fingerpicking style and a sensibility based on the Crescent City's Caribbean rhythms made him the king of New Orleans guitar. He first performed gospel in churches, before turning to blues and recording his debut album, *New Orleans Street Singer* (1959). Eaglin's music became more sophisticated through associations with Dave Bartholomew and Professor Longhair, and he remains a vital performer, although he rarely tours.

Left
In addition to his skilful saxophone playing, Eric Dolphy raised the profile of the flute and bass clarinet in jazz music.

Art Farmer

(Trumpet, flugelhorn, 1928–99)

Art Farmer was largely responsible for popularizing the mellow-toned flugelhorn as a solo jazz instrument. A wonderfully lyrical player, he came up in Los Angeles' Central Avenue jazz clubs in the 1940s and worked with Lionel Hampton, Horace Silver, Gerry Mulligan and alto saxophonist Gigi Gryce. In 1959–62 he and tenor saxophonist Benny Golson led the Jazztet, which had a hit with 'Killer Joe'. Farmer was based in Europe from 1968 onwards.

Below
Art Farmer (right), pictured with fellow leader of the Jazztet Benny Golson, was jazz music's main exponent of the flugelhorn.

see Clarence 'Gatemouth' Brown pp 218 *see* Professor Longhair pp 229 *see* Freddie Hubbard pp 256 *see* Keith Jarrett pp 307

Right
Stan Getz, a distinctive saxophonist and instigator of the early 1960s bossa nova trend.

Below
Guitarist Peter Green (centre) gave Fleetwood Mac a blues sound in the band's early days.

Fleetwood Mac

(Vocal/instrumental group, 1968–present)

Many fans who love Fleetwood Mac's string of 1970s hits are unaware of their earlier blues explorations. The band came into being when guitarist Peter Green, drummer Mick Fleetwood and bassist John McVie broke away from John Mayall's Bluesbreakers. In 1968, with Jeremy Spencer on second guitar, Fleetwood Mac debuted on Blue Horizon. A third guitarist, Danny Kirwan, joined in time for the band to gig in Chicago with Willie Dixon and Otis Spann. Their original tunes and covers of blues classics (e.g. 'I Need Your Love So Bad') testified to the band's aptitude.

In 1970, after the release of the album *Then Play On*, Green became burned out on LSD and was replaced by keyboardist Christine Perfect. Then, during the 1971 tour, Spencer joined the Children Of God cult. The blues content of Fleetwood Mac's music dwindled as they began to lean towards mainstream rock. By the time the band achieved superstar status in 1975, their blues days were over. The band has survived several personnel changes and break-ups, remaining a popular concert draw.

Stan Getz

(Tenor saxophone, 1927–91)

Stan Getz was one of many white tenor saxophonists influenced by Lester Young, but as he matured he developed a distinctive sound of his own. After working with Jack Teagarden, Stan Kenton, Jimmy Dorsey and Benny Goodman, Getz became one of the 'Four Brothers' in Woody Herman's Second Herd. From the 1950s onwards Getz led his own sessions, heading the massive bossa nova craze of the early 1960s. He initiated many original projects and was widely admired – by John Coltrane among others – for his lyrical virtuosity.

Charlie Haden

(Bass, b. 1937)

Charlie Haden's famed work with Ornette Coleman represents just one small facet of the versatile bassist's career. As a child in Iowa he performed on radio with his family's country and western band. At 15 he took up the bass while recovering from polio, acquiring a novel technique that makes his notes resonate deeply. Haden moved to Los Angeles in 1957 to find jazz work.

see Introduction pp 238 *see* Sources & Sounds pp 240 *see* Key Artists pp 248

He met pianist Paul Bley and altoist Ornette Coleman, who were trying out new ideas that formed the roots of free jazz.

After leaving the Coleman quartet, Haden began looking into folk music and assembled his politically inspired Liberation Music Orchestra in 1969. Haden has worked in a trio with saxophonist Jan Garbarek and guitarist Egberto Gismonti, and duetted with Pat Metheny; he has also collaborated with pianists Gonzalo Rubalcaba and Hank Jones. In the 1980s he formed his popular Quartet West.

John Hammond Jr.

(Guitar, harmonica, vocals, b. 1942)

The son of A&R genius John Hammond, this New York City native left home at the age of 19 to perform professionally. He remains primarily an acoustic player, in the tradition of the classic Delta musicians. Hammond cut a fine series of LPs during 1964–76, encapsulated on 2000's *Best Of The Vanguard Years*. He notably joined Mike Bloomfield and Dr. John for *Triumvirate* (1973). Hammond's career also got a boost from *Wicked Grin* (2001), an album of Tom Waits' songs that introduced him to a new audience.

Slim Harpo

(Harmonica, guitar, vocals, 1924–70)

Born James Moore in Lobdell, Louisiana, Harpo developed an upbeat style playing juke joints and parties before signing to Excello Records in 1955, where he was instrumental in defining the label's 'swamp-blues' sound. He had a profound influence on 1960s rockers including Van Morrison, the Kinks and the Rolling Stones, who covered Harpo's 'I'm A King Bee' and 'Shake Your Hips'. Harpo died from a heart attack in Baton Rouge, Louisiana.

Jimi Hendrix

(Guitar, vocals, 1942–70)

This left-handed Seattle, Washington native taught himself to play by flipping over a $5 acoustic guitar and copying licks from blues, R&B and rock'n'roll records. Hendrix apprenticed on the R&B circuit, backing up Little Richard among others, and mastered techniques from the stuttering ninth chords of James Brown sideman Jimmy Nolen to the epic string-bending of Albert King.

Hendrix's solo career ignited when he was discovered at Greenwich Village's Café Wha? by Animals' bassist Chas Chandler, who became his manager and moved Hendrix to London. The Jimi Hendrix Experience was formed and the group's debut LP *Are You Experienced?* (1967) became an international smash, fortified by Hendrix's flamboyant performing style. Throughout Hendrix's three brief years as an international pop star, his music became increasingly experimental, but even his incendiary version of the 'Star-Spangled Banner', recorded live at Woodstock and full of feedback explosions, showed his unswerving devotion to blues tonality.

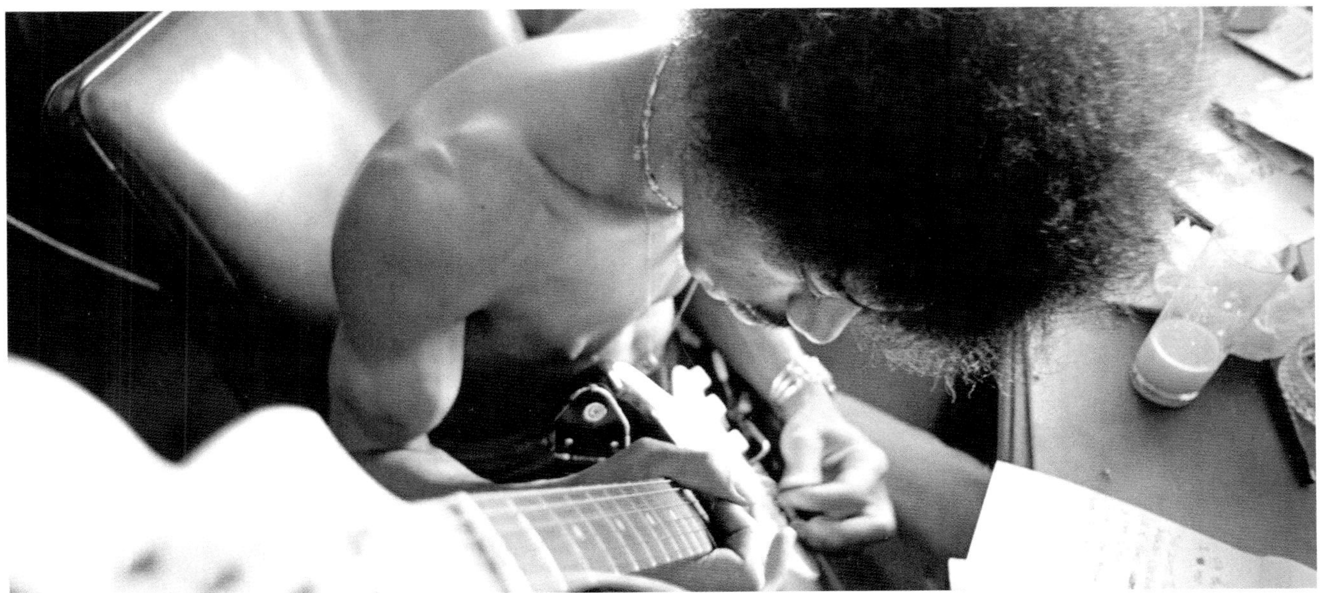

Left
Guitar legend Jimi Hendrix, whose love of the blues is evident in the blues-tinged rock music he produced.

see Lester Young pp 118 *see* Albert King pp 258 *see* Paul Bley pp 267 *see* Dr. John pp 298

Elvin Jones

(Drums, 1927–2004)

Powerhouse drummer Elvin Jones was the engine of John Coltrane's legendary quartet in the 1960s, appearing on most of the saxophonist's most popular recordings. He was the younger brother of pianist Hank and trumpeter Thad Jones and had worked with Bud Powell, Miles Davis, Sonny Rollins and J.J. Johnson prior to joining Coltrane. A masterful innovator of polyrhythms, after a brief stint with the Duke Ellington Orchestra, he formed Elvin Jones Jazz Machine and helmed it until his death. In his last years he also collaborated annually with pianist Cecil Taylor.

Above
After working extensively with John Coltrane's quartet, Elvin Jones led his own Jazz Machine band.

Janis Joplin

(Vocals, 1943–70)

Influenced by Bessie Smith, Joplin became a rock star while in San Francisco's Big Brother & the Holding Company, and enjoyed a meteoric solo career before her untimely death from a heroin overdose in Los Angeles. Nonetheless, she was perhaps the most commanding female blues singer of the modern era. Joplin's raw emotional expression and fiery presence overruled complaints about her straying intonation both in concert and on albums like Big Brother's *Cheap Thrills* (1968) and the posthumous *Pearl* (1971).

Freddie King

(Guitar, vocals, 1934–76)

Few bluesmen have possessed the bristling intensity of Freddie King, whose stinging vibrato and energetic, soaring vocal style influenced Eric Clapton. King was born in Gilmer, Texas and learned guitar from his mother at age six. He moved to Chicago in 1950, earning a reputation among peers like Buddy Guy and Otis Rush with his gritty approach.

His 1950s recordings for the Cobra label were not released, but King made his mark after signing with Cincinnati's Federal/King Records in 1960. His Federal/King sides included the oft-covered instrumentals 'Hideaway' and 'San-Ho-Zay', as well as 'Have You Ever Loved A Woman', subsequently made famous by Derek & the Dominos. Waning interest in blues left him without a contract in 1965, but King was soon accepted by white rock audiences and toured England extensively between 1967 and 1969. He played clubs and festivals and recorded for major labels until his heart failed after a Dallas concert.

Rahsaan Roland Kirk

(Saxophones, clarinet, flute, various invented instruments, 1936–77)

Reeds player Rahsaan Roland Kirk was one of jazz's most colourful figures, an eccentric who developed a method for playing two or three horns simultaneously. Accidentally blinded at the age of two, Kirk taught himself to play several instruments. At 15 he joined an R&B band, and at 20 he made his first record. He modified his unusual pawn-shop horns, the manzello and stritch, with extended keys, developed the skill

Right
Rahsaan Roland Kirk plays the saxophone at Ronnie Scott's jazz club in London.

see Introduction pp 238 *see* Sources & Sounds pp 240 *see* Key Artists pp 248

of circular breathing, enabling him to hold notes indefinitely, and eventually built the discipline to play two separate melodies at once.

In 1961 Kirk worked with Charles Mingus, then continued his solo career with exceptional recordings, such as *Rip, Rig And Panic* (1965). He regularly modified his instruments and took on the mysterious name 'Rahsaan' after a dream. Although partially paralyzed by a stroke at 40, Kirk kept playing his horns until his death in 1977.

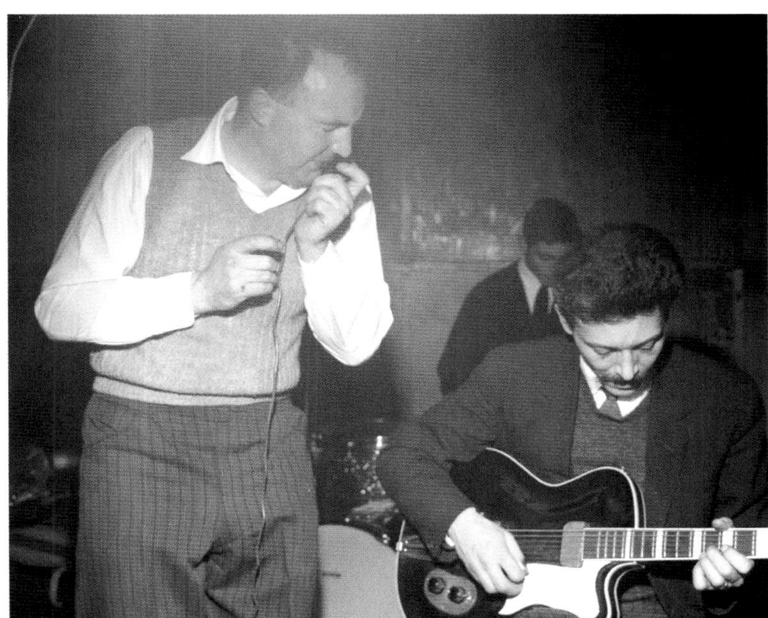

Left
Guitarist and blues promoter Alexis Korner (right) with harmonica player Cyril Davies and drummer Charlie Watts (seated behind) in Blues Incorporated.

Alexis Korner's Blues Incorporated

(Vocal/instrumental group, 1962–67)

Alexis Korner (guitar, piano, vocals), born in Paris, France in 1928, was considered to be the father of electric British blues. When he and Cyril Davies (harmonica, vocals) formed Blues Incorporated in 1962 with Dick Heckstall-Smith (saxophone), Andy Hoogenboom (bass), Ken Scott (piano) and Charlie Watts (drums), their amplified line-up met with resistance. So Korner and Davies opened their own venue, the Ealing Rhythm & Blues Club, beneath a London teashop in 1962; they were soon attracting large crowds of hipsters including Mick Jagger, Keith Richards and Brian Jones. Jack Bruce and Ginger Baker replaced Hoogenboom and Watts, and the group began a residency at the Marquee Club.

Their debut, the live *R&B From The Marquee* (1962), was the first British blues album. Yet commercial success evaded Korner, as the Rolling Stones, Bluesbreakers and other bands inspired and encouraged by him ascended. Korner remained musically active in the decades after Blues Incorporated, before dying of lung cancer in 1984.

Sammy Lawhorn

(Guitar, 1935–90)

Respected sideman Lawhorn began a nine-year stint with Muddy Waters' band in 1956 after working with harmonica players Sonny Boy Williamson II and Willie Cobbs, among others. Waters fired the Little Rock, Arkansas native in 1973 for excessive drinking. By then his razor-edged tone and imaginative soloing had already left an indelible mark on the blues. Lawhorn subsequently played on sides by James Cotton, Junior Wells and Koko Taylor. His death at the age of 54 was attributed to natural causes.

Sam Lay

(Drums, vocals, b. 1935)

Shuffle master Lay was an important figure in the racial integration of 1960s blues. He was born in Birmingham, Alabama and moved to Chicago, where he played with Little Walter, Howlin' Wolf and other Chess Records artists. He joined the Paul Butterfield Blues Band for its first two albums and played on Bob Dylan's *Highway 61 Revisited* as well as Dylan's electric debut at Newport in 1965. Lay leads his own band today and has also recently recorded with the Siegel-Schwall Band.

Little Milton

(Guitar, vocals, 1934–2005)

Born to sharecroppers in Inverness, Mississippi, the country music Milton Campbell heard in radio broadcasts from the Grand Ole Opry shaped his soulful sound as much as gospel and blues. After regional success, he signed to the Chess Records subsidiary Checker in 1961 and cut the classics 'If Walls Could Talk', 'Feel So Bad' and 'Grits Ain't Groceries', among others. Up until his death in 2005 he was a major artist on the chitlin circuit, recording for Jackson, Mississippi's Malaco Records.

see Bessie Smith pp 64 *see* Charles Mingus pp 230 *see* Rolling Stones pp 278 *see* Cecil Taylor pp 280

Above
Jazz-rock pioneer Herbie Mann was one of the first mainstream jazz players to make the flute his main instrument.

Charles Lloyd

(Various saxophones, b. 1938)

Charles Lloyd was an inspirational figure in 1960s jazz and was also enthusiastically embraced by the hippy culture. He moved from playing blues in Memphis to West Coast jazz with Gerald Wilson and Chico Hamilton. His quartet with pianist Keith Jarrett, bassist Ron McClure and drummer Jack DeJohnette was the first American jazz group to tour the Soviet Union. In 1969 he retired to teach transcendental meditation, before returning triumphantly at the 1982 Montreux Jazz Festival. Lloyd has since made a series of excellent albums for ECM.

Robert Lockwood Jr.

(Guitar, harmonica, vocals, 1915–2006)

Lockwood is thought to be the only musician given lessons by Robert Johnson, who was infatuated with Lockwood's mother. But Lockwood, who was raised in Helena, Arkansas, also assimilated jazz chords and swinging rhythms to become one of the most sophisticated guitarists to emerge from the Delta. After decades as a sideman and songwriter, Lockwood resided in Cleveland, Ohio, where until his death in 2006 he led a big band, and travelled the world playing solo in Johnson's style.

Magic Sam

(Guitar, vocals, 1937–69)

Along with peers Otis Rush and Buddy Guy, Mississippi native Samuel Maghett pioneered the ghetto-born mix of soul singing and guitar pyrotechnics that defined Chicago's West Side sound. 'Easy Baby' and 'All Your Love', cut for Cobra in the 1950s, are his signature tunes, but his Delmark LP *West Side Soul* (1967) is a classic example of raw, open-hearted emotional expression. He died unexpectedly of a heart attack just as his career was gaining momentum.

Herbie Mann

(Tenor saxophone, flute, 1930–2003)

Flautist Herbie Mann was a popularizer of the flute in jazz, an investigator of far-flung ethnic music traditions and a pioneer of jazz-rock fusion. Mann began as a tenor saxophonist but eventually became the most commercially successful of the few jazz players to concentrate exclusively on the flute. He fronted an Afro-Latin group in the late 1950s, then had a major crossover hit with 'Comin' Home Baby' and popular success with *Memphis Underground* (1968). Mann focused upon Brazilian-tinged jazz later in his career, and at the end of his life explored the music of his Central European Jewish ancestry.

John Mayall's Bluesbreakers

(Vocal/instrumental group, 1963–present)

Talented bandleader John Mayall (vocals, piano, organ, harmonica), born in Macclesfield, Cheshire in 1933, is largely responsible for igniting the popularity of British blues as well as the careers of famed guitarists Eric Clapton, Peter Green (Fleetwood Mac) and Mick Taylor (the Rolling Stones). Mayall's 1966 debut album *Blues Breakers*, using Chicago blues as a model, established the reputation of Clapton and also featured John McVie (bass) and Hughie Flint (drums). The album reached number six on the UK charts. Powerfully realized, it remains the seminal British electric blues album and began a streak of

Bluesbreakers classics, including *A Hard Road* (with Green, 1967) and *Crusade* (with Taylor, 1967).

Mayall began a parallel solo career with the underrated *The Blues Alone* (1968) that peaked the next year, following his relocation to California with *The Turning Point* and its FM-radio staple 'Room To Move'. Mayall continues to perform with a version of his Bluesbreakers and remains one of the few white blues performers whose songwriting equals that of his heroes Muddy Waters and J.B. Lenoir.

Wes Montgomery

(Guitar, 1925–68)

Wes Montgomery was a premier jazz guitarist; his unique guitar sound came from plucking octave figures with his thumb instead of a pick. Born into a musical family, Wes taught himself to play the guitar and toured with Lionel Hampton in the late 1940s. He performed with his brothers, bassist Monk and vibist Buddy, before beginning a solo career that brought him to the top of the jazz sales charts. He moved successfully into pop-jazz crossovers, under the direction of producer Creed Taylor, before his sudden death from a heart attack.

Lee Morgan

(Trumpet, 1938–72)

Born in Philadelphia, trumpeter Lee Morgan led one of the storybook lives in jazz. He joined Art Blakey's Jazz Messengers in 1958, having already worked with Dizzy Gillespie and John Coltrane. A magnificent hard-bop stylist who effectively utilized half-valve techniques and staccato blowing, Morgan was a star of the Blue Note Records roster, hitting the R&B top 10 in 1964 with the instrumental 'The Sidewinder'. Tragically, he was murdered by a woman who considered herself his wife outside a jazz club in 1972.

Sunny Murray

(Drums, b. 1937)

James 'Sunny' Murray is one of the quintessential free-jazz drummers. His most enduring legacy may be his many recordings with Cecil Taylor and Albert Ayler, which belie his beginnings with stride pianist Willie 'The Lion' Smith and swing era trumpeter Henry 'Red' Allen. Murray was as melodic on drums as Taylor was percussive on the piano, resulting in a stellar combination. He moved to France in the 1980s and has since led his own sessions.

Left
Self-taught guitarist Wes Montgomery created his own unique sound by using his thumb in place of a pick.

Below
One of hard-bop's greatest trumpeters, Lee Morgan was a regular on the Blue Note Records roster.

see J.B. Lenoir pp 228 *see* Albert Ayler pp 266 *see* Otis Rush pp 278 *see* British Blues pp 429

Right
Archie Shepp developed a distinctive tenor saxophone sound that drew inspiration from the jazz of his contemporaries as well as the jazz giants of the 1930s.

Joe Pass

(Guitar, 1929–94)

Although drug addiction nearly killed the promising career of Joe Pass, he became one of the most influential and beloved guitarists in jazz. As a young man Pass played with various swing bands, then fell into heroin abuse while in the military. He recorded his first album while in rehabilitation in 1962, showcasing his impressive technique of splitting melodic and accompanying figures. From the mid-1970s until his death from cancer, Pass was a true jazz star, particularly as a solo performer and in recordings with Ella Fitzgerald.

Pinetop Perkins

(Piano, guitar, b. 1913)

Belzoni, Mississippi's Perkins performed throughout the Delta until 1949, when he relocated to Chicago to play with Robert Nighthawk and Earl Hooker through the 1950s. In 1969 he replaced Otis Spann in Muddy Waters' band. Perkins stayed until 1980, when he, Calvin Jones (bass), Jerry Portnoy (harmonica) and Willie Smith (drums) left Waters to form the Legendary Blues Band. Perkins still works as a solo artist and with the Muddy Waters Tribute Band.

Below
Sam Rivers hosted free jazz sessions throughout the 1970s in his Studio RivBea, which served as a launch pad for the careers of many up-and-coming musicians.

Yank Rachell

(Mandolin, guitar, harmonica, violin, vocals, 1910–97)

Rachell and fellow Brownsville, Tennessee musicians Sleepy John Estes and Hammie Nixon played throughout the mid-South in the 1920s, eventually relocating to Memphis. Rachell and Estes partnered with pianist Jab Jones, recording for Victor as the Three J's Jug Band. During the 1930s and 1940s, Rachell played with John Lee 'Sonny Boy' Williamson. In 1962 he reunited with Estes and Nixon, recording and touring as Yank Rachell's Tennessee Jug-Busters on Chicago's Delmark label.

Sam Rivers

(Various saxophones, flute, b. 1923)

Sam Rivers boasts a most impressive résumé: bebop with Tadd Dameron and Dizzy Gillespie, hard bop with Miles Davis, free jazz with Cecil Taylor and Anthony Braxton, and Grammy consideration for his big band. Born in Oklahoma, Rivers played around Florida and Boston in the 1950s before settling in New York City. His 1960s Blue Note records were edgy and impressive. He hosted free jazz sessions at his loft Studio RivBea through the 1970s and helped to launch the careers of bassist Dave Holland and saxophonist Steve Coleman, among others.

Rolling Stones

(Vocal/instrumental group, 1962–present)

The Rolling Stones' original line-up comprised Mick Jagger (vocals, harmonica), Brian Jones and Keith Richards (guitars), Bill Wyman (bass) and Charlie Watts (drums). The band balanced R&B and blues with pop and psychedelia, releasing the heavily blues-influenced *Beggars Banquet* in 1968. Following the loss of Jones, who drowned in 1969, and the addition of Mick Taylor, the Stones released three more blues rock masterpieces: *Let It Bleed* (1969), *Sticky Fingers* (1971) and *Exile On Main Street* (1972). Now minus Wyman and Taylor, and with Ronnie Wood on guitar, the Stones continue to roll.

Otis Rush

(Guitar, vocals, b. 1934)

Rush, who was born in Philadelphia, Mississippi, was – along with Buddy Guy and Magic Sam – part of the defining trinity of Chicago's West Side sound. His 1950s Cobra Records singles 'All Your Love (I Miss Loving)' and 'I Can't Quit You Baby' became standards. Rush is undoubtedly a genius, with a big soulful voice and an unpredictable command of the

see Introduction pp 238 *see* Sources & Sounds pp 240 *see* Key Artists pp 248

guitar, but music-business troubles and his own erratic personality have impeded his career.

Archie Shepp

(Tenor and soprano saxophones, b. 1937)

Acid-toned saxophonist Archie Shepp was a principal figure in the second wave of free-jazz artists. Also recognized as a playwright and poet, Shepp was an articulate spokesman for Black Power. He emerged in 1960 as a member of Cecil Taylor's group, then collaborated with trumpeter Bill Dixon, Don Cherry and John Coltrane, most notably on Coltrane's powerful *Ascension*. In the late 1970s Shepp moved decisively away from free jazz into more mainstream projects, such as a programme of ballads and gospel songs in duet with pianist Horace Parlan.

Left
Saxophonist Wayne Shorter played and composed for Miles Davis's ambitious groups of the 1960s.

Wayne Shorter

(Tenor and soprano saxophones, b. 1933)

Wayne Shorter's most significant early position was in Maynard Ferguson's orchestra in 1958, where he met pianist Joe Zawinul. In 1959 Shorter joined Art Blakey's Jazz Messengers and soon thereafter made his debut as a leader. He gained prominence as a member of Miles Davis's ambitious groups from 1964–70, in which his unusual, compelling compositions were often featured, and as a Blue Note Records leader and sideman. Shorter teamed with Zawinul and bassist Miroslav Vitous in 1970 to form Weather Report, which became one of the world's most popular fusion bands.

Shorter's album *Native Dancer* (1974) introduced Brazilian singer Milton Nascimento to North America, and he was also in the repertory group VSOP with Herbie Hancock and Freddie Hubbard. Shorter left Weather Report in 1985, then toured with rock guitarist Carlos Santana and recorded with Joni Mitchell and Steely Dan. His own projects were intermittent until 1992, when a dying Miles Davis urged him to step forth. Shorter has led his own ensembles since then, acknowledged as a major, if still elusive, jazz voice.

Siegel-Schwall Band

(Vocal/instrumental group, 1964–present)

College mates Corky Siegel (harmonica, piano) and Jim Schwall (guitar) started out as a duo. They softened the electric blues they heard in Chicago with acoustic guitar and folk-music leanings. They expanded – adding Jos Davidson (bass, vocals) and Russ Chadwick (drums) – and made their debut album for the Vanguard label in 1966. They disbanded in 1974 following a unique blues *concerto grosso* by William Russo with the Chicago Symphony Orchestra, but reformed in 1988 and released the live *Siegel-Schwall Reunion Concert*.

Otis Spann

(Piano, vocals, 1930–70)

The finest post-war blues pianist, Spann learned to play at churches and parties around his Jackson, Mississippi birthplace. From 1952 until his death from cancer, he was house keyboardist at Chess Records, recording with Muddy Waters, Bo Diddley, Sonny Boy Williamson, Howlin' Wolf, Little Walter and others. Although Spann made a clutch of fine solo recordings, including the first Candid release, *Otis Spann Is The Blues* (1960) and duets with Robert Lockwood, he is best known as Waters' music director.

see Ella Fitzgerald pp 124 *see* Buddy Guy pp 254 *see* Don Cherry pp 269 *see* Steve Coleman pp 333

Taj Mahal

(Guitar, banjo, bass, harmonica, mandolin, piano, vocals, b. 1942)

Henry Saint Clair Fredericks' concept of the blues was formed partly by his West Indian father's diverse record collection and partly by his coming of age in the collegiate coffeehouses of western Massachusetts. Since Taj Mahal's eponymous debut in 1967, followed in 1968 by a role in *The Rolling Stones' Rock And Roll Circus*, he has challenged purists by employing the sounds and beats of Caribbean, African, Latin and American folk styles. He remains a tireless performer and champion of earlier artists.

Above

Fascinated by folk and world music, Taj Mahal incorporated their sounds and rhythms in his music.

Cecil Taylor

(Piano, b. 1929)

Since the late 1950s, pianist Cecil Taylor has maintained a prime position in the pantheon of free jazz. He was one of the first jazzmen to jettison standard chord changes, fixed rhythms and expected ensemble roles in the interest of musical democracy. Taylor developed his unorthodox style while studying at New England Conservatory. Duke Ellington, Thelonious Monk and Lennie Tristano were among his major influences. Taylor debuted in 1956 with *Jazz Advance!*.

He treats the piano as a percussion instrument, hammering out dissonant chords and long, sinuous melody lines, and has been both condemned and praised for his innovations. Besides leading magnificent ensembles – the best of which featured alto saxophonist Jimmy Lyons – and collaborating with artists ranging from Mary Lou Williams and Max Roach to the dancer Mikhail Baryshnikov, Taylor is also a commanding solo performer. He is tirelessly adept at forming beauty out of seeming chaos, and his performances can last for hours.

Ten Years After

(Vocal/instrumental group, 1967–present)

This UK rock band from Nottingham, comprising Chick Churchill (keyboards), Alvin Lee (guitar, vocals), Ric Lee (drums) and Leo Lyons (bass), emerged as a vehicle for Alvin Lee's speed-demon playing. Their sound was most notably captured on the Woodstock soundtrack in an 11-minute version of the group's signature song, 'Goin' Home'. They toured the US 28 times and are ably represented by the CD *Anthology 1967–1971*. The classic line-up lasted until 1975, when Alvin Lee left, however the band reformed in 1989.

Stan Tracey

(Piano, accordion, vibraphone, composer, arranger, b. 1926)

Stan Tracey is one of the UK's most original and talented jazz musicians, yet he has always remained underrated by critics; Sonny Rollins is quoted as asking 'Does anyone here realize how good he really is?'. Londoner Tracey was playing professionally from the age of 16, before landing the job of house pianist in Ronnie Scott's Soho jazz club. There he accompanied the big names of the day, including Zoot Sims, Stan Getz, Roland Kirk and Sonny Rollins, with whom he recorded the soundtrack for the film *Alfie* (1966). He played solo and in various line-ups ranging from duos to big bands, and had a big hit with his 1965 album *Under Milk Wood*, inspired by Dylan Thomas's audio play and featuring the breathy saxophone playing of Bobby Wellins.

Tracey has released over 45 albums and has received an OBE as well as various music awards. He has continued to compose, tour and record and has also taught for many years at London's Guildhall School of Music. Despite his long career and life in the jazz fast-lane,Tracey has remained refreshingly self-effacing and down-to-earth.

McCoy Tyner

(Piano, b. 1938)

McCoy Tyner will forever be remembered for his role in John Coltrane's great 1960s quartet. Born in Philadelphia and a member of jazz groups including the Jazztet, Tyner proved to be perfectly compatible with Coltrane until the saxophonist moved into free jazz, at which point the pianist left the band. Tyner worked

see Introduction pp 238 *see* Sources & Sounds pp 240 *see* Key Artists pp 248

as a sideman and leader for Blue Note during the rest of the decade, and gained further recognition after signing with Milestone Records. He has continued to lead his own sessions, ranging from solos, trios and larger combos to big bands.

Johnny 'Guitar' Watson

(Guitar, piano, vocals, 1935–96)

The self-proclaimed 'Gangster Of Love', Watson learned piano from his father in Houston, Texas but became known for his terse, stinging guitar, which influenced Frank Zappa and has been sampled by rappers. Etta James patterned her early singing after Watson's declarative vocals, best immortalized along with his wicked instrumental prowess on King and Federal singles from 1953 to 1963, including 'Motorhead Baby' and 'Space Guitar'. He suffered a fatal heart attack onstage in Japan.

Junior Wells

(Harmonica, vocals, 1934–98)

Amos Blackmore grew up in west Memphis, Arkansas under the sway of Sonny Boy Williamson II and began recording as a teenager in Chicago, playing with the innovative Four Aces before joining Muddy Waters' band. Wells created a personal style influenced by James Brown. In the mid-1960s he began a long association with guitarist Buddy Guy (who played on Wells's masterful 1965 debut LP *Hoodoo Man Blues*, Delmark Records), which lasted until Wells's death from cancer in 1998.

Tony Williams

(Drums, 1945–97)

Aged 14, Boston-born drum prodigy Tony Williams worked professionally with tenor saxophonist Sam Rivers. In 1962 he went to New York, played with Jackie McLean, then became part of one of Miles Davis's greatest bands. A dazzling colourist and dynamic rhythm-maker, Williams recorded two albums for Blue Note and played with many of the label's stars before establishing the breakthrough fusion band Lifetime. After a hiatus, Williams re-emerged in the late 1980s, leading a post-bop quintet of promising young players. He died of a heart attack in 1997 aged 51.

Left
Johnny 'Guitar' Watson, whose stinging guitar style complemented his declarative vocals.

Below
Harmonica ace Junior Wells dances onstage during a 1960s gig.

Yardbirds

(Vocal/instrumental group, 1963–68)

The Chicago blues-inspired Yardbirds, featuring Keith Relf (vocals, harmonica), Eric Clapton and Chris Dreja (guitars), Paul Samwell-Smith (bass) and Jim McCarty (drums), took over the Rolling Stones' residency at London's Crawdaddy Club and backed Sonny Boy Williamson II on tour in 1963. Clapton left after the release of their debut album in 1963 and was replaced by Jeff Beck; a succession of pop hits followed. Guitarist Jimmy Page joined in 1966 and after Beck departed, Page and Dreja formed the New Yardbirds (an ensemble which would eventually develop into Led Zeppelin). A version of the Yardbirds reformed after their 1992 induction into the Rock And Roll Hall Of Fame and continues to tour.

see Lennie Tristano pp 184 *see* Sonny Rollins pp 233 *see* Sonny Boy Williamson II pp 235 *see* Sam Rivers pp 278

List of Artists

Entries appear in the following order: name, music style, year(s) of popularity, instruments, country of origin.

AB Skhy, Blues Rock, 1960s–1970s, Various instruments, American
Aberg, Lennart, Modern Jazz; Jazz Rock; Free Jazz, 1960s–, Saxophones, bandleader, Swedish
Abrams, Muhal Richard, Free Jazz, 1960s–, Piano, clarinet, composer, American
Acklin, Barbara, Rhythm & Blues, 1960s–1970s, Vocals, composer, American
Adderley, Cannonball, Hard Bop; Soul Jazz, 1960s–1970s, Saxophone, American
Adler, Danny, Funk; Rhythm & Blues, 1960s–1990s, Guitar, vocals, composer, American
Alegre All Stars, Latin Jazz, 1960s, Various instruments, American
Alexander, Arthur, Rhythm & Blues, 1960s–1970s, Vocals, composer, American
Alexander, Monty, Modern Jazz; Hard Bop, 1960s–, Piano, bandleader, Jamaican
Alexander, Roland, Modern Jazz; Bebop; Free Jazz, 1960s–1990s, Saxophone, American
Ali, Muhammad, Free Jazz, 1960s–, Drums, American
Ali, Rashied, Free Jazz, 1960s, Drums, American
Alias, Don, Modern Jazz; Fusion, 1960s–, Drums, American
Allen, Byron, Free Jazz, 1960s, Saxophone, American
Allman, Duane, Blues Rock, 1960s–1970s, Guitar, American
Altschul, Barry, Free Jazz, 1960s–, Drums, American
Ambrosetti, Franco, Hard Bop; Modern Jazz, 1960s–, Trumpet, flugelhorn, Swedish
Amy, Curtis, Soul Jazz; Modern Jazz, 1960s–2000s, Saxophone, bandleader, American
Anderson, Jimmy, Chicago Blues, 1960s–, Harmonica, vocals, American
Anderson, Miller, Blues Rock, 1960s–1990s, Guitar, vocals, British
Animals, The, British Blues; Blues Rock, 1960s–1980s, Various instruments, British
Ardley, Neil, Modern Jazz, 1960s–, Composer, keyboards, British
Armatage, John, Swing, 1960s–, Drums, British
Aronov, Ben, Modern Jazz; Swing, 1960s–, Piano, American
Ashton, Gardner & Dyke, Blues Rock, 1960s–1970s, Various instruments, British
Atkinson, Lisle, Modern Jazz, 1960s–, Bass, American
Auger, Brian, Jazz Rock; Fusion, 1960s–, Keyboards, vocals, British
Ayers, Roy, Soul Jazz; Fusion; Jazz Funk, 1960s–, Vibraphone, American
Ayler, Albert, Free Jazz, 1960s–1970s, Saxophone, American
Aztecs, The, Blues Rock, 1960s–1970s, Various instruments, Australian
Baden Powell, Roberto, Brazilian Jazz, 1960s–, Guitar, Brazilian
Baltazar, Gabe, Hard Bop; Bebop; Big Band, 1960s–, Saxophone, American
Barone, Gary, Modern Jazz; Big Band, 1960s–, Trumpet, flugelhorn, American
Barone, Mike, Big Band; Modern Jazz, 1960s–, Trombone, composer, arranger, American
Bartkowski, Czeslaw, Modern Jazz; Jazz Rock, 1960s–, Drums, Polish
Bartz, Gary, Modern Jazz, 1960s–, Saxophone, American
Bass, Fontella, Rhythm & Blues, 1960s–1970s, Vocals, American
Bass, Mickey, Modern Jazz, 1960s–, Bass, American
Bastin, Bruce, Country Blues; East Cost Blues, 1960s–, Author, producer, British
Bates, Colin, Swing; Traditional Jazz; Modern Jazz, 1960s–1990s, Piano, Australian
Beck, Gordon, Modern Jazz, 1960s–, Piano, British
Beck, Jeff, British Blues; Blues Rock, 1960s–, Piano, guitar, British
Beckett, Harry, British Jazz; Big Band, 1960s–, Trumpet, flugelhorn, Barbadian
Benjamin, Sathima Bea, Modern Jazz, 1960s–, Vocals, South African
Benko, Sandor, Dixieland, 1960s–, Clarinet, saxophone, bandleader, Hungarian
Bennett, Duster, British Blues; Blues Rock, 1960s–1970s, Vocals, harmonica, British
Bennett, Lou, Modern Jazz; Hard Bop, 1960s–1990s, Organ, bandleader, American
Bennett, Wayne, Rhythm & Blues; Texas Blues, 1960s–1980s, Guitar, American
Bennink, Han, Free Jazz, 1960s–, Percussion, Dutch
Benson, George, Smooth Jazz; Hard Bop, 1960s–, Guitar, vocals, American
Benton, Buster, Modern Electric Blues; Chicago Blues, 1960s–1990s, Guitar, vocals, American
Berger, Karl, Free Jazz, 1960s–, Vibraphone, German
Berk, Dick, Modern Jazz, 1960s–, Drums, American
Bernhardt, Warren, Modern Jazz, 1960s–, Keyboards, composer, American
Bertles, Bob, Jazz Rock; Free Jazz, 1960s–, Saxophones, Australian
Bertoncini, Gene, Cool Jazz; Modern Jazz, 1960s–, Guitar, American
Betts, Richard 'Dickie', Country Blues, 1960s–1980s, Guitar, American
Big Brother & the Holding Company, Blues Rock, 1960s–1990s, Various instruments, American
Bishop, Walter Jr, Bebop; Hard Bop, 1960s–1990s, Piano, American
Bizor, Billy, Texas Blues, 1960s, Vocals, American
Blake, Ran, Free Jazz; Modern Jazz, 1960s–, Piano, composer, American
Bley, Carla, Free Jazz; Big Band; Modern Jazz, 1960s–, Keyboards, composer, bandleader, American
Bley, Paul, Free Jazz, 1960s–, Piano, keyboards, composer, Canadian
Blind Faith, Blues Rock; British Blues, 1960s, Artist, British
Blodwyn Pig, Blues Rock, 1960s–1990s, Various instruments, British
Bloomfield, Michael, Modern Electric Blues; Chicago Blues, 1960s–1980s, Guitar, American
Blues Incorporated, British Blues, 1960s, Various instruments, British
Blues Project, The, Blues Rock, 1960s–1970s, Various instruments, American
Blythe, Arthur, Free Jazz; Modern Jazz; World Fusion, 1960s–, Saxophone, bandleader, American
Bohanon, George, Big Band; Jazz Rock, 1960s–, Trombone, euphonium, American
Bond, Graham, British Blues; Blues Rock, 1960s–1970s, Saxophone, keyboards, British
Bookbinder, Roy, Country Blues, 1960s–, Guitar, American
Booker, Walter, Modern Jazz, 1960s–, Bass, American
Boone, Richard, Modern Jazz; Big Band, 1960s–, Trombone, vocals, American
Bowie, Lester, Free Jazz, 1960s–1990s, Trumpet, flugelhorn, vocals, percussion, American
Brackeen, Charles, Free Jazz, 1960s–, Saxophone, American
Brackeen, JoAnne, Modern Jazz, 1960s–, Piano, composer, American
Braith, George, Modern Jazz; Soul Jazz, 1960s–, Saxophone, American
Breau, Lenny, Modern Jazz, 1960s–1980s, Guitar, American
Breuker, Willem, Big Band; Free Jazz, 1960s–, Saxophone, clarinet, composer, Dutch
Bridgewater, Cecil, Hard Bop; Modern Jazz, 1960s–, Trumpet, flugelhorn, arranger, composer, American
Broberg, Bosse, Big Band; Bebop; World Fusion, 1960s–, Trumpet, composer, Swedish
Brooks, Roy, Modern Jazz; Hard Bop, 1960s–, Drums, American
Brosnan, Mike, Fusion; Blues Rock; Country Blues, 1960s–, Piano, New Zealander
Brötzmann, Peter, Free Jazz, 1960s–, Saxophones, clarinet, German
Brown, Andrew, Chicago Blues, 1960s–1980s, Guitar, American
Brown, Marion, Free Jazz, 1960s–1990s, Saxophone, American
Brown, Maxine, Rhythm & Blues, 1960s–1970s, Vocals, American
Bruce, Jack, British Blues, 1960s–, Bass, Scottish
Bruford, Bill, Jazz Rock; Jazz Funk, 1960s–, Drums, British
Brunious, Wendell, New Orleans Jazz; Latin Jazz; Big Band; Traditional Jazz, 1960s–, Trumpet, bandleader, American
Bryant, Bobby, Big Band; Modern Jazz, 1960s–1990s, Trumpet, saxophone, American
Buckley, Tim, Jazz Rock, 1960s–1970s, Vocals, composer, American
Buford, 'Mojo' George, Chicago Blues, 1960s–, Harmonica, American
Bull, Sandy, World Fusion, 1960s–1980s, Guitar, banjo, vocals, American
Burdon, Eric, Blues Rock, 1960s–1980s, Vocals, British
Burnap, Campbell, British Jazz; Traditional Jazz, 1960s–, Trombone, vocals, British
Burnett, Carl, Modern Jazz, 1960s–, Drums, American
Burrell, Dave, Free Jazz, 1960s–, Piano, American
Burris, J.C., Country Blues, 1960s–1980s, Vocals, harmonica, American
Burrowes, Roy, Jamaican Jazz; Hard Bop; Bebop, 1960s–, Trumpet, Jamaican
Burton, Ann, Modern Jazz, 1960s–1980s, Vocals, Danish
Burton, Gary, Modern Jazz, 1960s–, Vibraphonist, bandleader, American
Burton, Rahn, Hard Bop; Free Jazz, 1960s–, Piano, composer, American
Butterfield, Paul, Chicago Blues; Blues Rock, 1960s–1980s, Harmonica, American
Cage, James 'Butch', Delta Blues, 1960s–1970s, Violin, fife, guitar, American
Caliman, Hadley, Hard Bop; Modern Jazz, 1960s–, Saxophone, American
Campbell, Eddie C., Modern Electric Blues, 1960s–, Vocals, guitar, American
Canned Heat, Blues Rock; Modern Electric Blues, 1960s–, Various instruments, American
Capon, Jean-Charles, Free Jazz; Modern Jazz, 1960s–, Bass, French
Captain Beefheart, Blues Rock, 1960s–1980s, Vocals, harmonica, American
Carlsson, Rune, Modern Jazz, 1960s–, Drums, vocals, Swedish
Carlton, Larry, Fusion; Hard Bop; Soul Jazz; Smooth Jazz, 1960s–, Guitar, American
Carr, Barbara, Rhythm & Blues, 1960s–, Vocals, American
Carr, Ian, Modern Jazz; Jazz Rock; Fusion, 1960s–, Trumpet, flugelhorn, composer, bandleader, Scottish
Carr, Mike, Hard Bop; Modern Jazz, 1960s–, Organ, British
Carter, John, Free Jazz, 1960s–1990s, Clarinet, saxophone, composer, bandleader, American
Carter, Kent, Free Jazz; Modern Jazz, 1960s–, Bass, violin, keyboards, percussion, American
Carter, Levester 'Big Lucky', Modern Electric Blues; East Coast Blues, 1960s–2000s, Vocals, guitar, American
Carter, Ron, Hard Bop, 1960s–, Bass, cello, American
Carvin, Michael, Modern Jazz; Jazz Rock; Hard Bop, 1960s–, Drums, American
Chaix, Henri, Big Band; Swing, 1960s–, Piano, trombone, arranger, bandleader, French
Chambers, Joe, Free Jazz; Modern Jazz, 1960s–, Drums, vibraphone, composer, American
Charters, Samuel B., Country Blues, 1960s–, Author, producer, folklorist, American
Chenier, Clifton, Rhythm & Blues, 1960s–1980s, Vocals, accordion, harmonica, American
Cherry, Don, Free Jazz; World Fusion, 1960s–1990s, Trumpet, keyboards, vocals, American
Chicken Shack, British Blues; Blues Rock, 1960s–1980s, Various instruments, British
Christensen, Jon, Modern Jazz; Big Band; Jazz Rock, 1960s–, Drums, Norwegian
Christian, Jodie, Hard Bop; Free Jazz; Modern Jazz, 1960s–, Piano, bandleader, American
Cicero, Eugen, Free Jazz; Modern Jazz, 1960s–, Piano, Romanian
Clapton, Eric, British Blues; Blues Rock, 1960s–, Guitar, vocals, composer, British
Clark, Mike, Modern Jazz; Jazz Rock, 1960s–, Drums, American
Clarke, Stanley, Fusion, 1960s–1990s, Bass, American
Clarke-Boland Big Band, Big Band, 1960s–1970s, Various instruments, German
Clay, Otis, Rhythm & Blues, 1960s–, Vocals, American
Clempson, Dave, Jazz Rock, 1960s–, Guitar, British
Climax Blues Band, Blues Rock, 1960s–1990s, Various instruments, British
Cocker, Joe, Blues Rock, 1960s–, Vocals, British
Cohn, Larry, Country Blues, 1960s–, Producer, author, American
Cola, Kid Sheik, New Orleans Jazz; Traditional Jazz, 1960s–1990s, Trumpet, bandleader, American
Coleman, Ornette, Free Jazz, 1960s–, Saxophones, composer, American
Collier, Graham, British Jazz; Big Band, 1960s–, Composer, bass, author, British
Collins, Albert, Texas Blues; Modern Electric Blues, 1960s–1990s, Guitar, vocals, composer, American
Colon, Willie, Latin Jazz, 1960s–, Trombone, bandleader, American
Colosseum, Jazz Rock, 1960s–1970s, Various instruments, British
Coltrane, Alice, Free Jazz, 1960s–1980s, Piano, organ, harp, American
Coltrane, John, Modal Jazz; Free Jazz; Hard Bop, 1960s, Saxophones, composer, American
Cook, Marty, Free Jazz, 1960s–, Trombone, American
Cooke, Micky, New Orleans Jazz; Traditional Jazz, 1960s, Trombone, British
Cooper, Mike, Country Blues, 1960s–, Vocals, guitar, British
Corea, Chick, Fusion; Free Jazz, 1960s–, Piano, keyboards, composer, American
Cornford, Bob, Cool Jazz; Modal Jazz, 1960s–1980s, Piano, composer, arranger, Brazilian
Coryell, Larry, Fusion, 1960s–, Guitar, composer, American
Cotton, Mike, Dixieland; Jazz Rock; Rhythm & Blues, 1960s–, Trumpet, flugelhorn, harmonica, vocals, leader, British
Covey, Julian, Blues Rock, 1960s–, Drums, British
Cowell, Stanley, Hard Bop; Modern Jazz, 1960s–, Piano, composer, bandleader, producer, American
Coxhill, Lol, Free Jazz, 1960s–, Saxophone, British
Cranshaw, Bob, Hard Bop, 1960s–1990s, Bass, American
Cream, British Blues; Blues Rock, 1960s, Various instruments, British
Crockett, G.L., Rhythm & Blues, 1960s, Vocals, guitar, American
Cross, Earl, Free Jazz, 1960s–1980s, Trumpet, cornet, flugelhorn, mellophone, American
Crouch, Stanley, All Jazz Styles, 1960s–, Author, critic, drums, American
Crusaders, The, Hard Bop; Soul Jazz; Fusion, 1960s–, Various instruments, American
Cuber, Ronnie, Hard Bop, 1960s–, Saxophone, American
Cullum, Jim Jr, Dixieland Revival, 1960s–1990s, Cornet, American
Curson, Ted, Hard Bop, 1960s–, Trumpet, American
Cuscuna, Michael, Modern Jazz; Hard Bop, 1960s–, Producer, author, American
Cyrille, Andrew, Free Jazz, 1960s–, Drums, composer, American
D'Andrea, Franco, Hard Bop; Free Jazz; Jazz Rock; Modern Jazz, 1960s–, Keyboards, Italian
Dailey, Al, Hard Bop, 1960s–1980s, Piano, composer, American
Daniel, Ted, Free Jazz, 1960s–, Trumpet, American
Daniels, Eddie, Hard Bop, 1960s–, Saxophone, clarinet, American
Dapogny, James, Dixieland Revival; Swing, 1960s–1990s, Piano, bandleader, American
Dasek, Rudolf, Modern Jazz, 1960s–, Guitar, Czech
Dauner, Wolfgang, Modern Jazz; Jazz Rock, 1960s–, Piano, composer, bandleader, German
Davies, Cyril, British Blues, 1960s, Vocals, harmonica, British
Davis, Geater, Rhythm & Blues, 1960s–1980s, Vocals, American
Davis, Maxwell St. Jimmy, Country Blues, 1960s–1980s, Vocals, guitar, American
Davis, Nathan, Hard Bop; Free Jazz, 1960s–, Saxophone, American
Davis, Steve, Bebop; Hard Bop, 1960s–1980s, Drums, American
Davis, Tyrone, Rhythm & Blues, 1960s–2000s, Vocals, American
Dean, Elton, Free Jazz; Modern Jazz, 1960s–, Saxophone, saxello, bandleader, British
Dee, Brian, Modern Jazz, 1960s–, Piano, British
Dee, David, Modern Electric Blues; Rhythm & Blues, 1960s–, Vocals, bass, guitar, American
Degen, Bob, Modern Jazz; Hard Bop, 1960s–, Piano, American
DeJohnette, Jack, Fusion, 1960s–, Drums, piano, composer, American
Delaney & Bonnie, Blues Rock, 1960s–1970s, Vocals, American
Deodato, Brazilian Jazz; Soul Funk , 1960s–, Piano, arranger, Brazilian
Detroit Junior, Modern Electric Blues, 1960s–, Vocals, piano, American
Dickerson, Walt, Modern Jazz, 1960s–, Vibraphone, American
Dickie, Neville, Traditional Jazz, 1960s–, Piano, British
Dickinson, Jim, Memphis Blues, 1960s–, Guitar, songwriter, producer, American
Din, Hamza el, World Fusion, 1960s–1990s, Ud, African
Diorio, Joe, Modern Jazz, 1960s–, Guitar, American
Dixon, Bill, Free Jazz, 1960s–, Trumpet, flugelhorn, composer, American
Dixon, R.M.W., Country Blues, 1960s–, Author, British
Dolphy, Eric, Free Jazz, 1960s, Saxophone, flute, clarinet, American
Domanico, Chuck, Modern Jazz, 1960s–, Bass, American
Donato, João, Brazilian Jazz, 1960s–1970s, Piano, vocals, trombone, Brazilian
Dorge, Pierre, Free Jazz; Modern Jazz; Big Band, 1960s–, Guitar, bandleader, composer, Danish
Dorham, Kenny, Hard Bop, 1960s–1970s, Trumpet, composer, American
Dorsey, Lee, Rhythm & Blues, 1960s–1980s, Vocals, American
Dotson, Jimmy, Rhythm & Blues, 1960s–1980s, Vocals, guitar, drums, American
Douglas, Jim, Traditional Jazz; Chicago Jazz; Dixieland revival, 1960s–, Guitar, banjo, British
Dudas, Lajos, Modern Jazz, 1960s–, Clarinet, saxophone, composer, arranger, bandleader, Hungarian
Dudek, Gerd, Free Jazz, 1960s–, Saxophone, clarinet, flute, German
Duke, George, Fusion; Jazz Pop, 1960s–, Keyboards, composer, producer, American
Dunbar, Aynsley; Retaliation, Blues Rock, 1960s, Various instruments, British
Dunbar, Ted, Soul Jazz; Hard Bop, 1960s–, Guitar, American
Dupree, Cornell, Modern Electric Blues; Rhythm & Blues, 1960s–, Guitar, American
Durham, Bobby, Soul Jazz; Modern Jazz, 1960s–, Trombone, vibraphone, bass, American
Dyani, Johnny, Free Jazz, 1960s–1980s, Bass, vocals, South African
Eaglin, Snooks, Rhythm & Blues, 1960s–, Guitar, vocals, American
Earland, Charles, Soul Jazz; Hard Bop, 1960s–1990s, Keyboards, American
Electric Flag, Blues Rock, 1960s–1970s, Various instruments, American
Elgart, Billy, Free Jazz; Bebop, 1960s–, Drums, American
Ellis, Chris, Classic Jazz, 1960s–, Vocals, producer, British
Ellis, Don, Free Jazz; Modern Jazz; Big Band, 1960s–1970s, Trumpet, composer, bandleader, American
Embry, 'Queen' Sylvia, Delta Blues; Chicago Blues, 1960s–1980s, Vocals, bass, American
Erstrand, Lars, Swing, 1960s–, Vibraphone, Swedish
Escovedo, Pete, Latin Jazz; Fusion, 1960s–, Percussion, vibraphone, American
Evans, David, Country Blues, 1960s–, Author, producer, American
Evans, Margie, Rhythm & Blues; West Coast Blues, 1960s–, Vocals, American
Fame, Georgie, Rhythm & Blues, 1960s–, Vocals, piano, organ, British
Farmer, Art, Bebop; Hard Bop; Cool Jazz, 1960s–1990s, Trumpet, flugelhorn, American
Farrell, Joe, Hard Bop, 1960s–1980s, Saxophones, flute, American
Favors, Malachi, Free Jazz, 1960s–2000s, Bass, banjo, zither, percussion, American
Favre, Pierre, Hard Bop; Free Jazz, 1960s–, Drums, bandleader, Swiss
Felder, Wilton, Hard Bop; Soul Jazz; Fusion, 1960s–, Saxophone, bass, American
Ferre, Boulou, Swing; Bebop; Modern Jazz, 1960s–, Guitar, French
Fest, Manfredo, Brazilian Jazz; Latin Jazz, 1960s–1990s, Piano, bandleader, Brazilian
Few, Bobby, Hard Bop; Free Jazz, 1960s–, Piano, American
Feza, Mongezi, World Fusion, 1960s–1970s, Trumpet, South African
Fischer, Clare, Hard Bop; Latin Jazz, 1960s–, Piano, composer, arranger, bandleader, American
Fleetwood Mac, British Blues; Blues Rock, 1960s–, Various instruments, British
Forehand, Edward 'Little Buster', Soul Blues, 1960s–, Guitar, vocals, American
Fortune, Sonny, Free Jazz; Modern Jazz, 1960s–, Saxophone, American
Foster, Al, Hard Bop; Jazz Rock, 1960s–, Drums, American
Foster, Gary, Bebop; Cool Jazz, 1960s–, Saxophone, flute, American
Franklin, Aretha, Gospel; Soul Jazz, 1960s–1990s, Vocals, piano, American
Franklin, Guitar Pete, Chicago Blues, 1960s–1970s, Piano, guitar, American
Free, Jack, Dixieland, 1960s–, Trombone, British
Freeman, Von, Modern Jazz, 1960s–, Saxophone, bandleader, American
Frishberg, Dave, Swing; Bebop, 1960s–, Piano, vocals, composer, American
Gale, Eddie, Free Jazz, 1960s–, Trumpet, American
Gales, Larry, Hard Bop, 1960s–, Bass, American
Galloway, Jim, Swing; Dixieland, 1960s–, Saxophone, clarinet, Canadian
Garbarek, Jan, Free Jazz, 1960s–, Saxophone, composer, Norwegian
Gare, Lou, Free Jazz, 1960s–, Saxophone, British
Garnett, Carlos, Free Jazz; Hard Bop; Modern Jazz, 1960s–, Saxophone, Panamanian
Garon, Paul, Blues, 1960s–, Author, American
Garrett, Robert 'Bud', Electric Blues; Country Blues, 1960s–1980s, Guitar, American
Garrison, Jimmy, Free Jazz, 1960s–1980s, Bass, American
Gay, Al, Traditional Jazz; Dixieland Revival, 1960s–, Clarinet, saxophones, British
Geremia, Paul, Country Blues, 1960s–, Vocals, guitar, American
Getz, Jane, Hard Bop; Modern Jazz, 1960s–, Piano, American
Getz, Stan, Cool Jazz; Hard Bop, 1960s–1990s, Saxophone, American
Gibbs, Mike, Free Jazz; Fusion, 1960s–, Trombone, composer, arranger, bandleader, Rhodesian
Gibson, Lacy, Modern Electric Blues; Chicago Blues, 1960s–, Vocals, guitar, American
Gil, Gilberto, Modern Jazz; World Jazz, 1960s–, Guitar, accordion, composer, vocals, Brazilian
Gilberto, Astrud, Brazilian Jazz, 1960s–, Vocals, Brazilian
Gillespie, Dana, Blues Rock, 1960s–, Vocals, British
Gismonti, Egberto, Brazilian Jazz; World Fusion, 1960s–1990s, Guitar, piano, keyboards, vocals, Brazilian
Globe Unity Orchestra, Free Jazz; Big Band, 1960s–, Various instruments, German
Godding, Brian, Jazz Rock, 1960s–, Guitar, British
Godrich, John, Country Blues, 1960s–1990, Author, Australian
Gomez, Eddie, Modern Jazz, 1960s–, Bass, Puerto Rican
Goodwin, Bill, Modern Jazz; Bebop, 1960s–, Drums, American
Gordon, Bobby, Swing, 1960s–, Clarinet, American
Goykovich, Dusko, Hard Bop, 1960s–, Flugelhorn, trumpet, Slovenian
Graillier, Michel, Free Jazz, 1960s–2000s, Piano, composer, French
Granderson, John Lee, Chicago Blues, 1960s–1970s, Vocals, guitar, American
Gravenites, Nick, Blues Rock, 1960s–, Vocals, songwriter, American
Graves, Milford, Free Jazz, 1960s–, Percussion, American
Green, Al, Rhythm & Blues, 1960s–, Vocals, American
Green, Dave, Free Jazz, 1960s–, Double Bass, British
Greene, Burton, Free Jazz; Modern Jazz; World Fusion, 1960s–, Piano, composer, American
Greenwich, Sonny, Free Jazz, 1960s–, Guitar, Canadian
Gregorio, Guillermo, Free Jazz, 1960s–, Saxophone, clarinet, Argentinian
Grey Ghost, Texas Blues, 1960s; 1980s, Piano, American
Griffin, R.L., Dallas Blues; Modern Electric Blues, 1960s–, Drums, American
Griffin, Shirley, Country Blues, 1960s, Vocals, guitar, American
Grimes, Henry, Free Jazz; Hard Bop, 1960s, Bass, American
Grolnick, Don, Modern Jazz; Jazz Rock; Fusion, 1960s–1990s, Piano, keyboards, American
Grossman, Stefan, Country Blues, 1960s–, Vocals, guitar, author, American
Grossman, Steve, Hard Bop, 1960s–, Saxophone, American
Groundhogs, The, Blues Rock, 1960s–1990s, Various instruments, British
Gruntz, George, Modern Jazz; Big Band, 1960s–, Keyboards, composer, bandleader, Swiss
Grusin, Dave, Fusion, 1960s–, Piano, producer, composer, American
Guitar Junior (a.k.a. Lonnie Brooks), Chicago Blues, 1960s, Vocals, guitar, American
Guy, Buddy, Modern Electric Blues; Chicago Blues, 1960s–, Guitar, vocals, American
Haden, Charlie, Free Jazz; Hard Bop, 1960s–, Bass, American
Hahn, Jerry, Modern Jazz, 1960s–, Guitar, American
Hall, Bob, British Blues, 1960s–, Piano, British
Hammer, Jan, Fusion, 1960s–, Piano, keyboards, drums, Czech
Hammond, John Jr., Blues Rock; Rhythm & Blues, 1960s–, Producer, American
Hampel, Gunter, Free Jazz, 1960s–, Vibraphone, piano, flute, clarinet, German
Hardy, John 'Captain John', New Orleans Jazz, 1960s–1970s, Saxophone, American
Harley, Rufus, Hard Bop; Soul Jazz, 1960s–, Saxophone, flute, bagpipes, American
Harper, Billy, Cool Jazz; Fusion, 1960s–, Saxophone, flute, vocals, composer, American
Harpo, Slim, Jump Blues, 1960s, Guitar, harmonica, American
Harris, Beaver, Free Jazz, Modern Jazz, 1960s–1990s, Drums, bandleader, American
Harris, James 'Shakey Jake', Modern Electric Blues, 1960s, Vocals, harmonica, American
Harrow, Nancy, Modern Jazz, 1960s–, Vocals, American
Hart, Billy, Modern Jazz, 1960s–, Drums, American
Heckstall-Smith, Dick, British Jazz; World Jazz; Jazz Rock, 1960s–, Saxophone, British
Hemphill, Jessie Mae, Country Blues; Delta Blues, 1960s–, Vocals, guitar, American
Hemphill, Julius, Free Jazz, 1960s–1990s, Saxophone, composer, American
Henderson, Bugs, Blues Rock, 1960s–, Guitar, American
Henderson, Joe, Hard Bop, 1960s–1990s, Saxophone, flute, composer, American
Henderson, Wayne, Hard Bop; Soul Jazz; Fusion, 1960s–, Trombone, producer, American
Hendrix, Jimi, Blues Rock, 1960s–1970s, Guitar, composer, American
Henry Cow, Jazz Rock, 1960s–1970s, Various instruments, British
Hicks, John, Hard Bop; Modern Jazz, 1960s–, Piano, bandleader, American
Hill, Jessie, Rhythm & Blues, 1960s–1970s, Drums, vocals, American
Hill, Z.Z., Modern Electric Blues, 1960s–1980s, Vocals, American
Hino, Motohiko, Hard Bop; Fusion, 1960s–, Drums, Japanese
Hino, Terumasa, Hard Bop; Fusion, 1960s–, Trumpet, cornet, flugelhorn, bandleader, Japanese
Hiseman, Jon, Jazz Rock, 1960s–, Drums, British
Hodgkinson, Colin, British Blues; Blues Rock, 1960s–, Guitar, vocals, composer, British
Hogan, Silas, Modern Electric Blues; Louisiana Blues, 1960s–1990s, Vocals, guitar, harmonica, American
Hooper, Stix, Hard Bop; Soul Jazz; Fusion, 1960s–, Drums, bandleader, American
Howard, Noah, Free Jazz, 1960s–, Saxophone, American
Hubbard, Freddie, Hard Bop; Fusion, 1960s–, Trumpet, flugelhorn, composer, American
Humble Pie, Blues Rock; British Blues, 1960s–1980s, Various instruments, British
Hunter, Long John, Modern Electric Blues; Texas Blues, 1960s–1990s, Guitar, vocals, American
Hussain, Zakir, World Fusion, 1960s–, Percussion, Indian
Hutcherson, Bobby, Hard Bop, 1960s–, Vibraphone, marimba, American
Hyder, Ken, Free Jazz, 1960s–, Drums, percussion, vocals, British
Ironing Board Sam, Boogie-Woogie; Blues, 1960s–, Vocals, songwriter, American
Izenzon, David, Free Jazz, 1960s–1970s, Bass, composer, American
Jackson, Big Jack, Modern Electric Blues, 1960–, Vocals, guitar, American
Jackson, John, Country Blues, 1960s–1990s, Guitar, American
James, Bob, Fusion, 1960s–, Piano, composer, American
Jansch, Bert, British Blues; Folk Blues, 1960s–, Guitar, British
Jarman, Joseph, Free Jazz, 1960s–1990s, Saxophones, reeds, American
Jarreau, Al, Jazz Rock; Modern Jazz, 1960s–, Vocals, American
Jarvis, Clifford, Free Jazz, 1960s–1990s, Drums, American
Jazz Crusaders, The, Soul Jazz; Acid Jazz, 1960s, Various instruments, American
Johansson, Sven-Ake, Free Jazz, 1960s–, Drums, accordion, vocals, Swedish
Johnson, Bessie, Memphis Blues; Soul Blues, 1960s, Vocals, American
Johnson, Howard, Cool Jazz; Fusion, 1960s–, Saxophone, tuba, composer, arranger, flugelhorn, clarinet, American
Johnson, Jimmy, Modern Electric Blues, 1960s–, Vocals, guitar, American
Johnson, Larry, Modern Electric Blues, 1960s–1970s, Guitar, vocals, American
Johnson, Luther 'Georgia Boy' 'Snake', Modern Electric Blues, 1960s–1970s, Vocals, guitar, American
Johnson, Luther 'Guitar Jr', Chicago Blues, 1960s–, Guitar, vocals, American

see Introduction pp 238 *see* Sources & Sounds pp 240 *see* Key Artists pp 248 *see* A–Z of Artists pp 266

Johnson, Syl, Rhythm & Blues, 1960s–, Vocals, American
Jones, Andrew 'Jr. Boy', Modern Electric Blues; Texas Blues, 1960s–, Vocals, guitar, American
Jones, Eddie 'One String', Delta Blues, 1960s, Guitar, American
Jones, Elvin, Hard Bop, 1960s–2000s, Drums, composer, American
Jones, Joe 'Boogaloo', Soul Jazz, 1960s–1970s, Guitar, American
Jones, Paul, Rhythm & Blues, 1960s–, Vocals, British
Joos, Herbert, Hard Bop; Free Jazz, 1960s–, Flugelhorn, trumpet, alphorn, composer, arranger, German
Joplin, Janis, Blues Rock, 1960s–1970s, Vocals, American
Jordan, Sheila, Free Jazz; Modern Jazz, 1960s–, Vocals, composer, American
Katz, Dill, World Jazz; Jazz Rock, 1960s–, Guitar, double bass, British
K-Doe, Ernie, Rhythm & Blues, 1960s–1990s, Vocals, composer, American
Kellaway, Roger, Hard Bop; Bebop, 1960s–, Piano, arranger, composer, American
Kelly, Dave, Rhythm & Blues, 1960s–, Guitar, trombone, British
Kelly, Jo Ann, British Blues, 1960s–1990s, Vocals, British
Kelly, Paul, Rhythm & Blues, 1960s–, Vocals, composer, American
Kenyatta, Robin, Free Jazz; Hard Bop; World Fusion, 1960s–2000s, Saxophone, flute, American
Kidd, Kenneth, Chicago Blues; Rhythm & Blues, 1960s–1990s, Bass, American
Kikuchi, Masabumi, Hard Bop; Fusion, 1960s–, Piano, composer, Japanese
King, Albert, Modern Electric Blues; Rhythm & Blues, 1960s–1980s, Vocals, guitar, American
King, B.B., Modern Electric Blues; Rhythm & Blues, 1960s–, Vocals, guitar, American
King, Freddie, Texas Blues; Rhythm & Blues; Modern Electric Blues, 1960s–1970s, Vocals, guitar, American
King, Peter, Big Band; British Jazz, 1960s–, Saxophone, clarinet, British
Kirk, Rahsaan Roland, Free Jazz; Modern Jazz, 1960s–1970s, Saxophone, flute, clarinet, bandleader, American
Kirkland, Eddie, Modern Electric Blues, 1960s–1990s, Guitar, American
Klemmer, John, Smooth Jazz; Hard Bop; Modern Jazz; Fusion, 1960s–, Saxophone, flute, kalimba, keyboards, composer, American
Kloss, Eric, Hard Bop; Modern Jazz, 1960s–, Saxophone, bandleader, American
Koerner, Ray & Glover, Country Blues; Folk Blues, 1960s–1990s, Various instruments, American
Koerner, 'Spider' John, Folk Blues, 1960s–, Guitar, American
Korner, Alexis, British Blues; Blues Rock, 1960s–1980s, Guitar, Greek
Kottke, Leo, Country Blues, 1960s–, Guitar, American
Kowald, Peter, Free Jazz, 1960s–, Bass, German
Krivda, Ernie, Modern Jazz, 1960s–, Saxophone, American
Krog, Karin, Free Jazz, 1960s–, Vocals, Norwegian
Kuhn, Joachim, Modern Jazz; Hard Bop; Free Jazz, 1960s–, Piano, composer, German
Kuhn, Steve, Modern Jazz, 1960s–, Piano, composer, bandleader, American
Kynard, Charles, Soul Jazz, 1960s–1970s, Organ, American
LaBarbera, Pat, Hard Bop; Big Band, 1960s–, Saxophone, American
Laird, Rick, Bebop, 1960s–, Double bass, guitar, Irish
Lancaster, Byard, Free Jazz; Modern Jazz, 1960s–, Saxophone, flute, American
LaSalle, Denise, Rhythm & Blues, 1960s–, Vocals, composer, American
Lasha, Prince, Free Jazz, 1960s–, Flute, American
Latimore, Benny, Rhythm & Blues, 1960s–, Vocals, piano, American
Laurence, Chris, Free Jazz; Fusion, 1960s–, Double bass, British
Lawhorn, Sammy, Delta Blues; Chicago Blues, 1960s, Guitar, American
Lay, Sam, Chicago Blues, 1960s–, Drums, American
Leadbitter, Mike, Country Blues; Rhythm & Blues; Delta Blues, 1960s–1970s, Author, British
Leake, Brian, Swing, 1960s–1990s, Piano, saxophone, British
Leake, Lafayette, Boogie-Woogie, 1960s, Piano, American
Leavy, Calvin, Memphis Blues, 1960s, Vocals, guitar, American
Lee, Alvin, Blues Rock, 1960s–, Guitar, British
Lee, Dave, Bebop; Big Band; British Jazz, 1960s–, Piano, arranger, composer, vocals, leader, British
Lee, Jeanne, Free Jazz 1960s–, Vocals, American
Lee, Phil, British Jazz; Big Band, 1960s–, Guitar, British
Lemer, Pete, Free Jazz; Fusion, 1960s–, Piano, synthesizer, British
Leviev, Milcho, Bebop; Hard Bop; Fusion, 1960s–, Piano, arranger, Bulgarian
Levin, Tony, Free Jazz, 1960s–, Drums, British
Lightsey, Kirk, Hard Bop; Modern Jazz, 1960s–, Piano, American
Little Buster, Rhythm & Blues, 1960s–, Vocals, guitar, American
Little Milton, Modern Electric Blues; Rhythm & Blues, 1960s–, Guitar, American
Little Sonny, Modern Electric Blues, 1960s–, Vocals, harmonica, American
Littlejohn, Alan, British Jazz; Traditional Jazz; Dixieland, 1960s–, Trumpet, flugelhorn, leader, British
Littlejohn, John, Chicago Blues; Modern Electric Blues, 1960s–1990s, Guitar, vocals, American
Lloyd, Charles, Free Jazz; Hard Bop, 1960s–, Saxophone, flute, American
Lobo, Edu, Latin Jazz, 1960s–1990s, Vocals, composer, Brazilian
Lockwood, Robert Jr., Delta Blues; Chicago Blues, 1960s–, Guitar, vocals, American
Longo, Mike, Bebop, 1960s–, Piano, American
Lornell, Kip, Country Blues, 1960s–1980s, Producer, author, folklorist, American
Louiss, Eddy, Hard Bop, 1960s–, Piano, organ, bandleader, vocals, French
Love Sculpture, Blues Rock, 1960s–1970s, Various instruments, British
Lowry, Pete, Country Blues, 1960s–1970s, Producer, folklorist, American
Lowther, Henry, Free Jazz; Big Band, 1960s–, Trumpet, flugelhorn, cornet, violin, piano, British
Lusk, Professor Eddie, Modern Electric Blues; Chicago Blues, 1960s–1990s, Piano, American
Lynn, Barbara, Rhythm & Blues; Modern Electric Blues, 1960s–1990s, Guitar, vocals, American
Lyons, Jimmy, Free Jazz, 1960s–1980s, Saxophones, flute, American
Lytle, Johnny, Hard Bop; Soul Jazz; Bebop, 1960s–, Vibraphone, composer, American
Macintosh, Adrian, New Orleans Jazz; Chicago Jazz, 1960s–, Drums, British
Macon, John Wesley 'Shortstuff', Delta Blues, 1960s, Guitar, American
MacRae, Dave, Jazz Rock; British Jazz, 1960s–, Piano, synthesizer, New Zealander
Magic Sam, Modern Electric Blues; Chicago Blues, 1960s, Guitar, vocals, American
Malone, J.J., Modern Electric Blues, 1960s–2000s, Vocals, guitar, keyboards, American
Maneri, Joe, Free Jazz, 1960s–, Clarinet, saxophone, composer, American
Mangione, Chuck, Fusion, 1960s–, Trumpet, flugelhorn, composer, American
Mann, Herbie, Soul Jazz, 1960s–2000s, Flute, saxophone, composer, American
Mantler, Mike, Free Jazz, 1960s–, Trumpet, composer, bandleader, Austrian
Marcus, Steve, Hard Bop, 1960s–, Saxophone, American
Margolin, Bob, Modern Electric Blues, 1960s–, Guitar, American
Mars, Johnny, Chicago Blues; Modern Electric Blues, 1960s–, Harmonica, vocals, American
Marsalis, Ellis, Hard Bop; Modern Jazz, 1960s–, Piano, American
Marshall, Eddie, Hard Bop; Bebop, 1960s–, Drums, recorder, American
Marshall, John, British Jazz, 1960s–, Drums, British
Martin, Stu, Free Jazz; Hard Bop; Fusion, 1960s–1980s, Drums, American
Martino, Pat, Modern Jazz, 1960s–, Guitar, American
Masekela, Hugh, World Fusion; Soul Jazz, 1960s–, Trumpet, flugelhorn, South African
Mason, Phil, New Orleans Jazz, 1960s–, Cornet, British
Mason, Rod, New Orleans Jazz; Chicago Jazz, 1960s–, Trumpet, cornet, leader, British
Mathews, Ronnie, Hard Bop, 1960s–, Piano, American
Mathewson, Ron, Rhythm & Blues; Bebop; Modern Jazz, 1960s–, Double bass, guitar, British
Maupin, Bennie, Hard Bop; Modern Jazz; Fusion, 1960s–, Saxophone, clarinet, American
Mayall, John, British Blues; Blues Rock, 1960s–, Vocals, guitar, harmonica, keyboards, British
McBee, Cecil, Free Jazz; Modern Jazz, 1960s–, Bass, American
McCall, Cash, Rhythm & Blues, 1960s–, Vocals, guitar, composer, American
McCall, Steve, Free Jazz, 1960s–1980s, Drums, American
McCandless, Paul, Dixieland Revival; Hard Bop, 1960s–, Oboe, horn, clarinet, composer, American
McCann, Les, Soul Jazz; Hard Bop, 1960s–, Piano, vocals, American
McClain, Mighty Sam, Rhythm & Blues, 1960s–, Vocals, American
McClure, Ron, Jazz Rock, 1960s–, Bass, piano, composer, American
McConnell, Rob, Swing; Bebop, 1960s–, Trombone, arranger, bandleader, Canadian
McCoy, Ethel & George, Country Blues, 1960s–1970s, Vocals, guitar, American
McGregor, Chris, Free Jazz, 1960s–1990s, Piano, bandleader, South African
McGriff, Jimmy, Soul Jazz; Hard Bop, 1960s–, Organ, American
McIntyre, Kalaparusha Maurice, Free Jazz, 1960s, Saxophone, clarinet, percussion, American
McIntyre, Ken, Free Jazz; Modern Jazz, 1960s–2000s, Saxophone, flute, clarinet, oboe, American
McLevy, John, British Jazz, 1960s–, Trumpet, flugelhorn, British
McPhee, Joe, Free Jazz, 1960s–, Saxophone, trumpet, flugelhorn, American
Medicine Head, British Blues, 1960s–1970s; 1990s, Artist, British
Mehldau, Brad, Modern Jazz, 1960s–, Piano, bandleader, American
Mendes, Sergio, Latin Jazz; Brazilian Jazz, 1960s–, Piano, composer, arranger, bandleader, producer, Brazilian
Mengelberg, Misha, Free Jazz; Modern Jazz, 1960s–, Piano, composer, Ukrainian
Merryweather, Neil, Rhythm & Blues, 1960s–1970s, Bass, American
Meters, The, Rhythm & Blues, 1960s–1990s, Various instruments, American
Mighty Sam, Rhythm & Blues, 1960s–1980s, Vocals, American
Miller, Harry, Rhythm & Blues, 1960s–1970s, Bass, cello, South African
Mitchell, George, Country Blues, 1960s–1970s, Producer, folklorist, American
Mitchell, Grover, Swing; Big Band, 1960s–2000s, Trombone, arranger, bandleader, American
Mitchell, McKinley, Rhythm & Blues, 1960–1970s, Vocals, American
Mitchell, Roscoe, Free Jazz, 1960s–, Saxophones, reeds, vocals, American
Mitchell, Willie, Rhythm & Blues, 1960s–, Producer, arranger, composer, American
Moffett, Charles, Free Jazz, 1960s–1990s, Drums, American
Moncur, Graham III, Free Jazz, 1960s–, Trombone, American
Montgomery, Wes, Hard Bop, 1960s, Guitar, American
Moore, Glen, Modern Jazz, 1960s–, Bass, piano, American
Moreira, Airto, World Fusion; Brazilian Jazz, 1960s–, Drums, percussion, Brazilian
Morgan, Lee, Hard Bop, 1960s–1970s, Trumpet, composer, American
Morrison, Van, Jazz Rock, 1960s–, Vocals, composer, British
Morrissey, Dick, Jazz Funk; Jazz Rock, 1960s–2000s, Saxophone, British
Moses, Bob, Free Jazz; Modern Jazz, 1960s–, Drums, American
Motian, Paul, Free Jazz; Modern Jazz, 1960s–, Drums, composer, American
Mouzon, Alphonse, Modern Jazz; Fusion, 1960s–, Drums, American
Moye, Don, Free Jazz, 1960s–, Drums, marimba, miscellaneous percussion, horn, vocals, American
Moye, Famoudou Don, Free Jazz, 1960s–, Drums, percussion, American
Murray, Sunny, Free Jazz, 1960s–1990s, Drums, American
Naftalin, Mark, Modern Electric Blues, 1960s–, Piano, producer, American
Namyslowski, Zbigniew, Folk Jazz; Fusion, 1960s–, Saxophone, composer, flute, cello, trombone, piano, Polish
Napier, Simon, All Blues Styles, 1960s–1970s, Author, British
National Youth Jazz Orchestra, British Jazz, 1960s–, Various instruments, British
Nelson, Tracy, Country Blues, 1960s–, Vocals, American
Neville, Aaron, Rhythm & Blues, 1960s–, Keyboards, vocals, American
New Jazz Orchestra, British Jazz; Modern Jazz; Big Band, 1960s, Various instruments, British
Nicholls, Billy, British Blues, 1960s–1970s, Vocals, composer, British
Nichols, Maggie, Free Jazz, 1960s–, Vocals, piano, British
Nix, Don, Rhythm & Blues, 1960s–1970s, Saxophone, American
Nock, Mike, Jazz Rock; Fusion; Hard Bop, 1960s–, Piano, synthesizer, New Zealander
Numbers Band, The, Blues Rock, 1960s–1990s, Various instruments, American
Odom, Andrew 'Big Voice' 'B.B.', Chicago Blues, 1960s–1990s, Vocals, American
Olympia Brass Band, New Orleans Jazz, 1960s–1990s, Various instruments, American
Original Salty Dogs, The, Dixieland Revival, 1960s, Various instruments, American
Orsted Pedersen, Niels-Henning, Bebop; Hard Bop, 1960s–1990s, Bass, Danish
Osborne, Mike, Free Jazz; Bebop, 1960s–, Saxophone, clarinet, piano, British
Otis, Shuggie, Modern Electric Blues; Blues Rock, 1960s–, Guitar, American
Owens, Jack, Delta Blues; Country Blues, 1960s–1970s, Guitar, American
Owens, Jimmy, Bebop; Hard Bop, 1960s–, Trumpet, flugelhorn, composer, American
Oxley, Tony, Free Jazz; Fusion, 1960s, Drums, percussion, British
Palmieri, Eddie, Latin Jazz, 1960s–, Piano, arranger, American
Parker, Errol, Free Jazz, 1960s–1990s, Drums, piano, bandleader, Algerian
Parlan, Horace, Hard Bop, 1960s–, Piano, American
Pascoal, Hermeto, Latin Jazz; Brazilian Jazz, 1960s–1990s, Piano, flute, guitar, composer, Brazilian
Pass, Joe, Bebop; Hard Bop, 1960s–1990s, Guitar, American
Patterson, Don, Soul Jazz; Hard Bop, 1960s–1970s, Organ, piano, American
Patton, Big John, Soul Jazz; Hard Bop, 1960s–1990s, Organ, piano, American
Peacock, Annette, Free Jazz, 1960s–, Piano, keyboards, composer, vocals, American
Peacock, Gary, Free Jazz, 1960s–1990s, Bass, composer, American
Peebles, Ann, Rhythm & Blues, 1960s–, Vocals, American
Pena, Ralph, Cool Jazz; Bebop, 1960s, Bass, American
Pepper, Jim, Modern Jazz; World Fusion, 1960s–1990s, Saxophone, American
Perkins, Pinetop, Boogie-Woogie; Chicago Blues, 1960s–, Piano, American
Perry, P.J., Hard Bop; Bebop, 1960s–, Saxophone, Canadian
Person, Houston, Soul Jazz; Hard Bop; Swing, 1960s–, Saxophone, American
Peterson, James, Modern Electric Blues, 1960s–, Guitar, vocals, American
Phillips, Barre, Free Jazz, 1960s–, Bass, American
Phillips, Sonny, Soul Jazz, 1960s–1970s, Organ, piano, American
Phillips, Steve, Country Blues, 1960s–, Guitar, British
Piazza, Rod, West Coast Blues; Modern Electric Blues, 1960s–, Vocals, harmonica, American
Pike, Dave, Bebop, 1960s–, Vibraphone, marimba, composer, American
Polcher, Ed, Chicago Jazz; Swing; Big Band, 1960s–, Cornet, vibraphone, American
Ponder, Jimmy, Soul Jazz; Hard Bop, 1960s–, Guitar, American
Ponty, Jean-Luc, Fusion, 1960s–, Violin, American
Porter, Bob, Soul Jazz; Rhythm & Blues, 1960s, Producer, author, American
Powell, Baden, Latin Jazz, 1960s–, Guitar, composer, Brazilian
Power, Duffy, Rhythm & Blues, 1960s, Vocals, British
Priestley, Brian, All Jazz Styles, 1960s–, Piano, author, critic, British
Pucho & his Latin Soul Brothers, Latin Jazz, 1960s–1970s, Various instruments, American
Pukwana, Dudu, Free Jazz, 1960s–1990s, Saxophone, South African
Pullen, Don, Free Jazz, 1960s–1990s, Piano, organ, composer, American
Purdie, Bernard 'Pretty', Soul Jazz, 1960s–, Drums, American
Pyne, Chris, Free Jazz; Modern Jazz; Jazz Rock, 1960s–1990s, Trombone, piano, British
Pyne, Mick, Hard Bop; Modern Jazz; Free Jazz, 1960s–, Piano, trumpet, British
Rachell, Yank, Country Blues, 1960s–1980, Guitar, harmonica, American
Radcliff, Bobby, Funk; Soul Blues, 1960s–, Guitar, American
Rainey, Chuck, Soul Jazz; Hard Bop, 1960s–, Bass, American
Ranglin, Ernest, Jamaican Jazz, 1960s–, Guitar, arranger, composer, Jamaican
Redman, Dewey, Free Jazz, 1960s–1990s, Saxophones, clarinet, American
Reed, A.C., Rhythm & Blues; Modern Electric Blues, 1960s–2000s, Vocals, saxophone, American
Reed, Waymon, Hard Bop, 1960s–1980s, Trumpet, flugelhorn, American
Rhodes, Eugene, East Coast Blues, 1960s, Vocals, guitar, American
Rhodes, Sonny, Rhythm & Blues; Modern Electric Blues, 1960s–, Vocals, guitar, composer, American
Richmond, Kim, Big Band; Modern Jazz, 1960s–, Saxophone, clarinet, flute, arranger, composer, American
Riel, Alex, Free Jazz, 1960s–, Drums, Danish
Riley, Ben, Hard Bop, 1960s–, Drums, American
Riley, Howard, Free Jazz, 1960s–, Piano, British
Rimington, Sammy, New Orleans Jazz, 1960s–, Clarinet, saxophone, leader, British
Rising Sons, Blues Rock, 1960s, Various instruments, American
Rivers, Sam, Free Jazz, 1960s–, Saxophones, flute, piano, American
Roach, Freddie, Soul Jazz, 1960s–1970s, Organ, American
Robinson, Fenton, Texas Blues, 1960s–1980s, Guitar, vocals, American
Robinson, Jimmie Lee, Modern Electric Blues; Rhythm & Blues, 1960s–2000s, Vocals, guitar, composer, American
Robinson, Perry, Fusion, 1960s–, Clarinet, American
Rolling Stones, The, Blues Rock, 1960s–, Various instruments, British
Romano, Aldo, Free Jazz, 1960s–, Drums, guitar, Italian
Rosengren, Bernt, Free Jazz; Modern Jazz; Big Band, 1960s–, Saxophone, Swedish
Rubin, Ron, Traditional Jazz; Chicago Jazz; Dixieland Revival, 1960s–, Piano, double bass, British
Rusch, Bob, All Jazz Styles, 1960s–, Author, critic, American
Rush, Otis, Chicago Blues, 1960s–, Guitar, vocals, American
Rutherford, Paul, Free Jazz, 1960s–, Trombone, British
Sample, Joe, Hard Bop; Fusion; Soul Jazz, 1960s–, Piano, American
Sanders, Pharaoh, Free Jazz; Hard Bop, 1960s–, Saxophones, American
Santana, Carlos, Blues Rock, 1960s–, Guitar, American
Savoy Brown, Blues Rock; British Blues, 1960s–, Various instruments, British
Schiano, Mario, Free Jazz; Modern Jazz, 1960s–, Saxophone, vocals, bandleader, Italian
Schlippenbach, Alex, Free Jazz, 1960s, Piano, composer, bandleader, German
Schoof, Manfred, Free Jazz, 1960s–, Trumpet, flugelhorn, piano, composer, German
Schuller, Gunther, Ragtime; Modern Jazz, 1960s–, French horn, arranger, composer, author, American
Scott, Tom, Jazz Pop; Fusion, 1960s–, Saxophone, flute, bandleader, American
Scott-Adams, Peggy, Modern Electric Blues, 1960s–, Vocals, American
Sebesky, Don, Hard Bop; Jazz Rock, 1960s–, Trombone, arranger, composer, American
Shakey Vick, British Blues, 1960s, Various instruments, British
Shariff, Omar, Texas Blues, 1960s–, Piano, vocals, American
Sharrock, Sonny, Free Jazz, 1960s–1990s, Guitar, composer, American
Shaw, Eddie, Jump Blues; Modern Electric Blues, 1960s–, Vocals, saxophone, bandleader, American
Shaw, Marlena, Modern Jazz; Soul Jazz, 1960s–, Vocals, American
Shepherd, Jim, Traditional Jazz; Swing, 1960s–, Trombone, saxophone, British
Shepp, Archie, Free Jazz; Hard Bop, 1960s–, Saxophones, piano, vocals, composer, American
Shew, Bobby, Hard Bop; Big Band, 1960s–, Trumpet, flugelhorn, American
Shines, Johnny, Delta Blues; Chicago Blues, 1960s–1990s, Guitar, vocals, American
Shoemake, Charlie, Hard Bop; Bebop, 1960s–, Vibraphone, American
Shorter, Wayne, Modern Jazz; Hard Bop; Fusion, 1960s–, Saxophone, American
Shotham, Ramesh, Bebop, 1960s–, Percussion, Indian
Siegel-Schwall Band, Modern Electric Blues, 1960s–1980s, Various instruments, American
Silva, Alan, Free Jazz, 1960s–, Bass, cello, violin, piano, American
Simmons, Little Mack, Rhythm & Blues; Chicago Blues, 1960s–1990s, Vocals, harmonica, American
Simmons, Sonny, Free Jazz, 1960s–, Saxophone, American
Simpson, Martin, Modern Electric Blues, 1960s–, Guitar, British
Sirone, Free Jazz, 1960s–, Bass, American
Skeat, Len, Bebop, 1960s–, Bass, British
Skidmore, Alan, Bebop; Hard Bop, 1960s–, Saxophone, flute, drums, British
Smith, Brian, Jazz Rock, 1960s–, Saxophone, flute, New Zealander
Smith, Byther, Modern Electric Blues, 1960s–, Vocals, guitar, American
Smith, Colin, Traditional Jazz; New Orleans Jazz, 1960s–, Trumpet, British
Smith, Keith, Chicago Jazz; Swing; Big Band, 1960s–, Trumpet, vocals, leader, British
Smith, Lonnie, Soul Jazz; Hard Bop, 1960s–, Organ, American
Smith, Moses 'Whispering', East Coast Blues; Louisiana Blues, 1960s–1970s, Vocals, harmonica, American
Smith, Warren, Free Jazz, 1960s–, Percussion, American
Smither, Chris, Country Blues; Blues Rock, 1960s–, Guitar, vocals, American
Smoker, Paul, Bebop; Swing; Free Jazz, 1960s–, Trumpet, American
Smokey Babe, Country Blues, 1960s, Guitar, vocals, American
Smothers, Little Smokey, Modern Electric Blues, 1960s–1990s, Guitar, American
Smothers, Otis 'Big Smokey', Modern Electric Blues; Rhythm & Blues, 1960s–1990s, Vocals, guitar, American
Smythe, Pat, Free Jazz; World Jazz; Fusion, 1960s–1980s, Piano, composer, arranger, British
Soft Machine, The, Jazz Rock, 1960s–1990s, Various instruments, British
Soloff, Lew, Cool Jazz; Fusion, 1960s–, Trumpet, flugelhorn, piccolo, American
Spann, Otis, Chicago Blues, 1960s, Piano, American
Sparks, Melvin, Hard Bop; Soul Jazz, 1960s–, Guitar, American
Spellman, Benny, Rhythm & Blues, 1960s, Vocals, American
Spring, Bryan, Bebop; Hard Bop; Jazz Rock, 1960s–, Drums, British
Stackhouse, Houston, Country Blues; Delta Blues, 1960s–1970s, Vocals, guitar, American
Stanko, Tomasz, Free Jazz, 1960s–, Trumpet, Polish
Steampacket, British Blues, 1960s, Various instruments, British
Steig, Jeremy, Jazz Rock, 1960s–, Flute, piccolo, electronics, composer, American
Stevens, John, Free Jazz, 1960s–1990s, Drums, cornet, trumpet, British
Stewart, Louis, Swing; Modern Jazz, 1960s–, Guitar, Irish
Stubblefield, John, Free Jazz; Hard Bop; Modern Jazz, 1960s–, Saxophone, American
Sudhalter, Dick, Traditional Jazz; Swing, 1960s–, Cornet, horn, flugelhorn, piano, American
Sulzmann, Stan, Free Jazz; Modern Jazz, 1960s–, Saxophone, flute, clarinet, British
Sun Ra, Free Jazz, 1960s–1990s, Keyboards, composer, American
Sunshine, Monty, New Orleans Jazz; Chicago Jazz, 1960s–, Clarinet, British
Surman, John, Free Jazz; Jazz Rock, 1960s–, Saxophone, clarinet, British
Szabo, Gabor, Modern Jazz; Pop Jazz, 1960s–, Guitar, composer, arranger, bandleader, Hungarian
Tabackin, Lew, Hard Bop, 1960s–, Saxophone, flute, American
Taj Mahal, Country Blues, 1960s–, Vocals, piano, guitar, harmonica, American
Takayanagi, Masayuki, Free Jazz, 1960s–1990s, Guitar, Japanese
Tapscott, Horace, Free Jazz; Big Band, 1960s–1990s, Piano, arranger, composer, bandleader, American
Taylor, Cecil, Free Jazz, 1960s–, Piano, composer, American
Taylor, John, Free Jazz, 1960s–, Piano, British
Taylor, Mick, Blues Rock, 1960s–, Guitar, British
Tchicai, John, Free Jazz, 1960s–, Saxophones, flute, Danish
Ten Years After, British Blues; Blues Rock, 1960s–1990s, Various instruments, British
Texier, Henri, Hard Bop; Modern Jazz; Bebop, 1960s–, Bass, French
Thelin, Eje, Modern Jazz; Hard Bop, 1960s–1980s, Trombone, composer, Swedish
Them, British Blues; Blues Rock, 1960s, Various instruments, British
Themen, Art, Free Jazz; Hard Bop; Modern Jazz, 1960s–, Saxophone, British
Thilo, Jesper, Bebop; Swing, 1960s–, Saxophone, clarinet, Danish
Thomas, Irma, Rhythm & Blues, 1960s–, Vocals, American
Thomas, James 'Son', Delta Blues, 1960s–1980s, Guitar, American
Thomas, Leon, Free Jazz; Modern Jazz, 1960s–1990s, Vocals, American
Thompson, Butch, Traditional Jazz; Ragtime, 1960s–, Piano, clarinet, American
Thompson, Danny, Fusion; Folk Jazz, 1960s–, Double bass, British
Thompson, Don, Modern Jazz, 1960s–, Bass, piano, Canadian
Tippett, Keith, Free Jazz; Fusion, 1960s–1990s, Piano, composer, British
Togashi, Masahiko, Free Jazz; Hard Bop, 1960s–, Drums, composer, bandleader, Japanese
Tolliver, Charles, Hard Bop, 1960s–1980s, Trumpet, flugelhorn, American
Tomkins, Trevor, Bebop; Modern Jazz, 1960s–, Drums, percussion, British
Tommaso, Giovanni, Jazz Rock, 1960s–, Bass, Italian
Tompkins, Ross, Swing; Bebop; Cool Jazz, 1960s–, Piano, American
Tracey, Stan, Free Jazz; Hard Bop; Modern Jazz, 1960s–, Piano, composer, British
Tramp, British Blues, 1960s–1970s, Various instruments, British
Tucker, Luther, Modern Electric Blues; Chicago Blues, 1960s–1990s, Guitar, American
Tucker, Tommy, Rhythm & Blues, 1960s–1980s, Piano, clarinet, American
Turrentine, Stanley, Hard Bop; Fusion, 1960s–1990s, Saxophone, American
Tusques, Francois, Free Jazz, 1960s–, Piano, composer, bandleader, French
Twice as Much, British Blues, 1960s, Modern Electric Blues, British
Tyler, Charles, Free Jazz, 1960s–1990s, Saxophone, American
Tyner, McCoy, Modern Jazz; Hard Bop, 1960s–, Piano, composer, bandleader, American
VanHove, Fred, Free Jazz, 1960s–, Piano, Belgian
VanManen, Willem, Free Jazz, 1960s–, Trombone, composer, bandleader, Dutch
Vaughn, Jimmy, Boogie-Woogie, 1960s–1980s, Piano, arranger, American
Vick, Harold, Soul Jazz; Hard Bop, 1960s–1980s, Saxophones, American
Vitet, Bernard, Modern Jazz; Free Jazz, 1960s–, Trumpet, composer, French
Vitous, Miroslav, Free Jazz; Modern Jazz; Fusion, 1960s–, Bass, Czech
VonSchlippenbach, Alexander, Free Jazz; Big Bang, 1960s–, Piano, bandleader, German
Vuckovich, Larry, Modern Jazz, 1960s–, Piano, Montenegrin
Wallis, Bob, Traditional Jazz, 1960s–1990s, Trumpet, vocals, leader, British
Ward, Robert, Modern Electric Blues; Rhythm & Blues, 1960s–, Guitar, American
Warleigh, Ray, World Jazz; British Jazz, 1960s–, Saxophone, clarinet, flute, Australian
Washington, Albert, Rhythm & Blues; Modern Electric Blues, 1960s–1990s, Vocals, guitar, keyboard, American
Washington, Grover Jr, Soul Jazz, 1960s–1990s, Saxophones, clarinet, bass, piano, American
Washington, Leroy, Chicago Blues, 1960s, Vocals, American
Watanabe, Sadao, Jazz Pop, 1960s–, Saxophone, Japanese
Waterman, Dick, All Blues Styles, 1960s–, Photographer, promoter, manager, author, American
Watrous, Bill, Bebop, 1960s–, Trombone, composer, American
Watson, Johnny 'Guitar', Modern Electric Blues; Texas Blues; Rhythm & Blues, 1960s–1990s, Guitar, vocals, American
Watts, Charlie, Rhythm & Blues, 1960s–, Drums, British
Watts, Ernie, Modern Jazz; Jazz Rock, 1960s–, Saxophone, flute, American
Watts, Trevor, Free Jazz, 1960s–, Saxophone, piano, clarinet, British
Wells, Junior, Chicago Blues; Modern Electric Blues, 1960s–1990s, Harmonica, American
Weston, Harvey, Modern Jazz, 1960s–, Bass, British
Wheeler, Kenny, Free Jazz; Modern Jazz, 1960s–, Trumpet, flugelhorn, Canadian
Whigham, Jiggs, Swing; Big Band, 1960s–, Trombone, American
Willette, Baby Face, Soul Jazz; Hard Bop, 1960s, Organ, American
Williams, Buster, Hard Bop, 1960s–, Bass, American
Williams, Jackie, Swing, 1960s–, Drums, American
Williams, Johnny, Rhythm & Blues, 1960s–1970s, Vocals, American
Williams, Lee 'Shot', Modern Electric Blues, 1960s–, Vocals, guitar, American
Williams, Roy, Traditional Jazz; British Jazz, 1960s–, Trombone, British
Williams, Tony, Fusion; Hard Bop, 1960s–1990s, Drums, composer, American
Willis, Larry, Fusion, 1960s–, Pianist, arranger, composer, producer, American
Wilmer, Val, Jazz, 1960s–, Author, photographer, critic, British
Wilson, Nancy, Modern Jazz, 1960s–, Vocals, American
Wilson, Phillip, Free Jazz, 1960s–1990s, Drums, American
Wilson, Reuben, Soul Jazz; Hard Bop; Fusion, 1960s–1990s, Organ, American
Wilson, Smokey, Modern Electric Blues, 1960s–1980s, Guitar, American
Winstone, Norma, Free Jazz, 1960s–, Vocals, British
Winter, Edgar, Blues Rock, 1960s–1970s, Saxophone, American
Winter, Paul, World Fusion, 1960s–, Saxophones, producer, American
Wiseman, Val, Swing; Dixieland Revival, 1960s–, Vocals, British
Wofford, Mike, Modern Jazz, 1960s–, Piano, American
Woods, Johnny, Delta Blues, 1960s–, Harmonica, American
World's Greatest Jazz Band, Dixieland Revival, 1960s–1970s, Various instruments, American
Wrencher, Big John, Chicago Blues, 1960s–1970s, Harmonica, vocals, American
Wright, Frank, Free Jazz, 1960s–1990s, Saxophone, American
Yamashita, Yosuke, Free Jazz; Fusion; Hard Bop, 1960s–, Piano, composer, author, Japanese
Yardbirds, The, British Blues; Blues Rock, 1960s, Artist, British
Yoshizawa, Motoharu, Free Jazz, 1960s–1990s, Bass, Japanese
Young, Dave, Modern Jazz, 1960s–, Bass, Canadian
Young, Larry, Soul Jazz; Hard Bop; Fusion, 1960s–1970s, Organ, piano, American
Young, Mighty Joe, Chicago Blues, 1960s–1990s, Guitar, American
Zappa, Frank, Jazz Rock; Fusion, 1960s–1990s, Guitar, composer, American
Zeitlin, Denny, Hard Bop; Modern Jazz, 1960s–, Piano, American
Zoller, Attila, Modern Jazz, 1960s–1990s, Guitar, Hungarian

see Sun Ra pp 264 *see* Cannonball Adderley pp 266 *see* Fleetwood Mac pp 272 *see* Wayne Shorter pp 279

THE SEVENTIES

Of the entire century, the 1970s were the years of catching one's breath. Superficially, the promise of the 1960s had faded or failed, the victim of wretched excess and just plain bad taste. America's war in Vietnam sputtered to an end, international relations elsewhere seemed to stalemate in détente and economically the world suffered from stagflation: exhaustion beset with mixed signals.

Blues and jazz also reached some sort of crossroads. Several blues elders were still active, but their best days were behind them and their appearances often amounted to little more than valedictory trots. North American and European blues festivals sought these veterans as though they were holy men, by their presences condoning the appropriation of their lifelong works. A younger wave of true bluesmen had emerged from Chicago's South Side, but they did not gain much notoriety or respect. At the same time US jazz artists, disaffected by the turmoil of politics at home and the public's neglect of their accomplishments in favour of lesser but flashier sounds, sought other avenues in Europe and Japan, where government and corporate funding for jazz ran relatively high. Looking back, great music of the period is identifiable, but at the time such pop genres as progressive rock and disco seemed relatively content-free. The best jazz and blues existed beneath the radar, if not exactly underground. Part of the problem was media-related: FM radio programmed with imagination, but many recording companies had over-extended their investments without adequate gain. The mood was largely: May the seventies end! What's next?

LED ZEPPELIN

Sources & Sounds

KEY ARTISTS

Allman Brothers Band
Art Ensemble of Chicago
Dr. John
John McLaughlin

'The stuff they're doin' now – the disco and everything else – it's taken from the blues. The music they call "soul music", you know, it's the blues. So disco is not soul; rock'n'roll is not soul. The blues is soul.'

John Lee Hooker

In the 1970s, rock music continued to reign and infiltrate both jazz and blues. It could be said that the blues took a back seat to its own influence. The root sensibilities and typical three-chord structures of the blues could be detected in the music of hundreds of predominately rock artists and was in some ways a dominant force, but at the same time musicians who could genuinely claim the blues as their own territory were all but obscured from the public eye.

Above

Slide guitarist Ry Cooder was a key figure on the 1970s Los Angeles blues scene; his music reflected influences from other cultures, including Africa and Hawaii.

Crossing Over

The cross-pollination of blues and rock elements spread as the sounds of the British Blues scene crossed the Atlantic Ocean to re-inspire Americans. The Rolling Stones, the Yardbirds, Cream, John Mayall's Bluesbreakers and other British groups motivated younger artists like Johnny Winter (b. 1944), the Allman Brothers Band and ZZ Top to develop their own distinctive hybrids. American bands like the Eagles blended country and rock'n'roll influences with their personal takes on the blues, often achieving tremendous success. Although Duane Allman and ZZ Top's Billy Gibbons had little in common when it came to guitar techniques, both ranked among the most popular, influential players of the time. By mid-decade, their blues-enriched sounds were hotly competing with disco on the American music market.

Across America, young electric and acoustic blues artists swarmed from the woodwork. So many styles were formulated in so many regions that it was difficult to differentiate between them all. In Austin, Texas, while guitarist Jimmie Vaughan and the

see Introduction pp 284 *see* Key Artists pp 294 *see* A–Z of Artists pp 302 *see* List of Artists pp 312

Fabulous Thunderbirds were starting down the road to stardom in 1974, Jimmie's little brother Stevie Ray Vaughan (1954–90) was putting together his first band. Around the same time, Roy Buchanan (1939–88) was rocking the house in Washington, DC, Johnny Copeland (1937–97) was club-hopping in New York City, George Thorogood & the Destroyers were backing visiting blues acts in Boston, J.J. Cale (b. 1938) was continuing to lay down his lazy blues in Tulsa and down in New Orleans Dr. John (b. 1940) blended traditional jazz, rock'n'roll, Creole music, blues and voodoo weirdness into a heady, tantalizing stew.

The West Coast of the US boasted an innovative recording-studio blues community. In Los Angeles Ry Cooder (b. 1947) and Taj Mahal (b. 1940), who had played together in the Rising Sons, represented the global side of things as they tied together diverse threads of the blues, jazz, country, gospel and African and Hawaiian music. Elsewhere in town, a young, red-headed guitarist and singer named Bonnie Raitt (b. 1949) was turning heads with her slide abilities. Captain Beefheart – a truly idiosyncratic, inspired associate of canny and satirical composer, bandleader and rock-blues guitar virtuoso Frank Zappa – distilled the essence of Howlin' Wolf's (1910–76) gravelly blues into a cocktail of abstract lyrics and avant-garde guitars. Up in San Francisco, bassist Jack Casady and guitarist Jorma Kaukonen broke away from Jefferson Airplane to form Hot Tuna, a group of revolving personnel with a keen interest in acoustic blues traditions.

Rock Pervades The Jazz Scene

As far as the evolution of jazz was concerned, in many ways the 1970s can be seen as a transition period. The generational divide became evident with the ascendancy of young artists such as Jaco Pastorius (1951–87), George Benson and Chick Corea, and the deaths of veteran musicians Louis Armstrong (1901–71) and Duke Ellington (1899–74). Jazz musicians were in the pop-music charts for the first time since the 1950s, but this was a new breed of improvisers who were influenced as much by the Beatles or Motown/soul music as by Armstrong or Charlie Parker (1920–55), and they used electric instruments to express themselves. The free-jazz movement of the 1960s grew even more politicized and spread its branches to Chicago, St. Louis, Los Angeles and beyond. Artists who trod the middle ground between electricity and the avant-garde found it difficult to get live jobs, yet some still had a productive decade, recording some of their best work.

What Miles Hath Wrought

Trumpeter Miles Davis (1926–91) ushered in the new decade at New York City's Village Gate, in the middle of a month-long residency. The live shows bisected an intensive period of studio work that produced a stunning pair of albums, whose influence would continue to resonate three decades later: *Bitches Brew* (1969) and *Jack Johnson* (1970). While not the first jazz artist to use electric guitar, piano and bass, Davis was the highest-profile leader to adapt the popular approaches of Jimi Hendrix (1942–70), Sly Stone, James Brown and Stevie Wonder to his own ends. His imprimatur cannot be overrated.

Left
The 1980 film *The Blues Brothers* sparked a wide revival of interest in blues music.

CLASSIC RECORDINGS

1970
Ry Cooder: *Performance*
B.B. King: 'The Thrill Is Gone'

1971
J.J. Cale: 'After Midnight'
Keith Jarrett: 'In Front'

1972
Dave Holland Quartet: *Conference Of The Birds*
McCoy Tyner: *Echoes Of A Friend*

1973
Jimmy Dawkins: *All For Business*
Herbie Hancock: *Head Hunters*

1974
Jaco Pastorius: *Jaco*

1975
Led Zeppelin: *Physical Graffiti*

see Rolling Stones pp 278 *see* Jaco Pastorius pp 309 *see* ZZ Top pp 311 *see* Stevie Ray Vaughan pp 330

Above
Trumpeter Miles Davis revolutionized jazz yet again in the 1970s with his jazz-rock fusion.

Davis had been brewing up his new direction since 1968, and several of his collaborators from the period had ideas of their own about how to fuse elements of rock with jazz. Drummer Tony Williams (1945–97) formed Lifetime, which emulated the guitar-driven power trio sound of Cream and the Jimi Hendrix Experience; saxophonist Wayne Shorter (b. 1933) and keyboardist Joe Zawinul (b. 1932) started Weather Report to explore colour with amplified instruments; pianists Chick Corea and Herbie Hancock (b. 1940) put together their own distinctive electric bands. What these projects had in common was a greater emphasis on volume and individual expression through lengthy solos.

Marketing played a more important role, too. Gone was the underplayed artwork of Blue Note Records and Impulse!; in its place were rock-inspired themes and, in the case of Corea's Return To Forever, a series of grandiose sci-fi fantasies that seemed better suited to a British progressive rock band. Instead of nightclubs, the bands played university campuses and outdoor festivals. On FM radio, Weather Report was featured next to rockers like Pink Floyd and the Allman Brothers Band.

Electric Shock

Miles's musical progeny were making improvised instrumental music attractive and commercially viable. *Bitches Brew* and Hancock's *Head Hunters* (1973) set sales records for jazz. Rock artists, including guitarists Carlos Santana and Jeff Beck, blurred the lines between the genres from the opposite direction, while well-established jazz musicians such as Freddie Hubbard (b. 1938) and Donald Byrd, whether because of commercial pressures or artistic curiosity, began to add electric instruments and broaden their repertoire beyond jazz standards. Even musical iconoclast Ornette Coleman (b. 1930) went electric in the 1970s with his radical septet Prime Time.

However, as with all trends, the fascination wore off for many audiences as the second and third wave of participants arrived, and by the end of the 1970s jazz-rock fusion had become an artistic dead end of overlong solos and outdated, overblown imagery. As his former sidemen and acolytes delved into electric jazz rock, Davis moved deeper into dense, pan-cultural music that combined African rhythms, Indian instruments and distorted guitar. All but crippled by leg injuries, sickle-cell anaemia and drug abuse, Davis retreated from music completely in 1975.

Hard Times For Blues Musicians

Despite a definite resurgence of interest in the *idea* of blues music during the decade, many influential blues players found themselves pushed out of the marketplace altogether and the musicians who inspired the British Invasion now found themselves unable to make a living. At the start of the decade, the Rolling Stones had toured with Buddy Guy (b. 1936), Junior Wells (1934–98) and Bonnie Raitt, temporarily

see Introduction pp 284 *see* Key Artists pp 294 *see* A–Z of Artists pp 302 *see* List of Artists pp 312

expanding the blues audience. But by 1979, many of their fans were unaware of the primal southern roots of the Stones' beloved music; by the same token, the music that the Stones themselves were writing by this time showed less of their blues roots than had been discernible in their songs of the 1960s, although the material performed in their live shows would often pay tribute to the R&B greats that originally inspired them. Still, this did not stop a number of desperate, neglected blues artists from retreating into drug and alcohol abuse, further complicating their declines in popularity.

A few stalwarts kept their careers afloat. B.B. King (b. 1925) seemed to be an unstoppable force in the 1970s: he kicked off the decade with the tremendous pop crossover hit 'The Thrill Is Gone', which brought the blues to new audiences, collaborated several times with Bobby 'Blue' Bland (b. 1930), and released no fewer than 10 new records before the decade's end. Beloved worldwide and constantly busy, King was a beacon of hope that the bluesmen's stars would someday rise again. He has remained a pre-eminent blues musician into the twenty-first century, guesting with rock stars and appearing in commercials. Other blues artists continued to tour on the international festival and college circuits, but the audiences that had eagerly devoured their music in the previous decade were dwindling.

Above

Thad Jones (left) jams with Mel Lewis, 1976.

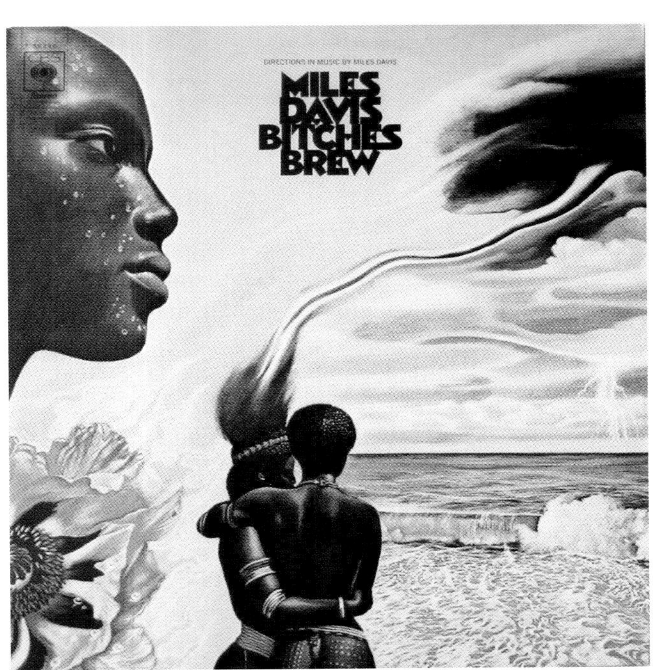

Left

Davis's 1969 *Bitches Brew* album set a new precedent; its influence is still felt in twenty-first century jazz releases.

Blues Lives On In Rock

Muddy Waters (1915–83) was moderately active at the time, although it was not until Johnny Winter produced Waters' *Hard Again* in 1977 on Columbia Records that he reclaimed a sizeable portion of his prior high profile. His powerful performance in the band's farewell concert also served to remind audiences that he was not only still going, but that he could at least equal if not upstage some of the best known musicians of the day. The Martin Scorsese-directed film of the event, *The Last Waltz* (1978), brought some stunning, mainly blues-based footage to the big screen; the performers represented a fine selection of the Band's friends, influences and contemporaries from both sides of the Atlantic, and included Dr. John, Paul Butterfield, Bob Dylan, Eric Clapton, Van Morrison, Pinetop Perkins and Bobby Charles.

see Miles Davis pp 200 *see* Muddy Waters pp 212 *see* B.B. King pp 260 *see* Herbie Hancock pp 305

Arthur 'Big Boy' Crudup (1905–74) – an R&B legend who had influenced Elvis Presley – and Albert King (1923–92) experienced rejuvenation in the early 1970s through music festivals and new recording opportunities. And, thanks to a contract with Leon Russell's Shelter label, Freddie King (1934–76) also kept relatively busy until his death in 1976. Howlin' Wolf had not performed much outside of a regular gig at Chicago's 1815 Club due to chronic health problems. His last performance was with B.B. King at the Chicago Amphitheatre in November 1975, two months before his death.

Above

The early 1970s was a prosperous time for some black blues artists, who were booked on package tours such as the American Blues Legends, presented by Big Bear music.

Around the middle of the decade, some British artists veered sharply away from the blues and headed deeper into mainstream rock. The phenomenon was not universal, as illustrated by the success of Eric Clapton, John Mayall and Rory Gallagher (1949–95), all three of whom stayed relatively faithful to the blues that had been their guiding light. But other influential British blues artists either faded away or irreversibly changed course.

Led Zeppelin was born from the ashes of the Yardbirds when guitarist Jimmy Page put together a 'ghost band' to honour the group's contracts. Its young fans loved the power of Page's sizzling guitar, Robert Plant's banshee voice, John Paul Jones's virtuoso bass licks and John Bonham's thunderous drums, but knew little about the proximity of certain Led Zeppelin numbers to early blues songs – especially as the band had a tendency to claim authorship. As the band assumed the throne of heavy-metal monarchy, fewer of its songs drew from the blues. A few platinum albums later, the covers of Otis Rush (b. 1934) and the hints of Muddy Waters and Elmore James (1918–63) that seasoned Zeppelin's early work had begun to waft away, although the occasional number, such as 'In My Time Of Dying' on 1975's *Physical Graffiti*, suggested that Led Zeppelin never completely abandoned its blues roots.

Coltrane's Children

The musicians that inspired the jazz of the 1970s were from the somewhat more recent past; if Davis's followers found commercial fortune in tracking his lead, the influence of John Coltrane (1926–67) was no less powerful. The concept of making music on your own terms and seeking freedom through your instrument was Coltrane's legacy, and there were many younger musicians ready to take up where he had left off. By the 1970s, Chicago had already launched the careers of several distinctive artists, including saxophonist Roscoe Mitchell and trumpeter Lester Bowie. With the Association for the Advancement of Creative Musicians (AACM), a musicians' collective that was formed by pianist Muhal Richard Abrams (b. 1930) and others in 1965, Chicago began to develop younger players such as saxophonists Henry Threadgill (b. 1944) and Chico Freeman, trombonist George Lewis and bassist Fred Hopkins, and to attract creative musicians from other Midwest cities, such as St. Louis saxophonists Oliver Lake and Julius Hemphill.

In California, Coltrane's influence also touched two young saxophonists who would make important contributions in the 1970s. Alto saxophonist Arthur Blythe grew up in San Diego and cut his musical teeth with influential pianist Horace Tapscott in Los Angeles. Further north, in Berkeley, David Murray was translating the harmonic freedom of Jimi Hendrix's guitar playing style to the saxophone. Studying with Blythe at Pomona College opened Murray's ears to the possibilities inherent in free jazz.

By the mid-1970s, many of these players had made the time-honoured trek to New York City, where

see Introduction pp 284 *see* Key Artists pp 294 *see* A–Z of Artists pp 302 *see* List of Artists pp 312

they found a common musical outlet in venues that collectively became known as 'the loft scene'. Cross-fertilization became commonplace, with musicians such as Murray, Freeman, drummer Philip Wilson, trumpeter Olu Dara and organist Amina Claudine Myers playing together frequently and influencing one another. In 1976, four of the most prolific reed players – Murray, Hemphill, Lake and Hamiet Bluiett – formed the World Saxophone Quartet. Along with Threadgill's trio Air – which included bassist Hopkins and drummer Steve McCall – Murray's thorny octet, the quartets led by multi-reed player Anthony Braxton and the Art Ensemble of Chicago, the World Saxophone Quartet pointed to a renewed period of creativity for avant-garde jazz.

Mainstream Struggles

While electric jazz-rock dominated live venues and the avant-garde became rejuvenated, the acoustic jazz that had characterized the 1960s was having a rough ride, with the exception of a few well-established names. So enthralled were the jazz media and the record-buying public by the flash and fire of fusion that numerous acoustic recordings gained lustre only in retrospect. Pianist McCoy Tyner (b. 1938) released several superb albums on Milestone – particularly *Sahara* (1972), *Echoes Of A Friend* (1972) and *Enlightenment* (1973) – while saxophone colossus Sonny Rollins (b. 1930), returning from a six-year recording hiatus, explored a range of approaches, from solo improvisation to all-star touring units. Alto player Phil Woods returned from

Above

Chicago's 1815 club, run by Eddie Shaw (centre, with Frank Weston and Mike Rowe), was an important blues venue in the 1970s.

see Sonny Rollins pp 233   *see* John Coltrane pp 250  *see* Jimi Hendrix pp 273  *see* Led Zeppelin pp 308

Above
Keyboardist Joe Zawinul, a co-founder of Weather Report – one of the most important electric-jazz combos of the decade.

four years in France and formed an outstanding quartet. Tenor giant Dexter Gordon (1923–90) returned from Europe to the US more than once, although it was his December 1976 stand in Greenwich Village that garnered the most attention, resulting in one of his best recordings – *Homecoming: Live At The Village Vanguard* (1976) – and a renewed belief in some quarters that acoustic jazz was back on solid ground.

In West Germany, meanwhile, former bassist Manfred Eicher was establishing a hybrid of electric and acoustic music on his nascent ECM label, using a signature crystalline studio sound that would be widely influential. The Canadian expatriate trumpeter Kenny Wheeler released two luminous LPs on ECM – *Gnu High* (1975) and *Deer Wan* (1977) – while Norwegian tenor player Jan Garbarek helped define the 'ECM sound' with his evocative *Witchi-Tai-To* (1974).

Rising Again

While acoustic blues was less prevalent than its jazz counterpart at this time, a number of promising enterprises arose to keep the blues flame flickering. *Living Blues*, one of the most purist magazines devoted to the music, published its first issue in 1970. It became the principal voice for blues artists and aficionados, touting new releases and reissues with equal zeal. In 1971, when producer Bruce Iglauer failed to get Chicago's Delmark Records to sign Hound Dog Taylor (1917–75) to a contract, he inaugurated his Alligator label specifically to document Taylor's music. Alligator was soon one of the most active blues imprints, issuing impressive albums by artists including Albert Collins (1932–93), Clifton Chenier (1925–87) and Son Seals (1942–2004), and later by Charlie Musselwhite (b. 1944), Johnny Winter and Delbert McClinton (b. 1940).

see Introduction pp 284 *see* Key Artists pp 294 *see* A–Z of Artists pp 302 *see* List of Artists pp 312

One of the greatest blessings to grace the blues came from an unlikely source. In 1977, comedians Dan Aykroyd and John Belushi unveiled their Blues Brothers characters on TV's *Saturday Night Live*. The skit was intended to spoof white blues enthusiasts who wore sunglasses and formed their own bands to play classics by Willie Dixon (1915–92), Jimmy Reed (1925–76) and Muddy Waters. Many in the show's audience missed the joke and fell in love with the Blues Brothers, giving birth to an explosive franchise. In 1980 their first feature film employed authentic blues and R&B artists such as Matt Murphy (b. 1927) and Steve Cropper as the Brothers' backing band and showcased performances by Aretha Franklin, Ray Charles (1930–2004), James Brown and Cab Calloway (1907–94), capturing the breadth of inspiration, influence and inherent entertainment imperatives of the blues. This ignited a widespread revival of interest in urban blues. Prior to Belushi's drug-related death they opened integrated blues clubs, from which came the franchise venue House of Blues. The blues had survived its toughest decade, and its future was looking brighter.

Left

Led Zeppelin's 1975 album *Physical Graffiti* included some tracks that relied heavily on traditional blues songs.

Below

The World Saxophone Quartet.

see Dexter Gordon pp 174 *see* Ray Charles pp 198 *see* Willie Dixon pp 221 *see* Hound Dog Taylor pp 310

Allman Brothers Band Key Artists

CLASSIC RECORDINGS

1969
The Allman Brothers Band, 'Dreams', 'Whippin' Post'

1970
Idlewild South, 'In Memory Of Elizabeth Reed', 'Midnight Rider'

1971
At Fillmore East, 'Statesboro Blues', 'You Don't Love Me'

1972
Eat A Peach, 'Melissa', 'One Way Out'

1973
Brothers And Sisters, 'Jessica', 'Ramblin' Man'

Above
The Allman Brothers Band, whose unique blend of blues and other musical styles began to dominate the 1970s American blues scene.

'Writing a good instrumental is very fulfilling because you've transcended language and spoken to someone with a melody.'

Dickey Betts, Allman Brothers Band

Few groups made as powerful an impression on American blues music in the early 1970s as the Allman Brothers Band. Its blend of blues, jazz, rock and country elements was a predominant sound on nascent FM radio and influenced countless bands that followed in their wake. The Allman Brothers Band have endured tragedies, periods of obscurity and personnel shifts to remain active in the new century.

Muscle Shoals To Macon

Guitarist Duane Allman (1946–71) and his brother, organist/vocalist Gregg Allman (b. 1947), grew up in Daytona Beach, Florida. Their first band, the Escorts, aped the Rolling Stones and the Beatles. They moved further into hard blues and soul with the Allman Joys and the Hour Glass, the latter of which recorded two albums for Liberty Records.

In the late 1960s Duane landed a job as a studio guitarist in Muscle Shoals, Alabama, the famed breeding ground of latter-day soul. He made his name backing King Curtis, Wilson Pickett and Aretha Franklin while framing his own approach to R&B, soul and blues. In 1969 manager Phil Walden urged Allman to put together a band of his own. He hired bassist Berry Oakley, lured guitarist Dickey Betts away from the band Second Coming and selected two drummers: Butch Trucks and Jai Johanny Johanson, a.k.a. Jaimoe. A long jam session proved the concept's viability, and eventually Gregg Allman was brought in on vocals and organ.

see Introduction pp 284 *see* Sources & Sounds 286 *see* A–Z of Artists pp 302

The Allman Brothers Band initially toured Georgia and Florida to build upon its blues-rock template. It first recorded in 1969 for Walden's label, Capricorn. The album did not sell well at first but impressed many of those who did hear it. Word of mouth and solid ticket sales earned the group a good reputation around the South. The Allmans settled in Macon, Georgia, where they worked more acoustic guitar and jazz flavourings into their sound. Duane Allman kept active as a sideman, working with Boz Scaggs, Otis Rush and Johnny Jenkins. He also teamed with Eric Clapton in Bonnie & Delaney, and later Derek & the Dominos.

Above
Gifted guitarist Duane Allman, who worked as a session musician and touring sideman in addition to his exquisite slide playing with the Allman Brothers Band.

Triumph And Tragedy

The group's fame spread on the strength of its second album, the hit tune 'Midnight Rider' and the powerful jam sessions that coloured their live concerts. While the musicians were capable of playing in odd keys and time signatures, their music was still accessible and rock-based enough to maintain its popular momentum.

In March 1971 the band played a series of shows at the Fillmore East, which were documented on its third album. Polydor Records churned up momentum for the record, which turned Duane Allman into America's newest guitar hero. But shortly after *At Fillmore East* was certified gold in October, Duane was killed in a motorcycle accident. Almost exactly one year later, following the success of the follow-up recording, *Eat A Peach*, Berry Oakley also died in a motorcycle crash. Rather than dissolve the group, Gregg Allman and Dickey Betts opted to press on. The first two albums were reissued as a double-LP set, and the next record moved away from the blues underpinnings for a more country-tinged flavour. 'Ramblin' Man' became another huge hit for the band.

The Road Goes On Forever

Around 1974 the group started to fall apart. Gregg Allman's tumultuous marriage to rock singer Cher, his solo career and problems with substance abuse made it hard for the band to stay consistent. Two years later the Allman Brothers Band broke up, with Betts going solo and the other members forming Sea Level. In 1978, cleaned up and ready to roll, Allman reformed the band but faced the spectre of irrelevance as New Wave and punk had staked their claims to rock radio. The band struggled through the 1980s, issuing moderate-selling albums that skirted its prior glory.

In 1989 the band reinvented itself again by bringing in two phenomenal musicians, guitarist Warren Haynes and bassist Allen Woody, whose skills were well beyond anything the Allmans had presented in years. The next album, *Seven Turns* (1990), proved that the band's rock-blues-country fusion was still viable 30 years on. The Allman Brothers Band soon returned to prominence, selling out arenas and concert halls as it has continued to do into the twenty-first century.

see Rolling Stones pp 278 *see* Otis Rush pp 278 *see* British Blues pp 428 *see* Blues Rock pp 431

Art Ensemble of Chicago Key Artists

CLASSIC RECORDINGS

1970
Les Stances a Sophie, 'Theme De Yoyo', 'Theme Libre'

1972
Live At Mandel Hall, 'Checkmate', *Bap-Tizum*, 'Immm', 'Odwalla', 'Ohnedaruth'

1978
Nice Guys, 'Dreaming Of The Master', 'JA'

1980
Urban Bushmen, 'New York Is Full Of Lonely People', 'Uncle'

Above
Art Ensemble of Chicago at AACM's twentieth anniversary festival in 1995. (l–r) Roscoe Mitchell, Famodon Don Moye, Lester Bowie, Malachi Favors and Joseph Jarman.

With its tribal masks, arcane percussion instruments and grand sense of theatre, the Art Ensemble of Chicago always seemed to be more than just a jazz band. Indeed, the group grew from the communal activities of the Chicago-based AACM, which quickly became a magnet and laboratory for freedom-seeking African-American musicians in the city, including saxophonists Roscoe Mitchell (b. 1940) and Joseph Jarman (b. 1937), trumpeter Lester Bowie (1941–99) and bassist Malachi Favors (1927–2004). AACM founder Muhal Richard Abrams' Experimental Band (est. 1961) and Mitchell's quartet, which formed two years later, were early models in the sprawling musical vision of the former and the latter's use of unusual timbres created by small percussion instruments.

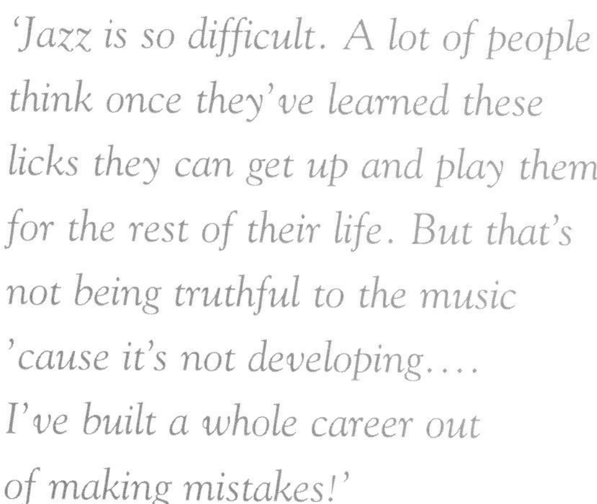

'Jazz is so difficult. A lot of people think once they've learned these licks they can get up and play them for the rest of their life. But that's not being truthful to the music 'cause it's not developing.… I've built a whole career out of making mistakes!'

Lester Bowie

French Sojourn

In June 1969, as the Roscoe Mitchell Art Ensemble, Mitchell, Bowie, Favors and Jarman travelled to Paris, where they re-christened themselves the Art Ensemble of Chicago. The band's impact was as much visual as musical; Favors and Jarman painted their faces and wore African robes and hats, while Bowie donned a white lab coat. Onstage, multiple saxophones and percussion devices surrounded the quartet. The effect was further heightened when drummer Don Moye (b. 1946) joined in September 1969. Moye called his array of drums, cymbals and hand-crafted instruments 'sun percussion' and liked to climax percussion movements by igniting magician's flash-paper between his fingers.

During its two years in Europe, the band recorded 11 albums and three film scores, and toured widely, frequently accompanied by soul singer Fontella Bass, Bowie's wife. The band's music escaped classification. The first three tracks on the 1969 album *A Jackson In Your House* capture part of the range: anthemic horn statements offset by a bicycle horn; antic vocal effects; melodies reminiscent of the Jazz Age; free-blown horn choruses that defy the shouted order to 'Get in line'; and a waltz performed at half-tempo with the horns stretching the melody line like taffy. The band also integrated Bowie's R&B background, with Moye laying down a backbeat and Favors switching to electric bass.

A Pragmatic Agenda

Returning to the US in 1971, the band's members determined that they would focus on building an audience through performances at jazz festivals, universities and large concert venues. Throughout the 1970s, the Art Ensemble steadily spread its name and its motto: 'Great Black Music, Ancient to the Future'. Two recordings for Atlantic Records exposed them to

see Introduction pp 284 *see* Sources & Sounds 286 *see* A–Z of Artists pp 302

a broader audience, and a breakthrough commercial contract with ECM initiated the band's most financially successful period. With *Nice Guys* (1978) and *Full Force* (1980) the band achieved a much higher profile and reached new levels of accessibility. During this period, several members – most notably Bowie and Mitchell – re-established recording and performing careers independent from the band.

Surviving Deaths

The Art Ensemble maintained a relatively high level of creativity and productivity through the 1980s, switching labels to the Japanese DIW company and touring only every other year in order to permit individual projects. In 1993, Jarman left the band to establish a martial arts and Buddhist spiritual centre in New York City, and the others carried on as a quartet. After Bowie's death from cancer in 1999, they re-formed again as a trio. Jarman returned to the fold in 2003, and the group recorded *The Meeting* (2003), as well as announcing an extended concert tour just prior to Favors' death. The remaining members kept the scheduled dates and have plans to continue as a trio or with younger AACM players.

Below

Trumpeter Lester Bowie was a co-founder of the Art Ensemble of Chicago and also led several of his own groups.

see Muhal Richard Abrams pp 266 *see* Free Jazz pp 394

Dr. John

CLASSIC RECORDINGS

1968
Gris Gris, 'Gris-Gris Gumbo Ya Ya', 'I Walk On Gilded Splinters', 'Mama Roux'

1972
Dr. John's Gumbo, 'Iko Iko', 'Junko Partner', 'Tipitina'

1973
In The Right Place, 'Life', 'Right Place, Wrong Time', 'Such A Night', 'Traveling Mood'

Malcolm John 'Mac' Rebennack Jr., a.k.a. 'Dr. John the Night Tripper', was born in New Orleans in November 1940. The singer and pianist began his professional career while he was still a teenager. He backed local favourites including Joe Tex and Professor Longhair on guitar and keyboards, produced and arranged sessions at Cosmio Studio, also frequented by Allen Toussaint, and issued a few singles of his own as Mac Rebennack. A hand injury caused him to abandon the guitar in the mid-1960s, and soon he migrated to Los Angeles for studio work.

'When I first came up, the blues I was playing was almost bebop orientated – very hip…. Now it's going back beyond that to some kind of roots….'

Dr. John

Voodoo Blues

The Dr. John persona emerged in the late 1960s, as Rebennack began to formulate his 'voodoo music', a unique fusion of blues, jazz, R&B and rock elements. His rough, drawling voice, combined with horn licks, deep blues, Mardi Gras funk and electric psychedelia, gave Dr. John an instantly recognizable sound. In live performances he draped himself and the stage with coloured beads, feathers, furs and exotic props, conducting a religious/musical ritual of sorts.

His stage theatrics were an amazing blend of authentic voodoo tradition and modern New Orleans hokum, perfectly complementing his otherworldly music; this was exemplified by 'I Walk On Gilded Splinters' and the title track of his debut album *Gris Gris* (1968), which Dr. John had recorded during studio time left over from a Sonny and Cher session on which he had worked. This album and its follow-up, *Babylon* (1969), were especially heavy on voodoo symbolism and social commentary, often with the sounds layered so densely that the lyrics were hard to discern. In tuneful, often swinging, sometimes sultry pieces, he drew from the standard New Orleans repertoire of jazz, Cajun, Creole and R&B tunes. He quickly integrated the electric piano and keyboards into his signature sound and challenged his generation of guitarists with the mock-heroic 'Lonesome Guitar Strangler'. His approach to music was so unusual and fresh that he built a small but loyal cult following. In the meantime, he also worked in support of artists such as Canned Heat, Jackie DeShannon, B.B. King, Buddy Guy, Albert Collins and John Sebastian.

Above
(l–r) Dr. John, Art Blakey and David 'Fathead' Newman in jazz combo Bluesiana Triangle.

see Introduction pp 284 *see* Sources & Sounds 286 *see* A–Z of Artists pp 302

In The Right Place

In 1972, on *Dr. John's Gumbo*, he garnered more attention by interpreting New Orleans standards, including 'Iko Iko' and 'Junko Partner', which had wider public appeal than his prior psychedelic fusions. The following year he broke out on to the mass market with an unlikely hit; on 'Right Place, Wrong Time', Dr. John was backed by the Meters, New Orleans' premier funk and soul band. The public ate up the infectious rhythms and his rasping voice, placing the tune high on the charts. It was the most substantial hit of his career and did well enough to seal his legacy.

He attempted to duplicate the winning formula without success on his next few recordings, and even tried a venture into disco. He made an appearance on the Band's *Last Waltz* show in 1977, playing 'Such A Night', but a collaboration with guitarists Mike Bloomfield and John Hammond did not draw much attention. He rose to prominence again in 1981 with an acclaimed solo acoustic album that showed off his authentic, rollicking New Orleans piano style. His debt to pianists such as Professor Longhair and Huey 'Piano' Smith became clearer once the voodoo trappings were removed.

Other Zones

More experiments followed for Dr. John: a recording of jazz and pop standards, then another jump into New Orleans history, interpretations of Duke Ellington and several career retrospectives. His more innovative pursuits were followed by rote-sounding returns to his comfort zone, giving Dr. John a rather patchy discography during this period.

In 1990 Dr. John dug deeper into jazz in the trio Bluesiana Triangle, with saxophonist David 'Fathead' Newman and bebop drummer Art Blakey. At his most ambitious, Dr. John collaborated with members of alternative rock bands like Portishead, Squeeze, Primal Scream and Supergrass, upon whom his murky early recordings had been a surprising influence. In 2000 he signed with Blue Note Records and founded his own reissue label, Skinji Brim. His 2001 album, *Creole Moon*, was well-received and saw him continuing to experiment with a melange of musical styles, including jazz, blues and funk.

Above
A youthful Dr. John back when he was still known as Mac Rebennack.

Left
Eccentric New Orleans bluesman Dr. John (left) with his band at London's Roundhouse.

see Duke Ellington pp 52 *see* Art Blakey pp 218 *see* Professor Longhair pp 229 *see* Huey 'Piano' Smith pp 234

John McLaughlin

CLASSIC RECORDINGS

1969
John McLaughlin: *Extrapolation*, 'Binky's Beam', 'Extrapolation'

1970
My Goal's Beyond, 'Goodbye Pork-Pie Hat', 'Peace One'

1971
The Mahavishnu Orchestra: *The Inner Mounting Flame*, 'Meetings Of The Spirit', 'The Noonward Race'

1972
Birds Of Fire, 'Birds Of Fire', 'One World'

1976
Shakti with John McLaughlin: *Shakti*, 'Joy', 'Lotus Feet'

By turns avant-garde adventurer, high-voltage rocker and Third World explorer, Yorkshire-born guitarist John McLaughlin has seldom repeated himself. Born in 1942, McLaughlin studied piano from the age of nine and taught himself guitar after becoming interested in country blues, flamenco and Django Reinhardt. A gig with Pete Deuchar's Professors of Ragtime in 1958 was his ticket to London, where the storm that would become the British Invasion of the US was brewing. He played with Georgie Fame, Graham Bond and Brian Auger, and picked up studio session jobs – ranging from Petula Clark to David Bowie.

Choosing Jazz

By 1967, McLaughlin had tired of session work and moved to Germany to play with vibraphonist Gunter Hampel. Occasionally, he returned to London to jam with musicians such as bassist Dave Holland and drummer Tony Oxley and, eventually, to record the album *Extrapolation* (1969), one of the most exciting debuts in contemporary jazz. Already in place were the remarkably fluid technical facility, diamond-hard tone and harmonic imagination that would set him apart from most jazz guitarists.

'McLaughlin to me is the most important, certainly the most influential voice in the last decade on the guitar, without a doubt.'
Pat Metheny

Concurrent with this recording, McLaughlin was invited by drummer Tony Williams to join his new band, Lifetime. Within hours of landing in the US, McLaughlin was jamming at Count Basie's club in front of an audience that included Miles Davis. Davis, several months into a two-year period of intensive recording activity, did not waste time; he invited McLaughlin to the studio on 18 February 1969 for what would form part of the seminal *In A Silent Way* (1969). While working with Lifetime, McLaughlin helped shape four other key Davis recordings: *Bitches Brew* (1969), *Jack Johnson* (1971), *Live-Evil* (1971) and *Big Fun* (1974).

Above
McLaughlin (second from left) with the Mahavishnu Orchestra, whose 1971 album *The Inner Mounting Flame* was a jazz landmark.

Following A New Leader

McLaughlin was extraordinarily prolific during his first 18 months in the US. In addition to the work with Davis and the Tony Williams Lifetime albums *Emergency!* (1969) and *Turn It Over* (1970), he recorded the rock-influenced *Devotion* (1970), the adventurous *Where Fortune Smiles* (1970) and the acoustic *My Goal's Beyond* (1970). The title and meditative mood of the latter album pointed to a major turning point in his life, a spiritual awakening that would find him pledging allegiance to a mystic, re-christening himself Mahavishnu John McLaughlin and launching a band that would set the bar much higher for instrumental prowess in the burgeoning jazz-rock movement.

The Mahavishnu Orchestra debuted in July 1971 and stunned listeners with rapid-fire unison melody lines played between McLaughlin, violinist Jerry Goodman and keyboardist Jan Hammer, unusual time signatures and advanced dynamics. The band's first recording, *The Inner Mounting Flame* (1971),

see Introduction pp 284 *see* Sources & Sounds 286 *see* A–Z of Artists pp 302

Above

McLaughlin (left) in Shakti, a group with its roots in traditional Indian music.

remains a landmark work of the era. McLaughlin continued to use the Mahavishnu Orchestra name for subsequent bands, but none matched the original for power and invention. The second group is notable for McLaughlin's collaboration with an ensemble conducted by Michael Tilson Thomas, documented on the album *Apocalypse* (1974).

Discovering Other Worlds

In 1976, McLaughlin surprised devotees by releasing *Shakti*, a recording of his acoustic encounter with four traditional Indian musicians. While McLaughlin's trademark lightning arpeggios were still there, the volume was reduced significantly. Never again could fans pin him down to a single style. His subsequent works included renewed interest in jazz rock, *Electric Dreams* (1978) and *Electric Guitarist* (1979); collaborations with classical pianist Katia Labéque, his then-partner; and spirited meetings with guitarists Paco de Lucía and Al DiMeola.

In the 1990s and the early years of the twenty-first century, McLaughlin continued his pattern of going wherever his imagination took him. He recorded and toured with organist Joey DeFrancesco in a trio, continued his occasional forays with De Lucía and DiMeola, and delved back into ragas with Shakti Remembered.

Left

Guitarist John McLaughlin, who worked as a session musician before playing with key jazz artists, including Miles Davis.

see Miles Davis pp 200 *see* Tony Williams pp 281 *see* Dave Holland pp 306 *see* Fusion & Jazz Rock pp 398

A-Z of Artists

Above
The Brecker Brothers, who led one of the most popular jazz-rock groups of the 1970s.

Luther Allison

(Guitar, vocals, 1939–97)

Luther Allison was an impressive electric bluesman whose guitar playing at times recalled Jimi Hendrix. After his brother taught him basic guitar techniques, Allison backed artists such as Muddy Waters, Jimmy Dawkins and Howlin' Wolf in Chicago clubs. Early records on Delmark and triumph at the Ann Arbor Festival led to Allison signing with Motown. He lived in France from 1984–94 and died of cancer in the midst of a strong comeback. His son Bernard carries on the family tradition.

Gato Barbieri

(Tenor saxophone, b. 1934)

An acerbic-toned saxophonist heavily influenced by John Coltrane, Barbieri is an enigmatic figure, best known for his trademark black borsalino and his successful excursions into commercial music. Argentinian by birth, he first surfaced in Paris as a member of trumpeter Don Cherry's group. After two years with Cherry, Barbieri began to actively seek ways to fuse Latin-American music and jazz. His soundtrack for *Last Tango In Paris* (1972) received widespread acclaim.

Carey Bell

(Harmonica, vocals, b. 1936)

Carey Bell is one of Chicago's most distinctive harmonica players. He began playing with pianist Lovie Lee in Mississippi at the age of 13 and moved to Chicago at 20. Sonny Boy Williamson II and Little Walter were key influences on his harmonica style, while tenures with Willie Dixon and Muddy Waters increased his profile in the business. Bell has led over a dozen sessions since his debut in 1969, some featuring his son, guitarist Lurrie Bell.

Anthony Braxton

(Various saxophones and clarinets, flute, piano, b. 1945)

'I've been isolated and kicked out of jazz as a black man who is not "black" enough, a jazz guy who is not "jazz" enough,' said Chicago native Braxton, looking back on a highly iconoclastic career that has been documented on more than 130 recordings. After military service, Braxton emerged in 1966 with a musical conception that, while influenced by older saxophonists like Roscoe Mitchell, Warne Marsh and John Coltrane, was wholly original.

see Introduction pp 284 *see* Sources & Sounds 286 *see* Key Artists pp 294

His debut recordings as a leader in 1968 – *Three Compositions Of New Jazz* and *For Alto* (both on Delmark) – were stunning in their conceptual maturity. In the 1970s, Braxton's music began to reflect his interest in composers Karlheinz Stockhausen and John Cage, as well as his love of marches by John Philip Sousa. His musical output includes solo works and compositions for massed orchestras of 160 players, but he is best known for his quartets, including the group Circle.

Brecker Brothers

(Randy Brecker, trumpet, flugelhorn, b. 1945; Michael Brecker, tenor and soprano saxophone, EWI, 1949–2007)
Philadelphia-born brothers Randy and Michael Brecker were already experienced players when they collaborated with drummer Billy Cobham in 1970 to form Dreams, one of the first groups to attempt combining elements of jazz and rock. In 1975 the siblings formed the Brecker Brothers. Over six years, the band was one of the most popular in jazz, featuring musicians such as David Sanborn, George Duke and Don Grolnick. The brothers reformed briefly in 1992, by which time Michael had established himself as one of jazz's pre-eminent soloists.

Roy Buchanan

(Guitar, vocals, 1939–88)
Roy Buchanan's use of harmonics and his melodic sense were incomparable. Raised on gospel and R&B, he performed with Johnny Otis, Johnny 'Guitar' Watson and Ronnie Hawkins' Hawks as a young man. A 1971 PBS documentary, *The Best Unknown Guitarist In The World*, together with adulation from the likes of John Lennon and Eric Clapton, kick-started Buchanan's rise. He retired in frustration for several years but returned in 1985. Sadly, Buchanan committed suicide while jailed for public drunkenness.

J.J. Cale

(Guitar, vocals, b. 1938)
Cale gigged around his native Tulsa, Oklahoma before moving to LA in 1964. He issued his first record in 1971, after Eric Clapton's hit with Cale's 'After Midnight'. Cale is still known to many only through covers of his songs and has always preferred to stay in the background of the blues scene; this is reflected in his music as he places his vocals way down in the mix, thereby drawing the listener's attention into the record.

Ry Cooder

(Guitar, mandolin, vocals, b. 1947)
Cooder is one of America's most versatile musicians, equally at home with blues, rock, jazz and various ethnic musics. In the mid-1960s he played guitar with Taj Mahal (in the Rising Sons) and Jackie DeShannon, then did studio work with Paul Revere & the Raiders. Especially gifted as a slide guitarist, he has filled that role on sessions with the Rolling Stones, Captain Beefheart, Little Feat, Randy Newman and other artists.

Cooder has also performed on and/or composed a large number of film scores, including *Performance* (1970), *Paris, Texas* (1984), *Streets Of Fire* (1984), *Cocktail* (1988) and *Steel Magnolias* (1989). On his first album, made in 1970, Cooder interpreted classic blues and folk songs as re-envisioned by arranger Van Dyke Parks. Since that time he has delved into jazz, Hawaiian music, Tex-Mex, Indian sitar music and other styles. Cooder gained particular acclaim for the 1997 album *Buena Vista Social Club*, made with various legendary Cuban musicians, and the subsequent documentary film of the same title.

Below
J.J. Cale was influential on the 1970s blues scene but has always shied away from the limelight.

see Don Cherry pp 269 *see* Johnny 'Guitar' Watson pp 281 *see* David Sanborn pp 337 *see* Lurrie Bell pp 352

Above
Guitarist Jimmy Dawkins on a 1972 European tour.

Jimmy Dawkins

(Guitar, vocals, b. 1936)

Guitarist Jimmy Dawkins came from Mississippi to the West Side of Chicago in 1955, formed a friendship with Luther Allison and slowly built a good reputation with his slow-burning expressiveness. He made his first recording, the award-winning *Fast Fingers*, in 1969 for Delmark Records and followed up with the equally serious *All For Business* (1973). In 1970 Dawkins toured and recorded in Europe with Clarence 'Gatemouth' Brown and Otis Rush. He has been a sideman with many key artists.

Robben Ford

(Guitar, vocals, b. 1951)

Robben Ford was born into a musical family on the coast of northern California. His father, Charles, was a guitarist who encouraged Robben to teach himself the instrument at the age of 13. Ford has two musical brothers, drummer Pat and harmonica player Mark. Influenced by Mike Bloomfield, Robben and Pat played in the Charles Ford Band in the late 1960s and were hired by Charlie Musselwhite in 1974.

Right
Blues, jazz and rock guitarist Robben Ford, pictured at the 2003 Yellowjackets reunion.

Robben Ford split his allegiances between playing blues with Jimmy Witherspoon, contemporary jazz with Tom Scott and Miles Davis, rock with Joni Mitchell and George Harrison, and leading his own bands. In 1977 his electric backing band, Yellowjackets, became a jazz group in its own right. Ford has continued to skirt the line between jazz and blues. In 1990 he rejoined his brother Pat in the Ford Blues Band, and he formed his acclaimed Blue Line in 1992.

Free

(Vocal/instrumental group, 1968–73)

Fronted by charismatic Paul Rodgers, Free was a catalyst in the popular shift from blues-dominated rock to heavy-metal forms. Rodgers left Brown Sugar to form Free with guitarist Paul Kossoff, whose playing on the hit 'All Right Now' sealed its popularity in 1970. Not long thereafter, tensions and drug abuse began to weaken the band. By 1973, Rodgers and drummer Simon Kirke had moved on to Bad Company; Kossoff died of heart failure in 1976.

Rory Gallagher

(Guitar, vocals, harmonica, 1949–95)

Irish blues musician Rory Gallagher fell in love with Delta and Chicago blues as a child, collecting as many records as he could get his hands on. In 1969 he formed the band Taste, receiving moderate acclaim, and a year later he released his own eponymous album

see Introduction pp 284 *see* Sources & Sounds 286 *see* Key Artists pp 294

to very good reviews. Gallagher became an extremely popular touring artist in the US and Europe and issued 14 albums in his lifetime, all with a strong flavouring of his personal blues sensibility.

Director Tony Palmer's documentary *Irish Tour* captures Gallagher performing live in 1974, while the live albums from the 1970s also successfully represent his energy and subtlety. He performed and recorded with Muddy Waters and Albert King at the height of his career, holding his own with the masters. Aside from a four-year hiatus in the 1980s, Gallagher stayed active as a touring musician until his death at the age of 46, following a failed liver transplant.

Herbie Hancock

(Piano, electronic keyboards, b. 1940)

A classical prodigy in Chicago, Hancock became one of the most versatile and influential jazz pianists of the post-war era. At the age of 20, he moved to New York City to play with trumpeter Donald Byrd. After his debut as a leader, *Takin' Off* (1962), he joined Miles Davis for a high-profile five years. In the 1970s, his Mwandishi sextet and jazz-funk unit Head Hunters were at the forefront of electric jazz, and he subsequently alternated between electric and acoustic music, becoming an articulate and much-quoted spokesperson for jazz.

Below

Pianist Herbie Hancock has continued to tour, record and explore the boundaries of jazz, electronics, pop music and the classics.

see Clarence 'Gatemouth' Brown pp 218 *see* Albert King pp 258 *see* Mike Bloomfield pp 267 *see* Yellowjackets pp 339

Dave Holland

(Bass, b. 1946)

A professional musician since the age of 13 in his native Wolverhampton, England, Holland became one of jazz's most in-demand bassists after Miles Davis persuaded him to emigrate to the US in 1968. Holland performed on two of Davis's seminal studio recordings, *In A Silent Way* (1969) and *Bitches Brew* (1969), before leaving to co-found the quartet Circle. His debut recording as a leader, *Conference Of The Birds* (1972), is one of the era's masterpieces. Having led two quintets and participated selectively in others' projects, he started a distinctive big band in 1999.

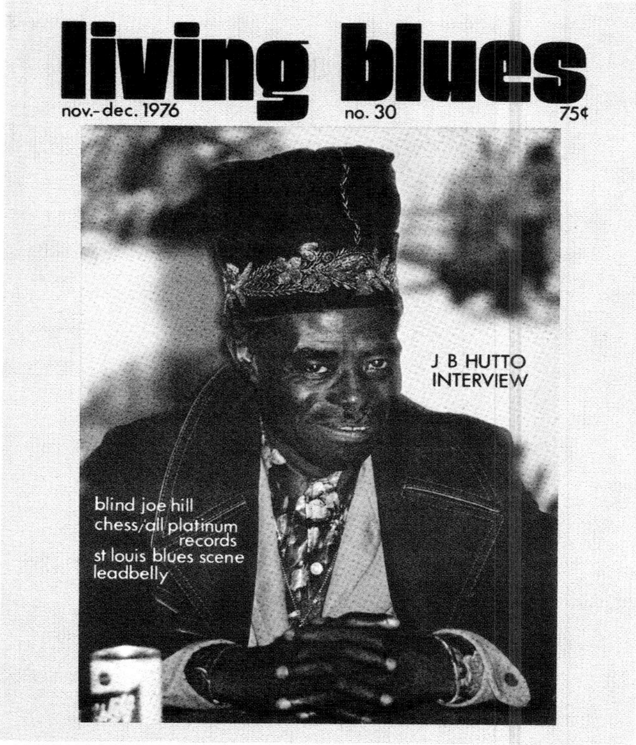

Right
J.B. Hutto graces the cover of a 1976 issue of *Living Blues*.

Hot Tuna

(Vocal/instrumental group, 1970–present)

Jefferson Airplane's Jorma Kaukonen (guitar, vocals) and Jack Casady (bass) – together with drummer Bob Steeler – formed Hot Tuna in San Francisco in order to satisfy their interest in acoustic blues. After an eponymous debut album, the group went electric, added fiddler Papa John Creach and expanded its range to become a staple of the jam-band scene spearheaded by the Grateful Dead. Many line-ups later, Kaukonen and Casady soldier on at Hot Tuna's fore, blending acoustic blues songs from the 1920s and 1930s with the occasional electric performance.

Above
Dave Holland was the pre-eminent bass player of the era, following a stint with Miles Davis.

J.B. Hutto

(Guitar, vocals, 1926–83)

The highly theatrical Joseph Benjamin 'J.B.' Hutto sang in the Golden Crowns Gospel Singers as a child and made his first records with his backup band, the Hawks, in 1954. Hutto then left the music business but returned, rejuvenated, 10 years later. He toured with various incarnations of the Hawks until Hound Dog Taylor's death in 1976, when Hutto briefly took over Taylor's band the Houserockers. He continued to perform with the New Hawks until his own passing.

Abdullah Ibrahim

(Piano, b. 1934)

Born Adolphe Johannes 'Dollar' Brand in Capetown, South Africa, Abdullah Ibrahim successfully fused African rhythms and lilting melodic lines with the piano styles of Duke Ellington and Thelonious Monk. In 1960, with trumpeter Hugh Masekela and others as the Jazz Epistles, he released the first contemporary South African jazz album. The racial climate in his country forced him and his wife, singer Sathima Bea Benjamin, to seek exile in Switzerland, where he met and recorded for Ellington.

Exposed to a wider audience through extensive jazz-festival work, the pianist played with Elvin Jones after the drummer left John Coltrane, and toured Europe with Don Cherry and others. Assuming his Muslim name in the 1970s, he worked frequently as a solo artist, but in 1976 he settled in New York City and established the sextet Ekaya; subsequently, he wrote soundtracks for French film director Claire Denis.

see Introduction pp 284 *see* Sources & Sounds 286 *see* Key Artists pp 294

Above

Trumpeter Thad Jones, whose collaboration with Count Basie lasted for nine years.

Keith Jarrett

(Piano, keyboards, flute, soprano saxophone, percussion, b. 1945)

Few artists are as demanding of themselves and their audiences as Allentown, Pennsylvania native Keith Jarrett. A child prodigy, Jarrett first caused a stir while playing in saxophonist Charles Lloyd's quartet. In 1970, he joined Miles Davis on electric piano and organ. Jarrett soon eschewed electronic keyboards and entered into a long relationship with the German-based label ECM.

In the 1970s he pursued three streams of jazz: improvised solo concerts; knotty, blues- and gospel-inflected works in a quartet with saxophonist Dewey Redman, bassist Charlie Haden and drummer Paul Motian; and more cerebral performances with saxophonist Jan Garbarek, bassist Palle Danielsson and drummer Jon Christensen. In 1983, Jarrett formed a trio with bassist Gary Peacock and drummer Jack DeJohnette to focus on the harmonic and melodic possibilities of the Great American Songbook. Work with this so-called Standards Trio dominated the following two decades, although he continued to pursue other projects, including some recordings of classical works.

Thad Jones

(Flugelhorn, cornet, valve trombone, 1923–86)

The middle brother in Detroit's musical Jones family, Thad Jones joined older sibling Hank at age 16 and, after wartime service, played with younger brother Elvin in Billy Mitchell's band. He rose to prominence with Count Basie during a nine-year tenure (1954–63), but he became best known for the 13-year period in which he co-led a big band with drummer Mel Lewis every Monday night at New York's Village Vanguard. In 1979 Jones moved to Denmark, where he formed the Thad Jones Eclipse.

see Count Basie pp 102 *see* Thelonious Monk pp 208 *see* Jack DeJohnette pp 270 *see* Elvin Jones pp 274

Volker Kriegel

(Electric guitar, 1943–2003)

As a sociology student in Frankfurt, Germany, Kriegel's playing caught the ears of older musicians, who convinced him to pursue music. After working with visiting US players he joined the nascent Dave Pike Set in 1968. Kriegel's *Spectrum* (1971) was an important step in the development of European jazz rock. In 1973, he formed Spectrum with bassist Eberhard Weber, and in 1976 co-founded the long-running United Jazz and Rock Ensemble.

Steve Lacy

(Soprano saxophone, 1934–2004)

Born Steven Lackritz in New York City, Lacy began his career playing Dixieland music with veterans Henry 'Red' Allen and Rex Stewart, but became best known as a highly lyrical and adventurous champion of the soprano saxophone. His adoption of the straight horn, neglected since the heyday of Sidney Bechet, inspired John Coltrane to double on the instrument. Lacy moved to Paris in 1970 and recorded extensively, often taking inspiration from poets and painters.

Above
Steve Lacy brought the straight soprano saxophone back to prominence and inspired John Coltrane to experiment with the instrument.

Right
Louisiana Red first recorded for Chess in 1949 and is equally at home on harmonica and guitar.

Led Zeppelin

(Vocal/instrumental group, 1968–80)

In 1968, after all the original members had left the Yardbirds, guitarist Jimmy Page had custody of the band's name and contracts. John Paul Jones, who had produced some of Page's side work, joined on bass, and Page hired singer Robert Plant away from Hobbstweedle. Drummer John Bonham, a friend of Plant's, rounded out the New Yardbirds to fulfil standing contractual obligations. After Keith Moon, drummer with the Who, quipped that their audacious, harder blues sound would 'go over like a lead zeppelin', the quartet took on a new name.

The group's love of the blues was explicit in its altered cover versions (generally left uncredited), which led to plagiarism charges. Led Zeppelin's self-titled debut album in 1969 was heavy on blues tunes with a psychedelic energy. As Led Zeppelin rose to superstardom it moved further away from the blues but never abandoned it completely. Bonham's death in 1980 effectively brought the premier heavy metal band to an end.

Louisiana Red

(Vocals, harmonica, guitar, b. 1936)

Iverson Minter, a.k.a. Louisiana Red, rose from childhood tragedy to build an impressive career. His mother had died and his father had been murdered by the Ku Klux Klan by the time Red was five years old. He first recorded for Chess in 1949, prior to his military service, and then played with John Lee Hooker before leading his own bands. Louisiana Red is a gifted guitarist, influenced by Elmore James and Muddy Waters.

see Introduction pp 284 *see* Sources & Sounds 286 *see* Key Artists pp 294

Albert Mangelsdorff

(Trombone, 1928–2005)

Although he played violin and guitar, Frankfurt native Albert Mangelsdorff did not take up the trombone until the age of 20. However, despite this relatively late start, he became a pioneer of multiphonics on the horn and a leader of the European avant-garde. Recordings with pianist John Lewis and sitarist Ravi Shankar in the 1960s helped to make his name, but it was as a member of the Globe Unity Orchestra, beginning in 1967, that he was perhaps best known.

Delbert McClinton

(Harmonica, vocals, b. 1940)

Delbert McClinton gigged around Fort Worth as a young man, playing with local acts like the Rondells. He moved to Los Angeles in the early 1970s, playing and writing songs with Glen Clark, but returned to Texas in 1975. As both a performer and songwriter, McClinton smoothly crosses the dividing lines between blues, country, rock and soul. He has enjoyed important collaborations with Roy Buchanan, Bonnie Raitt, Tanya Tucker, B.B. King, Vince Gill and others.

Matt Murphy

(Guitar, vocals, b. 1927)

Matt 'Guitar' Murphy came up in Memphis, playing with Howlin' Wolf, Little Junior Parker and Bobby 'Blue' Bland before gaining serious attention with Memphis Slim's band from 1952 to 1959. In the 1960s Murphy contributed to sessions by Sonny Boy Williamson II, Chuck Berry and Otis Rush, and was a crowd favourite while performing on the 1963 American Folk Blues Festival tour. Murphy's appearance in *The Blues Brothers* film in 1980 helped to seal his place in blues history.

Charlie Musselwhite

(Harmonica, vocals, guitar, b. 1944)

Often compared to his contemporary Paul Butterfield, Musselwhite has an exceptionally fluid and melodic harmonica style that places him head and shoulders above most competitors. He debuted on record in 1967 and has remained faithful to the Chicago style in his own projects and in supporting work for Elvin Bishop, Big Joe Williams, John Hammond Jr., Junior Watson and others. Musselwhite also gave brothers Robben and Pat Ford their start in the blues business in 1974. He staged a comeback in 2004 with a highly promoted album.

Oregon

(Instrumental group, 1971–present)

The antithesis of the fusion music of the 1970s, Oregon comprised Paul McCandless (oboe, English horn, tenor saxophone, bass clarinet), Glen Moore (bass, violin, piano, flute), Ralph Towner (guitar, piano, French horn, trumpet, flugelhorn) and Colin Walcott (tabla, sitar, clarinet, percussion). In some ways, Oregon resembled a chamber-music quartet more closely than a jazz combo, introducing diverse musical elements from far-flung cultures long before 'world music' came into vogue. After Colin Walcott was killed in a car accident in 1984, the group disbanded, but re-emerged in 1986 with Indian percussionist Trilok Gurtu and an even broader range of influences.

Jaco Pastorius

(Electric bass, piano, 1951–87)

The brash Pennsylvania native burst on to the music scene in 1974 with a debut recording, *Jaco*, which redefined the way in which the electric bass could be played. A veteran of R&B and pop bands in Fort Lauderdale by the age of 24, Pastorius collaborated with his good friend, guitarist Pat Metheny, before being hired to join the band Weather Report. In 1980 he formed his own group, Word of Mouth. Increasingly troubled by mental illness, Pastorius died homeless after being beaten by a bouncer outside a Florida nightclub.

Below
Jaco Pastorius, who redefined the role of the electric bass in jazz, played with Pat Metheny and Weather Report, among others.

see Henry 'Red' Allen pp 68 see Memphis Slim pp 179 see Paul Butterfield Blues Band pp 268 see Pat Metheny pp 328

Son Seals

(Guitar, vocals, drums, 1942–2004)

In 1973 dynamic guitarist Frank 'Son' Seals became one of the most exciting artists signed to the fledgling Alligator Records label. His choppy technique and hard-hitting vocals on original songs such as 'Your Love Is Like A Cancer' combine to create an extremely powerful sound. His finest albums include horn sections, which help to drive the energy level even higher. In 2000 Seals recorded *Lettin' Go* for Telarc, with Hammond organist Al Kooper of Blood, Sweat & Tears and guitarist Trey Anastasio of the jam band Phish.

Below
Dynamic guitarist Son Seals performs at London's Hammersmith Odeon in 1977.

Woody Shaw

(Trumpet, flugelhorn, composer, 1944–89)

A lyrical soloist, composer and bandleader, Shaw's career was cut tragically short by illnesses, including deteriorating vision, and a subway accident that cost him an arm. After early work with Willie Bobo and Eric Dolphy, Shaw played extensively in Europe with US expatriates Bud Powell, Kenny Clarke and Johnny Griffin. Returning to America, he worked with Horace Silver, Art Blakey and others. In 1976, he co-led a series of high-profile New York City gigs with Dexter Gordon and thereafter led his own combos, documented by Columbia Records.

Steve Swallow

(Electric bass, b. 1940)

One of a handful of electric-jazz bassists who have shaped the sound of the instrument, Swallow was a student at Yale University when he became attracted to music. An early apprenticeship with pianist Paul Bley grew into a long-term association and the two recorded frequently. Vibist Gary Burton provided another ongoing musical relationship. After a number of years teaching and playing in California, Swallow became involved with pianist-composer Carla Bley, and the pair co-lead numerous projects.

Hound Dog Taylor

(Guitar, vocals, 1915–75)

Many guitarists might sound as though they have extra fingers, but Theodore 'Hound Dog' Taylor, who did not become a full-time musician until he was well past 40, actually had an extra digit on each hand. Producer Bruce Iglauer founded the Alligator label in 1971 expressly to record the guitarist's energetic, raw almost to the point of primitive, 'house-rockin'' style. Taylor and his backing duo, the Houserockers, were among the label's hottest stars for four years until Taylor's death from cancer.

Right
Hound Dog Taylor, for whom producer Bruce Iglauer set up Alligator Records in 1971.

see Introduction pp 284 *see* Sources & Sounds 286 *see* Key Artists pp 294

Koko Taylor

(Vocals, b. 1935)

Singer Koko Taylor (née Cora Walton) earned the title 'The Queen of Chicago Blues' due to her no-nonsense, brazen vocal style. She writes much of her own material, songs that resonate with womanly power and assert her claim to blues royalty. Taylor grew up singing gospel in Memphis and switched to the blues after moving to Chicago in 1953. Bassist Willie Dixon signed her to Chess Records and wrote her big hit 'Wang Dang Doodle' in 1964.

After Chess folded in 1975 Taylor moved to Alligator, becoming one of the label's biggest stars. She was managed by her husband, Pops Taylor, who died in 1989 after an car accident in which Koko was also severely injured. Since her comeback in 1990 Koko Taylor has toured the world constantly, appearing at all the major blues and jazz festivals. Her later bands have often included a number of relatives.

Above

Powerful blues singer Koko Taylor, who recorded for Chess Records before signing with the 1970s-founded Alligator label.

Johnny Winter

(Guitar, vocals, harmonica, b. 1944)

Like his brother, keyboardist and saxophonist Edgar, Johnny Winter is a long-haired Caucasian albino from Texas who reshaped the face of the blues in the 1970s. A phenomenal guitar technician, particularly when using the slide, he rose to prominence in Texas bars and local studios. On his first album for Imperial Records, Winter explored psychedelic blues with middling success. Shortly thereafter he signed with Columbia, for whom he recorded between 1969 and 1974.

His group Johnny Winter And, with guitarist Rick Derringer, had a hit with 'Rock And Roll Hoochie Koo'. Winter is a great interpreter of classic material, covering blues and rock'n'roll tunes by Chuck Berry, B.B. King, Bob Dylan, the Rolling Stones and Van Morrison. *Second Winter* (1969) is one of his best recordings. He is also a gifted producer, working with Muddy Waters in the 1970s on such projects as *Hard Again* (1977). The album *Together – Live* (1976) presents the Winter brothers in fine form.

Joe Zawinul

(Piano, electronic keyboards, b. 1932)

Born in Vienna, Josef Zawinul was 27 when he arrived in the US on a music scholarship, but this relatively late start did not prevent him from becoming an enormously influential composer and bandleader. Following brief stints with Dinah Washington and Maynard Ferguson, Zawinul joined Cannonball Adderley's band as musical director and attracted the attention of Miles Davis, to whom he contributed compositions during the transition to electric jazz. In 1970, Zawinul and Wayne Shorter co-founded Weather Report. After 1985 he led a series of bands under the name Zawinul Syndicate.

ZZ Top

(Vocal/instrumental group, 1970–present)

ZZ Top is a perennial blues trio from Houston, Texas, as well known for their sunglasses, furry guitars and long beards as for their signature boogie beats. Guitarist Billy Gibbons, bassist Dusty Hill and drummer Frank Beard specialize in hard, shuffling electric blues, usually tinged with humour and double entendres. Hits like 'La Grange', 'Jesus Just Left Chicago', 'Tush', 'Legs' and 'Sleeping Bag' have kept the band in the studio and on the road since 1970.

see Muddy Waters pp 212 *see* Horace Silver pp 233 *see* Cannonball Adderley pp 266 *see* Gary Burton pp 267

List of Artists

Entries appear in the following order: name, music style, year(s) of popularity, instruments, country of origin.

Abarius, Gintautas, Modern Jazz; World Fusion, 1970s–1990s, Piano, Lithuanian
Abate, Greg, Fusion, 1970s–1990s, Saxophone, American
Abdullah, Ahmed, Modern Jazz, 1970s–1990s, Trumpet, American
Abe, Kaoru, Free Jazz, 1970s, Saxophone, Japanese
Abercrombie, John, Modern Jazz, 1970s–, Guitar, American
Abrahams, Mick, Blues Rock; Rhythm & Blues, 1970s–1990s, Guitar, British
Adaker, Ulf, Jazz Rock; Latin Jazz, 1970s–, Trumpet, composer, bandleader, Swedish
Adams, Arthur, Modern Electric Blues, 1970s–1990s, Guitar, vocals, American
Aebi, Irene, Free Jazz, 1970s–, Vocals, cello, violin, Swedish
Air, Free Jazz, 1970s–1980s, Various instruments, American
Aklaff, Pheeroan, Free Jazz, 1970s–, Drums, American
Allison, Luther, Chicago Blues; Modern Electric Blues, 1970s–1990s, Guitar, American
Allman Brothers Band, Blues Rock, 1970s–, Various instruments, American
Allman, Gregg, Blues Rock, 1970s–1990s, Keyboards, vocals, American
Altena, Maarten, Free Jazz; Modern Jazz, 1970s–, Bass, bandleader, Dutch
Andersen, Arild, Free Jazz; Modern Jazz, 1970s–, Double bass, electric bass, composer, Norwegian
Anderson, Jay, Modern Jazz; Big Band, 1970s–, Bass, American
Anderson, Little Willie, Modern Electric Blues; Chicago Blues, 1970s–1980s, Harmonica, American
Anderson, Ray, Free Jazz; Modern Jazz, 1970s–, Trombone, bandleader, American
Andersson, Krister, Hard Bop; Big Band, 1970s–, Saxophone, clarinet, Swedish
Arceneaux, Fernest, Rhythm & Blues; New Orleans Jazz; Blues, 1970s–, Accordion, American
Art Ensemble of Chicago, Free Jazz, 1970s–, Various instruments, American
Azymuth, Brazilian Jazz; Fusion, 1970s–1990s, Various instruments, Brazilian
Baars, Ab, Free Jazz, 1970s–, Saxophone, Dutch
Babbington, Roy, Jazz Rock, 1970s–, Bass, British
Backer, Steve, Modern Jazz, 1970s–, Producer, American
Bacon Fat, West Coast Blues, 1970s, Various instruments, American
Bad Company, Blues Rock, 1970s–1990s, Various instruments, British
Bailey, Judy, Modern Jazz, 1970s–, Piano, composer, New Zealander
Baker Gurvitz Army, Blues Rock, 1970s, Various instruments, British
Baker, Ginger, Jazz Rock; Fusion; Blues Rock, 1970s–, Drums, British
Balke, Jon, Jazz Rock; Modern Jazz, 1970s–, Piano, composer, arranger, Norwegian
Bang, Billy, Free Jazz; Fusion, 1970s–, Violin, composer, American
Barbieri, Gato, Latin Jazz; Jazz Pop, 1970s–1990s, Saxophone, flute, percussion, vocals, Argentinian
Barefield, Spencer, Free Jazz, 1970s–, Guitar, American
Barker, Stan, Eclectic Jazz, 1970s–, Piano, British
Barnes, Roosevelt 'Booba', Modern Electric Blues, 1970s–1990s, Guitar, harmonica, American
Baron, Joey, Free Jazz; Big Band, 1970s–, Drums, American
Barthelemy, Claude, Modern Jazz; Big Band, 1970s–, Guitar, composer, French
Battle, Bobby, Modern Jazz, 1970s–, Drums, saxophone, American
Bauer, Conrad, Free Jazz, 1970s–, Trombonist, German
Beckerhoff, Uli, Modern Jazz, 1970s–, Trumpet, German
Beirach, Richard, Free Jazz; Modern Jazz, 1970s–, Piano, composer, American
Belden, Bob, Big Band; Modern Jazz, 1970s–, Saxophone, arranger, record producer, American
Bell, Carey, Modern Electric Blues; Chicago Blues, 1970s–1990s, Harmonica, American
Bell, Kelvyn, Free Jazz, 1970s–, Guitar, vocals, American
Bell, Maggie, Blues Rock, 1970s–1980s, Vocals, British
Bem, Ewa, Modern Jazz, 1970s–, Vocals, Polish
Benoit, David, Fusion; Jazz Rock, 1970s–, Piano, producer, American
Beresford, Steve, Free Jazz, 1970s–, Piano, trumpet, trombone, guitar, violin, British
Berg, Bob, Modern Jazz; Hard Bop, 1970s–, Saxophone, American
Bergalli, Gustavo, Modern Jazz; Big Band, 1970s–, Trumpet, Argentinian
Bergin, Sean, Hard Bop; Modern Jazz; Big Band, 1970s–, Saxophones, composer, bandleader, South African
Bergman, Borah, Free Jazz, 1970s–, Piano, American
Bergonzi, Jerry, Hard Bop; Bebop; Modern Jazz, 1970s–, Saxophone, American
Berlin, Jeff, Jazz Rock, 1970s–, Electric Bass, American
Berne, Tim, Free Jazz, 1970s–, Saxophones, American
Betsch, John, Free Jazz, 1970s–, Drums, American
Big Bad Smitty, Modern Electric Blues, 1970s–1990s, Vocals, guitar, American
Big Time Sarah, Modern Electric Blues, 1970s–, Vocals, American
Big Town Playboys, Rhythm & Blues, 1970s–, Various instruments, British
Big Twist and the Mellow Fellow, Rhythm & Blues, 1970s–1990s, Various instruments, American
Binder, Roy Book, Country Blues, 1970s–1990s, Guitar, American
Bingert, Hector, World Fusion; Big Band, 1970s–, Saxophone, Uruguayan

Biscoe, Chris, Free Jazz; Big Band; Modern Jazz, 1970s–, Saxophone, clarinet, British
Blades, Reuben, Latin Jazz, 1970s–, Vocals, composer, Panamanian
Blake, Alex, Latin Jazz; Modern Jazz; Free Jazz; Jazz Rock, 1970s–, Bass, Panamanian
Blake, John, Modern Jazz; Smooth Jazz, 1970s–, Violin, bandleader, American
Bloom, Jane Ira, Free Jazz; Modern Jazz, 1970s–, Saxophone, composer, arranger, bandleader, American
Bluiett, Hamiet, Free Jazz; World Fusion, 1970s–, Saxophone, American
Boiarsky, Andres, Latin Jazz; Big Band; World Jazz, 1970s–, Saxophone, Argentinian
Boni, Raymond, Free Jazz, 1970s–, Guitar, French
Bonner, Joe, Modern Jazz; Big Band, 1970s–, Piano, American
Bottlang, Rene, Modern Jazz; Big Band, 1970s–, Piano, composer, Swedish
Boyle, Gary, Jazz Rock, 1970s–, Guitar, composer, British
Bramlett, Bonnie, Blues Rock, 1970s–, Vocals, American
Bramlett, Delaney, Blues Rock, 1970s, Vocals, American
Brand, Dollar, World Fusion, 1970s–1980s, Piano, South African
Braxton, Anthony, Free Jazz, 1970s–, Saxophones, clarinet, flute, percussion, vocals, American
Breakstone, Joshua, Cool Jazz; Modern Jazz, 1970s–, Guitar, American
Brecker, Michael, Fusion, 1970s–, Saxophones, flute, American
Brecker, Randy, Fusion; Hard Bop, 1970s–, Trumpet, piano, drums, American
Brennan, John Wolf, Jazz Rock; Fusion Jazz; Big Band, 1970s–, Piano, organ, keyboards, composer, Irish
Brett Marvin and the Thunderbolts, Loose Blues; Rhythm & Blues, 1970s–, Various instruments, British
Broadbent, Alan, Big Band, 1970s–, Piano, arranger, composer, Australian
Brooks, Elkie, Blues Rock, 1970s–, Vocals, British
Brotherhood of Breath, Free Jazz; Bebop, 1970s, Various instruments, British
Brown, Gerry, Modern Jazz; Jazz Rock, 1970s–, Drums, bandleader, American
Brubeck, Darius, Modern Jazz; World Fusion, 1970s–, Piano, keyboards, American
Bruninghaus, Rainer, Jazz Rock; Free Jazz, 1970s–, Piano, synthesizer, German
Bruton, Stephen, Blues Rock; New Orleans Rhythm & Blues, 1970s–, Guitar, American
Buchanan, Roy, Blues Rock; Modern Electric Blues, 1970s–1980s, Guitar, American
Bukovsky, Mike, Modern Jazz; Big Band, 1970s–, Trumpet, composer, bandleader, Czech
Bullock, Hiram, Jazz Rock, 1970s–, Guitar, Japanese
Burr, Jon, Modern Jazz; Big Band, 1970s–, Bass, American
Busch, Sigi, Modern Jazz, 1970s–, Bass, German
Butler, George 'Wild Child', Modern Electric Blues, 1970s–2000s, Vocals, harmonica, American
Cables, George, Hard Bop; Modern Jazz, 1970s–, Piano, keyboards, composer, American
Cale, Bruce, Modern Jazz; Big Band, 1970s–, Bass, composer, Australian
Cale, J.J., Blues Rock, 1970s–1990s, Guitar, vocals, composer, American
Camilo, Michel, Latin Jazz; Hard Bop, 1970s–, Piano, composer, bandleader, Dominican
Campbell, Roy, Hard Bop; Modern Jazz, 1970s–, Trumpet, American
Carl, Rudiger, Free Jazz, 1970s–, Saxophone, clarinet, accordion, German
Carroll, Baikida, Free Jazz, 1970s–, Trumpet, flugelhorn, American
Carter, Daniel, Free Jazz, 1970s–, Saxophone, clarinet, flute, trumpet, American
Castellucci, Bruno, Modern Jazz; Big Band; Bebop, 1970s–, Drums, Belgian
Castle, Geoff, Traditional Jazz; Jazz Rock; World Jazz, 1970s–, Piano, composer, British
Catherine, Philip, Modern Jazz; Jazz Rock, 1970s–, Guitar, Belgian
Ceccarelli, Andre, Modern Jazz, 1970s–, Drums, bandleader, French
Centipede, Jazz Rock, 1970s, Various instruments, British
Chadbourne, Eugene, Free Jazz; Fusion, 1970s–, Guitar, banjo, vocals, American
Chain, Blues Rock, 1970s, Various instruments, Australian
Chambers, Dennis, Fusion; Jazz Funk, 1970s–, Drums, American
Chancey, Vincent, Free Jazz, 1970s–, French horn, American
Chase, Tommy, Bebop; Soul Jazz, 1970s–, Drums, British
Chekasin, Vladimir, Free Jazz, 1970s–, Saxophone, keyboards, composer, Russian
Chiasson, Warren, Bebop, 1970s–, Vibraphone, Canadian
Childs, Billy, Modern Jazz, 1970s–, Piano, keyboards, composer, American
Christlieb, Pete, Bebop, 1970s–, Saxophone, American
Christmann, Gunter, Free Jazz, 1970s–, Trombone, bass, Polish
Cinelu, Mino, Modern Jazz; Jazz Rock; Fusion, 1970s–, Percussion, keyboards, vocals, French
Clark, Curtis, Free Jazz, 1970s–, Piano, American
Clark, John, Free Jazz; Modern Jazz; Big Band, 1970s–, French horn, bandleader, American
Clarke, Mick, British Blues; Blues Rock, 1970s–, Guitar, British
Clarke, William, Modern Electric Blues, 1970s–1990s, Harmonica, American
Clausen, Thomas, Hard Bop; Modern Jazz, 1970s–, Piano, composer, arranger, Danish
Clayton, Jay, Free Jazz, 1970s–, Vocals, American
Clayton, Willie, Rhythm & Blues, 1970s–, Vocals, composer, American
Cliff, Dave, Modern Jazz; Swing, 1970s–, Guitar, British
Cobham, Billy, Fusion, 1970s–, Percussion, American
Cochrane, Michael, Free Jazz; Modern Jazz, 1970s–, Piano, American
Codona, World Fusion; Free Jazz, 1970s–1980s, Various instruments, American
Coetzee, Basil, World Fusion; Free Jazz, 1970s–, Saxophone, South African
Cohelmec, Free Jazz, 1970s–1980s, Various instruments, French
Cohen, Alan, Swing; Big Band; Modern Jazz; Traditional Jazz, 1970s–, Composer, arranger, saxophone, British
Colaiuta, Vinnie, Jazz Rock; Modern Jazz, 1970s–, Drums, American
Cole, Richie, Bebop, 1970s–1990s, Saxophones, American
Collins, Cal, Swing; Modern Jazz, 1970s–2000s, Guitar, American
Colombo, Eugenio, Free Jazz; Modern Jazz, 1970s–, Saxophone, flute, composer, Italian
Colville, Randolph, Swing; Dixieland, 1970s–, Clarinet, saxophone, arranger, British
Concord Allstars, Swing; Bebop, 1970s–1990s, Various instruments, American
Connick, Harry Jr, Swing; Traditional Jazz; Big Band, 1970s–, Piano, vocals, bandleader, American
Connors, Bill, Modern Jazz; Fusion, 1970s–, Guitar, American
Connors, Norman, Fusion, 1970s–, Vocals, composer, producer, American
Conte, Luis, Fusion; Latin Jazz; Cuban Jazz, 1970s–, Percussion, Cuban
Cooder, Ry, Blues Rock, 1970s–1990s, Guitar, American
Cooper, Lindsay, Jazz Rock; Free Jazz, 1970s–, Saxophone, bassoon, composer, British
Copland, Marc, Hard Bop; Modern Jazz, 1970s–, Piano, saxophone, American
Cora, Tom, Free Jazz, 1970s–1990s, Cello, American
Costa, Paulinho Da, Brazilian Jazz; Latin Jazz; World Fusion, 1970s–1990s, Percussion, Brazilian

Coster, Tom, Free Jazz; Fusion; Jazz Rock, 1970s–, Piano, organ, keyboards, American
Crane, Ray, Big Band; Swing; Dixieland Revival, 1970s–1990s, Trumpet, piano, British
Crispell, Marilyn, Free Jazz, 1970s–, Piano, bandleader, American
Critchinson, John, Jazz Funk, 1970s–, Piano, British
Crook, Hal, Modern Jazz; Big Band, 1970s–, Trombone, piano, American
Crothers, Connie, Free Jazz; Modern Jazz, 1970s–, Piano, American
Crowbar, Rock Blues, 1970s, Blues band, Canadian
Crumly, Pat, Post-Bop; Blues Rock; Rhythm & Blues, 1970s–, Saxophone, flute, British
Curnow, Bob, Modern Jazz, 1970s–, Arranger, bandleader, American
Cutler, Chris, Jazz Rock; Fusion, 1970s–, Drums, American
Cuypers, Leo, Free Jazz, 1970s–, Piano, composer, Dutch
D'Ambrosio, Meredith, Cool Jazz, 1970s–, Vocals, American
D'Earth, John, Modern Jazz; Big Band, 1970s, Trumpet, American
Dagradi, Tony, Jazz Rock; Modern Jazz, 1970s–, Saxophone, bandleader, author, American
Damiani, Paolo, Free Jazz; Modern Jazz, 1970s–, Bass, cello, composer, bandleader, Italian
Danielsson, Palle, Modern Jazz, 1970s–, Bass, Swedish
Danko, Harold, Hard Bop; Modern Jazz, 1970s–, Piano, American
Darling, David, Modern Jazz; Fusion, 1970s–, Cello, composer, American
Dato, Carlo Actis, Hard Bop; Free Jazz, 1970s–, Saxophone, clarinet, bandleader, Italian
Davis, Anthony, Free Jazz; Modern Jazz, 1970s–, Piano, composer, American
Davis, Stanton, Free Jazz, 1970s–, Trumpet, American
Dawkins, Ernest, Free Jazz; Modern Jazz, 1970s–, Saxophone, flute, American
Dawkins, Jimmy, Modern Electric Blues; Chicago Blues, 1970s–1990s, Guitar, American
Dean, Roger, Free Jazz, 1970s–, Keyboards, bass, composer, British
DeGraaff, Rein, Modern Jazz; Hard Bop, 1970s–, Piano, Dutch
Dennard, Kenwood, Jazz Rock; Funk Jazz; Free Jazz, 1970s–, Drums, American
Derek & the Dominoes, British Blues; Blues Rock, 1970s, Various instruments, American
Derome, Jean, Free Jazz; Jazz Rock, 1970s–, Saxophone, flute, composer, Canadian
Dibango, Manu, World Fusion, 1970s–, Saxophone, piano, vibraphone, African
Dickerson, Dwight, Modern Jazz, 1970s–, Piano, American
Dikker, Loek, Free Jazz, 1970s–, Piano, composer, Dutch
DiMeola, Al, Fusion; Jazz Rock; World Fusion, 1970s–, Guitar, American
DiPasqua, Michael, Hard Bop; Modern Jazz, 1970s–, Drums, percussion, American
Dissidenten, World Fusion, 1970s–1990s, Various instruments, German
Doldinger, Klaus, Modern Jazz; Fusion, 1970s–, Saxophone, bandleader, German
Donato, Michel, Modern Jazz, 1970s–, Bass, Canadian
Doran, Christy, Free Jazz; Modern Jazz, 1970s–, Guitar, Irish
Downchild Blues Band, Modern Electric Blues; Jump Blues; Chicago Blues, 1970s–, Blues Band, Canadian
Downes, Bob, Free Jazz; Jazz Rock; World Jazz, 1970s–, Flute, saxophones, British
Downes, Wray, Modern Jazz; Bebop, 1970s–, Piano, Canadian
Dr. Feelgood, Blues Rock, 1970s–1990s, Various instruments, British
Dr. John, Rhythm & Blues; Jazz Rock; Funk, 1970s–, Piano, vocals, composer, American American
Drake, Hamid, Free Jazz; Cuban Jazz, 1970s–, Drums, tabla, American
Dresser, Mark, Free Jazz; Modern Jazz, 1970s–, Bass, composer, American
Drew, Martin, Bebop; Swing; Modern Jazz, 1970s–, Drums, British
Drummer, John, British Blues, 1970s, Drums, British
Dubin, Larry, Free Jazz, 1970s, Drums, Canadian
DuChaine, Kent, Delta Blues; Chicago Blues, 1970s–, Bass, guitar, American
Dudziak, Urszula, Modern Jazz; Fusion, 1970s–, Vocals, Polish
Dulfer, Hans, Free Jazz, 1970s–, Saxophone, Dutch
Dunmall, Paul, Free Jazz; Fusion, 1970s–, Saxophones, clarinets, bagpipes, other wind instruments, British
Dvorak, Jim, Fusion, 1970s–, Trumpet, American
Dykes, Omar, Blues Rock, 1970s–, Guitar, American
Easley, Bill, Hard Bop, 1970s–, Clarinet, saxophone, American
Eça, Luíz, Brazilian Jazz, 1970s–1990s, Piano, Brazilian
Ecklund, Peter, Traditional Jazz, 1970s–, Cornet, trumpet, whistle, American
Eduardo, Ze, Modern Jazz, 1970s–, Bass, piano, composer, arranger, bandleader, Portuguese
Edwards, Marc, Free Jazz, 1970s–, Drums, American
Egan, Mark, Modern Jazz; Fusion, 1970s–, Bass, composer, American
Ehrlich, Marty, Free Jazz; Modern Jazz, 1970s–, Saxophone, clarinet, bandleader, American
El'Zabar, Kahil, Free Jazz, 1970s–, Drums, American
Elias, Eliane, Brazilian Jazz; Latin Jazz, 1970s–, Piano, vocals, Brazilian
Elliot, Richard, Smooth Jazz, 1970s–, Saxophone, Scottish
Emborg, Jorgen, Fusion; Big Band, 1970s–, Piano, composer, bandleader, American
Emery, James, Free Jazz; Modern Jazz, 1970s–, Guitar, American
Engels, John, Modern Jazz; Hard Bop, 1970s–, Drums, Dutch
Enriquez, Bobby, Cuban Jazz, 1970s–1990s, Piano, American
Erquiaga, Steve, Modern Jazz; Hard Bop, 1970s–, Guitar, American
Erskine, Peter, Cool Jazz; Bebop; Fusion, 1970s–, Drums, American
Eschete, Ron, Modern Jazz, 1970s–, Guitar, American
Etheridge, John, Jazz Rock; Swing, 1970s–, Guitar, British
Eubanks, Kevin, Hard Bop; Modern Jazz, 1970s–, Guitar, bandleader, American

Evans, Sue, Cool Jazz, 1970s, Drums, percussion, American
Evans, Terry, Blues Rock; Rhythm & Blues, 1970s–, Vocals, American
Faddis, Jon, Bebop, 1970s–1990s, Trumpet, flugelhorn, American
Fahn, Mike, Swing; Big Band, 1970s–, Trombone, American
Fambrough, Charles, Hard Bop; Modern Jazz, 1970s–, Bass, American
Fasoli, Claudio, Modern Jazz; Jazz Rock, 1970s–, Saxophone, composer, bandleader, Italian
Fasteau, Zusaan Kali, World Fusion; Free Jazz, 1970s–, Vocals, various instruments, American
Ferguson, Sherman, Hard Bop; Modern Jazz, 1970s–, Drums, American
Ferris, Glenn, Jazz Rock; Big Band; Hard Bop, 1970s–, Trombone, American
Fine, Milo, Free Jazz, 1970s–, Piano, clarinet, percussion, critic, American
Fischer, John, Free Jazz, 1970s–, Piano, composer, bandleader, Belgian
Fleck, Bela, Modern Jazz; Fusion, 1970s–, Banjo, American
Flory, Chris, Swing, 1970s–, Guitar, American
Folds, Chuck, Traditional Jazz; Swing, 1970s–, Piano, American
Ford, Joe, Free Jazz; Modern Jazz, 1970s–, Saxophone, flute, American
Ford, Ricky, Hard Bop; Modern Jazz, 1970s–, Saxophone, American
Ford, Robben, Fusion, 1970s–, Guitar, American
Forman, Bruce, Bebop, 1970s–, Guitar, bandleader, American
Foster, Ronnie, Soul Jazz, 1970s–, Piano, keyboards, organ, American
Frampton, Roger, Free Jazz, 1970s–1990s, Piano, saxophone, composer, British
Francioli, Leon, Free Jazz, 1970s–, Bass, cello, Swiss
Franklin, Henry, Hard Bop; Modern Jazz, 1970s–, Bass, American
Free, Blues Rock, 1970s, Various instruments, British
Freeman, Chico, Modern Jazz, 1970s–, Saxophone, clarinet, flute, bandleader, American
Friedman, David, Hard Bop; Modern Jazz, 1970s–, Vibraphone, marimba, American
Friesen, David, Modern Jazz, 1970s–, Bass, American
Frith, Fred, Free Jazz, 1970s–, Guitar, composer, British
Gadd, Steve, Jazz Rock; Modern Jazz, 1970s–, Drums, American
Gaines, Roy, Modern Electric Blues, 1970s–, Guitar, American
Gale, Eric, Jazz Funk; Soul Jazz, 1970s–1990s, Guitar, American
Gallagher, Rory, British Blues; Blues Rock, 1970s–1980s, Guitar, Irish
Galliano, Richard, Modern Jazz, 1970s–, Accordion, composer, French
Galper, Hal, Modern Jazz, 1970s–, Piano, bandleader, American
Ganelin Trio, Free Jazz, 1970s–1990s, Various instruments, Russian
Gannon, Oliver, Swing; Jazz Rock; Modern Jazz, 1970s–, Guitar, Canadian
Garson, Mike, Modern Jazz, 1970s–, Piano, keyboards, American
Gatton, Danny, Blues Rock, 1970s–1990s, Guitar, songwriter, American
Giammarco, Maurizio, Free Jazz; Fusion; Hard Bop, 1970s–, Saxophone, Italian
Gibson, Banu, Dixieland Revival, 1970s–1990s, Vocals, American
Giddins, Gary, All Jazz Styles, 1970s–, Author, critic, American
Gilmore, Steve, Modern Jazz, 1970s–, Bass, American
Goldberg, Stu, Bebop; Fusion, 1970s–, Keyboards, composer, American
Golia, Vinny, Free Jazz, 1970s–, Saxophone, clarinet, flute, bassoon, arranger, composer, American
Gonzalez, Dennis, Free Jazz; Modern Jazz, 1970s–, Trumpet, flugelhorn, American
Gonzalez, Jerry, Latin Jazz; Cuban Jazz, 1970s–, Trumpet, flugelhorn, congas, bandleader, American
Goodrick, Mick, Modern Jazz, 1970s–, Bass, American
Goodwin, Jim, Traditional Jazz; Dixieland, 1970s–, Cornet, American
Gottlieb, Danny, Modern Jazz, 1970s–, Drums, American
Green, Peter, British Blues; Blues Rock, 1970s–, Guitar, British

Grusin, Don, Smooth Jazz, 1970s–, Keyboards, American
Guralnick, Peter, Rhythm & Blues, 1970s–, Author, American
Gurtu, Trilok, World Fusion; Fusion, 1970s–, Percussion, Indian
Guy, Barry, Free Jazz, 1970s–, Bass, composer, British
Hagans, Tim, Hard Bop, 1970s–, Trumpet, flugelhorn, American
Hall, Jimmy, Rhythm & Blues; Boogie-Woogie, 1970s–, Vocals, bandleader, saxophone, harmonica, British
Halliday, Lin, Hard Bop, 1970s–1990s, Saxophone, American
Hamilton, Jeff, Bebop, 1970s–, Drums, American
Hamilton, Scott, Swing; Modern Jazz, 1970s–, Saxophone, American
Hancock, Herbie, Modal Jazz; Hard Bop; Fusion, 1960s–, Keyboards, composer, American
Harney, Richard 'Hackshaw', Country Blues, 1970s, Guitar, American
Harrell, Tom, Hard Bop; Big Band, 1970s–, Trumpet, American
Harris, Craig, Free Jazz, 1970s–, Trombone, American
Harris, Hi Tide, Blues Rock; British Blues, 1970s–1980s, Guitar, vocals, American
Harrison, Wendell, Bebop, 1970s–, Saxophone, clarinet, American
Hashim, Michael, Swing, 1970s, Saxophone, American
Haurand, Ali, Modern Jazz, 1970s–, Bass, composer, German
Helias, Mark, Free Jazz; Modern Jazz, 1970s–, Bass, American
Hemingway, Gerry, Free Jazz; Modern Jazz, 1970s–, Drums, composer, bandleader, American
Henderson, Eddie, Modern Jazz; Fusion, 1970s–, Trumpet, American
Hersch, Fred, Modern Jazz, 1970s–, Piano, American
Hinton, Eddie, Rhythm & Blues, 1970s–1990s, Vocals, guitar, composer, American
Hinze, Chris, Jazz Rock; Fusion, 1970s–, Flute, composer, Dutch
Hiroshima, World Fusion, 1970s–1990s, Various instruments, American
Hoggard, Jay, Free Jazz, 1970s–, Vibraphone, American
Holdsworth, Allan, Jazz Rock; Fusion, 1970s–, Guitar, violin, composer, British
Holland, Dave, Free Jazz, 1970s–, Bass, cello, composer, British
Holley, 'Lyin" Joe, Blues Rock, 1970s, Piano, American
Hollywood Fats Band, Modern Electric Blues, 1970s, Various instruments, American

Hopkins, Fred, Free Jazz, 1970s–1990s, Bass, American
Hot Tuna, Blues Rock, 1970–, Various instruments, American
Hovington, Fred, Country Blues, 1970s, Guitar, American
Howard, George, Smooth Jazz, 1970s–1990s, Saxophones, American
Humphrey, Bobbi, Soul Jazz; Fusion, 1970s–1990s, Flute, American
Hunter, Chris, Cool Jazz; Fusion; Free Jazz, 1970s–, Saxophone, flute, British
Hunter-Randall, Ian, British Jazz; Traditional Jazz, 1970s–, Trumpet, British
Husband, Gary, Free Jazz; Fusion, 1970s–, Drums, piano, British
Hutto, J.B., Chicago Blues, 1970s–1980s, Guitar, vocals, American
Ibrahim, Abdullah, World Fusion; Modern Jazz, 1970s, piano, South African
Ingham, Keith, Swing; Dixieland Revival; Traditional Jazz, 1970s–, Piano, British
Inmates, Rhythm & Blues, 1970s–1980s, Various instruments, British
Irakere, Latin Jazz, 1970s–, Various instruments, Cuban
Irwin, Dennis, Hard Bop, 1970s–, Bass, American
J. Geils Band, Blues Rock, 1970s–1980s, Various instruments, American
Jackson, Chuck, Rhythm & Blues, 1970s–1980s, Vocals, American
Jackson, George, Rhythm & Blues, 1970s–, Vocals, piano, composer, producer, American
Jackson, Michael Gregory, Free Jazz; Jazz Rock, 1970s–, Guitar, American
Jackson, Ronald Shannon, Free Jazz; Hard Bop; Fusion, 1970s–, Drums, bandleader, American
Jacobsen, Pete, Fusion; Free Jazz; Modern Jazz, 1970s–, Piano, British
Jamal, Khan, Free Jazz; Modern Jazz, 1970s–, Vibraphone, American
James, John, Folk Blues, 1970s–, Guitar, British
James, Steve, Blues Rock, 1970s–, Bass, American
Jang, Jon, Free Jazz; World Fusion, 1970s–, Piano, composer, American
Jarrett, Keith, Fusion, 1970s–, Piano, composer, American
Jelly Roll Kings, The, Modern Electric Blues, 1970s–1990s, Artist, American
Jenkins, Leroy, Free Jazz, 1970s–1990s, Violin, viola, composer, American
Johnson, Henry, Hard Bop, 1970s, Vocals, American
Johnson, Marc, Modern Jazz, 1970s–, Bass, American
Jones, Bobby, Hard Bop, 1970s–1980s, Saxophone, flute, American
Jones, Leroy, Swing; Traditional Jazz; Big Band, 1970s–, Trumpet, American
Jones, Rodney, Modern Jazz; Fusion, 1970s–, Guitar, American
Jones, Thad, Bebop; Hard Bop, 1970s–1980s, Trumpet, arranger, composer, American
Jorgensmann, Theo, Free Jazz, 1970s–, Clarinet, German
Juris, Vic, Hard Bop; Modern Jazz, 1970s–, Guitar, American
Kent, Willie, Modern Electric Blues, 1970s–, Vocals, electric bass, American
Kerr, Brooks, Swing, 1970s–, Piano, American
Khan, Steve, Modern Jazz; Fusion, 1970s–, Guitar, American
King Biscuit Boy, Modern Electric Blues; Chicago Blues, 1970s–2000s, Vocals, harmonica, Canadian
Klugh, Earl, Fusion, 1970s–, Guitar, American
Koglmann, Franz, Free Jazz, 1970s–, Flugelhorn, trumpet, composer, Austrian
Kriegel, Volker, Hard Bop, 1970s–, Guitar, composer, German
Kuryokhin, Sergey, Free Jazz; Jazz Rock, 1970s–, Piano, multi-instrumentalist, composer, Russian
LA Four, Cool Jazz, 1970s–, Various instruments, American
Lacy, Steve, Free Jazz, 1970s–, Soprano saxophone, composer, American
Lake, Oliver, Free Jazz, 1970s–, Saxophone, flute, composer, American
Lande, Art, Free Jazz; Fusion, 1970s–, Piano, percussion, bandleader, American
Landreth, Sonny, Louisiana Blues, 1970s–, Guitar, American
Laswell, Bill, Free Jazz; Fusion, 1970s–, Guitar, producer, American
Lauer, Christof, Modern Jazz; Jazz Rock; Post-Bop, 1970s–, Saxophone, German
LaVerne, Andy, Modern Jazz, 1970s–, Piano, keyboards, American
Laws, Ronnie, Jazz Pop, 1970s–, Saxophone, American
Led Zeppelin, British Blues; Blues Rock, 1970s–1980s, Various instruments, British
Lee, Little Frankie, Rhythm & Blues, 1970s–, Vocals, American
Lemer, Pepi, Jazz Rock; Modern Jazz; Free Jazz; Fusion, 1970s–, Vocals, British
Levallet, Didier, Free Jazz, 1970s–, Double bass, composer, leader, French
Levy, Ron, Modern Electric Blues, 1970s–, Piano, organ, American
Lewis, George, Free Jazz, 1970s–, Trombone, composer, American
Liebman, Dave, Free Jazz; Modern Jazz, 1970s–, Saxophone, bandleader, American
Lindberg, John, Free Jazz, 1970s–, Bass, American
Linden, Colin, Modern Electric Blues, 1970s–, Guitar, composer, Canadian
Little Feat, Blues Rock, 1970s–, Various instruments, American
Litton, Martin, Swing; Chicago Jazz; New Orleans Jazz, 1970s–, Piano, British
Lockwood, Didier, Modern Jazz; Fusion, 1970s–, Violin, French
Loeb, Chuck, Fusion; Hard Bop, 1970s–, Guitar, arranger, composer, producer, American
Long, Joey, Texas Blues, 1970s–1990s, Guitar, American
Lorber, Jeff, Smooth Jazz, 1970s–, Keyboards, guitar, vibraphone, percussion, composer, American
Louisiana Red, Country Blues; Rhythm & Blues, 1970s–, Vocals, guitar, American
Lovens, Paul, Modern Jazz, 1970s–, Percussion, German
Lowe, Frank, Free Jazz, 1970s–1990s, Saxophone, American
Lowery, Robert, Country Blues; Delta Blues, 1970s–, Vocals, guitar, American
Lynn, Trudy, Rhythm & Blues, 1970s–, Vocals, American
Mack, Bobby, Blues Rock, 1970s–, Guitar, American
MacPherson, Fraser, Swing; Cool Jazz, 1970s–, Saxophone, Canadian
Maguire, Alex, Modern Jazz, 1970s–, Piano, composer, British
Mahavishnu Orchestra, Jazz Rock; Fusion, 1970s–1980s, Various instruments, American
Makowicz, Adam, Swing; Bebop, 1970s–, Piano, Czech
Mangelsdorff, Albert, Free Jazz, 1970s–, Trombone, bandleader, German
Manhattan Transfer, Smooth Jazz, 1970s–, Various instruments, American
Mason Jr., Harvey, Modal Jazz; Hard Bop; Fusion, 1970s–, Drums, percussion, piano, composer, American
Mason, Dutch, Modern Electric Blues, 1970s–, Vocals, guitar, Canadian
Mays, Lyle, Free Jazz; Modern Jazz; Fusion, 1970s–, Keyboards, composer, American

Mays, Bill, Modern Jazz, 1970s–, Piano, American
Mazur, Marilyn, Fusion, 1970s–, Percussion, vocals, composer, piano, American
McCauley, Jackie, Rhythm & Blues, 1970s–, Vocals, songwriter, Irish
McClinton, Delbert, Blues Rock; Modern Electric Blues, 1970s–, Harmonica, guitar, vocals, composer, American
McCorkle, Susannah, Modern Jazz, 1970s–2000s, Vocals, American
McLaughlin, John, Fusion; World Fusion, 1970s–, Guitar, composer, British
McNeely, Jim, Modern Jazz, 1970s–, Piano, arranger, American
Merchan, Chucho, Hard Bop; Modern Jazz; Free Jazz, 1970s–, Bass, guitar, Columbian
Midnite Follies Orchestra, Ragtime, 1970s–1980s, Various instruments, British
Miles, Butch, Swing; Big Band, 1970s–, Drums, bandleader, American
Miller, Marcus, Modern Jazz; Fusion; Jazz Funk, 1970s–, Bass, producer, American
Miller, Mark, All Jazz Styles, 1970s–, Author, critic, Canadian
Mingus Dynasty, Modern Jazz; Hard Bop, 1970s–1990s, Various instruments, American
Mintzer, Bob, Bebop; Hard Bop, 1970s–, Saxophone, clarinet, flute, American
Monk, T.S., Hard Bop, 1970s–, Drums, bandleader, American
Moondoc, Jemeel, Free Jazz, 1970s–, Saxophone, American
Moore, Gary, Blues Rock, 1970s–, Vocals, guitar, Irish
Moore, Ralph, Hard Bop; Bebop; Fusion, 1970s–, Saxophone, British
Morath, Max, Ragtime, 1970s–1990s, Piano, American
Morris, Butch, Free Jazz, 1970s–, Cornet, composer, American
Mossman, Michael, Cool Jazz, 1970s–, Trumpet, Flugelhorn, piano, American
Mraz, George, Hard Bop; Modern Jazz, 1970s–, Bass, Czech
Muhammad, Idris, Soul Jazz, 1970s–1990s, Drums, American
Mullen, Jim, Jazz Funk; Jazz Rock, 1970s–, Guitar, British
Murphy, Matt 'Guitar', Modern Electric Blues, 1970s–, Vocals, guitar, American
Murray, David, Free Jazz, 1970s–, Saxophone, clarinet, flute, American
Musselwhite, Charlie, Modern Electric Blues, 1970s–, Harmonica, American
Myers, Amina Claudine, Free Jazz, 1970s–, Piano, organ, vocals, American
Neil, Steve, Cool Jazz; Fusion; Bebop; Hard Bop, 1970s–, Saxophone, guitar, bass, drums, American
Newton, James, Free Jazz; Modern Jazz, 1970s–, Flute, composer, American
Nichols, Keith, Classic Jazz, 1970s–, Piano, trombone, reeds, accordion, arranger, leader, British
Nieman, Paul, Free Jazz; Fusion, 1970s–, Trombone, British
Nine Below Zero, Rhythm & Blues, 1970s, Various instruments, British
Nussbaum, Adam, Free Jazz; Modern Jazz, 1970s–, Drums, American
O'Neal, Jim, All Blues Styles, 1970s–, Author, American
Okoshi, Tiger, Jazz Rock; Fusion, 1970s–, Trumpet, synthesizer, composer, Japanese
Oquendo, Manny, Latin Jazz, 1970s–, Percussion, American
Oregon, Fusion, World Fusion, 1970s–1990s, Various instruments, American
Oscher, Paul, Modern Electric Blues, 1970s–, Vocals, harmonica, guitar, piano, American
Palmer, Robert, All Blues Styles, 1970s–1990s, Author, producer, American
Parker, Maceo, Soul Jazz, 1970s–, Saxophones, American
Parnell, Jack, Big Band; Swing, 1970s–, Drums, leader, British
Passport, Fusion, 1970s–, Various instruments, American
Pastorius, Jaco, Fusion, 1970s–1980s, Bass guitar, American
Pavone, Mario, Free Jazz; Modern Jazz, 1970s–, Bass, American
Peabody, Dave, British Blues; Folk Blues; Boogie-Woogie, 1970s–, Guitar, British
Pena, Paul, Rhythm & Blues, 1970s; 1990s, Vocals, piano, guitar, American
Perry, Bill, Modern Electric Blues, 1970s–, Guitar, vocals, American
Persson, Bent, New Orleans Jazz, 1970s–, Trumpet, cornet, leader, Swedish
Peterson, Marvin 'Hannibal', Free Jazz, 1970s–, Trumpet, American
Piccolo, Greg, Jump Blues, 1970s–, Saxophone, vocals, American
Ponomarev, Valery, Hard Bop, 1970s–, Trumpet, Russian
Pope, Odean, Modern Jazz, 1970s–, Saxophone, American
Portal, Michel, Contemporary Jazz, 1970s–, Clarinet, saxophone, French
Portnoy, Jerry, Country Blues; Chicago Blues, 1970s–, Vocals, harmonica, guitar, piano, American
Potts, Steve, Free Jazz, 1970s–, Saxophone, American
Primer, John, Modern Electric Blues, 1970s–, Guitar, American
Purim, Flora, Brazilian Jazz; Latin Jazz; Fusion, 1970s–, Vocals, guitar, percussion, Brazilian
Rainer, Blues Rock; Modern Electric Blues, 1970s–1990s, Guitar, German
Ramzy, Hossam, World Fusion, 1970s–, Drums, Egyptian
Raney, Doug, Cool Jazz, 1970s–, Guitar, American
Rayner, Alison, Fusion; Jazz Rock; Bebop; Cool Jazz, 1970s–, Bass, British
Reichel, Hans, Jazz Rock, 1970s–, Guitar, German
Reid, Rufus, Modern Jazz, 1970s–, Bass, bandleader, American
Reid, Steve, Free Jazz, 1970s–, Drums, American
Reijseger, Ernst, Free Jazz, 1970s–, Cello, Dutch
Remler, Emily, Swing; Modern Jazz, 1970s–1990s, Guitar, American
Return to Forever, Fusion, 1970s, Various instruments, American
Ricks, Jerry 'Philadelphia', Country Blues; Folk Blues, 1970s–, Vocals, guitar, American
Rifkin, Joshua, Ragtime, 1970s, Piano, American
Ritenour, Lee, Fusion, 1970s–1990s, Guitar, American
Robert, Yves, Free Jazz; Bebop, 1970s–, Trombone, French
Robertson, Sherman, Modern Electric Blues, 1970s–, Vocals, guitar, American
Rocket 88, Rhythm & Blues, 1970s–1980s, Various instruments, British
Rockin' Sidney, Cajun, 1970s–1990s, Vocals, accordion, harmonica, guitar, organ, American
Roditi, Claudio, Hard Bop, 1970s–, Trumpet, flugelhorn, Brazilian
Romao, Dom Um, Latin Jazz; Brazilian Jazz; World Fusion, 1970s–, Drums, percussion, Brazilian
Rosengarden, Bobby, Dixieland Revival, 1970s–, Drums, percussion, American
Rosewoman, Michele, Free Jazz, 1970s–, Piano, American
Rothenberg, Ned, Free Jazz; World Fusion, 1970s–, Saxophone, clarinet, bandleader, American
Rova Saxophone Quartet, Free Jazz, 1970s–1980s, Saxophone, American
Ruegg, Mathias, Big Band, 1970s–, Composer, piano, Swiss

Ruiz, Hilton, Latin Jazz; Bebop, 1970s–1990s, Piano, Cuban
Rushen, Patrice, Smooth Jazz; Modern Jazz, 1970s–, Vocals, keyboards, arranger, composer, American
Rypdal, Terje, Fusion, 1970s–1990s, Guitar, flute, Norwegian
Samuels, David, Cool Jazz, 1970s–, Vibraphone, marimba, American
Sanchez, Poncho, Latin Jazz, 1970s–, Percussion, bandleader, American
Sandoval, Arturo, Latin Jazz, 1970s–, Trumpet, flugelhorn, keyboards, percussion, Cuban
Scott, Isaac, Modern Electric Blues, 1970s–, Guitar, American
Scott-Heron, Gil, Modern Jazz; Jazz Rock, 1970s–, Vocals, composer, keyboards, American
Seals, Son, Modern Electric Blues, 1970s–2000s, Guitar, vocals, composer, American
Seifert, Zbigniew, Free Jazz, 1970s–, Violin, saxophone, Polish
Sellars, Roger, Modern Jazz; Jazz Rock, 1970s–, Drums, percussion, Australian
Shakti, World Fusion; Fusion, 1970s, Various instruments, American
Shankar, Lakshminarayana, World Fusion; Fusion, 1970s–1990s, Violin, composer, Indian
Shaw, Charles 'Bobo', Rhythm & Blues, 1970s–1980s, Drums, American
Shaw, Woody, Hard Bop, 1970s–1980s, Trumpet, flugelhorn, composer, American
Sidran, Ben, Smooth Jazz; Cool Jazz, 1970s–, Piano, vocals, American
Smith, Carrie, Swing, 1970s–, Vocals, American
Smith, Hal, Traditional Jazz, 1970s–, Drums, American
Smith, Lonnie Liston, Fusion, 1970s–1990s, Piano, keyboards, American
Smith, Ruthie, Free Jazz, 1970s–, Saxophone, vocals, cello, British
Smith, Wadada Leo, Free Jazz, 1970s–, Trumpet, flugelhorn, flute, American
Soprano Summit, Swing, 1970s, Various instruments, American
Spencer, Jeremy, British Blues; Blues Rock, 1970s, Guitar, British
Spyro Gyra, Smooth Jazz; Fusion, 1970s–, Various instruments, American
Steely Dan, Jazz Rock, 1970s–, Various instruments, American
Stern, Mike, Jazz Rock, 1970s–, Guitar, American
Stewart, Bob, Free Jazz, 1970s–, Tuba, American
Stivin, Jiri, Free Jazz, 1970s–, Flute, saxophone, composer, Czech
Strother, Percy, Modern Electric Blues, 1970s–, Vocals, guitar, harmonica, American
Sugar Blue, Modern Electric Blues, 1970s–1990s, Harmonica, American
Supersax, Bebop, 1970s, Saxophones, American
Suzuki, Yoshio, Hard Bop, 1970s–, Bass, piano, Japanese
Swainson, Neil, Modern Jazz, 1970s–, Bass, Canadian
Swallow, Steve, Modern Jazz, 1970s–, Bass, composer, American
Swartz, Harvie, Modern Jazz, 1970s–, Bass, American
Sweet Substitute, Traditional Jazz; Swing, 1970s–1990s, Vocals, British
Swift, Duncan, New Orleans Jazz; Chicago Jazz, 1970s–1990s, Piano, trombone, British
Tacuma, Jamaaladeen, Free Jazz; Free Funk, 1970s–, Bass, American
Takase, Aki, Free Jazz; Modern Jazz, 1970s–, Piano, bandleader, Japanese
Talley, James, Country Blues; Modern Electric Blues, 1970s–, Guitar, vocals, composer, American
Taylor, Hound Dog, Chicago Blues, 1970s, Guitar, vocals, American
Taylor, Koko, Modern Electric Blues; Chicago Blues; Rhythm & Blues, 1970s–, Vocals, American
Taylor, Martin, Swing; Cool Jazz; Bebop, 1970s–, Guitar, British
Terenzi, Danilo, Free Jazz; Big Band, 1970s–, Trombone, composer, Italian
Termos, Paul, Free Jazz, 1970s–, Saxophone, composer, Dutch
Thackery, Jimmy, Modern Electric Blues, 1970s–, Vocals, guitar, American
Theesink, Hans, Folk Blues; Modern Electric Blues, 1970s–, Vocals, guitars, mandolin, harmonica, Dutch
Thompson, Barbara, Free Jazz; Fusion, 1970s–1990s, Saxophones, flute, British
Thompson, Malachi, Free Jazz; Modern Jazz, 1970s–, Trumpet, bandleader, American
Thompson, Ron, Modern Electric Blues, 1970s–1980s, Piano, bandleader, American
Tibbetts, Steve, Fusion, 1970s–, Guitar, American
Tilbrook, Adrian, Free Jazz; Modern Jazz, 1970s–, Drums, British
Tiso, Wagner, Brazilian Jazz; Latin Jazz, 1970s–1990s, Piano, keyboards, arranger, composer, Brazilian
Towner, Ralph, Modern Jazz, 1970s–, Guitar, American

Toyama, Yoshio, New Orleans Jazz; Dixieland, 1970s–, Trumpet, vocals, bandleader, Japanese
Tracey, Clark, Free Jazz; Hard Bop; Modern Jazz, 1970s–, Drums, British
Tucker, Mickey, Hard Bop; Modern Jazz, 1970s–, Piano, American
Turre, Steve, Latin Jazz; Hard Bop; Bebop, 1970s–, Trombone, American
Tyson, Willie, Country Blues, 1970s, Piano, American
Urbani, Massimo, Free Jazz, 1970s–, Saxophone, Italian
Urbaniak, Michal, Fusion, 1970s–, Violin, saxophones, composer, Polish
Vache, Warren Jr, Swing; Chicago Jazz, 1970s–, Cornet, flugelhorn, American
Valente, Gary, Free Jazz; Big Band, 1970s–, Trombone, American
VanDeGeyn, Hein, Bebop; Big Band; Modern Jazz, 1970s–, Bass, Dutch
VanDenBroeck, Rob, Free Jazz; Jazz Rock, 1970s–, Piano, Dutch
Varner, Tom, Cool Jazz, 1970s–, French horn, composer, American
Vasconcelos, Nana, Latin Jazz; World Fusion, 1970s–, Percussion, Brazilian
Vesala, Edward, Contemporary Jazz, 1970s–, Drums, percussion, multi-instrumentalist, composer, Finnish
Wachsmann, Phil, Free Jazz, 1970s–, Violin, electronics, Ugandan
Wadud, Abdul, Free Jazz, 1970s–, Cello, American
Walcott, Colin, World Fusion, 1970s–1980s, Sitar, percussion, vocals, American
Waldo, Terry, Ragtime, 1970s–1980s, Piano, vocals, arranger, American
Walker, Eddie, Ragtime; Country Blues, 1970s–, Vocals, guitar, songwriter, British
Walker, Philip, Modern Electric Blues, 1970s–1990s, Vocals, American
Wallace, Bennie, Modern Jazz, 1970s–, Saxophone, American
Walrath, Jack, Modern Jazz, 1970s–, Trumpet, composer, arranger, bandleader, American
Walters, John, Jazz Rock, 1970s–, Composer, arranger, lyricon, computer, synthesizers, saxophone, flute, British
Ward, Carlos, Rhythm & Blues; Funk, 1970s–, Saxophone, flute, composer, Panama
Ware, David S., Free Jazz, 1970s–, Saxophone, American
Washington, Kenny, Bebop; Hard Bop, 1970s–, Drums, American
Washington, Toni Lynn, Rhythm & Blues, 1970s–, Vocals, American
Wasserman, Rob, Fusion, 1970s–, Bass, American
Watkins, John 'Mad Dog', Jump Blues; Chicago Blues, 1970s–1980s, Bass, drums, guitar, American
Watson, Bobby, Hard Bop; Modern Jazz, 1970s–, Saxophone, bandleader, American
Weather Report, Fusion, 1970s–1980s, Various instruments, American
Weber, Eberhard, Modern Jazz; World Fusion, 1970s–, Bass, cello, composer, bandleader, German
Weller, Don, Jazz Rock, 1970s–, Saxophone, clarinet, British
Werner, Kenny, Modern Jazz, 1970s–, Piano, American
Westbrook, Kate, Free Jazz; Big Band, 1970s–, Vocals, horn, piccolo, flute, British
Weston, John, Country Blues; Modern Electric Blues, 1970s–, Harmonica, vocals, American
Whispering Smith, Rhythm & Blues, 1970s, Harmonica, vocals, American
White, Andrew, Fusion; Hard Bop, 1970s–, Saxophone, American
White, Artie 'Blues Boy', Rhythm & Blues, 1970s–, Vocals, American
White, Josh Jr, Country Blues, 1970s–1980s, Vocals, guitar, composer, American
White, Lynn, Rhythm & Blues, 1970s–, Vocals, American
Whitehead, Tim, British Jazz; Big Band, 1970s–, Saxophone, clarinet, British
Wiggins, Phil, Country Blues, 1970s–, Harmonica, American
Wikström, Rolf, Country Blues, 1970s–, Guitar, Swedish
Wilkerson, Ed, Hard Bop; Free Jazz, 1970s–, Saxophone, clarinet, piano, composer, bandleader, American
Wilkinson, Alan, Free Jazz, 1970s–, Saxophone, vocals, British
Williams, James, Modern Jazz; Hard Bop, 1970s–2000s, Piano, composer, American
Williams, Jessica, Modern Jazz, 1970s–, Piano, American
Winter, Johnny, Blues Rock; Modern Electric Blues, 1970s–, Guitar, American
World Saxophone Quartet, Free Jazz, 1970s–, Saxophones, American
Zawinul, Joe, Fusion; World Fusion; Soul Jazz; Hard Bop, 1970s–1990s, Piano, keyboards, composer, Austrian
Zingaro, Carlos, Free Jazz; Fusion, 1970s–, Violin, Portuguese
Zottola, Glenn, Traditional Jazz, 1970s–, Trumpet, saxophone, American
Zwingenberger, Axel, Boogie-Woogie, 1970s–1980s, Piano, German
ZZ Top, Blues Rock, 1970s–1990s, Various instruments, American

see John McLaughlin pp 300 *see* Brecker Brothers pp 303 *see* Herbie Hancock pp 305 *see* Johnny Winter pp 311

THE EIGHTIES

As the end of the twentieth century approached, the United States – its culture included – entered a rare period of recapitulation, retrieval and, ultimately, renewal. The election as President of ageing Ronald Reagan, ex-movie star and California governor, introduced unexpected neo-conservatism, an ideology that looked back to a rosy, though mythical, Golden Age. Declaring 'It's morning in America', Reagan spoke for ways of life that had little to do with blues and jazz (or rock, classical and the newly surging rap/hip hop styles). Blues and jazz reacted by themselves, returning to the past. They were aided by the institution of a whole new recording format, the compact disc.

The CD, a palm-sized digital medium developed by German BMG and Japanese Sony corporations and introduced in 1983, re-energized the teetering recording industry as music devotees rushed to replace favourite LPs with the wondrous new product. Reissues of blues and jazz classics outnumbered but also financed new albums by younger artists. Those younger artists, however, also looked back to the glories of the 1950s and early 1960s for inspiration, polishing the past to a streamlined sheen. The new bluesmen still sang of love's pangs, but more often at white college fraternity parties than for black and hipster crowds in low-rent venues. The new jazz instrumentalists were sharply suited 'Young Lions', led by Wynton Marsalis, a virtuoso with classical chops as well as a post-bop background. There were fusion revisionists too – electric guitarist Pat Metheny, and Miles Davis staging a final comeback. Also, jazz voices from overseas announced themselves with a fervour that would not be denied. By the 1980s' end, home computers had transformed how people lived; Communism, the Iron Curtain and the USSR itself were gone, and the global economy had a running start into the contemporary era.

Second
B
B
KINGS
BLUES
CLUB
ONE WAY
GREETINGS FROM
AUSTIN
Capitol
TEXAS
VIOLET CROWN
Roadhouse
RELICS
VISIT OUR GALLERY
VINTAGE NEON
SIGNS & DECOR
(512) 442-NEON

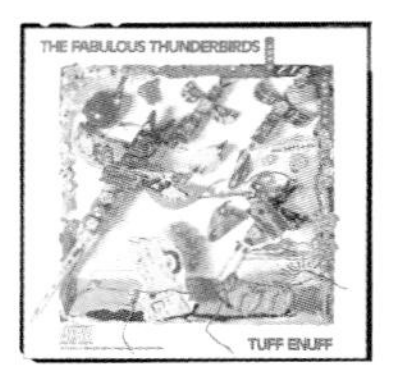

Sources & Sounds

KEY ARTISTS

Robert Cray

Wynton Marsalis

Pat Metheny

Stevie Ray Vaughan

The 1980s, in contrast to the decade that preceded them, were years of prosperity and decadence, and witnessed many important advances in science and technology; the music business was one of the many industries to benefit from these developments. The first compact disc was developed by Phillips and Sony and was released in the US in 1982 (or 1 March 1983 in the UK), with the first CD players following shortly afterwards. Compact discs were presented as being virtually indestructible, with a crystal-clear sound that enabled the listener to hear each high-quality audio track in minute detail.

Right
A mural in Austin, Texas, which boasted a lively blues scene during the 1980s.

'Whatever avenue you choose, whatever you have to say to the world, it comes down to that basic thing. It's your own voice … that's what music is – somebody's point of view about the world.'

David Sanborn

The Rise And Rise Of The Compact Disc

The general public was not immediately converted to the wonders of the compact disc. The discs were very expensive at first, and there were only a limited amount of titles available. Replacing an extensive vinyl collection promised to be extremely expensive, and in many cases, impossible. Furthermore, many listeners thought – and indeed still think – that the sparkling-clean digital sound of a CD loses some of the soul and warmth of the vinyl equivalent. Nevertheless, following gradual initial sales, by 1988 the CD became the dominant music medium. CD sales figures far surpassed those of vinyl and cassettes, which began to rapidly decline.

A wealth of reissues of old material ensued, including some previously unavailable recordings. One of the most important CD packages of the decade for blues fans was Columbia's *Robert Johnson: The Complete Recordings*, comprising 41 tracks that represented every single master and alternate take that the great man recorded during his 1936–37 sessions. Meanwhile, Australian broadcaster and sound engineer Robert Parker developed a technique of digitally remastering the classic jazz recordings of the 1920s and 1930s, resulting in his *Jazz Classics In Digital Stereo* series, which boasted a vastly improved clarity of sound and triggered a surge of renewed interest in the early days of jazz music.

Music In Your Pocket Or On Your TV

Another invention that changed the way in which people listened to music in the 1980s was the growing accessibility of portable music players. Sony's Walkman II was launched in 1981 and was smaller and cheaper than its predecessor, ensuring massive sales figures. Now people could continue to listen to music while on the move. Portable CD players were also introduced, with Sony releasing its Discman in 1984, but these gadgets had a tendency to skip at the slightest movement, and so they did not really take off until the next decade, by which time this problem had been largely rectified. Of course, in years to come MP3 players would revolutionize the portable music market, but the humble Walkman was the highly significant first step in this evolution.

The third major development in the music business as the 1980s began was the launch of MTV (Music Television) on 1 August 1981. Showing back-to-back music videos, this brought a new dimension to every pop music release thereafter. Artists would now have to create an original, interesting or catchy video to accompany their songs, and the pressure to look good increased immeasurably. Previously, singles would occasionally be accompanied by a short promotional film, but this was far from the norm; now, however, the viewers – the 'MTV generation' – had the power.

Stevie Ray Vaughan Arrives

Texas was a hotbed of rockin' blues in the mid- to late 1970s. Austin-based bands, heavily influenced by the British blues scene, such as the Cobras – featuring guitar sensation Stevie Ray Vaughan (1954–90) – and the Fabulous Thunderbirds – formed by Stevie Ray's older brother Jimmie Lee Vaughan – were gathering strong regional followings with their tough brand of roots-oriented roadhouse blues. These potent groups, as well as others such as the Nightcrawlers, Omar & the Howlers and the Electromagnets, spearheaded a 1980s blues-rock boom that paralleled the trend towards blues rock sparked in the late 1960s by Texas guitarist Johnny Winter (b. 1944).

The Fabulous Thunderbirds went on to build a national following in the 1980s in the wake of their major crossover success with 1986's *Tuff Enuff* (the title track was released by Epic Records as a single with accompanying video and received heavy play on MTV). Stevie Ray Vaughan went on to form his own band, Double Trouble, which quickly became one of the most popular bands in Texas and by 1982 began to receive national recognition. Stevie Ray's appearance with Double Trouble at the Montreux Jazz Festival in the summer of 1982 caught the attention of pop star David Bowie; he recruited the flashy Texan to lay down stinging lead-guitar tracks on his 1982 album *Let's Dance*, bringing Vaughan further into the public eye. Legendary record producer John Hammond (1910–86), who had significantly influenced the careers of everyone from Charlie Christian (1916–42) and Billie Holiday (1915–59) to Bob Dylan and Bruce Springsteen, signed Stevie Ray to a contract with Epic; his 1983 debut, *Texas Flood*, became an unqualified hit, crossing over to the pop market and earning two Grammy nominations.

CLASSIC RECORDINGS

1980
David Sanborn: *Hideaway*

1982
Rory Block: *High Heeled Blues*
Jaco Pastorius: *Word Of Mouth*
George Thorogood & the Destroyers: 'Bad To The Bone'

1983
George Adams: *Live At The Village Vanguard*
Wynton Marsalis: *Think Of One*
Lonnie Mack: *Strike Like Lightning*

1986
Kenny G: *Duotones*
Fabulous Thunderbirds: *Tuff Enuff*

1988
Bobby McFerrin: 'Don't Worry Be Happy'

Left
The Vaughan brothers Jimmie Lee (left) and Stevie Ray were key figures on the circuit.

see Robert Cray pp 324 *see* Stevie Ray Vaughan pp 330 *see* Fabulous Thunderbirds pp 335 *see* David Sanborn pp 337

Rock & Soul

The combined successes of the Vaughan brothers invigorated the blues-rock genre and also led to a renewed appreciation of blues-rock pioneers such as Lonnie Mack (b. 1941), Johnny Winter and Roy Buchanan (1939–88), all of whom signed with Chicago-based Alligator Records in the mid-1980s. The momentum that the Vaughan brothers had created paved the way for 1990s blues-rock players, including Kenny Wayne Sheppard, Jonny Lang, Coco Montoya, Tinsley Ellis (b. 1957), Sonny Landreth, Chris Duarte, Bryan Lee, Little Jimmy King, Larry McCray, Charlie Sexton and British blues-rock guitar hero Gary Moore.

Below
The legendary Beale Street in Memphis, Tennessee, which was regenerated in the 1980s.

Elsewhere in America, other forms of blues music were developing or resurrecting. In Jackson, Minnesota, a selection of artists were working together to create a type of blues with a more relaxed approach than that of their Texas peers. Soul blues was recorded by a number of artists signed to the Malaco label, including guitarist and vocalist Little Milton, who had been recording R&B and funk since the 1950s. Meanwhile, in Memphis, the legendary Beale Street – immortalized itself in a blues song – was going through a regeneration process, and a new wave of blues artists were rising up from its depths. In the UK, singer and saxophonist Joe Jackson was experimenting with a range of styles; from a new wave and jazz background, Jackson also meddled with R&B and in 1981 released the album *Jumpin' Jive*, which recreated the 1940s jump blues sound of Louis Jordan to great effect.

New Fusion Vs Neo-Traditionalists

By the late 1970s, the jazz-rock fusion movement – which had been ushered in at the outset of the decade with raw, tumultuous abandon by the likes of the Tony Williams Lifetime, Miles Davis and the Mahavishnu Orchestra – had become codified and diluted. Groups and individual artists such as the Crusaders, Chuck Mangione, Bob James, George Benson, Ramsey Lewis, Grover Washington Jr., Spyro Gyra and Jeff Lorber began smoothing off the rough edges, producing a more palatable strain of pop-influenced jazz that sought to cross over to a mainstream audience by appeasing rather than provoking. This tamer brand of fusion from the late 1970s – alternately derided by musicians and critics alike as 'happy jazz', 'fuzak' and 'hot-tub jazz' – paved the way for New Adult Contemporary (NAC) in the 1980s and the smooth-jazz movement of the 1990s.

Meanwhile, with the rise to prominence in the early 1980s of Wynton Marsalis – a gifted young trumpeter from New Orleans who took an earnest stand to play strictly acoustic jazz in the face of the electrified funk and fusion that dominated the era – a major schism had been set in place in jazz. Marsalis, through the sheer force of his talent and personality, along with his two Grammy Awards for both jazz and classical performance in 1983, quickly became leader of the so-called 'Young Lions'

see Introduction pp 314 *see* Key Artists pp 324 *see* A–Z of Artists pp 332 *see* List of Artists pp 340

movement, which sought a return to jazz's acoustic roots. This swinging, neo-conservative (neo-con) trend developed in parallel with a trend towards smooth jazz, marked by simpler, more melodious and accessible radio-friendly sounds, and represented by the movement's leader Kenny G (b. 1956), whose 1986 breakthrough album, *Duotones*, became an international multi-million seller. One further factor that altered the sound of some jazz musicians in the 1980s and beyond was that many of its exponents came to it through study, rather than from first-hand experience as many of their predecessors had.

Developing Jazz Styles

Other jazz styles also began to develop around this time. Acid jazz – which described bands such as the Brand New Heavies, the James Taylor Quartet, Jamiroquai and Incognito – began as a mainly UK-based style that ran alongside the acid-house dance movement of the late 1980s. Taking elements from diverse types of music styles, including disco, swing, rock, and electronic dance music such as techno, the specific blend of influences determined each band's sound; some included rock instruments within jazz combos, while some blended their jazz with dance music by merging looped samples into the mix, among live improvisations.

Jazz rap, a relation of hip hop and influential on the developing rap genres, also came to the fore during the late 1980s. The first stirrings of this movement began with the poet, keyboard player and vocalist Gil Scott-Heron (b. 1949), who had been performing and recording his politically charged poetry, with and without musical accompaniment, since the mid-1970s. Some of the diverse themes discussed in his lyrics included political corruption, nuclear power, poverty, drink and drug abuse and racism, while his music blended influences of jazz and blues – specifically John Coltrane, Billie Holliday and Robert Johnson – as well as soul and Latin music, which had surrounded him in the Hispanic-dominated area where he went to school in Chelsea, New York. Scott-Heron had been publishing his poems and novels since the age of 19, but it was not until he met pianist and composer Brian Jackson at Lincoln University that the music really began to flow. Classic tracks such as 'The Revolution Will Not Be Televised' (on which Ron Carter played bass), 'The Bottle' and '"B" Movie' had an influence on acid jazz and laid the groundwork for jazz rap, a genre that included Gang Starr, the Jungle Brothers and De La Soul. In return, rap and hip hop music would also feed back into the jazz scene, inspiring artists such as saxophonists Maceo Parker and Courtney Pine.

Above
Gil Scott-Heron's politically charged poetry influenced jazz rap.

see Wynton Marsalis pp 326 see Kenny G pp 335 see Lonnie Mack pp 336 see Acid Jazz pp 400

Above
Pianist Chick Corea (foreground), shown here with tenor saxophonist Bob Berg, was a major force in electronic jazz in the 1980s with his Elektric Band.

Fusion Holds Its Own

A few fusion renegades persisted in the face of both neo-con and smooth-jazz factions during the 1980s, notably drummer and Ornette Coleman disciple Ronald Shannon Jackson, whose Decoding Society accounted for some of the most fiercely uncompromising music of the decade. Alongside him were harmolodic guitarist James 'Blood' Ulmer (b. 1941), alto saxophonist Steve Coleman (b. 1956, founder of the cutting-edge M-Base Collective) and former Weather Report bassist Jaco Pastorius (1951–87), who blended big-band jazz, rock bombast, free-jazz abstractions and Stravinsky-esque dissonance on his 1982 recording *Word Of Mouth*. Fusion pioneers Chick Corea and John McLaughlin (b. 1942) both returned to the electronic arena with a vengeance in the mid-1980s – Corea with his Elektric Band, and McLaughlin with a new edition of his Mahavishnu Orchestra. Another fusion pioneer, Herbie Hancock (b. 1940), scored a massive radioplay hit in 1983 with 'Rock It', a streetwise melding of techno and funk that updated his own early 1970s jazz-funk hit 'Chameleon' while presaging the hip hop/jazz movement of the 1990s. 'Rock It' was also worthy of note for having an MTV video, signalling the arrival of jazz into a wider musical field.

An influential and widely imitated musician of the decade was guitarist-composer Pat Metheny (b. 1954), whose refreshingly original sound affected a generation of listeners and players alike. Another successful jazz guitarist was Stanley Jordan, who developed a tapping technique that enabled him to accompany himself while playing intricate countermelodies in the upper registers. The 1980s also marked the return of Miles Davis (1926–91) from the retirement that he imposed upon himself in 1975. Davis's comeback band of 1980 included bassist Marcus Miller, guitarist Mike Stern and saxophonist

see Introduction pp 314 see Key Artists pp 324 see A–Z of Artists pp 332 see List of Artists pp 340

Left
Tenor saxophone legend Dextor Gordon portrays lonely musician Dale Turner in the 1986 film *Round Midnight*.

Bill Evans (1929–80), each of whom became a bandleader in his own right later in the decade.

The Stalwarts Of Jazz

Other jazz giants still active on the scene in the 1980s included trumpeter and bebop pioneer Dizzy Gillespie (1917–93), tenor saxophonist and Gillespie protégé James Moody (b. 1925), alto sax burner Jackie McLean (1931–2006), former Miles Davis collaborator Ron Carter (b. 1937), who was leading his own ensemble, tenor saxophonist Johnny Griffin, drummer Mel Lewis, who continued to lead his orchestra every Monday night at the Village Vanguard through the 1980s, and tenor sax titan Dexter Gordon (1923–90), who appeared in the 1986 film *Round Midnight* (which also boasted a score written by Herbie Hancock). Other significant figures in this period were vocalist/talent scout Betty Carter – whose band served as a training ground during the 1980s for promising young talent including pianists Benny Green, Marc Cary and Stephen Scott, saxophonists Don Braden and Craig Handy, drummers Winard Harper and Gregory Hutchinson, and bassists Curtis Lundy and Taurus Mateen – and the great drummer Art Blakey (1919–90), who continued to tour with his Jazz Messengers. The group's ranks during this period included future bandleaders Wynton and Branford Marsalis, trumpeters Terence Blanchard, Philip Harper and Brian Lynch, saxophonists Bobby Watson, Billy Pierce, Donald Harrison and Javon Jackson, pianists James Williams, Donald Brown, Mulgrew Miller and Geoff Keezer, and bassists Charles Fambrough and Lonnie Plaxico. Blakey led his Messengers in typically dynamic fashion right up until his death in 1990.

Below
Blues-rock artists such as Lonnie Mack enjoyed renewed fame following the Vaughans' success.

see John McLaughlin pp 300 see Herbie Hancock pp 305 see Jaco Pastorius pp 309 see James 'Blood' Ulmer pp 338

Above
Chuck Berry celebrates his sixtieth birthday onstage in St. Louis with Keith Richards.

It was also possible to see legendary jazzmen, such as trumpeters Clark Terry and Doc Cheatham (1905–97), saxophonists Stan Getz (1927–91), Sonny Rollins (b. 1930), Benny Carter (1907–2003) and Jimmy Heath (b. 1926), guitarists Barney Kessel (1923–2004) and Joe Pass (1929–94), trombonist J.J. Johnson (1924–2001), violinist Stephane Grappelli (1905–97), pianists Oscar Peterson (b. 1925), Dave Brubeck (b. 1920) and Eubie Blake (1883–1983), drummers Kenny Clarke (1914–85), Buddy Rich (1917–84) and Max Roach (b. 1924), and bandleaders Count Basie (1904–84), Benny Goodman (1909–86), Cab Calloway (1907–94) and Woody Herman (1913–87).

Paying Tribute To The Old Blues

In Chicago, the city where the blues once thrived, the music was now suffering from neglect. Throughout the 1970s and into the early 1980s the old blues greats, including Muddy Waters and John Lee Hooker, had continued to play there, but no recordings were being made and little interest was being taken in the scene. It was as though music history was being lost as soon as it was happening. As the 1980s marched on, the older bluesmen began to die, and many of the established blues clubs were taken over or fell into disrepair. It was as a result of this unhappy period for the blues that the Chicago Blues Foundation would be founded in 1996, dedicated to restoring, preserving and archiving the remaining photographs, posters, recordings and artefacts that recall the great heroes of Chicago blues and the venues in which they played. Some of the masters, of course, were still recording, and John Lee Hooker's 1989 album *The Healer*, recorded in collaboration with guest musicians that included Carlos Santana and Robert Cray, re-established him as a major blues force to be reckoned with.

see **Introduction pp 314** *see* **Key Artists pp 324** *see* **A–Z of Artists pp 332** *see* **List of Artists pp 340**

Tributes to early blues figures cropped up throughout the decade; in 1983 Bob Dylan recorded the song 'Blind Willie McTell' for his album *Infidels*, in which Dylan laments that he will never be able to compete vocally with the sweet-voiced Georgia bluesman. A beautifully rendered, powerful blues song in itself, fans continue to be baffled as to why Dylan left it out of the final track selection for the album. Three years later, on 18 October 1986 Keith Richards joined R&B legend Chuck Berry and a supporting cast of blues, R&B and soul musicians, including Linda Ronstadt, Etta James, Eric Clapton, Johnnie Johnson and Robert Cray, onstage in St. Louis to celebrate Berry's sixtieth birthday. The concert, held in St. Louis, was televised and became the film *Hail! Hail! Rock 'N' Roll*. Although Richards and the notoriously difficult Berry did not always see eye-to-eye during rehearsals, the film was a success and Richards came away from the experience feeling no less warmth and respect towards his hero.

Slide specialist Ry Cooder (b. 1947), who worked with Richards in the late 1960s, played his own part in reawakening blues interest in the 1980s. His work on film soundtracks brought the blues to new audiences; particular cases in point are the beautiful slide work that he recorded for the 1984 BAFTA-winning Wim Wenders film *Paris, Texas*, starring Harry Dean Stanton, and 1986's *Crossroads*, which featured Ralph Macchio and was loosely based on the life of Robert Johnson. Cooder also worked on the scores of *The Long Riders* (1980), *Southern Comfort* (1981) and *Alamo Bay* (1985).

Below

Ry Cooder's work on film soundtracks brought blues music to new audiences.

see John Lee Hooker pp 158 *see* Muddy Waters pp 212 *see* Ry Cooder pp 303 *see* Robert Cray pp 324

Robert Cray

CLASSIC RECORDINGS

1980
Who's Been Talkin', 'Nice As A Fool Can Be', 'That's What I'll Do', 'The Score', 'Too Many Cooks'

1983
Bad Influence, 'Bad Influence', 'Phone Booth', 'So Many Women, So Little Time'

1985
False Accusations, 'I've Slipped Her Mind'

1986
Strong Persuader, 'Right Next Door', 'Smoking Gun'

Although Robert Cray's clean, good looks, precise guitar lines and slick presentation earned him some knocks from critics early on in his career (hardcore blues aficionados tended to dismiss him as 'blues lite' for yuppies), he later gained their respect for his smart songwriting and razor-sharp guitar licks, along with an intensely passionate vocal style reminiscent of the great 1960s R&B singer O.V. Wright.

A Promising Debut

Born on 1 August 1953 in Columbus, Georgia, Cray moved around frequently until the age of 15, when his family finally settled in Tacoma, Washington. Inspired by Texas guitarslinger Albert Collins (who played at Cray's high-school graduation), he taught himself to play guitar and formed his first band in 1974 with bassist Richard Cousins. After playing around the Pacific Northwest during the 1970s, even joining Collins's backing band on a few West Coast gigs, Cray's band made its recording debut in 1980 with *Who's Been Talkin'* (on Tomato Records). That first album set the tone for Cray's recording career, reflecting an equal allegiance to blues and R&B in his faithful covers of O.V. Wright's 'I'm Gonna Forget

'I walked into a record store, and they were playing Robert Cray's new record … the music just grabbed me … I said, "Man, it's time for me to get back into this music!".'

Joe Fonda

Right
Singer, songwriter and razor-sharp guitarist Robert Cray lets rip onstage during a 1987 UK tour.

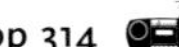 *see* Introduction pp 314 *see* Sources & Sounds pp 316 *see* A–Z of Artists pp 332

About You', Freddie King's 'The Welfare (Turns Its Back On You)' and the Willie Dixon-penned title track. But it was Cray's originals 'Nice As A Fool Can Be' and 'That's What I'll Do' that pointed to a future direction for this talented singer, songwriter and guitarist.

Cray followed up with two solid outings on the High Tone label – 1983's *Bad Influence*, which contained the chilling original 'Phone Booth', and 1985's *False Accusations* – before finally breaking through to mainstream acceptance following the release of his superb 1986 Mercury Records debut, *Strong Persuader* (containing his hit original song 'Smoking Gun'). In 1985 Cray appeared on a guitar summit meeting, the aptly named *Showdown!* (Alligator Records), with fellow blues six-stringers Albert Collins and Johnny 'Clyde' Copeland.

Above
Cray (right) with blues legend B.B. King in 1992.

A Southerly Direction

During the 1990s, Cray took more of a southern soul direction on recordings such as 1990's *Midnight Stroll*, 1992's *I Was Warned* and 1995's *Some Rainy Morning* (all on Mercury), while continuing to blossom as a songwriter with a knack for minor-key confessionals. In 1999 he collaborated with drummer Steve Jordan, who produced and played on the Memphis-flavoured *Take Your Shoes Off* (Rykodisc). Also appearing on that retro-soul outing was drummer-producer Willie Mitchell of Hi Records fame; he co-wrote and also created the horn arrangements for the opening track, which has the distinct feel of an early 1970s Al Green number. Elsewhere on the album, Cray offers faithful renditions of Mack Rice's '24-7 Man' and Solomon Burke's 'Won't You Give Him (One More Chance)'.

Time Will Tell

Cray has continued to expertly blend relaxed, good-feeling southern soul and urgent blues on 2001's Stax/Volt-flavoured *Shoulda Been Home* (again produced in Memphis by drummer Steve Jordan) and 2003's *Time Will Tell* (Sanctuary), his thirteenth recording as a leader. That most recent release is easily his most ambitious to date and is in some ways uncharacteristic of his style. Not only does it contain two stridently anti-war songs in 'Survivor' and 'Distant Shore', it also features Cray in an odd turn on electric sitar, playing with the Turtle Island String Quartet on 'Up In The Sky', a psychedelic number that sounds like an outtake from Prince's *Around The World In A Day* (1985). Regardless of the context, however, Cray remains a commanding vocal presence and an assertive six-stringer. After 30 years of constant gigging, he has become one of the seasoned veterans on the contemporary blues scene.

see Willie Dixon pp 221 *see* B.B. King pp 260 *see* Albert Collins pp 270 *see* Johnny 'Clyde' Copeland pp 334

Wynton Marsalis

CLASSIC RECORDINGS

1982
Wynton Marsalis, 'Hesitation'

1983
Think Of One, 'Knozz-Moe-King', 'Melancholia'

1984
Hot House Flowers, 'I'm Confessin'', 'When You Wish Upon A Star'

1985
Black Codes From The Underground, 'Black Codes', 'Chambers Of Tain'

1986
J Mood, 'Insane Asylum', 'Skain's Domain'

1989
The Majesty Of The Blues, 'The Majesty Of The Blues'

Above
Wynton Marsalis (right) and saxophonist brother Branford were important figures in the neo-conservative revival of traditional jazz values.

In the 1980s, trumpeter Wynton Marsalis leapt from jazz-steeped New Orleans to international artistic prominence. In 1979 he was enrolled in New York City's Juilliard School and was jamming with Art Blakey's Jazz Messengers, and 10 years later he had seeded what has become an unrivalled international jazz performance centre. In between, Marsalis established himself as a hot soloist, bandleader, composer and recording artist, as well as an eager educator, media charmer and ad-hoc ambassador of American values.

'I try to play whatever I'm hearing. And that's part of jazz music. That's what it is.'
Wynton Marsalis

A Musical Family

Born in New Orleans on 18 October 1961, Marsalis is the second of six sons of jazz pianist and educator Ellis Marsalis. His elder brother Branford is a saxophonist while younger siblings Delfaeyo and Jason play the trombone and drums respectively. At the age of eight Wynton was in the Fairview Baptist Church band, organized by veteran jazz banjoist and guitarist Danny Barker. He also played in marching bands and classical youth orchestras, performing the Haydn Trumpet Concerto with the New Orleans Philharmonic at the age of 14. He left his studies in 1980 for the front line of Blakey's Messengers with Branford. In July 1981, Wynton toured Japan with Miles Davis's famed 1960s rhythm section – pianist Herbie Hancock, drummer Tony Williams and bassist Ron Carter. Their recording *Quartet* (1982) was released as Marsalis's debut on Columbia Records.

The Neo-Conservative Style

Marsalis's youth, energy, technical facility, directness of expression, breadth of repertoire and articulation of a neo-conservative aesthetic were in strong contrast with Davis's flagging health and fading iconoclasm. He was promoted as king of the Young Lions – a fresh crop of skilled, musically educated instrumentalists who abjured free jazz and commercial fusion to stand for the achievements and ambitions of an African-American middle class. Marsalis proclaimed the primacy of blues, swing, bebop, Louis Armstrong, Duke Ellington, Blakey, mid-period Davis and Thelonious Monk, but he scorned jazz rock, funk and fusion (music Miles was playing at the time).

After leaving Blakey, Marsalis formed a quintet (with Branford, Kenny Kirkland on piano, and Jeff 'Tain' Watts on drums) that expanded on post-bop conventions. Marsalis's *Think Of One* (1983) and his

see Introduction pp 314 *see* Sources & Sounds pp 316 *see* A–Z of Artists pp 332

first album of classical trumpet fare both won Grammy Awards, an unprecedented feat he repeated with *Hot House Flowers* and *Baroque Music* in 1984. His *Black Codes (From The Underground)* from 1985 is another early peak. Subsequently, Marsalis recorded two three-volume sets of jazz standards and of original, intertwined material entitled *Soul Gestures In Southern Blues* (1988). As Branford launched his own career (the brothers still appear together, and occasionally *en famille*), Wynton discovered other collaborators, including pianist Marcus Roberts, drummer Herlin Riley and trombonist Wycliffe Gordon.

Marsalis At Lincoln Center

In summer 1987 Marsalis presented a concert series, Classical Jazz, under the auspices of Lincoln Center, New York's premier performing-arts institution. So began a unique collaboration between artist and establishment that has developed far-reaching jazz education programmes, jazz collaborations with chamber-music ensembles, orchestras and ballet troupes, countless radio and television productions, the globe-trotting Lincoln Center Jazz Orchestra, and Wynton himself.

Marsalis is a celebrity, but he has never sold out. He has consistently applied serious efforts to his ensembles, film scores, chamber works and art songs. His oratorio *Blood On The Fields* (1995), featuring vocalists Cassandra Wilson, Miles Griffith and Jon Hendricks, was the first jazz piece awarded the Pulitzer Prize, and he wrote *All Rise* for a big band, 100-voice choir and the New York Philharmonic Orchestra to celebrate the turn of the twenty-first century.

In October 2004, Marsalis realized a fondly nurtured dream – the opening of Jazz@Lincoln Center's state-of-the-art Rose Hall, a multi-venue, multi-use facility billed as the first ever specifically designed for jazz. By 1990, Wynton Marsalis was already as he remains today: a tireless advocate for jazz (particularly its African-American strains), a communicator of jazz principles and a virtuoso instrumentalist, credibly interpreting diverse genres and styles, and able to improvise deeply affecting personal statements.

Below
Marsalis's Lincoln Center Jazz Orchestra, which is based in New York but tours festivals and concert halls worldwide.

see Miles Davis pp 200 *see* Thelonious Monk pp 208 *see* Art Blakey pp 218 *see* Jeff 'Tain' Watts pp 367

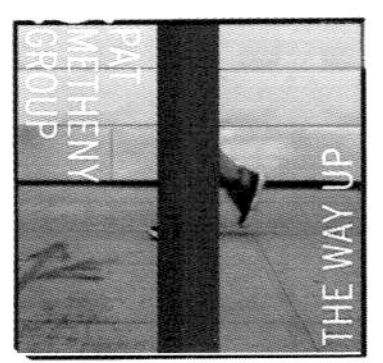

Pat Metheny

CLASSIC RECORDINGS

1979
American Garage, 'American Garage'

1982
Off Ramp, 'Are You Going With Me?', 'James', 'The Bat'

1984
First Circle, 'End Of Game', 'If I Could', 'Yolanda, You Learn'

1987
Still Life (Talking), 'Last Train Home', 'So May It Secretly Begin', 'Third Wind'

Above
The line-up for 1986's *Song X* included (l–r) Metheny, Jack DeJohnette and Ornette Coleman.

'To me if it's anything, jazz is a verb – it's more like a process than it is a thing.'
Pat Metheny

Guitarist Pat Metheny emerged in the mid-1970s with a fully realized approach to his instrument that was wholly unique for its time, offering a refreshing alternative to both bop and fusion styles. His sweeping, warm-toned, reverb-soaked lines and liquid phrasing, once described by *Down Beat* magazine as 'the sound of wind through the trees', had a huge impact on a generation of guitarists and forged a new direction in jazz in the late 1970s. Metheny also made a significant impact as a composer, with original, genre-stretching music that artfully blended his own folk influences with elements of rock, Brazilian music, bebop, new age and free jazz.

A Precocious Student

Born on 12 August 1954 in the small midwestern town of Lee's Summit, Missouri, Metheny started on trumpet aged eight before switching to guitar at the age of 12. By 15, he was already a local legend in Kansas City, where he gained invaluable bandstand experience working with veteran players on the jazz scene. In 1972 he moved to Florida and at 18 became the youngest teacher ever at the University of Miami. In 1973 he joined the faculty at the Berklee College of Music in Boston and became the youngest musician ever to be on the staff there (he received an honorary doctorate at Berklee in 1996).

Metheny established his reputation through his work as a sideman with Gary Burton's group – he is

see Introduction pp 314 see Sources & Sounds pp 316 see A–Z of Artists pp 332

featured on Burton's ECM albums *Dreams So Real* (1975) and *Passengers* (1976) – and as a leader of such acclaimed recordings as his 1976 ECM debut, *Bright Size Life* (a trio date with bassist Jaco Pastorius and drummer Bob Moses) and two powerful follow-up recordings for the label: 1977's *Watercolors* (which established his long-running partnership with keyboardist Lyle Mays) and 1978's *Pat Metheny Group* (which introduced the band featuring Mays on keyboards, Mark Egan on electric bass and Danny Gottlieb on drums).

Left
Pat Metheny took jazz guitar in a new direction and was refreshingly open to the influence of other musical styles.

Metheny Meets The Mainstream

Metheny broke into mass-market acceptance with 1979's *American Garage*, a far more rock-oriented recording than the typically introspective and searching ECM fare. He achieved mainstream popularity and attained gold-record status (sales of 500,000 copies) during the 1980s with a string of melodic, Brazilian-tinged albums, including 1983's *Travels*, 1984's *First Circle*, 1987's *Still Life (Talking)* and 1989's *Letter From Home*. And yet he never stopped taking risks and expanding his musical boundaries throughout the decade, as evidenced by such uncompromising side projects as 1980's free-boppish *80/81* with bassist Charlie Haden, drummer Jack DeJohnette and the twin tenors of Michael Brecker and Dewey Redman; 1981's ethereal duet with keyboardist Mays on *As Falls Witchita, So Falls Wichita Falls*; 1982's abstract *Off Ramp* (which introduces his use of guitar synthesizer); 1983's *Rejoicing*, a subdued guitar-trio setting with bassist Haden and drummer Billy Higgins; 1984's film soundtrack *The Falcon And The Snowman*, which included a collaboration with pop star David Bowie on 'This Is Not America'; and 1986's provocative *Song X*, an historic collaboration with one of his boyhood idols – free-jazz icon Ornette Coleman.

An Experimental Superstar

By the end of the 1980s, Metheny was a bona-fide jazz superstar whose name was on a par with Miles Davis, Keith Jarrett, Herbie Hancock, Joe Zawinul and Wayne Shorter. Through the 1990s, he continued to release recordings of consistently high quality that appealed to his massive fan base (particularly 1992's *Secret Story*, 1994's *We Live Here* and 1997's *Imaginary Day*) while also indulging in purely experimental projects such as 1992's solo guitar synth noise onslaught *Zero Tolerance For Silence* and 1997's *The Sign Of 4*, an edgy free-jazz collaboration with British avant-garde guitar pioneer Derek Bailey, recorded live at New York's Knitting Factory with drummers Paul Wertico and Gregg Bendian.

Over the years, Metheny has won countless polls as 'Best Jazz Guitarist', as well as earning three gold records and 15 Grammy Awards. His Pat Metheny Group, now in its twenty-fifth year, remains one of the longest-standing acts in jazz.

Left
Vibist Gary Burton, in whose group Metheny established his original playing style.

see Ornette Coleman pp 248 *see* Gary Burton pp 267 *see* Keith Jarrett pp 307 *see* Jaco Pastorius pp 309

Stevie Ray Vaughan

CLASSIC RECORDINGS

1983
Texas Flood, 'Love Struck Baby', 'Pride And Joy', 'Rude Mood'

1984
Couldn't Stand The Weather, 'Cold Shot', 'Scuttle Buttin''

1985
Soul To Soul, 'Look At Little Sister', 'Say What!'

1989
In Step, 'The House Is Rockin'', 'Tightrope', 'Wall Of Denial'

Above
Stevie Ray Vaughan – the greatest guitar virtuoso since Jimi Hendrix – who died tragically young in a helicopter crash.

The premiere torch-bearer for the blues-rock boom of the 1980s, Texan guitar wizard Stevie Ray Vaughan galvanized a generation of players and fans alike with his pyrotechnic licks and flamboyant stage presence. Connecting deeply with both the psychedelic, 'voodoo chile' mystique of Jimi Hendrix and the down-home roadhouse grittiness of his biggest guitar influence, Albert King, Vaughan fashioned a sound that reached out and grabbed listeners with its combination of raucous rock-fuelled abandon, string-bending intensity, gut-level directness and real-deal, bluesy authority.

'I've said that playing the blues is like having to be black twice. Stevie Ray Vaughan missed on both counts, but I never noticed.'
B.B. King

His meteoric rise to fame during the mid-1980s, over the course of four recordings and countless gigs, was fuelled by self-destructive cocaine-and-alcohol binges that led to a physical collapse and subsequent rehabilitation in 1987. Stevie Ray ultimately mustered the courage to overcome his addictions, returning to the scene in 1988 with a clean bill of health and a renewed sense of conviction. He continued touring and recording and was at his peak when he died in a tragic helicopter crash after a concert in the summer of 1990.

The Vaughan Brothers

Born in the Oak Cliff area of Dallas, Texas on 3 October 1954, Stevie Ray Vaughan grew up under the influence of his older brother Jimmie, an accomplished blues and R&B guitar player and vintage record collector. Stevie Ray got his first guitar at the age of seven and began copying licks from brother Jimmie's records by the likes of Lonnie Mack, Albert King, Freddie King, B.B. King, Buddy Guy, T-Bone Walker, Otis Rush and Jimmy Reed. Although the Vaughan brothers had a competitive relationship, Stevie Ray idolized Jimmie and closely followed his progress through a succession of early bands, including the Swinging Pendulums, the Chessmen and Texas Storm. Stevie Ray formed his own band, Blackbird, in 1970.

In 1971, aged 17, he dropped out of high school to concentrate on music. On New Year's Eve of 1971, Stevie Ray and his Blackbird bandmates all moved to Austin and began working on the thriving blues scene there. In 1973 Steve Ray joined the Nightcrawlers and by the end of 1974 was playing his first gig with Paul Ray's popular Cobras. After leaving the Cobras in July 1977 he formed his own Triple Threat Revue, featuring singer Lou Ann Barton, guitarist W.C. Clark, drummer Freddy 'Pharoah' Walden and keyboardist Mike 'Cold Shot' Kindred. After Triple Threat imploded due to inner bickering between Vaughan and Barton, Stevie Ray formed Double Trouble (named after one of Vaughan's favourite Otis Rush tunes) in May of 1978. The band built a strong regional following for the next few years, culminating in a triumphant appearance at

see Introduction pp 314 *see* Sources & Sounds pp 316 *see* A–Z of Artists pp 332

the Montreux International Jazz Festival on 17 July 1982. Pop stars Jackson Browne and David Bowie were in the audience at that galvanizing performance; Browne later offered his studio to record Double Trouble, while Bowie hired Stevie Ray to play on his recording *Let's Dance* (1983), considerably elevating the guitarist's profile.

A Brilliant Career

Vaughan and Double Trouble were signed to an Epic Records contract by legendary producer and talent scout John Hammond. Stevie Ray's 1983 debut, *Texas Flood*, was an immediate hit and led to a triple award from *Guitar Player* magazine for Best New Talent, Best Electric Blues Guitar Player and Best Guitar Album, as well as W.C. Handy Blues Awards for Entertainer of the Year and Blues Instrumentalist of the Year. Stevie Ray's virtuoso playing and Hendrix-inspired mystique (for a generation of young fans who missed out on the 1960s, he provided a bridge to Jimi through his faithful covers of 'Voodoo Chile [Slight Return]' and 'Third Stone From The Sun', replete with wild guitar-thashing stage antics) helped to fuel subsequent successes with 1984's *Couldn't Stand The Weather* and 1985's *Soul To Soul*. Following an extensive tour in 1986, which yielded the double LP *Live Alive* and culminated in an onstage collapse in London, Vaughan entered a rehabilitation hospital in Georgia. After taking a year out he returned to the scene, re-energized and with a new outlook on life. By the end of 1988, he had begun writing the material that would make up the bulk of 1989's *In Step*, which went gold (500,000 copies sold) within six months of its release and later won a Grammy Award for Best Contemporary Blues Recording. Vaughan co-headlined a 1989 tour of America with rock guitarist Jeff Beck, and in the spring of 1990 he recorded an album with his brother Jimmie entitled *Family Style*.

An Untimely Death

On 26 August 1990 Stevie Ray and Double Trouble played a gig at the Alpine Valley Music Theater in Easy Troy, Wisconsin. The concert culminated with an all-star encore jam featuring special guests Eric Clapton, Buddy Guy, Jimmie Vaughan and Robert Cray. After the concert, Vaughan boarded a helicopter bound for Chicago; minutes after its 12:30 a.m. takeoff, the helicopter crashed into hills, killing the blues guitar hero instantly. At his funeral in Dallas, Stevie Wonder sang 'Amazing Grace' at the gravesite. Jimmie and Stevie Ray's *Family Style* was released posthumously in October 1990 and won two Grammy Awards for Best Rock Instrumental ('D/FW') and Best Contemporary Blues Recording. Other posthumously released recordings by Stevie Ray Vaughan include 1992's *In The Beginning*, which documents a 1980 concert by Double Trouble, and 2000's four-CD boxed set *SRV*.

Below
Vaughan's well-travelled guitar case.

see Buddy Guy pp 254 see Albert King pp 258 see Jimi Hendrix pp 273 see Otis Rush pp 278

A-Z of Artists

Above

Passionate saxophonist George Adams performing at the North Sea Jazz Festival in The Hague, 1982.

George Adams

(Tenor saxophone, flute, 1940–92)

A passionate voice on tenor sax in Charles Mingus's last band (1973–76), Adams co-led one of the most dynamic quartets of the 1980s with pianist Don Pullen; it also featured Mingus drummer Dannie Richmond and bassist Cameron Brown. In a series of 12 recordings through the 1980s for the Soul Note and Timeless labels, the Adams-Pullen band brilliantly straddled the inside-outside aesthetic, perhaps most successfully on 1983's two-volume *Live At The Village Vanguard*.

Marcia Ball

(Piano, vocals, b. 1949)

One of the leading exponents of the Professor Longhair school of piano playing, East Texas-born 'Long Tall' Marcia Ball was also greatly influenced by R&B divas Irma Thomas and Etta James, and zydeco king Clifton Chenier. Her infectious blend of modern Texas roadhouse blues, boogie-woogie and Louisiana swamp rock is best exemplified on a series of Rounder recordings, including 1984's *Soulful Dress*, 1986's *Hot Tamale Baby* and 1989's *Gator Rhythms*. Ball still tours continuously and is an annual attraction at the New Orleans Jazz & Heritage Festival.

Rory Block

(Guitar, vocals, b. 1949)

An interpreter of classic country blues, Block took guitar lessons from Rev. Gary Davis, Mississippi John Hurt and Son House before moving to California and working on the folk-blues coffeehouse circuit. She recorded for small labels before signing with Rounder Records and debuting with 1982's *High Heeled Blues*. She is featured in the Robert Mugge film *Hellhounds On My Trail* (2000), celebrating Robert Johnson's posthumous entry into the Rock And Roll Hall Of Fame. Her most recent recordings are 2003's *Last Fair Deal* and 2004's *From The Dust* (both on Telarc Blues).

The Blues Band

(Vocal/instrumental group, 1979–present)

Blues aficionados Paul Jones (vocals, harmonica), Dave Kelly (vocals, guitar), Tom McGuiness (guitar), Gary Fletcher (bass) and Hughie Flint (drums) formed the Blues Band in 1979, purely for their own enjoyment. Initial success on the pub and club circuit swiftly led to greater things and their first album was released in 1980. Flint was replaced in 1981 by Rob Townsend and the band has continued to perform and record prolifically. Ex-Manfred Mann star Jones also plays an important role in keeping the blues alive as Britain's premier blues DJ.

 *see* Introduction pp 314 *see* Sources & Sounds pp 316 *see* Key Artists pp 324

Left
Piedmont blues exponents John 'Bowling Green' Cephas (right) and 'Harmonica' Phil Wiggins perform in Knoxville, Tennessee in 1982.

Cephas & Wiggins

(Vocal/instrumental group, 1978–present)

The W.C. Handy Award-winning duo patterned itself after Sonny Terry & Brownie McGhee. Guitarist John 'Bowling Green' Cephas (b. 1930) and 'Harmonica' Phil Wiggins (b. 1954) met at a jam session in Washington, DC and began performing together in 1978. They toured the globe on a US State Department tour and recorded throughout the 1980s, while their most recent recordings for the Alligator label are 1996's *Cool Down*, 1999's *Homemade* and 2003's *Somebody Told The Truth*. They remain the leading exponents of the Piedmont blues style.

Eddy Clearwater

(Guitar, vocals, b. 1933)

Mississippi-born Eddy Harrington left the South in 1950 and established himself on Chicago's West Side as a Chuck Berry imitator named Guitar Eddy. He later took the stage name Clear Waters as a takeoff on Muddy Waters, but finally settled on Eddy 'The Chief' Clearwater, a nickname he got from his penchant for wearing Native American headdresses onstage. His tough, slashing, southpaw guitar attack is best documented on 1980's Rooster Blues debut, *The Chief*.

Steve Coleman

(Alto saxophone, b. 1956)

Chicago native Coleman worked in funk and R&B bands before switching to jazz and learning under tenor sax great Von Freeman. He moved to New York in 1978 and worked with the Thad Jones–Mel Lewis Orchestra and Sam Rivers. He had a key tenure in the early to mid-1980s with Dave Holland before forming his own group, Five Elements, which blended solid funk rhythms with odd time signatures and Ornette Coleman-influenced angular lines.

Coleman was also a co-founder (with Greg Osby) of the Brooklyn-based M-Base Collective (short for 'Macro-Basic Array Of Structured Extemporization'), whose ranks included such forward-thinking players as trumpeter Graham Haynes, bassist Lonnie Plaxico, tenor saxophonist Gary Thomas, trombonist Robin Eubanks, keyboardist Geri Allen and vocalist Cassandra Wilson. While enjoying high-profile sideman work with artists such as Sting and Abbey Lincoln, he went on to spearhead adventurous hybrid collaborations with rappers, Cuban percussionists and singers, with his bands Mystic Rhythm Society, Council of Balance and Five Elements.

Below
Guitarist Eddy Clearwater has a distinctive playing style that combines the blues with elements of Chuck Berry's hit songs.

see Rev. Gary Davis pp 173 see Brownie McGhee pp 179 see Sonny Terry pp 183 see Charles Mingus pp 230

Above

Guitarist Johnny 'Clyde' Copeland's hit 'Bringin' It All Back Home' fused blues with African music.

Johnny 'Clyde' Copeland

(Guitar, vocals, 1937–97)

The Houston guitarist played with bluesman Joe 'Guitar' Hughes before forming his own band in the late 1950s. Relocating to New York in 1974, Copeland debuted on Rounder Records with 1977's *Copeland Special.* In 1985 he recorded a guitar summit meeting with Albert Collins and Robert Cray (*Showdown!*) and in 1986 recorded *Bringin' It All Back Home*, an adventurous hybrid of African music and blues. He continued this fusion on his last recording – 1996's *Jungle Swing* (Verve), featuring jazz pianist Randy Weston. Singer Shemekia Copeland is his daughter.

Paquito D'Rivera

(Saxophone, clarinet, b. 1948)

Growing up in Havana, D'Rivera saw many legendary Cuban musicians, but it was a Benny Goodman recording that inspired him to play jazz. He performed with the National Theater Orchestra of Havana at the age of 10, and in 1973 joined with eight other musicians to form Irakere, which fused jazz, rock and Cuban music in an exhilarating hybrid. In 1981, D'Rivera defected to the US and made his recording debut as a leader with *Paquito Blowin'*. He released a string of recordings during the decade and in 1988 joined Dizzy Gillespie's 15-piece United Nations Orchestra. Since then he has led small group recordings that highlight his virtuosity.

Dirty Dozen Brass Band

(Instrumental group, 1975–present)

Drawing from the age-old parade-band tradition of

see Introduction pp 314 *see* Sources & Sounds pp 316 *see* Key Artists pp 324

New Orleans, the Dirty Dozen Brass Band revolutionized the form by drawing on the bebop repertoire and incorporating elements of contemporary R&B into the joyful mix. The innovative group revitalized the brass-band tradition in the 1980s, inspiring a new generation of brass bands to incorporate popular themes of the day into those infectious grooves. During the 1980s the DDBB recorded for Concord, Rounder and Columbia.

Ronnie Earl

(Guitar, b. 1953)

New York City native Ronald Horvath began playing in Boston blues clubs during the 1970s, and in 1980 replaced Duke Robillard in Roomful of Blues. After eight years with the band, he struck out on his own with the Broadcasters, which prominently showcased his passionate Magic Sam meets T-Bone Walker guitar style. One of the jazziest of blues guitarists, he combines finesse and fire on his best outing, 1987's *Smokin'* (on Black Top Blues).

Fabulous Thunderbirds

(Vocal/instrumental group, 1974–present)

Fusing straight blues, early rock'n'roll and classic R&B, the Texas roadhouse band – formed by guitarist Jimmie Vaughan and harpist/vocalist Kim Wilson – built a cult following throughout the 1970s and early 1980s, before breaking through commercially in 1986 with *Tuff Enuff*. While the band's early Chrysalis recordings appealed mainly to blues and rock'n'roll purists, their late 1980s output for Epic, including 1987's *Hot Number* and 1989's *Powerful Stuff*, brought wider recognition and helped to absorb rock fans into the blues arena.

Digby Fairweather

(Cornet, trumpet, b. 1946)

The Essex-born trumpeter worked as both a sideman and a leader in a wide variety of settings throughout the 1970s, before later branching out as a jazz educator, author and radio broadcaster. A key figure in establishing the jazz section of Britain's Musician Union, he also founded the National Jazz Foundation Archive. Fairweather led his own small groups in the 1980s, including the Jazz Superkings, and from 1994 has worked with the Great British Jazz Band.

Kenny G

(Soprano and alto saxophones, b. 1956)

Kenny Gorelick came up as a sideman in Jeff Lorber's fusion band of the 1970s, before releasing his first R&B-flavoured recordings as a leader in the early 1980s. He hit pay dirt in 1986 with his phenomenally successful *Duotones*, which sold millions on the strength of his huge radioplay hit 'Songbird'. His lyrical, emotive soprano sax playing has come to define smooth jazz, earning him a huge following (as well as hordes of detractors).

Stanley Jordan

(Guitar, b. 1959)

In the early 1980s, Chicago native Jordan developed a revolutionary approach to the guitar, in which he sounded notes by tapping on the fretboard with the fingers of both hands. This technique allowed Jordan to play completely independent lines on the guitar simultaneously. His dazzling polyphony soon captured the attention of Blue Note Records, which released his debut, *Magic Touch*, in 1985. He continued to interpret both jazz and pop standards, recording six more albums for Blue Note before switching to Arista Records in 1994. He continues to perform in solo and trio settings and in 2003 collaborated with the Italian pop group Novecento.

Far Left Bottom
The Dirty Dozen Brass Band combine bebop and contemporary R&B to revitalize a New Orleans tradition.

Below
Stanley Jordan's innovations on the guitar allow him to play two lines simultaneously.

see Benny Goodman pp 110 *see* Albert Collins pp 270 *see* Magic Sam pp 276 *see* Robert Cray pp 324

Above

With his vocal range and eclectic musical tastes, Bobby McFerrin carved a unique role for himself in the 1980s jazz scene.

Lil' Ed & The Blues Imperials

(Vocal/instrumental group, 1975–present)

Chicago native Ed Williams learned slide guitar from his uncle, renowned bluesman J.B. Hutto. During the early years of the Blues Imperials, flamboyant frontman Ed continued working at his day job in a local car wash, but by the early 1980s the band had established a substantial regional following. Their 1986 Alligator Records debut, *Roughhousin'*, and 1989 follow-up, *Chicken Gravy & Biscuits*, are prime examples of their raucous, rough-edged party music, in the tradition of Hound Dog Taylor.

Lonnie Mack

(Guitar, vocals, b. 1941)

Mack's 1964 debut album, *The Wham Of That Memphis Man* – chock-full of lightning-fast licks, vibrato-drenched lines and whammy-bar techniques on his Flying V guitar – captured the imagination of a young Stevie Ray Vaughan growing up in Dallas. Two decades later, Vaughan would produce Mack's 1985 comeback album on Alligator Records, *Strike Like Lightning*. The Indiana native followed up with two offerings on Alligator, before moving to the Epic label with *Road Houses & Dance Halls* (1988).

Magic Slim

(Guitar, b. 1937)

Born Morris Holt in Grenada, Mississippi, Slim began playing on Chicago's West Side in the mid-1960s. In 1976, when Hound Dog Taylor passed away, Slim took over his Sunday afternoon gig at Theresa's on the South Side. Slim's band the Teardrops was featured on the 1970 Alligator anthology series *Living Chicago Blues*. Throughout the 1980s, Slim recorded for the Alligator and Rooster Blues labels, highlighting his stinging licks and gruff vocals.

Bobby McFerrin

(Vocals, b. 1950)

A vocal gymnast and daring improviser, McFerrin is one of the most distinctive and uncategorizable singers in contemporary music. His remarkable range (he makes uncanny leaps from deep bass tones to the highest falsetto zone), elastic delivery and incredibly open-minded nature allow him to convincingly cover everything from pop, R&B, jazz and rock to demanding classical pieces. His 1982 self-titled debut on Elektra introduced an extraordinary talent, while his 1984 follow-up, *The Voice*, was a milestone in jazz – the first time a singer had recorded an entire album without any accompaniment.

His Blue Note debut, *Spontaneous Inventions* (1986), earned him respect from the jazz community and 1988's *Simple Pleasures* made him a household name on the strength of his surprise hit 'Don't Worry, Be Happy'. McFerrin continued to challenge himself through the 1990s with his vocal group Voicestra and his duet collaborations with classical cellist Yo-Yo Ma and pianist Chick Corea, and has also been a conductor and performer at the BBC Proms in London's Royal Albert Hall.

Courtney Pine

(Tenor and soprano saxophones, bass clarinet, b. 1964)

Starting out in reggae and funk bands in school, the British saxophonist became interested in jazz in the early 1980s and eventually gravitated towards the music of his biggest influences, Sonny Rollins and John Coltrane. He began playing with John Stevens's Freebop band and by the mid-1980s had formed the Jazz Warriors, an adventurous big band that combined

see Introduction pp 314 *see* Sources & Sounds pp 316 *see* Key Artists pp 324

elements of reggae, calypso and ska with jazz. Pine later formed a sax quartet called the Saxophone Posse and made his recording debut as a leader with 1986's *Journey To The Urge Within* on Island Records. Through his work as a composer-bandleader and virtuosic player – along with his high-profile guest appearances in the UK with the George Russell Orchestra, Art Blakey's Jazz Messengers and the Elvin Jones Jazz Machine – Pine became a role model for a generation of young black jazz musicians in London in the mid-1980s.

Bonnie Raitt

(Guitar, vocals, b. 1949)

During the 1960s, while attending college in Cambridge, Massachussetts, Raitt learned the ropes firsthand from slide masters Son House and Mississippi Fred McDowell. She began appearing on the folk and blues festival circuit in the late 1960s, sometimes encouraging elderly, rediscovered blues legends (such as Sippie Wallace) to join her onstage, and in 1971 recorded her self-titled debut for Warner Bros., featuring bluesmen Junior Wells and A.C. Reed. Her blues sensibility has graced gold-selling and Grammy-winning recordings from the 1980s to the present.

Roy Rogers

(Guitar, vocals, b. 1950)

An exponent of acoustic and electric blues, California-based slide guitarist Rogers played with John Lee Hooker's Coast To Coast band from 1982–86, before releasing his debut recording as a leader, *Chops Not Chaps* (1986). He followed up with 1988's *Slidewinder* and in 1990 produced Hooker's Grammy-winning comeback album *The Healer*. Rogers maintained an acoustic duo in the 1990s with harmonica maestro Norton Buffalo. He is also featured in the Robert Mugge film *Hellhounds On My Trail* demonstrating Robert Johnson's slide-guitar techniques.

Above
David Sanborn is an influential alto saxophonist with a distinctive tone and unusual phrasing.

Roomful Of Blues

(Vocal/instrumental group, 1967–present)

The nine-piece, horn-based outfit from Westerly, Rhode Island was formed by guitarist Duke Robillard and pianist Al Copley and has been a swinging institution in the Northeast since 1967. The band concentrates on jump blues, boogie-woogie and slow blues numbers. Roomful's self-titled debut on Island Records in 1979 began a rich recorded legacy, which has included Grammy-nominated collaborations with blues greats Big Joe Turner, Eddie 'Cleanhead' Vinson and Earl King. Roomful released its eighteenth album, *Standing Room Only* (Alligator), in 2005.

David Sanborn

(Alto saxophone, b. 1945)

One of the most instantly recognizable and widely imitated voices in jazz during the 1980s, Sanborn emerged from the New York studio session scene – and a seat in Gil Evans's orchestra – to gain crossover success worldwide on the strength of seven R&B-infused outings for Warner Bros., beginning with 1980's breakthrough album *Hideaway*. His intensely expressive phrasing, marked by leaps into the altissimo register, remains a Sanborn signature, while his pungent tone and urgent attack are indebted to Hank Crawford's bluesy alto playing.

Left
Bonnie Raitt was well known on the blues scene many years before she was signed to Warner Bros.

see Son House pp 126 *see* John Lee Hooker pp 158 *see* Sonny Rollins pp 233 *see* J.B. Hutto pp 306

John Scofield

(Guitar, b. 1951)

A masterful improviser who is equally adept at funk, fusion, bebop and ballads, Scofield came up in the mid-1970s with the Billy Cobham/George Duke fusion band before recording as a sideman with Charles Mingus, Gary Burton and Dave Liebman. In 1982–85 he worked with Miles Davis, and through the 1980s made six powerhouse recordings as a leader for Gramavision. His 1990s Blue Note recordings established him as one of the premier guitarists in jazz. His sixth recording for Verve, 2005's *That's What I Say*, is a tribute to the late Ray Charles.

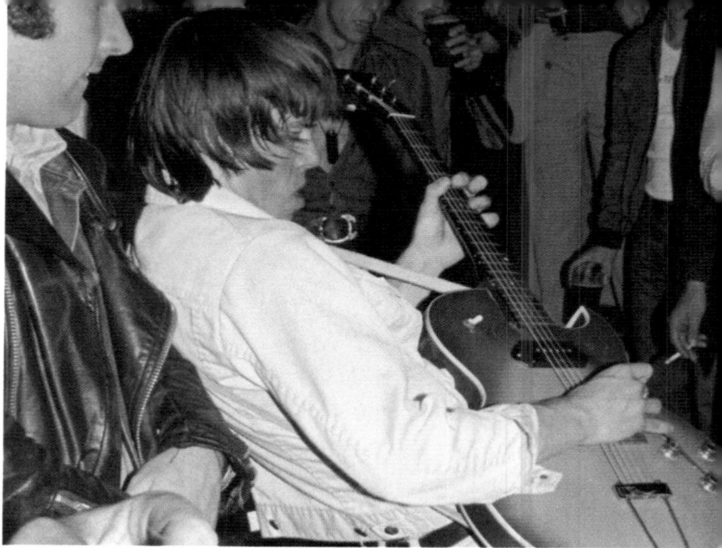

Right
George Thorogood's energetic guitar playing and gruff vocals gave his band an enduringly popular down'n'dirty blues-rock sound.

Above
John Scofield (right), shown here with fellow guitarist Pat Metheny, has recorded with many great jazz artists.

Steps Ahead

(Instrumental group, 1979–present)

Originally an acoustic jazz quintet led by vibist Mike Mainieri and featuring tenor saxophonist Michael Brecker, pianist Don Grolnick, bassist Eddie Gomez and drummer Steve Gadd, Steps changed personnel through the early 1980s, changed its name to Steps Ahead in 1983 and by 1985 had become a high-tech fusion outfit, with Mike Stern on electric guitar and both Brecker and Mainieri playing MIDI controllers. Mainieri continued to lead the band with new personnel through the 1990s.

George Thorogood & The Destroyers

(Vocal/instrumental group, 1973–present)

Thorogood's energetic, Delaware-based band drew inspiration from Elmore James and Hound Dog Taylor. Flash guitarist and raw vocalist Thorogood moved the band to Boston in 1974 and gained popularity on the blues circuit there, leading to its 1978 self-titled debut on Rounder Records. The 1979 album *Move It On Over* was a commercial breakthrough and the band's popularity was further enhanced after opening a Rolling Stones tour in 1981. The band continue to play no-nonsense, rocking boogie into the twenty-first century.

Henry Threadgill

(Alto saxophone, flute, composer, b. 1944)

One of the most prolific and original composers of his generation, Chicago native Threadgill was a charter member of the Association for the Advancement of Creative Musicians (AACM) in the mid-1960s. During the 1970s he collaborated with several AACM colleagues and also worked with Air, his trio with drummer Steve McCall and bassist Fred Hopkins. After moving to New York, he began composing through the 1980s for his acclaimed Sextet and Very Very Circus. He has also written ambitious works for symphonic forces and uncategorizable ensembles such as his Make A Move quintet.

James 'Blood' Ulmer

(Guitar, b. 1941)

Drawing on systems that are both ancient (the blues) and modern (free jazz), this experimental guitarist forged an original vocabulary on his instrument that has rarely been imitated and remains one of the most strikingly individual approaches in jazz. Ulmer began his career working in organ bands around the Midwest in the 1960s, before moving to New York in 1973. Hooking up with Ornette Coleman that same year introduced him to the harmolodic theory of musical composition and improvisation, altering his approach for all time.

see Introduction pp 314 *see* Sources & Sounds pp 316 *see* Key Artists pp 324

Through the 1980s Ulmer led three record dates for Columbia, which helped to expose his music to a wider audience. He also worked with tenor saxophonist David Murray and drummer Ronald Shannon Jackson in the Music Revelation Ensemble, and then in 1987 formed the edgy co-operative group Phalanx with tenor saxophonist George Adams, bassist Sirone and drummer Rashied Ali.

Joe Louis Walker

(Guitar, vocals, b. 1949)

A passionate, gospel-influenced singer, Walker came up in the 1960s on the San Francisco blues scene. In 1975 he began singing with the Spiritual Corinthians, remaining on the gospel circuit until 1985 when he formed his own band, the Boss Talkers. He recorded some strong albums during the 1980s for the High Tone label, such as his 1986 debut *Cold Is The Night* and 1988's *The Gift*. Walker continued to turn out consistently good recordings in the 1990s – including 1994's *JLW*, 1995's *Blues Of The Month Club* and 1997's *Great Guitars* – and remains active.

Walter 'Wolfman' Washington

(Guitar, vocals, b. 1943)

This New Orleans guitarist started out accompanying R&B singers, but as a leader in the 1970s he developed a strong local following and gradually crossed over to wider audiences through appearances at the New Orleans Jazz & Heritage Festival. He debuted on Rounder Records in 1986 with the funky *Wolf Tracks*, following up with 1988's *Out Of The Dark* and 1991's *Wolf At The Door*. After recording for other labels (Virgin/Pointblank and Artelier), Washington returned to Rounder with 1998's *Funk Is In The House* and 2000's *On The Prowl*. He continues to tour worldwide with his band, the Roadmasters.

Katie Webster

(Piano, organ, 1939–99)

This Texas native was active on the southern Louisiana swamp-blues scene in the late 1950s and early 1960s, recording for various regional labels. She spent the 1970s and early 1980s playing her unique brand of boogie-woogie piano around Louisiana – including at the New Orleans Jazz & Heritage Festival – before being 'discovered' by Alligator Records in 1987. She debuted in 1988 with *Swamp Boogie Queen* and followed up with two strong offerings, *Two-Fisted Mama!* (1990) and *No Foolin!* (1991), before suffering a stroke in 1993.

Above
James 'Blood' Ulmer has a highly original approach to jazz music and plays a blend of blues and free jazz.

Yellowjackets

(Instrumental group, 1981–present)

Bassist Jimmy Haslip and keyboardist Russell Ferrante joined drummer Will Kennedy as the backing band for a 1979 recording by guitarist Robben Ford. By 1981, that same quartet recorded its debut for Warner Bros. under the band name Yellowjackets. When Ford left the band the following year, he was replaced by alto saxophonist Marc Russo. Through the 1980s they pursued a Zawinul-influenced sound; saxophonist Bob Mintzer brought more jazz credibility to the group in the 1990s.

see Elmore James pp 226 *see* Charles Mingus pp 230 *see* Ornette Coleman pp 248 *see* Joe Zawinul pp 311

List of Artists

Entries appear in the following order: name, music style, year(s) of popularity, instruments, country of origin.

3 Mustaphas 3, World Fusion, 1980s–, Various instruments, Balkan
Abou-Khalil, Rabih, World Fusion, 1980s–, Ud, composer, Lebanese
Abrahams, Brian, Free Jazz, 1980s–, Vocals, drums, percussion, South African
Abrahams, Chris, World Fusion; Jazz Rock; Free Jazz, 1980s–, Piano, Australian
Actis Dato, Carlo, Free Jazz; World Jazz, 1980s–, Saxophones, clarinet, bandleader, Italian
Adams, George, Hard Bop; Modern Jazz, 1980s–1990s, Saxophone, flute, American
Afrika, Mervyn, World Fusion; Soul Jazz, 1980s–, Piano, composer, arranger, African
Akagi, Kei, Modern Jazz, 1980s–, Piano, keyboard, Japanese
Albright, Gerald, Smooth Jazz; Jazz Pop, 1980s–, Saxophone, American
Alden, Howard, Swing; Big Band; Traditional Jazz, 1980s–, Guitar, bandleader, American
Allen, Carl, Modern Jazz, 1980s–, Drums, bandleader, American
Allen, Eddie, Free Jazz; Jazz Rock; Big Band, 1980s–, Trumpet, American
Allen, Harry, Swing; Modern Jazz, 1980s–, Saxophone, American
Allen, Pete, Classic Jazz, 1980s–, Clarinet, alto and soprano sax, leader vocals, British
Amsallem, Frank, Modern Jazz, 1980s–, Piano, composer, Algerian
Anderson, Clifton, Hard Bop; Big Band, 1980s–, Trombone, American
Anderson, Wessell, Hard Bop; Modern Jazz; Swing, 1980s–, Saxophone, American
Aoki, Tatsu, Free Jazz, 1980s–, Bass, Japanese
Apfelbaum, Peter, World Fusion; Free Jazz, 1980s–, Tenor sax, piano, drums, composer, American
Argüelles, Julian, Free Jazz; Modern Jazz, 1980s–, Saxophone, woodwind, composer, British
Argüelles, Steve, World fusion; Free Jazz, 1980s–, Drums, British
Ascione, Joe, Swing, 1980s–, Drums, American
Back Bay Ramblers, Dixieland Revival, 1980s–, Various instruments, American
Bailey, Victor, Modern Jazz, 1980s–, Electric bass, American
Baker, Fred Thelonious, British Jazz, 1980s–, Guitar, British
Bakr, Rashid, Free Jazz, 1980s–, Drums, American
Ball, Marcia, Modern Electric Blues, 1980s–, Piano, American
Ballamy, Iain, Modern Jazz; Big Band, 1980s–, Saxophone, British
Balzar, Robert, Modern Jazz, 1980s–, Bass, bandleader, Czech
Barker, Guy, Modern Jazz; Big Band, 1980s–, Trumpet, British
Barlow, Dale, Hard Bop; Fusion, 1980s–, Saxophone, Australian
Barnes, Alan, Modern Jazz, 1980s–, Saxophone, clarinet, British
Barrett, Dan, Swing; Dixieland; Big Band, 1980s–, Trombone, cornet, bandleader, American
Barth, Bruce, Modern Jazz, 1980s–, Piano, American
Barton, Lou Ann, Blues Rock; Texas Blues, 1980s–, Vocals, American
Basia, Trzetrzelewska, Contemporary Jazz, 1980s–, Vocals, Polish
Bates, Django, Free Jazz; Fusion, 1980s–, Piano, keyboards, trumpet, composer, bandleader, British
Batish, Ashwin, World Fusion; Fusion, 1980s–1990s, Sitar, Indian
Bauer, Johannes, Free Jazz, 1980s–, Trombonist, German
Bauer, Stefan, Free Jazz, 1980s–, Vibraphone, marimba, German

Beard, Jim, Modern Jazz; Jazz Rock, 1980s–, Piano, keyboards, American
Beier, Chris, Free Jazz, 1980s–, Piano, composer, German
Belmondo, Lionel, Modern Jazz; Big Band, 1980s–, Saxophone, clarinet, composer, bandleader, French
Belmondo, Stephane, Modern Jazz; Big Band, 1980s–, Trumpet, flugelhorn, trombone, bandleader, French
Benita, Michel, Modern Jazz, 1980s–, Bass, composer, French
Bent, Phillip, Acid Jazz, 1980s–, Flute, piccolo, keyboard, British
Bentzon, Nikolaj, Funk Jazz; Hard Bop; Modern Jazz, 1980s–, Keyboards, arranger, composer, Danish
Bergcrantz, Anders, Hard Bop; Modern Jazz, 1980s–, Trumpet, Swedish
Bernstein, Peter, Modern Jazz, 1980s–, Guitar, American
Berry, Steve, Big Band; British Jazz, 1980s–, Bass, guitar, cello, British
Beuf, Sylvain, Modern Jazz; Bop; Big Band, 1980s–, Saxophones, composer, French
Bex, Emmanuel, Free Jazz; Modern Jazz, 1980s–, Piano, organ, composer, bandleader, French
Bhatt, Vishwa Mohan, World Fusion, 1980s–1990s, Guitar, Indian
Bijma, Greetje, Free Jazz, 1980s–, Vocals, Dutch
Bisio, Michael, Modern Jazz; Free Jazz, 1980s–, Bass, American
Bjorkenheim, Raoul, Free Jazz, 1980s–, Guitar, composer, Finnish
Blackman, Cindy, Hard Bop; Big Band, 1980s–, Drums, bandleader, American
Blake, Ron, Free Jazz; Modern Jazz, 1980s–, Saxophone, Puerto Rican
Blanchard, Terence, Hard Bop; Modern Jazz, 1980s–, Trumpet, composer, American
Block, Rory, Country Blues; Delta Blues, 1980s–, Vocals, guitar, American
Blues Band, British Blues, 1980s–1990s, Various instruments, British
Bluesbusters, The, Blues Rock, 1980s, Various instruments, American
Bolberg-Pedersen, Henrik, Big Band; Bebop, 1980s–, Trumpet, Danish
Bollenback, Paul, Soul Jazz; Fusion, 1980s–, Guitar, American
Bollin, Zuzu, Texas Blues, 1980s, Guitar, American
Bolognesi, Jacques, Big Band, 1980s–, Trombone, piano, accordion, bandleader, French
Bonafede, Salvatore, Modern Jazz, 1980s–, Piano, Italian
Bop Brothers, Hard Bop, 1980s–1990s, Various instruments, British
Bourde, Herve, Modern Jazz; Big Band, 1980s–, Saxophone, flute, composer, French
Bourelly, Jean-Paul, Free Jazz; World Fusion; Jazz Rock; Blues Rock, 1980s–, Guitar, American
Boussaguet, Pierre, Modern Jazz, 1980s–, Bass, composer, French
Boutte, Lillian, New Orleans Jazz; Dixieland; Rhythm & Blues, 1980s–, Vocals, American
Box of Frogs, Blues Rock, 1980s, Various instruments, British
Braden, Don, Hard Bop; Modern Jazz, 1980s–, Saxophone, flute, American
Bramhall, Doyle, Texas Blues; Modern Electric Blues, 1980s–1990s, Drums, vocals, composer, American
Bromberg, Brian, Hard Bop; Modern Jazz; Fusion, 1980s–, Bass, American
Brooks, Cecil, Modern Jazz; Soul Jazz, 1980s–, Drums, bandleader, American
Broom, Bobby, Jazz Funk; Jazz Rock; Modern Jazz, 1980s–, Guitar, American
Brown, Angela, Chicago Blues, 1980s–, Vocals, American
Brown, Ari, Free Jazz, 1980s–, Saxophone, piano, American
Brown, Donald, Modern Jazz; Hard Bop, 1980s–, Piano, composer, American
Brown, Rob, Free Jazz, 1980s–, Saxophone, American
Browne, Allan, Traditional Jazz; Modern Jazz, 1980s–, Drums, bandleader, Australian
Browne, Tom, Rhythm & Blues; Funk; Free Jazz; Modern Jazz, 1980s–, Trumpet, American
Brozman, Bob, Country Blues, 1980s–, Guitar, American
Bruning, Uschi, Free Jazz, 1980s–, Vocals, German
Bruno, Jimmy, Modern Jazz, 1980s–, Guitar, American
Buck, Tony, Free Jazz; Jazz Rock, 1980s–, Drums, composer, Australian
Buckwheat Zydeco, Zydeco, 1980s–1990s, Accordion, various instruments, American
Bunnett, Jane, Bebop; World Fusion; Latin Jazz, 1980s–, Saxophone, flute, bandleader, Canadian
Burrage, Ronnie, Modern Jazz, 1980s–, Drums, American
Burton, Aron, Chicago Blues, 1980s–, Bass, American
Butler, Henry, Modern Jazz; Rhythm & Blues, 1980s–, Piano, American
Butman, Igor, Modern Jazz, 1980s–, Saxophone, Russian
Cain, Chris, Modern Electric Blues, 1980s–, Vocals, guitar, American
Cain, Michael, Free Jazz; Modern Jazz, 1980s–, Piano, keyboards, American
Calderazzo, Joey, Modern Jazz, 1980s–, Piano, keyboards, American
Campbell, John, Modern Electric Blues, 1980s–1990s, Vocals, guitar, American
Campbell, Tommy, Modern Jazz; Big Band; Hard Bop, 1980s–, Drums, American
Caratini, Patrice, Swing; Big Band, 1980s–, Bass, composer, bandleader, French
Carmichael, Judy, Swing, 1980s–, Piano, American
Carrington, Terri Lyne, Hard Bop; Funk, 1980s–, Drums, American
Cartwright, Deirdre, Jazz Rock; Bebop; Cool Jazz, 1980s–, Guitar, British
Castronari, Mario, Fusion; Big Band, 1980s–, Bass, composer, German
Catfish Keith, Delta Blues; World Fusion, 1980s–, Guitar, vocals, American
Caumont, Elisabeth, Swing; Modern Jazz, 1980s–, Vocals, composer, French
Celea, Jean-Paul, Free Jazz, 1980s–, Drums, Algerian
Cephas & Wiggins, East Coast Blues, 1980s–, Various instruments, American
Chapin, Thomas, Free Jazz; Modern Jazz, 1980s–1990s, Saxophone, flute, bandleader, American
Chase, Allan, Free Jazz, 1980s–, Saxophone, bandleader, American
Cheatham, Jeannie, Swing, 1980s–, Piano, vocals, American
Cheatham, Jimmy, Swing, 1980s–, Trombone, bandleader, American
Chenier, C.J., Zydeco, 1980s–, Saxophone, accordion, American
Cherry, Ed, Soul Jazz; Big Band, 1980s–, Guitar, American
Christi, Ellen, Free Jazz, 1980s–, Vocals, American
Clark, W.C., Texas Blues; Modern Electric Blues, 1980s–1990s, Guitar, American
Clayton, Jeff, Swing; Big Band, 1980s–, Saxophone, American
Clearwater, Eddy, Modern Electric Blues; Rhythm & Blues; Chicago Blues, 1980s–, Guitar, vocals, American
Clifford, Winston, Modern Jazz, 1980s–, Drums, British
Cline, Alex, Free Jazz; Modern Jazz, 1980s–, Percussion, American
Cline, Nels, Free Jazz; Modern Jazz, 1980s–, Guitar, American
Cohen, Greg, Free Jazz; Jazz Rock, 1980s–, Bass, American
Cohn, Joe, Modern Jazz, 1980s–, Guitar, American
Coke, Alex, Free Jazz; Modern Jazz, 1980s–, Saxophone, flute, American
Cole, Holly, Swing; Traditional Jazz, 1980s–, Vocals, Canadian
Coleman, Anthony, Modern Jazz, 1980s–, Piano, keyboards, composer, American
Coleman, Gary 'B.B.', Modern Electric Blues, 1980s–1990s, Vocals, keyboards, bass, producer, American
Coleman, Michael, Modern Electric Blues; Chicago Blues; Rhythm & Blues, 1980s–, Vocals, guitar, American
Coleman, Steve, Modern Jazz; Free Jazz; Big Band, 1980s–, Saxophone, bandleader, American
Colianni, John, Modern Jazz, 1980s–, Piano, American
Colley, Scott, Modern Jazz, 1980s–, Bass, American
Connor, Joanna, Modern Electric Blues, 1980s–, Guitar, vocals, composer, American
Copeland, Johnny 'Clyde', Modern Electric Blues; Texas Blues, 1980s–1990s, Guitar, vocals, American
Coscia, Gianni, Swing, 1980s–, Accordion, composer, Italian
Cottle, Laurence, Jazz Rock; Big Band, 1980s–, Bass, composer, Welsh
Courtois, Vincent, Modern Jazz, 1980s–, Cello, composer, French
Cox, Anthony, Free Jazz; Hard Bop, 1980s–, Bass, American
Cray, Robert, Modern Electric Blues, 1980s–, Guitar, vocals, American
Croft, Monte, Modern Jazz, 1980s–, Vibraphone, American
Crosby, Gary, Jamaican Jazz, 1980s–, Bass, bandleader, Jamaican
Cugny, Laurent, Big Band; Modern Jazz; Jazz Rock, 1980s–, Piano, arranger, author, French
Cunliffe, Bill, Hard Bop; Modern Jazz; Fusion Jazz, 1980s–, Piano, arranger, composer, American
D'Agaro, Daniele, World Fusion; Free Jazz, 1980s–, Saxophone, clarinet, Italian
Dalla Porta, Paolino, Modern Jazz, 1980s–, Bass, composer, Italian
Dalseth, Laila, Modern Jazz, 1980s–, Vocals, Norwegian
Danielsson, Lars, Free Jazz, 1980s–, Bass, cello, composer, bandleader, Swedish
Dankworth, Alec, Bebop; Big Band; British Jazz, 1980s–, Bass, composer, British
Dara, Olu, Free Jazz, 1980s–, Trumpet, cornet, American
Darriau, Matt, World Fusion; Modern Jazz, 1980s–, Saxophone, clarinet, American
Davies, Debbie, Modern Electric Blues, 1980s–, Vocals, guitar, American
Davis, Jesse, Hard Bop, 1980s–, Saxophone, American
Dean, Joanna, Blues Rock, 1980s–, Vocals, American
Debriano, Santi, Free Jazz; Latin Jazz, 1980s–, Bass, Panamanian
Deffaa, Chip, All Jazz Styles, 1980s–, Author, critic, American
Delay, Paul, Modern Electric Blues, 1980s–, Vocals, harmonica, American
DelFra, Riccardo, Modern Jazz, 1980s–, Bass, composer, arranger, bandleader, Italian
Demierre, Jacques, Free Jazz; Modern Jazz, 1980s–, Piano, Swiss

Denley, Jim, Free Jazz, 1980s–, Saxophone, flute, Australian
Dennerlein, Barbara, Hard Bop; Modern Jazz, 1980s–, Organ, German
Deppa, Claude, Free Jazz; Bebop; Big Band, 1980s–, Trumpet, South African
Dial, Garry, Modern Jazz, 1980s–, Piano, keyboards, American
DiCastri, Furio, Modern Jazz, 1980s–, Bass, Italian
Dick, Robert, Free Jazz; Modern Jazz, 1980s–, Flute, American
Dirty Dozen Brass Band, New Orleans Jazz, 1980s–, Bandleader, American
Donald, Barbara, Free Jazz, 1980s–, Trumpet, American
Dresch, Mihaly, Free Jazz, 1980s–, Reeds, composer, bandleader, Hungarian
D'Rivera, Paquito, Latin Jazz, 1980s–, Saxophones, clarinet, flute, Cuban
Drummond, Ray, Hard Bop, 1980s–, Bass, American
Dulfer, Candy, Smooth Jazz, 1980s–, Saxophone, Dutch
Eade, Dominique, Modern Jazz, 1980s–, Vocals, composer, British
Ealey, Robert, Texas Blues, 1980s–1990s, Drums, vocals, American
Earl, Ronnie, Blues Rock; Modern Electric Blues, 1980s–, Guitar, American
Edwards, Archie, Modern Electric Blues, 1980s, Guitar, American
Elf, Mark, Modern Jazz; Bebop, 1980s–, Guitar, American
Ellis, Lisle, Free Jazz; Modern Jazz, 1980s–, Bass, Canadian
Endresen, Sidsel, Jazz Rock; Modern Jazz, 1980s–, Vocals, composer, Norwegian
Eneidi, Marco, Free Jazz, 1980s–, Saxophone, American
Eskelin, Ellery, Free Jazz; Modern Jazz, 1980s–, Saxophone, American
Eubanks, Robin, Hard Bop; Modern Jazz, 1980s–, Trombone, bandleader, American
Evans, Bill, Jazz Rock; Fusion, 1980s–, Saxophone, American
Evans, Sandy, Fusion; Free Jazz, 1980s–, Saxophone, composer, Australian
Faber, Johannes, Jazz Rock, 1980s–, Trumpet, flugelhorn, piano, violin, composer, German
Fabulous Thunderbirds, The, Blues Rock, 1980s–, Various instruments, American
Fairweather, Digby, British Jazz, 1980s–, Cornet, author, British
Farnham, Allen, Hard Bop; Modern Jazz, 1980s–, Piano, producer, American
Fattburger, Smooth Jazz, 1980s–, Various instruments, American
Fay, Rick, Dixieland, 1980s–, Saxophone, clarinet, American
Felder, Dale, Modern Jazz, 1980s–, Saxophone, American
Feldman, Mark, Free Jazz, 1980s–, Violin, American
Ferrell, Rachelle, Modern Jazz, 1980s–, Vocals, American
Fields, Brandon, Modern Jazz, 1980s–, Saxophone, American
Fieldstones, Delta Blues; Chicago Blues, 1980s, Various instruments, American
Filiano, Ken, Free Jazz, 1980s–, Bass, American
Fioravanti, Ettore, Hard Bop; Free Jazz, 1980s–, Drums, composer, Italian
Flores, Luca, Free Jazz, 1980s–1990s, Piano, Italian
Forman, Mitchel, Modern Jazz; Fusion, 1980s–, Piano, keyboards, American
France, Martin, British Jazz, 1980s–, Drums, British
France, Nic, British Jazz, 1980s–, Drums, percussion, piano, steel pan, British
Franck, Tomas, Hard Bop, 1980s–, Saxophone, Swedish
Fraser, Hugh, Free Jazz; Modern Jazz; Hard Bop; Big Band, 1980s–, Trombone, piano, composer, bandleader, Canadian
Funderburgh, Anson, Modern Electric Blues, 1980s–, Guitar, American
Futterman, Joel, Free Jazz, 1980s–, Piano, American
G, Kenny, Smooth Jazz, 1980s–, Saxophones, American
Gambale, Frank, Fusion, 1980s–, Guitar, Australian
Gardony, Laszlo, Modern Jazz, 1980s–, Piano, composer, Hungarian
Garland, Tim, Modern Jazz, 1980s–, Saxophones, woodflute, synthesizer, British
Garrett, Kenny, Modern Jazz, 1980s–, Saxophone, American
Gatto, Roberto, Fusion; Hard Bop, 1980s–, Drums, Italian
Gayle, Charles, Free Jazz, 1980s–, Saxophone, clarinet, piano, American
Gebbia, Gianni, Free Jazz, 1980s–, Saxophone, bandleader, Italian
Gertz, Bruce, Free Jazz, 1980s–, Bass, American
Gewelt, Terje, Fusion; Jazz Rock; Modern Jazz, 1980s–, Bass, Norwegian
Ghiglioni, Tiziana, Free Jazz, 1980s–, Vocals, Italian
Giordano, Vince, Dixieland Revival, 1980s–1990s, Bass, tuba, saxophone, American
Glerum, Ernst, Free Jazz, 1980s–, Bass, piano, Dutch
Goldings, Larry, Modern Jazz, 1980s–, Piano, organ, American
Gonzales, Ruben, Latin Jazz, 1980s–, Piano, Cuban
Gordon, Jimmie, Chicago Blues, 1980s, Vocals, piano, American
Graewe, Georg, Free Jazz; Big Band, 1980s–, Piano, German
Grand, Otis, Modern Electric Blues, 1980s–, Guitar, bandleader, British
Granelli, Jerry, Modern Jazz, 1980s–, Drums, bandleader, American
Green, Benny, Modern Jazz, 1980s–, Piano, American
Gress, Drew, Free Jazz; Modern Jazz, 1980s–, Bass, pedal steel, American
Grossman, Richard, Free Jazz, 1980s–, Piano, American
Gustafsson, Mats, Free Jazz, 1980s–, Saxophone, Swedish
Guy, Phil, Modern Electric Blues, 1980s–, Vocals, guitar, American
Hale, Simon, Jazz Rock, 1980s–, Piano, composer, British
Hamsters, Blues Rock, 1980s–, Various instruments, British
Hanrahan, Kip, World Fusion; Fusion, 1980s–1990s, Bandleader, American
Haque, Fareed, Modern Jazz; Fusion, 1980s–, Guitar, American
Hardcastle, Paul, Fusion, 1980s–, Keyboards, British
Hardy, Craig, Hard Bop, 1980s–, Saxophone, American
Harle, John, Traditional Jazz; Jazz Rock; Modern Jazz, 1980s–, Saxophone, composer, British
Harman, James, Modern Electric Blues, 1980s–, Vocals, harmonica, American
Harper Brothers, The, Hard Bop, 1980s–, Various instruments, American
Harrison, Donald, Modern Jazz, 1980s–, Saxophone, American
Hart, John, Hard Bop; Modern Jazz, 1980s–, Guitar, American
Haslam, George, Free Jazz, 1980s–, Saxophone, British
Hathaway, Martin, Free Jazz, 1980s–, Saxophone, clarinet, flute, piano, vocals, composer, arranger, British
Hauser, Fritz, Free Jazz; World Fusion, 1980s–, Drums, Swiss
Hawkins, Ted, Rhythm & Blues, 1980s–1990s, Guitar, vocals, American
Haynes, Graham, Modern Jazz, 1980s–, Cornet, American
Haynes, Phil, Free Jazz, 1980s–, Drums, bandleader, American
Hays, Kevin, Modern Jazz, 1980s–, Piano, American
Healey, Jeff, Blues Rock, 1980s–, Guitar, vocals, Canadian
Hedges, Chuck, Swing; Dixieland, 1980s–, Clarinet, American
Henderson, Scott, Fusion, 1980s–, Guitar, American
Herring, Vincent, Hard Bop; Modern Jazz, 1980s–, Saxophone, American
Herwig, Conrad, Latin Jazz; Modern Jazz, 1980s–, Trombone, bandleader, American
Hidalgo, Giovanni, Latin Jazz; World Fusion, 1980s–1990s, Percussion, Puerto Rican
Ho, Fred, World Fusion, 1980s–, Saxophone, composer, American
Holland, Jools, Boogie-Woogie, 1980s–, Piano, bandleader, British
Holloway, Ron, Hard Bop, 1980s–, Saxophone, American
Hollyday, Christopher, Hard Bop, 1980s–, Saxophone, American
Holmes Brothers, Modern Electric Blues, 1980s–, Various instruments, American
Horiuchi, Glenn, Free Jazz; World Fusion, 1980s–1990s, Piano, keyboards, American
Horvitz, Wayne, Free Jazz; Jazz Funk; Modern Jazz, 1980s–, Organ, piano, keyboards, American
Hunter, James, Chicago Blues; Rhythm & Blues, 1980s–, Vocals, British
Hurst, Robert, Hard Bop, 1980s–, Bass, American
Incognito, Acid Jazz, 1980s–, Various instruments, British
Jackson, Javon, Hard Bop, 1980s–, Saxophone, American
Jacque, Beau, Modern Electric Blues, 1980s–1990s, Vocals, accordion, American
Jazz Passengers, Modern Jazz, 1980s–, Group, American
Jazz Warriors, The, Acid Jazz, 1980s, Various instruments, British
Jenkins, Billy, Jazz Rock; Free Jazz, 1980s–, Guitar, composer, British
Johnston, Phillip, Free Jazz; Modern Jazz, 1980s–, Saxophone, American
Jones, Oliver, Bebop, 1980s–, Piano, Canadian
Jordan, Stanley, Modern Jazz; Jazz Bop, 1980s–, Guitar, American
Joseph, Julian, British Jazz, 1980s–, Piano, composer, British
Katon, Michael, Blues Rock, 1980s–, Guitar, vocals, American
Keezer, Geoff, Hard Bop, 1980s–, Piano, American
Kerr, Anthony, Free Jazz; Big Band, 1980s–, Vibraphone, marimba, Irish
Kibwe, Talib Qadir, Modern Jazz, 1980s–, Saxophone, flute, American
Kikoski, Dave, Fusion; Hard Bop, 1980s–, Piano, composer, American
Kilgore, Rebecca, Swing, 1980s–, Guitar, vocals, American
Kimbrough, Frank, Modern Jazz, 1980s–, Piano, American
King, Eddie, Modern Electric Blues, 1980s–, Vocals, guitar, American
Kinsey, Lester 'Big Daddy', Modern Electric Blues, 1980s–2000s, Vocals, guitar, harmonica, American
Kirkland, Kenny, Modern Jazz; Latin Jazz, 1980s–1990s, Piano, keyboards, American
Kisor, Ryan, Trumpet; Modern Jazz, 1980s–, Trumpet, American
Kopinski, Jan, British Jazz; Hard Bop, 1980s–, Saxophone, composer, British
Lagrene, Bireli, Swing; Modern Jazz; Fusion, 1980s–, Guitar, French
Laka Daisical, Funk; Bebop; Free Jazz, 1980s–, Piano, vocals, British
Lalama, Ralph, Hard Bop, 1980s–, Saxophone, flute, American
Last Exit, Free Jazz, 1980s–1990s, Various instruments, American
Laws, Johnny, Modern Electric Blues; Rhythm & Blues, 1980s–, Vocals, guitar, composer, producer, American
Lee, Lovie, Chicago Blues; Modern Electric, 1980s–1990s, Vocals, piano, American
Legendary Blues Band, Modern Electric Blues, 1980s–, Various instruments, American
Leitch, Peter, Hard Bop, 1980s–, Guitar, bandleader, Canadian
Lil' Ed & the Blues Imperials, Modern Electric Blues, 1980s–, Various instruments, American
Little Charlie & the Nightcats, Modern Electric Blues, 1980s–1990s, Various instruments, American
Lofsky, Lorne, Cool Jazz, 1980s–, Guitar, Canadian
London, Frank, Free Jazz, 1980s–, Keyboards, cornet, trumpet, American
Loose Tubes, British Jazz; Big Band; Jazz Fusion, 1980s, Various instruments, British
Lucas, Robert, Rhythm & Blues, 1980s–, Harmonica, guitar, American
Lundy, Carmen, Modern Jazz; Bebop, 1980s–, Vocals, American
Lynch, Brian, Hard Bop, 1980s–, Trumpet, American
Mack, Lonnie, Modern Electric Blues; Rhythm & Blues, 1980s–, Guitar, American
Madsen, Peter, Free Jazz; Hard Bop, 1980s–, Piano, arranger, American
Magic Slim, Modern Electric Blues, 1980s–, Guitar, American
Malone, Russell, Swing; Bebop, 1980s–, Guitar, American
Man Called Adam, A, Acid Jazz, 1980s–1990s, Various instruments, British
Manhattan Jazz Quintet, Swing, 1980s, Various instruments, American
Maria, Tania, Brazilian Jazz; Modern Jazz; Latin Jazz; Jazz Pop, 1980s–, Piano, vocals, Brazilian
Marienthal, Eric, Smooth Jazz, 1980s–, Saxophone, American
Marsalis, Branford, New Orleans Jazz; Hard Bop, 1980s–, Saxophones, American
Marsalis, Wynton, New Orleans Jazz; Swing, 1980s–, Trumpet, American
Martin, Claire, Traditional Jazz, 1980s–, Vocals, British
May, Tina, British Jazz, 1980s–, Vocals, British

see Introduction pp 314 see Sources & Sounds pp 316 see Key Artists pp 324 see A–Z of Artists pp 332

McFerrin, Bobby, Modern Jazz, 1980s–, Vocals, American
Meirelles, Pascoal, Brazilian Jazz, 1980s–1990s, Drums, percussion, composer, Brazilian
Melford, Myra, Free Jazz, 1980s–, Piano, composer, American
Metheny, Mike, Hard Bop, 1980s–, Flugelhorn, bandleader, American
Metheny, Pat, Fusion, 1980s–, Guitarist, composer, American
Miller, Mulgrew, Hard Bop; Modern Jazz, 1980s–, Piano, American
Moffett, Charnett, Modern Jazz, 1980s–, Bass, American
Mondesir, Mark, Modern Jazz, 1980s–, Drums, British
Mondesir, Michael, Modern Jazz, 1980s–, Bass, composer, British
Moore, Johnny B., Chicago Blues; Modern Electric Blues, 1980s–, Vocals, bass, American
Morris, Joe, Free Jazz; Modern Jazz, 1980s–, Guitar, American
Mseleku, Bheki, World Jazz, 1980s–, Piano, saxophone, vocals, South African
Murley, Mike, Modern Jazz, 1980s–, Saxophone, Canadian
Nabatov, Simon, Free Jazz, 1980s–, Piano, composer, Russian
Neal, Kenny, Modern Electric Blues; Louisiana Blues, 1980s–, Vocals, guitar, harmonica, American
Nelson, Steve, Hard Bop, 1980s–, Vibraphone, American
Newton, Dave, British Jazz, 1980s–, Piano, British
Nicholson, Reggie, Free Jazz, 1980s–, Drums, American
O'Higgins, Dave, Neo-Bop, 1980s–, Saxophone, flute, keyboard, drums, composer, British
Omar & the Howlers, Modern Electric Blues; Blues Rock, 1980s–, Various instruments, American
Ozone, Makoto, Modern Jazz, 1980s–, Piano, composer, arranger, Japanese
Page, Jimmy, British Blues, 1980s–, Guitar, composer, producer, British
Paladins, Blues Rock, 1980s–, Various instruments, American
Parker, Eddie, Jazz Rock; Jazz Fusion, 1980s–, Flute, composer, British
Patitucci, John, Fusion, 1980s–, Bass, American
Peplowski, Ken, Swing; Traditional Jazz; Dixieland, 1980s–, Clarinet, saxophone, American
Petrucciani, Michel, Modern Jazz, 1980s–1990s, Piano, French
Pine, Courtney, Modern Jazz, 1980s–, Saxophone, clarinet, British
Pitchford, Lonnie, Delta Blues; Chicago Blues, 1980s–, Guitar, American
Pizzarelli, John, Swing, 1980s–, Guitar, vocals, bandleader, American
Plaxico, Lonnie, Modern Jazz, 1980s–, Bass, American
Plimley, Paul, Free Jazz, 1980s–, Piano, Canadian
Previte, Bobby, Free Jazz, 1980s–, Drums, bandleader, American
Raitt, Bonnie, Blues Rock, 1980s–, Guitar, vocals, composer, American
Rascoe, Moses, Country Blues, 1980s, Vocals, guitar, American
Red Devils, Blues Rock, 1980s–1990s, Various instruments, American
Remy, Tony, Jazz Rock; Fusion; Funk, 1980s–, Guitar, vocoder, composer, British
Rey, Del, Country Blues, 1980s–, Vocals, guitar, American
Ribot, Marc, Free Jazz; Jazz Rock, 1980s–, Guitar, American
Richards, Tim, Free Jazz; Fusion, 1980s–, Piano, composer, British
Rippingtons, The, Smooth Jazz, 1980s–, Various instruments, American
Roberts, Hank, Free Jazz, 1980s–, Cello, American
Roberts, Marcus, Hard Bop; Modern Jazz, 1980s–, Piano, American
Robertson, Herb, Free Jazz, 1980s–, Trumpet, flugelhorn, cornet, American
Robinson, Orphy, Funk; Modern Jazz, 1980s–, Vibraphone, marimba, composer, British
Robinson, Spike, Swing; Cool Jazz, 1980s–, Saxophone, American
Rogers, Roy, Blues Rock, 1980s–, Guitar, producer, American
Roney, Wallace, Hard Bop; Modern Jazz, 1980s–, Trumpet, American
Roomful of Blues, Jump Blues; Modern Electric Blues, 1980s–, Various instruments, American
Rosnes, Renee, Hard Bop; Modern Jazz, 1980s–, Piano, Canadian
Rucker, Ellyn, Swing; Cool Jazz, 1980s–, Piano, vocals, American
Salgado, Curtis, Modern Electric Blues, 1980s–, Vocals, harmonica, American
Sanborn, David, Smooth Jazz, 1980s–, Saxophone, flute, American
Sanchez, David, Bebop, 1980s–, Saxophone, Puerto Rican
Sandke, Randy, Swing, 1980s–, Trumpet, flugelhorn, American
Satan & Adam, Modern Acoustic Blues; Folk Blues, 1980s–, Vocals, guitar, harmonica, American
Schulz, Bob, Dixieland Revival, 1980s–, Cornet, American
Schuur, Diane, Modern Jazz, 1980s–, Vocals, piano, American
Scofield, John, Fusion, 1980s–, Guitar, composer, American
Sharpe, Avery, Free Jazz, 1980s–, Bass, American
Shaw, Ian, Jazz Pop, 1980s–, Vocals, British
Sheppard, Andy, Modern Jazz, 1980s–, Saxophone, flute, composer, bandleader, British
Silveira, Ricardo, Brazilian Jazz; Fusion, 1980s–1990s, Guitar, Brazilian
Slater, Ashley, Free Jazz; Modern Jazz; Big Band, 1980s–, Trombone, tuba, vocals, Canadian
Smith, Marvin 'Smitty', Hard Bop; Modern Jazz, 1980s–, Drums, American
Smith, Tommy, Modern Jazz, 1980s–, Saxophone, flute, British
Sons of Blues, Chicago Blues, 1980s–, Various instruments, American
Speake, Martin, Modern Jazz, 1980s–, Saxophone, composer, British
Specter, Dave, Modern Electric Blues; Jump Blues, 1980s–, Guitar, American
Steps Ahead, Modern Jazz; Fusion, 1980s–, Group, American
Stereo MCs, Acid Jazz, 1980s–, Various instruments, British
Strehli, Angela, Modern Electric Blues, 1980s–, Vocals, American
Stroman, Scott, All Jazz Styles, 1980s–, Trombone, vocals, composer, educator, American
Swanton, Lloyd, Fusion, 1980s–, Bass, composer, Australian
Taylor, James, Acid Jazz; Soul Jazz, 1980s–, Keyboards, British
Thomas, Gary, Hard Bop; Modern Jazz, 1980s–, Saxophone, flute, American
Thorogood, George, Blues Rock, 1980s–1990s, Guitar, American
Threadgill, Henry, Free Jazz, 1980s–, Saxophone, flute, composer, bandleader, American
Todd, Phil, Jazz Rock, 1980s–, Saxophone, clarinet, flute, British
Tommaso, Bruno, Free Jazz; Big Band; Modern Jazz, 1980s–, Bass, Italian
Tonolo, Pietro, Free Jazz, 1980s–, Saxophone, Italian
Tononi, Tiziano, Free Jazz; Modern Jazz; Big Band, 1980s–, Drums, composer, bandleader, Italian
Tuncboyaciyan, Arto, World Fusion, 1980s–, Percussion, Armenian
Twenty-Ninth Street Saxophone Quartet, Hard Bop; Latin Jazz; Funk, 1980s, Saxophone, American
Ulmer, James Blood, Free Jazz, 1980s–, Guitar, flute, vocals, American
Vaughan, Jimmie, Modern Electric Blues; Blues Rock, 1980s–, Guitar, American
Vaughan, Stevie Ray, Texas Blues; Modern Electric Blues; Blues Rock, 1980s–1990s, Guitar, American
Vaughn, Maurice John, Chicago Blues, 1980s–, Vocals, guitar, saxophone, American
VonEssen, Eric, Free Jazz; Modern Jazz, 1980s–1990s, Bass, cello, American
Vukan, George, Modern Jazz, 1980s–, Piano, composer, arranger, bandleader, Hungarian
Vysniauskas, Petras, Free Jazz, 1980s–, Saxophone, clarinet, Lithuanian
Walker, Joe Louis, Modern Electric Blues, 1980s–, Guitar, American
Washington, Walter 'Wolfman', Rhythm & Blues; Modern Electric Blues, 1980s–, Vocals, guitar, American
Webster, Katie, Rhythm & Blues, 1980s–1990s, Piano, American
Weckl, Dave, Fusion, 1980s–, Drums, American
Wellington, Valerie, Modern Electric Blues, 1980s–1990s, Vocals, piano, American
Wertico, Paul, Fusion; Big Band; Jazz Rock, 1980s–, Drums, American
West Jemond Rhythm Kings, Dixieland Revival, 1980s–1990s, Various instruments, American
Westbrook, Mike, Free Jazz; Big Band, 1980s–, Piano, bandleader, British
Whalum, Kirk, Smooth Jazz, 1980s–, Saxophone, American
White, Michael, Dixieland Revival; New Orleans Jazz, 1980s–, Violin, American
Whitehead, Annie, Bebop; Hard Bop; Free Jazz, 1980s–, Trombone, vocals, British
Williamson, Steve, Free Jazz; Bebop, 1980s–, Saxophone, British
Willis, Chick, Modern Electric Blues, 1980s–, Vocals, guitar, American
Wilson, Kim, Modern Electric Blues, 1980s–, Vocals, harmonica, American
Winterschladen, Reiner, Free Jazz, 1980s–, Trumpet, flugelhorn, German
Wood, Mark, Modern Jazz; Jazz Rock, 1980s–, Guitar, British
Woodard, Rickey, Hard Bop; Swing, 1980s–, Saxophone, American
Woods, Mitch, Boogie-Woogie; Jump Blues, 1980s–, Piano, American
Yellowjackets, The, Smooth Jazz; Fusion, 1980s–1990s, Various instruments, American
Zadeh, Aziza Mustafa, Folk Jazz, 1980s–, Piano, vocals, Azerbaijani

see Wynton Marsalis pp 326 *see* Stevie Ray Vaughan pp 330 *see* Bonnie Raitt pp 337 *see* David Sanborn pp 337

THE CONTEMPORARY ERA

By definition, a contemporary era defies summary. No one living in it has the conclusive perspective to discern the prevailing character of our times, even though we all know what we're going through, and can hear what we hear. The reductive view is: Americans, after a burst stock-market bubble and terrorist attacks, live in uncertainty, tinged with denial. Newly unified Europe, with the UK at some slight distance, is quite possibly on the rise. The large and small states of the former Soviet Union are in disarray, Japan's economy stands still and China has become a production behemoth despite political isolation. Africa remains beset with under-development and internal conflicts. South and Central America, the Caribbean, the South Pacific, including Australia, and Canada exist almost unto themselves. Nice places to visit, they're heard from now and then.

Blues and jazz in the contemporary era, on the other hand, is known everywhere. The musics seem creatively robust, though no more fiscally secure than usual. Blues is the more endangered species, the conditions of its birth fading into history, its fundamental assertions obscured by aggressive and ironic attitudes, digital electronics and the unforgiving beat. As blues is being prepared, we hope prematurely, for museum display, jazz is simultaneously institutionalizing and subverting itself. No one agent is responsible for the tug-of-war: forces of industry, philanthropy, individuals' aesthetics and career choices lead to both jazz classicism and jazz debasement (neither always where you'd expect them), standardization and extreme makeover. Future blues and jazz is unpredictable. The contemporary era is what's happening now.

Sources & Sounds

KEY ARTISTS

Joey DeFrancesco
Chris Thomas King
Diana Krall
Hubert Sumlin
Otis Taylor
Walter Trout
Jeff 'Tain' Watts

Right
French gypsy guitarist Birelli Lagrene is one of the many bringing new flavours to jazz music.

In the first decade of the twenty-first century, musical culture is blown every which way and some feel that jazz and blues music bears the brunt of the storm. Blues is still present somewhere deep in the roots of the new generations of rock bands, but the increased corporate consolidation of the media means that celebrity vocalists mouthing formulaic pop songs rule the airwaves, while vapid, mid-tempo fantasies dominate commercial, 'lite' jazz. Record companies race to catch up with the changes in how music is captured, heard and sold; they recycle hit songs from eons ago, re-arranged for the latest or the longest-surviving of vocalists, and repackage classic albums with newly added attractions or in new formats, rarely channelling the funds into new artists.

'If an art form doesn't evolve, it dies. If blues wants to survive, it's got to do something fresh and it's got to reach the youth.'
Otis Taylor

A Decrease In Record Sales

We are now in one of the most exciting yet frustrating periods of the blues' long history. The music has become a living continuum, with artists whose ages range from early teens to late-eighties performing everything from field hollers and fife-and-drum band songs to Delta slide guitar, barrelhouse piano, Chicago, Texas and jump blues, improvisational blues rock, blues rap and even more experimental hybrids. At the same time, the proliferation of CD reissues allows listeners to investigate the music of virtually every significant blues artist who ever recorded. It is potentially a Garden of Eden for the genre, but certain factors prevent many musicians from enjoying its rewards.

A worldwide decrease in album sales and opportunities for musicians has occurred in all genres, but the blues' already slim margin has been hit especially hard. At the turn of the millennium, blues CDs accounted for little more than two per cent of overall sales, according to the Blues Music Association. Since then, that figure has fallen to less than one per cent. Without the emergence of a major crossover artist to spark interest in the music within the mainstream, there is little immediate hope for reversal.

Furthermore, the reissue explosion means that contemporary artists who are lucky enough to hold recording contacts find themselves competing against releases by the likes of Muddy Waters (1915–83) and Robert Johnson (1911–38) for sales, press and airplay. In the US in particular, they do so in an environment that has also been shaken by the closings of many clubs and music shops, declining spending on live entertainment.

see Introduction pp 342 *see* A–Z of Artists pp 352 *see* List of Artists pp 368

Internet radio has been a bright spot in the marketplace, with UK programmes such as *Shade Of Blues* on Swindon FM and Paul Jones's BBC Radio 2 show, *Good Time Blues* in Buenos Aires, *Messaround* in Bonn and *Triple R Blues Radio* in the Netherlands bringing blues to a worldwide audience.

A Lack Of Exposure

At its inception, commercial radio was highly diversified and characterized by local programming; it was perfect for exposing short recordings by regionally known artists to a larger audience. It has since become centrally owned and operated, promulgating a limited playlist. Blues and jazz seldom, if ever, makes that list. Only non-commercial, government-supported 'public radio' in the US and Britain, and the newly burgeoning satellite radio systems (sold to subscribers in a similar way to cable TV networks), seek to serve niche markets, of which the audience for jazz is one. A couple of generations ago, adults on a given night might have danced to a swing band in a ballroom or relaxed at a nightclub; today, their grandchildren are transfixed by home entertainments, watching music videos or downloading favourite songs, often for free. So far, jazz has not proved very telegenic, nor has the downloading of jazz music via the Internet proved particularly popular or profitable.

With each death of a jazz veteran – from the demise of the still-provocative Miles Davis (1926–91) through the close of the swing era with the passings of the indefatigable Lionel Hampton (1908–2004) and the scornful, long-retired Artie Shaw (1910–2004) – direct links of jazz to its prior golden ages are lost. At every turn, economic factors and new trends threaten not only the maintenance, but the very growth and development of jazz.

Jazz Raises Its Profile

And yet simultaneously, jazz education at high school and college levels, as well as in prestigious conservatories, has never enjoyed higher enrolment. Jazz has been embraced by musicians and audiences around the globe, with the European Union, West and South Africa, the Caribbean, South America, Russia and the Far East advancing gifted musicians, as well as stalwart support networks (Jazz Institute of

CLASSIC RECORDINGS

1993
Geri Allen: *Feel The Fire*
Cassandra Wilson: *Blue Light 'Til Dawn*

1994
R.L. Burnside: *Too Bad Jim*

1996
Keb' Mo': *Just Like You*

2000
Paul Rishell & Annie Raines: *Moving To The Country*

2001
Otis Taylor: 'My Soul's In Louisiana'

2002
Chris Thomas King: 'Tha Real'
Susan Tedeschi: *Wait For Me*

2004
Elliott Sharp: *Do The Don't*

2005
Hubert Sumlin: *About Them Shoes*

Left
The New Orleans Jazz & Heritage Festival – proof that the jazz spirit lives on in the city where the music was born.

see Robert Johnson pp 112 *see* Lionel Hampton pp 125 *see* Miles Davis pp 200 *see* Muddy Waters pp 212

Above
Corey Harris, who appeared in Scorsese's 2003 film *From Mississippi To Mali*, has dedicated himself to keeping the blues alive.

Far Right
Guitarist Otis Taylor blends the roots of blues music with 1960s-style psychedelic sounds.

volumes on figures as disparate as Django Reinhardt (1910–53) and Wayne Shorter (b. 1933), and jazz's rich, associative legacy has been tapped for literary purposes by the likes of Toni Morrison, Roddy Doyle, Geoff Dyer and Edgardo Vega Yunqué, and in films by Robert Altman, Clint Eastwood, Taylor Hackford and Spike Lee.

The Blues Train Rolls On

As influential labels such as Rooster Blues withdrew from the market and journeyman players scuffled for a living, even a chart-topping collaboration between Eric Clapton and B.B. King (b. 1925), *Riding With The King* (2000), failed to produce a trickle-down of interest in other artists. Likewise, the high-profile public television series *Martin Scorsese Presents: The Blues* had little effect on overall attention for the genre or on record sales, save for the handful of musicians most prominently featured. Both of those events came in 2003, proclaimed the 'Year of the Blues' by the US Congress in order to celebrate the music's centennial.

Chicago, San Francisco Jazz, New Orleans Jazz & Heritage Foundation, Monterey Jazz Festival, Earshot Jazz, Northsea Jazz Festival, Umbria Jazz Festival, etc.), which comprise entrepreneurs and semi-professionals alike.

In autumn 2004 Wynton Marsalis (b. 1961) presided over the opening of the first major performance facility ever designed specifically for jazz. Rose Hall, home of Jazz@Lincoln Center, the world's leading multi-purpose jazz institution, offers three venues, classrooms, rehearsal space, an art gallery and production facilities in a glamorous site in New York City, with an ambitious calendar of staged shows, big band concerts and combo bookings. Jazz – and Wynton himself – was celebrated in a 19-hour series by video documentarian Ken Burns; biographers are publishing

Yet, as many of the style's elder statesmen have repeated over the decades, the blues will never die. The ever-silver lining of the style is its durability and strength, born of its roots in struggle and spirituality. Corey Harris (b. 1969), who was featured in the Scorsese series, has dedicated himself to exploring every traditional avenue of the genre, and spoke not just for himself when he declared: 'It's a sacrifice for me to do this music, but I'm dedicated to its sounds and words and I take my path in it very seriously'. Harris made that statement after a long day at the

see Introduction pp 342 *see* A–Z of Artists pp 352 *see* List of Artists pp 368

carpentry job he must work to support his family, despite his international standing as a performer.

Traditional Artistry Thrives

There are blues musicians, such as the New Englanders Duke Robillard (b. 1948) and Ronnie Earl (b. 1953), who can play with the linear eloquence of swinging, single-note guitar soloist T-Bone Walker (1910–75). Others, including Doug MacLeod and Louisiana Red (b. 1936) evoke the raw complexity of the Texas acoustic virtuoso Blind Lemon Jefferson (1897–1929) or the early Delta masters Charley Patton (1891–1934) and Son House (1902–88). Regardless of approach, what the finest of today's traditional blues artists share is a drive for mastery combined with personal expression, including a desire to write original songs that – while in keeping with the sounds and stylistic tics of their chosen idioms – use modern or timeless themes to speak meaningfully to contemporary listeners.

Some are astonishingly eclectic, dipping into every font of the blues with grace and authenticity. An example is Paul Rishell & Annie Raines, a guitar and harmonica duo from Massachusetts that won the Blues Foundation's W.C. Handy Award for Acoustic Blues Album of the Year in 2000 for *Moving To The Country*. Their repertoire embraces the ballads of Patton, the gospel of Washington Phillips and the laconic playfulness of the Memphis Jug Band, but also extends to include Little Walter (1930–68) instrumentals and the Chicago ghetto blues of Magic Sam (1937–69) as well as their own songs.

Keeping The Blues Alive

Otis Taylor (b. 1948) follows tradition even further back, albeit with modern instrumentation. Using digital effects and electric banjos in Appalachian folk tunings, he is able to evoke the sounds of ancient African instruments such as the kora and the n'jarka. Then Taylor, who may be the finest blues lyricist to emerge since Sonny Boy Williamson II (1899–1965) and Willie Dixon (1915–92), ups the ante by returning the blues to the realm of visceral protest music, which it inhabited in the rural South through the era of jim crow. His song 'My Soul's In Louisiana', about a lynching, is a blood-chilling example of his art.

see Wayne Shorter pp 279 see Wynton Marsalis pp 326 see Corey Harris pp 357 see Paul Rishell & Annie Raines pp 363

Above
Pianist Bill Charlap, who has played with Benny Carter, Clark Terry and Gerry Mulligan, among others.

Then there are artists who focus on a single type of blues with laser precision. English harmonica virtuoso Paul Lamb (b. 1955), who fronts the King Snakes, and his US counterpart Kim Wilson, who performs both as a solo artist and with his Fabulous Thunderbirds, are at the forefront of this camp, playing first-generation-style electric blues so authentic that it sounds as though it has been transported from a Chicago steelworkers' bar of the late 1950s.

Blues rock, the brushfire ignited by Cream in the 1960s, has by now existed long enough to fall into tradition's camp. While many artists from the 1960s and 1970s groups are still at the style's forefront, newcomers Walter Trout (b. 1951), the Black Crowes and Government Mule have also carved their place in the subgenre.

The Meaning Of 'Jazz' Today

Blues, then, seems to have a certain invincibility, but is jazz a thriving art or a fading pastime? That's a troubling question facing those who love the music, which exhibits both tendencies. Is jazz, in 2005, still fundamentally the realm of black Americans (who are now exploring the much higher profile and higher profit genres of rap, hip hop and old-school soul)? Or does jazz belong to a worldwide elite whose members add their own accents to jazz's trademark themes, rhythms, strategies and variations?

The jazz industries – businesses involved with recording, performing, promoting and marketing the music – can accurately be described as threatened, but jazz itself, the art of a functional culture, may be securing itself through consolidation.

see Introduction pp 342 *see* A–Z of Artists pp 352 *see* List of Artists pp 368

Virtuosic saxophonists such as Bobby Watson and Kenny Garrett, steeped in hard swing and deep blues, and sophisticated pianists such as Mulgrew Miller and Bill Charlap (b. 1966) define the young to middle-aged mainstream.

Diverse Influences

Neo-conservatives such as the Marsalis brothers canonize the very greatest names of the jazz past, although with selectivity, and many musicians pay homage to jazz repertoire by launching tribute projects (such as pianist Michael Wolff's Children on the Corner) or by stylistically emulating their heroes, such as alto saxophonist Vincent Herring taking off from Cannonball Adderley (1928–75), and trumpeter Nicholas Payton from Louis Armstrong (1901–71). Direct 'quotes' of historic jazz also proliferate, due to hip hop's rage for digital samples. Turntable artists recycle licks of soul jazz artists of the 1950s and 1960s to make new hits from scraps of the old.

The bland noodlings of soprano saxophonist Kenny G (b. 1956) remain the bestselling recordings by an instrumentalist of all time. The quasi 'chamber jazz' of pianist Bob James's Fourplay, the fleet, light fingerings of fusion-focused guitarists Lee Ritenour and Larry Carlton, the California glitz of put-together studio ensembles such as the Rippingtons, the innocuous effusions of Canadian singer-pianist Diana Krall (b. 1964) and the youthful moxie of British pianist-singer Jamie Cullum all top jazz CD sales lists. However, with purer forms of jazz struggling in the US but thriving abroad, audiences have been more willing to lend an ear to far-flung ensembles. The Ganelin Trio, darlings of the 1980s Russian avant-garde, have reconvened sporadically since the fall of the Soviet Union, despite the pianist-leader's emigration to Israel. Pierre Dorge's New Jungle Orchestra of Denmark has gained renown, as Denmark has become famous for bestowing the world's most prestigious and remunerative jazz honour, the annual JazzPar Award.

New Directions In Blues

Some of the most interesting musicians in contemporary blues are those nudging it towards its future. Blues industry pundits agree that the music must find a younger audience to gain sales and avoid further marginalization and fossilization. The blues-pop blendings of Keb' Mo' (b. 1951) and Eric Bibb (b. 1951), popular as they are, do not speak

Below
Wynton Marsalis at the opening procession for the Rose Hall jazz venue at New York's Lincoln Center.

see Kenny G pp 335 *see* Diana Krall pp 359 *see* Paul Lamb & The King Snakes pp 359 *see* Walter Trout pp 366

Blues Hybrids

King may become a true touchstone for this hybrid, which has grown in underground popularity to the extent that the Mississippi juke joint label Fat Possum has built hip hop-oriented tracks around its musical patriarch R.L. Burnside (1926–2005) for college audiences. Chuck D., leader of the rap group Public Enemy, dabbled in this arena in 2003 when he led a union of rappers and blues session players into the Chess studios in *Godfathers And Sons* – part of the *Martin Scorsese Presents: The Blues* series – and thrashed John Lee Hooker's 'Boom Boom' in a well-intentioned yet poorly executed performance in the *Lightning In A Bottle* concert film. Other mainstream rappers, notably Arrested Development and Michael Franti of the group Spearhead, have explored blues themes with more satisfying results.

Several years ago Chris Thomas King started his own record label dedicated to the blues. Among his signings is England's Nublues, an interracial group that blends acoustic textures with singing, rapping, sampling and turntable manipulation. There are other smart hybridizers at work, too. The North Mississippi

Above
Chris Thomas King combines his blues roots with hip hop influences and often samples standard blues records.

Right
Musicians such as saxophonist and composer John Zorn continue to question the limits of jazz.

to the under-25 or even the under-35 crowd in the same way that John Mayall's Bluesbreakers did in the 1960s. A new breed of daring artists are banking their hopes on infusing blues with the electronic rhythms and blunt vocal cadences of hip hop. Foremost among them is Chris Thomas King (b. 1964), who grew up playing traditional electric blues in his father's juke joint in Baton Rouge, Louisiana, but whose imagination was inflamed by the potent words and music of this comparatively new urban sound. Inspired by hip hop's anti-authority stance, King has also delved into the realms of protest music with his stories of hard ghetto life and racial discrimination. Like other rappers, he uses sampling as part of his palette, but on his albums he often samples the likes of Son House, or his own acoustic slide guitar.

Allstars, for example, have built a niche within the jam-band audience for their live blend of Delta sounds, 1970s blues rock, rap and small cloudbursts of electronic noise. Occasionally, Medeski Martin & Wood and John Scofield (b. 1951), jazz artists who also court the jam-band crowd, make similar excursions.

The Effects Of Other Cultures

Other jazz artists ensure that individuality, originality and iconoclasm still exist within their genre. Experimentalists such as tenor and soprano saxophonist Evan Parker (b. 1944), American reedsmen Charles Gayle and Roscoe Mitchell and saxophonist-composer John Zorn (b. 1953) continue to test the bounds of their instruments and poke at the lines between structured or spontaneous improvisation. Lawrence Douglas 'Butch' Morris, William Parker (b. 1952) and Walter Thompson conduct large ensembles through instant, scoreless compositions. Folkloric elements from Spain and Latin American settlements in the Western Hemisphere have been embraced as basic to jazz – in the words of Jelly Roll Morton (1890–1941), 'the Spanish tinge' – so Panamanian-born pianist Danilo Perez, Dominican pianist Michel Camilo and Nuyorican trumpeter-conguero Jerry Gonzalez with his *piratas del flamenco* attain full measures of respect and influence.

A Brighter Future?

Jazz continues to mirror contemporary society as does no other art form. Culture is fragmented; so is jazz. Communications are global, and jazz is a worldwide phenomenon. Values everywhere are in dispute; jazz has its internal debates, feuds and competitions. The best news is that the music hasn't been fixed, even for the most comprehensive encyclopedia, or frozen for museum display. Fertile, free of untoward constraints and fighting as always for self-definition, jazz lives!

Out on the very horizon of blues music, a few dedicated experimenters are pushing the style further into the digital age while still honouring its deepest traditions. Foremost among them may be Elliott Sharp (b. 1951), who spent years at the front of avant-garde rock. He was a key figure in the downtown Manhattan art-music scene before returning to blues in the early 1990s with his group Terraplane – as well as a laptop computer, deft programming skills and an acute tonal sensibility. All of these artists and many others guarantee that the future of the blues will be musically bright. However, whether the style will again enjoy the kind of prominence, economic success and wide appeal that it did in the 1930s, 1960s and, briefly, the 1980s, remains to be seen.

Above
Elliott Sharp has helped to modernize the blues.

see Jelly Roll Morton pp 60 see R.L. Burnside pp 354 see Chris Thomas King pp 358 see Elliott Sharp pp 364

A-Z of Artists

Above
Geri Allen's lyrical compositions and accomplished piano playing have made her a respected jazz figure.

Geri Allen

(Piano, b. 1957)

Raised in Detroit, pianist-composer Allen emerged in New York City with older midwestern avant-gardists such as Lester Bowie and Oliver Lake, and hometown colleagues including saxophonist Kenny Garrett. Her albums feature elusive but lyrical compositions for small ensembles. She toured briefly and recorded *Feel The Fire* (1993) with singer Betty Carter, and has worked with her husband, trumpeter Wallace Roney. Allen performed as Mary Lou Williams in Robert Altman's film *Kansas City* (1996).

Fred Anderson Jr.

(Tenor saxophone, b. 1929)

Admired by post-1960s Chicago improvisers as a founding member of the Association for the Advancement of Creative Musicians, tenor saxophonist Fred Anderson's reputation spread after his first trip to Europe in 1977, but he was very sparsely recorded until the 1990s. Since then his huge tone and gutsy, freely associative statements have been captured on numerous albums, and his music club, the Velvet Lounge, has become an internationally renowned venue.

Derek Bailey

(Guitar, 1932–2005)

The British guitarist was uncompromisingly, spontaneously cerebral, exploring atonal, anti-melodic, arhythmic yet associative 'sound', abjuring musical conventions. Yet his solos and collaborations with master improvisers of jazz and beyond were compelling. The author of *Improvisation: Its Nature And Practice In Music* (1993), Bailey considers traditions from Africa and India as well as the West. In the early 1990s he produced the television series *On The Edge* for Britain's Channel 4.

Lurrie Bell

(Guitar, vocals, b. 1958)

Bell grew up among Chicago legends, including his harmonica-playing father Carey Bell. The self-taught guitarist was 17 when he joined Willie Dixon's band and 19 when he toured with Koko Taylor. He had already built a reputation for wiry, envelope-pushing improvisations when he formed Sons of Blues with Billy Branch in the mid-1970s. He has since recorded several solo albums, including 1995's superb *Mercurial Son*, but his career has been interrupted periodically by homelessness and health issues.

see Introduction pp 342 *see* Sources & Sounds pp 344

Steven Bernstein

(Trumpet, composer, arranger, b. 1961)

A member of several populist-experimental-fun jazz bands since the late 1980s (including Hieroglyphics Ensemble, Kamakazi Ground Crew, Lounge Lizards, Spanish Fly, Sex Mob and the Millennial Territory Orchestra), Bernstein continues to perform on slide trumpet (or soprano trombone), cornet and other standard brass instruments, and to compose and arrange film soundtracks. His projects include adaptations of Jewish folk and liturgical themes with Cuban mambo and New Orleans R&B rhythms.

Eric Bibb

(Guitar, vocals, b. 1951)

Folk-bluesman Bibb blends deep roots with pop influences, occasionally incorporating African and Afro-Cuban sounds. He resides in Sweden but was born in New York City, where his father, Leon, performed in musical theatre and on the folk scene. His uncle was John Lewis of the Modern Jazz Quartet, while Odetta, Pete Seeger and Paul Robeson were among his family's friends. Bibb's finest album to date, 2004's *Friends*, features Odetta, Guy Davis, Martin Simpson, Harry Manx and his role model Taj Mahal.

Elvin Bishop

(Guitar, vocals, b. 1942)

This Tulsa, Oklahoma native's return to his roots as a blues player has been characterized by barnstorming live sets and albums for the Alligator label in the Chicago electric tradition, at times approximating the sound of Elmore James's bands. Bishop, who became a charter member of the Paul Butterfield Blues Band while attending college in Chicago in the 1960s, stopped making music for nearly a decade following his Elvin Bishop Group's US number-three pop hit 'Fooled Around And Fell In Love' in 1976. Today he resides in San Francisco.

Billy Branch

(Harmonica, vocals, b. 1951)

Branch began playing harmonica at the age of 10, before polishing his onstage technique in Chicago with Big Walter, James Cotton, Junior Wells and Carey Bell. In 1975 he became a sideman for Willie Dixon and then formed Sons of Blues with Lurrie Bell (guitar). Branch continues to front the band and is a respected blues educator. He also appears in the Robert Mugge-directed concert film *Hellhounds On My Trail: The Afterlife Of Robert Johnson* (1999) and has made cameo appearances in the Hollywood movies *Adventures In Babysitting* (1987) and *Next Of Kin* (1989).

Left
Trumpeter Steven Bernstein has played in various experimental jazz ensembles.

Below
Blues harpist Billy Branch, with guitarist Kenny Neal.

see Willie Dixon pp 221 *see* Elmore James pp 226 *see* Taj Mahal pp 280 *see* Junior Wells pp 281

Above
Dee Dee Bridgewater has lent her vocals to jazz groups, Broadway musicals and tribute projects.

Above Right
R.L. Burnside remained relatively unknown until the 1991 documentary *Deep Blues*.

Dee Dee Bridgewater

(Vocals, b. 1950)

First heard in the 1970s with the Thad Jones-Mel Lewis Orchestra, then in the Broadway musicals *The Wiz* and *Sophisticated Ladies* and later in pop/jazz contexts, Bridgewater relocated to Paris in 1983. Leading a trio, she regained career momentum in the 1990s with tribute projects commemorating Billie Holiday, Horace Silver and Ella Fitzgerald, and has also performed hard-swinging, scat-laden performances of jazz-related standards.

R.L. Burnside

(Guitar, vocals, 1926–2005)

Sharecropper Rural 'R.L.' Burnside was inspired to learn guitar by his north Mississippi neighbours Fred McDowell and Ranie Burnette, as well as John Lee Hooker records. He first recorded in the 1960s, but his career ignited after he appeared in the documentary *Deep Blues* (1991) and released *Too Bad Jim* (1994) on Fat Possum, a label based in Burnside's birthplace of Oxford, Mississippi. Along with Junior Kimbrough, this potent rhythm and slide guitarist and singer was responsible for the 1990s juke-blues revival.

Uri Caine

(Piano, b. 1956)

Born in Philadelphia, Caine pursued classical studies and performances with locally based jazz stars (Philly Joe Jones, Grover Washington Jr.) prior to moving to New York in the late 1980s and commencing an international career. He has productive associations with clarinetist Don Byron and trumpeter Dave Douglas, among others, and his output ranges from mainstream and electric piano trios to neo-klezmer, to post-modern revisions of works by Mahler, Wagner and Bach, and a concept album depicting early twentieth-century Tin Pan Alley.

John Campbell

(Guitar, vocals, 1952–93)

Campbell, who was born in Louisiana and grew up in Texas, combined the traditional approach of Lightnin'

see Introduction pp 342 *see* Sources & Sounds pp 344

Hopkins with his own swampy, electrified New Orleans hoodoo spiritualism. His debut, the Ronnie Earl-produced *A Man & His Blues* (1988), is a superb summation of his acoustic roots, but its two electric follow-ups, *One Believer* (1991) and *Howlin' Mercy* (1993), which introduced rock flourishes, had him poised for a commercial breakthrough when his heart failed.

James Carter

(Various saxophones, b. 1969)

A musical prodigy from Detroit's Creative Arts Collective, saxophonist James Carter toured Europe at the age of 16, worked with Wynton Marsalis and starred in Julius Hemphill's saxophone opera *Long Tongues*. Since 1990, his New York ensemble has recorded a variety of 'quiet storm' romantic jazz, Django Reinhardt-style gypsy jazz, hard-core fusion and jazz standards. At the fiftieth anniversary Newport Jazz Festival he upped the stakes by improvising 33 choruses of Duke Ellington's 'Diminuendo And Crescendo In Blue' – topping Paul Gonsalves's 1956 benchmark of 26 choruses.

Regina Carter

(Violin, b. 1966)

Violinist Regina Carter has stabilized her instrument's precarious role in jazz after advanced work in classical, jazz-pop and experimental formats. From childhood Suzuki lessons (a method of teaching music that stresses listening over reading skills), she joined the Detroit-based band Straight Ahead, then the String Trio of New York. She was a featured soloist in Wynton Marsalis's Pulitzer Prize-winning *Blood On The Fields* oratorio (1995) and was the first jazz musician, person of colour or woman to play and record on Paganini's Stradivarius, 'the Cannon'.

Bill Charlap

(Piano, b. 1966)

The son of Broadway composer Moose Charlap and singer Sandy Stewart, Bill Charlap was inducted into professional jazz by Gerry Mulligan and has been critically acclaimed for his deft playing, superb taste and unfailing swing feel. In 2004 he succeeded pianist Dick Hyman as director of the long-established, prestigious jazz series at New York's 92nd Street Y (Young Men's and Young Women's Hebrew Association).

Ravi Coltrane

(Tenor and soprano saxophones, b. 1965)

Ravi Coltrane, the son of John and Alice Coltrane, faces problematic expectations to which he has responded with modesty and genuine accomplishment. Raised by his spiritually devout mother, Ravi joined Coltrane drummer Elvin Jones's band in his early 20s. The loosely organized Brooklyn M-Base Collective supported his individuality and, while touched by the influence of his parents, he mines a progressive rather than radical musical style.

Shemekia Copeland

(Vocals, b. 1979)

This Harlem-born daughter of Texas bluesman Johnny 'Clyde' Copeland apprenticed onstage with her father. She emerged as a solo artist in 1997, beginning a run of albums that made her one of the most popular artists in contemporary blues. Nevertheless, it wasn't until 2002's Dr. John-produced *Talking To Strangers* that the quality of Copeland's songs matched that of her powerful shouter's voice and live charisma.

Left
The violin has made a comeback on to the jazz scene in the hands of Regina Carter.

see Mississippi Fred McDowell pp 130 *see* Billie Holiday pp 156 *see* Thad Jones pp 307 *see* Johnny 'Clyde' Copeland pp 334

Joey DeFrancesco

(Organ, b. 1971)

The son of jazz organist Papa John DeFrancesco, Joey's keyboard skill and enthusiasm were well-recognized even before 1987, when he was a finalist in the annual Thelonious Monk Competition. Indebted in style to Jimmy Smith, DeFrancesco played with Miles Davis and recorded on Columbia Records prior to his graduation from high school. His prodigious youthful energy has attracted audiences and revitalized an interest in jazz organ.

Dave Douglas

(Trumpet, b. 1963)

Dave Douglas spans musical abstraction and gutsiness in acclaimed albums and a busy, international touring schedule. After attending Berklee School of Music, New England Conservatory and New York University, he studied with classical trumpeter Carmine Caruso and toured with Horace Silver. He has recorded for a variety of small labels, as well as BMG-RCA Victor, and is known for his Tin Hat Trio (jazzing Balkan music) and John Zorn's Sephardic-tinged jazz quartet Masada. In 2005 Douglas introduced his own record label with *Mountain Passages*.

Tinsley Ellis

(Guitar, vocals, b. 1957)

Blues rocker Ellis grew up in Florida and emerged in the 1980s from Atlanta, Georgia, where he led the Heartfixers, whose albums include a disc featuring blues shouter Nappy Brown. Ellis blends the dynamic technique of B.B. King, Freddie King, Albert King, Otis Rush and Magic Sam with the Cream-era pyrotechnics of Eric Clapton. His evolution as a songwriter and musical pluralist, incorporating elements of funk and soul, is captured best on 2000's *Kingpin*.

Bill Frisell

(Guitar, b. 1951)

A distinctive electric guitar stylist, Frisell evokes longing and wonder through melodic selectivity, *legato* attack and strategic outbursts. Originally a clarinetist, then inspired by Wes Montgomery, he studied at Boston's Berklee School of Music and with Jim Hall. He recorded for ECM and won fame in the New York

Below

Inspired by Wes Montgomery, Bill Frisell (second from right) is one of the most sought-after jazz guitarists of his generation.

see Introduction pp 342 *see* Sources & Sounds pp 344

noise/improv scene, exploring pastoral Americana imagery in his own projects. Besides playing in Paul Motian's trio with Joe Lovano, Frisell has recorded colouristic accompaniments for rock and pop singers.

Left
Roy Hargrove plays both ballads and funk tracks in a clean, hard bop-influenced trumpet style.

Roy Hargrove

(Trumpet, b. 1969)

Encouraged by Wynton Marsalis while in high school in Dallas, Texas, Hargrove has a jauntier approach to trumpet than his mentor. He principally employs hard-bop vocabulary, but has also led the Latin jazz band Crîsol with Cuban pianist Chucho Valdés, recorded with hip hop/soul singer D'Angelo, and co-starred in Herbie Hancock's New Standards quintet with saxophonist Michael Brecker. In his own programmes, Hargrove plays both tender ballads and R&B/funk hits.

Corey Harris

(Guitar, vocals, b. 1969)

Harris was discovered on the streets of New Orleans playing acoustic blues. Soon after his debut, 1995's *Between Midnight And Day*, the Denver, Colorado native began incorporating rock, Afro-Cuban, Afro-Caribbean and African influences into his repertoire, creating a distinctive fusion. The electric *Greens From The Garden* (1999) and *Mississippi To Mali* (2004), a collaboration with musicians from Mississippi and Africa, tied to his appearance in a similarly titled 2003 Martin Scorsese documentary, capture his soulful versatility.

Michael Hill

(Guitar, vocals, b. 1952)

Michael Hill's Blues Mob earned an international cult following with a gritty, aggressive, expansive style well-tailored to Hill's lyrics, which often focus on urban social issues. Born in the south Bronx into a family with roots in North Carolina and Georgia, Hill began playing blues after hearing Jimi Hendrix and Cream. He worked in cover bands and as a sideman before he started making original music in 1987. In 1993 he formed Blues Mob and recorded *Bloodlines*, the first of five strong albums that fuse his rock-fuelled instincts with pop, African and Caribbean flourishes.

Shirley Horn

(Vocals, piano, b. 1934)

Shirley Horn was successful from 1954 through the mid-1960s in her hometown of Washington, DC. She was promoted by Miles Davis and Quincy Jones and owned a club called the Place Where Louie Dwells, but gradually turned full attention to her family. She returned with records, club dates and concert tours in the mid-1980s, and is admired for her unadorned, expressive ballad singing and self-accompaniment. Horn suffered a diabetic foot amputation in 2004 but continues to perform.

Charlie Hunter

(Guitar, b. 1967)

The leading exponent 'acid jazz', guitarist Charlie Hunter has learned to emulate the organ-bass runs of his inspiration, Larry Young, on a customized guitar. Raised in Berkeley, California, the son of a guitar repairer, he was a street musician in Europe prior to founding Disposable Heroes of Hiphoprisy in the early 1990s – the first of his series of popular combos, which draw on the R&B, soul, alternative rock and reggae repertoires. His fingerpicking is ingenious and his melodic playing intrigues young audiences.

Below
Charlie Hunter is a flexible guitarist and was a key figure in the acid-jazz movement.

 *see* Horace Silver pp 233 *see* Quincy Jones pp 227 *see* Wes Montgomery pp 277 *see* Herbie Hancock pp 305

Vijay Iyer

(Piano, composer, b. 1971)

Raised in Rochester, New York, Vijay Iyer started Suzuki violin lessons at the age of three and taught himself to play piano. He performed professionally while pursuing advanced studies at Yale and the University of California, Berkeley and moved to New York in 1998, having released two albums and toured with saxophonist Steve Coleman. Iyer incorporates socio-political concerns and South Asian musical elements into his cross-genre projects, frequently in collaboration with saxophonist Rudresh Mahanthappa.

Norah Jones

(Vocals, piano, b. 1979)

An overnight sensation, Norah Jones's debut album *Come Away With Me* (2002) won numerous Grammy Awards and its sales revitalized Blue Note Records. Introduced by her mother to Billie Holiday's music, Jones won *Down Beat* Student Music Awards in 1996 and 1997 and studied jazz piano at North Texas State University prior to arriving in New York City in 1999. Her warm voice and intimate delivery lend compelling inflections to pop, folk and country songs in basic arrangements with 'jazz' content from sidemen.

Below

Norah Jones's debut album *Come Away With Me* made her an overnight sensation.

Junior Kimbrough

(Guitar, vocals, 1931–98)

Along with Fat Possum labelmate R.L. Burnside, David 'Junior' Kimbrough, from Holly Springs, Mississippi was a leader of the 1990s juke-blues revival and had also played a part in creating the 'Sun sound' by influencing early rockers in the 1950s, including Charlie Feathers. Kimbrough's approach was rooted in traditional African drum groups and he functioned much like a drum master, establishing the band's rhythms on his guitar. His later recordings include *All Night Long* (1993), the first Fat Possum Records release, and he appeared in the documentary *Deep Blues* (1991).

Chris Thomas King

(Guitar, bass, keyboards, drums, vocals, b. 1964)

Multi-talented King began in the footsteps of his father – Baton Rouge, Louisiana juke bluesman Tabby Thomas. King has mastered traditional electric and acoustic blues. He also performs and records rock- and rap-blues hybrids. In 2000 he appeared as Tommy Johnson in *O Brother, Where Art Thou?*. He also played Lowell Fulson in the Ray Charles biopic *Ray* (2004) and Blind Willie Johnson in *The Soul Of A Man*, the Wim Wenders-directed episode of *Martin Scorsese Presents: The Blues*. In 2002 Chris Thomas King established his own New Orleans-based label, 21st Century Blues.

The Kinsey Report

(Vocal/instrumental group, 1984–present)

Gary, Indiana's Kinsey brothers formed the Kinsey Report to support their father, Lester 'Big Daddy' Kinsey. In 1985 they recorded *Bad Situation* as Big Daddy Kinsey & the Kinsey Report. Led by Donald

see Introduction pp 342 *see* Sources & Sounds pp 344

(guitar, vocals), who had been a sideman for Albert King and Bob Marley, the brothers signed with Alligator Records and released *Edge Of The City*, the first of three snarling, blues-rock Kinsey Report albums, in 1987. Big Daddy Kinsey went on to make fine solo recordings, including 1993's *I Am The Blues*, until his death from cancer in 2001.

Diana Krall

(Vocals, piano, b. 1964)

From western Canada, Diana Krall attended Berklee School of Music, was encouraged to sing by Los Angeles-based pianist-singer Jimmy Rowles and was mentored by bassist Ray Brown. Her first trios, co-led by guitarist Russell Malone, emulated Nat 'King' Cole's. Her accessible stylings led to international festival tours, bestselling recordings and increasingly nuanced vocal shadings. In 2004 Krall married British singer-songwriter Elvis Costello and released her first album of all-original material.

Birelli Lagrene

(Guitar, b. 1966)

A French gypsy, Lagrene was hailed as Django Reinhardt's heir upon the release of his first album at the age of 13. He has performed gypsy jazz in the company of swing veterans Benny Carter, Benny Goodman and Stephane Grappelli, but has also developed a personal, fusion-oriented style and mixes both approaches in collaborations with guitarists John McLaughlin, Al Di Meola, Paco de Lucia, Larry Coryell, Philip Catherine, Christian Escoudé and Stanley Jordan, among others.

Paul Lamb & The King Snakes

(Vocal/instrumental group, 1989–present)

English harmonica virtuoso Lamb (b. 1955) initially learned to play from recordings, but was mentored by Sonny Terry after they met at the World Harmonica Championships when Lamb was 15. He performed with other blues legends, including Buddy Guy and Junior Wells, before forming the five-piece Paul Lamb & the King Snakes. They released the first of their nine albums in 1990 and play nearly 300 dates annually, faithfully recreating the sound of late 1950s Chicago blues.

Above
Harmonica virtuoso Paul Lamb, who tours extensively with his band the King Snakes.

Abbey Lincoln

(Vocals, composer, b. 1930)

Lincoln caps her long, diversified singing and acting career as an iconic songwriter and performer. Her first record, in the 1950s, was with Benny Carter's orchestra; in the 1960s she recorded politicized material with then-husband Max Roach. In the mid-1980s she re-emerged, paying tribute to Billie Holiday and embodying an African-American feminism. Employing top younger instrumentalists in her bands, she has also become a model for younger vocalists such as Cassandra Wilson, Erika Badhu and Lizz Wright.

Below
Abbey Lincoln has become a mentor for younger musicians and vocalists.

see Benny Carter pp 122 *see* Billie Holiday pp 156 *see* Buddy Guy pp 254 *see* Steve Coleman pp 333

Joe Lovano

(Various saxophones, clarinet, drums, b. 1952)

The son of Cleveland saxophonist Tony 'Big T' Lovano, Joe Lovano attended Berklee School of Music before working in organ groups. He was in Woody Herman's 1970s Thundering Herd and Mel Lewis's Vanguard Jazz Orchestra, freelanced extensively and joined drummer Paul Motian's trio with Bill Frisell in 1990. He has become a leading voice of mainstream modernism, applying himself to diverse contexts. He has collaborated with his vocalist wife, Judi Silvano, various saxophonists and rhythm sections, and composer Gunther Schuller.

Above

Joe Lovano is one of the most prolific saxophonists on the current jazz scene.

Right

Keb' Mo's accessible, poppy blues style has ensured him several successful albums.

Medeski, Martin & Wood

(Instrumental group, 1991–present)

In the 1990s John Medeski (keyboards, b. 1965), Billy Martin (drums, b. 1963) and Chris Wood (bass, b. *c.* 1969) established an energized form of lengthy improvisations over powerful grooves, playing student venues and festivals. All three members have impressive résumés, including conservatory training and experience with experimental jazz leaders. Their recordings have taken increasing liberties with the basic jam band formula, adding DJs, vocalists, compositional complexity and collage effects.

Keb' Mo'

(Guitar, vocals, b. 1951)

Songwriter Kevin Moore spent the 1970s and 1980s in his native Los Angeles, playing studio sessions and in mainstream funk and blues bands. Committing himself to blues, he travelled to the Mississippi Delta to study with the late guitarist Eugene Powell. Moore then combined blues with pop hooks and instrumental sweetening, and has released eight easy-listening, semi-acoustic albums, including his eponymous 1994 debut and the 1996 Best Contemporary Blues Grammy-winner *Just Like You*.

John Mooney

(Guitar, vocals, b. 1955)

Born in East Orange, New Jersey, Mooney grew up in Rochester, New York, where he joined Joe Beard's group at 15 and studied slide with Delta giant Son House. In 1976 he moved to New Orleans, where he began to concoct an electric style that blended Crescent City funk rhythms with traditional blues, gelling on his 2000 album *Gone To Hell*. Today Mooney performs and records both with his upbeat band and as a solo acoustic artist.

see Introduction pp 342 *see* Sources & Sounds pp 344

Neville Brothers

(Vocal/instrumental group, 1977–present)

The Neville Brothers – Art (keyboards, vocals), Aaron (percussion, vocals), Charles (saxophone, vocals) and Cyril (percussion, vocals) – have been one of New Orleans' foremost musical families since 1954. Art led Allen Toussaint's house band (the Meters) from the late 1960s, before convening his brothers into a unit in 1976. They released the successful *Fiyo On The Bayou* in 1981 and since then have made consistently good albums including *Yellow Moon* (1989), produced by Daniel Lanois. Their album *Walkin' In The Shadow Of Life* (2004) focuses on family ties, cultural heritage and spiritual identity.

Arturo O'Farrill

(Piano, orchestra leader, b. 1960)

Arturo O'Farrill is the pianist and music director of the Latin jazz orchestra his father, Chico O'Farrill, organized upon his comeback in the mid-1990s; he has also worked with keyboardist-composer-bandleader Carla Bley, trumpeter Lester Bowie and the Fort Apache Band. Upon Chico's death in 2000, Arturo inherited his bandbook and legacy. In 2003 he was named leader of Jazz@Lincoln Center's Afro-Latin Jazz Orchestra.

Greg Osby

(Alto and soprano saxophones, b. 1960)

After playing in R&B bands in St. Louis, Greg Osby studied at Washington, DC's Howard University, with classmates including pianist Geri Allen. He quit Berklee School of Music to tour with Dizzy Gillespie, then moved to New York City and joined Steve Coleman's M-Base Collective. At first their styles were mirror images, but Osby gradually found a unique voice based on phrase displacements. He has recorded with Cassandra Wilson, older iconoclasts and acoustic groups with new talents such as pianist Jason Moran.

Evan Parker

(Tenor and soprano saxophones, b. 1944)

Bristol-born Evan Parker has been an important experimentalist in the UK and continental Europe for 40 years with the Spontaneous Music Ensemble, Music Improvisation Company, London Jazz Composer's Orchestra, Brotherhood of Breath, Dutch-based ICP and Globe Unity Orchestra. His mastery of circular breathing and alternate fingerings have resulted in inimitable, multi-levelled, atonal improvisations. Live shows by his Electro-Acoustic Ensemble feature interactive electronics.

William Parker

(Bass, b. 1952)

William Parker apprenticed with major bassists in New York City's Jazzmobile programme, studied privately with Jimmy Garrison and Wilber Ware, and performed with Cecil Taylor's group at the age of 21. He has anchored many ensembles, including the David S. Ware Quartet. His prodigious work ethic, instrumental steadiness, dependability and selflessness have made Parker central to activities that culminate annually in a week-long interdisciplinary Vision Festival, produced by his wife, dancer-choreographer Patricia Parker.

Above

The Neville Brothers worked as the house band for Allen Toussaint before going their own way in the 1970s.

see Son House pp 126 *see* Dizzy Gillespie pp 152 *see* Woody Herman pp 154 *see* Chico O'Farrill pp 181

Lucky Peterson

(Keyboards, guitar, bass, drums, trumpet, vocals, b. 1963)

Born Judge Kenneth Peterson in Buffalo, New York, this child prodigy keyboardist had played on *The Ed Sullivan Show* by the age of six. His father is soul bluesman James Peterson. At 17, Lucky became Little Milton's bandleader and then played with Bobby Bland. In 1988 he focused on guitar and began a solo career that has become increasingly experimental, culminating in the racial themes and heavy rock and funk of 2003's visceral *Black Midnight Sun*, produced by Bill Laswell.

Above

Lucky Peterson performing at 2001's Monterey Jazz Festival.

Right

Like his father Dewey, Joshua Redman is a versatile and successful jazz reedsman.

Chris Potter

(Various saxophones, b. 1971)

A Chicago native, Chris Potter emerged professionally in bebop trumpeter Red Rodney's combo, before moving on to featured roles in the Mingus Big Band and bassist Dave Holland's quintet and big band. Potter became the youngest musician to win Denmark's prestigious and financially valuable Jazzpar Prize in 2000. Personally self-effacing, Potter is a virtuosic instrumentalist with an adventurous frame of melodic mind, equal to any musical challenge.

Enrico Rava

(Trumpet, b. 1939)

Raised in Turin, Italy and taught piano by his conservatory-graduate mother, Rava began playing traditional jazz on trombone as a teenager but, inspired by Miles Davis, switched to trumpet. He worked with expatriate American jazzmen in Rome and travelled throughout Europe and around South America and New York. Through broad perspective and international experience he has arrived at a distinctive sound, with a melodic style that embraces both conventional and radical gestures.

Joshua Redman

(Tenor and soprano saxophones, b. 1969)

Joshua Redman neé Shedroff grew up in Berkley, California and played reeds throughout high school. He was accepted by Yale Law School, but his victory at the 1991 Thelonious Monk competition persuaded him to take up music professionally. He was quickly accepted by jazz elders, peers and audiences due to his strong, blunt tone, populist taste, articulate manner and voracious style. In 2000 he was appointed artistic director and

see Introduction pp 342 see Sources & Sounds pp 344

artist-in-residence of the San Francisco Jazz Festival, and continues to record and tour widely.

Dianne Reeves

(Vocals, b. 1956)

Dianne Reeves's parents were musicians and her cousin, pianist George Duke, encouraged her, as did trumpeter Clark Terry. She sang in Los Angeles studio sessions in the late 1970s and 1980s, and with pop/jazz groups Caldera, Night Flight and Sergio Mendes's troupe. Her albums blend jazz, gospel, African and Brazilian accents with pop-music production. She has recorded a tribute to Sarah Vaughan and in 2002 was appointed Creative Chair for Jazz by the Los Angeles Philharmonic, to curate jazz bookings and educational workshops at the Hollywood Bowl and the Walt Disney Concert Hall.

Paul Rishell & Annie Raines

(Vocal duo, 1993–present)

This Cambridge, Massachusetts-based duo embrace vintage music styles with absolute authenticity. Brooklyn-born Rishell (b. 1950, vocals, guitar) discovered traditional blues in the 1960s and played with Son House and Johnny Shines. He began leading bands and performing solo in 1975, releasing his debut *Blues On Holiday* in 1990. He then met Raines (b. 1969, harmonica, mandolin, vocals), whose influences included Little Walter and Sonny Boy Williamson I. Their first recording together was 1996's *I Want You To Know*, while *Moving To The Country* (2000) won a W.C. Handy Award for Acoustic Blues Album of the Year.

Duke Robillard

(Guitar, vocals, b. 1948)

Robillard's grasp of blues and jazz has kept him in demand since he founded Roomful of Blues in 1967. He was born in Woonsocket, Rhode Island and was influenced by Bill Doggett, T-Bone Walker and many others, absorbing the fine details of playing and arranging. He left Roomful in 1979 for a stint with rockabilly singer Robert Gordon and then ignited his solo career, which he interrupted briefly in 1990 to replace Jimmie Vaughan in the Fabulous Thunderbirds. In the late 1990s he began producing albums for Ruth Brown, Jay McShann, Eddy Clearwater and others.

Above

Mighty Mo Rodgers is a gifted songwriter who has absorbed both blues and soul influences.

Mighty Mo Rodgers

(Keyboards, vocals, b. 1942)

Maurice Rodgers grew up sneaking into chitlin circuit clubs in his native Chicago and nearby Gary, Indiana. His distinctive songwriting combines funky arrangements with explorations of the metaphysics of the blues, notably on his 1999 debut *Blues Is My Wailin' Wall*. He began performing in the mid-1960s in Los Angeles with T-Bone Walker, Albert Collins and others; his sound is influenced by the Memphis Stax stable of stars.

see Sonny Boy Williamson pp 138 *see* Sarah Vaughan pp 184 *see* Little Milton pp 275 *see* Dave Holland pp 306

Gonzalo Rubalcaba

(Piano, keyboards, b. 1963)

A pianist with Romantic sensibilities, Rubalcaba is from a revered musical family and studied at Havana's Amadeo Roldan Conservatory. He led an electric Grupo Proyecto on tours of Europe and Asia in the 1980s, representing triumphs of Castro-era Cuba, but the US denied him entry until 1993. Bassist Charlie Haden sponsored his first Blue Note Records albums and remains an important collaborator, while Rubalcaba has continued to compose lush yet abstract works for trio, quartet and quintet, occasionally employing electronics.

Below

Bobby Rush is a popular figure on the modern chitlin circuit.

Bobby Rush

(Guitar, bass, harmonica, b. 1940)

Rush's mix of vaudeville stage antics and soul-blues grooves has made him the king of the modern chitlin circuit. Born in Homer, Louisiana, Rush moved with his family to Chicago in 1953, already mesmerized by Muddy Waters and Louis Jordan. He emerged from the West Side blues scene in the 1960s and his career took off with 1971's 'Chicken Heads', after which he spent the next two decades touring and recording. Increasing press coverage and a starring role in an episode of 2003's *Martin Scorsese Presents: The Blues* series have introduced him to a wider audience.

Saffire – The Uppity Blues Women

(Vocal/instrumental group, 1984–present)

Formed in Virginia by virtuoso Ann Rabson (piano, guitar, vocals) and her guitar student Gaye Adegbalola, Saffire burst out internationally in 1990 with the release of their eponymous debut. Andra Faye replaced original bassist Earlene Lewis in 1992. The band has a knack for framing contemporary songs with twists of novelty humour, written from a feminist perspective in traditional acoustic settings reminiscent of Bessie Smith and Ma Rainey. Rabson and Adegbalola also have solo careers.

Maria Schneider

(Composer, arranger, bandleader, b. 1960)

Schneider studied several instruments and composition prior to an internship with arranger Gil Evans in New York City in 1985. After further work with Bob Brookmeyer and Mel Lewis, she established a jazz orchestra that performed weekly in Greenwich Village from 1993–98 and recorded three albums. In 2004 she self-produced *Concert In The Garden* and distributed it over the Internet. She has written for orchestras in Paris, Denmark and Stockholm, and for the Pilobolus Dance Theater company.

Elliott Sharp

(Guitar, bass, reeds, programming, vocals, b. 1951)

Cleveland, Ohio-born Sharp is on the cutting edge, combining his experience as an improviser – he was a cornerstone of Manhattan's 1980s downtown, avant-garde music scene – with deep tradition.

see Introduction pp 342 *see* Sources & Sounds pp 344

Sharp's earliest gigs were with blues bands. After 20 years of sophisticated experimentation with other styles, he formed his own blues band, Terraplane, in 1994. Sharp's playing pushes the envelope of blues tonality and incorporates digital programming and other unconventional elements. It is best heard on 2004's *Do The Don't*, which features guest guitarist Hubert Sumlin.

Matthew Shipp

(Piano, b. 1960)

A prolific recording artist, Shipp considers himself to be a follower of bassist William Parker, with whom he has worked on many projects including the David S. Ware's Quartet. His keyboard style is rhythmically propulsive; he lays dense harmonic accompaniments for single-note instruments. In 1999 he contracted with Thirsty Ear Records to produce his own imprint, Series Bleu, featuring himself with associates including hip hop DJs and punk-rock bands.

Kim Simmonds

(Guitar, harmonica, piano, vocals, b. 1947)

Simmonds emerged as the leader of early British blues-rock band Savoy Brown in 1965. Although the Welsh-born guitarist's group grew louder and heavier into the 1970s, he never lost his interest in the acoustic country blues that had sparked his playing. Savoy Brown soldiers on, but in 1997 Simmonds began a parallel solo career with the all-acoustic *Solitaire*, and continues to perform and record in that vein.

Angela Strehli

(Vocals, b. 1945)

This raw-edged songstress emerged from the same Austin, Texas scene that yielded Stevie Ray Vaughan, with her 1986 debut *Stranger Blues*. Strehli, who was born in Lubbock, perfected her slow phrasing and dynamic attack at the famed Antone's nightclub, learning from visiting artists Muddy Waters, Otis Rush, Albert Collins and Albert King. She helped to start the influential Antone's record label. In recent years Strehli has incorporated more 1940s and 1950s R&B influences into her music.

Hubert Sumlin

(Guitar, vocals, b. 1931)

Sumlin's distinctive riffs are all over Howlin' Wolf's classic Chess recordings; Wolf plucked the Greenwood, Mississippi innovator from a band he had started with James Cotton, and Sumlin became an integral part of Wolf's sound. After Wolf's death in 1976, Sumlin joined saxophonist Eddie Shaw in his Wolf Gang band and ventured out on his own in 1980, but excessive drinking kept his performances and albums patchy. However, Sumlin sobered up in the late 1990s and has since recorded several successful solo albums, including 2005's brilliant *About Them Shoes*.

Above
Howlin' Wolf's erstwhile guitarist Hubert Sumlin plays a gig at London's Borderline club in 2000.

Otis Taylor

(Guitar, banjo, mandolin, harmonica, vocals, b. 1948)

Colorado's Otis Taylor is the most inventive blues songwriter to emerge in recent decades. The Chicago native revives the genre's role as protest music, often telling stories of lynchings, racial injustice and homelessness. His use of archaic Appalachian banjo tunings, droning progressions and digital delay creates a sound that reflects the blues' African roots and echoes 1960s psychedelia. It is a wise, timeless combination, best captured on his potent albums *Respect The Dead* (2002) and *Truth Is Not Fiction* (2003).

Susan Tedeschi

(Guitar, vocals, b. 1970)

Tedeschi was introduced to blues and gospel via her parents' record collection. While singing in the Berklee College of Music gospel choir, she performed at blues jams around her native Boston and formed her own group. Her international debut, 1998's *Just Won't Burn*, was mostly blues rock with hints of emotionalism; it earned her a Grammy nomination and sold 700,000 copies. She seemed poised for a crossover career until the follow-up, 2002's far superior, soul-steeped *Wait For Me*, failed to generate much attention outside blues circles.

see Louis Jordan pp 176 *see* James Cotton pp 220 *see* Howlin' Wolf pp 225 *see* Charlie Haden pp 272

Walter Trout

(Guitar, vocals, b. 1951)

In a BBC radio poll, blues rocker Trout was ranked number six among the top 20 guitarists of all time. Not bad for an Ocean City, New Jersey native who worked for decades as a sideman with John Lee Hooker, Big Mama Thornton, Canned Heat and John Mayall before forming his own band in 1990. Since then he has recorded a dozen albums, heavy on guitar, and earned an international reputation for his fiery live performances.

Chucho Valdés

(Piano, b. 1941)

Chucho remained in Cuba after his father, pianist Bebo Valdés, defected in the late 1950s. In his mid-20s Chucho established Orquesta Cubana de Musica Moderna, which became the much-recorded, internationally touring jazz showband Irakere; he turned it over to his son in 1998. A large man with huge hands, Valdés is capable of sweeping ballads as well as dazzling fast display. He teaches at Havana's Beny Moré School of Improvised Music and at the Banff Center for the Arts in Canada, and directs the annual Cuban Jazz festival.

Ken Vandermark

(Tenor saxophone, clarinet, b. 1961)

Ken Vandermark studied film before turning to music with a trio in Boston in the mid-1980s. He moved to Chicago in 1989, playing reeds with a flinty, aggressive sound. His investigations of free improvisation won him a five-year MacArthur Foundation 'genius' grant in 1999

Above

Mali musician Ali Farka Toure found widespread fame following a 1994 collaboration with guitarist Ry Cooder.

Ali Farka Toure

(Guitar, gurkel, n'jarka, vocals, 1939–2006)

Toure based his distinctive style on the music of his native Mali and on American blues and R&B – in particular John Lee Hooker, whose simple yet inimitable hypnotic drones are echoed in Toure's songs. Five earlier albums had made Toure a cult favourite when his 1994 Grammy-winning collaboration with slide guitarist Ry Cooder, *Talking Timbuktu*, elevated him to *éminence grise* of the world music scene.

see Introduction pp 342 *see* Sources & Sounds pp 344

and he has used the funding to invest in further recordings and his international career, including membership in saxophonist Peter Brotzmann's high-energy Tentet.

Jeff 'Tain' Watts

(Drums, b. 1960)

Watts played timpani in the Pittsburgh Youth Symphony Orchestra during his teens and vibraphone at Berklee School of Music, where he met the Marsalis brothers. He recorded with Wynton Marsalis from 1981 and then with Branford, following him into the house band of the televised *Tonight Show*. An explosive polyrhythmist who can also provide restrained accompaniment, 'Tain' is much in demand for sessions by many jazz modernists.

Cassandra Wilson

(Vocals, composer, b. 1955)

Raised in Mississippi, smoky contralto Wilson sang R&B and folk music, but emerged in New York in the early 1980s as a member of the M-Base Collective and with Henry Threadgill's band. Her breakout album *Blue Skies* (1988) reprised jazz standards and she starred in Wynton Marsalis' oratorio *Blood on the Fields*, but the cornerstone of her mature style is *Blue Light 'Til Dawn* (1993), in which she performs original songs, famous blues and unusual rock/pop choices with interesting arrangements.

John Zorn

(Alto saxophone, composer, b. 1953)

New Yorker John Zorn deconstructed bebop themes in the late 1970s and created musical games that dictated improvisational structures. He plays assertively in bands such as Masada, purveying electric funk, Japanese pop and punk rock. Zorn has encouraged other renegade musicians by establishing music policies at venues and curating international festivals. As principal of Tzadik Records, he jump-started the avant-garde klezmer and 'Radical Jewish Culture' movements. He remains a prolific composer and has also branched into film soundtracks and chamber music.

Above

Cassandra Wilson's mellow vocals are ideally suited to jazz- and blues-tinged material.

Far Left Bottom

Accomplished jazz drummer Jeff 'Tain' Watts has forged a career working with legendary musicians such as B.B. King and Wynton Marsalis.

see John Lee Hooker pp 158 *see* Ry Cooder pp 303 *see* Wynton Marsalis pp 326 *see* Henry Threadgill pp 338

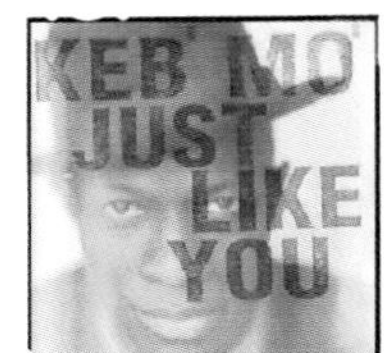

List of Artists

Entries appear in the following order: name, music style, year(s) of popularity, instruments, country of origin.

Affif, Ron, Hard Bop; Jazz Rock, 1990s–, Guitar, American
Albion Jazz Band, Dixieland Revival, 1990s, Various instruments, Canadian
Alexander, Eric, Modern Jazz, 1990s–, Saxophone, American
Allen, Geri, Free Jazz; Modern Jazz, 1990s–, Piano, American
Alvim, Cesarius, Modern Jazz, 1990s–, Bass, piano, composer, Brazilian
Anderson, Fred, Free Jazz, 1990s–, Saxophone, American
Arc Angels, The, Blues Rock, 1990s, Various instruments, American
Armstrong, James, Modern Electric Blues, 1990s–, Vocals, guitar, composer, American
Arriale, Lynne, Modern Jazz, 1990s–, Piano, bandleader, American
Assad, Badi, Brazilian Jazz, 1990s, Guitar, Brazilian
Avery, Teodross, Modern Jazz, 1990s–, Saxophone, American
Bailey, Derek, Free Jazz, 1990s–, Guitar, British
Barretto, Carlos, Modern Jazz, 1990s–, Bass, composer, Portuguese
Battaglia, Stefano, Free Jazz; Modern Jazz, 1990s–, Piano, bandleader, Italian
Batuque, Grupo, Brazilian Jazz, 1990s, Various instruments, Brazilian
Bedard, George, Blues Rock, 1990s, Vocals, guitar, American
Bell, Lurrie, Modern Electric Blues; Chicago Blues, 1990s, Guitar, American
Bell, T.D., Texas Blues; Modern Electric Blues, 1990s, Guitar, American
Benoit, Tab, Modern Electric Blues, 1990s–, Guitar, vocals, composer, American
Bernstein, Steven, World Fusion; Modern Jazz, 1990s–, Trumpet, composer, arranger, American
Bibb, Eric, Folk Blues; Modern Acoustic Blues, 1990s–, Vocals, guitar, composer, American
Big Dave & the Ultrasonics, Blues Rock; Modern Electric Blues, 1990s, Various instruments, American
Big Sugar, Blues Rock, 1990s, Various instruments, Canadian
Bishop, Elvin, Modern Electric Blues, 1990s–, Guitar, American
Blade, Brian, Modern Jazz; Jazz Rock; Fusion, 1990s–, Drums, American
Blake, Seamus, Hard Bop; Modern Jazz, 1990s–, Saxophone, Canadian
Blakeslee, Rob, Free Jazz, 1990s–, Trumpet, flugelhorn, clarinet, American
Bluebirds, The, Blues Rock, 1990s–, Various instruments, American
Blues Traveler, Blues Rock, 1990s–, Various instruments, American
Boney James, Fusion; Smooth Jazz, 1990s–, Saxophone, American
Botti, Chris, Smooth Jazz, 1990s–, Trumpet, American
Braam, Michiel, Modern Jazz, 1990s–, Piano, bandleader, Dutch
Branch, Billy, Chicago Blues, 1990s–, Vocals, harmonica, American
Brand New Heavies, Acid Jazz, 1990s–, Various instruments, British
Breaux, Zachary, Soul Jazz, 1990s, Guitar, American
Bridgewater, Dee Dee, Modern Jazz, 1990s–, Vocals, American
Brown, Carlinhos, Brazilian Jazz, 1990s–, Percussion, Brazilian
Brown, Jeri, Bebop; Modern Jazz, 1990s–, Vocals, American
Buena Vista Social Club, Latin Jazz, 1990s–, Various instruments, Cuban
Burks, Eddie, Modern Electric Blues, 1990s–2000s, Vocals, harmonica, American
Burnside, R.L., Delta Blues; Modern Electric Blues, 1990s–, Guitar, vocals, American
Burton, Abraham, Hard Bop; Modern Jazz, 1990s–, Saxophone, bandleader, American
Butler Twins, Modern Electric Blues, 1990s–2000s, Various instruments, American
Byron, Don, Free Jazz; Modern Jazz, 1990s–, Clarinet, bandleader, American
Caine, Uri, Free Jazz; Modern Jazz, 1990s–, Piano, composer, American
Campbell, John, Modern Jazz, 1990s–, Piano, American
Cardenas, Steve, Modern Jazz, 1990s–, Guitar, American
Carter, James, Hard Bop, 1990s–, Saxophones, American
Carter, Regina, Jazz Funk; Modern Jazz, 1990s–, Violin, American
Cary, Marc, Modern Jazz, 1990s–, Piano, American
Catney, Dave, Modern Jazz, 1990s–, Vocals, piano, American
Charlap, Bill, Modern Jazz, 1990s–, Piano, American
Cheek, Chris, Free Jazz; Fusion, 1990s–, Saxophone, American
Chestnut, Cyrus, Hard Bop; Modern Jazz, 1990s–, Piano, American
Clarvis, Paul, Free Jazz, 1990s–, Percussion, British
Cleaver, Gerald, Free Jazz; Modern Jazz, 1990s–, Drums, American
Cohen, Avishai, Hard Bop; Modern Jazz; Fusion, 1990s–, Bass, Israeli
Coleman, Deborah, Modern Electric Blues, 1990s–, Guitar, vocals, American
Coltrane, Ravi, Hard Bop; Modern Jazz, 1990s–, Saxophone, American
Coolbone Brass Band, Acid Jazz, 1990s–, Various instruments, American
Copeland, Shemekia, Modern Electric Blues, 1990s–, Vocals, American
Corduroy, Acid Jazz, 1990s–, Various instruments, British
Courvoisier, Sylvie, Free Jazz, 1990s–, Piano, Swiss
Cox, Bruce, Jazz Funk; Free Jazz, 1990s–, Drums, American
Croce, A.J., All Jazz Styles, 1990s–, Piano, vocals, composer, American
Cusic, Eddie, Country Blues, 1990s–, Vocals, guitar, American
D*Note, Acid Jazz, 1990s–, Various instruments, British
D'Influence, Acid Jazz, 1990s–, Various instruments, British
Dahl, Carsten, Modern Jazz; Hard Bop, 1990s–, Piano, Danish
Davis, Guy, Country Blues; Folk Blues, 1990s, Vocals, guitar, harmonica, American
Davis, Xavier, Modern Jazz, 1990s–, Piano, American

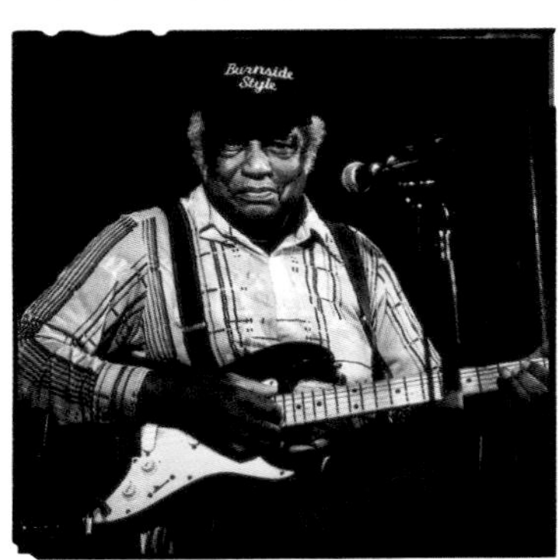

DeBethmann, Pierre, Modern Jazz, 1990s–, Piano, French
DeFrancesco, Joey, Soul Jazz; Hard Bop, 1990s–, Organ, piano, trumpet, American
Delbecq, Benoit, Free Jazz; Modern Jazz, 1990s–, Piano, keyboards, French
Delius, Tobias, Modern Jazz, 1990s–, Saxophone, British
DiBattista, Stefano, Modern Jazz; Hard Bop, 1990s–, Saxophone, Italian
Dickey, Whit, Free Jazz, 1990s–, Drums, American
DJ Greyboy, Acid Jazz, 1990s, DJ, producer, American
DKV Trio, Free Jazz, 1990s–, Various instruments, American
Dobbins, Bill, Modern Jazz, 1990s–, Piano, American
Doky Brothers, Hard Bop, 1990s, Various instruments, Danish
Domancich, Sophia, Free Jazz, 1990s–, Piano, composer, French
Doneda, Michel, Free Jazz, 1990s–, Saxophone, bandleader, French
Dorsey, Leon Lee, Modern Jazz, 1990s–, Bass, American
Douglas, Dave, Free Jazz; Modern Jazz, 1990s–, Trumpet, bandleader, American
Dread Flimstone, Acid Jazz, 1990s, DJ, producer, American
Drew, Kenny Jr, Hard Bop; Modern Jazz, 1990s–, Piano, American
Drummond, Billy, Hard Bop, 1990s, Drums, American
Duarte, Chris, Blues Rock, 1990s–, Guitar, vocals, American
Ducret, Marc, Free Jazz, 1990s–, Guitar, French
Dupree, Big Al, Modern Electric Blues, 1990s–2000s, Vocals, piano, saxophone, American
Duval, Dominic, Free Jazz; Modern Jazz, 1990s–, Bass, American
Dyer, Ann, Free Jazz, 1990s–, Vocals, American
Elling, Kurt, Modern Jazz, 1990s–, Vocals, American
Ellis, Tinsley, Modern Electric Blues, 1990s–, Guitar, American
Erickson, Craig, Modern Electric Blues, 1990s–, Guitar, American
Farnsworth, Joe, Hard Bop, 1990s–, Drums, American
Farr, Deitra, Modern Electric Blues; Jump Blues; Chicago Blues, 1990s–, Vocals, American
Faulk, Dan, Hard Bop, 1990s–, Saxophone, American
Fields, Scott, Free Jazz, 1990s–, Guitar, composer, American

Flynn, Billy, Modern Electric Blues, 1990s–, Guitar, American
Foley, Sue, Modern Electric Blues, 1990s–, Vocals, guitar, Canadian
Formanek, Michael, Free Jazz; Modern Jazz, 1990s–, Bass, composer, American
Fourplay, Smooth Jazz, 1990s–, Various instruments, American
Freelon, Nnenna, Modern Jazz, 1990s–, Vocals, American
Fresu, Paolo, Free Jazz, 1990s–, Trumpet, flugelhorn, composer, bandleader, Italian
Friedlander, Erik, Free Jazz, 1990s–, Cello, American
Frisell, Bill, Fusion, 1990s–, Guitar, American
Froman, Ian, Modern Jazz; Hard Bop, 1990s–, Drums, Canadian
Fryland, Thomas, Modern Jazz; Big Band, 1990s–, Trumpet, Danish
Fujii, Satoko, Free Jazz; Big Band, 1990s–, Piano, Japanese
Galliano, Acid Jazz, 1990s, Various instruments, British
Garner, Larry, Modern Electric Blues, 1990s–, Vocals, guitar, composer, American
Garzone, George, Modern Jazz, 1990s–, Saxophone, American
Gjerstad, Frode, Free Jazz, 1990s–, Saxophone, Norwegian
Gogo, David, Modern Electric Blues, 1990s–, Vocals, guitar, Canadian
Goldberg, Ben, Hard Bop; Free Jazz, 1990s–, Clarinet, bandleader, American
Grassy Knoll, The, Acid Jazz, 1990s, Various instruments, American
Greyboy Allstars, Acid Jazz, 1990s, Various instruments, American
Groove Collective, Acid Jazz, 1990s–, Various instruments, American
Haddix, Travis, Modern Electric Blues, 1990s–, Vocals, guitar, American
Hargrove, Roy, Hard Bop, 1990s–, Trumpet, American
Harris, Allan, Swing, 1990s–, Vocals, American
Harris, Corey, Delta Blues; Modern Electric Blues, 1990s–, Vocals, guitar, American
Harris, Stefon, Free Jazz; Modern Jazz, 1990s–, Vibraphone, American
Hart, Alvin Youngblood, Country Blues, 1990s–, Vocals, guitar, American
Hart, Antonio, Hard Bop; Modern Jazz, 1990s–, Saxophone, American
Hatch, Provine Little, Modern Electric Blues, 1990s–2000s, Vocals, harmonica, American
Hill, Michael, Blues Rock, 1990s–, Guitar, American
Hoax, The, British Blues; Blues Rock, 1990s–, Various instruments, British
Hobgood, Laurence, Free Jazz; Modern Jazz, 1990s–, Piano, American
Hole, Dave, Modern Electric Blues, 1990s–, Vocals, guitar, Australian
Horn, Shirley, Traditional Jazz, 1990s–, Piano, vocals, American
Hornbuckle, Linda, Modern Electric Blues, 1990s–, Vocals, American
Houle, Francois, Free Jazz, 1990s–, Clarinet, Canadian
Hunter, Charlie, Jazz Rock; Fusion, 1990s–, Guitar, American
Ibarra, Susie, Free Jazz, 1990s–, Drums, American
Iyer, Vijay, World Fusion, 1990s–, Piano, composer, American
Jackson, D.D., Modern Jazz, 1990s–, Piano, bandleader, Canadian
Jackson, Fruteland, Country Blues, 1990s–, Vocals, guitar, American
James, Colin, Modern Electric Blues; Jump Blues, 1990s–, Vocals, guitar, Canadian
Jamiroquai, Acid Jazz, 1990s–, Various instruments, British
Jensen, Ingrid, Hard Bop, 1990s–, Trumpet, Canadian
Jhelisa, Acid Jazz, 1990s, Vocals, British
Johnson, Luther 'Houserocker', Modern Electric Blues, 1990s–, Guitar, vocals, American
Jones, Norah, Smooth Jazz, 1990s–, Vocals, piano, American
Jones, Tutu, Modern Electric Blues, 1990s–, Guitar, drums, American
Jordan, Ronny, Acid Jazz, 1990s–, Guitar, British
Jumpin' The Gunn, Blues Rock; British Blues, 1990s, Various instruments, British
Karayorgis, Pandelis, Free Jazz, 1990s–, Piano, Greek
Keb' Mo', Blues Rock, 1990s–, Guitar, songwriter, American

Keene, Steven, Contemporary Blues; Folk Blues; Blues Rock, 1990s–, Guitar, harmonica, American
Keller, Sue, Ragtime, 1990s–, Piano, American
Kelly, Vance, Modern Electric Blues; Chicago Blues, 1990s–, Vocals, guitar, American
Kessler, Siegfried, Free Jazz, 1990s–, Piano, German
Kimbrough, Junior, Modern Electric Blues; Delta Blues; Country Blues, 1990s, Guitar, composer, American
King, Chris Thomas, Modern Electric Blues; Louisiana Blues, 1990s–, Vocals, guitar, American
King, Little Jimmy, Modern Electric Blues, 1990s–2000s, Vocals, guitar, American
King, Nancy, Modern Jazz, 1990s–, Vocals, American
King, Shirley, Modern Electric Blues, 1990s, Artist, American
Kinsey Report, Modern Electric Blues; Chicago Blues, 1990s, Various instruments, American
Knock-Out Greg & Blue Weather, Modern Electric Blues; Chicago Blues; Delta Blues, 1990s–, Various instruments, Swedish
Krall, Diana, Swing, 1990s–, Vocals, piano, Canadian
Kubek, Smokin' Joe, Modern Electric Blues, 1990s–, Guitar, American
Lagrene, Birelli, Gypsy Jazz; Fusion, 1990s–, Guitar, French
Lamb, Paul, Chicago Blues, 1990s–, Harmonica, British
Lang, Jonny, Modern Electric Blues, 1990s–, Vocals, guitar, American
Lee, Bonnie, Chicago Blues, 1990s–, Vocals, American
Lincoln, Abbey, Free Jazz; Modern Jazz, 1990s–, Vocals, composer, American
Lloyd, Jon, Free Jazz; Modern Jazz, 1990s–, Saxophone, British
Locke, Joe, Modern Jazz; Smooth Jazz, 1990s–, Vibraphone, arranger, American
Louis, Big Joe, & his Blues Kin, British Blues, 1990s, Various instruments, British
Lovano, Joe, Hard Bop, 1990s–, Saxophones, American
Lundgren, Jan, Hard Bop; Bebop, 1990s–, Piano, Swedish
Madcat & Kane, Rhythm & Blues, 1990s, Harmonica, guitar, American
Magic Dick, Blues Rock; Modern Electric Blues, 1990s, Harmonica, American
Manfreds, The, Blues Rock; Rhythm & Blues, 1990s–, Various instruments, British
McBride, Christian, Hard Bop, 1990s–, Bass, bandleader, American
McCray, Larry, Modern Electric Blues, 1990s–, Vocals, guitar, American
Medeski, Martin & Wood, Modern Jazz; Funk, 1990s–, Various instruments, American
Memphis Sheiks, Country Blues, 1990s, Various instruments, American
Messer, Mike, British Blues, 1990s–, Guitar, British
Mingus Big Band, Big Band, 1990s–, Various instruments, American
Mondo Grosso, Acid Jazz, 1990s–, Various instruments, Japanese
Mooney, John, Ragtime; Delta Blues, 1990s–, Guitar, vocals, American
Morgan, Mike, Modern Electric Blues; Texas Blues, 1990s–, Guitar, American
Morganfield, 'Big' Bill, Chicago Blues, 2000s–, Vocals, guitar, American
Neville Brothers, The, Rhythm & Blues, 1990s–, Various instruments, American
Nocturne, Johnny Band, Jump Blues; Modern Electric Blues, 1990s–, Various instruments, American
Nulisch, Darrell, Texas Blues; Modern Electric Blues, 1990s–, Vocals, harmonica, American
O'Farrill, Arturo, Lating Jazz, 1990s–, Piano, leader, Cuban
Okey Dokey Stompers, British Blues, 1990s–, Various instruments, British
Osby, Greg, Free Jazz; Modern Jazz, 1990s–, Saxophone, American
Outback, World Fusion, 1990s, Various instruments, British
Palm Skin Productions, Acid Jazz, 1990s–, Producer, British
Parker, Evan, Free Jazz, 1990s–, Saxophones, British
Parker, William, Free Jazz, 1990s–, Bass, American
Parrish, Michael, Country Blues, 1990s, Piano, guitar, American
Payton, Nicholas, New Orleans Jazz; Modern Jazz, 1990s–, Trumpet, bandleader, American
Peterson, Giles, Acid Jazz, 1990s–, DJ, British
Peterson, Lucky, Modern Electric Blues, 1990s–, Vocals, guitar, keyboard, American
Peterson, Ralph, Free Jazz, 1990s–, Drums, composer, American
Pollock, Marilyn Middleton, New Orleans Jazz, 1990s–, Singer, American
Popa Chubby, Blues Rock, 1990s, Guitar, American
Potter, Chris, Modern Jazz, 2000s–, Saxophones, American
Primrich, Gary, Modern Electric Blues, 1990s–, Vocals, harmonica, American
Qualls, Henry, Texas Blues; Modern Electric Blues, 1990s–2000s, Guitar, American
Rava, Enrico, Free Jazz; Modern Jazz, 1990s–, Trumpet, Italian
Rebello, Jason, Modal Jazz; Hard Bop; Fusion, 1990s–, Piano, British
Red Snapper, Acid Jazz, 1990s–, Various instruments, British

Redman, Joshua, Modern Jazz, 1990s–, Saxophone, bandleader, American
Reed, Eric, Modern Jazz, 1990s–, Piano, American
Reeves, Dianne, Modern Jazz, 1990s–, Vocals, American
Rishell, Paul & Annie Raines, Country Blues, 1990s–, Guitar, vocals, harmonica, American
Roach, Michael, Country Blues; Folk Blues, 2000s, Vocals, guitar, American
Roberts, David Thomas, Ragtime, 1990s–, Composer, American
Robillard, Duke, Modern Electric Blues, 1990s–, Vocals, guitar, American
Robinson, Reginald R., Ragtime, 1990s–, Piano, American
Rodgers, Paul, Blues Rock, 1990s–, Vocals, British
Rodgers, Mighty Mo, Soul Blues; Rhythm & Blues, 1990s–, Keyboards, vocals, American
Rubalcaba, Gonzalo, Latin Jazz, 1990s–, Keyboards, Cuban
Rush, Bobby, Rhythm & Blues, 1990s–, Vocals, guitar, harmonica, American
Saffire; The Uppity Blues Women, Country Blues, 1990s–, Various instruments, American
Sandals, Acid Jazz, 1990s, Various instruments, British
Schneider, Maria, Big Band, 1990s–, Piano, composer, arranger, bandleader, American
Scott, E.C., Soul Blues; Rhythm & Blues; Modern Electric Blues, 1990s–, Vocals, American
Sease, Marvin, Rhythm & Blues, 1990s–, Vocals, composer, American
Shannon, Mem, Modern Electric Blues, 1990s–, Vocals, guitar, American
Shannon, Preston, Modern Electric Blues; Rhythm & Blues, 2000s–, Vocals, guitar, American
Sharp, Elliott, Contemporary Blues; Modern Electric Blues; Modern Delta Blues, 1990s–, Guitar, bass, reeds, programming, vocals, American
Sharpe, B.J., Blues Rock, 1990s, Vocals, American
Shepherd, Kenny Wayne, Modern Electric Blues, 1990s–, Vocals, guitar, American
Shields, Lonnie, Modern Electric Blues; Rhythm & Blues, 1990s–, Vocals, guitar, American
Shipp, Matthew, Free Jazz, 1990s–, Piano, composer, American
Silva, Robertinho, Brazilian Jazz, 1990s, Drums, percussion, Brazilian
Simmonds, Kim, Blues Rock, 1990s–, Guitar, harmonica, piano, vocals, British
Slide Five, Acid Jazz, 1990s, Various instruments, American
Smith, Willie 'Big Eyes', Modern Electric Blues, 1990s–, Drums, American
Spady, Clarence, Modern Electric Blues, 2000s, Vocals, guitar, American
Stern, Peggy, Hard Bop, 1990s–, Piano, American
Storyville, Blues Rock, 1990s, Various instruments, American
Strehli, Angela, Modern Electric Blues, 1990s–, Vocals, American
Sumlin, Hubert, Chicago Blues; Modern Electric Blues, 1990s, Guitar, American
Sweet Pain, Rhythm & Blues, 1990s–, Various instruments, British
Taylor, Melvin, & the Slack Band, Modern Electric Blues, 1990s, Various instruments, American
Taylor, Otis, Folk Blues; Modern Acoustic Blues, 2000s, Vocals, guitar, banjo, harmonica, composer, American
Taylor, Sam, Jump Blues, 1990s, Guitar, composer, American
Tedeschi, Susan, Modern Electric Blues, 2000s, Vocals, guitar, American
Terrasson, Jacky, Modern Jazz, 1990s–, Piano, keyboards, bandleader, German
Thomas, Earl, Rhythm & Blues, 1990s–, Vocals, composer, American
Toure, Ali Farka, Modern Electric Blues, 1990s–, Guitar, vocals, percussion, Malinese
Tramontana, Sebi, Free Jazz, 1990s–, Trombone, Italian
Trout, Walter, Blues Rock, 1990s–, Guitar, American
United Future Organization, Acid Jazz, 1990s–, Various instruments, Japanese
Valdes, Chucho, Latin Jazz, 1990s–, Piano, Cuban
Vandermark, Ken, Free Jazz, 1990s–, Saxophones, clarinet, American
Vicari, Andrea, Modern Jazz, 1990s–, Piano, composer, American
Watson, Junior, West Coast Blues, 1990s, Guitar, vocals, American
Watts, Jeff 'Tain', Modern Jazz, 1990s–, Drums, American
Weathersby, Carl, Modern Electric Blues, 1990s–, Guitar, American
Welch, Mike, Contemporary Blues, 1990s–, Guitar, American
West Coast All Stars, Traditional Jazz, 1990s, Various instruments, American
White, Charles, West Coast Blues, 1990s–, Vocals, American
Wilson, Cassandra, World Fusion, 1990s–, Vocals, American
Willson, Michelle, Jump Blues, 1990s–, Vocals, American
Wilson, U.P., Texas Blues; Modern Electric Blues, 1990s–2000s, Vocals, guitar, American
Wong, Francis, Modern Jazz, 1990s–, Saxophone, American
Yeoh, Nikki, Fusion, 1990s–, Piano, composer, British
Young, Zora, Modern Electric Blues, 1990s–, Vocals, American
Zorn, John, Free Jazz, 1990s–, Saxophone, composer, bandleader, American

see Chris Thomas King pp 358 see Walter Trout pp 366 see Jeff 'Tain' Watts pp 367 see John Zorn pp 367

THE STYLES

JAZZ STYLES

The diversity and flexibility of jazz music is due in part to the high calibre of its artists. A long line of hugely talented and inventive players and bandleaders through the decades, such as Louis Armstrong, Jelly Roll Morton, Count Basie, Coleman Hawkins, Lester Young, Dizzy Gillespie, Charlie Parker, Miles Davis, Bill Evans and John Coltrane, have ensured that jazz has continued to move along and develop at an extraordinary rate and in unprecedented directions, never remaining in one place long enough to become stale or uninteresting.

From the syncopated rhythms of ragtime to the unrestricted outpourings of free jazz; from the stripped-back, simple musical structures of the Dixieland revival to the outlandish sounds of jazz rock and from the often minimalist recordings of cool jazz to the passionate invocations of Latin jazz, this multi-faceted genre embraces an incredibly wide range of different styles, reflecting the changing times and the many cultural, social and geographical influences that informed its creators. The fact that conflicting factions exist within the jazz scene (e.g. the Modernists v Moldy Figs debate of the 1950s) is surely testament to the enormous musical variety that it encompasses.

This section of the book examines in detail each of the main styles of jazz, describing the circumstances, people and events that helped to develop the music, as well as discussing the most important artists, composers and recordings and looking at the defining features of the style's sound.

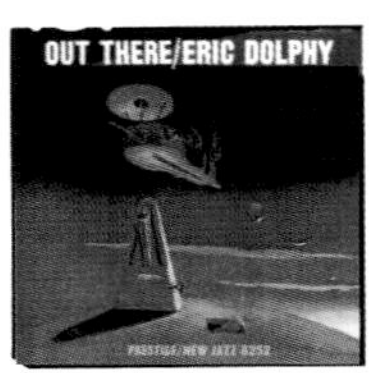

Introduction

STYLES

- Ragtime
- New Orleans
- Chicago
- Swing
- Bebop
- Dixieland Revival
- Cool Jazz
- Hard Bop
- Free Jazz
- Soul Jazz
- Fusion & Jazz Rock
- Acid Jazz
- Smooth Jazz
- Latin Jazz
- Brazilian Jazz

Like a great river that runs endlessly, forming numerous tributary streams as it flows, jazz continues to evolve over time. And no matter how far the River Jazz may flow from its source – whether through stylistic evolution or technological innovation – the essential spirit of the music remains intact.

Granted, the more academic and esoteric extrapolations of avant-gardists such as Anthony Braxton and Cecil Taylor may, on the surface of it, appear to be light years away from the early innovations and earthy expressions of Louis Armstrong and Sidney Bechet. In essence, however, both widely divergent approaches are imbued with that spirit of spontaneous creativity, risk-taking and discovery that is at the core of all jazz. Regardless of what instruments are being used; whether the general tone is harshly electric or purely acoustic; and whether the form is defined by straight 4/4 time, or more intricate rhythmic variations, or no time at all; jazz is, in all of its manifestations, fundamentally about improvising and the art of playing without premeditation – or, in the parlance of Louis Armstrong, 'taking a scale and making it wail'.

'Jazz has got to have that thing. You have to be born with it. You can't learn it, you can't buy it and no critic can put it into any words. It speaks in the music. It speaks for itself.'

Miles Davis

Cool jazz or fusion, swing-era big bands or bebop quintets, Dixieland or the avant-garde: the music thrives on a collective spirit of interplay and the daring chances taken by the participants individually or as a group, and strictly in the moment. Jazz is, as the noted critic Whitney Balliett once called it, 'the sound of surprise'. The phrase could be applied as accurately to Armstrong's 1928 duets with Earl Hines as it could to Charlie Parker's pyrotechnic excursions in 1945 with kindred spirit Dizzy Gillespie; or to Eric Dolphy's 1960 opus *Out There*, the Art Ensemble of Chicago's 1973 classic *Fanfare For The Warriors*, alto-saxophonist Steve Coleman's radical M-Base experiments of the mid-1980s, or trumpeter Dave Douglas's compelling, Middle Eastern-flavoured offering from 2001, *Witness*.

Jazz has been called the quintessential American music, the ultimate in rugged individualism and the creative process incarnate. In its infancy, it was

Above Right
Innovative jazz legend, Louis Armstrong, one of the twentieth century's most famous performers.

Right
Two of the greatest innovators in jazz, Charlie Parker (centre) and Miles Davis (right), with bass player Tommy Potter. Parker and Davis were instrumental in bringing jazz forward to a new era.

see Jazz Styles Introduction pp 372 *see* New Orleans Jazz pp 380 *see* Bebop pp 386 *see* Fusion & Jazz Rock pp 398

dismissed by one pointed newspaper editorial as 'a manifestation of a low streak in man's taste that has not yet come out in civilization's wash'. In more modern times, it has been hailed as one of the noblest forms of human expression, with a deep and direct connection to the soul. It is about individuals filling space with invention while negotiating their agendas within a group; an improvisational art that thrives on freedom of expression yet demands selfless collaboration.

New Orleans was the nexus for its genesis. A cultural melting pot where people of all nationalities lived side by side, New Orleans was one of the richest, most cosmopolitan cities in America during the early 1800s. It was in this integrated society that strains of melodies from the West Indies began to mingle with traces of African polyrhythms, carried over by slaves and European classical music played by Creoles (the free and prosperous light-skinned descendants of French and Spanish colonists and their African wives and mistresses). Many of these Creole musicians, who identified with their European and not their African ancestors, were classically trained. Added to the mix were minstrel tunes and plantation songs, work songs and spirituals, along with the constant sound of brass bands parading around the Crescent City at weddings, funerals and picnics, as well as during the six- to eight-week carnival season leading up to Mardi Gras. This incredible hodgepodge of sound would eventually lead to ragtime at the outset of the 1890s.

In 1896, a landmark decision by the US Supreme Court would change the face of New Orleans music forever. This 'separate but equal' ruling institutionalized segregation between the races, effectively forcing classically trained Creole musicians into the black community, where they merged their technical fluency on various instruments with the blues-inflected music of black bands. Together, they would create a new music that began to emerge at the dawn of the new twentieth century. Something beyond ragtime or blues, it was initially called 'hot music', to convey its fiery nature, and later dubbed 'jass' (a name that came from the jasmine perfume favoured by prostitutes in Storyville). By 1907, around the time that the pianist-composer Jelly Roll Morton began to blend ragtime with minstrel songs, the blues and habañera dance rhythms from the Caribbean (which he described as the all-important 'Spanish tinge'), the term had eventually morphed into 'jazz' and it has remained there to this day.

Above
It was in New Orleans that Creole and African musical influences combined to create the musical style we know as jazz. This scene shows Canal Street in 1924, when New Orleans jazz was well under way.

While the facts of where jazz came from and how it evolved over time are indisputable, the question of where jazz is going – or, indeed, should be headed – is a topic of heated debate. On the one hand, staunch traditionalists believe jazz to be a precious, homemade American art music that ought to be preserved and disseminated intact. This 'curator' notion has led to the formation of various repertoire bands in the United States, chief among them the Lincoln Center Jazz

see Louis Armstrong pp 44 *see* Jelly Roll Morton pp 60 *see* Sidney Bechet pp 69 *see* Anthony Braxton pp 302

Orchestra in New York (for which the trumpeter Wynton Marsalis serves as artistic director). Since its formation in 1988, the LCJO has taken on the task of presenting the works of jazz masters such as Duke

Above
Sidney Bechet played the clarinet and soprano saxophone with a clear, penetrating tone that soared above the other instruments in the band. As a young man Bechet played in Bunk Johnson's Eagle Band.

Ellington, Sidney Bechet, Jelly Roll Morton, Thelonious Monk and others to largely subscription audiences at the prestigious Alice Tully Hall in the Lincoln Center complex.

Others maintain that the jazz tradition is one of innovation itself, and that the music must adapt to new times in order to survive. Indeed, many movements that came along throughout the course of jazz history were direct reactions to some previous, prevailing movement: as bebop was to swing, as hard bop was to the cool school, as the avant-garde movement was to mainstream jazz, and so on. Rather than supplanting a previous style, each new movement is an extension, that builds on the past while retaining some inherent qualities of previous styles. So, in Dizzy Gillespie's pyrotechnic trumpet work at the height of the bebop era in the late 1940s we can still hear something of Louis Armstrong; in Cecil Taylor's turbulent piano work we can still hear traces of his heroes Duke Ellington, Bud Powell and Fats Waller; in revolutionary, alto saxophonists such as Ornette Coleman and Eric Dolphy we can hear a direct connection to Charlie Parker.

Through the miracle of technology, we are now hearing something of the past masters (quite literally) in new hybrid forms such as hip hop jazz and smooth jazz. Countless beats from early 1960s Blue Note and Prestige soul-jazz recordings have been digitally sampled and looped to create the foundation for rhythm tracks on modern-day, cutting-edge recordings. The smooth jazz saxophone star Kenny G went one step further by brazenly 'dueting' with Louis Armstrong (via sampling) on 'What A Wonderful World', from his 1999 CD, *Classics In The Key Of G*.

Whether jazz remains an exclusive or inclusive art form, there is no denying the impact of other cultures on this quintessentially American music as it reaches ever outward. From its earliest manifestations at the turn of the twentieth century in the cultural gumbo of New Orleans, to the Afro-Cuban jazz collaborations of Dizzy Gillespie and Machito in the 1940s, to the groundbreaking cross-pollination efforts of Stan Getz in the early 1960s with *Jazz Samba* and *Getz/Gilberto*, to the incorporation of Eastern rhythms and scales during the 1970s by fusion groups such as the Mahavishnu Orchestra and Weather Report, jazz has a history of embracing other cultural expressions.

Today, numerous jazz artists (such as trumpeter Roy Hargrove, alto saxophonist Steve Coleman and soprano saxophonist Jane Bunnett, among others) have travelled to Havana to soak up and document the authentic Afro-Cuban vibe in their music. Others, such as Panamanian pianist Danilo Pérez, Argentine pianist-composer-arranger Guillermo Klein, Czech bassist

see Jazz Styles Introduction pp 372 *see* Swing pp 384 *see* Cool Jazz pp 390 *see* Smooth Jazz pp 402

George Mraz, Cameroonian bassist Richard Bona, Cuban trumpeter Arturo Sandoval, Norwegian alto saxophonist Jan Garbarek, Armenian percussionist Arto Tuncboyaçyin, Lithuanian pianist Vyacheslav Ganelin, Cuban piano sensation Gonzalo Rubalcaba, Tunisian oud player Anouar Brahem, Chinese pianist/composer Jon Jang, Indian alto saxophonist Rudresh Mahanthappa, Pakistani guitarist Fareed Haque, Chinese baritone saxophonist Fred Ho, Vietnamese guitarist Nguyên Lê, Swedish keyboard player Esbjörn Svensson, Cuban saxophonist/clarinetist Paquito D'Rivera, Swiss-Dutch vocalist Susanne Abbuehl, Japanese pianist/composer/arranger and big-band leader Toshiko Akiyoshi, Indian percussionist Zakir Hussain, Japanese pianist Satoko Fujii, Norwegian keyboard player Bugge Wesseltoft, Puerto Rican saxophonist David Sanchez, Brazilian percussionist Airto Moreira, Australian bassist Nicki Parrott, Irish guitarist David O'Rourke and Indian percussionist Trilok Gurtu (the list goes on and on) have mined the richness of their own cultural heritages to come up with other new and exciting hybrid forms of jazz. In the process, all have advanced the cause of jazz, taking the essence of the music to a new place through their bold experimentation and honest expression.

This living drama continues to unfold. Every trumpeter today, 100 years after the birth of jazz, still carries a little piece of Buddy Bolden, or King Oliver, or Louis Armstrong with him; every alto sax player a bit of Bird, every pianist something of Jelly Roll, every drummer a touch of Baby Dodds and so it goes on. Like Olympians carrying the eternal flame across the ages, they represent the past while charging full steam ahead into the future. In his own time and in his own way, each has made a unique contribution. This is the nature of jazz – continually flowing and changing, like the never-ending river.

Above
After experimenting with the 'jungle sound', involving the heavily muted trumpet of Bubber Miley, the Duke Ellington Orchestra found nationwide fame by accepting the position of house band at New York's Cotton Club.

Left
On *Blues & Roots*, Charles Mingus concentrated on the blues and gospel elements of his musical heritage.

see Duke Ellington pp 52 *see* Warren 'Baby' Dodds pp 72 *see* Charlie Parker pp 162 *see* Stan Getz pp 272

Ragtime

KEY ARTISTS

Tom Turpin
James Scott
Scott Joplin
Eubie Blake
Joseph Lamb
Max Morath
Joshua Rifkin
Reginald R. Robinson
David Thomas Roberts
Marcus Roberts

A forerunner of jazz, ragtime was derived from brass-band music and European folk melodies, African-American banjo music and spirituals, minstrel songs, military marches and European light classics.

The 'raggy' style, or ragged-time feeling, of this jaunty, propulsive, toe-tapping piano music refers to its inherent syncopation, where loud right-hand accents fall between the strong beats of the left-hand rather than on top of them. One noted practitioner, the pianist Eubie Blake (composer of the 1920s hit song 'I'm Just Wild About Harry'), summed it up simply: 'Ragtime is syncopation and improvising and accents'.

'Scorned by the Establishment as ephemeral at best, trashy at worst, ragtime was the fountainhead of every rhythmic and stylistic upheaval that has followed in a century of ever-evolving American popular music.'

Max Morath

While this highly syncopated style involved only limited improvisation and lacked a jazz-swing feel, it directly informed the work of the early jazz giant Jelly Roll Morton and served as a precursor to the Harlem stride piano movement of the 1920s, pioneered by James P. Johnson, Willie 'The Lion' Smith and Fats Waller. Ragtime could be heard as early as the 1880s in camps of workers building the great railroads across the American continent, as well as in travelling minstrel shows and vaudeville shows. By 1892, the composer Charles Ives had come across it in his hometown of Danbury, Connecticut. At the Chicago World's Fair that same year, many people heard ragtime for the first time. By 1896, the first pieces labelled 'ragtime' were published. The following year, some 20 rags were published. By 1899, 120 rags were issued in New Orleans.

Above
Scott Joplin wisely secured a royalty contract on 'Maple Leaf Rag', one of his most successful compositions. He received one cent for each copy sold, which, although hardly a princely sum, provided him with a steady income.

As piano rolls and sheet music appeared at the turn of the century, a ragtime fad swept the nation. Hordes of young people shocked their parents by kicking up their heels to this infectious new music, which was described alternately by critics and newspaper columnists as 'syncopation gone mad' and 'the product of our decadent art culture'.

The Ragtime King

Although Scott Joplin became the figurehead for this burgeoning new American music movement, there were several ragtime piano players who preceded him, including Walter Gould (known as One Leg Shadow), Tom Turpin, James Scott and One-Leg Willie Joseph, along with other ivory-tinkling 'professors' who plied their trade in brothels, gambling joints, saloons and private clubs. Following the phenomenal success of Joplin's 'Maple Leaf Rag', which sold 75,000 copies of sheet music in 1899 for the publisher John Stark and 500,000 copies within 10 years, he was dubbed 'King of Ragtime Writers' and presided over ragtime's reign as the main popular musical style of the US for nearly 20 years.

The son of a former slave, born in Texarkana, a town in the northeast corner of Texas, on 24 November 1868, Joplin was a piano prodigy with a musical education financed by his mother's work as a domestic servant. With aspirations to become a classical concert pianist, he played at the Chicago World's Fair in 1892 and later enrolled at the George R. Smith College for Negroes in Sedalia, Missouri (where he would write 'Maple Leaf Rag'). In 1901, Joplin moved to St. Louis to begin working with Stark, where he began to expand his writing from ragtime tunes to full-length pieces such as ballets and operas. The first of these, *A Guest Of Honor*, emerged in 1903.

see The Early Years Sources & Sounds pp 14 *see* The Twenties Sources & Sounds pp 36 *see* Jazz Styles Introduction pp 372

Left
Eubie Blake and Noble Sissle began writing songs together in 1915 and went on to have a successful writing and performing partnership, calling themselves 'The Dixie Duo'. They made their last recording together in 1968.

Rather than being improvised, Joplin's music was as formally composed and carefully worked out as any of Frédéric Chopin's études. And while he easily enchanted the masses with catchy numbers such as 'Maple Leaf Rag' and 'The Entertainer' (an infectious quality that Irving Berlin strived to emulate in 1911 with his 'Alexander's Ragtime Band'), Joplin longed to be taken seriously as a composer. He saw himself as a black American counterpart to Chopin or Strauss, a composer of new music for a new century. Joplin's death in 1917, just before the end of the First World War, effectively marked the beginning of the end of ragtime's supremacy in America. And although Zez Confrey had some success in the early 1920s with tunes such as 'Kitten On The Keys' and 'Dizzy Fingers', by the second decade of the twentieth century, attention had shifted dramatically to the new phenomenon of 'hot music' or 'jazz'. By 1930, ragtime was largely extinct. The legacy of the early ragtime pioneers lived on only through sheet music and piano rolls of their compositions: there were no recordings of any of the music. In fact, the year Joplin died was the same year in which the Original Dixieland Jass Band made the first jazz recording.

Ragtime Revival

More than half a century after Joplin's death, this rollicking, syncopated music enjoyed a revival in the early 1970s, sparked by three significant events. In 1971, the musicologist and pianist Joshua Rifkin recorded an album of Joplin's pieces for Nonesuch, which caught on with critics and the public alike. The following year, Joplin's 1915 ragtime opera, *Treemonisha*, was resurrected and staged at Atlanta's Memorial Arts Center. Then, in 1973, the pianist-composer Marvin Hamlisch used Joplin's 'The Entertainer' as the main theme for the Hollywood blockbuster *The Sting*, starring Paul Newman and Robert Redford. That Academy Award-winning film made Joplin a household name, helping to trigger renewed interest in his jaunty and sophisticated music.

Treemonisha was again staged by the Houston Grand Opera in May 1975 and brought to Broadway that October, contributing to Joplin being posthumously awarded a special Pulitzer Prize in 1976 for his contribution to American music. Joplin's legacy has been kept alive through the 1980s and 1990s by ragtime piano interpreters such as Terry Waldo, Butch Thompson, Dick Hyman and Marcus Roberts, as well as by prominent jazz instrumentalists such as Anthony Braxton, Archie Shepp, Ran Blake, Ron Miles, Bill Frisell and Wynton and Branford Marsalis. Original composers in the ragtime style, such as Mississippi's David Thomas Roberts and Chicago's Reginald Robinson, have helped to keep this nearly extinct music alive on the concert and recording scene over the past 10 years.

Below
Thomas 'Fats' Waller, along with his one-time piano tutor James P. Johnson, pioneered the stride piano style that grew out of ragtime. Stride (originally called 'shout') shared the basic structure of ragtime but was rhythmically looser.

see Eubie Blake pp 70 see James P. Johnson pp 76 see Fats Waller pp 85 see Wynton Marsalis pp 326

New Orleans

KEY ARTISTS

Buddy Bolden
Freddie Keppard
King Oliver
Jelly Roll Morton
Louis Armstrong
Kid Ory
Sidney Bechet
Johnny Dodds
Jimmie Noone
Original Dixieland Jass Band

Conditions were ripe for jazz to evolve in New Orleans at the turn of the twentieth century. A thriving port of immigration, where Africans and Creoles lived side by side with Italians, Germans, Irish, French, Mexicans and Cubans, New Orleans' unprecedented ethnic diversity allowed for a free and easy mingling of musical ideas between cultures.

Other factors contributed to the coalescing of jazz as a cultural expression unique to New Orleans. The call-and-response tradition of West African music was retained in many Baptist churches of the South, particularly in New Orleans, while concepts of polyrhythm and improvisation within group participation (qualities inherent in African drumming ensembles) were kept alive in the Crescent City at Congo Square, an authorized venue where slaves would gather to recreate their drumming and dancing traditions. These African drumming concepts, and indeed the very notion of percussiveness as musical expression, would seep into the cultural consciousness of New Orleans.

'Arguably the happiest of all music is New Orleans jazz. The sound of several horns all improvising together on fairly simple chord changes with definite roles for each instrument but a large amount of freedom cannot help but sound consistently joyful.'

Scott Yanow

Let The Good Times Roll

The foundation for a new hybrid music was set by a combination of the African notion of rhythm that swings, or has a propulsive motion, with the European classical influences brought into the mix by ragtime and sophisticated Creole musicians. Add a thriving brass band tradition, which developed in the late-nineteenth century from the plentiful supply of cheap brass band instruments left behind after the Civil War, blend in rhythmic and melodic elements from Cuba, the West Indies and the Caribbean, and factor in the slightly decadent and pervasive 'party time' atmosphere of the City That Care Forgot (typified by the pageantry of Mardi Gras, as well as the city's unofficial motto, 'Laissez les bons temps rouler' or 'Let the good times roll'), and you have a potent recipe for jazz.

Out of this rich cultural gumbo came Charles 'Buddy' Bolden, the first bona fide jazz star of the twentieth century. A cornetist of unparalleled power, Bolden's innovative approach took the essence of ragtime and put a looser, hotter, bluesier spin on it, grabbing dancers in the process. By 1895, Bolden was leading his own group in residence at New Orleans' Globe Theater, where he held court as 'King' Bolden. By 1901, his popularity spread from playing dance halls scattered throughout the city and in outlying communities, including Preservation Hall, the Tin Roof Café and Funky Butt Hall. In 1903, he began to fade from the scene, plagued by spells of dementia and drunkenness, until he was committed to the East Louisiana State Mental Hospital on 5 June 1907: the first jazz casualty.

Above
Kid Ory's 'tailgate' playing style – in which the trombone plays a rhythmic line beneath the band's trumpets and cornets – may have been influenced by his earlier experiences as a banjo player.

see The Early Years Sources & Sounds pp 14 *see* Jazz Styles Introduction pp 372 *see* Chicago Jazz pp 382

Left
The Red Hot Peppers sessions, led by pianist, composer and bandleader Jelly Roll Morton represent some of the finest recordings in the New Orleans style.

Succeeding Bolden as the cornet king of New Orleans was Freddie Keppard, who, in 1906, led the Olympia Orchestra. Legend has it that Keppard, leery of having other cornet players 'steal his stuff', turned down an offer from the Victor Talking Machine Company to become the first New Orleans musician to record. Another prominent cornetist was Joe Oliver, who began playing in local dance bands and with the Onward Brass Band in 1907. By 1917, he became the star cornetist in a popular band led by the trombonist Edward 'Kid' Ory, who billed him as 'King' Oliver. An early master of mutes, Oliver pioneered the 'wah-wah' and other vocal effects on his horn, which would later become a signature of the Ellington trumpeter Bubber Miley. When Oliver went north to Chicago in February 1919, Ory hired the 18-year-old Louis Armstrong as his replacement on cornet.

The Jazz Age

Oliver's contemporary on the New Orleans scene was the Creole clarinetist Sidney Bechet. A child prodigy, Bechet held his own with Freddie Keppard's band at the age of 10. He left school at 16 and began working with various bands, thrilling audiences and players alike with his forceful attack, soaring passion and unusually fast vibrato. Bechet relocated to Chicago in 1918 and, a year later, became one of the first Americans to spread jazz to Europe as a member of the travelling Southern Syncopated Orchestra. It was while he was in London that he ran across the instrument with which he would eventually make jazz history: the soprano saxophone.

A key figure in New Orleans jazz was the pianist, composer, entertainer and raconteur Jelly Roll Morton. A natural extrovert who bragged that he had invented jazz, Morton began embellishing on ragtime, blues and light classics while performing at the 'sporting houses' of the Storyville red-light district as early as 1902. By 1907, he began touring in vaudeville shows throughout the Gulf Coast and the Midwest. He settled in Chicago in 1914, then relocated to the West Coast from 1917 to 1922. He had composed numerous works by that time, including his classic 'King Porter Stomp' and 'Winin' Boy Blues', but remained unrecorded until 1923.

A plethora of jazz musicians were active in New Orleans during the first decade of the twentieth century, but the first jazz recording was not made until 1917. That honour went not to pioneers such as Keppard, Ory, Oliver, Bechet or Morton (all of whom went unrecorded until after they had left New Orleans), but to a group of five young, white New Orleans musicians calling themselves the Original Dixieland Jass Band. Led by Sicilian-American cornetist Nick LaRocca, the ODJB assembled in the Victor studio in New York City on 26 February 1917 to record 'Livery Stable Blues'. A lively novelty number that featured passages where the instruments imitated barnyard animals, it immediately caught on with the public. Following the extraordinary success of their recording debut (it would eventually sell 1.5 million copies), the ODJB toured British variety theatres, where they audaciously billed themselves as 'The Creators of Jazz'. The ODJB later introduced such Dixieland standards as 'Margie', 'Indiana' and 'Tiger Rag', spawning a number of copy bands and sparking a craze that quickly swept America, as well as setting the stage for what the writer F. Scott Fitzgerald characterized as 'The Jazz Age' of the 1920s.

Below
King Oliver's Creole Jazz Band made some of the most important jazz recordings of the 1920s. The band, including such greats as Louis Armstrong, Johnny Dodds and King Oliver himself, took group improvisation to new heights.

see Kid Ory pp 22 *see* Original Dixieland Jass Band pp 31 *see* Jelly Roll Morton pp 60 *see* King Oliver pp 62

Chicago

KEY ARTISTS

New Orleans Rhythm Kings
King Oliver
Louis Armstrong
Jimmy McPartland
Frank Teschemacher
Joe Sullivan
Bix Beiderbecke
Max Kaminsky
Cutty Cutshall
Bud Freeman
Jess Stacy
Miff Mole

Jazz was the by-product of cultures coming together in New Orleans at the turn of the twentieth century. the music, along with some of its greatest practitioners, moved north by 1917. That year Storyville, the red-light district, was forced to close and jazz musicians headed north to Chicago, where jazz matured into a fine art form.

Chicago held the promise of a new life for the Southern black population, which migrated from the fields of the cotton industry to the blast furnaces and factories of big Northern cities. A centrally located, active transportation hub that provided easy access to Los Angeles and New York, Chicago was an attractive destination for working jazz musicians, many of whom worked in the gangster-owned speakeasies created by the Volstead Act of 1919 (outlawing the manufacture and sale of alcohol in the United States).

'Armstrong plays with such bravura and rhythmic intensity that when you listen to it you hear the future. At that moment you know that something is in the works and it's never going to be contained.'

Gary Giddins, critic

Blow The Way You Feel

While the North Side of Chicago had its famous clubs – the Green Mill, College Inn, Blackhawk, Kelly's Stables and Friar's Inn – the hottest jazz bands of the early 1920s could, primarily, be found on a nine-block stretch of State Street on the city's predominantly black South Side, known as 'The Stroll'. There, jazz lovers could choose between the Pekin Inn, Dreamland Café, Plantation Café, Elite Café and Sunset Café. Among the patrons who frequented The Stroll was a group of jazz-hungry, white teenage students who attended Chicago's Austin High School – cornetist Jimmy McPartland, tenor saxophonist Bud Freeman, drummer Dave Tough and reedman Frank Teschemacher. Along with developing young players, such as guitarist Eddie Condon, pianist Joe Sullivan, cornetists Muggsy Spanier and Leon 'Bix' Beiderbecke, clarinetist Benny Goodman and drummer Gene Krupa, this next generation of jazz musicians originated the

Above
Eddie Condon never took solos, preferring to work as a steady rhythm player. He played an important part in the desegregation of jazz, as well as in moving jazz performances from underground clubs to concert halls.

'Chicago style', building on the rhythmic innovations of the New Orleans pioneers while injecting a frenetic intensity and reckless spirit that reflected the city itself.

Hypnosis At First Hearing

The Austin Gang and other architects of the extrovert Chicago style were fans of the Original Dixieland Jass Band, but they quickly fell under the spell of another white group from New Orleans, playing in Chicago in 1920 under the name of the New Orleans Rhythm Kings. They made their recording debut in 1922, and a year later teamed up in the studio with Jelly Roll Morton for one of the first-ever integrated sessions. Another focal point for the Austin Gang's adulation, and a great source of inspiration for aspiring cornetists McPartland and Beiderbecke, was the dazzling cornet virtuoso Louis Armstrong, who came to town in 1922 to join his mentor King Oliver in the ranks of the Creole Jazz Band. (The band also included the great New Orleans clarinetist Johnny Dodds and his younger brother Warren 'Baby' Dodds on drums, along with

see The Twenties Sources & Sounds pp 36 *see* Jazz Styles Introduction pp 372 *see* New Orleans Jazz pp 380

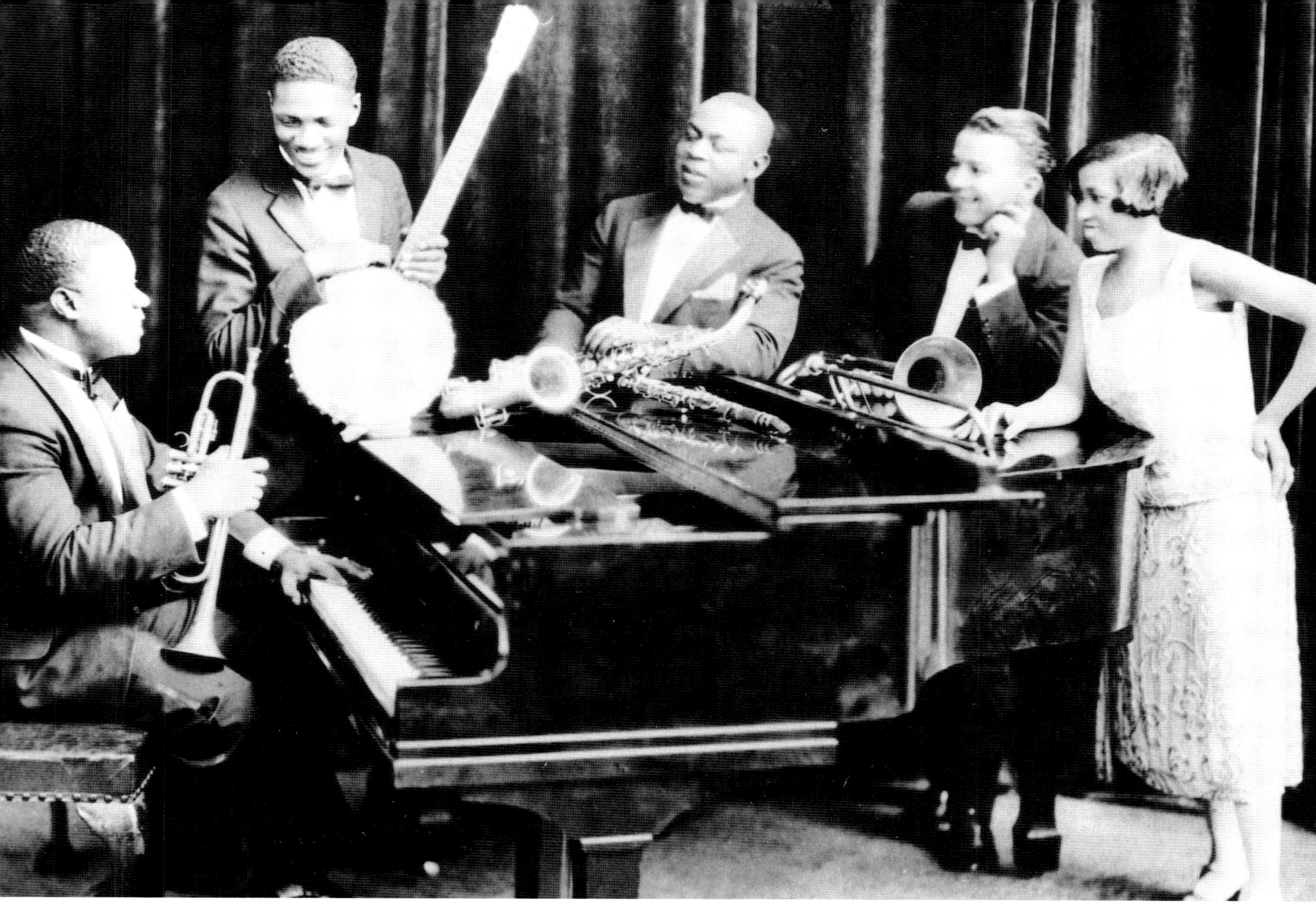

Honoré Dutrey on trombone, Bill Johnson on bass and banjo, and Lil Hardin on piano.) With its two-cornet frontline, underscored by an intuitive call-and-response chemistry between its leader and 22-year-old star, the impact of King Oliver's Creole Jazz Band on young audiences was devastating. As guitarist Eddie Condon recalled in his memoirs, *We Called It Music: A Generation of Jazz* (Henry Holt): 'It was hypnosis at first hearing. Armstrong seemed able to hear what Oliver was improvising and reproduce it himself at the same time. Then the two wove around each other like suspicious women talking about the same man'.

In the early part of 1923, Oliver's pace-setting group went into a rickety studio in Richmond, Indiana, and cut its first historic recording ('Chimes Blues') for the small but influential Gennett label.

Armstrong left Chicago in 1924 to join Fletcher Henderson's band in New York. The following year, he returned to Chicago to lead a band organized by his new wife, Lil (Hardin) Armstrong, at the Dreamland Café. Soon afterward, he began doubling with Erskine Tate's Vendome Theater Orchestra, where he was the featured hot soloist. Then, on 12 November 1925, he went into the Okeh studios in Chicago to make the first of a series of five dozen tracks recorded between 1925 and 1928, which have come to be known as the Hot Fives and Hot Sevens sessions. With these revolutionary recordings, Armstrong single-handedly shifted the focus from jazz as an ensemble music to a soloist's art form. As noted critic Gary Giddins put it, 'It's the moment when jazz becomes an art form. With these pivotal recordings, he virtually codifies what jazz is going to be for the next half century'.

By 1929, Armstrong shifted his home base from Chicago to New York, where jazz was poised for its next evolution.

Above

Featuring ex-members of King Oliver's band, Louis Armstrong's Hot Five recordings may represent the greatest jazz of all time. Pictured from left to right are Armstrong, Johnny St. Cyr, Johnny Dodds, Kid Ory and Lil Hardin-Armstrong.

see Louis Armstrong pp 44 *see* Bix Beiderbecke pp 48 *see* Eddie Condon pp 71 *see* Jimmy McPartland pp 78

Swing

KEY ARTISTS

- Fletcher Henderson
- Count Basie
- Duke Ellington
- Chick Webb
- Cab Calloway
- Benny Goodman
- Artie Shaw
- Glenn Miller
- Tommy Dorsey
- Jimmy Dorsey
- Woody Herman
- Harry James
- Gene Krupa
- Bunny Berigan
- Charlie Barnet

The popularity of jazz hit a peak after the Depression years of 1929–1933. By the end of 1934, huge numbers were tuning in to the NBC radio series Let's Dance, which broadcast performances by the Xavier Cugat, Kel Murray and Benny Goodman orchestras. Goodman's orchestra in particular caught on with the public and created a demand for live performances.

When Goodman went on tour in the US, scoring his first big success before a packed house of ecstatic teenagers at the Palomar Ballroom in Los Angeles on 21 August 1935, it signalled the beginning of a new national youth craze to rival the turn-of-the-century ragtime fad. Symbolically, it was the birth of the swing era, the predominance of big bands in jazz.

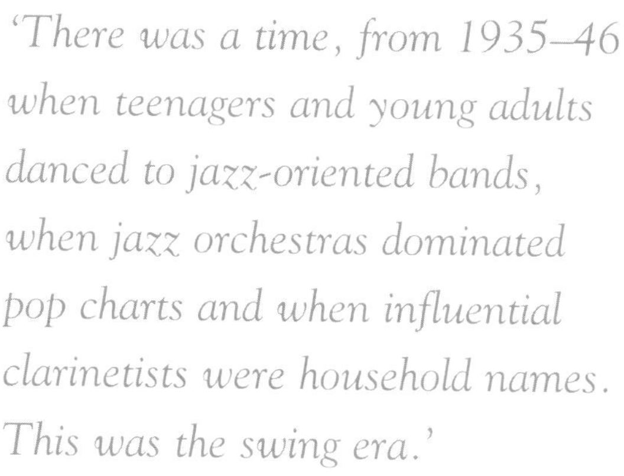

'There was a time, from 1935–46, when teenagers and young adults danced to jazz-oriented bands, when jazz orchestras dominated pop charts and when influential clarinetists were household names. This was the swing era.'

Scott Yanow

Reaching Fever Pitch

Following Goodman's triumph at the Palomar Ballroom, the floodgates opened wide and several bands followed in his wake. By 1937, Kansas City pianist and bandleader William 'Count' Basie had recorded his first swinging sides, including the anthemic 'Jumpin' at the Woodside' and 'One O'Clock Jump', both featuring the tenor saxophonist Lester Young and the all-American rhythm section of bassist Walter Page, drummer Papa Jo Jones and guitarist Freddie Green. That same year, Jimmy Dorsey scored hits with 'Marie' and 'Song of India', featuring classic trumpet solos by Bunny Berigan. Shortly after, Berigan formed his own big band and had a hit in August 1937 with 'I Can't Get Started', still part of the standard jazz repertoire to this day. Swing-era momentum reached fever pitch with Benny Goodman's historic Carnegie Hall concert in New York in January 1938, which was recorded for posterity and included the classic instrumental version of Louis Prima's 'Sing, Sing Sing', the frantic number that made drummer Gene Krupa such a star that he left the BG Orchestra to form his own big band.

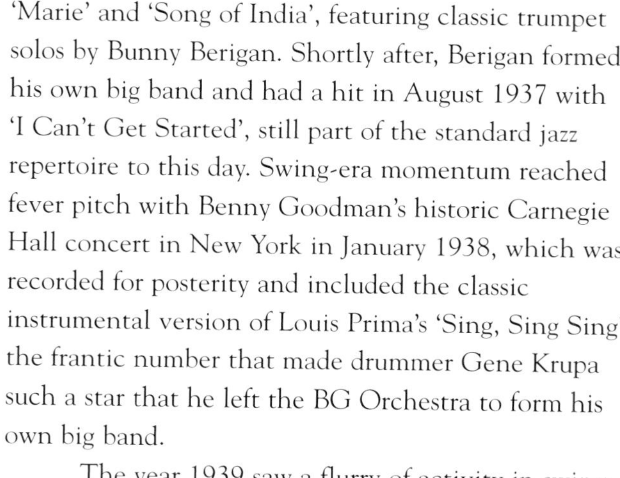

The year 1939 saw a flurry of activity in swing: Harry James, an outstanding trumpeter in the Goodman organization, formed his own orchestra. The clarinetist Woody Herman scored his first big band hit with 'At the Woodchopper's Ball'. The saxophonist Charlie Barnet became a household name that same year on the strength of his big band hit 'Cherokee'. Singer Ella Fitzgerald took over the

Above
Count Basie was taught piano in the Harlem stride tradition by Fats Waller. He worked in the vaudeville circuit for a number of years before going on to become one of the world's greatest big-band leaders.

see The Thirties Sources & Sounds pp 92 *see* Jazz Styles Introduction pp 372 *see* Bebop pp 386

Chick Webb Orchestra following the drummer-bandleader's death that summer. Glenn Miller's Orchestra rose to prominence by blending pop elements with the highly polished big band formula, scoring several top 10 hits in 1939 and 1940 with popular recordings such as 'Little Brown Jug', 'In The Mood' and 'Pennsylvania 6-5000'. In that same year, trumpeter Dizzy Gillespie joined the Cab Calloway Orchestra; tenor-sax great Coleman Hawkins recorded his immortal 'Body And Soul'; and bassist Jimmy Blanton and tenor saxophonist Ben Webster joined the great orchestra led by Duke Ellington. Ellington's orchestra had been a monumental force in jazz since the early 1920s and he remained a major name during the swing era on the strength of anthemic hits such as 'It Don't Mean A Thing If It Ain't Got That Swing', 'Rockin' in Rhythm' and 'Drop Me Off In Harlem'.

Swing Is The Thing

As the 1930s came to a close, one thing was eminently clear: swing had become as commercially viable and lucrative as rap music is today. While the swing era dance bands enjoyed unprecedented popularity, there was never any attempt at playing to the lowest common denominator. The general level of musicianship had risen incrementally in the early 1930s due to the towering influence of Louis Armstrong, whose pyrotechnic playing on the Hot Five sessions of 1925 and collaboration with Earl Hines in 1928 (particularly on anthemic showpieces like 'Weather Bird' and 'West End Blues') had raised the bar for instrumental virtuosity in jazz. The combination of Armstrong-influenced hot soloing, well-honed ensemble playing and an infectious 4/4 beat proved irresistible for listeners and dancers through the 1930s and into the early 1940s.

With the size of the ensembles ranging from 10 to 20 pieces or more, big band music flowed smoothly on a steady 4/4 pulse, propelled by a foundation of string bass 'walking' in synch with the drums, which kept time on the high-hat cymbal and bass drum while providing syncopated accents on snare and tom-toms. The distinctive big band quality came from the use of separate trumpet, trombone and saxophone (alto, tenor, baritone) sections to provide chordal or contrapuntal blocks of sound or add rhythmic punch to an arrangement. Over the top of these intricately voiced, highly polished arrangements was room designated for individual soloists to tell their story. That juxtaposition of discipline and freedom is a hallmark of big band music.

Above
Virtuoso clarinetist Benny Goodman messes around with Gene Krupa, a drummer so innovative that he was able to upstage Goodman, leading to a falling out between the pair in the late 1930s.

From A Flurry To A Fall

By 1942, the first full year of American participation in the Second World War, the swing era had suffered some setbacks. Key players and bandleaders like Glenn Miller and Artie Shaw had enlisted in the Armed Services and a recording strike by the Musicians Union from 1942–44 effectively halted the documenting of this new music's development. By the end of the Second World War in 1945, the swing era was feeling competition from the Dixieland revival and the advent of bebop, creating a kind of Civil War that split the jazz audience into three factions. By 1946, many of the big bands had broken up. Combos were the wave of the future. Name-orchestras like Duke Ellington's, Count Basie's and Woody Herman's persisted in the face of changing times but the swing era as a cultural force was clearly over.

Far Left Bottom
Django Reinhardt was a key player in European jazz during the swing era. After losing two fingers on his fretting hand in a caravan fire, Reinhardt developed his own unique style of playing which became hugely influential.

see Duke Ellington pp 52 *see* Count Basie pp 102 *see* Benny Goodman pp 110 *see* Glenn Miller pp 180

Bebop

KEY ARTISTS

Charlie Parker
Dizzy Gillespie
Thelonious Monk
Kenny Clarke
Max Roach
Bud Powell
Roy Haynes
Miles Davis
Fats Navarro
Dexter Gordon
Oscar Pettiford

Right
The bebop movement established the saxophone as the future sound of modern jazz.

Though it was often referred to as a musical revolution, bebop was actually a natural evolution of jazz, involving innovative approaches to harmony and rhythm that advanced the music forward to a modern era.

Traces of bebop began to emerge during the early 1940s, in orchestras led by Earl Hines and Billy Eckstine. Those adventurous impulses were further developed in Harlem nightspots such as Minton's Playhouse and Clark Monroe's Uptown House, where the architects of an iconoclastic new movement conducted experiments with time, tempo and extended techniques.

An Iconoclastic New Movement

It was there that drummer Kenny Clarke began to employ new methods on the kit – implying time, accenting in unpredictable ways and generally colouring and embellishing the music spontaneously from measure to measure, rather than keeping strict metronomic time in the manner of swing-era drummers. It was there that pianist Thelonious Monk began to map out sophisticated harmonic modulations and new melodic contours around familiar songs. In the same spirit of discovery, the trumpeter Dizzy Gillespie and alto saxophonist Charlie Parker began to effectively eliminate bar lines by soaring over the chord changes with impunity, injecting their lines with a stream-of-consciousness creativity that cascaded effortlessly through their horns. These young modernists were, largely, reacting to clichés that had begun to saddle big bands towards the end of the swing era. Their ambitious efforts at developing a new lexicon of expression coalesced into a new kind of music that was publicly unveiled on 'Swing Street', the vibrant strip of nightclubs that lined 52nd Street between Fifth and Seventh Avenues in Midtown Manhattan.

'"Bebop" was a label that certain journalists later gave it, but we never labeled the music. It was just modern music, we would call it. We wouldn't call it anything, really, just music.'
Bebop drummer Kenny Clarke

A Divisive Movement

With the emergence of bebop around 1945, the jazz world was suddenly divided into opposing (and at times hostile) camps: those who thrived on the new music and those threatened by its incursion. Some old-guard icons, such as trumpeter Louis Armstrong and bandleader Cab Calloway, readily dismissed bebop, branding its frantic tempos, eccentric rhythms, advanced harmonies and discordant melodies as undanceable and indecipherable. But others, such as tenor saxophonists Coleman Hawkins and Don Byas, successfully made the transition from the old into the new.

John Birks 'Dizzy' Gillespie, with his outrageous stage persona, became a figurehead of the rebellious new movement. Aside from his peerless virtuosity as a trumpeter, Dizzy was also a beloved showman

Right
Earl Hines, a jazz pianist who had played on Louis Armstrong's Hot Five sessions, led a big band throughout the 1930s and 1940s that served as a launch pad for the up-and-coming bebop movement.

see The Forties Sources & Sounds pp 144 *see* Jazz Styles Introduction pp 372 *see* Swing pp 384 *see* Cool Jazz pp 390

throughout his long and illustrious career. Gillespie, along with his kindred spirit and musical partner Charlie 'Yardbird' Parker, whose blinding speed and dazzling facility placed him a cut above every other improviser of his day, unleashed a torrent of new ideas (some of which were based on pre-existing chord patterns from swing-era standards) that set a new standard for instrumental virtuosity and changed the course of jazz.

Born in South Carolina in 1917, Gillespie began playing trombone at the age of 14, before switching to trumpet the following year. He played with Philadelphia's Frank Fairfax Band, before he joined Teddy Hill's Orchestra in 1937, filling a spot formerly held by his trumpet-playing idol, Roy Eldridge. In 1939, Gillespie found himself in fast company on a Lionel Hampton all-star date for Victor. He distinguished himself with some singular, muted trumpet work on 'Hot Mallets', which showed a distinct departure from Eldridge's influence and pointed to a new path for jazz trumpet. Following a two-year stint in Cab Calloway's band, Gillespie worked in a succession of bands led by musicians including Ella Fitzgerald, Benny Carter, Duke Ellington and, in 1943, Earl Hines. In January 1944, he put together the Hepsations, the first bebop-oriented jazz group to play on 52nd Street. In June 1944, he joined Billy Eckstine's all-star big band, and by spring 1945 he had teamed up with Parker at The 3 Deuces on Swing Street. Together, they dominated the bop era from 1945–49.

A Jazz Messiah

With remarkable technical proficiency, coupled with the sheer force of his charismatic personality, Charlie Parker became a jazz messiah in the mid-1940s. His solos were sermons to a faithful flock, hungering for a hipper alternative to Benny Goodman and Glenn Miller. Parker's virtuosic flights on alto sax, marked by an uncanny fluidity, an inherent bluesy quality and an intuitive harmonic logic that was complex yet crystal clear, earned him a lofty status among critics, fans and contemporaries alike. An early apprenticeship with the Jay McShann Orchestra in 1937 helped him hone his technique, and by the time he first visited New York City in 1939 as an eager 19-year-old, he was prepared to deal with the advanced playing of Art Tatum and take the next step in his musical journey. Parker met and began exchanging ideas with Gillespie as early as 1940. The two later met in Earl Hines' band in 1943 and, for a few months, in Billy Eckstine's Orchestra in 1944. But it was not until late 1944 that they worked together on 52nd Street, startling the world with bop anthems such as 'Groovin' High', 'Hot House' and 'Shaw 'Nuff'.

Above
Dizzy Gillespie's incredibly varied and unpredictable playing style created a feeling of excited suspense. Charlie Parker may have developed bebop beyond all expectations, but without Diz it would never have begun.

In the wake of landmark small group recordings by Bird & Diz, documented in May 1945 on the Guild label, other modernists would add to the bebop canon, including pyrotechnic virtuosos such as pianist Bud Powell, trumpeters Howard McGhee and Fats Navarro, saxophonists Dexter Gordon and Edward 'Sonny' Stitt, trombonist J.J. Johnson, and pianists Tadd Dameron and Al Haig, all of whom placed a premium on speed of thought and execution in their music. By 1950, bebop had run its course as a burgeoning new movement. Some of its early practitioners and disciples had evolved, and were already experimenting with two new jazz tributaries – hard bop and cool jazz.

see Dizzy Gillespie pp 152 *see* Charlie Parker pp 162 *see* Kenny Clarke pp 172 *see* Thelonious Monk pp 208

Dixieland Revival

KEY ARTISTS

Bunk Johnson
Kid Ory
George Lewis
Eddie Condon
Muggsy Spanier
Bob Crosby
Bob Scobey
Lu Watters Yerba
Buena Jazz Band
Louis Armstrong
Yank Lawson
Wingy Manone
Bob Haggart
Doc Cheatham
Bud Freeman
Pee Wee Russell

By the end of the 1930s, the swing era was in full force, ushered in by big bands led by Benny Goodman, Chick Webb, the Dorsey brothers (Jimmy and Tommy) and Glenn Miller. New Orleans jazz and its stylistic off-shoot, Dixieland, had both largely faded from popularity.

New Orleans pioneers King Oliver and Jelly Roll Morton drifted into obscurity. Original Dixieland Jass Band leader Nick LaRocca left music altogether and became a building contractor, while New Orleans trombonist-bandleader Edward 'Kid' Ory (once a mentor to the teenage Louis Armstrong in New Orleans and later appearing on Armstrong's revolutionary Hot Five and Hot Seven sessions from 1925–28) had gone into chicken farming.

'By the mid-1930s the word 'dixieland' was being applied freely to certain circles of white musicians, first by the trade press, then by the public. By the end of the decade it had all but lost any direct 'Southern' association.'

Richard Sudhalter

Goodtime Music From The Past

By 1939, Dixieland was making a solid comeback. A generation of players, including clarinetists Pee Wee Russell and Joe Marsala, saxophonist Bud Freeman, trumpeters Bobby Hackett, Muggsy Spanier, Max Kaminsky and Wild Bill Davison, guitarist Eddie Condon and others, began reinvestigating the extroverted collective improvisational style of early New Orleans music and Chicago-style jazz of the 1920s. Part of the impetus for the revival of Dixieland came in 1938, when New York record store owner Milt Gabler launched his Commodore Records label to document these prominent Dixieland revivalists. Responding to the renewed interest in old-style New Orleans music, Jelly Roll Morton (who had made only one appearance on record between 1931–37 on a little-known Wingy Manone date) led sessions in 1939 with such notable New Orleans sidemen as Sidney Bechet, Red Allen and Albert Nicholas. Ironically, Morton's music became popular again after his death in July 1941, just as the Dixieland revival really started to take off.

Another figure who spearheaded the Dixieland revival was Bob Crosby. A former singer in the Dorsey Brothers' band from 1934–35, Crosby led a band through the late 1930s and early 1940s that revived such New Orleans evergreens as 'South Rampart Street Parade', 'Sugarfoot Strut' and 'Muskrat Ramble' while also interpreting popular hits of the day in a Dixieland two-beat style. Following the example of Tommy Dorsey (who in 1935 formed his Dixieland-flavoured Clambake Seven as a featured smaller group within his big band), Crosby formed the Bobcats from the ranks of his own big band. This smaller Dixieland ensemble featured several New Orleans-born musicians performing faithful renditions of classic fare by Louis Armstrong, King Oliver and the Original Dixieland Jass Band.

Spirited Ensemble Music

By the early to mid-1940s, New Orleans jazz pioneers like Kid Ory, Bunk Johnson and George Lewis were being persuaded to return to recording studios and concert halls, which touched off renewed interest in the original New Orleans-style jazz and placed more emphasis on interactive ensemble playing and less on extroverted soloing, as was the style of the Dixielanders. Their pure, spirited playing directly inspired the British cornetist and trumpeter Ken Colyer, who would spearhead a wave of traditional New Orleans jazz throughout England in the 1950s.

A primary force for a West Coast Dixieland revival was Lu Watters' Yerba Buena Jazz Band,

Above
Ken Colyer helped to keep traditional New Orleans-style jazz alive in Britain.

see The Forties Sources & Sounds pp 144 *see* Jazz Styles Introduction pp 372 *see* New Orleans Jazz pp 380

Left
Humphrey Lyttleton, a self-taught trumpeter, is one of Britain's leading revivalists. His engaging style earned praise from Satchmo himself, who proclaimed Lyttleton 'the top trumpet man in England'.

which issued its first records in 1942. This revivalist octet emulated the two-cornet approach of King Oliver's Creole Jazz Band with trumpeters Watters and Bob Scobey on the frontline alongside trombonist Turk Murphy and clarinetist Ellis Horne. By the mid- to late 1940s, with the advent of the modernist bebop movement, traditional New Orleans jazz and Dixieland players were being dismissed by progressives as 'moldy figs'. Yet the music was carried on in the late 1940s and through the 1950s by its figurehead, Louis Armstrong, who broke up his big band in 1947 and spent the rest of his career leading an all-star sextet which specialized in playing old New Orleans jazz and Dixieland standards like 'Basin Street Blues', 'Royal Garden Blues', 'Sleepy Time Down South', 'Tiger Rag', 'Indiana' and 'Struttin' With Some Barbecue'.

Guitarist Eddie Condon, a major propagandist for the Dixieland cause, recorded prolifically throughout the 1940s and 1950s with notable Dixieland players such as trumpeters Wild Bill Davison and Max Kaminsky, trombonists Jack Teagarden and Cutty Cutshall, and clarinetists Pee Wee Russell and Peanuts Hucko. Other Dixieland revivalists during the 1950s included trumpeter Adolphus 'Doc' Cheatham, New Orleans clarinetist George Lewis, trombonist Wilbur de Paris (whose band featured the great New Orleans-born clarinetist Omer Simeon), San Francisco trumpeters Bob Scobey and Turk Murphy and former Bobcats bandmates trumpeter Yank Lawson and bassist Bob Haggart (who would team up in the late 1960s to form their Dixieland-inspired World's Greatest Jazz Band).

In 1961, Preservation Hall opened in New Orleans to keep the tradition alive and provide steady work for old-time New Orleans jazzmen, such as the trumpeters Kid Thomas Valentine and Punch Miller, clarinetist Willie Humphrey and, on trumpet, his older brother Percy. Trumpeter Al Hirt and clarinetist Pete Fountain also brought greater visibility to Dixieland with their popular recordings and frequent television appearances throughout the 1950s and 1960s.

This spirited ensemble music is still being championed today by New Orleans clarinetists Dr. Michael White and Pete Fountain, New Orleans-based singer-bandleader Banu Gibson, soprano saxophonist Bob Wilber (whose Bechet Legacy group was active in the early 1980s), cornetists Jim Cullum Jr. and Warren Vaché, New Orleans trumpeter Wynton Marsalis and the current edition of the Preservation Hall Jazz Band.

Below
New Orleans jazzman Bunk Johnson ceased playing in 1931 after a fellow trumpeter was stabbed to death onstage. He was rediscovered in the early 1940s by two jazz biographers, who encouraged him to make his first recordings.

see Bunk Johnson pp 28 *see* Bud Freeman pp 72 *see* Bobby Hackett pp 125 *see* Pee Wee Russell pp 133

Cool Jazz

KEY ARTISTS

Claude Thornhill
Miles Davis
Gerry Mulligan
Lee Konitz
Gil Evans
John Lewis/
Modern Jazz Quartet
Lennie Tristano
Shorty Rogers
Howard Rumsey
Bud Shank
Jimmy Giuffre
Chet Baker
Paul Desmond
Dave Brubeck
Chico Hamilton

In the wake of the pyrotechnic manifesto that Charlie 'Bird' Parker and Dizzy Gillespie jointly issued on their first recording together in 1945, most musicians on the New York jazz scene began fanning the flames of bebop. Tempos picked up speed, intensity increased on the bandstand and blazing virtuosity became a means to an end, in a fiery pursuit of Bird and Diz.

And yet, the task of topping the two trendsetters who originated and mastered the art of bebop seemed insurmountable to many of their disciples, who, at best, might be considered great imitators but never originators. This frustrating fact caused several forward-thinking musicians to break from the extroverted bebop mould and forge a new, more reflective and deliberate musical path. Like pouring water on the flames of the bebop movement, these thoughtful young player-composers came to epitomize a 'cool school' in jazz.

'It was an ethereal, drifting cloud music that used French horns as well as regular jazz instruments, highly wrought arrangements and rich tone colours, through which the soloists played in a measured, walking-on-eggshells manner.'

John Fordham

Velvety, Sensuous And Swinging

The roots of this antidote to the hyperactivity of bebop can be heard in the work of Claude Thornhill & His Orchestra, a dreamy-sounding ensemble from the early 1940s that utilized such unusual instrumentation as French horns and tuba as melodic voices. Some of the finest charts in the band's book, circa 1946–47, were contributed by the composer-arranger Gil Evans, who brought his own boppish inclinations to the ensemble's softer, inherently sweet quality. By the end of 1947, Evans had become acquainted with Miles Davis, a promising 22-year-old trumpeter from East St. Louis who had apprenticed alongside Parker at the height of the bebop craze.

While Davis did not possess the dazzling, high-note virtuosity of his idol Dizzy Gillespie, he began developing a sparser, middle-register approach to trumpet soloing, contrasting with the explosive bravura of the beboppers. This quieter, cooler style finally came to fruition on Davis' *Birth Of The Cool*, the 1949 recording that helped usher in a new musical movement in jazz.

Above
Percy Heath of the Modern Jazz Quartet, a band led by John Lewis, employed classical musical forms, such as the fugue.

Davis' landmark nonet sessions of 1949–50 were characterized by a relaxed yet disciplined integration of elements, featuring cool-toned soloists such as alto saxophonist Lee Konitz, trombonists J.J. Johnson and Kai Winding, and baritone saxophonist Gerry Mulligan. Working with the larger canvas of a nonet, the arrangers Evans ('Boplicity', 'Moon Dreams'), Mulligan ('Venus De Milo', 'Darn That Dream'), Johnny Carisi ('Israel'), John Lewis ('Move') and Davis ('Deception') incorporated the lush tones of French horns, trombone and tuba in creating a velvety, sensuous yet swinging body of work, that has stood the test of time.

Offshoots Of The Cool School

Key participants in the seminal *Birth Of The Cool* sessions went on to incorporate various musical precepts of the Davis nonet experience in their own work: Gerry Mulligan with his celebrated, pianoless quartet, featuring trumpeter and kindred spirit Chet Baker; John Lewis with the chamber like Modern Jazz Quartet; Lee Konitz in his mid-1950s work with tenor saxophonist Warne Marsh. So pervasive was the influence of *Birth Of The Cool* among musicians that it spawned a separate movement, known as 'West Coast Jazz'. Some of the leaders of this West Coast branch of the cool school

see The Fifties Sources & Sounds pp 190 *see* Jazz Styles Introduction pp 372 *see* Bebop pp 386

included bassist Howard Rumsey and his Lighthouse All-Stars, trumpeter-arranger Milton 'Shorty' Rogers and his Giants, alto saxophonist Bud Shank with his tenor saxophonist partner Bill Perkins, valve trombonist Bob Brookmeyer, trumpeter Conte Candoli, multi-reedman Jimmy Giuffre, vibist Teddy Charles, tenor saxophonist-oboeist Bob Cooper, trombonist Frank Rosolino and drummer-composer Chico Hamilton, who introduced a group in 1955 that featured the unusual instrumentation of cello (Fred Katz), guitar (Jim Hall), flute (Buddy Collette) and bass (Carson Smith).

Another leading light of West Coast Jazz was the alto saxophonist Paul Desmond, whose tone was once described as 'sounding like a dry martini'. In 1951 Desmond teamed up with the pianist Dave Brubeck, a protégé of the contemporary classical composer Darius Milhaud, who had led an experimental third-stream octet during the late 1940s. Together Desmond and Brubeck found phenomenal success on college campuses, reaching new audiences and turning a younger generation on to jazz. In the wake of 1954's *Jazz Goes To College*, the Dave Brubeck Quartet was so popular that its leader appeared on the cover of *Time* magazine. From the quartet's million-selling 1959 album, *Time Out*, Desmond's anthemic 'Take Five' remains an oft-covered jazz classic.

While the rich tonal colours, highly wrought arrangements and relaxed, measured solos of West Coast or cool jazz emerged in reaction to the urgency and all-out burn of bebop, it in turn triggered another movement that followed in the mid-1950s and prospered through to the mid-1960s: hard bop.

By 1959 Miles Davis, who had helped usher in the cool jazz movement a decade earlier with *Birth Of The Cool*, was already on to other groundbreaking work. His landmark album of that year, the influential and bestselling *Kind Of Blue*, would popularize modal jazz – a system of improvising based on modes or scales rather than running chord progressions – and pave the way for the free jazz movement of the 1960s.

Above
Chet Baker's ethereal, melodic playing style, combined with his androgynous vocals, introduced a fragile element to cool jazz.

Left
The Dave Brubeck Quartet experimented with unusual time signatures on tracks such as the now-classic 'Take Five'. They were advised that such records would not sell, as they were too difficult to dance to.

see Miles Davis pp 200 *see* Gerry Mulligan pp 210 *see* Dave Brubeck pp 219 *see* John Lewis pp 229

Hard Bop

KEY ARTISTS

Art Blakey
Sonny Rollins
Horace Silver
John Coltrane
Miles Davis
Wes Montgomery
Max Roach
Art Farmer
Freddie Hubbard
Cannonball Adderley

Above
Sonny Rollins (left) and Max Roach (standing, centre) played some incredible music together that was not always popular with the critics, but was admired by peers such as Miles Davis.

Hard bop evolved out of bebop during the early 1950s but its rhythms were more driving and syncopated. Hard bop also tended to have a more full-bodied sound, a bluesy feel with darker textures and shorter improvised lines, and its chord progressions were usually composed rather than borrowed from popular tunes.

'If Art Blakey's old-fashioned, I'm white.'
Miles Davis

Although Miles Davis made an early foray into hard bop with *Walkin'* (1953), the style did not become established until drummer Art Blakey and pianist Horace Silver joined forces later that year. They played with the trademark hard-driving grooves and gospel-inspired phrasings that would later be associated with the genre.

The Fathers Of Hard Bop

Many listeners underestimate the impact Horace Silver had on contemporary mainstream jazz: the hard bop style he and Art Blakey developed in the 1950s is still one of the dominant forms of the genre. Silver studied piano at school in Connecticut, where he formed a trio for local gigs. They impressed tenor saxophonist Stan Getz, who immediately hired them and brought them over to New York in 1950. Silver worked with Getz for a year there and also began to play with other top jazzers, including the saxophonists Coleman Hawkins and Lester Young. In 1953 he joined forces with Art Blakey to form a band under their joint leadership. Their first album, *Horace Silver And The Jazz Messengers* (1955), proved to be a milestone in the development of hard bop, with some of the tunes Silver penned for the recording later becoming jazz standards. Silver left the band in 1956 to record a series of albums that showcased his original, funky piano style. His recordings throughout the ensuing five decades have featured many jazz notables, including the trumpeters Donald Byrd, Art Farmer and Randy Brecker, as well as the saxophonists Hank Mobley and Michael Brecker.

Art Blakey began as a pianist before he switched to the drums in the 1940s. He drummed with Mary Lou Williams, Fletcher Henderson's Swing Band and Billy Eckstine's band before forming the original Jazz Messengers in 1955. The band varied in size, and there were countless personnel changes over the next 40 years (a list of the band's alumni is basically a who's who of mainstream jazz from the 1950s onwards), but they always delivered top-notch jazz, powered by Blakey's driving drums. His accompaniment style was relentless, and even the best players in his bands had to be on their toes to keep up with him. He was never really the jazz world's most subtle or versatile drummer, but what he played, he played exceedingly well and with spirit, until his death in 1990.

see The Fifties Sources & Sounds pp 190 *see* Jazz Styles Introduction pp 372 *see* Bebop pp 386

Other Hard Bop Players

Max Roach was another hugely influential bebop and hard bop drummer. He and Kenny Clarke were the first drummers to spell out the pulse of a groove with the ride cymbal to get a lighter texture. This gave them more freedom to explore their drum kits, and to drop random snare 'bombs' while allowing the frontline virtuosos to play with greater freedom at faster speeds. Roach possessed a broader range than Blakey; he was capable of creating a furious drive, but also drum solos with storylines. He was also very creative with his use of silence, using cymbals as gongs and handling the brushes as deftly as the sticks.

Sonny Rollins, one of jazz's most influential and most loved saxophonists, also played a key role in the development of hard bop. Rollins started out on the piano before he permanently switched to the tenor sax in the mid-1940s. After a recording debut with Babs Gonzales in 1949, he worked with Miles Davis from 1951, Thelonious Monk from 1953 and the classic Max Roach-Clifford Brown quintet from 1955. He became a bandleader in 1956 and produced a series of brilliant recordings for Blue Note, Prestige, Contemporary and Riverside, including *Saxophone Colossus* (1956), *Tour De Force* (1957), *A Night At The Village Vanguard* (1957) and *Our Man In Jazz* (1962).

Above
Art Blakey's style of drumming set a new precedent for jazz percussionists. During the other musicians' solos, Blakey would spur them on with a drum roll when they seemed to be running out of inspiration.

Left
Wes Montgomery's mellow tone was a result of his picking technique; whereas other guitarists tended to use a plectrum, Wes used his thumb, which one recording engineer described as 'the fastest thing I've ever seen'.

Rollins was such a good soloist that Miles Davis once called him 'the greatest tenor ever', and a sax player cannot get a better compliment than that! Other notable hard bop saxophonists who helped to expand the style included Julian 'Cannonball' Adderley, John Coltrane and, more recently, Michael Brecker.

The trumpet was also a prominent instrument in hard bop, and some of the trumpeters who played it were exceptional musicians. Freddie Hubbard, one of the all-time great trumpeters, made a number of acclaimed recordings with Sonny Rollins, Philly Joe Jones (drummer) and Slide Hampton (trombonist), while Art Farmer's trumpet gave a lyrical feel to recordings by the Horace Silver Quintet and the Gerry Mulligan Quartet during the mid-to-late 1950s. The electric guitar was not originally a prominent instrument in hard bop, but Wes Montgomery's great soloing on *The Incredible Jazz Guitar Of Wes Montgomery* (1960) and *Smokin' At The Half Note* (1965) influenced a later generation of jazz guitar giants, including Pat Metheny and Mike Stern.

see Max Roach pp 182 *see* Art Blakey pp 218 *see* Sonny Rollins pp 233 *see* Horace Silver pp 233

Free Jazz

KEY ARTISTS

Ornette Coleman
Cecil Taylor
John Coltrane
Lennie Tristano
Anthony Braxton
Eric Dolphy
Albert Ayler
Sun Ra
Derek Bailey
Keith Tippett
Elton Dean
Peter Bratzman
Misha Mengleberg

Free jazz is seen by many as an avant-garde art form rather than a type of jazz, with its unpredictable rhythm and chord progressions. Evolving out of bebop in the 1940s and 1950s the exponents of free jazz abandoned traditional forms to expand the music's creative possibilities, challenging mainstream listeners and players alike.

The first documented free jazz recordings were made by the pianist Lennie Tristano and his band for Capitol Records in 1949. He asked the other players to ignore keys, chord structures, time signatures and melodies for the sessions, and just focus on 'reading into each others' minds'. Capitol were not exactly happy about this, but they released the sessions as *Crosscurrents* (1949). Tristano was a pioneer; his unique contrapuntal and improvisational ideas inspired other bebop musicians to try expanding the boundaries of jazz.

'I have always wanted musicians to play on a multiple level with me. I don't want them to follow me. I want them to follow themselves, but to be with me at the same time.'

Ornette Coleman

Coleman And Taylor

Although Tristano and his fellow musicians had been indulging in free jazz improvisation in the 1940s, the term free jazz was not used in earnest until the saxophonist Ornette Coleman released his first album in 1958. Coleman started out by playing Charlie Parker-style alto sax in Fort Worth, Texas, during the 1940s, before he moved to Los Angeles in 1950. He worked there as a lift operator, studied music theory and developed some radical ideas about jazz composition. Although these ideas were initially rejected by most of LA's jazz elite, Coleman eventually found enough allies to form a band: Don Cherry (trumpet), Don Payne (bass), Walter Norris (piano) and Billy Higgins (drums). They recorded *Something Else!!!!* (1958), an original collection of atonal jazz compositions, for Contemporary Records, and it took the jazz world by storm. Coleman's next record, *The Shape Of Jazz To Come* (1959), featured himself, Cherry and Higgins with bassist Charlie Haden. This trimmed-down band line-up showed more focus and a better realization of Coleman's vision. The next offering, *Free Jazz* (1960), was the album that gave the style its name, although Coleman denied later that he had any intention of naming the new type of music he had been developing.

Coleman's music was revolutionary. He used traditional instrumentation and his music swung in a relatively conventional way, but the manner in which he dealt with tonality was extremely unusual. His tunes were based around quirky bebop motifs, and he would use the overall tonality of these to create space for unusually free and expressive solos. Traditional jazz critics initially dismissed this music as 'anti-jazz' because it did not fit in with their conceptions of what jazz should sound like. Nowadays, though, Coleman is seen as a true jazz pioneer, on a par with the likes of Charlie Parker, Louis Armstrong and Miles Davis.

A seminal figure in the free jazz movement was Cecil Taylor who was inspired by Fats Waller's

Above

Cecil Taylor was a leading figure in free jazz until his success was eclipsed by the advent of Ornette Coleman in 1959.

see The Sixties Sources & Sounds pp 240 *see* Jazz Styles Introduction pp 372 *see* Bebop pp 386

single-note melodies and Dave Brubeck's chord clusters, and went on to develop what many critics consider to be one of the most extraordinary jazz piano techniques ever heard; recordings such as *Jazz Advance* (1956), *Looking Ahead!* (1958) and *The World Of Cecil Taylor* (1960) featured highly original versions of standards and atonal tunes, the likes of which had never been heard before. Taylor's approach was very different to Coleman's, as Whitney Balliett once observed in the *New Yorker*: 'Coleman's music is accessible, but he is loath to share it; Taylor's music is difficult, and he is delighted to share it'. 'The American aesthetic landscape is littered with idiosyncratic marvels – Walt Whitman, Charles Ives, D.W. Griffith, Duke Ellington, Jackson Pollock – and Taylor belongs with them,' Balliett continued.

Left

Rumour has it that when gigging with Pee Wee Crayton's band in 1953, Ornette Coleman was paid to forfeit his solos, as audiences would stop dancing when he began to play.

From Coltrane To Braxton

Possibly the most influential free jazz player to emerge during the late 1950s was John Coltrane. Unlike Coleman, 'Trane was already a well-known figure in the mainstream jazz scene; he had played on seminal recordings by Dizzy Gillespie and Miles Davis. While Coleman was defining his art by reducing jazz's tonal base to its bare essence, Coltrane increased the complexity of jazz harmony many times over with his *Giant Steps* (1959) recording. He also began to explore modal jazz concepts, and recorded a series of more progressively 'free' jazz albums up until his premature death at the age of 40 in 1967. Other notable free jazz musicians from this period include multiple reed player Eric Dolphy, saxophonist Albert Ayler and the eccentric keyboard playing bandleader, Sun Ra, who claimed to have arrived here on Earth from Saturn on a date that cannot be revealed because of its mystical astrological significance!

Free jazz developed throughout the early 1960s and 1970s as a growing number of new players such as the Art Ensemble of Chicago and David Murray in the US; Keith Tippett, Steve Beresford, Elton Dean, Trevor Watts, Ian Coxhill and Maggie Nichols amongst others in the UK; Peter Brotzman and Peter Kowald in Germany; and in the Netherlands' Willem Breuker, Misha Mengleberg and Han Bennick decided to follow in the footsteps of Coleman, Coltrane and Taylor, throwing original ideas into the ever-filling free-jazz pot. Derek Bailey, an eccentric guitarist from the UK, pioneered the use of unusual guitar effects and developed a highly idiosyncratic style, completely avoiding conventional melodies, chords or rhythms while Anthony Braxton and Steve Lacy coaxed extraordinary textures out of saxophones and clarinets, on solo and ensemble recordings. These and other free jazz exponents are continuing to produce original and challenging music.

Below

John Coltrane's eagerness to experiment with chords and musical structure led to his being labelled 'eccentric' and even 'unmusical'.

see Lennie Tristano pp 184  see Ornette Coleman pp 248 see John Coltrane pp 250 see Cecil Taylor pp 280

Soul Jazz

KEY ARTISTS

Horace Silver
Jimmy Smith
Cannonball Adderley
Ronnie Foster
Ramsey Lewis
Lou Donaldson
Jack McDuff
Grover Washington Jr.
Big John Patton

Soul jazz stood out from other previous jazz forms. Its melodies were simpler and more rhythmic compared to hard bop, and influences from gospel and R&B were evident. In more traditional jazz forms, soloists would follow walking bass lines or metric cymbal rhythms. In soul jazz, they followed a whole groove, which encouraged a different style of phrasing.

Soul jazz, also known as jazz-funk, can be traced back as far as the early 1950s, when Horace Silver was writing groovy jazz numbers for his now famous trio. One of their recordings, *Horace Silver Trio & Art Blakey* (1952), featured one of the earliest recorded jazz-funk tunes, 'Opus de Funk', which even helped to name the emerging style. The much celebrated hard-bop classic, *Horace Silver And The Jazz Messengers* (1954), also boasts a couple of funky little numbers, including 'The Preacher', one of Silver's most well-known tunes.

The music developed during the 1960s and 1970s within both the jazz and soul music fraternities, although the more modern sounds of fusion and smooth jazz were to overshadow it by the 1980s.

'Funky means earthy and blues-based. It might not be blues itself, but it does have that "down-home" feel to it. Soul is basically the same, but there's an added dimension of feeling and spirit.'
Horace Silver

King Of The Organ

One of the first musicians to be associated with soul jazz was the legendary organist Jimmy Smith. Both of Jimmy's parents played the piano, so it was not long before he did too; he worked with his father in clubs during the 1940s and formed his own trio in 1955. His brand of 'late night' soul jazz met with almost instant success, and albums such as *Home Cookin'* (1958), *Back At The Chicken Shack* (1960) and *Bashin'* (1962) inspired countless other Hammond B3 maestros, including 'Brother' Jack McDuff, Jimmy McGriff, Richard 'Groove' Holmes and Big John Patten. Smith's influence also extended to many major figures in rock and pop, including Steve Winwood, John Mayall, Georgie Fame, Brian Auges and Jon Lord of Deep Purple. After a string of hits in the 1960s, he went off the boil and recorded a series of unremarkable albums in the 1970s and 1980s. By then, though, his reputation as an influential pioneer of soul-jazz organ was assured.

Right
Jimmy Smith has remained faithful to the Hammond organ sound despite advances in keyboard technology. His pioneering, bluesy style was influenced more by saxophonists than fellow keyboard players.

Another soul jazz pioneer was the saxophonist Julian 'Cannonball' Adderley. Nicknamed 'Cannibal' at school because of his capacious liking for food, Julian changed this to 'Cannonball' during his early jazz years. He directed a local high school band during the early 1950s, formed his own jazz combo in 1956, and signed to Riverside Records in 1958. They produced a series of albums, often live, that contributed greatly to the soul jazz style. The first of these, *Somethin' Else* (1958), featured the legendary trumpeter Miles Davis as a sideman. In turn, Cannonball played alto sax on Miles's universally acclaimed *Kind Of Blue* (1959). The most influential Adderley soul jazz recordings were made a few years later, with keyboardist Joe Zawinul in the band; *Jazz Workshop Revisited* (1963) spawned a soul jazz

Far Right
Horace Silver's relationship with the innovative Blue Note label lasted for 28 years. Blue Note is the most famous and influential jazz label and has remained open-minded about emerging jazz styles since it began in 1939.

see The Fifties Sources & Sounds pp 190 *see* Jazz Styles Introduction pp 372 *see* Smooth Jazz pp 402

Left
Cannonball Adderley's impassioned, open-hearted playing style ensured that he quickly shook off the early comparisons to Charlie Parker and established his own role in the jazz scene.

classic in 'Mercy, Mercy, Mercy', penned by Zawinul. The keyboard player's electric piano sound became another recognizable texture in jazz-funk and fusion (he later formed Weather Report with the saxophonist Wayne Shorter).

The guitar also began to appear in soul jazz music during the 1960s, and the velvet-toned Wes Montgomery, an exceptional soloist, often appeared with Jimmy Smith. Wes picked out melodies with his right thumb and fingers, a soft style which originally developed out of trying not to upset his neighbours! His albums were among the first jazz recordings to appeal to a non-jazz public, but in 1968, at the peak of his popularity and aged only 43, he died suddenly of a heart attack. Kenny Burrell was another cool-toned player who graced countless soul jazz recordings during the 1960s and 1970s. His successful career, spanning six decades, has also encompassed hard bop and jazz funk, and his most popular album, *Midnight Blue* (1963), was cited as the main influence for Van Morrison's jazz-pop classic, *Moondance* (1970).

The Next Generations

Many new soul jazz and jazz funk artists began to appear during the 1970s. As the decade progressed, the music became more dance oriented. The guitarist/singer George Benson effortlessly switched between soulful and smooth jazz styles, and the organist Ronnie Foster emerged as a talented mainstream funk keyboardist, whose Blue Note records later became cult items among a younger generation of listeners raised on acid jazz.

A number of soul jazz hits appeared during the 1970s, one of the most famous of which is The Crusaders' 1979 classic 'Street Life'. The guest vocalist on the song was Randy Crawford, who also sang on Cannonball Adderley's *Big Man* (1975), released after the great saxophonist's death. Artists such as the pianist Ramsey Lewis and saxophonist Grover Washington Jr. also produced a lot of lighter instrumental soul jazz during the 1970s and 1980s. Although jazz purists dismissed most of this as borderline muzak, it introduced soul jazz – and, indeed, jazz itself – to a wider audience.

see Jimmy Smith pp 234 *see* Cannonball Adderley pp 266 *see* Wes Montgomery pp 277 *see* Joe Zawinul pp 311

Fusion & Jazz Rock

KEY ARTISTS

Weather Report
Mahavishnu Orchestra
Return To Forever
Tony Williams' Lifetime
Al Di Meola
Pat Metheny
Frank Zappa
Jean-Luc Ponty
Allan Holdsworth
John Scofield

'Fusion' can be applied to any music that blends two or more different styles, though it is normally used to describe the electronic jazz rock movement that emerged in the late 1960s. Some of the musicians expanded the boundaries of both jazz and rock, while others focused on producing sophisticated, but shallow, 'background' music.

Although fusion records have never sold in huge quantities, the style has remained popular within the musical community during the past 30 years. The term 'musician's musician' is often used to describe the top exponents.

It is widely accepted that Miles Davis's *Bitches Brew* (1969) album was the first influential jazz rock recording. It combined modal jazz with rock guitar and drum sounds, and introduced jazz to a wider rock audience. The album featured an extraordinary selection of musicians, including Joe Zawinul and Chick Corea (keyboards), Wayne Shorter (saxophone), John McLaughlin (electric guitar) and Lenny White (drums). These players went on to form three of the most celebrated and influential fusion bands in the early 1970s: Weather Report (Zawinul and Shorter), Return To Forever (Corea and White) and the Mahavishnu Orchestra (McLaughlin).

Right
The Fender Jazz Bass has a warm but punchy sound and sounds not unlike an upright string bass. Jaco Pastorius of Weather Report used a fretless version on the track 'Night Passage'.

'Bitches Brew *has a kind of searching quality because Miles was onto the process of discovering this new music and developing it.*'

Dave Holland (bass player on *Bitches Brew*)

Weather Report And Mahavishnu

Weather Report was one of the most successful fusion bands, with albums reaching the Top 50 charts on both sides of the Atlantic. Their earliest recordings were patchy, but *Black Market* (1976) featured strong compositions and introduced the legendary Jaco Pastorius on bass guitar. The combination of strikingly original tunes, Shorter's searing sax lines, Zawinul's colourful synth passages (played on Arp and Oberheim instruments) and Pastorius's jaw-dropping bass work (ranging from 'singing' melodic passages to unusual harmonics and ultra-fast riffs) proved to be an even bigger success with their next album, *Heavy Weather* (1977). Further recordings, such as *Mr. Gone* (1978), *Night Passage* (1980) and *Weather Report* (1982), confirmed the band's status as a top-flight jazz act, although Pastorius left in 1982 and the band eventually split in 1986. Sadly, Pastorius died in 1987 after he was beaten up outside a nightclub in Fort Lauderdale, Florida.

The Mahavishnu Orchestra was more rock-oriented than Weather Report. Formed by John McLaughlin during the early 1970s and influenced by Eastern mysticism, the original band featured McLaughlin on electric guitar, along with Jan Hammer (keyboards), Jerry Goodman (violin), Rick Laird (bass) and Billy Cobham (drums). Their explosive creativity broke new boundaries in jazz, both in terms of virtuosity and complexity, and their albums *The Inner Mounting Flame* (1971) and *Birds of Fire* (1972) are widely regarded as fusion classics. Hammer, Goodman and Cobham left to work on their

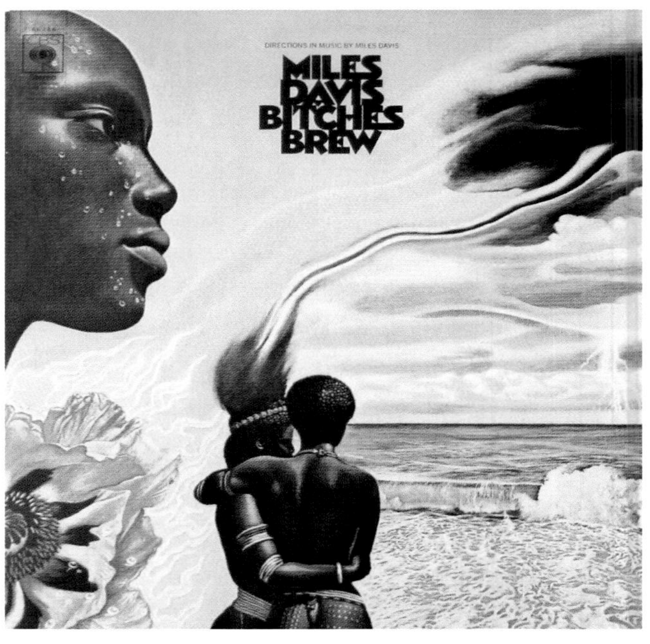

Right
The groundbreaking *Bitches Brew* marked an irrevocable change in the development of jazz. The dark but fiery combination of Miles Davis's horn and Wayne Shorter's saxophone on the album blew away all who heard it.

see The Seventies Sources & Sounds pp 286 *see* Jazz Styles Introduction pp 372 *see* Free Jazz pp 394

own projects a year later, and McLaughlin reformed the band with various other line-ups for the next two decades. He also formed Shakti, an exploratory 'Eastern' acoustic fusion band, with renowned Indian classical musicians such as L. Shankar (violin) and Zakir Hussain (tablas) during the mid-1970s, as well as a much-celebrated acoustic guitar trio with flamenco virtuoso Paco de Lucía and fusion ace Al Di Meola. The trio's live recording, *Friday Night In San Francisco* (1980), features some breathtakingly fleet guitar work that has to be heard to be believed.

Other Influential Bands

The other primary 1970s fusion band to directly emerge out of the *Bitches Brew* scene was Chick Corea's Return To Forever. Their first line-up was a Latin-style band led by Chick on keyboards, but by 1975 the group had developed into an all-out fusion outfit featuring Al Di Meola (guitar), Stanley Clarke (bass) and Lenny White (drums). Their *Romantic Warrior* (1976) recording was a landmark jazz-rock album, featuring six complex, intricately crafted instrumentals that were to inspire rock and jazz musicians for years to come. It also acted as a launching pad for Di Meola's solo career; he went on to record *Land Of The Midnight Sun* (1976), *Elegant Gypsy* (1976), *Casino* (1977) and *Splendido Hotel* (1979), which resulted in *Guitar Player* magazine readers voting him Best Jazz Player for five consecutive years.

There were a number of other seminal fusion recordings made during the 1970s: *Believe It* (1975) by Tony Williams introduced Allan Holdsworth's unique but influential legato lead-guitar style; Frank Zappa's *Roxy & Elsewhere* (1974) fused jazz and rock with a warped, but much-loved sense of humour; and the Pat Metheny Group with its self-titled album (1978) forged a new, earthy jazz style that eventually earned the group huge audiences, critical acclaim and Grammy awards. Across the Atlantic, Brand X's *Unorthodox Behaviour* (1976) and Soft Machine's *Third* (1970) proved that British bands were also capable of producing world-class fusion, while the French and Belgians also showed their fusion mettle with violinist Jean-Luc Ponty's *Enigmatic Ocean* (1977) and Marc Moulin's *Placebo* (1973).

By contrast, the 1980s were relatively quiet for fusion, although Corea, Holdsworth and the American guitarist John Scofield made some significant recordings during this period. In more recent years, Tribal Tech, led by guitarist Scott Henderson and bass virtuoso Gary Willis, has kept the fusion flag flying. Their recent recordings, *Thick* (1999) and *Rocket Science* (2000), show that jazz rock is still alive and kicking. The latest platform for 'jazz rock' has evolved into the 'jam band scene'.

Above
An incredibly talented and versatile pianist, Chick Corea made forays into fusion jazz that were only a part, albeit an important one, of his musical output. He also peformed Latin and free jazz and music from the classical repertoire.

see Wayne Shorter pp 279 *see* Tony Williams pp 281 *see* John McLaughlin pp 300 *see* Jaco Pastorius pp 309

Acid Jazz

KEY ARTISTS

The Brand New Heavies
Jamiroquai
Galliano
Groove Collective
James Taylor Quartet
Courtney Pine
United Future Organisation
Stereo MC's

'Acid jazz was the most significant jazz form to emerge out of the British music scene.'
Q magazine, UK

Acid jazz is a lively, groove-oriented music style that combines elements from jazz, funk and hip hop, with an emphasis on jazz dance. The term 'acid jazz' was first used during the late 1980s, both as the name of an American record label and the title of a British jazz funk, 'rare groove' compilation series.

Interest had originally been sparked by a thriving London club scene, where hip DJs were playing rare 1970s jazz funk records. This encouraged British and American underground musicians such as The Brand New Heavies, Jamiroquai, Stereo MC's, Galliano and Groove Collective, who began to popularize the style by the 1990s.

Above
N'Dea Davenport, as a member of the Brand New Heavies, was an important figure in the development of acid jazz. After leaving the band in 1994, she embarked on a solo career, releasing her debut album four years later.

One of the first DJs to be identified with acid jazz was the London-based Gilles Peterson, who began broadcasting jazz funk sets from his garden shed at home and DJing at London clubs in the late 1980s. He teamed up with Eddie Piller, who had previously released a debut album by a young, contemporary Hammond organ virtuoso, James Taylor, to form Acid Jazz Records. The label's first releases were a series of compilations titled *Totally Wired*, which alternated jazz funk obscurities from the 1970s with updated tracks from the new acid jazz movement. Peterson later formed his own acid jazz label, Talkin' Loud Records.

Mainstream Acid Jazz

Acid jazz entered into the mainstream in 1990, after The Brand New Heavies released their self-titled debut album on the Acid Jazz label. Formed in 1985 by drummer Jan Kincaid, guitarist Simon Bartholomew and bassist/keyboardist Andrew Levy – old school friends from London – they were originally an instrumental band inspired by James Brown and The Meters, whose records were getting extensive play around the rare groove scene. The band began recording their own material, added a singer and a brass section, and gained exposure via the club circuit. Their first album was a success and it was followed by a string of hit singles in 1991 in the UK and US. Then came *Heavy Rhyme Experience, Vol. 1* (1992), featuring guest appearances by the rappers Main Source, Gang Starr, Grand Puba and The Pharcyde. The following album, *Brother Sister* (1994), went platinum in Britain, and the band's success has since continued on both sides of the Atlantic with *Original Flava* (1994) and *Delicious* (1997).

After the emergence of the Heavies, Galliano and a few smaller UK acid jazz bands, a spate of compilations were launched en masse by record labels, leaving many consumers confused over exactly what the style was or who played it. The confusion increased when even more independent acid jazz communities began to spring up all over the US during the early 1990s. By then, the term could refer to anything from Jamiroquai's commercial soul funk to the James Taylor Quartet's rendering of the 'Starsky And Hutch Theme', or from the ethnic eclecticism of the Japanese producers United Future Organisation to the hip hop poetry of New York's Groove Collective.

see The Eighties Sources & Sounds pp 316 *see* Jazz Styles Introduction pp 372 *see* Soul Jazz pp 396

Left
Jason Kay has been largely responsible for bringing the acid jazz sound into the musical mainstream. The themes explored in his songs include the environment, government incompetence and space travel.

The creation of the UK singer/songwriter Jason Kay, Jamiroquai has perhaps popularized acid jazz more than any other band. Although some listeners today dismiss them as mere Stevie Wonder imitators, the band has experienced chart success all over the world with an irresistible blend of house rhythms and 1970s-era soul/funk. As he did not originally have a band to back up his songs, Jay came up with his own project and coined its moniker by adding the name of an American Indian tribe, Iroquois, to the music term 'jam'. He assembled a group of musicians and produced some demos, which impressed the Acid Jazz label enough to issue the debut single 'When You Gonna Learn?' in late 1992. A hit, it led to a long-term and lucrative recording contract with Sony, who released *Emergency On Planet Earth* (1992) and *The Return Of The Space Cowboy* (1994), both major hit albums in the UK. This success spread to America with Jamiroquai's third effort, *Travelling Without Moving* (1996), which contained the worldwide hit 'Virtual Insanity'. The band is still going strong, although they now appear to be past their prime.

Cutting-Edge Jazz

A number of more 'serious' jazz artists, including the UK's Courtney Pine, the American veteran Pharaoh Sanders (saxophonists) and the American Pat Metheny (guitarist), were also associated with acid jazz forms during the 1990s. Pine and Sanders both contributed to a British compilation series titled *Rebirth Of The Cool* (named after the classic Miles Davis album *Birth Of The Cool*), while The Pat Metheny Group used hip hop-style grooves to great effect on their *We Live Here* (1995) album.

Nu Jazz

Since the 1990s, acid jazz has moved more left-field, evolving into the nu jazz (nu-fusion or future-jazz) movement via the house music-led club dance floor. The cutting edge, springing from the underground, has been exploited commercially by France's St. Germain and even the 'establishment's' Herbie Hancock (*Future2Future*, 2002). A serious jazz vibe is being combined with percussion-led, acousto-electric keyboards and programmed beats transfused with the hip hop/drum 'n' bass repetitions of house music, Afro-Brazilian beats and live jazz. Leading the nu jazz field are labels such as Germany's Compost (Jazzanova, Beanfield, Les Gammas, Kyoto Jazz Massive and Minus 8) and UK's 'West London collective' working with producer-DJ IG Culture and artists such as Kaidi Tatham, Modaji and Seiji. In nu jazz, vocalists are coming into their own again, high in both profile and mix – Vikter Duplaix, Robert Owens, Peven Everett and Ursula Rucker in the US, Victor Davies, Joseph Malik, Kate Phillips (Bembé Segué) and Marcus Begg in the UK and Europe. Producers collaborating with live musicians are mixing (today's technological equivalent of scoring/arranging), remixing and sampling to brilliant effect, and new technology is opening up even more possibilities for jazz. Indeed, as Sun Ra predicted as long ago as 1972, 'Space Is The Place', especially for the MP3 generation.

Below
The James Taylor Quartet has kept acid jazz alive through continual gigging and recording. They have also been involved in writing film music, including the theme to *Austin Powers: International Man Of Mystery*.

see Sun Ra pp 264 *see* Herbie Hancock pp 305 *see* Pat Metheny pp 328 *see* Courtney Pine pp 336

Smooth Jazz

KEY ARTISTS

George Benson
Yellowjackets
Steely Dan
Kenny G
Larry Carlton
Spyro Gyra
The Rippingtons

Slick, 'radio-friendly' smooth jazz emerged in the 1970s, and it has continued to evolve ever since. The most artful examples can make for rewarding listening, while blander compositions can be recognized by any combination of musical clichés: light funk grooves, cool jazz chords, slapped bass lines, corny horn accompaniments and predictable solos.

The style has drawn fierce criticism from jazz purists, but its unobtrusiveness has often made it popular with restaurants, wine bars and other public places where sophisticated-sounding background music is required to give clients or customers a chill-out vibe.

'Kenny G has long been the musician many jazz listeners love to hate.'

All Music Guide

Above

The musically open-minded guitarist George Benson infuriated jazz fans with his covers of pop records, but he refuses to be constricted by what is expected of him, explaining that his first duty is as an entertainer.

Many would use the term 'fusion' to describe smooth jazz, even though the same word is more commonly used to describe the more exploratory jazz rock scene that emerged out of Miles Davis's *Bitches Brew* period. This seems rather contradictory, as smooth jazz is normally cool background music while jazz rock is often complex and demanding. But it probably explains why jazz rock fans tend to pour scorn over even the most distinguished smooth jazz acts whenever they are mentioned.

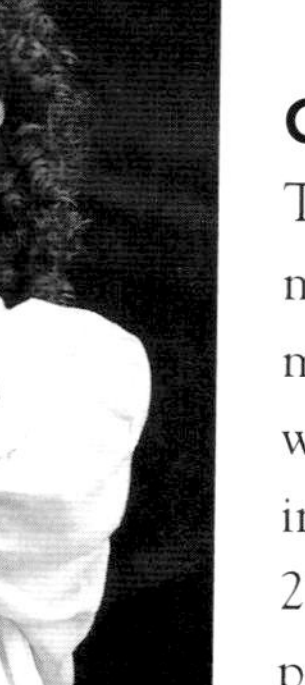

Cool Sounds In The 1970s

The earliest smooth jazz artists were musicians who wanted to make more commercial, accessible music without losing their jazz roots. Born in Pittsburgh, Pennsylvania on 22 March, 1943, George Benson is perhaps the best example of this. His stepfather was a musician who taught him to play the ukulele and guitar, and after being enticed by the jazz sounds of saxophonist Charlie Parker and guitarist Grant Green, he decided to become a jazz guitarist. He emerged as a popular soloist in the style of Wes Montgomery, and played alongside top artists such as Herbie Hancock, Jack McDuff and Ron Carter during the 1960s. In the 1970s, he switched over to a more commercial, jazz funk style, and was rewarded with serious album sales. *Breezin'* (1976) sold more than two million units and was the first of several Grammy-winning recordings with Warner Brothers, while *In Flight* (1976) was a polished album that featured Benson – an accomplished vocalist – 'scat' singing in unison with his trademark cool solos. He switched to a more overtly pop vocal sound during the 1980s, to the disgust of some jazz purists, but he later compensated by recording with Count Basie's old band in 1990.

Benson's popularity inspired other jazz guitarists to go 'smooth' during the 1970s. Earl Klugh appeared with acoustic guitar albums, including the acclaimed *Earl Klugh* (1976) and *Finger Painting* (1977), while Lee Ritenour produced Latin-influenced recordings such as *Guitar Player* (1976) and *Captain Fingers* (1977),

see The Eighties Sources & Sounds pp 316 *see* Jazz Styles Introduction pp 372 *see* Fusion & Jazz Rock pp 398

and Larry Carlton delighted listeners with his excellent soloing on *Larry Carlton* (1977). Keyboard players were at it too, with Herbie Hancock using electronically synthesized vocals on *Sunlight* (1977), Ramsey Lewis producing slick recordings such as *Tequila Mockingbird* (1978) and George Duke recording many albums, including his critically acclaimed *Solo Keyboard Album* (1976). On the band side, Spyro Gyra delivered the infectious *Morning Dance* (1979) and even jazz rock heroes Steely Dan fully developed their own unique and sophisticated brand of jazz pop on the albums *Aja* (1977) and *Gaucho* (1980).

Further Refinements

Some of the most polished, artistic and commercial examples of smooth jazz emerged during the 1980s and 1990s. Perhaps the most respected band in this period was the Yellowjackets. They formed in 1977, when the guitarist Robben Ford assembled a group of veteran session musicians to work on one of his albums. Ford and the trio of musicians – keyboardist Russell Ferrante, bassist Jimmy Haslip and drummer Ricky Lawson – enjoyed working together, hence the Yellowjackets. Ford and Lawson left after two well-received albums, but the band continued to refine its sound: by the late 1980s, recordings such as *Politics* (1988) and *The Spin* (1989) demonstrated that they were already a cut above most other smooth jazz bands in terms of artistry. By the mid-1990s, they had developed a definitive smooth jazz sound on the albums *Greenhouse* (1991), *Like A River* (1992) and *Blue Hats* (1997). They are still going strong, and their lively 2002 *Mint Jam* album (Heads Up label) featured among the 2003 Grammy nominations.

At the more commercial end of the musical spectrum, Kenny Gorelick (Kenny G) has been introducing larger pop audiences to smooth jazz. He began playing professionally with Barry White in 1976, and, after graduating from the University of Washington, worked with the keyboardist Jeff Lorber before signing to Arista as a solo artist in 1982. His first three albums were moderately successful, but his fourth, *Duotones* (1986), hit the big time with a hugely popular instrumental hit, 'Songbird'. Since then, he has released a succession of popular smooth jazz albums, which have sold more than 30 million copies and annoyed jazz purists who consider them innocuous and one-dimensional. Various other smooth jazz bands, such as the Rippingtons, Fattburger and Acoustic Alchemy, as well as solo artists such as Joyce Cooling, Dave Koz and Boney James, have helped to maintain the popularity of this style.

Above
Donald Fagan, whose distinctive vocals added an unusual dimension to Steely Dan. Their music is an obscure but strangely accessible combination of jazz, rock and pop, with a hint of country.

Far Left
There are many who would dispute the music of Kenny G deserving the name jazz; to his credit he prefers to describe his music as 'instrumental pop'. His records are popular as relaxing background music.

see Ron Carter pp 268 *see* Wes Montgomery pp 277 *see* Kenny G pp 335 *see* Yellowjackets pp 339

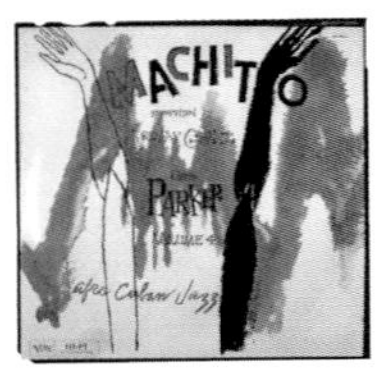

Latin Jazz

KEY ARTISTS

Machito
Mario Bauzá
Chano Pozo
Dizzy Gillespie
Israel 'Cachao' López
Arturo Sandoval
Paquito D'Rivera
Eddie Palmieré
Danilo Pérez
David Sánchez
Tito Puente
Patato Valdés

Latin jazz is commonly defined as the fusion of American jazz melodies, improvisation and chords with Latin American rhythms, predominantly those of Afro-Cuban origin. How this marriage of styles occurred is also one of the most significant cultural, musical exchanges in history.

Mention the birth of Latin jazz to any aficionado of the art form and they will invariably reply with two names: Machito and Mario Bauzá. The former was born Francisco Raul Gutiérrez Grillo on 16 February 1912, in Cuba. The young vocalist/maraca man hit New York City in 1937, where he played stints with Xavier Cugat and Noro Morales before forming his own band, Machito's Afro-Cubans. By 1940, Machito asked his brother-in-law, Mario Bauzá (who was married to his sister Estella), a trumpeter, pianist, arranger and composer who had already worked with the likes of Dizzy Gillespie and Chick Webb, to be his band's musical arranger. It was this orchestra that two American musicians – one in Los Angeles, one in New York City – would hear, and the musical world would never be the same again.

'We play jazz with the Latin touch, that's all, you know.'

Tito Puente

The Night That Changed Dizzy's Life

On 31 May 1943, the already legendary Gillespie went to the Park Place Ballroom in New York. There, he heard Machito and his orchestra perform 'Tanga' (meaning marijuana), a dazzling new Afro-Cuban composition written by Bauzá during a rehearsal. The piece is widely recognized to be a breakthrough in the creation of a new style of music, which has been called Afro-Cuban jazz, Cubop and Latin jazz, a term Bauzá reportedly hated. Still, Gillespie would often recall that night as one that changed his life. The trumpet virtuoso was so taken with the conga, bongos, and 'clave' rhythms that he immediately incorporated them into his own group.

In January 1946, the influential American pianist/bandleader Stan Kenton was awestruck when he heard the same 'Tanga' at a club in Los Angeles. Soon, he too added Latin elements to virtually all of his music. Gillespie made Latin music history himself with his 30 December 1947 recording of 'Manteca' on RCA Victor, which he co-wrote with a musician introduced to him by Bauzá. It was the master *conguero* Chano Pozo, another seminal figure in the birth of Latin jazz and the key figure in Gillespie's continued 'latinization' of jazz. 'Manteca' would subsequently become Gillespie's signature tune and one of the most covered standards in the history of the genre.

Following closely behind Machito, Pozo, Gillespie and Kenton is master *timbalero*, bandleader and composer Tito Puente, also known as El Rey del Timbal and The Mambo King. Born in New York to Puerto Rican parents, Puente was instrumental in taking jazz to a broader audience thanks to his big band orchestrations and his onstage flourish. And, of course, he wrote and recorded 'Oye Cómo Va', later popularized by Carlos Santana, which incorporated a *coro* section and used other eminently Latin elements, such as a *charanga*-style flute and, of course, the characteristic syncopated piano cha-cha riff.

Another pioneer who took Latin jazz to the mainstream was master *conguero* Ramón 'Mongo' Santamaría, best known for his hit rendition of Herbie Hancock's 'Watermelon Man' and for authoring jazz standard 'Afro Blue'. It was with Santamaria's band, that a then-young Chick Corea first received major exposure, while present-day *conguero* Poncho Sánchez cites Santamaría as his mentor and major influence.

Above
Harlem-born Puerto Rican Tito Puente's arrangements of the mambo and cha-cha earned him admiration across a wide cultural sphere. He recorded over a hundred albums and has a star on the Hollywood Walk of Fame.

see The Forties Sources & Sounds pp 144 *see* Jazz Styles Introduction pp 372 *see* Fusion & Jazz Rock pp 398

has renewed interest in the genre. Currently, pianist Valdés is the elder statesman of a new generation of highly virtuosic Latin jazz pianists, including Gonzalo Rubalcaba, who freely blend American standards with Cuban rhythms and are also highly experimental in their own compositions.

Other current leaders of the movement include Sandoval and countryman Paquito D'Rivera, who, like Valdés, were once members of experimental Cuban jazz ensemble Irakere, and are currently living in the US. D'Rivera in particular, expanded beyond his brand of Afro-Cuban jazz to delve extensively in to other styles of Latin jazz, incorporating rhythms from Venezuela, Peru and Puerto Rico into his music.

The openness to rhythms outside of Cuba is congruent with the rise of several Latin jazz musicians from other countries, including pianists Danilo Pérez (Panama) and Michel Camilo (Dominican Republic).

Left
Machito (right) inspired players such as Dizzy Gillespie and Stan Kenton to experiment with Latin sounds. Kenton described him as the 'greatest exponent of Afro-Cuban jazz' and even named a track after him.

A New Generation

Other direct descendants of Latin jazz's founding fathers include brothers Charlie and Eddie Palmieri, born in New York to Puerto Rican parents. Both of them pianists, composers, bandleaders and arrangers, they created their separate bands and helped shape the New York salsa sound. While Eddie is best known for his work with his band La Perfecta, which incorporated trombones and trumpets, Charlie revived the concept of the *descarga* (Latin jam session) originally popularized by veteran Cuban bassist Israel López 'Cachao'. Largely forgotten in the 1980s, Cachao lived a brilliant revival in the mid-1990s when he was rediscovered by Cuban-born Hollywood film star Andy García, who directed a documentary on Cachao's life, *Cachao: como su ritmo no hay dos*. Later on, García would also be involved in a film project based on the life of another Cuban musician, trumpeter Arturo Sandoval. Those two projects, coupled with the 2000 film *Calle 54*, which features a series of Latin jazz performances by the likes of Jerry González and the Fort Apache Band, Cuban percussionist Patato Valdés and fellow countryman and pianist Chucho Valdés,

Below
Mario Bauzá started out as a professional clarinet and oboe player in the Havana Philharmonic before moving to New York in 1930. It was there, while playing with Noble Sissle, that he took up the trumpet.

see Mario Bauzá pp 170 *see* Machito pp 178 *see* Paquito D'Rivera pp 334 *see* Chucho Valdés pp 366

Brazilian Jazz

KEY ARTISTS

Laurindo Almeida
Bud Shank
João Gilberto
Antonio Carlos Jobim
Luiz Bonfá
Charlie Byrd
Stan Getz
Astrud Gilberto
Hermeto Pascoal
Baden Powell

In the mid-1950s, a cultural crossfertilization of Brazilian samba rhythms, American cool jazz and sophisticated harmonies led to the development of bossa nova. In the early 1960s the bossa nova movement swept through the United States and Europe producing a strain of Brazilian-influenced jazz that remains a vital part of the jazz scene.

By the early 1950s, a few pioneering Brazilian composers began listening seriously to American jazz, particularly the limpid-toned West Coast variety practised by Chet Baker, Gerry Mulligan and Shorty Rogers. In absorbing that cool influence, composers such as Antonio Carlos Jobim, João Gilberto, Baden Powell and Luiz Bonfá stripped the complex polyrhythms of Afro-Brazilian samba down to their undulating essence and offered a more intimate approach, in which melodies were caressed rather than belted out in the raucous Carnival fashion.

'I just thought it was pretty music. I never thought it would be a hit.'

Stan Getz on his first involvement with Brazilian music, the album *Jazz Samba*

Blame It On The Bossa Nova

Around the same time, American jazz saxophonist Bud Shank (from the West Coast branch of cool jazz) had joined forces with Brazilian guitarist Laurindo Almeida in a quartet that blended Brazilian rhythms and folk melodies with cool jazz improvising. Recorded five years before the term 'bossa nova' was even coined, their 1953 collaboration on the World Pacific label, *Brazilliance*, would have a significant impact on the ultimate architects of the bossa nova movement.

In 1956, the Bahian guitarist/composer João Gilberto relocated from Salvador to Rio de Janeiro, where the colourful cultural mix was inspiring another brilliant guitarist/composer, Antonio Carlos Jobim. The two began to collaborate, and in July 1958, Gilberto recorded Jobim and Vinícius de Moraes's 'Chega de Saudade' ('No More Blues'), which became the hit single (backed by his own 'Bim Bom') widely considered to be responsible for launching the bossa nova movement in Brazil. Their follow-up single, Jobim's 'Desafinado' ('Off-Key') was a fully formed masterpiece that floated on Gilberto's distinctive, syncopated guitar rhythm, which would become the basis for this new, hybrid form. Momentum for the movement picked up the following year with the popularity of the Oscar-winning film *Black Orpheus*, a romance set in Rio de Janeiro during Carnival, featuring a beguiling score by Jobim and fellow Brazilian guitarist/composer Luiz Bonfá, and introducing such enduring bossa nova anthems as 'Manhã de Carnaval' and 'Samba de Orfeo'. Then, in 1960, Gilberto and Jobim recorded 12 original bossa nova pieces on the largely overlooked Capitol release, *Samba de Uma Note So*.

Meanwhile, this 'quiet revolution' continued to unfold. In 1961, the US State Department sponsored a good-will jazz tour of Latin America that included American guitarist Charlie Byrd. A swing through Brazil on that tour was a revelation to Byrd, igniting the guitarist's love affair with bossa nova. Back in the States, Byrd played some bossa nova tapes to his friend, the soft-toned tenor saxophonist Stan Getz, who then convinced Creed Taylor at Verve to record an album of the alluring Brazilian music with himself and Byrd. Their historic 1962 collaboration, *Jazz Samba*,

Right
Black Orpheus was an updating of the Orpheus & Eurydice myth, set against the background of a Brazilian Carnival. The intense vitality of the music in the film fascinated viewers and the soundtrack sold in the millions.

see The Sixties Sources & Sounds pp 240 *see* Jazz Styles Introduction pp 372 *see* Cool Jazz pp 390

introduced the bossa nova sound to mass North American audiences. *Jazz Samba* enjoyed immense popularity on the strength of the hit single, Jobim's 'Desafinado' ('Off-Key'), prompting a rush by American jazz record labels to repeat its success, which produced a flood of copycat releases between 1962 and 1963, including Gene Ammons's *Bad! Bossa Nova*, Dave Brubeck's *Bossa Nova USA*, Herbie Mann's *Do The Bossa Nova With Herbie Mann* and Eddie Harris's *Bossa Nova*.

A Universally Appealing Message

In 1963, Jobim and Gilberto came to New York to collaborate with Stan Getz on another bossa nova classic, *Getz/Gilberto*. The album made Gilberto an international superstar and also introduced his then-wife, the singer Astrud Gilberto, whose seductive vocals graced the mega-hit single, 'The Girl From Ipanema', written by Jobim and Vinícius de Moraes. At this time, de Moraes was also working with the influential guitarist Baden Powell, composing a number of important Afro-sambas, paying tribute to the African tradition in Brazilian music.

Getz's recorded output for Verve during the bossa nova craze also included a collaboration with bandleader/arranger Gary McFarland (1962's *Big Band Bossa Nova*), guitarist/composer Luiz Bonfá (1963's *Jazz Samba Encore!*) and guitarist/bossa nova pioneer Laurindo Almeida (1963's *Stan Getz With Guest Artist Laurindo Almeida*). All of Getz's important recordings in this genre have been compiled on a five-CD set by Verve, entitled *The Bossa Nova Years (Girl From Ipanema)*.

While Getz passed away in 1991, Gilberto continues to perform and record. Today, the veteran architect of Brazil's bossa nova movement is known in his native country as simply *O Mito* (The Legend). His 2000 recording, *João Voz E Violão*, is stripped down to the bare essentials – João's magnificent voice and his silky-sounding guitar accompaniment.

The alluring sound of bossa nova has continued to thrive over the past four decades. Its universally appealing message has been and is continuing to be spread by prominent Brazilian artists such as singer-composers Milton Nascimento and Ivan Lins; pianist/composer/orchestrator Hermeto Pascoal; pianist/vocalist Eliane Elias; vocalists Joyce and Flora Purim; guitarists Toninho Horta, Carlos Barbosa-Lima, Oscar Castro-Neves and Baden Powell; percussionist Airto Moreira; and the group Trio da Paz (comprised of guitarist Romero Lubambo, bassist Nilson Matta and drummer Duduka da Fonseca), as well as by scores of jazz artists all over the world.

Left

Versed in rural blues as a boy, Charlie Byrd turned to jazz in 1945 after meeting Django Reinhardt in Paris.

Below

Jobim's prolific songwriting and adaptability to concert hall performances led to comparisons with George Gershwin. His studio albums showcase his gentle strumming technique and haunting vocals.

see Chet Baker pp 216 *see* João Gilberto pp 222 *see* Antonio Carlos Jobim pp 227 *see* Stan Getz pp 272

BLUES STYLES

One of the great things about blues music is its simplicity; its recognizable 12-bar structure, often repetitive lyrics and familiar instrumentation create an instantly accessible sound that has a powerful emotional effect on the listener. However, the inventiveness of countless performers over the years has sent the blues in many different directions and has transformed it into the wide-ranging genre that it has become.

This section of the book examines the various styles of blues music that have arisen from musicians delivering their own take on the standard blues formula. A number of factors can inform the development of music: in some cases the very landscape in which the musicians live may provide a key influence (consider the beautiful yet desolate music inspired by the Mississippi Delta); in other cases the cultural mix might alter the sound (for example, the unique blues style that grew out of the cultural melting pot of New Orleans, with its Creole and Hispanic influences).

The variety of instruments and instrumental techniques available to the players has a major influence on the development of different blues styles, in addition of course to the individual ingenuities of the artists, producers and bandleaders involved. The influences of other developing musical styles tend to have an irreversible effect on the genres that surround them; in its global spread since its early days in localized pockets of America, the blues has absorbed aspects of other musical styles, while continuing to have a heavy influence on other genres such as rock music. However, whether from Chicago, Texas or London; whether jump, R&B or rock, the raw power of blues music remains constant.

BLUE OASIS
Jeff
BECK'S
GUITAR SHOP

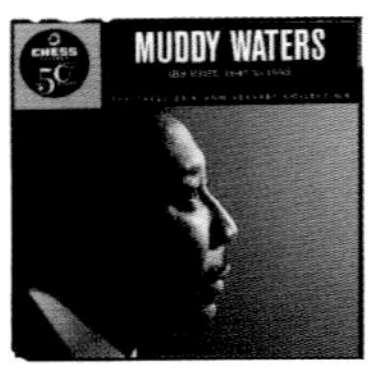

Introduction

STYLES

Work Songs
Delta/Country Blues
Louisiana Blues
Texas Blues
Boogie-Woogie
Chicago Blues
Piedmont Blues (East Coast Blues)
Jump Blues
British Blues
Rhythm & Blues
Blues Rock
Modern Electric Blues

Few would deny that the blues has played a more important role in the history of popular culture than any other musical genre. As well as being a complete art form in itself, it is a direct ancestor to the different types of current popular music we know and love today. Without the blues there would have been no Beatles or Jimi Hendrix, no Led Zeppelin or Nirvana, Louis Armstrong or Miles Davis, James Brown or Stevie Wonder, Pink Floyd or Frank Zappa, Oasis or Blur … the list is endless.

The blues emerged out of the hardships endured by generations of African American slaves during the late nineteenth and early twentieth centuries. By 1900, the genre had developed to a three-line stanza, with a vocal style derived from southern work songs. 'Call and response' songs were a fundamental part of African slave labour, with the gang leader singing a line and the other workers following in response. This style was developed further by early blues guitar players, who would sing a line and then answer it on the guitar. They would often sing when they were feeling depressed, or 'blue', and by 1910, the word 'blues' was commonly used in southern states to describe this musical tradition. Capitalizing on its popularity, the music industry published 'Memphis Blues' by the black composer W.C. Handy in 1912.

'The blues is a low-down, aching chill; if you ain't never had 'em, I hope you never will.'
Robert Johnson

Above
Bessie Smith's powerful, roaring voice brought intense misery and despair to numbers such as 'Nobody Knows You When You're Down And Out'.

By the 1920s, rural African-Americans had migrated to the big cities in search of work, bringing their music with them. Mamie Smith, a New York vaudeville singer, made the first known blues recording, 'Crazy Blues', with Okeh Records in 1920. Its success convinced singers such as Bessie Smith and Ma Rainey to follow suit. Louis Armstrong accompanied them on their recordings, absorbing some of their blues vibes into his jazz singing and trumpeting styles. Street musicians such as Blind Lemon Jefferson also started to make recordings, which inspired a whole generation of blues guitar players.

The 1930s were a crucial period in the development of the blues, for it was then that early Mississippi Delta blues performers Charley Patton, Son House and Robert Johnson travelled throughout the southern states, singing about their woes, freedom, love and sex to community after community. Johnson, who allegedly made a pact with the Devil in order to become a better guitar player, was the first true blues performance artist. On the East Coast, musicians such as Blind Boy Fuller, Sonny Terry and the Rev. Gary Davis developed a more folky, 'Piedmont' blues style. In Kansas City, Count Basie was absorbing the blues and reinjecting it into the big band jazz style of the swing era. And in New York, Billie Holiday, one of the most famous blues/jazz singers of all time, began captivating audiences with her haunting, sensuous voice.

As urban blues grew and developed in cities all over the country, the 1940s witnessed the birth of a wide range of new musical styles. In Los Angeles, bandleaders Louis Jordan and Tiny Bradshaw pioneered jump blues, an energetic style based around singers and saxophone players. They still used the traditional call-and-response blues approach, but this time it was the singers ('shouters') and saxophonists ('honkers') who

Above

It was in Mississippi bars such as this one that the blues began to take shape.

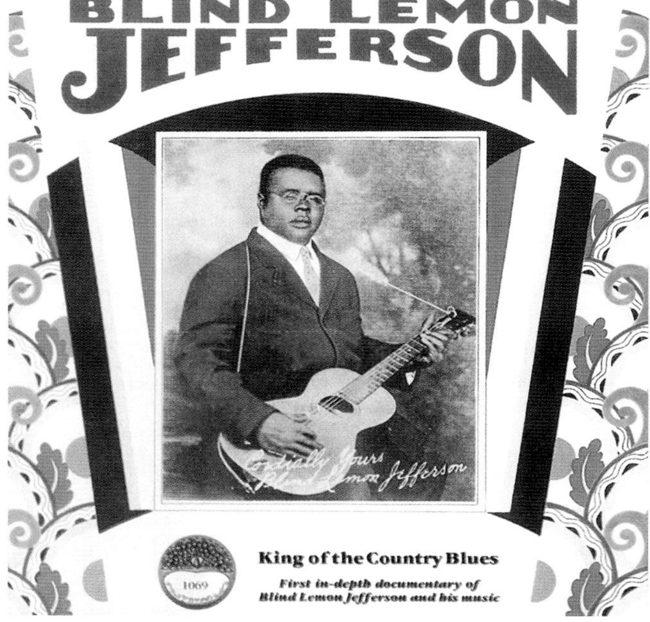

Left

Blind Lemon Jefferson was one of many successful blind bluesmen. Their lack of sight heightened their other senses, leading to expressive playing and vocals, while being unable to work gave them plenty of practice time.

see Louis Armstrong pp 44 *see* Bessie Smith pp 64 *see* Robert Johnson pp 112 *see* Billie Holiday pp 156

vibrato and note-bending techniques on his beloved guitar, 'Lucille'; these are now used today by all blues lead-guitar players. Hooker developed a different style, where he stomped continuously with his right foot while singing and playing. Wolf injected more power and frustration into the blues and Walker jazzed things up, but it was perhaps Muddy Waters, with his passionate singing and biting guitar tones, who popularized the style more than anyone else from this period. Some bluesmen, including Big Bill Broonzy, visited England, where their performances inspired local musicians to adopt the style. Chris Barber, a jazz bandleader, assembled his own blues outfit with guitarist Alexis Korner and harmonica player Cyril Davies; they went on to become Blues Incorporated.

The 1960s witnessed a musical and cultural revolution, as British guitar players such as Eric Clapton and Peter Green began to mimic American bluesmen, using solid body guitars and more powerful amps to get a harder, more driving sound than their American mentors. The Rolling Stones (named after a Muddy Waters' song) developed a blues-influenced style, injecting rawness and attitude into mainstream chart music. These Brits had enormous worldwide success with their anglicized blues, much to the surprise of the American traditionals. But what went around came around, and the success of British bluesmen encouraged more listeners to check out some of the earlier, more authentic blues artists, whose audience numbers began to swell. 'They stole my music,' Muddy Waters said of the Rolling Stones, 'but they gave me my name.' Another musical phenomenon of the 1960s was Jimi Hendrix, an avant-garde bluester who expanded the boundaries of the electric lead-guitar style. His and Clapton's guitar tones prompted the birth of a number of other styles, including blues rock, hard rock and heavy metal.

From the 1970s onwards, fewer and fewer dedicated blues musicians have appeared, as more singers and players have adopted the spin-off styles that

Above

Muddy Waters was first recorded by Alan Lomax on a Mississippi plantation before heading to Chicago in the 1940s and hitting the big time with songs like Willie Dixon's 'Hoochie Coochie Man'.

Far Right

The Rolling Stones were inspired by the likes of Muddy Waters, Howlin' Wolf and Jimmy Reed. They started out playing covers of blues songs, which were largely unknown to British audiences at the time.

were exchanging phrases and passages. By the end of the decade, jump blues developed into rhythm and blues (R&B), in which more emphasis was placed on the singers than the instrumentalists. In Chicago, electric blues began to develop, as local bluesmen took Mississippi Delta ideas, amplified them and put them into a small-band context. The harmonica also became a more prominent instrument, thanks to players such as Little Walter and Otis Rush.

By the 1950s, electric blues was in full swing, with B.B. King, Muddy Waters, John Lee Hooker, T-Bone Walker and Howlin' Wolf playing to packed houses in major cities. King pioneered across-the-string

see **Jump Blues pp 426** *see* **British Blues pp 428** *see* **Rhythm & Blues pp 429** *see* **Blues Rock pp 431**

emerged out of it. However, Stevie Ray Vaughan and Gary Moore still managed to inject energy into it, Robben Ford expanded the blues-jazz chops repertoire and Robert Cray introduced the genre to a larger, more mainstream audience throughout the 1980s and 1990s. Other artists, including Bernard Allison, Walter Trout, Dave Hole and Susan Tedeschi, continue to play the blues to enthusiastic audiences around the world.

It might seem paradoxical that a music born out of loneliness, misery, poverty and depression should give so many listeners so much joy, but in reality the first blues songs were sung to raise the spirits of impoverished African-American slaves. The earliest blues singers empathized with their audiences because they had been through the same experiences. It seems fitting that such a sincere and worthy art form has endured to this day, spawning numerous musical children of its own.

Left

The harmonica is one of the most expressive blues instruments. The Marine Band was used by such greats as Sonny Terry, Little Walter, Sonny Boy Williamson II and Paul Butterfield.

see Muddy Waters pp 212 *see* B.B. King pp 260 *see* Rolling Stones pp 278 *see* Walter Trout pp 366

Work Songs

KEY ARTISTS

Sid Hemphill

Ervin Webb

Ed Young

Miles Pratcher

Fred McDowell

Below

Alan Lomax made these recordings in 1959, when the African-American music of the century's early years was still alive in the South. The collection includes field hollers, Delta blues, spirituals and prison recordings.

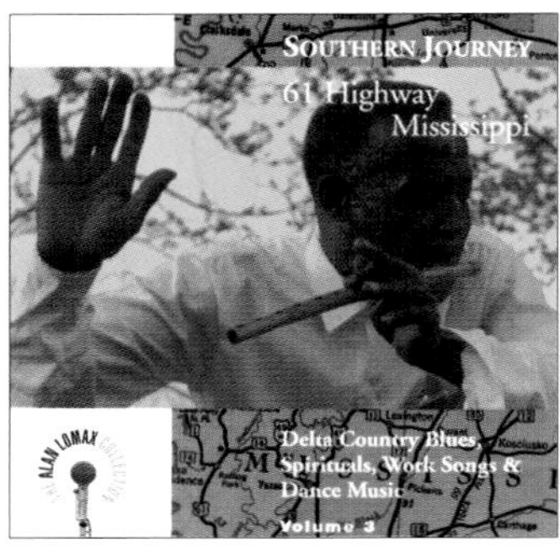

'These long, mournful, antiphonal songs accompanied the work on cotton plantations, under the driver's lash.'

Tony Palmer, *All You Need Is Love: The Story Of Popular Music*

Right

Work songs, often secular and usually relating to the slaves' predicament, helped the slaves in the cotton fields to pick in rhythm and also served to lift their spirits, relieving the pain and boredom of their labour.

Jazz, blues, spirituals and gospel music, were rooted in the work songs of black labourers of the South. As Chet Williamson wrote 'These were songs and chants that kept a people moving and advancing through dreadful oppression. These are the voices of those who harvested the fields, drove the mules, launched the boats, and hammered the rails.'

Based on the compelling rhythms, sliding-pitch intonation and overlapping call-and-response traditions of West African music, which persevered in North America during the time of slavery, these work songs resounded in the South during the Reconstruction years following the Civil War, which ended in 1865. Whether sung by slaves and, later, sharecroppers picking cotton or husking corn, workers laying track on the railroad line, prisoners on the chain gang breaking rocks and draining swamps or coal miners with pickaxes, work songs were structured in a very similar way to West African percussion ensembles.

A Fount Of Creativity And Personal Expression

In a typical drum ensemble of Ghana, the leader/drummer would give signals or motifs to the rest of the group, which would then respond in overlapping call-and-response fashion. The leader, in effect, poses a question and the group offers an answer (the overlap occurring where the call is still in the air when the response begins, or the call begins again before the response is done). Responsorial singing follows this same procedure, with the leader often improvising above a rhythmic pulse by varying the timing, pitch, attack or decay of words at the beginning or end of a phrase. The leader might also toy with the phrasing by employing rhythmic displacement or a slight altering of the phrases in relation to the underlying beat.

In most work songs, the rhythm was tied into the pattern of the work itself – the swinging back and down and the blow of a sledgehammer or pickaxe, the hoisting of ropes on a block and tackle – while the lead chanter acted as a coach, directing the teamwork until the job was done. Each new line was often punctuated by a grunt as the axe or hammer found its mark:

'Dis ole hammer – hunh!
Ring like silver – hunh!
Shine like gold, baby – hunh!
Shine like gold – hunh!'

Field hollers, work songs and the cries of street vendors advertising their wares all incorporated imaginative vocal sounds and various pitch-altering decorations of a note, including the use of 'blue notes'. A good example of this can be heard on an Alan Lomax recording from 1959 of 'Louisiana', sung by prisoner Henry Ratcliff, who was serving time at the Mississippi State Penitentiary at Parchman Farm. Other examples from Lomax's recording include 'Stewball', sung by Ed Lewis leading a group of prisoners at the Lambert State Penitentiary in Mississippi, and 'Berta Berta', sung by Leroy Miller leading a hoeing group at Parchman Farm. Another well-known field holler is 'Mama Lucy', sung by Leroy Gary and recorded by Lomax in 1959, also at Parchman Farm.

The work song was fluid and organic and never repeated exactly the same way twice. This idea of an endless fount of creativity and personal expression within a simple, finite structure, through the use of vocal slurs, falsetto leaps and patches of melisma, is an inherently African device also readily apparent in the blues idiom.

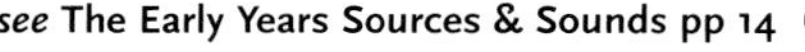

see The Early Years Sources & Sounds pp 14 *see* Blues Styles Introduction pp 408

Delta/Country Blues

It was in the rich cotton-producing delta stretching from Mississippi to Tennessee that black labourers working the plantations gave ferment to an earthy style of music born out of African songs, chants, spirituals and gospel tunes that had been handed down for generations. They called it the blues.

The man usually recognized as the first star of Delta country blues is Charley Patton. An acoustic guitarist of impressive facility with a hoarse, impassioned singing style, Patton was a house-rocking entertainer who played plantation dances and juke joints throughout the Mississippi Delta during the early 1920s. Combined with a high-energy performance style, the strong rhythmic pulse of his music was so galvanizing that he held emotional sway over audiences everywhere he played. Legend has it that workers would often leave crops unattended to listen to him play guitar.

Patton's Prototype

When he finally documented his entertaining tunes in the studio (beginning with 'Pony Blues', for the Paramount label, in 1929), his records could be heard on phonographs throughout the South. And while he did not invent the form (nor was he the first Delta bluesman to record), Patton was the genre's most popular attraction: a genuine celebrity whose appetite for food, liquor and women were legendary, and who travelled from one engagement to the next with a flashy, expensive-looking guitar fitted with a custom-made strap and case. In essence, he was the prototypical rock star. When Patton died in 1934, he left behind a total of only 60 recorded tracks but his legacy was a colourful one, thoroughly addressed in 2001's Grammy-winning seven-CD box set, *Screamin' And Hollerin' The Blues: The Worlds Of Charley Patton*, on the Revenant label.

By the late 1920s, at the time of Patton's first recordings, other Mississippi bluesmen were also making their mark on records, including Patton contemporaries such as Tommy Johnson and Son House. While Johnson emulated Patton's powerful, rough-hewn vocal delivery and showboating style – playing the guitar behind his neck and the like – he lacked the ambition that drove Patton to the pinnacle of stardom in the late 1920s. Instead, Johnson spent most of the 1920s drinking, gambling and womanizing, until his slow descent into alcoholism started to take its toll. Canned Heat, the popular, California-based boogie-blues band of the 1960s, took its name from the title of a Johnson song about drinking Sterno-denatured alcohol used for artificial heat.

The Major Innovators

Another major innovator of the Delta blues style, Eddie James 'Son' House brought an extraordinary degree of emotional power to his singing and slide guitar playing on his first recordings in the early 1930s

KEY ARTISTS

Charley Patton
Tommy Johnson
Son House
Robert Johnson
Bukka White
Skip James
Mississippi John Hurt
Mississippi Fred McDowell
Johnny Shines
Robert Lockwood Jr.
Junior Kimbrough
R.L. Burnside
Big Jack Johnson
Roosevelt 'Booba' Barnes
Paul 'Wine' Jones

'Blues actually is around you every day. Downheartedness and hardship. You express it through your song.'

Arthur Lee Williams

Above
After the death of his blues partner Willie Brown, Son House gave up the guitar. It wasn't until years later, in 1965, that he played and recorded once more.

see Charley Patton pp 23 *see* Son House pp 126 *see* John & Alan Lomax pp 129 *see* Mississippi Fred McDowell pp 130

for the Paramount label. A main source of inspiration for both Robert Johnson and Muddy Waters, Son (unlike his contemporary Charley Patton) lived long enough to experience his own rediscovery during the folk blues revival of the mid-1960s. A one-time Baptist preacher, House imbued his blues with an almost demonic intensity on recordings such as 'My Black Mama', 'Preachin' The Blues' and 'Walkin' Blues'. His 1965 recording of 'Death Letter' (cut while in his 60s for the Columbia label) is one of the most anguished and emotionally stunning laments in the Delta blues oeuvre and has been covered in dramatic fashion by a diverse list of artists such as David Johansen, Cassandra Wilson, Diamanda Galas, James Blood Ulmer, Derek Trucks and the White Stripes. In 1965, he played Carnegie Hall in New York and subsequently became an attraction on the folk blues coffeehouse network, where he was rightly hailed as the greatest living Delta singer still actively performing.

Perhaps the most celebrated and mythic figure in Delta blues was Robert Johnson, a guitarist of dazzling technique who could simultaneously juggle independent rhythms and pianistic-type lines by employing the unique finger-style approach he developed. Legend has it that one night Johnson met the Devil at the crossroads and exchanged his everlasting soul for the gift of unparalleled virtuosity on the guitar. Whether that is folklore or not, Johnson's incredible skills as both a player and a profoundly blue singer soon became apparent to all around the Delta, including elders and inspirations such as Son House, who marvelled at his talent. An itinerant performer, Johnson had a wandering nature that took him well beyond the Delta to places like St. Louis, Chicago, Detroit and New York. His only recordings were made between 1936 and 1937.

Though Johnson died on 16 August 1938 at the age of 27, his approach to playing guitar and singing had a profound effect on a generation of blues musicians, including Jimmy Reed, Elmore James, Hound Dog Taylor and hundreds of others. His most famous songs, such as 'Sweet Home Chicago', 'Crossroads' and 'Love In Vain', have become blues standards, covered endlessly by the likes of the Rolling Stones, Led Zeppelin, Cream, Eric Clapton, Steve Miller and Cassandra Wilson. Other key, early country blues players include the idiosyncratic Skip James, Bukka White, Mississippi John Hurt, Mississippi Fred McDowell and Robert Johnson partners and disciples Robert Lockwood Jr. (Johnson's step-son and taught by the master himself) and Johnny Shines.

In recent years, renewed interest in Delta or country blues has been triggered by the spirited work of guitarists/singer-songwriters like Corey Harris, Keb' Mo', Guy Davis, Eric Bibb and Alvin Youngblood Hart, who have blended in touches of Delta-style acoustic blues along with their more contemporary pop-oriented offerings on record and in concert appearances all over the world. Present-day exponents of an edgier, electrified version of the raw, uncut Delta blues sound include Mississippi-based guitarists-singers R.L. Burnside, Big Jack Johnson, Paul 'Wine' Jones, Roosevelt 'Booba' Barnes and James 'Super Chikan' Johnson.

Above
Mississippi John Hurt's delicate picking style in fact had more in common with the East Coast ragtime guitarists than the Delta guitar sound.

Right
Out of all the Delta bluesmen, Robert Johnson probably had the most direct impact on the generations that followed. His intricate guitar work and use of unusual tunings have frustrated budding guitarists for decades.

see The Early Years Sources & Sounds pp 14 *see* Blues Styles Introduction pp 408

Louisiana Blues

New Orleans is widely acknowledged as the birthplace of jazz, but it also produced its own indigenous brand of blues, which borrowed from Texas and Kansas City while also making use of cajun and Afro-Caribbean rhythm patterns.

A mix of croaking and yodelling, floating over the top of the music in an independent time scheme, Professor Longhair's singular vocals added to his idiosyncratic charm. Influenced by New Orleans barrelhouse pianists Tuts Washington, Kid Stormy Weather and Sullivan Rock, Longhair developed his unique conception and made his recording debut in 1949 with the anthemic 'Mardi Gras In New Orleans', for the Dallas-based Star Talent label. In typically enigmatic fashion, he named his band the Shuffling Hungarians and scored a hit in 1950 for the Mercury label with 'Bald Head', which combined his rolling piano with some good-time bounce and hilarious lyrics.

Rolling Piano And Good-Time Bounce

In 1953, Longhair recorded another New Orleans anthem, 'Tipitina', for the Atlantic label, and in 1959 he revived his 'Mardi Gras In New Orleans' (retitled 'Go To The Mardi Gras') for the regional Ron imprint. After fading from the scene in the 1960s, his performance at the first New Orleans Jazz & Heritage Festival in 1971 ignited a comeback, leading to a slew of recordings and international festival appearances. His last recording, the triumphant *Crawfish Fiesta* (Alligator Records), was released after his death on 30 January 1980. Longhair's irrepressible piano style was carried on by such Crescent City disciples as James Booker, Allen Toussaint, Fats Domino, Dr. John (Mac Rebennack) and Henry Butler.

An accompanist to Longhair during his comeback years, Snooks Eaglin distinguished himself as a guitarist who could cover any style of music convincingly. Blind since birth, he developed a dazzling finger-style approach, which allowed him to shift easily from Delta-style blues to flamenco, to gospel, R&B, rock, surf guitar or jazz. His earliest recordings, for the Folkways label in 1958, present him in an acoustic folk blues setting, accompanied only by harmonica and washboard. His early 1960s sides for the Imperial label show him excelling at New Orleans R&B, while his output for the Black Top label from the late 1980s onward highlight his blistering, rock-tinged guitar work in funky, New Orleans-style settings. He remains a top attraction in the Crescent City, at both the Jazz & Heritage Festival and showcase venues such as Tipitina's.

'Black or white, local or out-of-town, they all had Longhair's music in common, just that mambo-rhumba boogie thing.'

Allen Toussaint

KEY ARTISTS

- Champion Jack Dupree
- Tuts Washington
- Professor Longhair
- James Booker
- Dr. John
- Guitar Slim
- Snooks Eaglin
- Earl King
- Slim Harpo
- Lightnin' Slim
- Lazy Lester
- Raful Neal
- Kenny Neal

Above

Roy Byrd (a.k.a. Professor Longhair) started out as a street musician in the 1930s. He went on to influence countless musicians with catchy songs like 'Mardi Gras In New Orleans', which features his trademark whistling.

see Mississippi John Hurt pp 28 *see* Robert Johnson pp 112 *see* Professor Longhair pp 229 *see* Snooks Eaglin pp 271

Swamp And Gospel

Another significant figure on the New Orleans blues scene was Eddie Jones (a.k.a Guitar Slim). Hailing from the Delta, he turned up in New Orleans at the age of 24, heavily influenced by Texas guitarist Clarence 'Gatemouth' Brown. His 1951 debut on the Imperial label featured the eerily distorted, nasty-toned guitar work and gospel-drenched vocals that would become his trademark. In 1954, his swampy, gospel-tinged track 'The Things I Used To Do', cut in New Orleans for the Specialty label, topped the R&B charts for 14 weeks and influenced a generation of young players, including the guitarist-songwriter Earl King. After recording throughout the 1950s for the Savoy, Specialty and Ace labels, King scored his biggest hits in the 1960s with Imperial, including 1960's rock-flavoured 'Come On' (later covered by Jimi Hendrix), 1961's funky 'Trick Bag' and 1962's 'Always A First Time'.

King also wrote for Fats Domino, Professor Longhair and Lee Dorsey during the 1960s. Following a lull in the 1970s, his career was revived in the 1980s through a series of first-rate releases for the Black Top label. He remains a top attraction in the Big Easy, thrilling fans with his scintillating showmanship, as well as his irresistible blend of high-energy jump blues and second-line rhythms.

A swampy side of the blues can be heard in the music of Baton Rouge artists such as harmonica aces Slim Harpo and Lazy Lester, as well as guitarists Silas Hogan and Lightnin' Slim, the latter scoring a national hit in 1959 with 'Rooster Blues'. The Baton Rouge style was characterized by reverb-laden production, laid-back beats, relaxed vocals, snakey guitar riffs and raw, wailing harmonica. That tradition was continued by the harmonica player Raful Neal in the 1970s, and is being continued today by his son, the talented harmonica player/guitarist/songwriter Kenny Neal.

Accordion player Clifton Chenier melded traditional French Cajun dance music with R&B, rock'n'roll and the blues, originating the southwestern Louisiana hybrid known as zydec. He made his first recordings in 1955, for the Los Angeles-based Specialty label. By the mid-1970s, Chenier's Red Hot Louisiana Band was an international touring act. He recorded regularly throughout the 1980s for the blues/folk revival label Arhoolie, winning a Grammy in 1982 for the album *I'm Here!* and maintained a relentless touring schedule on the international festival circuit until his death in 1987. Chenier's zydeco heirs include such blues-drenched accordionists and bandleaders as his son C. J. Chenier, Boozoo Chavis, Buckwheat Zydeco and Rockin' Dopsie.

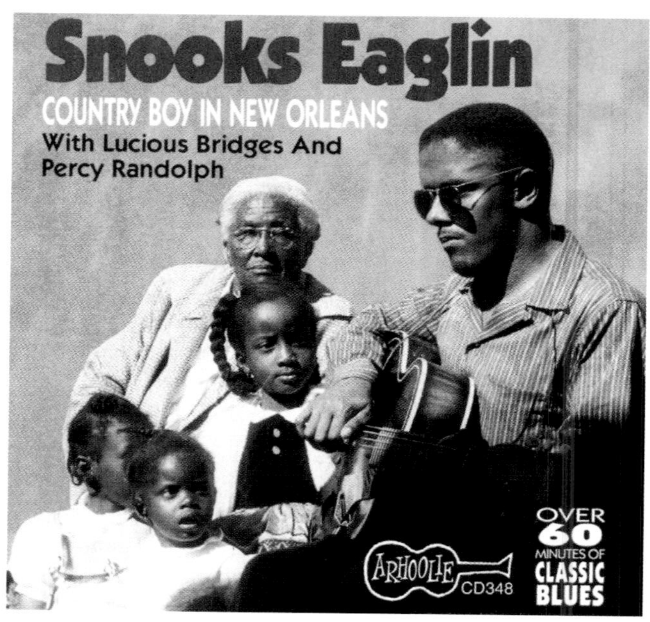

Right
Blind finger-picker Snooks Eaglin was Longhair's favourite guitarist and can be heard on many 'Fess tracks, as well as on Sugar Boy Crawford's rocking Mardi Gras anthem 'Jock-A-Mo'.

Below
As 'Dr. John Creaux, The Night Tripper', Mac Rebennack was a flamboyant performer and wore outrageous Mardi Gras carnival costumes. Today, he is the main torchbearer for the classic New Orleans sound.

see The Forties Sources & Sounds pp 144 *see* Blues Styles Introduction pp 408

Texas Blues

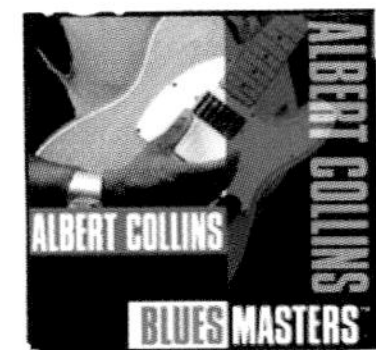

Although Texas has a rich legacy of acoustic country blues artists, its primary contribution to the blues was electric. An inordinate number of dazzling electric guitarists hailed from the Lone Star state, including T-Bone Walker, Clarence 'Gatemouth' Brown, Albert Collins, Freddie King and scores of hotshot six-stringers still on the scene.

Often accompanied by flamboyant showmanship, the Texas electric-guitar style has always been overtly aggressive and rhythmically driving. As Billy Gibbons, of the Texas blues rock band ZZ Top, put it: 'The Texas sound could be described as heavier than light and bluesier than anything else…. And the flamboyancy of most Texans, which is now an established fact throughout the world, has created the flashiness that goes right along with the technical skills of most musicians'.

Aggressive Showmanship

That flamboyance was perhaps best exemplified by the archetypal blues guitarist/vocalist/showman Aaron Thibeaux (T-Bone) Walker. Although Walker made his mark in Los Angeles in the late 1930s, before spearheading the West Coast blues movement following his 1947 signature tune 'Stormy Monday', his roots were in Texas. Born on 28 May, 1910 in Linden, Texas, the young T-Bone learned all the stringed instruments – including mandolin, violin, ukulele, upright bass and banjo – but gravitated toward guitar. As a teenager, he often served as 'lead boy' for the Texas acoustic blues master Blind Lemon Jefferson, while the older, sightless man walked the Dallas streets playing for tips.

Walker later worked in touring carnivals and medicine shows with the blues singers Ida Cox and Bessie Smith, sharing the bill with stars such as Bill 'Bojangles' Robinson and Cab Calloway, who had a major impact on T-Bone's concept of showmanship. He formed his own group in 1928 and recorded his first single for Columbia a year later, billed as Oak Cliff T-Bone (named after the Dallas neighbourhood where he grew up). When he relocated to Los Angeles in 1934, Walker vacated a position in the 16-piece, Dallas-based Lawson Brooks Band, which was promptly filled by his younger friend and jamming partner, the guitarist Charlie Christian. At the height of his popularity in the late-1940s, Walker exuded star quality. His audacious stage act – doing splits while playing his newly amplified Gibson electric guitar behind his head, with his teeth or under his leg – made him the Jimi Hendrix of his day.

Clarence 'Gatemouth' Brown's big break came in the mid-1940s, when he filled in for an ailing T-Bone at the Bronze

KEY ARTISTS

- Blind Lemon Jefferson
- Blind Willie Johnson
- Johnny Winter
- Lightnin' Hopkins
- T-Bone Walker
- Clarence 'Gatemouth' Brown
- Albert Collins
- Johnny 'Guitar' Watson
- Freddie King

'In East Texas … guitar accompanied blues tended to be rhythmically diffuse, with guitarists like Blind Lemon Jefferson playing elaborate, melodic flourishes to answer their vocal lines.'

Robert Palmer

Left
Sam 'Lightnin'' Hopkins took up his name after pairing up with pianist Wilson 'Thunder' Smith.

see T-Bone Walker pp 168 *see* Clarence 'Gatemouth' Brown pp 218 *see* Guitar Slim pp 223 *see* Clifton Chenier pp 269

Above
Clarence 'Gatemouth' Brown was an extremely versatile musician; he played a wide variety of instruments and his compositions embraced a range of musical styles.

Above Right
T-Bone Walker's electric lead guitar play and singing set a precedent for future musicians.

Peacock Lounge in Houston's Fifth Ward and thrilled the audience with his crowd-pleasing boogie-woogie and blistering finger-picked riffs. He was leading his own 25-piece band by 1947, and in 1949, scored a hit with 'My Time Is Expensive' on the Peacock label. His next hit, the influential 'Okie Dokie Stomp', came in 1951. In the mid-1960s, Brown served as musical director for the house band on *The!!!Beat*, a groundbreaking syndicated blues and R&B television show (a black alternative to *American Bandstand*), broadcast out of Dallas and hosted by the influential WLAC radio DJ Bill 'Hoss' Allen. Up until his death in 2005, Gatemouth continued to pay tribute to his two biggest influences, jump blues master Louis Jordan and fellow Texan T-Bone Walker, while also blending in bits of country, Cajun and swinging, Count Basie-styled small band arrangements.

Stinging Intensity

Albert Collins emulated both T-Bone's patented licks and his flamboyant stage presence. While his stinging intensity earned him the nickname 'Master of the Telecaster', Collins also engaged the audience by jumping off the stage and strolling through the house with a 46 m (150 ft) guitar cord.

His first hit came in 1962 with the million-selling 'Frosty'. He cut his classic sides for the Imperial label from 1968 to 1970. Collins had signed to the Chicago-based Alligator label by 1977, while the late 1980s saw him releasing a string of well-received recordings, including the Grammy-winning *Showdown!*, a 1987 collaboration with the guitarists Robert Cray and his fellow Texan Johnny Copeland.

Two other Texas guitar slingers of note are Houston's Johnny 'Guitar' Watson and Gilmer's Freddie King. A flamboyant showman and nasty-toned picker in the T-Bone Walker tradition, Watson recorded throughout the 1950s before hitting it big in 1961 with his 'Gangster Of Love'. He reinvented himself as a raunchy disco-funkster in the 1970s, scoring hits with popular numbers such as 'A Real Mother For Ya', 'Ain't That A Bitch' and 'Superman Lover'. Freddie King, nicknamed 'The Texas Cannonball' for his dynamic stage presence and intense attack on his Gibson guitar, made a great impact on a generation of players with his electrified output from the 1960s and early 1970s. His signature tune, the 1961 instrumental hit 'Hideaway', remains a staple in the modern blues repertoire.

see The Thirties Sources & Sounds pp 92 *see* Ragtime pp 378 *see* Blues Styles Introduction pp 408

Boogie-Woogie

A rollicking, fast piano style characterized by repetitive eighth-note bass figures in the left hand, meshed with sharp, bluesy single-note runs in the right hand, boogie-woogie was an infectious form that had an immediate appeal to dancers.

KEY ARTISTS

Pine Top Smith
Albert Ammons
Meade 'Lux' Lewis
Pete Johnson
Jimmy Yancey
Amos Milburn
Floyd Dixon

While the left hand remained tied to the task of covering driving bass lines in a kind of 'automatic pilot' approach through chord changes (repeating continuous eighth-note bass figures in each different harmony), the right hand was liberated to explore, express and create with bluesy impunity.

Although the boogie-woogie fad swept the nation in the late 1930s, its roots go back much further. Jelly Roll Morton and W.C. Handy recalled hearing boogie-woogie-style piano in the American South during the first decade of the twentieth century. By the 1920s, boogie-woogie pianists were making their mark in saloons, juke joints, honky-tonks and at rent parties throughout both the South and North, where their powerfully rhythmic attack could cut through the din of a good time.

A Powerfully Rhythmic Attack

One of the pioneers of this raucous, rapid-fire, eight-to-the-bar piano style was Jimmy Yancey. Born in 1894 in Chicago, he worked in vaudeville as a singer and tap dancer – starting at the age of six – before taking up the piano in 1915. Although he did not make a recording until 1939, his most famous student, Meade 'Lux' Lewis, would become one of the first to document the boogie-woogie piano style on record with his 1927 'Honky Tonk Train Blues', a masterpiece of intricate cross-rhythms that highlights Lewis's remarkable independence between hands. That same year, Pine Top Smith garnered widespread attention with his catchy 'Pine Top's Boogie-Woogie', in which the pianist shouts instructions to dancers over the top of his rolling keyboard work. The hit tune, covered by several artists – including Bing Crosby with the Lionel Hampton Orchestra – also featured the rhythmic 'breaks' that were an essential part of early ragtime.

'They played a rolling rhythm in the left hand so that they could reach for a drink or a sandwich with the right hand.'

Donald Clark, *The Rise and Fall of Popular Music*

From Spirituals To Swing

In 1938, a single event helped bring boogie-woogie to wider public exposure. Jazz impresario John Hammond, a producer and talent scout who had a keen interest in boogie-woogie piano (and particularly in Meade Lux Lewis), arranged to have Lewis and fellow boogie-woogie pianists Albert Ammons and Pete Johnson appear on the bill of his 'From Spirituals To Swing' concert, held at Carnegie Hall on 23 December 1938. The gala event (which also featured Count Basie's Orchestra, gospel singer-guitarist Sister Rosetta

Above

Albert Ammons (left) was a flexible enough player to record with his son Gene Ammons, the founder of the 1940s Chicago saxophone sound. Pete Johnson (right) found success playing piano for the great Joe Turner.

see Meade 'Lux' Lewis pp 128 *see* Jimmy Young pp 139 *see* Albert Collins pp 270 *see* Johnny 'Guitar' Watson pp 281

Tharpe, blues shouters Jimmy Rushing and Big Joe Turner, blues harmonica ace Sonny Terry, soprano sax genius Sidney Bechet and his New Orleans Feet Warmers and the Kansas City Six featuring tenor saxophonist Lester Young on the bill) not only helped launch the boogie-woogie boom but also led directly to the formation of Blue Note Records by the German immigrant Alfred Lion.

As Michael Cuscuna wrote in *The Blue Note Years* (Rizzoli): 'Lion attended the legendary "From Spirituals To Swing" concert at Carnegie Hall. He was so moved by the pulsating, dazzling boogie-woogie artistry of pianists Albert Ammons, Meade Lux Lewis and Pete Johnson that he scraped up enough money for one day's rental on a studio. Exactly two weeks later on 6 January 1939, he recorded Ammons and Lewis. By that evening, Alfred Lion found himself in the record business – Blue Note Records was born'.

Below
John Hammond kick-started the careers of the key boogie-woogie players as well as discovering Bessie Smith, Billie Holiday, Bob Dylan and Robert Johnson.

Lion pressed 50 copies each of two 78rpm singles, one by Ammons, the other by Lewis. There followed other sessions with the two boogie-woogie pianists, including an innovative 1941 session with Lewis on celeste, Charlie Christian on guitar, Edmond Hall on clarinet and Israel Crosby on bass. Ammons recorded in the 1940s with the blues singer Sippie Wallace and in 1949 he cut a session with his son, the great tenor saxophonist Gene Ammons, before passing away later that year. Lewis continued playing after the boogie-woogie craze died down, relocating to Los Angeles and recording until 1962. Pete Johnson, the third member of the Big Three of boogie-woogie (the others being Albert Ammons and Meade Lux Lewis), forged a musical rapport with his Kansas City compatriot, blues shouter Big Joe Turner, releasing popular recordings such as 'Roll 'Em Pete' and 'Cafe Society Rag'. He spent 1947–49 in Los Angeles before moving to Buffalo in 1950 and, subsequently, drifting into obscurity.

Down-Home Double Entendre And Humour

Born the year Meade Lux Lewis cut his first tracks, Amos Milburn was a jovial boogie-woogie disciple who picked up the torch and ran with it. The Houston-born pianist pounded out some of the most explosive boogie grooves of the post-war era, beginning in 1946 on the Los Angeles-based Aladdin label. His first hits included the driving, countrified boogie of 'Down The Road Apiece' (covered in 1960 by Chuck Berry and in 1965 by the Rolling Stones). Milburn excelled at good-natured, upbeat romps about booze and partying, imbued with a vibrant sense of humour and double entendre, as well as vivid, down-home imagery in his lyrics. He scored successive Top 10 R&B hits with 1948's 'Chicken Shack Boogie', 1949's 'Roomin' House Boogie', 1950's 'Bad, Bad Whiskey' and 1953's 'One Scotch, One Bourbon, One Beer'.

Milburn's frantic piano-pumping style would have a profound effect on seminal rock'n'rollers such as Floyd Dixon, Fats Domino, Little Richard and Jerry Lee Lewis in the early 1950s. That boogie-woogie piano lineage continues today with explosive players such as Marcia Ball, Billy C. Wirtz and Mitch Woods.

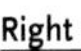

Right
Amos Milburn (piano) & his Chicken Shackers, as the group called themselves after the runaway success of their hit 'Chicken Shack Boogie'.

see The Fifties Sources & Sounds pp 190 *see* Blues Styles Introduction pp 408 *see* Delta/Country Blues pp 415

Chicago Blues

Chicago blues is a raw, rough-and-tumble music, defined by slashing, Delta-rooted electric slide guitars, raunchy-toned harmonicas overblown into handheld microphones to the point of distortion, uptempo shuffle drummers, insistently walking bass players and declamatory, soulful vocalists who imbued the tunes with Southern gospel fervour.

It became a universally recognized sound by the 1960s, fuelling the British blues movement in the early part of the decade (spearheaded by Alexis Korner, Cyril Davies, John Mayall and the Rolling Stones) and the American blues boom of the late 1960s (spearheaded by blues rock pioneers such as Paul Butterfield, Michael Bloomfield, Elvin Bishop and Johnny Winter, and bands such as the Blues Project and Canned Heat).

Urban And Amplified

Just as a generation of New Orleans jazz musicians had migrated from the source of the music to Chicago in the 1920s, a generation of Mississippi bluesmen migrated from the fertile Mississippi Delta region to Chicago in the 1940s. Mississippians such as Sunnyland Slim, Bukka White, Robert Nighthawk, Arthur 'Big Boy' Crudup, Muddy Waters, Otis Spann, Otis Rush, Homesick James, Johnny Young, Eddie Taylor, Jimmy Reed and Hound Dog Taylor were among the Delta blues musicians who came north to the Windy City, where they helped forge an urban, amplified take on the Delta sound. A second wave, including Howlin' Wolf, Hubert Sumlin, Elmore James, Sonny Boy Williamson II, Buddy Guy, Pinetop Perkins, Big Walter 'Shakey' Horton, James Cotton, Magic Sam, Magic Slim, David Honeyboy Edwards and Carey Bell, followed that same path north in the early 1950s, contributing to the post-war Chicago blues explosion.

By the 1960s, Chicago's south side was a bustling hub of blues activity. Bands led by Muddy Waters, James Cotton, Otis Rush, Homesick James, J.B. Hutto, Otis Spann, Junior Wells and Howlin' Wolf performed regularly at South Side nightclubs such as Peppers Lounge, Turner's Blue Lounge, Theresa's, the J&C Lounge and Curley's. A significant recording from 1965 documented this vital scene and helped spread

KEY ARTISTS

- Muddy Waters
- Howlin' Wolf
- Big Walter Horton
- Little Walter Jacobs
- Elmore James
- Willie Dixon
- James Cotton
- Jimmy Reed
- Buddy Guy
- Junior Wells
- Hound Dog Taylor
- Hubert Sumlin
- Magic Sam
- Otis Rush

'Muddy Waters, Howlin' Wolf and Elmore James were already seeming "old", but their dynamism, their fierce shouting … expressed the swelling anger of the younger blacks.'

Paul Oliver

Above
Howlin' Wolf's primitive style of blues did not at first go down as well as the more sophisticated recordings of his contemporaries. The Rolling Stones helped to popularize his music.

see Albert Ammons pp 100 *see* Pete Johnson pp 128 *see* Howlin' Wolf pp 225 *see* Otis Rush pp 278

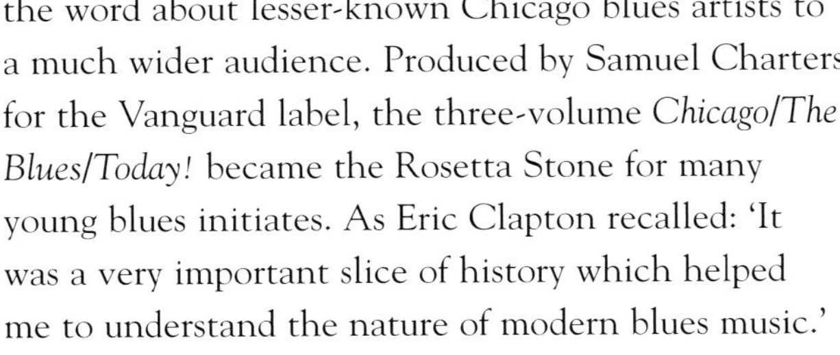

the word about lesser-known Chicago blues artists to a much wider audience. Produced by Samuel Charters for the Vanguard label, the three-volume *Chicago/The Blues/Today!* became the Rosetta Stone for many young blues initiates. As Eric Clapton recalled: 'It was a very important slice of history which helped me to understand the nature of modern blues music.'

The acknowledged father of the Chicago blues scene was McKinley Morganfield (a.k.a. Muddy Waters). A product of the fertile Mississippi Delta, he grew up in Clarksdale on Stovall's plantation, where he emulated the passionate slide-guitar stylings of Delta patriarch Son House. In 1941, the musicologist Alan Lomax made important field recordings of Waters at Stovall's under the auspices of the Library of Congress, documenting for all time the intensity and unfettered expression of the Mississippi Delta bluesman. Two years later, Waters moved to Chicago, where he sharpened his slide-guitar skills. He took up with the pianist Sunnyland Slim, who played a large role in launching Muddy's career by inviting him to provide guitar accompaniment for his 1947 Aristocrat session. That same day in the studio, Waters cut his own first recordings for Aristocrat. A year later, he had his first national hit with the 78 'I Can't Be Satisfied' backed with 'I Feel Like Going Home'.

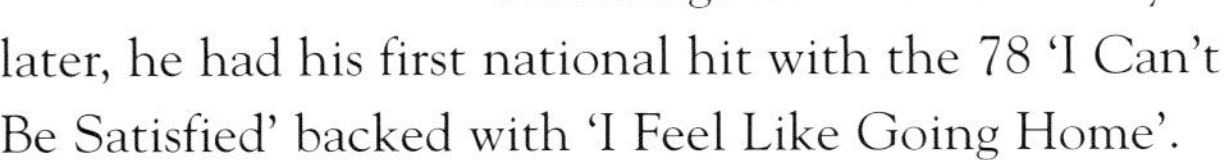

Above
Elmore James took the Delta blues and brought it closer to rock'n'roll.

Waters enjoyed a string of chart-toppers throughout the 1950s, backed by a tight band of superior musicians that included harmonica ace Little Walter, guitarist Jimmy Rogers and pianist Otis Spann. His supremacy continued through the first half of the 1960s, until the emerging psychedelic rock movement rendered his old-school Chicago sound passé. After a relatively low profile in the 1970s, Muddy's recording career was resuscitated in the later part of the decade by his disciple Johnny Winter, who produced a triumphant triumvirate of hard-hitting Chicago blues albums announcing the great man's comeback.

Right
Former boxer Willie Dixon was a man of many talents: he was a singer, musician, composer, producer, arranger, manager and promoter. As a composer, he was able to turn a simple blues into a catchy, memorable tune.

A Thriving Blues Centre

Other important players on the Chicago blues scene include Elmore James, the most influential slide guitarist of the post-war period; Little Walter (Marion Walter Jacobs), the king of amplified blues harp and a key man in Muddy Waters' powerful band of the late-1940s and 1950s; harmonica ace Junior Wells, who replaced Little Walter in Waters' band and later formed a potent partnership with the guitarist Buddy Guy; and Howlin' Wolf (a.k.a. Chester Arthur Burnett), who migrated to Chicago from Mississippi in 1953 and would be challenging Muddy Waters' blues supremacy in the Windy City by 1958.

No summary of Chicago blues can be written without mentioning the ubiquitous session bassist-producer and Chess Records songwriter Willie Dixon, who penned numerous hits for Muddy Waters, Howlin' Wolf, Little Walter, Bo Diddley and Koko Taylor among others. His most famous tunes, including 'Hoochie Coochie Man', 'Evil', 'My Babe', 'Wang Dang Doodle' and 'Spoonful', are staples of the blues repertoire, having been covered countless times by rock and blues bands.

Chicago remains a thriving blues centre, boasting several vibrant nightclubs on the city's south and west sides, as well as two important blues labels in Alligator Records and Delmark. The city also hosts an annual, free summer blues festival in Grant Park, which draws fans from around the world.

see The Twenties Sources & Sounds pp 36  *see* Blues Styles Introduction pp 408  *see* Delta/Country Blues pp 415

Piedmont Blues (East Coast Blues)

While the Mississippi Delta gave birth to guitar-based acoustic blues, in the area known as the Piedmont region – which stretches along the Atlantic seaboard from Virginia to Florida – a wide range of blues styles flourished, from the backwoods sound of the Appalachian foothills of Virginia to the more urbane sound of big cities such as Atlanta.

The characteristic that these varying Piedmont styles have in common, distinguishing them from the Delta blues style, is an emphasis on a sophisticated, syncopated kind of rhythm playing, with a complex fingerstyle technique that closely emulated a pianistic or ragtime approach on the guitar. Some of the earliest and most famous practitioners of the Piedmont style include three virtuosic sightless players: Blind Blake (whose signature ragtime guitar piece 'Diddie Wah Diddie' was covered nearly 50 years later by Leon Redbone), Blind Boy Fuller (famed for 'Step It Up And Go' and 'Rag Mama Rag') and the formidable 12-string dazzler Blind Willie McTell (whose 'Broke Down Engine' was covered in the 1960s by blues guitar star Johnny Winter and whose 'Statesboro Blues' is still being performed as a blues-rock anthem to this day by the Allman Brothers Band). Other Piedmont pioneers included Curley Weaver and Robert 'Barbecue Bob' Hicks, both of whom recorded in the late 1920s.

In the late-1950s, a folk revival swept college campuses from coast to coast, helping to revive the careers of many Piedmont bluesmen. Pink Anderson, John Jackson, Etta Baker and the duo of harmonica ace Sonny Terry and guitarist Brownie McGhee were rediscovered and soon performing on college campuses and in coffeehouses. Budding folk artists such as Bob Dylan, Taj Mahal, Joan Baez and Bonnie Raitt championed the cause of Rev. Gary Davis, while Ry Cooder, David Bromberg and Jorma Kaukonen studied with him.

A Uniquely American Artist

Also a blind artist and strictly self-taught on guitar, Davis developed remarkably quickly and, by his twenties, had an advanced technique that was unmatched in the blues field. Davis recorded for the first time in the early 1930s and became an ordained minister in 1937. An appearance at the 1958 Newport Folk Festival helped bring greater attention to Davis, leading to his becoming one of the most popular figures of the folk and blues revival scenes. Some of his signature tunes include 'Cocaine Blues', 'Samson and Delilah', 'Twelve Gates to the City' and 'Lovin' Spoonful'.

One of the most outstanding exponents of the Piedmont style today is the Washington DC based duo of guitarist John Cephas and harmonica player Phil Wiggins.

KEY ARTISTS

Blind Blake
Blind Boy Fuller
Blind Willie McTell
Rev. Gary Davis
Sonny Terry
Brownie McGhee

Left
Brownie McGhee's smooth sound contrasted perfectly with the rough harmonica style of Sonny Terry.

'...Emphasis on good execution, rhythmically free-flowing, lighter in texture ... it had a distinct flavour which mingled with that of the hillbilly and mountain singers of the white rural tradition.'

Paul Oliver

Left
Joan Baez's admiration of Rev. Gary Davis was presumably mutual, judging by the poster on his wall. Davis's musical experimentations showed him to be musically ahead of his time.

see Blind Willie McTell pp 79 *see* Rev. Gary Davis pp 173 *see* Muddy Waters pp 212 *see* Elmore James pp 226

Jump Blues

KEY ARTISTS

Louis Jordan
T-Bone Walker
Roy Milton
Jimmy Liggins
Joe Liggins
Pee Wee Crayton
Johnny Otis
Wynonie Harris
Big Joe Turner
Roy Brown
Charles Brown

Infectiously swinging, full of good humour and hugely popular for its time, the jump blues movement of the pre- and-post-Second World War years was a precursor to the birth of both R&B and rock'n'roll.

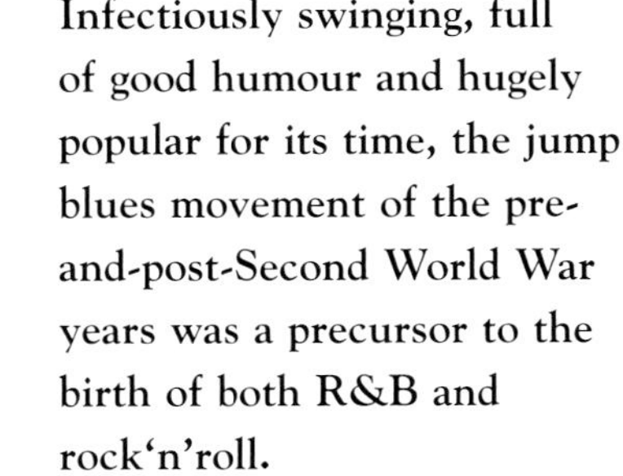

Kansas City was an incubator for jump blues in the late 1930s, via the infectious, rolling rhythms of Walter Page's Blue Devils and the Bennie Moten and Count Basie bands. But in the years following America's involvement in the Second World War, Los Angeles became a major breeding ground for a West Coast branch of this new sound, characterized by shuffling uptempo rhythms, raucously upbeat spirits, honking tenor saxophones and swaggering vocalists who shouted about partying, drinking and good times. It was there, in the clubs that lined Central Avenue in Los Angeles, that a bevy of saxophonists dubbed 'honkers' for their piercing, squealy tones and frantic showmanship helped to define the scene. Among them were Big Jay McNeely, Chuck Higgins and Joe Houston, all players influenced by Illinois Jacquet's rambunctious tenor soloing on Lionel Hampton's huge 1942 hit, 'Flying Home'.

'Louis Jordan was a great musician and, in my opinion, he was way ahead of his time.'

B.B. King

Setting The Pattern

The undisputed heavyweight champion of the jump blues movement was Louis Jordan, who with his Tympany Five came to personify the spirit of the times with his theme song 'Let The Good Times Roll'. From 1941 to 1952, Jordan reigned as the 'King of Jukeboxes', with a string of catchy, uptempo boogie-woogie influenced hits like 'Caldonia', 'Choo Choo Ch'Boogie', 'Ain't Nobody Here But Us Chickens', 'Five Guys Named Mo' and 'Saturday Night Fish Fry'. Jordan's infectious rhythms, aggressive alto sax playing and dynamic stage presence set the pattern for jump blues.

Many of the most popular West Coast performers who followed in the wake of Jordan's success based themselves in Los Angeles during the 1940s but originally hailed from Texas. Chief among them were pianist-singer Charles Brown, whose ultra-mellow style made a big impact in 1945 with 'Driftin' Blues' and again in 1947 with the Yuletide classic 'Merry Christmas Baby' (both cut with Johnny Moore's Three Blazers) and the pioneering electric guitarist T-Bone Walker, whose inherent soulfulness and jazzy dexterity on the instrument would influence generations of bluesmen from B.B. King, Lowell Fulson and Pee Wee Crayton to proto-rocker Chuck Berry and blues rock pioneers like Duane Allman, Johnny Winter and Eric Clapton.

Above
The jump king Louis Jordan (centre) with his band. Jordan helped bring about the musical transition from big band swing and early R&B to the rock'n'roll sound of artists like Little Richard.

Pioneer Spirit

Walker arrived in Los Angeles in 1934 and by 1939 was singing in Les Hite's popular Cotton Club Orchestra. After striking out on his own in 1941, he signed with Capitol Records and cut 'Mean Old World'

 *see* The Forties Sources & Sounds pp 144 *see* Blues Styles Introduction pp 408

backed with 'I Got A Break Baby' for the fledgling label. The momentum of his recording career was halted by the American Federation of Musicians' recording band which lasted from 1942–44. After spending two years in Chicago, Walker returned to Los Angeles in 1946 and signed with Black & White Records. His third session for the label, the anthemic 'Call It Stormy Monday', became an immediate and huge hit in 1947, leading to a string of other successful recordings like 'T-Bone Shuffle' and 'West Side Baby'. Walker's success directly inspired guitarist Pee Wee Crayton, another transplanted Texan who relocated to Los Angeles, signed with the Bihari brothers in 1948 and hit big with 'Blues After Hours'.

Another successful bandleader on the West Coast blues scene was drummer/singer Roy Milton, who followed both Jordan's and Walker's example with his Solid Senders, a lively jump blues small combo. Milton's steady backbeat and infectious, Jo Jones-styled ebullience behind the kit provided the kinetic pulse behind such mid-1940s hits as 'R. M. Blues', 'Milton's Boogie' and 'Hop, Skip, Jump'. By late 1947, at the peak of the West Coast blues boom, Roy Milton & his Solid Senders became the number two jump blues band in the land, second only to Louis Jordan & his Tympany Five. Camille Howard, an outstanding boogie-woogie pianist, was the group's secret weapon and was heavily featured in the band throughout the Specialty label years, which ended in 1954.

Above

This image of Big Jay McNeely really sums up the spirit of jump blues – the raw, dirty sound of the sax, the performer putting everything into the swinging soul of the music and, above all, the audience going wild.

The Liggins Brothers

Two other key figures on the West Coast blues scene were brothers Joe and Jimmy Liggins. In 1945, pianist-bandleader Joe Liggins had a two-million-seller hit with 'The Honeydripper'. After joining Specialty in 1950, he hit big again with 'Pink Champagne', which became his signature song and was promptly covered by both Tommy Dorsey and Lionel Hampton. Jimmy's younger and more frantic brother Joe (who was originally the bus driver for the Honeydrippers), jumped into the recording business himself after signing with Specialty in 1947, and scored a hit the following year with 'Cadillac Boogie'. After leaving Specialty in 1953, he cut some sessions for Aladdin that anticipated the coming rock'n'roll movement, including the rousing novelty number 'I Ain't Drunk' (later covered by Texas blues guitarist Albert Collins). Joe's wild stage presence and manic delivery also had a direct and lasting impact on rock'n'rollers like Little Richard, Chuck Berry, Bill Haley and Elvis Presley.

Left

A Clarksdale juke joint in 1939. Blacks went to juke joints to drink and dance and it was in these venues that jump blues gained popularity, due to its raucous, danceable, feel-good sound.

Another key figure on the West Coast blues scene was bandleader, producer and talent scout Johnny Otis. By 1947, with the decline of the big bands, Otis downsized his larger ensemble to a septet, patterning his new band after the wildly successful examples of Louis Jordan & his Tympany Five and Roy Milton & his Solid Senders. In 1958 he scored a hit with 'Willie and the Hand Jive' and in 1972 formed the Blues Spectrum label to document many of the living jump blues legends of the day like Big Joe Turner, Roy Milton, Roy Brown and Pee Wee Crayton.

see T-Bone Walker pp 168 *see* Louis Jordan pp 176 *see* Roy Milton pp 180 *see* Johnny Otis pp 181

British Blues

KEY ARTISTS

John Mayall's Bluesbreakers
The Rolling Stones
Blues Incorporated
Eric Clapton
Cyril Davies
Peter Green
Alexis Korner
Ten Years After
The Yardbirds

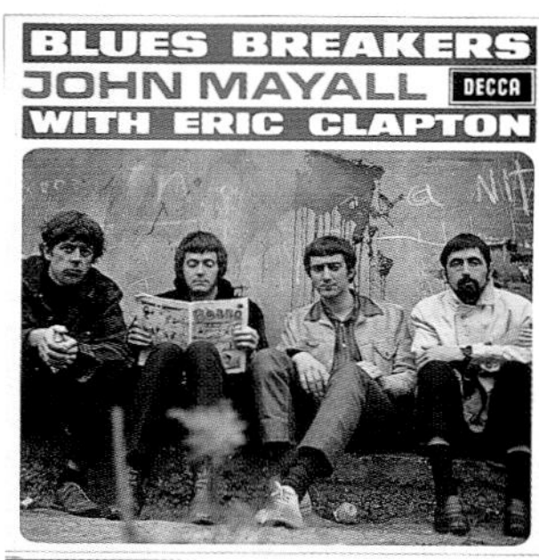

Above
On this album the inclusion of Eric Clapton, fresh from the Yardbirds, helped British blues to reach a wider audience. Clapton's incredible guitar work on the record inspired 'Clapton Is God' graffiti across London.

British blues was born when British musicians attempted to emulate Mississippi and Chicago bluesmen during the 1960s. Led by Eric Clapton and The Rolling Stones, these musicians copied the styles of Big Bill Broonzy, Muddy Waters, Howlin' Wolf and B.B. King, and, aided by powerful amplifiers, developed a sound of their own.

In the early 1950s, the first American blues musician to appear in England was Big Bill Broonzy. Although he was a popular, Chicago-style bluesman, his UK performances consisted of acoustic folk blues and protest songs. It was Muddy Waters' visit to the country in 1958 that really sparked off the beginning of the British blues movement. Muddy played with an electric, solid-body Fender guitar, backed by Chris Barber's British blues group featuring guitarist Alexis Korner and blues harpist Cyril Davies. They played at a volume that shocked folk purists, but delighted a growing younger audience.

'I spent most of my teens and early twenties studying the blues – the geography of it and the chronology of it, as well as how to play it.'
Eric Clapton

Inspiration For A New Generation

After Muddy's tour, Korner and Davies pursued their musical ambitions even more passionately and formed Blues Incorporated, the first of the British blues bands. By 1962, the group had a regular slot at London's Marquee Club and a recording contract with Decca. Blues Incorporated inspired a younger generation of musicians, who then formed the three most influential British blues bands: John Mayall's Bluesbreakers featuring Eric Clapton, the Rolling Stones and the original Fleetwood Mac, with Peter Green.

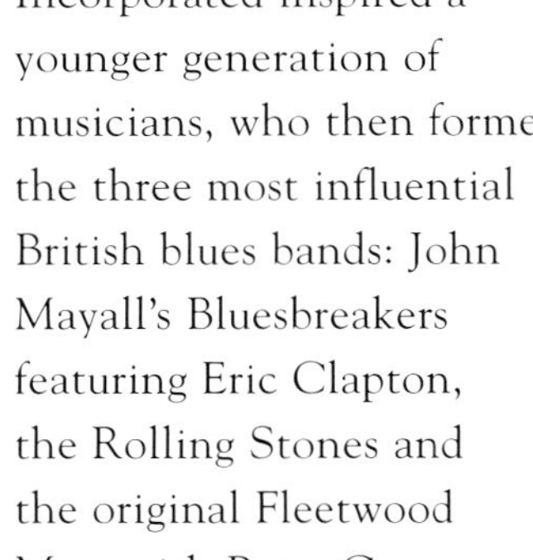

Right
Alexis Korner was the main man behind the 1960s British blues scene.

Clapton was a phenomenon with the Bluesbreakers – he turned his amp up to gig volume for recordings and obtained a more modern electric sound that influenced the likes of Jimi Hendrix and also Jimmy Page, who went on to form Led Zeppelin.

Sex, Drugs And Rock'n'Roll

The Rolling Stones were perceived to be the definitive British blues band. They made a stream of hit records during the mid-1960s, including a chart-topping version of Willie Dixon's 'Little Red Rooster' (1964). They also covered songs by Muddy Waters and Howlin' Wolf, even insisting that Howlin' was a featured guest at a special US appearance. Their legendary 'sex, drugs and rock'n'roll' lifestyle contrasted sharply with the Beatles' squeaky-clean image during the 1960s.

By 1966, British blues was in full flight: the legendary *John Mayall's Bluesbreakers With Eric Clapton* album was released that year; bands such as Fleetwood Mac, the Yardbirds (with Jeff Beck) and Ten Years After (with Alvin Lee) were forming, and the Animals started to develop their inimitable brand of blues pop. By the end of the decade, the British blues movement was carried back across to the United States, where it was reabsorbed by larger audiences than the original Chicago and Mississippi bluesmen had enjoyed. The success of the British blues bands also encouraged early American blues rock bands such as the Allman Brothers and ZZ Top, who had already developed their own unique styles.

Although British blues is now seen by many as an early step in the conversion of blues into rock and heavy metal, it was a distinct style in its own right. Even today, musicians such as John Mayall, Eric Clapton and Aynsley Lister are waving the British blues flag.

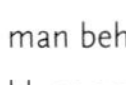

see The Sixties Sources & Sounds pp 240 *see* Blues Styles Introduction pp 408 *see* Jump Blues pp 426

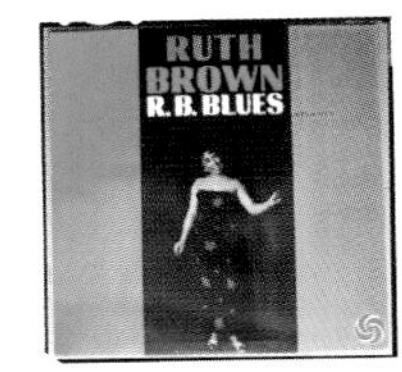

Rhythm & Blues

Rhythm & blues (R&B) music evolved out of jump blues rhythms during the late-1940s, but it also had riffs and lyrics that were beginning to point more towards the emergence of rock'n'roll. Using sparser instrumentation than jump blues, R&B was based upon traditional blues chord changes played over a steady backbeat.

R&B placed more emphasis on the singer and the song than on the band's instrumentalists. Although it branched out into rock'n'roll during the 1950s, and soul during the 1960s, it always retained its own following, and R&B artists continue to draw large audiences all over the world.

Legendary R&B Singers

As rock'n'roll continued to emerge, R&B branched out into further distinct styles, including doo wop, electric blues and New Orleans. Each of these exerted its influence on other R&B forms, as well as popular music in general.

During the late 1940s and early 1950s, a number of great singers began to emerge from the R&B scene. Ruth Brown was perhaps the first of these. Initially inspired by jazz singers such as Sarah Vaughan, Billie Holiday and Dinah Washington, Ruth developed her own expressive tone and was recommended to the bosses of a fledgling Atlantic Records in 1948. After she was promptly signed up, they produced a string of R&B classics, including 'So Long' (1949), 'Teardrops From My Eyes' (1950), 'I'll Wait For You' (1951), '(Mama) He Treats Your Daughter Mean' (1953) and 'Mambo Baby' (1954). She became well known as 'Miss Rhythm', appeared on the TV program *Showtime At The Apollo* with Miles Davis and Thelonious Monk, and proved to be a big influence on subsequent female R&B singers.

Ray Charles was another hugely influential figure in the 1950s R&B movement, and one of the forefathers of soul music. Born Ray Charles Robinson in Albany, Georgia, on 23 September 1930, and blind since the age of seven, he studied composition and learned to play a number of musical instruments at the St. Augustine School for the Deaf and the Blind in Florida. He drew from gospel and Southern blues music to develop a unique singing and songwriting style, which encouraged Atlantic Records to sign him up in 1953. Charles and Atlantic hit the jackpot: 'I Got A Woman' was a number two R&B hit in 1955, and Charles followed it with a string of other chart-toppers, combining his unmistakably soulful vocal delivery with R&B rhythms. Ray influenced countless R&B singers and became one of the first soul superstars in the 1960s. He later worked with many popular artists, including Aretha Franklin and Michael Jackson.

Another important name in early R&B music is Clyde McPhatter. Originally a gospel singer with the Mount Lebanon Singers in New York, Clyde switched over to R&B when he joined the Dominoes in 1950. They signed to Syd Nathan's King label and recorded 'Sixty Minute Man' (1951), the biggest R&B hit of the year and, according to some, the earliest identifiable example of a rock'n'roll song. He quit the Dominoes in early 1953 and

KEY ARTISTS

Ray Charles
Ruth Brown
Clyde McPhatter
Johnny 'Guitar' Watson
Bo Diddley

'I was born with music inside me. That's the only explanation I know of.'

Ray Charles

Above
Owing to the seemingly endless string of hits enjoyed by Ruth Brown on Atlantic Records, the then fledgling label came to be known as 'The House That Ruth Built'.

Left
Clyde McPhatter's compelling vocals combined blues and gospel influences, giving a stunning, emotionally charged tenor voice that served as a forerunner to the 1960s and 1970s soul sounds.

see Ruth Brown pp 198 *see* Ray Charles pp 219 *see* Alexis Korner's Blues Incorporated pp 275

undeservedly, faded into obscurity. Other notable R&B singers from the 1950s included Jackie Wilson and James Brown, who both became soul superstars during the 1960s.

R&B Guitar Icons

Other R&B artists, such as Bo Diddley and Johnny 'Guitar' Watson, were associated with their instruments as much as their singing. Diddley developed an unorthodox, 'hambone' rhythm guitar style, which he played on a trademark rectangular guitar. Perhaps his most famous hit was the two-sided 'Bo Diddley'/'I'm A Man' (1955), which he recorded for Chess records. Watson grew up listening to bluesmen T-Bone Walker and Clarence 'Gatemouth' Brown and developed a biting, high-treble guitar tone, which he used to strong effect on albums such as *Gangster Of Love* (1958) and *Johnny Guitar Watson* (1963). An eccentric performer, he was reputed to have played the guitar standing upside-down, using a 46m (150 ft) cord so he could get on top of the auditorium with his instrument. 'Those things Jimi Hendrix was doing; I started that shit!' he said to a music journalist.

Above
Although undoubtedly a key influence in R&B, Ray Charles has successfully turned his hand to a number of musical styles, including blues, gospel, pop, country, jazz, and early rock'n'roll.

Right
A plectrum, as used by Bo Diddley to create his distinctive, percussive guitar sound.

formed his own band, the Drifters, the same year. They recorded 'Money Honey' (1954) and several other big R&B hits for Atlantic Records during the mid-1950s and McPhatter's extremely versatile tenor voice proved capable of handling both sensitive ballads and raucous rock'n'roll. He left the band for a solo career and released several other hits during the late-1950s, but he had less success in the following decade and,

Although R&B branched off into a number of different music styles between the 1950s and 1970s, countless blues and soul stars have released R&B hits over the past 40 years. Recent R&B revival artists, such as Big Boy Bloater & his Southside Stompers, continue to ensure that the genre is very much alive.

see The Sixties Sources & Sounds pp 240 *see* Blues Styles Introduction pp 408 *see* British Blues pp 428

Blues Rock

Blues rock grew out of the British blues movement that started during the late 1950s, which was in turn developed in the 1960s. The Brits used more powerful amplification than their American counterparts, resulting in a harder, more imposing sound. Jimi Hendrix, Led Zeppelin and other artists developed this into a riff-oriented rock style.

Among the earliest blues rock bands were Cream, the Paul Butterfield Blues Band and Canned Heat. Cream were formed when Ginger Baker, drummer with the Graham Bond Organisation, decided to start his own band with guitarist Eric Clapton and bassist Jack Bruce. 'Things were going badly with Graham', Baker told music journalist Chris Welch, 'so I decided to get my own thing together. I was unaware that Eric had such a huge following. I just dug his playing, so I went to a Bluesbreakers gig in Oxford. In the interval Eric asked if I'd play a number with them, and it really took off! So I told him I was getting a band together and was wondering if he'd be interested. He said that he was and recommended Jack as the bass player.'

As all three band members were well known around the British blues circuit when they formed, each with a reputation for being a virtuoso on his respective instrument, Cream was, effectively, the first 'supergroup'. They were louder and more riff-oriented than previous blues-influenced bands, and their style incorporated extended solos – a regular feature for subsequent blues rockers. Despite only lasting for three years, Cream's first three albums, *Fresh Cream* (1966), *Disraeli Gears* (1967) and *Wheels Of Fire* (1967), are widely accepted as both blues rock classics and milestones in the birth of rock music. Influential American bands had also developed blues rock styles by the late 1960s: the Paul Butterfield Blues Band, with Mike Bloomfield and Elvin Bishop on guitars, and Canned Heat, a white blues band formed by singer Bob 'The Bear' Hite and harmonica player Alan 'Blind Owl' Wilson, were the most notable of these.

KEY ARTISTS

Cream
The Paul Butterfield Blues Band
Canned Heat
Jimi Hendrix
The Rolling Stones
Led Zeppelin
The Allman Brothers Band
Free
Carlos Santana
Rory Gallagher

'I had a Les Paul before Eric but I didn't have a Marshall. And when Eric got all of that together he was a delight to listen to. He really understood the blues.'

Jimmy Page

Above
Jeff Beck's *Guitar Shop*, released in 1989, is a showcase for Beck's incredible guitar skills.

Left
The brilliant Cream fused blues and rock.

see Paul Butterfield Blues Band pp 268 *see* Canned Heat pp 268 *see* Cream pp 270 *see* Johnny 'Guitar' Watson pp 281

Above

Led Zeppelin star Jimmy Page initially refused to join his first band, the Yardbirds, thinking he would make more money as a session musician.

A Dazzling Showman

Another key figure in the transition from blues to rock was the legendary Jimi Hendrix. Born Johnny Allen Hendrix in Seattle on 27 November 1942, he later changed his name to James (Jimi) Marshall Hendrix. Influenced by legendary bluesmen such as Robert Johnson and B.B. King as a schoolboy, he taught himself to play guitar before working with musicians such as Little Richard in the early 1960s. His break came when Chas Chandler, the bassist with the Animals, heard him play in New York's Greenwich Village. Chas persuaded him to move over to London, where the Jimi Hendrix Experience was formed, with Jimi on guitar, Noel Redding on bass and Mitch Mitchell on drums.

Jimi was a dazzling showman, playing the guitar behind his head and with his teeth, but it was his extraordinary soloing and mastery of controlled feedback that set a new standard in electric blues lead guitar playing. His best albums, *Are You Experienced?* (1967), *Axis: Bold As Love* (1968) and *Electric Ladyland* (1968), demonstrate that something seriously interesting was happening to the blues by the late-1960s. Although he tragically died in 1970, Jimi was to influence countless blues and rock players for many years to come.

see The Seventies Sources & Sounds pp 286 *see* Blues Styles Introduction pp 408

Broadening Out

By the end of the 1960s, blues rock began to diversify into heavy metal in the UK and southern blues rock in the US. Led Zeppelin was, perhaps, the first band to be described as heavy metal, but the group's blues roots are apparent in all of its recordings, including the hugely popular *Led Zeppelin II* (1969) and *Led Zeppelin IV* (1971) albums. The band's guitarist, Jimmy Page, grew up listening to blues and rock'n'roll recordings, but one of his biggest influences was hearing Eric Clapton's Gibson Les Paul guitar through a cranked-up Marshall amp at a Bluesbreakers gig. 'I had a Les Paul before Eric but I didn't have a Marshall,' Page recalled. 'And when Eric got all of that together he was a delight to listen to. He really understood the blues.'

Meanwhile, in the States, the Allman Brothers Band was fusing electric blues with country and folk elements, to form what is now known as 'southern rock'. Albums such as *The Allman Brothers Band* (1969), *Idlewild South* (1970) and *Live At The Fillmore East* (1971) paved the way for a whole family of southern rock bands, including Lynyrd Skynyrd and Black Oak Arkansas. ZZ Top, a trio from Texas, also emerged out of the blues rock scene. Led by the bearded Billy Gibbons (guitar, vocals) and Dusty Hill (bass, vocals), the trio developed their own style of boogie-style blues rock, which became hugely popular in the 1970s and 1980s.

Meanwhile, over in the UK, the group Free inspired generations of British blues rockers with major hits like 'All Right Now' (1970) and 'Wishing Well' (1973). Many other notable blues rock artists have since appeared on both sides of the Atlantic, including Bernard Allison, Bonnie Raitt, Walter Trout, Dave Hole and Ronnie Earl.

Left
Jimi Hendrix helped to popularize the use of feedback and wah-wah, as well as widening the rock palette by his use of unusual intervals (e.g. the diminished fifths in the 'Purple Haze' intro) and chords (the so-called 'Hendrix chord' of E7#9, also used in 'Purple Haze').

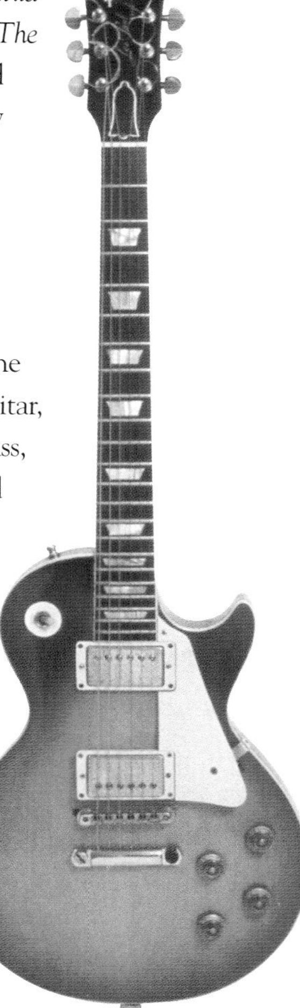

Below
The Gibson Les Paul is the most famous and sought-after guitar in the world and was the first solid-bodied Gibson.

see Jimi Hendrix pp 273 *see* Allman Brothers Band pp 294 *see* Free pp 304 *see* Led Zeppelin pp 308

Modern Electric Blues

KEY ARTISTS

Stevie Ray Vaughan
Robben Ford
Roy Buchanan
Johnny Winter
Robert Cray
Jimmie Vaughan

Although the first generations of electric bluesmen played louder and more flamboyantly than their acoustic forefathers, their music was still traditional in its delivery and structure. The British blues players who emulated them during the 1960s were also fairly traditional in their approach to the genre.

Jimi Hendrix opened things up a bit more when he first appeared on the scene in 1967, but the musicians he in turn influenced tended to lean towards the rock side of the musical spectrum.

Another group of electric bluesmen also began to emerge during the late-1960s and early 1970s – guitar players such as Roy Buchanan and Johnny Winter, who had taken on board the new sounds of rock but were steeped in the traditions of the blues.

Blues Got Them Early

The son of a Pentecostal preacher, Roy Buchanan grew up in California and, as a teenager, joined Dale Hawkins' band in 1958. After a stint as a session player in the 1960s, he decided to try his luck as a solo artist with *Roy Buchanan* (1972), an accomplished album highlighting his distinctive, treble-sounding Fender Telecaster tone. He was asked to join the Rolling Stones after Brian Jones died but, surprisingly, he turned the offer down. His career, like that of many other blues musicians, was plagued by booze and drug problems, and, after a number of unsuccessful suicide attempts, he hung himself in a police cell in 1988.

'Stevie Ray Vaughan is the best friend I've ever had, the best guitarist I ever heard and the best person anyone will ever want to know.'
Buddy Guy

Johnny Winter, an albino bluesman who grew up in Texas, also began playing and singing the blues early in life; he cut his first record at the age of 15, and produced a demonstration disc known as *The Progressive Blues Experiment* in 1968. An excellent review in *Rolling Stone* magazine led to lucrative management and recording deals. His first proper album, *Johnny Winter* (1969), established his standing as an outstanding performer with an exceptionally dexterous guitar style and paved the way for more than 20 further, critically acclaimed Winter blues albums.

Blues Fusions

Robben Ford is another great blues artist who emerged during the early 1970s. He also showed a mastery of jazz, unlike most blues guitar players, and his music developed into a compelling blend of the two styles. Inspired by Eric Clapton and Mike Bloomfield, Robben learned blues guitar during the 1960s and performed with Charlie Musselwhite in 1970. He also toured and recorded with George Harrison and Joni Mitchell in the mid-1970s and with Miles Davis in the 1980s. His *Talk To Your Daughter* album (1988) was nominated for a Grammy, while later, *Robben Ford And The Blue Line* (1992) won considerable acclaim for its original, earthy approach to the blues. Robben's soloing is more sophisticated than that of most other blues players and his chord progressions are often laced with rich jazz harmonies.

Right
Robert Cray was largely responsible for the 1980s blues guitar revival and his versatile playing style ensured a wide crossover success. He even had videos played on MTV, which was unheard of for a blues artist.

see The Eighties Sources & Sounds pp 316 *see* Blues Styles Introduction pp 408 *see* British Blues pp 428

Left
Robben Ford started out as a saxophonist and it was his love for this instrument – and its masters, such as John Coltrane and Wayne Shorter – that helped to shape his unique jazz-tinged blues guitar sound.

Another musician who effortlessly fused jazz with the blues is the Connecticut-born John Scofield. Although John spent many of his early years studying the work of jazz and fusion players such as Jim Hall and John McLaughlin, his *Still Warm* (1986) and *Blue Matter* (1987) albums are full of original, angular blues-style licks.

The two blues giants of the 1980s were undoubtedly Robert Cray, from Georgia, and Stevie Ray Vaughan, from Texas. Cray formed his first band in 1974, but did not really hit the big time until his *Bad Influence* album was released to critical and commercial acclaim in 1983. A mainstream fusion of blues, soul and rock, his style was particularly popular throughout the 1980s, introducing a wider pop audience to the blues. He was invited to play with Eric Clapton during the ex-Bluesbreaker's famous series of concerts at London's Albert Hall in 1989.

A Recent Legend

Stevie Ray Vaughan was heavily influenced by his older brother, Jimmie Vaughan (of the Fabulous Thunderbirds), as well as by Albert King and Hendrix. He played in various local bands in Austin, Texas before forming Double Trouble (named after an Otis Rush song), with bassist Tommy Shannon and drummer Chris 'Whipper' Layton. In 1982 the ensemble played at the Montreux Jazz Festival, where Vaughan's stunning, high-energy blues style was noted by David Bowie, who poached him for his *Let's Dance* album (1983). The same year, Double Trouble also recorded *Texas Flood* with the legendary blues producer John Hammond, to critical and commercial acclaim. The second Double Trouble album, the Hendrix-influenced *Couldn't Stand The Weather* (1984), was an even bigger success – it went platinum.

Vaughan battled with alcohol and drug problems during the mid-1980s, and was admitted to a rehabilitation centre in Georgia, but he straightened out to make the Grammy-winning *In Step* (1989). Tragically, he died in a helicopter accident in 1990, after playing at an Eric Clapton concert in Milwaukee. As with Hendrix, Vaughan's reputation has grown since his death, with recent guitar magazine reader polls indicating that he is one of the most popular blues artists of all time.

Thanks to players such as Vaughan and Ford, modern electric blues evolved during the 1980s and 1990s and, like every current musical style, continues to do so. Players including Walter Trout, Susan Tedeschi, Dave Hole, Tinsley Ellis and Bernard Allison continue to delight audiences.

Below
Stevie Ray Vaughan's amazing guitar technique and understanding of the blues won him two W.C. Handy National Blues Awards in 1984: Entertainer of the Year and Blues Instrumentalist of the Year. He was the first white person to win either award.

see Roy Buchanan pp 303 see Robben Ford pp 304 see Johnny Winter pp 311 see Stevie Ray Vaughan pp 330

THE INSTRUMENTS

The instruments used to play blues and jazz have ranged from the jew's harp to the bagpipes, but convention has favoured a fairly set group of brass, reed, string and percussion instruments. While the instruments originated largely in Europe in the early decades, blues and jazz musicians distinguished themselves by emphasizing vocal and rhythmic aspects with roots in African traditions, funnelled through the unique American slave and pre-jazz experiences.

Vocal emulation and rhythmic variation have dominated the evolution of both blues and jazz, whether the music has been played on the bottleneck guitars of the earliest Mississippi Delta bluesmen or on the turntables of contemporary jazz improvisers. Another constant has been innovation; since the earliest years, blues and jazz musicians have demonstrated their ability to push instruments past their traditional limits in search of personal expression. This experimentation encompasses the entire span of the music – from the rips and slurs that marked Louis Armstrong's repertoire of trumpet techniques to Little Walter Jacobs' amplification of the harmonica, and from Cecil Taylor's percussive approach to piano to Bobby McFerrin's use of the human body itself in making music.

Blues musicians and, to a greater extent, jazz musicians have also been responsible for exposing some new or neglected instruments to a wider audience. Examples include the electric guitar and its cousin the electric bass in blues, and the bottom-most members of the saxophone family in avant-garde jazz. Beginning in the 1970s, jazz players also helped to broaden the interest in instruments from other cultures, particularly those from India, Africa and South America.

From washtub bass to djembe drum, and from kazoo to iBook, the language of blues and jazz is spoken in many ways.

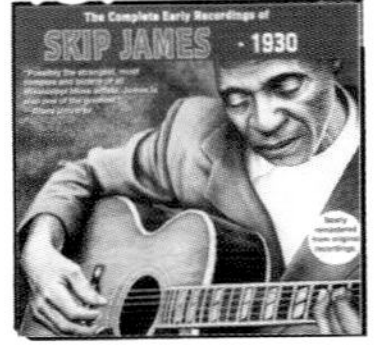

Blues

Bass: Early blues bands often utilized large earthenware jugs or an upturned metal washtub, broom handle and baling twine to create a rudimentary bass line. In his role as A&R man and house songwriter for Chess Records, Willie Dixon made the double bass a dominant instrument in Chicago blues. The invention of the electric bass made it a standby for blues combos beginning in the early 1950s.

Drum Kit: Like the bass, drum kits were little used in early blues groups. Rudimentary kits began to appear in the 1930s, and drummers such as Fred Below, Elga Evans and Francis Clay provided propulsive drive and rhythmic accents to the electric-blues movement based in Chicago.

Guitar: Cheap, portable and highly expressive – particularly when played with a glass or metal slide – the guitar was the itinerant bluesman's meal ticket. Many southerners bought their instruments from mail-order catalogues, although some, like Bukka White, preferred metal-bodied resonator guitars manufactured by National, for their volume and sturdiness. The electric guitar gained dominion when blues players moved north and formed bands, with Muddy Waters setting the pace. In the 1950s, T-Bone Walker and B.B. King popularized horn-like *legato* lines that utilized the sustained capability of modern amplification.

Harmonica: Invented by a German clockmaker in 1821, the harmonica – or 'blues harp' – was first mass-produced in the US in 1857. The diatonic harmonica, with reeds that produce the natural notes of a single scale, lends itself well to the bent notes, slurs and other vocal effects of blues. Players like Little Walter Jacobs and Sonny Boy Williamson II (Rice Miller) also used the larger chromatic harmonica, which contains complete 12-note octaves. Amplified, the harmonica offers a wide range of tonal effects.

Organ: Although musicians like Jimmy Smith and Johnny Hammond popularized bluesy jazz playing on the Hammond B-3 and other lesser-known models, the organ is something of a rarity in true blues settings. Robert Hooker and Gregg Allman are notable exceptions.

Piano: Blues songs were a key part of the repertoire for pianists who spanned ragtime and the early jazz era. The canon expanded with the compositions of W.C. Handy, and pianists held a prominent place as accompanists of blues singers such as Bessie Smith in the 1920s. Leroy Carr and Jay McShann were among the first to introduce a more urban style of blues piano, and artists such as Memphis Slim (Peter Chatman) and Big Maceo (Major Merriweather) were major forces on the Chicago blues scene. Otis Spann redefined the role of blues piano as the longtime sideman of Muddy Waters. In New Orleans, players such as Professor Longhair (Henry Roy Byrd) and James Booker were pioneering other styles still.

Saxophone: Although primarily used in ensemble settings in blues, particularly in the jump-blues bands that dominated on the US West Coast, the saxophone did find a few standout solo performers in tenorists J.T. Brown – a frequent sideman with Elmore James – and his protégé A.C. Reed, as well as alto player Eddie 'Cleanhead' Vinson.

Trumpet: While almost every jazz trumpeter has played blues forms, and the trumpet has often been featured in larger blues ensembles, few trumpet soloists have worked in traditional blues settings. One notable exception is Olu Dara, a Mississippi-born New Yorker who also plays guitar and sings.

see The Twenties Sources & Sounds pp 36 *see* The Fifties Sources & Sounds pp 190

Jazz

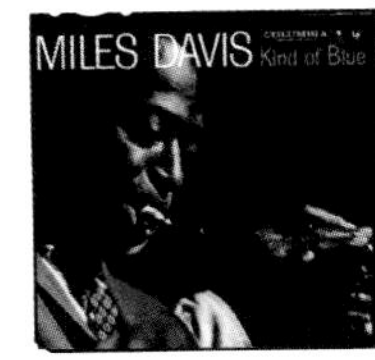

BRASS

Cornet: Pitched in B♭ or occasionally in C, the three-valved cornet was invented in 1830 and adapted by New Orleans brass bands later in the century. Manuel Perez is credited by some as the first jazz cornetist, although Buddy Bolden may have in fact preceded him. The dominant brass instrument in jazz until the late 1920s, the cornet has continued to be favoured by some players, including Bobby Bradford and Graham Haynes.

Trumpet: Usually pitched in B♭, the trumpet supplanted the slightly smaller cornet thanks largely to Louis Armstrong's use of the instrument on his revolutionary recordings of 1926–27 and, along with the tenor saxophone, has become jazz's dominant solo instrument. It has been the voice of many of the genre's leading improvisers – including Armstrong, Dizzy Gillespie, Fats Navarro, Clifford Brown, Miles Davis and Freddie Hubbard – and an expressive tool for stylists such as Bubber Miley, Maynard Ferguson and Lester Bowie. Major advancements include King Oliver's use of mutes, Don Ellis's experiments with electronics and extra valves for microtonality, and Davis's popularization of amplification and processing.

Flugelhorn: Pitched in B♭, the flugelhorn (with a bell and bore that are slightly larger than the trumpet's) is favoured as an alternate instrument by many trumpeters for its dark, burnished tone. Joe Bishop introduced the flugelhorn to jazz with Woody Herman's band in 1936, and Miles Davis helped to popularize it on *Miles Ahead* (1957). Chuck Mangione is one of the few musicians to concentrate on flugelhorn alone, but others such as Kenny Wheeler, Art Farmer and Thad Jones have used it extensively.

Trombone: The B♭ tenor slide trombone became the most commonly used in jazz, although some players prefer the B♭/F or B♭/F/E instruments, which have valves to alter the pitch. Various models also have trumpet-like valves or a combination of valves and slide. Capable of a wide range of vocal effects, the trombone was a standby in the early New Orleans bands, where its function was largely rhythmical or as a supporter of the lead instruments, at least until the advent of Jack Teagarden and his virtuoso solo playing. The trombone then went on, in the hands of Joe 'Tricky Sam' Nanton, to become a staple of Duke Ellington's orchestra in the swing era. During the bebop revolution, J.J. Johnson introduced a new dexterity and fluidity to the trombone, and avant-gardists such as Albert Mangelsdorff and George Lewis created new techniques to expand the instrument's sound.

Tuba: A carry-over from marching bands, this large, valved instrument carried the bass line in early jazz groups. Subsequently supplanted by the double bass, the tuba fell from popularity until being revived by Gil Evans in arrangements for Claude Thornhill and Miles Davis, usually played by Bill Barber for the latter. In the 1980s, Howard Johnson and Bob Stewart brought the tuba back to prominence as a solo instrument.

KEYBOARDS

Clavichord: Developed as early as the fourteenth century, the clavichord features metal tangents that strike the strings from below and stay in contact as long as the keys are depressed. This design allows the player to alter the pitch of notes or produce a narrow *glissando* or controlled vibrato. Oscar Peterson – *Porgy & Bess* (1976) – and Keith Jarrett – *Book Of Ways* (1986) – have used the instrument to good effect.

Electric Piano: Earl Hines recorded on an early version of the electric piano in 1940, but it was not until the late 1950s that artists such as Sun Ra and Joe Zawinul began to incorporate the Wurlitzer electric piano. The invention of the highly portable Fender Rhodes piano in 1965 coincided with the growing interest in tonal variation, and the sound of the instrument dominated the 1970s. Interest waned in the 1980s, but the distinctive sound of the vintage instruments made a comeback in the late 1990s.

Organ: Until 1935, when Hammond created its first electronic organ, the use of the instrument was limited to recordings using church-based pipe organs or theatre organs. Fats Waller recorded extensively on organ in the 1920s and Count Basie included organ on some recordings and live performances in suitably equipped venues. Waller adopted the Hammond organ immediately, taking it on tour in the late 1930s. Glenn Hardman, Wild Bill Davis and Milt Buckner were also early converts, but it was Jimmy Smith who used the electronic organ to change the sound of jazz when he formed his first trio in 1955. The organ-guitar-drums trio became a standby in nightclubs in the 1950s and 1960s. Larry Young adapted the organ for use in free jazz, and latter-day players such as John Medeski and Larry Goldings continued to keep it in the forefront in to the twenty-first century.

Piano: From James P. Johnson to Art Tatum to Bud Powell to Cecil Taylor to Keith Jarrett, the piano has constantly been in the vanguard of change and innovation in jazz. The diversity of other major influential pianists, including Earl Hines, Duke Ellington, Oscar Peterson, Thelonious Monk and Herbie Hancock, shows the range that jazz piano can cover.

see Dizzy Gillespie pp 152 *see* Muddy Waters pp 212 *see* Sonny Boy Williamson II pp 235 *see* Keith Jarrett pp 307

Synthesizer: Developed by electronics engineers in the early 1950s, synthesizers cover a very broad range of devices that generate and process sound, from keyboard-triggered systems that emulate strings to touchpad-controlled digital samples of actual sounds. Sun Ra and Paul Bley were early proponents of the synthesizer in jazz, and various versions became a standby during the jazz-rock fusion era. As advances in digital technology occurred, synthesizers became much more flexible. They continue to be used extensively by many players, including Herbie Hancock, Joe Zawinul and Lyle Mays.

PERCUSSION

African, Asian, Indian and Latin Percussion: One of the major innovations in jazz after the Second World War was the integration of elements of music from other parts of the world, and nowhere was this more evident than in the rhythm section. The rise in interest in Afro-Cuban music that Dizzy Gillespie and Chano Pozo spearheaded in 1947 introduced congas to jazz, and opened the way for a range of Caribbean and Central and South American percussive devices, such as bongos, maracas and the cuica, or Brazilian friction drum. In the 1970s and 1980s some musicians, such as trumpeter Don Cherry, began introducing various ancient African instruments, for example the berimbau and various talking drums. Indian devices like the tabla also gained prominence with bands and musicians, including Oregon and Miles Davis in the 1970s. Drummers have long sought out exotic sounds, for instance Chinese gongs; in the 1980s, this expanded to include instruments such as traditional gamelan gongs from Bali and unusually pitched cymbals and bells from other parts of Asia.

Drum Kit: The drum kit, or trap set (from 'contraption'), evolved to serve the needs of orchestral percussionists during the late nineteenth century. The main elements – bass (or kick) drum mounted with a foot pedal, snare drum, floor- or rack-mounted tom-tom, foot-controlled hi-hat cymbals and assorted other accent cymbals – have not changed beyond advancements in materials. But, from the early years of jazz, drummers have augmented their kits with other percussive devices, including cowbells, wooden blocks and drums of various sizes. Sonny Greer had an extensive kit – featuring timpani, tubular bells and Chinese gongs – when he was in Duke Ellington's orchestra, and in the 1970s jazz-rock drummers added double-bass drums and a wide array of cymbals. Techniques have evolved to encompass hand drumming and the use of chopsticks and multi-pronged wooden sticks. In the 1980s, synthesizers were incorporated into drum kits, allowing the drummer to alter the sound of his instruments or trigger a variety of digitized sounds. Major advances in technique were introduced by Papa Jo Jones, Kenny Clarke, Max Roach, Ed Blackwell, Han Bennink and Gerry Hemingway.

REEDS

Bassoon: The double reed bassoon is relatively rare in jazz. Used as early as 1928 by Frankie Trumbauer in Paul Whiteman's band, it held a very small role until the 1960s, when Yusef Lateef began to incorporate it into his work. More recently, Karen Borca has become a prominent soloist in avant-garde music.

Clarinet: Like saxophones, clarinets cover the musical range from the E♭ sopranino to the B♭ contrabass, but it is the B♭ soprano that is most commonly used by jazz musicians. The clarinet was the dominant woodwind in jazz until it was supplanted by the saxophone in the 1930s; however the instrument remained in the forefront because of its use by high-profile players such as Benny Goodman, Artie Shaw and Buddy DeFranco. Jimmy Giuffre and John Carter used the clarinet in more modern types of improvised music, and Anthony Braxton, Marty Ehrlich and Don Byron have ensured that it remains a highly contemporary instrument.

Bass Clarinet: Among the clarinet family, the B♭ bass version is the other reed to gain prominence in jazz, largely for its warm, woody tonal quality. Eric Dolphy alternated bass clarinet with flute and alto saxophone, and helped to extend the range normally associated with the instrument. Anthony Braxton, David Murray and Marty Ehrlich are other important proponents.

Oboe: This double reed woodwind is rarely used in jazz, although players from Don Redman in the 1920s to Paul McCandless in the 1970s have found effective uses for it.

Sopranino Saxophone: The highest pitched of Adolphe Sax's family of single reed instruments, the sopranino's range is about an octave above the alto saxophone. Little used in jazz until the 1960s, it gained some popularity when avant-gardists Joseph Jarman and Anthony Braxton played it.

Saxello/Manzello: A variant of the B♭ soprano saxophone, the saxello was invented in the 1920s. Forty years later, Rahsaan Roland Kirk modified the horn and renamed it the manzello.

Soprano Saxophone: Manufactured as either a straight or curved horn, the soprano was popularized by Sidney Bechet and used widely as a secondary instrument in the big bands of the 1930s and 1940s. Steve Lacy revived interest in the soprano, but it was John Coltrane who made it a featured solo instrument again with his recording of 'My Favorite Things' (1960).

Alto Saxophone: Popularized by Jimmy Dorsey, Frankie Trumbauer and Johnny Hodges in the 1920s, the alto was frequently used by big-band arrangers as the lead voice in the saxophone section. In the 1940s, Charlie Parker revolutionized the sound of the alto with his speed, dexterity and harmonic sophistication. Ornette Coleman and Eric Dolphy introduced subsequent innovations on the instrument.

 *see* The Seventies Sources & Sounds pp 286 *see* The Eighties Sources & Sounds pp 316

Stritch: A variation of the straight E♭ alto horn, developed by Rahsaan Roland Kirk.

Tenor Saxophone: All things considered, the tenor remains the dominant saxophone voice of jazz. In the hands of Coleman Hawkins, Lester Young, Sonny Rollins, John Coltrane and Joe Lovano – to name a few of the instrument's many outstanding virtuosi through the ages – the tenor has shown itself to be remarkably versatile and expressive.

C-melody Saxophone: Pitched in C, this version of the tenor saxophone was the principal horn used by Frankie Trumbauer in the 1920s, but it faded from use until revived in the 1980s by Bob Wilber and Kenny Davern.

Baritone Saxophone: Used primarily for colour in large ensembles until the 1950s, the baritone was popularized as a solo instrument by Gerry Mulligan and Pepper Adams. Latter-day players Hamiet Bluiett, John Surman and James Carter extended the upper range of the horn by using the technique called 'overblowing'.

Contrabass Saxophone: An octave below the baritone, the contrabass saxophone was little used until Anthony Braxton began to feature it on recordings in the 1970s.

Bass Saxophone: Something of a novelty when played by Adrian Rollini in the 1920s, the largest of the saxophone family continued to be employed by musicians such as Charlie Ventura in the post-war era, often to supplement or replace the double bass. In the 1960s and 1970s, Roscoe Mitchell, Anthony Braxton and Vinny Golia took up the unwieldy instrument – which stands approximately 1.5 m (5 ft) high – and James Carter featured it on a 2000 tribute to Django Reinhardt.

STRINGS

Banjo: This five-string fretted instrument was popular in ragtime and fulfilled a rhythm role in early jazz bands. Banjoist Johnny St. Cyr was a prominent member of Louis Armstrong's Hot Five and Hot Seven bands. Briefly revived in the 1940s with the renewed interest in New Orleans jazz, the banjo is now only occasionally used as a textural device by string musicians such as Vernon Reid.

Bass: The double (string, or upright) bass was prominently featured in ragtime and early jazz groups, although frequently as a bowed, rather than plucked, instrument. John Lindsay and Pops Foster were two of the earliest stars of the instrument, introducing various effects such as slapping the strings for percussive effect. Later developments were introduced by Jimmy Blanton with Duke Ellington, Oscar Pettiford and Ray Brown. Charles Mingus, Scott LaFaro and Charlie Haden have been important for their contribution in moving the bass beyond its traditional role in the rhythm section. The introduction of the Fender Precision electric bass in 1951 gave the instrument more tonal variety and volume, but major developments that separated the electric and acoustic instruments did not occur for more than 20 years, when players such as Jaco Pastorius, Stanley Clarke, Steve Swallow and Jamaaladeen Tacuma revolutionized the electric bass through advancements in electronics and extended playing and improvisational techniques.

Cello: As the string instrument pitched closest to the human voice, the cello has grown in popularity in improvised music. Bassist Oscar Pettiford used the instrument occasionally in the 1950s, as did Ron Carter in the 1970s. In the later years of the twentieth century artists such as Hank Roberts, Tom Cora, Diedre Murray, David Eyges, Erik Friedlander and Peggy Lee helped to make the cello a legitimate jazz instrument.

Guitar: Largely a rhythm instrument in the hands of many of jazz's early players, with notable exceptions including Lonnie Johnson, Eddie Lang and Django Reinhardt, the guitar gained prominence when amplification was introduced. Charlie Christian popularized flowing *legato* lines and Wes Montgomery expanded the vocabulary through his expressive use of octaves. From the 1970s onwards, the guitar became one of the genre's dominant instruments, in the hands of players like George Benson, John McLaughlin, Pat Metheny, John Scofield and Bill Frisell.

Violin: Prominent in the society orchestras of New Orleans, the violin was used sparingly in jazz until the late 1920s. Among the early US standouts on the instrument were Joe Venuti, Stuff Smith, Ray Nance and Claude 'Fiddler' Williams, while in Europe Stephane Grappelli played a key role in the Quintet of the Hot Club of France. Players such as Leroy Jenkins and Billy Bang have made important contributions to free jazz, and Ornette Coleman used the violin as a textural device beginning in the early 1960s. The violin's amplification gave it a prominent spot in the jazz-rock fusion movement, with Jean-Luc Ponty, Jerry Goodman and Michal Urbaniak making notable contributions.

WIND

Flute: Despite Wayman Carver's work with Benny Carter and Chick Webb in the 1930s, the flute was a rarity in jazz, more often heard soloing in Latin dance bands, until the 1950s, when Frank Wess (also a talented saxophonist) became a featured soloist in Count Basie's band and several California-based composers began to utilize the instrument. Although several other saxophonists have doubled on flute effectively – particularly Eric Dolphy, Charles Lloyd and Jane Bunnett – it was the specialists, such as Herbie Mann, Hubert Laws and James Newton, who legitimized the instrument as a solo voice.

see Frankie Trumbauer pp 84  *see* John Coltrane pp 250  *see* Anthony Braxton pp 302 *see* Pat Metheny pp 328

Glossary

African-American Also known as Afro-Americans or Black Americans; an ethnic group in the United States of America whose ancestors, usually in predominant part, were indigenous to Sub-Saharan and West Africa.

Arrangement The reworking or recomposing of a musical **composition** or some part of it (such as the **melody**) for a medium or **ensemble** other than that of the original; also the resulting version of the piece.

Ballad Properly, a sentimental love song; also used in reference to any slow piece.

Barrelhouse A bar, originating in the late 1800s, serving liquor straight from the barrel; also, the loud, rough style of piano-playing initially practised in these establishments.

Bebop Style of **jazz** developed in the 1940s and characterized by jagged **rhythms**, asymmetric phrases and fast **tempi**.

Blue note A **note** that is flattened for expressive effect; most commonly the third or seventh degree of the **scale**.

Blues Most commonly, a musical **form** consisting of a repeated 12-bar pattern with standardized **harmony**; also a **melodic** style and a particular mood.

Boogie-Woogie Originally a style of dance performed to piano accompaniment; later the style of piano-playing itself, characterized by continuous, repeated patterns in the left hand and **blues harmonies**.

Break A **solo** passage played during a break in the accompaniment, most often occurring at the end of a phrase.

Bridge Generally applied to a passage of music that links two sections of a piece. In **jazz** it often refers to the contrasting middle section of a **tune** (the B section of an AABA **form**, for example).

Burlesque A humorous piece involving parody through exaggeration. In late nineteenth- and early twentieth-century America, it referred to a variety show in which the main attraction was striptease.

Cadence A recognizable **harmonic progression** or **melodic** formula occurring at the end of a phrase or piece, which indicates whether the piece is to continue or has concluded. It also establishes the tonality of a section or piece.

Chase A competition between two or more **soloists** playing in turn.

Chord A group of two or more **notes** sounded simultaneously. There are many descriptors that can be attached to 'chord' to indicate the **notes** included, for example 'added sixth chord').

Chorus In **jazz**, one complete cycle of a **tune** or of the harmonies that make up that **tune**. More generally a chorus is the section of a song that is repeated with identical words and **melody** in between verses.

Chromatic Based on an **octave** divided into 12 **semitones**, as opposed to the seven-**note diatonic scale**. Chromatic has its root in the Greek word 'chromatikos' meaning 'coloured'.

Composition The act of creating a piece of music, and the product of that process. In **jazz**, the product is generally referred to as a '**tune**'.

Cool Applied to many styles of **jazz** that focus on simplicity and understated lyricism. Particularly used in reference to musicians in the late 1940s and early 1950s that followed the examples of Miles Davis and Lester Young.

Creole Ill-defined term often referring to descendants of French and Spanish settlers in the southern United States and Louisiana in particular. Used by several early **jazz** bands made up of Creole musicians from **New Orleans**.

Dectet See *Ensemble*

Diatonic Based on an **octave** divided into seven steps of **tones** and **semitones** in various configurations, as opposed to **chromatic**. The major, natural minor **scale**, and Church modes are diatonic. Diatonic **harmony** is, most loosely, that which contains only **notes** from the **scale** on which a piece is based.

Ditty A short, simple song; also a short poem, often humorous in nature.

Dixieland The original **form** of **jazz** as appeared in **New Orleans** in the early 1900s. Also referred to as **New Orleans jazz** and **trad jazz**.

Duo See *Ensemble*

Ensemble From the French meaning 'together'. A group of two or more instrumentalists and/or singers performing together. Various sizes of ensemble have specific names, e.g. duo (2 musicians), trio (3), quartet (4), quintet (5), sextet (6), septet (7), octet (8), nonet (9), dectet (10). In **jazz** the instrumental line-up of an ensemble is not fixed.

Fake book A collection of **tunes** made illegally (hence 'fake'). Most often sold by word of mouth, or belonging to a particular band for use of the members only. Better presented, legal collections were later published as 'real books'.

Folk music A term that has no clear definition but essentially refers to the traditional music of an indigenous population. Generally lacks an identifiable composer, is passed on aurally (i.e. not notated) and is performed by non-professionals.

Form The structure or organization of a piece of music; usually related to recognizable sections of **melody** and/or **harmony**.

Free jazz A style of **jazz** typified by Ornette Coleman and late-era John Coltrane and characterized by a lack of predetermined **harmonic** and **melodic** structures and a focus on both individual and group **improvisation**. Very often high-octane in mood.

Fusion Loosely describes a musical style begun in the 1960s that combined the **harmonic** language and **improvisatory** techniques of **jazz** with the instrumentation and idioms of rock music. Well-known exponents include Wayne Shorter, Herbie Hancock and Chick Corea. The style was originally known as 'jazz rock'; the term 'fusion' was only applied from the mid-1970s.

Gospel music Religious song deriving from evangelical Protestant groups in the United States, both white and **African-American**, that came to prominence in the early twentieth century. African-American gospel music had a profound impact on **jazz** both musically and spiritually.

Groove A regular, repeated pattern. Also an aesthetic judgment; a piece that is said to 'groove' has an instinctive feeling of 'rightness'.

Harmony The combining of a succession of **chords** to produce a harmonic **progression**. There are systems governing such **progressions** which help to create recognizable harmonic structures.

Hot jazz Used to describe any **jazz** but particularly early jazz and **swing** that is energetic and vigorous in character.

Improvise To invent with little or no preparation. In **jazz**, improvisation generally takes place over an existing **harmonic** structure and often uses **melodic** shapes and ideas from a set **tune**.

Jam session An informal gathering of **jazz** musicians playing for their own pleasure, free from the constraints of public performance. Jam sessions came to be organized for audiences in the 1930s, thus losing their essence, but in the 1970s the original jam session made a comeback.

Jazz A style of music characterized by **rhythmic syncopation**, repeated **harmonic** structures and **improvisation** that has its roots in performing conventions brought to the United States by **African-Americans**.

Jazz rock See *Fusion*

Jug band An instrumental **ensemble** developed amongst **African-Americans** in the early twentieth century consisting of a variety of home-made instruments, such as kazoos and washboards. The jug of the name was used as a bass instrument.

Key In western tonal music, describes an arrangement of **pitches** and the relationships between them.

Latin Applied to **jazz** in which elements of Latin-American music are conspicuous, particularly dance **rhythms** and percussion instruments such as claves, bongos and cowbells.

Lyrics The words written for a song.

Mainstream Loosely refers to the type of **jazz** using **solos improvised** over a set **harmonic** structure. Specifically coined by Stanley Dance in the 1950s to refer to the **swing** music of the 1930s and 1940s.

Melody An organized group of **pitches**, each sounded subsequently.

Metre Generally, a **rhythmic** pattern of stressed and unstressed sounds. In music it is used as a way of organizing sounds to create a framework in time. Also used to refer to time signature.

Minstrel show An indigenous **form** of American entertainment consisting of comic sketches and songs performed by actors in blackface.

Modern jazz Used to describe collectively the **jazz** styles developed between the 1940s and 1960s.

Mouldy fig Used derisively by practitioners of bebop to describe fans of older styles of **jazz**; one whose tastes are out-of-date.

New Orleans See *Dixieland*

Nonet See *Ensemble*

Notation A means of describing musical sounds visually through symbols representing instructions to the performer.

Note Specifically, the graphical representation of a sound; also used in reference to the sound itself.

Obbligato Refers to an essential line in a **composition** that is not the principal **melody**.

Octave The interval between two **pitches** 12 **semitones** apart. Acoustically these **pitches** are very similar, seeming to differ only in **register**, and as such have played a central role in the development of tonal systems.

Octet See *Ensemble*

Pentatonic Literally, 'five **tones**'. Applied to **scales** constructed of five different **pitches**. Most commonly used for the **scale** C-D-E-G-A.

Pitch The quality of a sound that fixes its position in a **scale**. Sounds that do not belong in a **scale** (usually percussive sounds) are said to be unpitched.

Pop Applied to a particular group of musical styles that are popular. As a result, the term is subject to constant redefinition.

Progression See *Harmony*

Pulse A regular, **rhythmic** beat related to but not necessarily the same as the time signature.

Quartertone See *Tone*

Quartet See *Ensemble*

Quintet See *Ensemble*

Ragtime A style of music popular in America between the 1890s and 1920s. Most often played on the piano, it is distinguished by a **syncopated** (or 'ragged') **melody** set against a straight-moving bass.

Real book See *Fake book*

Recording Used to mean any method for storing visual images and/or sound. Audio recording was invented in 1877 by Thomas Edison.

Register Relative height of a pitch or group of pitches. The violin, for example, plays in a higher register than the cello.

Rhythm The variation in the duration of sounds in time. The perception of rhythm in music is related to the use of metre and **pulse**.

Riff A short, recognizable phrase. Also, a pre-prepared **melodic** phrase used in **improvisation**.

Scale A sequence of **notes** arranged in ascending or descending order of **pitch**.

Semitone The smallest commonly used division, a 12th, of the **octave**. A step comprising two semitones is known as a tone. The division of the semitone in half is known as a quartertone.

Septet See *Ensemble*

Sextet See *Ensemble*

Solo In **jazz**, a continuous **improvisation** by one player, normally over several repetitions of a **tune**'s **harmony**.

Standard A **tune** that has become established in the repertory.

Stride A style of piano-playing that developed from **ragtime**, particularly associated with Harlem, New York. Takes its name from the distinctive 'stride bass', characterized by strong leaping left-hand figures. Typified by Fats Waller and, later, Thelonious Monk.

Swing A style of **jazz** from the 1930s characterized by big bands, **solo improvisation** and a strong **rhythmic pulse**. A **rhythmic** manner of playing first heard in the swing style. Also, an indefinable quality associated with great **jazz** perhaps best described as having the x-factor.

Syncopation The effect of **rhythmic** displacement through accents on weak beats or in between beats.

Tailgate A style of trombone-playing typical of **New Orleans jazz** and characterized by *glissandi* (sliding **notes**). Bands at the time played on wagons and the only place with enough room for the trombonist was the tailgate.

Tempo The speed at which a piece is played. In the plural 'tempi'.

Third stream Term coined by Gunther Schuller for a type of music that synthesized elements of classical music and **jazz**.

Timbre The tonal quality of an instrument or voice.

Tone See *Semitone*

Traditional (or trad) A style of **jazz** practised in the UK in the 1950s and 1960s that revived the style and instrumentation of turn-of-the-century **New Orleans jazz**, typified by Acker Bilk and Kenny Ball. Also, the original **jazz** style of the early 1900s, otherwise known as **Dixieland**.

Trio See *Ensemble*

Tune A **jazz composition** or performance.

Vamp A short, simple passage of accompaniment repeated freely until the **soloist** is ready to begin or continue.

Vaudeville Originally a satirical French song. In the nineteenth century it came to indicate a musical comedy or musichall variety show.

Virtuoso An instrumentalist or singer (or indeed any craftsman) of extraordinary technical skill.

Acknowledgments

Picture Credits

Arbiter Group plc: 386 (tr); Fender Musical Instruments Inc.: 398 (tr)

Corbis: 1, 59; Jeff Albertson: 134; BBC: 53, 75; Bettmann: 12, 26 (b), 55 (r), 113, 133 (r), 164, 165, 230 (b), 437; Lee Celano/Reuters: 358; Terry Cryer: 174, 214, 217, 220; Pierre Fournier: 203; Gavin Hellier: 315, 318; Hulton-Deutsch Collection: 5 (bl), 47, 202, 239, 262, 274 (b), 437; Steve Jennings: 143, 161; Craig Lovell: 362 (l), 436; Darrin Zammit Lupi: 352 (b); Alen MacWeeney: 143, 160 (r); Mosaic Images: 128 (r), 230 (t), 233 (b), 238, 239, 252, 253 (t), 277 (r), 279, 307, 312 (tr); Neal Preston: 315, 322, 323, 337 (b), Reuters: 343, 364; Bradley Smith: 35, 46, 437; John Springer Collection: 120 (b); Ted Streshinsky: 280; Derick A. Thomas/Dat's Jazz: 315, 319; John Van Hasselt: 315, 332 (b); Pierre Vauthey: 263; David H. Wells: 334 (t); Ted Williams: 128 (l), 223 (b)

Lauren Deutsch: 296 (r)

Foundry Arts: 4 (tl), 8 (tl), 10 (tl), 14 (tl), 14 (b), 22 (tl), 23 (tr), 24 (tl), 25 (tr), 26 (tl), 32 (tl), 36 (tl), 44 (tl), 48 (tl), 50 (tl), 52 (tl), 56 (tl), 56 (r), 58 (tl), 60 (tl), 62 (tl), 64 (tl), 68 (tl), 88 (tl), 92 (tl), 100 (tl), 102 (tl), 104 (tl), 104 (b), 106 (tl), 108 (tl), 110 (tl), 112 (tl), 112 (r), 116 (tl), 117 (l), 118 (tl), 120 (tl), 133 (l), 135, 138 (t), 140 (tl), 144 (tl), 152 (tl), 154 (tl), 156 (tl), 158 (tl), 162 (tl), 166 (tl), 168 (tl), 170 (tl), 186 (tl), 190 (tl), 197 (b), 198 (tl), 200 (tl), 204 (tl), 206 (tl), 208 (tl), 210 (tl), 212 (tl), 215 (b), 216 (tl), 236 (tl), 239, 240 (tl), 248 (tl), 250 (tl), 254 (tl), 256 (tl), 258 (tl), 260 (tl), 264 (tl), 266 (tl), 267, 282 (tl), 285, 286 (tl), 289 (b), 293 (t), 294 (tl), 296 (tl), 298 (tl), 300 (tl), 302 (tl), 312 (tl), 316 (tl), 324 (tl), 326 (tl), 328 (tl), 330 (tl), 332 (tl), 340 (tl), 344 (tl), 352 (tl), 368 (tl), 373, 374 (tl), 377 (b), 378 (tl), 380 (tl), 381 (t), 382 (tl), 384 (tl), 384 (b), 386 (tl), 388 (tl), 390 (tl), 392 (tl), 394 (tl), 396 (tl), 398 (tl), 398 (b), 400 (tl), 402 (tl), 404 (tl), 406 (tl), 409, 410 (tl), 411 (b), 413 (t), 414 (tl), 414 (l), 415 (tr), 417 (tr), 418 (t), 419 (tr), 421 (tr), 423 (tr), 425 (tr), 426 (tl), 428 (tl), 428 (tr), 429 (tr), 430 (b), 431 (l), 431 (tr), 434 (tl), 438 (tl), 438 (c), 438 (bl), 438 (br), 439 (all), 440 (all), 441 (all), 442 (tl), 443 (tr), 444 (tl), 446 (tl)

Getty Images: 9 (t); Hulton Archive: 65, 114; Michael Ochs Archives: 13, 16 (t), 17 (t), 35, 38 (b), 39, 49 (b), 51, 55 (b), 60 (r), 64 (r), 71 (b), 77 (r), 79, 87, 89, 90, 91, 94, 95, 100 (r), 103 (t), 107, 116 (b), 117 (r), 118 (r), 119, 121 (b), 122 (l), 123, 127 (l), 129, 137 (t), 139, 140 (tr), 143, 146 (r), 156 (r), 158 (r), 163, 167, 169 (t), 170 (b), 171, 173 (t), 175, 176, 177 (t), 177 (b), 178 (r), 179, 181 (b), 184 (t), 186 (b), 187, 189, 194, 195, 197 (t), 205, 210 (b), 216 (l), 218, 219 (r), 221 (t), 222, 223 (t), 224, 225 (t), 225 (b), 227, 233 (t), 239, 253 (b), 256 (r), 258 (r), 270, 273, 285, 299 (t), 308 (r), 313 (t), 321 (b), 370, 373, 377 (t), 378 (r), 379 (t), 381 (b), 391 (t), 391 (b), 393 (b), 409, 410 (r), 416 (l), 421 (b), 422 (r), 423 (l), 426 (r), 429 (r), 429 (b), 430 (t), 431 (b), 433 (l), 437; Photodisc: 438 (cl)

Todd S. Jenkins: 304 (b), 313 (bl)

Mary Evans Picture Library: 375

Redferns Music Picture Library: 31, 62 (b), 63, 72, 74 (b), 143, 155, 395 (b); Bob Baker: 397 (b); Glenn A. Baker Archives: 67, 170 (r), 213, 379 (b), 409, 420 (l); Dave Bennett: 45 (l), 88 (b); Paul Bergen: 246, 315, 337 (t), 338 (l), 343, 362 (r), 369, 373, 403, 435 (t), 437; Keith Bernstein: 285, 309; Carey Brandon: 343, 354 (l); Henrietta Butler: 343, 366 (l); Pete Cronin: 329 (l); Geoff Dann: 433 (r); Frank Debaeker: 395 (t); Deltahaze Corporation: 13, 19, 23 (b), 25 (l), 27 (b), 28, 50 (b), 68 (b), 78, 81 (r), 82, 409, 416 (r); Ian Dickson: 315, 325, 340 (l); Alan Dister: 5 (br), 268 (r), 315, 330 (r), 338 (r), 437; James Dittiger: 354 (r), 368 (bl); Rico D'Rozario: 373, 405 (b); Amanda Edwards: 365, 368 (br); Colin Fuller: 389 (t); GAB Archives: 69, 130 (l), 137 (b), 239, 281 (r); GEMS: 268 (l), 278 (b), 295, 303; Steve Gillett: 255 (b); William Gottlieb: 13, 29, 35, 68 (l), 74 (t), 91, 109, 122 (r), 126, 131, 132, 138 (b), 140 (b), 147, 148, 389 (b), 405 (t), 437; William Gottlieb/Library of Congress: 4 (bl), 34, 36 (r), 153, 208 (b), 374 (b), 376; Carry Hammond: 76; Tom Hanlet: 299 (b); Olivia Hemingway: 373, 401 (t); Paul Hoeffler: 157, 231, 234 (t), 239, 271 (t), 272 (t); Richie Howell: 216 (b); Max Jones Files: 13, 18, 20, 22 (r), 24 (b), 30, 32–3, 35, 41, 45 (r), 48 (r), 49 (t), 61, 71 (t), 73 (b), 77 (l), 83 (t), 84, 85, 86, 91, 96, 102 (r), 110 (b), 124, 135 (r), 140 (r), 200 (r), 221 (b), 285, 310 (r), 372, 373, 374 (tr), 380 (r), 382 (r), 383, 385, 386 (b), 407 (r); K&K: 428 (b); Ivan Keeman: 272 (b); Robert Knight: 317, 331, 409, 432; Elliott Landy: 159, 186 (r), 242; Herman Leonard: 91, 97, 108 (r), 142, 143, 149, 154 (r), 172, 181 (t), 182, 183, 184 (b), 189, 196, 219 (l); Andrew Lepley: 9 (b), 293 (b), 308 (l), 314, 335, 339, 343, 348, 353 (l), 353 (r), 355, 357 (r), 360 (l), 366 (r); Robin Little: 356; Marc Marnie: 239, 269; Steve Morley: 294 (r), 313 (br); Keith Morris: 3, 239, 260 (b), 261; Leon Morris: 11 (t), 66, 297, 334 (b), 342, 350 (l), 361; Jan Persson: 166 (r); Andrew Putler: 241 (b), 247, 285, 289 (t), 292, 301 (t), 394 (r); RB: 413 (b); David Redfern: 168 (r), 180, 189, 201, 206 (r), 207, 209, 211, 226 (t), 226 (b), 235, 239, 241 (t), 249, 257, 264 (r), 266, 274 (t), 275, 276, 277 (l), 287 (t), 284, 285, 288, 300 (r), 301 (b), 302 (b), 305, 306 (l), 312 (b), 327, 329 (r), 343, 344 (r), 350 (r), 357 (l), 363, 367, 368 (tr), 368 (c), 371, 373, 384 (tr), 388 (r), 390 (r), 392 (b), 393 (t), 396 (r), 397 (t), 402 (tr), 402 (b), 407 (l), 409, 418 (b), 437; David Redfern/USA Post Office: 208 (tr); Adam Ritchie: 250 (r); Ebet Roberts: 285, 298 (r), 315, 316 (r), 326 (r), 328 (r), 341, 351, 422 (l); Philip Ryals: 343, 360 (r); Philippe Schneider: 373, 404 (r); Nicky J. Sims: 401 (b); Chuck Stewart: 185, 232, 248 (b); Colin Streater: 400 (b); Gai Terrell: 239, 243, 271 (b); Toby Wates: 373, 399, 437; Bob Willoughby: 91, 111, 136, 320, 336, 340 (br), 359 (b), 373, 387, 427 (t); Graham Wiltshire: 285, 286 (r); Charlyn Zlotnik: 285, 311

Sylvia Pitcher Photo Library: 4 (br), 6, 32 (b), 35, 38 (t), 57, 58 (r), 91, 105, 115, 127 (r), 130 (r), 143, 144 (r), 160 (l) 169 (b), 173 (b), 188, 189, 191 (b), 204 (r), 215 (t), 228, 239, 244 (t), 254 (r), 255 (t), 259, 285, 290, 291, 304 (t), 310 (l), 312 (r), 315, 333 (t), 333, (b), 340 (tr), 408, 409, 411 (t), 412, 415 (l), 417 (l), 420 (r), 424 (l), 424 (r), 425 (tl), 425 (b), 437; B. Fisher: 178 (l), 189, 198 (b), 199 (b), 437; Tony Mottram: 371, 435 (b); Brian Smith: 11 (b), 234 (b), 281 (l), 324 (r), 343, 359 (t), 409, 419 (b), 434 (b); The Weston Collection: 13, 16 (b), 17 (b), 27 (t), 70, 88 (tr), 104 (r), 245, 306 (r), 414 (r)

Telarc & Heads Up: Tim Jackson 343, 347

Topham Picturepoint: 10 (b), 13, 15, 21, 33, 35, 37 (t), 37 (b), 40, 42 (l), 42 (r), 43, 44 (r), 52 (b), 54, 73 (t), 80, 81, 83 (b), 88 (c), 91, 92 (r), 93 (t), 93 (b), 101, 103 (b), 106 (b), 118 (b), 121 (t), 125, 141, 143, 145, 146 (l), 150, 151, 152 (r), 189, 191 (t), 192 (l), 192 (r), 193, 212 (b), 229, 251, 265, 285, 287, 427 (b); Arena PAL: 143, 162 (r), 190 (r), 210 (tr), 244 (b), 321 (t), 343, 346; Arena PAL/Christina Burton: 98; Mark Godfrey/The Image Works: 240 (r); Jeff Greenberg/The Image Works: 99; The Image Works: 343, 349; Michael Schwarz/The Image Works: 343, 345

Universal/The Kobal Collection: 189, 199 (t); DISPATFILM/GEMMA/TUPAN: 406 (b)

Author Biographies

Jeff 'Tain' Watts (Foreword)
One of the most in-demand jazz drummers in the world today, Jeff Watts initially studied classical percussion at Pittsburgh's Duquesne University, where he was primarily a timpanist. Following this he enrolled at the Berklee School of Music. Jeff joined the Wynton Marsalis Quartet in 1981 and proceeded to win three Grammy Awards with the ensemble. After leaving Wynton in 1988 he went on to work with George Benson, Harry Connick Jr. and McCoy Tyner. In 1989 Jeff joined the Branford Marsalis Quartet. As of 2007, he is the only musician to appear on every Grammy Award-winning jazz record by both Wynton and Branford Marsalis. In addition he was voted Best Acoustic Jazz Drummer by *Modern Drummer* magazine in both 1988 and 1993. Jeff has worked in the film and television industries as both a musician on the *Tonight Show* with Jay Leno and as an actor, playing Rhythm Jones in Spike Lee's *Mo' Better Blues*. After three years in LA on the *Tonight Show*, Jeff returned to New York in 1995 and joined Kenny Garrett's band. He also continued to record and tour with Branford Marsalis as well as Michael Brecker, Courtney Pine, Geri Allen, Alice Coltrane, Greg Osby, Steve Coleman, Gonzalo Rubalcaba and Ravi Coltrane. Jeff has an extensive discography as a sideman as well as five albums as a leader: *Citizen Tain* (1999), *Bar Talk* (2002), *Megawatts* (2004), *Detained* (2004) and *Folk's Songs* (2007).

Julia Rolf (General Editor; Sources & Sounds)
Julia Rolf developed a love of jazz at a young age after hearing Robert Parker's BBC Radio 3 series *Jazz Classics in Digital Stereo*, and has retained a particular interest in the New Orleans and Chicago jazz of the pre-swing era. She was turned on to the blues at the tender age of eight via her dad's record collection, counting Elmore James and Robert Johnson among her early heroes. She has worked as an author and editor on a wide range of music books, with an emphasis on jazz and blues titles. Her recent projects include *Bob Dylan: Highway 61 Revisited* and *The Rolling Stones: Beggars Banquet*, both from Flame Tree Publishing's *Legendary Sessions* series, *Blues: The Complete Story* and *Jazz: The Complete Story*.

Cliff Douse (The Styles)
Cliff Douse has written hundreds of articles and columns during the past 10 years for many of the UK's foremost music and computer magazines including *Guitarist*, *Guitar Techniques*, *Total Guitar*, *Computer Music*, *Future Music*, *Rhythm* and *Mac Format*. He is also the author and co-author of several music books published by IMP, Music Sales, Music Maker and Thunder Bay. He is currently the editor of *Guitarist Icons* magazine (a quarterly special issue of *Guitarist* magazine) and is working on a number of new books and music software projects.

Ted Drozdowski (Blues 1960s; Blues Contemporary)
Ted Drozdowski is a freelance journalist and musician living in Boston, Massachusetts. He writes about popular culture, specializing in music. His writing has appeared internationally in a wide variety of publications including *Tracks*, *Rolling Stone* and *Musician*. He is co-author of *The Best Music CD Art and Design* and appears on television and radio offering commentary on music. He was a research consultant for Martin Scorsese's PBS-TV series *The Blues* and has been awarded the Blues Foundation's Keeping the Blues Alive Award for Journalism. He leads the Mississippi-informed blues band Scissormen.

James Hale (Jazz 1970s; The Instruments)
Based in Ottawa, Canada, James Hale is a feature writer, Critics Poll jury member and a frequent CD reviewer for *Down Beat*. He is also a frequent feature and review contributor to *Coda*, *Planet Jazz* and the *Ottawa Citizen*, and his work has appeared in *Jazziz*, *Pulse!*, *The Jazz Report*, *Modern Drummer*, *Words & Music* and *RhythmMusic*. In 2002 and 2003, he was nominated for a Canadian National Jazz Award as Best Journalist. A member of the Jazz Journalists Association, Hale is managing editor of the organization's website – www.jazzhouse.org – and associate editor of their newsletter, *JazzNotes*.

Todd Jenkins (Jazz 1960s; Blues 1970s)
Todd S. Jenkins is a contributor to *Down Beat*, *All About Jazz*, *Signal To Noise*, *The ZydE-Zine* and *Route 66* magazines. He is the author of *Free Jazz and Free Improvisation: An Encyclopedia* (Greenwood Press), *Eclipse: The Music of Charles Mingus* (Praeger), and an upcoming biography of pianist Jimmy Rowles. A resident of San Bernardino, California, Todd is a member of the American Jazz Symposium and the Jazz Journalists Association.

Howard Mandel (Introduction; Chapter openers; Jazz Contemporary)
Howard Mandel is a writer and editor specializing in jazz, blues, new and unusual music. Born in Chicago, now living in New York City, he is a senior contributor for *Down Beat*, produces arts features for National Public Radio, teaches at New York University, is president of the Jazz Journalists Association and edits its website www.Jazzhouse.org. Mandel's *Future Jazz* (Oxford University Press, 1999) ranges from the AACM to John Zorn; he has written for *Musical America*, *The Wire* (UK), *Swing Journal* (Tokyo), *Bravo* (Rio de Janeiro), and many other periodicals.

Kenny Mathieson (Jazz 1940s; Jazz 1950s)
Kenny Mathieson lives and works in Boat of Garten, Strathspey, Scotland. He studied American and English Literature at the University of East Anglia, graduating with a BA (First Class) in 1978 and a PhD in 1983. He has been a freelance writer on various arts-related subjects since 1982, specializing in music, primarily jazz, classical and folk. He contributes to *The Herald*, *The Scotsman*, *The List*, *Times Educational Supplement Scotland*, *Jazzwise* and other publications. He has contributed to a variety of reference books. He is the author of two books on jazz, *Giant Steps* and *Cookin'* (both Canongate), and edited and co-wrote *Celtic Music – A Listener's Guide* (BackbeatUK). He writes on arts for the *Inverness Courier*, and is the commissioning editor for the HI-Arts online arts journal (www.hi-arts.co.uk).

John McDonough (Jazz 1930s)
John McDonough has been critic and contributing editor at *Down Beat* since 1968, and a contributor on jazz and other cultural topics to *The Wall Street Journal* since 1986. A three-time Grammy nominee for Best Album Notes, he has written biographies on Lester Young, Pee Wee Russell and Coleman Hawkins for Time-Life Books as well as the book accompanying the Grammy-winning *The Complete Ella Fitzgerald Song Books* on Verve. He has also contributed other notes for Mosaic, Pablo, Columbia, Victor, et al. McDonough is also editor of *The Encyclopedia of Advertising* (2003) and a long-time contributor to *Advertising Age* and National Public Radio, for which he writes and produces historical pieces in partnership with former CBS anchor Walter Cronkite. He lives near Chicago with his wife and son.

Bill Milkowski (Jazz 1920s; Blues 1980s; Jazz 1980s)
Bill Milkowski is a regular contributor to *Jazz Times*, *Jazziz*, *Bass Player*, *Modern Drummer*, *Guitar Club* (Italy) and *Jazzthing* (Germany) magazines. He was named the Jazz Journalists Association's Writer of the Year for 2004. He is also the author of *JACO: The Extraordinary Life of Jaco Pastorius* (Backbeat Books), *Rockers, Jazzbos & Visionaries* (Billboard Books) and *Swing It! An Annotated History of Jive* (Billboard Books).

Jim O'Neal (Blues Early Years)
Jim O'Neal is based in Kansas City and is founding editor of *Living Blues*, America's first blues magazine. He co-edited *The Voice of the Blues: Classic Interviews from Living Blues Magazine* (Routledge, 2002), and he collects and sells soul, R&B, funk, jazz, country, folk, world/ethnic, gospel, soundtrack and rock'n'roll records as well as blues. His website, BluEsoterica.com, is a research forum for discussing new, obscure or overlooked details on blues.

Bob Porter (Blues 1930s; Blues 1940s; Blues 1950s)
Bob Porter is a discographer, record producer and award-winning broadcaster and writer based in New Jersey. His syndicated blues program *Portraits in Blue* began its 24th year in autumn 2004. As well as serving on the board of directors of the Blues Foundation and being on the nominating committee for the Rock And Roll Hall of Fame, he has won two Grammies for his liner notes and produced more than 150 jazz and blues albums for artists such as Big Joe Turner and Illinois Jacquet. Porter has written for *Jazz Times Magazine*, *Down Beat*, *Jazz Journal* and *Discographical Forum*, amongst others. He contributed to the *Oxford Companion to Jazz*, and in 1992 was awarded the New Jersey Jazz Society's Outstanding Service Award.

William Schafer (Jazz Early Years)
Since gaining a Phd at the University of Minnesota, William Schafer has worked as editor and publications designer for the military and USDA, and taught at Berea College, Kentucky, where he is Chair of the English Department and head of the humanities program. His many publications include *The Art of Ragtime* (with Johannes Reidel, LSU Press), *Rock Music* (Augsburg Press), *Brass Bands and New Orleans Jazz* (LSU Press), *The Truman Nelson Reader* (ed., University of Massachusetts Press) and *Mapping the Godzone* (University of Hawaii Press). William has also contributed to *Contemporary Novelists* (St. Martin's Press), *Contemporary Short Stories* (St. Martin's Press), *The Encyclopedia of Southern Culture* (University of North Carolina Press) and Grove's dictionaries of American Music and Jazz. He is also a contributing editor of *Mississippi Rag*.

David Whiteis (Blues 1920s)
David Whiteis, an internationally published critic and journalist with over 25 years of experience writing about blues, jazz and other essential issues, currently writes on a regular basis for the *Chicago Reader*, *Down Beat*, *Living Blues*, *Juke Blues* and others. He is the recipient of the Blues Foundation's 2001 Keeping the Blues Alive Award for Achievement in Journalism. His book, *I Mean It From The Heart: Stories and Portraits in Chicago Blues*, was published by University of Illinois Press in 2005.

Resources

Further Reading

Abbott, L. & Seroff, D., *Out of Sight: The Rise of African American Popular Music, 1889–1895*, University of Missouri Press, 2003

Alexander, C. (ed.), *Masters of Jazz Guitar*, Balafon Books, 1999

Appel, A., *Jazz Modernism*, Alfred A. Knopf, 2002

Badger, R., *A Life in Ragtime: A Biography of James Reese Europe*, American Philological Association, 1995

Balliett, W., *Jelly Roll, Jabbo & Fats*, Oxford University Press, 1983

Barlow, W., *Looking Up At Down*, Temple University Press, 1989

Bascom, W.R. & Herskovits, M.J., *Continuity And Change In African Cultures*, University of Chicago Press, 1962

Basie, C. & Murray, A., *Good Morning Blues*, Random House, 1985

Berger, M. & E. & Patrick, J., *Benny Carter, A Life in American Music*, Scarecrow Press, 1982

Berry, P., *Up From the Cradle of Jazz*, University of Georgia Press, 1986

Blesh, R. & Janis, H., *They All Played Ragtime*, Schirmer, 1974

Bogdanov, V. (ed.), *All Music Guide to the Blues: The Definitive Guide to the Blues*, Backbeat, 2003

Britt, S., *Long Tall Dexter: A Critical Musical Biography*, Quartet Books, 1989

Brooks, T., *Lost Sounds: Blacks and the Birth of the Recording Industry 1890–1919*, University of Illinois Press, 2004

Brovan, J., *Walking To New Orleans*, Blues Unlimited, 1974

Brunn, H.O., *The Story of the Original Dixieland Jazz Band*, Louisiana State University Press, 1960

Brunning, B., *Blues: The British Connection: The Stones, Clapton, Fleetwood Mac and the Story of Blues in Britain*, Helter Skelter, 2003

Carr, I., *Miles Davis: The Definitive Biography*, HarperCollins, 1999 (new edition)

Carr, I., *The Rough Guide to Jazz*, Rough Guides, 2000

Castro, R., *Bossa Nova: The Story of the Brazilian Music that Seduced The World*, A Cappella Publishing, 2000

Catalano, N., *Clifford Brown: The Life and Art of the Legendary Jazz Trumpeter*, Oxford University Press, 2000

Charters, S., *Sweet As The Showers Of Rain*, Oak Publications, 1977

Charters, S., *The Blues Makers*, Da Capo Press, 1991

Charters, S., *The Country Blues*, Da Capo Press, 1975

Charters, S. & Kunstadt, L., *Jazz: A History of the New York Scene*, Da Capo Press, 1981

Chilton, J., *Let The Good Times Roll: The Story of Louis Jordan & His Music*, University of Michigan Press, 1997

Chilton, J., *Sidney Bechet: Wizard of Jazz*, Da Capo Press, 1996

Clayson, A., *The Yardbirds*, Backbeat Books, 2002

Cohn, L. (ed.), *Nothing But the Blues: The Music and the Musicians*, Abbeville Press, 1993

Cohodas, N., *Spinning Blues Into Gold: The Chess Brothers and the Legendary Chess Records*, St. Martin's Press, 2000

Cook, B., *Listen to the Blues*, Charles Scribner's Sons, 1973

Crease, S.S., *Gil Evans: Out of the Cool*, A Cappella Publishing, 2002

Cuscuna, M. & Lourie, C., *The Blue Note Years*, Rizzoli, 1995

Dance, H., *Stormy Monday: The T-Bone Walker Story*, Louisiana State University Press, 1987

Dance, S., *The World of Swing*, Da Capo Press, 1974

Daniels, D.H., *Lester Leaps In: The Life and Times of Lester 'Pres' Young*, Beacon Press, 2002

Davis, F., *Bebop and Nothingness: Jazz and Pop at the End of the Century*, Schirmer Books, 1996

Davis, F., *The History Of The Blues*, Hyperion, 1995

Davis, M. & Troupe, Q., *Miles: The Autobiography*, Simon and Schuster, 1989

Deffaa, C., *Traditionalists & Revivalists in Jazz*, Scarecrow Press, 1993

DeVeaux, S., *The Birth of Bebop: A Social and Musical History*, University of California Press, 1997

Dixon, R.M.W., Godrich, J. & Rye, H. (eds.), *Blues & Gospel Records, 1890–1943*, Clarendon Press, 1997

Dixon, W., with Snowden, D., *I Am The Blues: The Willie Dixon Story*, Da Capo Press, 1989

Edwards, D., *The World Don't Owe Me Nothing*, Chicago Review Press, 1997

Ekkehard, J., *Free Jazz*, Da Capo Press, 1981

Erlewine, M. et al (ed.), *All Music Guide To The Blues*, Backbeat, 1996

Eyre, B., *In Griot Time: An American Guitarist in Mali*, Temple University Press, 2000

Ferguson, O. et al, *The Otis Ferguson Reader*, December Press, 1982

Ferris, W., *Blues From The Delta*, Anchor Press/Doubleday, 1978

Firestone, R., *Swing Swing Swing: The Life and Times of Benny Goodman*, W.W. Norton & Co., 1993

Fraher, J., *The Blues Is A Feeling: Voices and Visions of African-American Bluesmen*, Face To Face Books, 1998

Friedman, M., *Buried Alive: the Biography of Janis Joplin*, Harmony, 1973

Gara, L., *The Baby Dodds Story*, Louisiana State University Press, 1992 (revised edition)

Gavin, J., *Deep in a Dream: The Long Night of Chet Baker*, Chatto & Windus, 2002

Gelly, D. (ed), *Masters of Jazz Saxophone*, Balafon Books, 2000

Giddins, G., *Celebrating Bird: The Triumph Of Charlie Parker*, Beechtree Books, 1987

Giddins, G., *Visions of Jazz: The First Century*, Oxford University Press, 1998

Gillespie, D. & Fraser, A., *To Be Or Not To Bop: Memoirs, The Autobiography Of Dizzy Gillespie*, Doubleday, 1979

Gillet, C., *The Sound of the City*, Da Capo Press, 1996

Gitler, I., *Jazz Masters Of The Forties*, Da Capo Press, 1966

Goggin, J. & Clute, P., *The Great Jazz Revival: A Pictorial Celebration of Traditional Jazz*, Donna Ewald Publishing, 1994

Goldberg, J., *Jazz Masters Of The Fifties*, Da Capo Press, 1965

Gordon, R., *Can't Be Satisfied: The Life & Times of Muddy Waters*, Little, Brown and Company, 2002

Gourse, L., *Straight, No Chaser: The Life and Genius of Thelonious Monk*, Schirmer Books, 1997

Gurlanick, P., *Lost Highway*, Harper & Row, 1979

Hammond, J., *John Hammond On Record*, Summit Books, 1977

Handy, W.C. (ed.), *Blues: An Anthology*, Applewood Books, 2001

Handy, W.C., *Father of the Blues*, Da Capo Press, 1991

Harris, S., *Blues Who's Who*, Da Capo Press, 1978

Hasse, J.E. (ed.), *Jazz: The First Century*, William Morrow, 2000

Henderson, D., *'Scuse Me While I Kiss the Sky: The Life of Jimi Hendrix*, Doubleday, 1978

Hotchner, A.E., *Blown Away: the Rolling Stones and the Death of the Sixties*, Simon and Schuster, 1990

Jenkins, T.S., *Free Jazz and Free Improvisation: An Encyclopedia*, Greenwood Press, 2004

Jost, E., *Free Jazz*, Da Capo Press, 1994

Kahn, A., *Kind of Blue: The Making of the Miles Davis Masterpiece*, Da Capo Press, 2000

Keepnews, O., *The View From Within: Jazz Writings, 1948–1987*, Oxford University Press, 1987

Kimball, R., *Reminiscing with Sissle and Blake*, Cooper Square Books, 2000

King, B.B. with Ritz, D., *Blues All Around Me: The Autobiography of B.B. King*, Avon Books, 1996

Kirchner, B. (ed.), *The Oxford Companion To Jazz*, Oxford University Press, 2000

Klinkowitz, J., *Listen: Gerry Mulligan*, Schirmer Books, 1991

Knight, R., *The Blues Highway: New Orleans to Chicago*, Trailblazer Publications, 2001

Kofsky, F., *Black Nationalism and the Revolution in Music*, Pathfinder Press, 1970

Kooper, A., *Backstage Passes & Backstabbing Bastards*, Billboard, 1998

Lees, G., *Leader of the Band: The Life of Woody Herman*, Oxford University Press, 1995

Levinson, P., *Trumpet Blues: The Life of Harry James*, Oxford University Press, 1999

Leymarie, I., *Cuban Fire: The Saga of Salsa and Latin Jazz*, Continuum International Publishing Group, 2002

Lincoln Collier, J., *The Making Of Jazz: A Comprehensive History*, Houghton Mifflin Company, 1978

Litweiler, J., *The Freedom Principle: Jazz After 1958*, William Morrow, 1984

Lomax, A., *The Land Where the Blues Began*, Random House, 1993

Lotz, R.E., *Black People: Entertainers of African Descent in Germany and Europe*, Birgit Lotz Verlag, 1997

Lydon, M., *Ray Charles: Man and Music*, Riverhead Books, 1998

Lyons, L., *The 101 Best Jazz Albums*, William Morrow, 1980

Maggin, D., *Stan Getz: A Life in Jazz*, William Morrow, 1996

Mandel, H., *Future Jazz*, Oxford University Press, 1999

Mathieson, K., *Cookin': Hard Bop and Soul Jazz, 1954–65*, Canongate Books Ltd, 2002

Mathieson, K., *Giant Steps: Bebop and the Creators of Modern Jazz, 1945–65*, Payback Press, 1999

McStravick, S. & Roos, J., (eds.), *Blues-Rock Explosion: From The Allman Brothers To The Yardbirds*, Old Goat Publishing, 2002
Mercer, M., *Footprints: The Life and Work of Wayne Shorter*, Tarcher/Penguin, 2004
Mezzrow, M. & Wolfe, B., *Really The Blues*, Doubleday, 1946
Milkowski, B., *Jaco: Jaco Pastorius*, Backbeat, 1998
Milkowski, B., *Rockers, Jazzbos & Visionaries*, Billboard Books, 1998
Milkowski, B., *Swing It! An Annotated History Of Jive*, Billboard Books, 2001
Mongran, N., *The History of the Guitar in Jazz*, Oak Publications, 1983
Morgan, T. & Barlow, W., *From Cakewalks to Concert Halls: An Illustrated History of African-American Popular Music from 1895 to 1930*, Black Belt Press, 1992
Murray, C.S., *Boogie Man: The Adventures of John Lee Hooker in the American Twentieth Century*, St. Martin's Press, 2000
Neville, A. & Ritz, D., *The Brothers: An Autobiography*, Da Capo Press, 2001
Newman, R., *Blues Breaker: John Mayall And The Story Of The Blues*, Sanctuary Publishing, 1995
Nicholson, R., *Mississippi the Blues Today!*, Da Capo Press, 1999
Nicholson, S., *Billie Holiday*, Gollancz, 1995
Nicholson, S., *Jazz-Rock: A History*, Schirmer Books, 1998
Nisenson, E., *Open Sky: Sonny Rollins and His World of Improvisation*, St. Martin's Press, 2000
O'Neal, J. & van Singel, A. (eds.), *The Voice of the Blues*, Routledge, 2002
Oakley, G., *The Devil's Music: A History of the Blues*, Da Capo Press, 1997
Obrecht, J., *Rollin' and Tumblin': The Postwar Blues Guitarists*, Backbeat Books, 2000
Odum, H.W. & Johnson, G.B., *The Negro and His Songs: A Study of Typical Negro Songs in the South*, Greenwood Press
Oliver, P., *Songsters & Saints: Vocal Traditions on Race Records*, Cambridge University Press, 1984
Oliver, P., *The Story of the Blues: The Making of a Black Music*, Pimlico, 1997
Owens, T., *Bebop: The Music and Its Players*, Oxford University Press, 1995
Page, C.I., *Boogie Woogie Stomp: Albert Ammons & His Music*, Northeast Ohio Jazz Society, 1997
Palmer, R., *Deep Blues*, Viking Press, 1981
Patoski, J.N. & Crawford, B., *Stevie Ray Vaughan: Caught in the Crossfire*, Little, Brown and Company, 1993
Pepper, A., *Straight Life*, Schirmer Books, 1979
Pessanha, R. & McGowan, C., *The Brazilian Sound: Samba, Bossa Nova and the Popular Music of Brazil*, Temple University Press, 1998
Peterson, O., *A Jazz Odyssey*, Continuum, 2002
Pettinger, P., *Bill Evans: How My Heart Sings*, Yale University Press, 1998
Porter, L., *John Coltrane: His Life and Music*, University of Michigan Press, 1998
Raccuglia, D., *Darker Blues*, Fat Possum Records, 2003
Reich, H. & Gaines, W., *Jelly's Blues*, Da Capo Press, 2003
Roberts, J.S., *Black Music of Two Worlds*, Allen Lane, 1973
Roberts, J.S., *The Latin Tinge*, Oxford University Press, 1998
Rosalsky, M., *Encyclopedia Of Rhythm And Blues And Doo Wop Vocal Groups*, Scarecrow Press, 2000
Rosenthal, D.H., *Hard Bop: Jazz and Black Music, 1955–1965*, Oxford University Press, 1994
Rowe, M., *Chicago Blues: The City And The Music*, Da Capo Press, 1973
Rowe, M., *Chicago Breakdown*, Drake Publishers, 1975
Russell, R., *Bird Lives!*, Charterhouse, 1972
Salem, J., *The Late, Great Johnny Ace*, University of Illinois Press, 1999
Sallis, J. (ed.), *The Guitar in Jazz: An Anthology*, University of Nebraska Press, 1996
Sallis, J., *The Guitar Players*, University of Nebraska Press, 1982
Santelli, R., *The Big Book of Blues: A Biographical Encyclopedia*, Penguin, 1994
Santoro, G., *Highway 61 Revisited: The Tangled Roots of American Jazz, Blues, Rock & Country Music*, Oxford University Press, 2004
Santoro, G., *Myself When I Am Real: The Life and Music of Charles Mingus*, Oxford University Press, 2000
Sargeant W., *Jazz, Hot and Hybrid*, E.P. Dutton & Co., 1938
Sawyer, C., *B.B. King: the Authorized Biography*, Quartet Publishing, 1982
Schafer, W.J. & Reidel, J., *The Art of Ragtime*, Louisiana State University Press, 1973
Schuller, G., *Early Jazz*, Oxford University Press, 1986
Schuller, G., *The Swing Era*, Oxford University Press, 1989
Schumacher, M., *Crossroads: The Life And Music Of Eric Clapton*, Citadel Press, 2003
Segrest, J. & Hoffman, M., *Moanin' at Midnight: The Life and Times of Howlin' Wolf*, Pantheon Books, 2004
Shaw, A., *Honkers and Shouters: The Golden Years of Rhythm and Blues*, Macmillan, 1978
Sheridan, C. (ed.), *Dis Here: A Bio-discography of Julian 'Cannonball' Adderley (Discographies)*, Greenwood Press, 2000
Shipton, A., *Groovin' High: The Life of Dizzy Gillespie*, Oxford University Press, 1999
Silvester, P.J., *A Left Hand Like God*, Da Capo Press, 1988
Simon, G.T., *The Big Bands (4th ed.)*, Schirmer Books, 1981
Simosko, V., *Artie Shaw: A Musician Biography and Discography*, Scarecrow Press, 2000
Southern, E., *The Music Of Black Americans: A History*, Norton, 1983
Stowe, D.W., *Swing Changes: Big Band Jazz in New Deal America*, Harvard University Press, 1994
Sudhalter, R.M., *Lost Chords: White Musicians And Their Contributions To Jazz, 1915–1945*, Oxford University Press, 1999
Szwed, J., *Jazz 101: A Complete Guide to Learning and Loving Jazz*, Hyperion, 1999
Szwed, J., *So What: The Life of Miles Davis*, Heinemann, 2002
Tingen, P., *Miles Beyond: The Electric Explorations of Miles Davis 1967–1991*, Billboard Books, 2001
Tipaldi, A., *Children of the Blues: 49 Musicians Shaping a New Blues Tradition*, Backbeat Books, 2002
Tisserand, M., *The Kingdom of Zydeco*, Avon Books, 1998
Titon, J.T., *Early Downhome Blues: A Musical and Cultural Analysis*, Atlantic Books, 1995
Waldo, T., *This Is Ragtime*, Da Capo Press, 1976
Waller, M. & Calabrese, A., *Fats Waller*, Schirmer Books, 1997
Ward, G., *The Rough Guide To The Blues*, Rough Guides, 2000
Wardlow, G.D., *Chasin' That Devil Music*, Miller Freeman Books, 1998
Waterman, D., *Between Midnight and Day: the Last Unpublished Blues Archive*, Thunder's Mouth Press, 2003
Wein, G. with Chinen, N., *Myself Among Others: A Life in Music*, Da Capo, 2003
Wexler, J. & Ritz, D., *Rhythm and the Blues: A Life in American Music*, Alfred A. Knopf, 1993
Wilcox D.E. & Guy, B., *Damn Right I've Got the Blues/Buddy Guy and the Blues Roots of Rock-and-Roll*, Woodford Press, 1993
Wilder, A., *American Popular Song: The Great Innovators, 1900–50*, Oxford University Press, 1972
Wilmer, V., *As Serious As Your Life*, Serpent's Tail, 1992 (2nd edition)
Woideck, C., *Charlie Parker: His Music and Life*, University of Michigan Press, 1996
Wolfe, C. & Lornell, K., *The Life and Legend of Leadbelly*, HarperCollins, 1992
Wolkin, J.M. & Keenom, B., *Michael Bloomfield: If You Love These Blues*, Miller Freeman Books, 2000
Wondrich, D., *Stomp and Swerve: American Music Gets Hot 1843–1924*, A Capella Publishing, 2003
Wyman, B., *Bill Wyman's Blues Odyssey: A Journey To Music's Heart And Soul*, Dorling Kindersley, 2001
Zabor, R., *The Bear Comes Home*, Norton, 1998
Zorn, J. (ed.), *Arcana: Musicians on Music*, Granary Books, 2000

Websites

http://www.allaboutjazz.com
http://www.allmusic.com
http://www.allofmp3.com
http://www.aloud.com
http://www.apassion4jazz.net
http://www.apple.com/itunes/
http://www.archive.org/details/etree
http://www.bbc.co.uk/music
http://www.bbc.co.uk/radio
http://www.bigmouth.co.uk
http://www.billboard.com
http://www.blueprint-blues.co.uk
http://www.blues.org
http://www.bluesandrhythm.co.uk
http://www.bluesandstuff.com
http://www.bluesfestivalguide.com
http://www.bluesmatters.com
http://bluesnet.hub.org
http://www.bluespeak.com
http://www.bluesworld.com
http://www.channel4.com/music
http://www.chicagojazz.com
http://www.clickmusic.com
http://www.downbeat.com
http://www.earlyblues.com
http://www.efestivals.co.uk
http://www.emusic.com
http://www.extraplay.com
http://www.fly.co.uk
http://www.hob.com
http://www.jass.com
http://www.jazz-blues.com
http://www.jazz-clubs-worldwide.com
http://www.jazzconnect.com
http://www.jazzcorner.com
http://www.jazzfm.com
http://www.jazzgrrls.com
http://www.jazzhouse.org
http://www.jazzonline.com
http://www.jazzpromo.com
http://www.jazzreview.com
http://www.kingbiscuittime.com
http://www.legendsofjazz.net
http://www.live365.com
http://www.livedaily.com
http://www.mary4music.com
http://www.modernmusicians.com
http://www.mudcat.org
http://www.musicfirebox.com
http://www.musicsearch.com
http://www.musictoday.com
http://www.musicweek.com
http://www.napster.com
http://www.play.com
http://www.realbluesmagazine.com
http://www.recordcollectormag.com
http://www.redhotjazz.com
http://www.rhapsody.com
http://www.riverwalkjazz.org
http://www.roughstock.com
http://www.smoothjazzlinks.com
http://www.sonymusic.com
http://www.sortmusic.com
http://www.soul-sides.com
http://www.spin.com
http://www.thebluehighway.com
http://www.thejazz.com
http://www.thisdayinmusic.com
http://www.tunes.com
http://www.vh1.com

Index

Page references in **bold** refer to major articles, and page references in *italics* to illustrations.